THE
COWBOY
DICTIONARY

The Chin Jaw Words and Whing-Ding Ways of The American West

RAMON F. ADAMS

A Perigee Book

*Dedicated to all outdoor men, especially those old-timers
who tamed the frontier for those who followed them*

Perigee Books
are published by
The Putnam Publishing Group
200 Madison Avenue
New York, NY 10016

First Perigee Edition 1993
This book was previously published under the title *Western Words*.
Published by arrangement with the University of Oklahoma Press.
Copyright © 1968 by The University of Oklahoma Press,
Norman, Publishing Division of the University.
All rights reserved. This book, or parts thereof,
may not be reproduced in any form without permission.
Published simultaneously in Canada

Library of Congress Cataloging-in-Publication Data

Adams, Ramon F. (Ramon Frederick), date.
   [Western words]
   The cowboy dictionary : the chin jaw words and whing-ding ways of
the American West / Ramon F. Adams.
      p.   cm.
   Originally published: Western words. New ed., rev. and enl. Norman
University of Oklahoma Press, 1968.
   ISBN 0-399-51866-5
   1. Cowboys—West (U.S.)—Language (New words, slang, etc.)—Dictionaries.
2. English language—Dialects—West (U.S.)—Dictionaries.   3. West (U.S.)—Popular
culture—Dictionaries.   4. Americanisms—West (U.S.)—Dictionaries.   I. Title.
PE3727.C6A4   1994   93-30210   CIP
427'.978'088636—dc20

Drawing on title page by Nick Eggenhofer
Cover design copyright © 1993 by Honi Werner

Printed in the United States of America
1   2   3   4   5   6   7   8   9   10

Introduction
to the New Edition

"A little hoss is soon curried"

The first edition of *Western Words* was devoted strictly to the cowman's language, as indicated by its subtitle: *A Dictionary of the Range, Cow Camp, and Trail*. This revision came about as the result of countless requests to add words and phrases used in other western vocations. To satisfy these requests, I have added not only many words used by the cowman that did not appear in the original edition (including rodeo terminology) but also the more common words of the vocabulary of the sheepman, the freighter and packer, the trapper, the buffalo hunter, the stagecoach driver, the western-river boatman, the logger, the sawmill worker, the miner, the western gambler—and the Indian.

There will still be omissions. Each vocation has a vocabulary of its own, and it is beyond the scope of this book to include a complete lexicon of each one.

It is my hope that this compilation will be of benefit to those interested in western vocations and to writers of western life and that it will provide enjoyment for those who cherished a fondness for the West.

RAMON F. ADAMS

Dallas, Texas

Introduction
to the First Edition

"There ain't much paw and beller to a cowboy"

They say a good range cook never misses a rock when "herding" his teams across the country. I hope that, like him, I have not missed many words from the cowman's vocabulary in compiling this lexicon. My greatest pleasure in collecting the material has been in associating with the cowboy in his native haunts. Never loquacious around strangers, he has attained the reputation of being about as talkative as a Piegan Indian. But I learned as a small boy, that when one becomes intimate with him, he "don't depend entirely on the sign language." Among his own kind he is never "hog-tied when it comes to makin' chin music." In fact, if he accepts you, his tongue gets "plumb frolicsome."

From first youthful impressions, my interest in his speech has grown until recording it has become the hobby of a lifetime. When a tenderfoot hears this range vernacular—distinctive, picturesque, and pungent —he is as surprised as a dog with his first porcupine. After he recovers from the shock of such unconventional English, the more he listens the more refreshing it becomes, because, like a fifth ace in a poker deck, it is so unexpected.

Never having had a chance to "study the higher branches of information through book learnin'," the native cowman forged his own language. Like other men of the soil, he created similes and metaphors, salty and unrefined, but sparkling with stimulating vigor. In the early days, many men with college degrees came west, fell in love with the freedom of range life, and remained. Not bound by conventions, they were not long in "chucking" their college grammar and drifting into the infectious parlance of the cow country. I have never yet met a cowman who didn't use it naturally and unconsciously, be he educated or otherwise.

With the cowman's figures of speech lie the rich field of his subtle humor and strength—unique, original, full-flavored. With his usually limited education he squeezes the juice from language, molds it to suit his needs, and is a genius at making a verb out of anything. He "don't have to fish 'round for no decorated language to make his meanin' clear," and has little patience with the man who "spouts words that run eight to the pound."

Perhaps the strength and originality in his speech are due to the solitude, the nearness of the stars, the bigness of the country, and the far horizons—all of which give him a chance to think clearly and go into the depths of his own mind. Wide spaces "don't breed chatter-boxes." On his long and lonely rides, he is not forced to listen to the scandal and idle gossip that dwarf a man's mind. Quite frequently he has no one to talk to but a horse that can't talk back.

William MacLeod Raine told me that he once heard his friend Gene Rhodes call a man a "rancid, left-handed old parallelogram." Who but a Westerner could put so much punch into a phrase? Who but a cowman would say of a gesticulating foreigner that "he couldn't say 'hell' with his hands tied"? Or think of a better figure for hunger than "hungrier'n a woodpecker with the headache"?

"The frontiersman, like the Indian," says Edward Everett Dale, "was a close observer. He saw every detail and in speaking of something he did not describe it. Rather he painted a picture in a single apt phrase—a picture so clear and colorful that description was unnecessary. He did not tell the listener—he preferred to show him—and show him he did with one pungent, salty phrase that often meant more than could long and detailed explanation."[1]

Unlettered men rely greatly upon comparisons to natural objects with which they are familiar to express their ideas and feelings. Mental images are a part of the life of a cowman. His comparisons are not only humor-ous, but fruity and unfaded. One cowhand spoke of a friend who had gone into a city barbershop to experience his first manicure with, "He's havin' his forehoofs roached and rasped by a pink and white pinto filly." A certain fiery old-timer was said to be "gettin' 'long in years, but his horns ain't been sawed off."

"Calm as a hoss trough," "pretty as a red heifer in a flower bed," "soft as a young calf's ears," "useless as a knot in a stake rope," "a heart in his brisket as big as a saddle blanket," "noisy as a calf corral," and "gals in them days didn't show much of their fetlocks" are but a few of the many examples of homely comparisons cowmen create.

[1] "Speech of the Frontier," an address at the Association Banquet, Central States Speech Association, Oklahoma City, April 1, 1941.

One of the inherent characteristics of the cowboy is exaggeration. Not only does he have a talent for telling tall tales, but he has a genius for exaggeration in ordinary conversation. In the following examples the ordinary man would be content to use the unitalicized words, but the cowman wants more strength and he adds words such as the italicized ones to gain this potency: "so drunk he couldn't hit the ground with his hat *in three throws*," "raised hell *and put a chunk under it*," "his tongue hangin' out a foot *and forty inches*," and "he'd fight y'u till hell freezes over, *then skate with y'u on the ice.*"

Another pronounced trait is the pithy, yet robust humor which continually crops out in his speech. Struthers Burt writes, " . . . this closeness with nature makes the cowboy exceedingly witty. They are the wittiest Americans alive. Not wisecracking like the city man, but really witty."[2]

The cowman has always reserved control of his spelling and pronunciation, completely ignoring the dictionary. He pronounces his Spanish as it sounds to his ear, and thus new words have been created; for instance, *hackamore* (from *jáquima*) and *hoosgow* (from *juzgado*).

"Just as the cowboy 'borrowed' much of his traditional 'riggin' ' from the *vaquero*," wrote S. Omar Barker, "and adapted it to his own needs, so, too, he borrowed freely from this *vaquero*'s word supply, which he also adapted. He borrowed 'by ear,' of course, and so plentifully that today much typical western terminology owes its origin to Spanish, however little it sometimes resembles the original either in spelling or pronunciation."[3]

Like all other Americans, the cowman is in a hurry and employs our typical shortening of words and phrases. His grammar is rough and rugged like his hills and canyons, but his short cuts are practical. Thus he creates words such as *lariat*, from *la reata*; *chaps*, from *chaparreras*; and *dally*, from *dar vuelta*.

Yet in his actions he is not hurried, but takes time to examine small things. He gets the habit of "usin' his eyes a lot and his mouth mighty little." He catalogs each detail and stores it away in his mind for future use, squeezing out all significant items and adding their essence to his refreshing philosophy. He has a talent for "sayin' a whole lot in a mighty few words," and "don't use up all his kindlin' to get his fire started."

2 Struthers Burt, *Powder River* (New York, Farrar & Rinehart, 1938), 229.

3 S. Omar Barker, "Sagebrush Spanish," *New Mexico Magazine*, Vol. XX, No. 12 (December, 1942), 18.

Not only did the cowman borrow from the Spanish, but he took what he wanted from the Indian, the trapper, and the freighter who preceded him, and from the gambler, the gunman, and others who came after him.

The terms recorded in this volume have been gathered from every part of the range. There are genuine cowmen who may disclaim ever having heard of certain ones. This can easily be true, just as throughout our country one section is unfamiliar with the colloquialisms of another. When the East-Sider ridicules the Southerner's *you-all*, he doesn't stop to think that his own *youse guys* is just as comical and ridiculous south of Mason and Dixon's line.

Different sections of the West also have their own peculiar argot. As Will James said, "A feller wrote a review of my books one time, without being asked, and he said something about my language not being true cowboy language. As I found out afterwards, that feller had been a cowboy all right enough, but I also found out that he'd only rode in one state all his life. He'd compared his language with mine and mine had been picked up and mixed from the different languages from the different parts of the whole cow country. The language of the cow country is just as different as the style of the rigs and ways of working."[4]

The Texan says *pitch*; the northern cowboy says *buck*; yet they mean the same thing. Likewise, the Texan's *stake rope* becomes *picket rope* on the northern range, and *cinch* in the North becomes *girth* when it hits the South. These are but a few examples of many that could be mentioned. California, Oregon, Utah, Nevada, and Idaho use terms rarely heard in the rest of the range country.

When Texas first went into the cattle business, it adopted the Mexican's methods and equipment—big-horned saddles, spade bit, rawhide rope, system of "dallying," and all the rest. The massacre at the Alamo stirred in Texans a fierce hatred of all things Mexican and brought changes in following the customs of the Spanish *vaquero*. The long rope and system of "dallying" disappeared, and Texas became a "tie-fast" country. The grazing bit was substituted for the spade and ring bits, and the Spanish rig gave way to the double-rigged saddle.

But the language of the Mexican had deeper roots. This the Texan kept and corrupted to suit his needs. The cattle business of California was also born under Spanish influence, but it had no Alamo, no Goliad.

4 Will James, *Lone Cowboy* (New York, Charles Scribner's Sons, 1930), 226.

Today it still uses the Spanish rig, the long rope, the spade bit, and the dally. Many other Spanish customs dominate, and the language has been less corrupted.

When the Texan rode over the long trails north, he carried his customs and his manner of working all the way to the Canadian line. Montana, Wyoming, and other northern and central states adopted much of his Spanish-influenced language. In exchange, the northern cowman gave the Texan that which he had appropriated from the northern Indian and the French-Canadian, words strange to the man from the Rio Grande.

Many cowmen, yearning to see what was "on the other side of the hill," or being forced to go where they "could throw a rope without gettin' it caught on a fence post," were like a tumbleweed drifting before a wind. They scattered their language until it no longer remained a "boggy crossin'" for a cowman from another section.

Yet, even today, there are some who have never been off their home range; and to them portions of this collection will seem strange. One old-timer told me that he had never heard the word *cowpuncher* until he was an old man. Of course, it is a comparatively recent word, having come into use with the moving of cattle by train and the closing of the trails. Now the majority prefer it to *cowboy*, for the word *cowboy* has more or less borne a stigma for many years. Yellow journalists, during the trail days, spread the cowboy's reputation for woolliness far and wide. He was pictured as a demon of death and disaster. Mothers even threatened their unruly offspring with the coming of this evil one.

And so almost every cowman chooses to be called *puncher, cowhand,* or just plain *hand*. But no matter by what name he is called, the working cowhand is called "plenty early in the mornin'."

Cowhands are neither so plentiful nor so picturesque as they were in the days of the open range, and with the passing of its customs, many of their terms are becoming obsolete. This volume has been prepared to help preserve this lingo for posterity. As long as we are a nation of meat-eaters, I am not afraid that the cowboy himself will become extinct, but some of his older language may die with the passing years. However, he will create new idioms typical of the range as long as he forks a horse. Furthermore, living in the tradition of men who rode semiwild horses to work obstinate, unruly cattle, he will never become so soft that he will *pack* a lunch, wear his sleeves rolled up, and say *my gracious* instead of *goddam* when he is mad.

Acknowledgments

"A pat on the back don't cure saddle galls"

In compiling this new edition, I wish to acknowledge help from various issues of *American Speech* and *Dialect Notes* magazines; H. L. Mencken's *American Speech*; *A Dictionary of Americanism*, edited by Mitford M. Mathews; Mark Twain's *Life on the Mississippi*; *Dictionary of Gambling*, by John S. Salak; *Sucker's Progress*, by Herbert Asbury; and *Pack Transportation*, by H. W. Daly. My thanks also go to such westerners as Dan Cushman, of Montana, and S. Omar Barker, of New Mexico.

RAMON F. ADAMS

In Appreciation
(First Edition)

"A full house divided don't win no pots"

Many years ago, my "roundup" of the lingo of the cowboy became so copious that I arrived at the decision to move some of it, grass finished though it was, to shipping pens, and thence to market. Riding herd over it had been a keen but solitary pleasure for nearly twenty years. It seemed to me, as it must to most cowmen, that a reasonably well filled-out herd is not for the keeping, but for the sharing. My *Cowboy Lingo*, published in 1936, was the result. Its reception was sufficiently gratifying to justify my previous course in pasturing the stuff out of sight for so long. Since its publication, many of its terms have been used in stories by writers of "westerns"; and western story magazines are reflecting current interest in the subject by conducting columns and departments on this jargon of the range, cow camp, and trail.

Letters from philologists, authors, and editors asking for more examples of this lusty speech have encouraged the preparation of *Western Words*. Yet the completed volume would not have been possible without the help of others, who contributed expressions, defined words, gave other definitions, dug up sources of phrases, and added colorful anecdotes.

First, I want to thank the host of sun-tanned, grin-wrinkled cowhands I have met upon the range and the old-timers with whom I have talked at cowmen's conventions throughout the West. They are too many to name. Besides, they are of the breed whose mention in a book would make them as uncomfortable as a camel in the Klondike. To them I can only say *muy gracias*. This volume is largely theirs, and I hope it will serve as a monument to their picturesque speech.

The authors I quote are not those "town-gaited" writers who have never been closer to a cow than a milk wagon. They have lived the life, and you may have confidence in their knowledge. I extend thanks to the following writers, each of whom I am proud to list as a personal friend: J. Frank Dobie, W. S. Campbell (Stanley Vestal), Edward

Everett Dale, J. Evetts Haley, Foster-Harris, William MacLeod Raine, Agnes Wright Spring, Jack Potter, John M. Hendrix, and the late George Saunders.

I am also grateful to these writers with whom I have corresponded and whose co-operation has been most helpful: Philip A. Rollins, Harold W. Bentley, the late Will James, Agnes Morley Cleaveland, Dick Halliday, W. M. French, Bruce Clinton, and "Don," who wishes to remain anonymous.

I am no less grateful to Eugene Cunningham, Ross Santee, E. W. Thistlewaite, the late Will C. Barnes, and all others whom I have quoted in citations.

I especially wish to thank *Cattleman* magazine and its former editor, Tad Moses; *Western Horseman* magazine and its former editor, Paul Albert; and all other publishers who so generously allowed me to quote from books in their lists.

Last, but by no means least, I wish to acknowledge a debt of grateful obligation to Elizabeth Ann McMurray, bookdealer and lover of all literature of the West, for her continued interest, faith, and encouragement. She has been unceasing in her efforts to spur my own energies to the riding of the "final horse." Thanks are extended, also, to E. DeGolyer for his sustained and stimulating interest. Without the urging of such good friends, this volume would have perhaps been hazed into the "cut backs" until the old man with the hay hook "come along."

Rounding up this bunch of strays, driving them to the home range, and cutting them into the proper herds has been a long, hard work. The brush has been thick, the coulees rough, and the quicksands boggy. Yet all my saddlesores are healed by the thought that this bob-tail may fill some hand long after I've "sacked my saddle." You can now ride the same trail at a high lope without rope or running iron, but you'll miss the fun I had in dragging these mavericks to the branding fire.

RAMON F. ADAMS

Dallas, Texas
September 15, 1944

THE
COWBOY
DICTIONARY

A

"A wink's as good as a nod to a blind mule"

abajador
In mining, the workman in charge of tools furnished to miners underground; from the Spanish, meaning *helper*.

Aberdeen Angus
A breed of black, hornless beef cattle originated in Scotland.

access road
In logging, a road built into isolated stands of commercial timber so that they can be reached by loggers, fire fighters, and others.

ACCIDENTS
See hung up, wedding, yoking.

ace-high
In poker, a hand with an ace but no pair or better.

ace in the hole
A shoulder holster; a man's ace in the hole might take various forms, such as the carrying of his gun in the waistband, in a bootleg, or in some other unexpected place. A hideout.

ace kicker
In draw poker, an ace held with a pair in a two-card draw.

acequia
An irrigation ditch; from the Spanish, meaning *trench* or *channel*.

aces up
In poker, a hand of two pairs including a pair of aces.

ación
Stirrup leather; from the Spanish; some-times used on the southern border and in California.

acorn calf
A runty calf; a weakling.

ACTION
See cut his wolf loose, first rattle out of the box, get down to cases, nimble-blooded, throw one's leg.

Ada from Decatur
In dice, eight as a point; also called *Ada Ross, the stable hoss.*

Ada Ross, the stable hoss
See *Ada from Decatur.*

added money
In rodeo, the purse put up by the rodeo committee. The total prize money in any rodeo event consists of the contestants' entry fee and the committee's purse. If an event is canceled for lack of entries, the purse for the canceled event is added to the prize money for other events.

adiós
Good-bye, So long, or *I'll see you later;* from the Spanish, meaning literally *to God;* commonly used in the border cattle country as an expression of friendly leave-taking.

adit
In mining, a nearly horizontal passage from the surface of a mine. Usually called a *tunnel,* though the latter, strictly speaking, passes entirely through a hill and is open at both ends.

adobe
A mud brick made from clay that adheres compactly when wet. After being mixed with water and straw, it is cast into wooden

molds about 18 by 6 by 10 inches in dimension. When taken from the molds, the bricks are placed in the hot sun and allowed to dry and bake. They are common building material in regions of Spanish influence. The word is also used in referring to a house built of adobe—usually shortened to *'dobe*. It is also used by the cowboy in referring to something of inferior quality. (Harold W. Bentley, *Dictionary of Spanish Terms in English* [New York, Columbia University Press, 1932], 87.) The Mexican silver dollar is sometimes spoken of as a *'dobe* because the cowman holds it to be of little value.

adobe furnace

In mining, a primitive furnace made of mud bricks, in which ore was smelted before the advent of modern machinery and of large-scale treatment of ore.

advance growth

In logging, young trees which have become established naturally in a forest before cutting or regenerating operations are begun.

advance workings

In mining, workings that are being advanced into the solid rock ahead and from which no pillars are being removed.

ADVANTAGE

See big casino, covering, deadwood, hold the high card.

advertising a leather shop

Said of a tenderfoot dressed up in exaggerated leather "trimmin's," such as boots, chaps, cowhide vest, leather cuffs, etc. Charlie Nelms pointed out to me one dressed in hairy chaps and vest with the remark that "from the hair he's wearin' you'd think it's cold 'nough to make a polar bear hunt cover, and here it's hot as hell with the blower on."

afoot

Said of a man without a horse in the cattle country. A man afoot on the range is looked upon with suspicion by most ranchers and is not welcome when he stops for food or shelter, unless he can prove that he belongs to the country and that his being afoot is the result of some misfortune. It has always been the custom of the range country to regard a man as "a man and a horse"—never one without the other. Even cattle have no fear of a man on foot, and he is in danger of being attacked by them. One of the old sayings of the West is, "A man afoot is no man at all." He cannot do a man's work without a horse and is useless in cow work. Teddy Blue Abbott used to say, "There's only two things the old-time puncher was afraid of, a decent woman and bein' left afoot."

agua ardiente

A variety of strong drink that originated at San Fernández de Taos; from the Spanish, meaning *burning water*. It was often referred to as *Taos lightnin'* or just *Touse*, by the early trappers. Another word for distilled spirits was *taffe*, which has been traced to the West Indies in the form of *tafia*, molasses rum.

aguardiente

Any one of various alcoholic drinks, especially a fiery, strong one; from the Spanish.

air hoist

In mining, a hoisting machine operated by compressed air.

air hole

In mining, a hole drilled in advance to improve ventilation by communication with other workings or with the surface.

airin' the lungs

What the cowboy calls "cussin'," which seems to be a natural part of his language; and he has a supply of words and phrases that any mule skinner "would be happy to get a copy of." As one cowman said, "The average cowhand ain't pickin' any grapes in the Lord's vineyard, but neither's he tryin' to bust any Commandments when he cusses. It jes' sets on his tongue as easy as a hoss-fly ridin' a mule's ear, and he can shore cram plenty o' grammar into it."

airin' the paunch

What the cowboy calls vomiting.

air shaft

A shaft used for ventilating a mine; it may either receive or discharge the circulating current.

air-tights

What the cowboy called canned goods. The open-range cowboy rarely saw any canned foods other. than corn, tomatoes, peaches, and milk.

à la Comanche

Hanging on the side of a horse as the Comanche Indian did in battle.

albino

A horse ranging in color from a pure white, with a blue, or "glass," eye, to a cream too light to be considered a palomino.

alcalde

In regions of Spanish influence, an administrative officer, such as a mayor, judge, or justice of the peace.

alcaldía

The territory in which an *alcalde (q.v.)* has jurisdiction; also, the office in which he conducts business.

alegría

Pigweed, an herb used as a cosmetic; from the Spanish. The leaves can be chewed or squeezed to produce a bright-red juice.

alfalfa desperado

A cowboy's name for a hay hand.

alfaloofee

A humorous name for alfalfa used by Wyoming cowhands.

alforja

From the Spanish, meaning *saddlebag* or *portmanteau*. Americanized, it is a wide leather or canvas bag, one of which hangs on each side of a packsaddle from the crosses on the top of the saddle. English modifications of the word are *alforge, alforche, alforki,* and *alforka.* (Philip A. Rollins, *The Cowboy* [New York, Charles Scribner's Sons, 1936], 155.)

ALIAS

See summer name, under a flag.

alkalied

Acclimated to the country; said of one who has lived in the country a long time, and also of one who drinks alkaline water. Most of the men considered old-timers had been living in the country so long that, in the language of the cowboy, "they knowed all the lizards by their first names, except the younger set."

all-around cow horse

A horse good at performing any duty, such as cutting, roping, etc.

All hands and the cook!

A phrase used in an emergency when every hand is called to guard the herd, when the cattle are unusually restless or there is imminent danger of a stampede.

all horns and rattles

Said of someone displaying a fit of temper. A man in this mood, as one cowboy said, "maybe don't say nothin', but it ain't safe to ask questions."

alligator

In logging, a boat provided with windlass and cable for hauling logs. A sled, often the fork of a tree, used in skidding logs. In mining, a rock breaker operated by jaws, used in early days.

All's set!

The call of the freighting teamster in answer to the wagon master's *Catch up!* signifying that the teamster is ready to pull out.

alluvium

In mining, the sediment of streams and floods.

amalgam

In mining, a compound of mercury or quicksilver with another metal; any metallic alloy of which mercury is an essential constituent. A native compound of mercury and silver found in fine crystals in mines in which veins of copper and silver cross each other.

amalgamate

In mining, to make an amalgam of, as one metal with another. Compounded with quicksilver; blended; coalesced.

amalgamation

In mining, a process based in the power of mercury to attract gold and hold it fast. The compounding of mercury with another metal; applied particularly to the

5

process of separating gold and silver from their ores by means of mercury.

amble

A cowboy's term meaning *to go*. To go leisurely, as, "I'm goin' to amble over to the north pasture."

ambulance

A passenger vehicle that somewhat resembles a hospital ambulance; a prairie wagon.

ambush

To attack someone, especially from a hidden position.

AMBUSH

See bushed, bushwhack, bushwhacker, dry-gulch, gunman's sidewalk, lay for.

amigo

Friend, good fellow, or companion; commonly used in the Southwest; from the Spanish.

amole

The root of a soap plant, or the soap obtained from it; from the Spanish.

among the willows

Dodging the law; on the dodge.

AMOUNT

See burro load, caboodle, peco, units of measure, whole shebang.

amygdaloid

A lava bed that contains almond-shaped cavities filled with mineral deposits.

anchor

A miner's pick.

anchor cattle

Cattle used on a roundup as the nucleus for another herd.

anchor man

In blackjack, the last player to play his card hand—the player sitting to the dealer's right.

andale

An expression commonly used by Spanish-speaking cowboys, meaning *hurry up, get a move on, get going*; from the Spanish *andar*, meaning *move, stand out of the way*, plus *le*, meaning *you (thou)*. Because it is easier on the vocal organs than longer English phrases, cowboys frequently yell this word at cattle being driven.

ANGER

See all horns and rattles, arching his back, cabin fever, dig up the tomahawk, easy on the trigger, fawche, frothy, get a rise from, get hard-nosed, get his back up, get his bristles up, horning the brush, horn-tossin' mood, on the peck, on the warpath, paint for war, red-eyed, riled, ringey, sharpen his horns, snorty, sod-pawin' mood, techy as a teased snake, wash off the war paint.

angoras

Chaps made of goat hide with the hair left on.

animal

A bull. The cowboy will use any word to avoid calling a spade a spade in the presence of ladies. In earlier times *bull* was a word unsuited for parlor use.

ANIMAL PARTS

See belly fleece, boss, buffalo cider, dewclaw, fiddle, frog, git-up end, mountain oyster, pastern.

ANIMALS

See badger, beaver, bed-slat ribs, beef, birds, blacktail, bologna bulls, buffaloes, buffalo wolf, bull head, bulls, calves, cat, cattalo, cattle, cattle breeds, cimarrón, colts, cows, donkeys, goat, hinny, hooter, horses, jack, javelina, jenny, ketch dog, lobo, medicine wolf, mountain lamb, mules, nutria, otie, oxen, pack rat, painter, prairie dog, prairie lawyer, prairie tenor, rooter, sheep eater, short-handled pup, skunks, snakes and lizards, stag, stand, timber wolf, wolf, woosher.

ankle express

The feet. To walk.

anquera

A round covering for the hindquarters of a horse; semilunar tailpiece of a saddle; from the Spanish. Americans use this term for the broad leather sewn to the base of the cantle when there is no rear jockey and extending beyond the cantle.

ante

In poker, a bet or contribution to the pot before a deal. To put up such a contribution.

antelope dance

An Indian ceremonial dance.

ANTICS

See cut a shine, cut his wolf loose.

anti-godlin

The cowboy's description of diagonal or roundabout movement.

anvil

Said when a traveling horse strikes his forefeet with his hind ones, especially if he is shod all around. See *forging*.

anxious seat

At frontier revival meetings, a seat near the front reserved for those who were concerned about their spiritual welfare. Also called *anxious bench*.

aparejo

A packsaddle consisting of a large leather pad about 28 inches wide by 36 inches long, stuffed to a thickness of 2 or 3 inches. Attached to it is a wide cinch and an exceptionally wide breeching that fits close under the animal's tail, like a crupper. Since it is not equipped with sawbucks like the ordinary packsaddle, kyacks cannot be used with it. It is especially designed for heavy, awkward loads that cannot be handled on ordinary packsaddles. Today it is becoming scarce, and consequently good aparejo men are rare. From the Spanish.

The aparejo is believed to be of Arabian origin, dating back to the earliest use of animals as beasts of burden.

aparejo cover

A canvas covering attached to the aparejo to protect the leather from wear and tear. Also called *sombre-jalma, q.v.*

aparejo hay

Hay used to stuff an aparejo saddle. The hay must have the life and spring of curled hair so that it will not pack together and can be added to old packing in the aparejo. It should be fine, soft, and elastic.

apex

In mining, the top of a vein of ore.

apishamore

A saddle blanket made of buffalo-calf skin; from the Indian.

appaloosa

A breed of horse whose distinguishing characteristics are the color spots on the rump, a lack of hair on the tail and inside the thigh, a good deal of white in the eye, and pink on the nose. This particular breed was developed by the Nez Percé Indians in the Palouse, or Pelouse, River country. There are several explanations of the origin of the word *appaloosa*. Some writers contend that the word comes from the Spanish noun *pelusa* (an unlikely origin since this feminine noun means *down which covers plants or fruits* and is certainly not applicable); others claim that the spelling is *Appaluchi* and, with vivid imagination, connect it with the Appalachian Mountains.

Yet it is easy to discover the origin of the word. In the early days no one had occasion to write the word, and as a spoken term the two words *à Pelousé* were corrupted into *appalousy*, which in turn became *appaloosa*. The spelling is merely an endeavor to follow the Nez Percé pronunciation and stress the final *e*. (F. D. Haines, "The Appaloosa, or Palouse Horse," *Western Horseman*, Vol. II, No. 1 [January–February, 1938], 30–31; Robert M. Denhardt, "Peculiar Spotted Ponies," *Cattleman*, Vol. XXVI, No. 6 [November, 1939], 19–23.)

appalos

A trapper's term for alternate cuts of fat and lean meat skewered on a sharpened stick and roasted.

APPEAR

See bulge, show up on the skyline.

apple

A saddle horn.

apple-horn

The name given the style of saddle used in the eighties. It was so named from the small horn whose top was round like an apple, compared to the broad, flat horns of the saddles it replaced.

apron-faced horse

A horse with a large white streak on the forehead.

Arbuckle

In ranching, a green hand. So called on the assumption that the boss sent off Arbuckle coffee premium stamps to pay for the hand's "extraordinary" services.

Arbuckle's

The brand of coffee so common on the range that most cowmen never knew there was any other kind. Coffee is the first thing on the fire at the cook's call, "Roll out!" long before day; and throughout the day and night, if camp is not to be moved, the pot nests on hot coals so that the hands can have a cup of coffee at the change of guard. Nothing else the cook can do will make the cowboy hold him in such high esteem as keeping the coffee hot and handy.

The old-time wagon cook loved to tell the tenderfoot his favorite recipe for making cowboy coffee. With the greatest secrecy he would say, "Take two pounds of Arbuckle's, put in 'nough water to wet it down, boil for two hours, and then throw in a hoss shoe. If the hoss shoe sinks, she ain't ready." The cowman likes his coffee to "kick up in the middle and pack double."

arch

In logging, a piece of equipment used to hold up one end of the logs. A sled, often the fork of a tree, used in skidding logs.

arching his back

Said of an angry person or of a horse preparing to buck.

arch irons

The irons connecting the saddle boards at both front and rear.

arena director

The person responsible for seeing that a rodeo goes off smoothly and according to the rules. He supervises all jobs and details in and connected with the rodeo arena itself, such as loading the chutes, keeping the arena clear, etc. He may be hired by the rodeo committee, the producer, or the stock contractor. Frequently the stock contractor or producer works as the arena director.

Are you ready?

In mining, the question asked by the wagon driver of the miners to determine whether the mine wagons are full and ready to be hauled away and replaced by empties.

argentiferous

Silver-bearing; containing silver; said of ore.

Argonaut

A person who went to California to hunt gold during the gold rush of 1848–49. From the Greek legend, one of the men who sailed with Jason in the *Argo* in quest of the golden fleece.

Arizona nightingale

A prospector's burro. So called because of its extraordinary bray.

Arizona tenor

A coughing tubercular.

Arizona trigger

A cattle trap consisting of a kind of chute leading into a watering place, which is left wide open at first so that the cattle will get used to going into it. Then, when the cattle are to be caught, the chute is narrowed at the inside so that the cattle can get in but cannot get out.

Arkansas toothpick

A large sheath knife; a dagger.

Arkie

In logging, a worker from Arkansas, also, a term of disparagement.

ARMED

See heeled.

armed to the teeth

Fully armed.

armitas

Well-cut aprons, usually made of home-tanned or Indian buckskin and tied around the waist and knees with thongs; from the Spanish *armar*, meaning *to arm* or *to equip*. Armitas protect the legs and clothes and are cooler to wear in summer than chaps. Their use practically ceased with the passing of old-time range customs, although they are still used to some extent, especially in southern California. Also called *chigaderos* and *chinkaderos* (Dick Halliday to R. F. A.)

arrastrar

In mining, a rude machine formerly used for ore crushing; from the Spanish, meaning *to drag*. See *arrastre*.

arrastre

The English form of *arrastrar*. In mining, a crude contrivance, consisting essentially of a heavy stone dragged around on a circular stone bed, used for pulverizing gold or silver ore. It was an early Mexican device and was usually pulled by mules. Quicksilver was often added to the ore in the arrastre to help recover gold or silver. The ore was kept wet while being crushed.

arreador

In mining, a mule driver on a hoisting whim; from the Spanish.

arriero

A muleteer or packer; a man who packs loads on mules; from the Spanish.

ARRIVE

See blow in, blow in with the tumbleweeds.

ARROWS

See dogwood switch.

arroyo

A creek; from the Spanish, meaning *rivulet*. The word is used almost exclusively in the Southwest, where a small stream can cut a deep channel in the soft earth; the word has come to mean a narrow gorge with precipitous dirt walls.

arroyo seco

A dry *arroyo*, q.v.

artillery

Pistols; personal weapons. I heard one cowhand say of a heavily armed man, "He's packin' so much artillery it makes his hoss swaybacked."

as full of arrows as a porcupine

Said of one who received many arrows in his body during an Indian fight or ambush.

ASHORE

See up the hill.

ash well

In river steamboating, a pipe, usually about 6 or 8 inches in diameter, leading from the ashpan at the base of a steamboat furnace down through the interior of the hull and out through the bottom. Live coals and ashes are sloshed down this pipe into the river. Also called *ash chute*.

assay

To test samples of ores or minerals to determine the proportion or value of precious metal. Hence, by extension, the substance to be assayed or the act of assaying. Tests may involve chemical or blowpipe examination or smelting. For gold and silver an additional process, called *cupeling*, is required to separate them from the base metals.

assay balance

A sensitive balance used in assaying gold and silver.

assayer

An expert in analyzing ore for its mineral content; one who performs assays.

assay master

The chief or official assayer.

assay value

In mining the amount of gold and silver, in ounces per ton of ore, as shown by assay of any given sample.

assessment work

In mining, the annual labor required to hold a claim; the work necessary to maintain title to an unpatented mining claim in the public domain.

asshole

In logging, a kink in the logging cable.

assistant pit boss

In mining, the assistant to the mine foreman. Each assistant has a section of the mine to look after; also called *pennydog*, because he gets all the blame when anything goes wrong.

assistant wagon boss

In freighting, the second in command. He rides at the end of the train, while the wagon boss rides at the head.

Association saddle

The saddle adopted by rodeo associations in 1920. Its use is now compulsory at all large contests. Built on a modified Ellenburg tree, medium in height, with a 14-inch swell and a 5-inch cantle, it has nothing about it to which the rider can anchor himself. As the cowboy says, "It gives the hoss all the best of it." The original Association saddle was made with small, round skirts, three-quarter-rigged, with a flank rig set farther back than on a regular-rigged saddle. It was full-basket-stamped and had stirrup leathers made to buckle for quick and easy adjustment. Also called *Committee saddle* and *contest saddle*.

atajo

See *hatajo*.

atol

A kind of corn meal, or gruel or porridge made of corn meal; from the Spanish.

attle

In mining, waste rock.

augur

A cowboy's term for the boss. A big talker. To talk.

augurin' match

A talking contest such as held nowhere else except in the early West. In the language of the cowman, an augurin' match was "jes' a case of two loose-tongued humans a-settin' cross-legged, knee to knee and face to face, talkin' as fast as they can to see which one can keep it up the longest without runnin' out of words and wind. There's jes' a constant flow of words that don't make no sense a-tall, both of 'em talkin' at the same time and each one's got so much to say that it gets in his way. At the start they talk fast and furious, but after an hour or so they slow down to a trot to be savin' of both words and wind. By the time it's over, neither one of 'em's got 'nough vocal power left to bend a smoke ring."

auriferous

Gold-bearing; containing gold; said of ore.

aux aliments du pays

In trapping, to live off the land; from the French, meaning *nourishment of the land*. Employees of fur companies were sometimes required to subsist *aux aliments du pays*—that is, with such food as the country provided.

avant-courier

A runner or scout used by fur trappers; from the French.

average

In rodeo, the average points or times in all go-rounds of an event. Contestants in rodeos with more than one go-round are paid off in prize money for the best ride or time in each go-round and for the best average of all the go-rounds. The winner of the average is the winner of the event.

awerdenty

In trapping, an early name for whisky. Undoubtedly a corruption of *aguardiente*, *q.v.*

axle grease

A cowboy's term for butter.

azotea

A flat roof; from the Spanish.

azurite

In mining, a beautiful blue carbonate of copper.

B

"Brains in the head saves blisters on the feet"

baa-a-ah

A cowboy's contemptuous name for sheep. If you want to start a fight, just blat this at a cowboy.

baby beef

Young cattle killed for market.

BACHELORS

See lone ranger, sourdough.

back

In mining, the roof of a drift, stope, or other working.

back-and-belly

In steamboating, the method by which two men can most conveniently carry a large box of freight when loading a boat; the man in front backed up to it, and the man behind stood right up against it.

backbreakers

In logging, tree stumps.

backfire

A fire set counter to an advancing fire; used in fighting prairie or forest fires. The fire is controlled on the advancing side and driven toward the oncoming blaze until the two meet and burn themselves out.

back in

In poker, to come into the betting after *checking, q.v.*

back jockey

The top skirt of a saddle; the uppermost broad leathers joining behind the cantle.

back to back

In stud poker, said of the hole card and the first upcard when they are a pair.

back trail

A trail just traversed. To go back over a trail.

badger

A carnivorous mammal living in a burrow, nocturnal in habits, and feeding upon vegetables and small quadrupeds. To ridicule; to tease.

bad Indian

An Indian who continually stirred up trouble against the whites.

badlander

An inhabitant of the *badlands, q.v.*

badlands

A section of country with little vegetation, composed principally of buttes, peaks, and badly eroded soil. A cowboy's name for a red-light district.

bad medicine

Bad news. A man considered dangerous. Some bad men, said one cowboy, "were so tough they'd growed horns and was haired over." Tom Kirk spoke of one as being "a wolf, and he ain't togged out in no sheep's wool either."

BAD MEN

See bad medicine, bandido, bugheway, cabrón, cat-eyed, curly wolf, Daniel Boones, gunmen, high-line rider, holdup man, killer, long rider, outlaw, road agent, short-trigger man, snake, wanted, wool in his teeth.

bag pannier

A flat, oblong bag of canvas or leather with a long flap, lashed to the packsaddle and used to carry camp equipment.

BAGS

See sacks, traveling bags.

baile

In the Southwest, a dance, especially one conducted under Mexican or mixed auspices. From the Spanish.

bait

Food; a meal.

bait can

A logger's term for his lunch pail.

baja

A descent, usually severe, as at Raton Pass.

bake

To ride in such a way as to overheat a horse.

baldface

A cowboy's word for a stiff-bosomed shirt, sometimes called *boiled*. A horse with the white on its head, including one or both eyes. Sometimes white-faced cattle are called *baldfaced*.

baldface dishes

A cowboy's term for china dishes. He is used to eating out of granite or tin plates or bowls.

baldy
A treeless mountaintop.

BALKING
See bulling, bull-windy.

ball hooter
In logging, a person who rolls logs down a hillside.

ball hooting
Rolling logs free down an incline.

ballin' the jack
A logger's expression meaning *going fast*.

balloon
A logger's name for his pack or bedroll.

baloney
A large wire rope used in logging.

band
A group of horses. The word is used in referring to horses only; cattle or livestock are spoken of as a *herd* or *bunch* of cattle or as a *bunch* of livestock.

bandido
A bandit; an outlaw. Used near the Mexican border to refer to a Mexican outlaw. *Bandit* is the more common word for an American outlaw.

band wagon
A range-peddler's wagon, usually loaded with clothing, cinches, stirrup leathers, and other cowboy supplies.

bang juice
A miner's term for nitroglycerin. A logger's term for dynamite.

bangtail
A mustang or wild horse. Later used in the East in speaking of race horses, as, "playing the bangtails."

banjo
A miner's name for his short-handled shovel.

bank
In logging, to pile logs along a railroad track. In mining, the surface of the mouth of a mine pit.

banking ground
A log landing.

banksman
In mining, the man at the shaft mouth who handled the bucket.

baquero
See *buckaroo*.

barbed brand
A cattle brand with a short projection from any part.

barbed wire
Wire with barbs, commonly used to fence the range.

barber
A name sometimes given to a sheep-shearer.

barber chair
In logging, a stump on which is left standing a slab that splintered off the tree as it fell. It generally indicates careless felling. Also, a *goose-pen tree*, a tree in danger of collapsing because of a hole burned in the center.

bar bit
A horse's mouthpiece, a straight or slightly curved round bar with a ring at each end for attaching the rein and headstall.

barboquejo
A halter for the back part of the under-jaw of a horse; from the Spanish, meaning *chin strap*. Also, a chin strap for a cowboy's hat (see *bonnet strings*). The term is used almost exclusively near the Mexican border.

barbs
An earmark with sharp V-shaped angles on the ends of splits and slashes.

bar diggings
Gold washing on river bars. Bars are worked when the water is low or with the aid of cofferdams.

bar dog
A cowboy's term for a bartender. Many bartenders were former cowboys too stove-up for riding. A bar-dog's favorite occupation, as one cowhand said, was "yawnin' on

the glasses to give 'em a polish." When he reached for your bottle and hammered the cork home with the heel of his hand, he was telling you more plainly than words that your credit had run out.

bareback riding

One of the five standard rodeo events. The rider has no saddle, stirrups, bridle, or rein; instead, a simple leather *bareback rigging (q.v.)* with a leather handhold is cinched around the horse.

bareback rigging

In rodeo, a piece of leather shaped roughly like a shallow triangle with two points trimmed off. It is approximately 18 inches long on the back side and cannot exceed 11 inches in width at the place where the handhold leather is, approximately in the center. The rigging is cinched on the horse. It is usually owned by the contestant.

barefoot

Said of an unshod horse.

barge

A river boat built somewhat after the style of a ship's longboat and closely resembling a keelboat. It was from 30 to 70 feet long and 7 to 12 feet wide and had a mast, sails, and rudder. Its downstream progress was accelerated either by the wind or by four of the crew, who wielded long oars; the motive power for upriver movement was supplied by a number of men using iron-tipped poles.

Barge passengers were accommodated in covered enclosures, sometimes in the shape of a houseboat built in the center of the boat, supported by timbers at the four corners and covered with a gable roof.

bark

An old trapper's word meaning *to scalp.*

barker

In logging, a machine used to peel bark from trees.

barkin' at a knot

A cowman's expression for trying to accomplish the impossible. One cowman might express the same thought with, "like tryin' to scratch your ear with your elbow,"

or with, "like huntin' for a whisper in a big wind."

bark mark

In logging, a mark on the bark of a log by which the owner identifies his timber. This mark is used in addition to a stamp brand on the end of the log. When the stream or pond is crowded, a bark mark is easier to see.

barney

In mining, a small car or truck attached to a rope and used to push cars up a slope or incline. Also called *bullfrog, donkey, ground hog, Larry, mule, ram,* and other names.

barranca

A ravine; a deep break or hole made by a heavy rain; from the Spanish.

barricade

In river boating, a platform, built between the main deck and the boiler deck of a packet, upon which light articles of freight were stowed.

barrier

In a rodeo arena, a rope stretched across the front end of the box from which the roper's or steer wrestler's horse comes when the barrier flagman drops the flag. According to the arena conditions, the stock is given a predetermined head start, or score, marked by a score line. After the stock is far enough out of the chute or has passed the score line, the barrier flagman lowers his flag, signaling the start of time, and simultaneously pulls a rope that releases the barrier.

barrow pit

A ditch alongside a road.

bar shoe

A horseshoe with a metal piece welded across the heel.

BARTENDERS

See bar dog.

base burner

A cowboy's term for a drink of whisky.

basket hitch

A packer's knot made by passing sling

ropes across the bottom of the pannier and around the rear cross of the packsaddle and then bringing the loose end up under the pannier and tying it down.

Basque barbecue

A lamb barbecue; so called because a large percentage of southwestern sheepmen are of Basque ancestry.

bastard quartz

Valueless quartz with no accessory minerals.

basto

The skirt of a saddle; from the Spanish, meaning *saddle pad*. The word is a technical term restricted to the saddle industry and to horsemen.

bastonero

A word used by early traders for a master of ceremonies; from the Spanish, meaning *cane maker* or *cotillion leader*.

batch

An unmarried man, short for *bachelor*. To live alone; to cook one's own food.

BATHING

See washing his profile, washing out the canyon.

bathin' his countenance

A cowboy's term for washing his face.

bateau

A flat-bottomed boat; from the French. It was clumsily constructed in the shape of a huge box, with the square ends given enough rake to prevent impeding headway. It measured from 50 to 75 feet in length. Principally a downstream craft, when moved upstream it was propelled by pole, oar, or sail or was pulled by rope from the shore.

bat-wings

Chaps made of heavy bullhide with wide, flapping wings. They have become the most popular chaps on the range because they snap on. Every cowboy lives with a pair of spurs on his heels, and when wearing bat-wings, he does not have to pull his spurs off to shed his chaps, as he does with *shotgun chaps (q.v.)*. These chaps are commonly decorated with nickel or silver conchas down each leg. Also called *buzzard-wings*.

bay

A horse of light-red color, always having a black mane and tail.

bayo coyote

In the Southwest, a dun horse with a black stripe down its back.

Bayou Salade

A trapper's term for *salt marsh*—what is now South Park, the tableland of central Colorado; so called because of the salt rock found in the region.

bean eater

A cowboy's term for a Mexican.

bean master

A cowboy's term for the cook.

bearded

Said of cattle having abscessed sores in the mouth, caused by cheat-grass beards, grain beards, etc. The ailment quite often requires surgery. The term is used in eastern Washington.

B.B.'s

The lumberjack's abbreviation for *bridge builders*.

bear fighter

In lumbering, the man who separates strips from boards in a sawmill. See *fighting the bear*.

bear sign

The cowboy's term for doughnuts. The logger's term for berry jam.

bear trap

A cowboy's term for a certain style of saddle. A severe bit. In river boating, a section of movable dam about 100 feet wide with concrete piers on either side and a gate that can be lowered or raised by compressed air. When the pool level maintained at the dam becomes a little too high, the bear trap is lowered and the excess water is allowed to run off; then it is raised again.

beast with a bellyful of bedsprings

A good bucking horse. Sometimes a poor

rider would let someone else *top off (q.v.)* his horse "to see that there ain't no bed-springs loose."

beat the board

In stud poker, to have a higher combination than the exposed cards of any other player.

beaver

A fur trapper's name not only for the animal he trapped but also for money.

beavering down

Trapping for beavers.

bed

In mining, a horizontal seam or deposit of ore.

bedded

In the cowman's language, said of a roped animal that has been thrown full length with such force as to cause it to lie still.

bedding

In logging, a bed into which large trees are felled to prevent breakage, made by leveling the ground surface through excavating or filling in or both.

BEDDING CATTLE

See bedding down, bed ground, father the herd, herd ground, riding 'em down.

bedding down

The forming of a herd of cattle for their night's rest—a scientific job requiring that the herd not be crowded too closely nor be allowed to scatter over too much territory. As the sun began to sink in the west, the men in charge of a trail herd would carefully and gradually work the cattle into a more compact space and urge them toward open, level ground selected for the bed ground. If the herd had been well grazed and watered during the day, they would stop, and gradually a few would lie down to their contented cud chewing. The cowboys would stay patiently with the cattle until relieved by the men of the first guard.

bedding out

Sleeping in the open; an expression often used in connection with the roundup season, when the cowboy does all his sleeping outdoors.

bed ground

The place where cattle are held at night; also called *herd ground*. It is the duty of the day herders to have the cattle on the bed ground and bedded down before dusk. The bed ground is chosen in an open space when possible, away from ravines or timber, in ordering to avoid anything that might frighten the cattle.

bed him down

A cowboy's expression meaning *to kill a man*. Also, to put a drunk to bed.

bedrock

The solid rock underlying *auriferous (q.v.)* gravel, sand, clay, etc., and upon which the alluvial gold rests.

bedrock 'im

An expression used in the mountain-range country to mean *ride a horse down* or *break his heart*.

bedroll

The cowboy's bedding and other equipment rolled up for carrying. It consists of a tarpaulin 7 by 18 feet, made of No. 8 white ducking, weighing 18 ounces a square yard, and thoroughly waterproofed. It is equipped with rings and snaps so that the sleeper can pull the flap over him and fasten it. In the bed proper will be, perhaps, two heavy quilts, or *soogans*, a couple of blankets, and a war bag, which the cowboy uses for a headrest. In such a bed placed on well-drained ground, he can sleep as dry as inside a house, even in a heavy rain. (John M. Hendrix, "The Bed-roll," *Cattleman*, Vol. XX, No. 4 [September, 1934], 10.)

Next to his horse and saddle, his bedroll is the cowboy's most valued possession. It serves as his safe-deposit box, and it is not healthy to be caught prowling through another man's bedroll.

Such a bed is warm in winter. The tarp keeps out snow, sleet, and wind; even when it is covered with snow and ice, the extra weight helps keep the sleeper warm. In the morning when he awakens, he dresses *à la* Pullman before quitting the blankets.

For a cowhand to leave his bed unrolled and not packed for loading into the wagon when camp is to be moved is a very serious breach of etiquette. The cook will be sure to call him names that would "peel the hide off a Gila monster." If the careless puncher commits this offense more than once, the cook is certain to drive off and leave his bed behind.

BEDS AND BEDDING

See balloon, bedroll, bed wagon, bindle, bunk, cama, carry the balloon, cootie cage, crumb incubator, crumb roll, donkey's breakfast, dream sack, fleabag, flea trap, flop, gear, goose hair, hen skin, hippin's, hot roll, lay, Missouri feather bed, Mormon blanket, mule's breakfast, muzzleloader, parker, prairie feathers, rildy, shakedown, skunk boat, spool your bed, star-pitch, sugan, tarp, three-point, Tucson bed, turkey, velvet couch.

bed-slat ribs

Said of an animal in poor condition. A cowhand in New Mexico told me of a drought when "them bed slats got so pore their shadows developed holes in 'em."

bed wagon

A wagon used to carry bedding, branding irons, war bags, hobbles, and corral ropes. It generally contained all that the cowboy truly valued, and was also used as a hospital to carry the injured or sick until they could be taken to town or to headquarters. Only the larger outfits provided a bed wagon, the smaller ones piling their beds into the chuck wagon.

beef

Any cow or steer over four years old. To kill an animal for food. To bellyache. To knock a man down.

BEEF

See baby beef, beef, beef cut, beefing, beef roundup, big antelope, jerky, slow elk, wohaw.

beef book

A tally book in which the records of the ranch are kept. See *tally sheet*.

beef cut

Roundup parlance for cattle cut out of a herd for shipment to market. See also *cut*.

beef head

A Texan.

beefing

Slaughtering. Bellyaching.

beef issue

The issue of beef for reservation Indians at a government agency.

beef plumb to the hocks

Said of a fat or heavy person.

beef roundup

Roundup of cattle for shipment to market, occurring in the fall of the year. Also called *fall roundup*.

beefsteak

To ride so that a horse's back becomes galled and sore.

beef tea

The old-time cowman's term for shallow water in which cattle have stood—usually green, stagnant, and full of cow urine.

beeline

A trader's word for a straight line, as, "He made a beeline for camp."

BEHAVIOR

See wagon manners.

behind the six

In faro, the money drawer, often located behind the six card on the faro layout; also, broke or short of funds, since one's money has gone into the drawer.

bell

In packing, ordinarily a sheep bell attached by a strap to the neck of a horse leading a pack train of mules; also, the packer's name for a horse wearing such a bell; alluded to in such expressions as *get the bell, lead the bell, stop the bell*, and *call the bell*. In sheepherding, a bell used as a marker. There are usually ten or more black sheep in every thousand and about the same number of belled sheep. No considerable number of sheep could stray without taking some markers along; if all markers are present, the herder can be reasonably sure that no sheep have strayed.

bell cord

In steamboating, a sash cord rigged in the pilothouse near the pilot wheel and connected by wire to a signal bell in the engine room. Sometimes bell cords are braided and adorned in a fancy manner and, when suspended from overhead, terminate in brass rings called *bell pulls, q.v.* Also, the rope connecting the tapper of the roof bell to a convenient location on the forecastle or to the side of the hurricane deck.

belled snake

A rattlesnake.

bell horse

See *bell.*

bell man

In logging, the man in charge of the high line. The operations of the crews of the skidder machines are guided by a bell system on a separate signal line, and it is the bell man who operates this system. He is never approached or talked to when on duty because the workers' lives depend upon his delivering the right signal.

bell mare

A mare with a bell around her neck, used in some sections of the cattle country to keep the saddle horses together. Some cowmen contend that the bells warn them if the horses become frightened in the night and leave in a hurry. But most cowmen object to a bell in the remuda because it sounds too many false alarms and awakens a sleeping outfit needlessly.

bell on his tail

The cowmen's term for the rattles on a rattlesnake's tail.

bell pulls

In steamboating, two varieties of pulls: a brass ring attached to the end of a bell cord suspended from overhead in the pilothouse, and a brass handle attached to the end of a bell cord on the *bell stand, q.v.* The pilot uses either pull to ring signal bells to the engineer in the engine room.

bell sharp

Said of a mule that becomes especially attached to the *bell horse, q.v.*

bell stand

In steamboating, an upright post in the pilothouse just aft of the pilot wheel on which are rigged the bell pulls for signal bells in the engine room.

bellwether

A belled sheep that leads the flock and is also a marker. See *bell.*

belly bunches

A puffing of the skin on the belly of a pack mule. This condition indicates that too much padding has been used in the boots of the aparejo and from the boots to the "hand hole." Too much hay causes the boots of the aparejo to flare out from the body of the mule and prevents proper shaping or bending of the aparejo to the conformation of the mule's body. The result is that in cinching the aparejo to the animal too much pressure is placed on the belly, the circulation is slowed, and on removal of the cinch the skin puffs up. Also called *body bunches* and *bunches.*

belly buster

A Texan's term for the long stick or pole that serves as a latch for wire gates. If you have ever tried to open one of these gates and let the pole slip from your hand, you will know that it is well named.

belly cheater

A cowman's name for the cook. Many cooks were merely cooks and not cowhands. One cowhand informed me that the cook with his outfit "didn't savvy *cow* unless it was dished up in a stew."

belly fleece

The thin layer of flesh on the belly of an animal.

belly gun

A gun carried in the waistband of the pants instead of in a holster. The gun is naked and is drawn with a single motion similar to the regulation cross draw. See *border draw.*

belly robber

A logger's name for the camp cook.

belly rope

A roper's loop that is too large and slips

over the shoulders of the roped animal and tightens around its belly. This act is always funny to everyone except the man doing the roping.

belly through the brush

A cowboy's expression meaning to hide and dodge the law.

belly up

Said of something dead. To drink at a bar. Old Cap Mulhall had nothing but contempt for the younger punchers when they "raised hell" in town after a few drinks. I have often heard him utter the philosophy, "It don't take backbone to belly up to a bar."

belly-wash

What the cowboy calls weak coffee. What the logger calls a soft drink.

bench

A plain rising above a lowland.

bench brand

A brand resting upon a horizontal bracket with its feet downward like a bench.

bend

In cattle driving, to turn a stampede or the general movement of animals; used in some sections of the Northwest. In gambling, to fold a card slightly to facilitate various cheating tricks.

bender

A drinking frolic; a big drunk.

bendin' an elbow

Drinking whisky. One old rancher, who had no patience with a drinking man, used to hold to the philosophy that "a corkscrew never pulled no one out of a hole."

bends

A miner's disease caused by too swift a decrease in air pressure after a prolonged stay deep in a mine; *caisson disease, q.v.*

bent

A measure of bulk hay; a pile as long, as wide, and as high as can be stacked by a derrick on a single setting.

BEST

See nickel-plated, top, worthiness.

better count ribs than tracks

A trapper's maxim, meaning that when one was moving from place to place and was unable to carry hay for the horses it was necessary for them to find forage along the way.

BETTING

See gambling.

bet the limit

In gambling, to wager the maximum amount permitted by the bookmaker or by the game or house rules.

bet the top

To make a bet of the same number of chips or amount of money as the pot holds at the time.

between a rock and a hard place

Bankrupt; in a tight.

between hay and grass

The time between winter and spring, when hay has gone and grass has not yet come up. Difficult times. Also, *between grass and hay*, between summer and winter. Between boyhood and manhood.

Bible

A cowboy's name for his book of cigarette papers.

Bible "Two"

The Texas Rangers' fugitive list, published annually; read by them more often than the real Bible; also called *black book.*

bicycle

In logging, a pulley device used in a two-spar tight-line high lead. Also, a steel piece to which logs are fastened and drawn to the railroad.

bicycling

Riding a bucking horse by scratching with first one foot and then the other in the manner of riding a bicycle.

biddy

A sheepman's name for an old ewe.

biddy bridle

An old-fashioned bridle with blinders.

big antelope

An animal belonging to someone else and killed for food. It was the custom in the old days for a ranchman never to kill his own cattle for food, and many an old-timer was accused of never knowing how his own beef tasted. One ranchwoman was heard to say, "I would just as soon eat one of my own children as one of my yearlings."

big augur

A cowboy's name for the big boss.

big blue

In logging, a large butt log, particularly one with a taper. See *butt*.

big boss

In mining, one high in authority, usually of higher rank than the superintendent; for example, one who owned large shares in the mine.

big bull

In logging, a camp foreman or general superintendent; especially used by the loggers of the Northwest.

big casino

Any idea or physical asset that is expected to bring success. (Philip A. Rollins, *The Cowboy* [New York, Charles Scribner's Sons, 1936], 80.)

big cat

In poker, a hand with a king high, an eight low, and no pair; also called *big tiger*.

big dick

In dice, ten as a point; to throw a ten.

big digger

In poker, the ace of spades.

big dog

In poker, a hand with an ace-high, a nine low, and no pair.

big fifty

The .50-caliber Sharps rifle used by buffalo hunters.

bighead

Osteoporosis, a bone disease of horses and cattle, caused by eating poisonous plants and resulting in an enlargement of the head.

big hole

A logger's term for the lowest gear of a logging truck.

big house

The cowboy's name for the home of the ranch owner.

big jaw

Actinomycosis, a disease of cattle; also called *lump* or *lumpy jaw*.

big Joe from Boston

In dice, ten as a point.

big jump

A cowman's reference to death. When a person died, he was said to have taken the *big jump*, and a good many cowmen were "weighted down with their boots."

big loop

A cattle thief's rope. When a man is suspected of stealing cattle, it is said that he "throws a big loop."

Big Muddy

The Missouri River, so called because of its muddy water.

big natural

In dice, a throw of eleven.

big pasture

What the cowboy sometimes calls the penitentiary.

big pay

In mining, comparatively large salary.

big-pond boom

Logs or timbers fastened together end to end and used to hold floating logs.

big savage

A logger's name for the general superintendent.

big sticks

A logger's name for the woods.

big sugar

A cowboy's name for the owner of the ranch.

big swimmin'

A high river.

big talk

A freighter's name for a conference.

big tiger

In poker, a hand in which the king is the highest card, the eight is the lowest, and there is no pair. Also called *big cat.*

big 'uns

What the logger calls extra-large trees.

big-wheel rigs

In logging, the huge carts that carried logs suspended beneath their 15-foot-high wheels.

bigwig

A logger's name for foreman or boss.

billet

A wide leather strap looped through the tree on the off side of a saddle. Holes are punched in the strap to accommodate the tongue of the cinch buckle.

bill of lading

In steamboating, a printed form used in connection with a shipment of freight, usually listing the shipper, the consignee, addresses, date and place of origin, description of the shipment, the weight of each article, and other pertinent data for the rate clerk, the shipping clerks, and others concerned.

Bill-show

A wild West show, such as Buffalo Bill's or Pawnee Bill's.

Bill-show cowboy

A show-off cowboy of the Buffalo Bill–show type.

binder

In logging, a piece of chain or cable bound around a load of logs or lumber on a truck.

bindle

A logger's blanket roll. *Gear* is now a more popular term.

bindle stiff

A logger who carries his blankets with him.

bird cage

The frayed or ragged strands of wire rope, or a rope that resembles a cage. In gambling, the name used in some regions for *chuck-a-luck (q.v.)* because of the metal cage used in the game, which is shaped like an hourglass and turns on an axle.

bird's eye

In logging, a small, localized area in the lumber where the fibers are indented and otherwise contorted to form circular figures; not considered a defect if the wood is sound.

Birds

See blue-jay camp meeting, camp robber, chaparral bird, hooter, magpie, paisano, road runner, whisky jack.

birling

Log rolling; the traditional game of the *river driver, q.v.*

biscuit

The saddle horn.

biscuit roller

The ranch cook.

biscuit shooter

The ranch cook. A waitress in a restaurant.

bit

A metal bar that fits into the horse's mouth. There are many kinds of bits, some of them extremely cruel when misused. Yet it is rare that a cowboy uses a bit for cruelty. His idea of a bit is that it is merely to hang in the horse's mouth. When turning to the right, for example, he does not pull the right rein; he merely moves his bridle hand a couple of inches to the right, bringing the left rein against the horse's neck. It is merely a signal. The well-trained horse turns himself; he does not have to be pulled around. Many cowboys do not use bits but ride with a hackamore instead.

bitch

A tin cup filled with bacon grease and, with a twisted rag wick, used in place of a lamp or candle. A cowhide stretched under a wagon from axle to axle for carrying wood or other fuel. See *cuna.*

bitch chain

In logging, a short chain used to fasten the lower end of a gin pole to the car or sled when loading logs.

bitches

In mining, a set of chairs used to support pipes in a mine shaft.

bite-'em lip

Said of a rodeo bulldogger when he leans over and fastens his teeth in the upper lip of the bulldogged steer. This stunt was originated by Bill Pickett, a famous Negro bulldogger.

bite the dust

To be thrown from a horse. When Hawk Nance once got thrown, he got up, gingerly tested his bones, and then remarked with a grin, "I reckon I didn't break nothin', but all the hinges and bolts are shore loosened." Also to be killed. The expression originated in the Indian days; when an Indian was shot from his horse during a battle, it was said that "another redskin had bit the dust."

bite the ground

To be killed.

bit ring

The metal ring to which a horse's reins are fastened.

bits

An earmark for cattle, formed by removing small sections from the ear to produce a simple design.

Bits

See bar bit, bear trap, bit, bit ring, bridles, broken bit, chain bit, Chileno, cricket, curb bit, curb strap, freno, grazing bit, halfbreed bit, Kelly's, port, riding equipment, ring bit, snaffle bit, spade bit, Spanish bit, stomach pump, straight bit, tasters, tool chest, war bridle.

bittin' ring

Fastening the rein of the bridle to the belly strap to make the horse bridle-wise before the rider mounts. When the rein is fastened, the horse will gallop in a circle with little danger of crashing through a fence.

bitts

In steamboating, sturdy wooden posts on the forecastle of a boat used to attach mooring lines. The term is used in the plural because the posts are invariably used in pairs. They are set upright, securely braced in the stem, and extend above the forecastle to a height of 3 feet. They are spaced about 2 or 3 feet apart and are connected by a horizontal crosspiece securely bolted to each pole.

blab

A thin board, 6 by 8 inches in size, clipped on a calf's nose at the center of one of the long sides. This device is used for weaning; the calf can graze and drink but cannot suck. Also called *blab board* and *butterboard weaner*. To clip such a board to a calf's nose. Also, a piece of stiff leather worn by an early-day *rep (q.v.)*. It was worn around the neck and bore the brand of the outfit the cowboy represented, serving as his identification card.

blab board

The full name for the *blab, q.v.*

blackballed outfit

A ranch or outfit barred from sending a *rep (q.v.)* to the general roundup, the term being especially applied to small ranchers suspected of rustling or of being friendly to rustlers.

black book

See *Bible "Two."*

black chaparral

A very thorny brush peculiar to the Southwest.

black diamonds

A logger's term for poles dipped in creosote.

black-eyed Susan

A cowboy's term for a six gun.

blackface

Any one of several shire breeds of sheep.

blackjack

In mining, sphalerite, a dark variety of zinc blende. In logging, coffee; also called *blackstrap.* In gambling, the private variety of the game generally called *twenty-one (vingt-et-un)* in gambling houses. The main difference between the two games lies in the betting systems; the basis of the play is practically the same.

An ordinary fifty-two-card deck is used. Card values are as follows: ace counts one or eleven, as the holder wishes; king, queen, jack, and ten count ten; the other cards count according to their numbers. The object of the game is to hold two or more cards that have a total value of twenty-one or as close to twenty-one as possible without exceeding it. Each player, including the dealer, is dealt two cards. Each one may draw one or more additional cards or "stand," i.e., make his first score his final one. In the gambling-house game the dealer must take additional cards when his score is sixteen or less and must stand when his total is seventeen or more. In private games the dealer is not bound by these rules. A player whose cards have a value of more than twenty-one loses and is out of the game. A player whose first two cards are an ace and a face card or a ten has a *black-jack* or *natural* and wins the game.

blackjack steer

A scrawny steer from the timber country.

black Mike

A logger's term for stew.

black robe

An Indian's name for a priest.

blacksmithing

What the cowboy calls pimping or procuring for a woman of easy virtue; a polite way of giving information about such activity, as, "Bill is blacksmithin' for Bertha."

black snake

A long whip, like those used by ox-team freighters.

black spot

What the cowboy calls a piece of shade. Also used in another sense, as when one cowman speaks of another by saying, "His past was full of black spots," in this characteristic cowboy manner letting one know of the man's shady reputation.

blackstrap

The cowboy's name for thick, black molasses.

blacktail

Black-tailed deer.

black water

A freighter's term for weak coffee.

blade man

A sheepshearer.

blanc-bec

Greenhorn; from the French, meaning *white-face.* A name used by French-Canadian trappers for a Missouri *voyageur (q.v.)* who had never passed the Platte River. Upon his first passing, a *blanc-bec* was subjected to an initiation like that given sailors when they first cross the equator.

blanket tables

In mining, long, narrow tables used for washing gold.

blanket veins

In mining, horizontal, flat veins of ore.

blast furnace

A furnace for melting ore. The furnace is charged with fuel mixed with the ore, and combustion is forced by a blast of air introduced near the bottom of the column.

blattin' cart

See *calf wagon.*

blaze

A white mark on a horse's nose running upward to join the *star strip (q.v.).* In herding and logging, a mark on a tree trunk, made by painting or chipping off a spot with an ax, to indicate a trail, a boundary, the location of a road, a tree to be cut, etc.; also, to make such a mark. In trapping and freighting, to fire a shot. In faro, a hand of five count cards, which beats two pairs.

blazer

One who blazes trees. See *blaze.*

blazing

In gambling, marking playing cards with the fingernails or a needle point embedded in a ring. Cards so marked are called *scratch paper*.

blazing star

In freighting, a stampede of pack mules or other animals from a central point.

blende

In mining, a sulphide of zinc.

blind

A leather hood used to cover the eyes of a pack mule when loading the animal or tightening the load.

blind as a snubbing post

Undiscerning. One cowhand described such a person with, "He couldn't see through a bob-wire fence."

blind bridle

A harness bridle with blinders. The homesteader used it, and therefore it was considered an insult to say of a cowboy that "he rides for a blind bridle."

blind bucker

A horse that loses his head when ridden and bucks into or through anything.

blind canyon

See *box canyon*.

blinder

A sack or cloth used to cover a horse's eyes when saddling or shoeing the animal.

blinding

Covering a horse's eyes with a sack or cloth to keep him quiet for saddling.

blind lead

In mining, a lead, or lode, that has no surface outcrop and cannot be detected from the surface. Also called *blind lode*.

blind level

In mining, a level, or passage, not yet connected with other workings. Also, a level for drainage, having a shaft at either end and acting as an inverted siphon.

blind lode

See *blind lead*.

blind opening

In gambling, the compulsory opening of the pot with a blind bet, as in one form of draw poker.

blind stope

In mining, a secret working to remove ore.

blind the trail

To conceal tracks or give them the appearance of going in a different direction.

blind trail

A trail with indistinct markings, or sign.

blind trap

A hidden corral for trapping cattle or wild horses.

blind vein

In mining, a vein that does not continue to the surface.

blizzard

A high, cold, searching wind, accompanied by blinding sleet and smothering snow. When riding through a blizzard, you would think, as one cowboy of my acquaintance did, that you were "ridin' on the knob of the North Pole."

blizzard-choked

Said of cattle caught in a corner or draw or against a drift fence during a blizzard.

blocker loop

An extra-large loop, named for John Blocker, a well-known roper of Texas, who originated and used it. It is turned over when thrown and goes over the steer's shoulders and picks up both front feet. It is started like the straight overhead loop, being taken around the head to the left. The cast is made when the loop is behind the right shoulder, the right arm being whipped straight forward across the circle it has been describing. At the same time the hand and wrist give the loop a twist toward the left. The loop goes out in front of the roper, appears to stop, stand up, and then roll to the left, showing the honda to be on the side of the loop opposite its position when the throw was started. (W. M. French, "Ropes and Ropers," *Cattleman*, Vol. XXVI, No. 12 [May, 1940], 17–30).

block heads

What the miner calls the bulwarks of a mine.

blond Swede

What the loggers call an elderly man.

blood bay

A horse of darker red than the bay.

blossom

In mining, decomposed outcropping of a vein of ore or coal.

blossom rock

In mining, quartz stained with metallic oxides that indicate the proximity of mineral deposits, differing but little in gold and silver lodes.

blot

To deface a cattle brand.

blow a stirrup

To lose a stirrup, which in a rodeo contest, disqualifies the rider.

blower

In mining, a shallow receptacle for weighing gold dust. Made of tin or sheet iron, it is 6 inches wide at one end and 3 inches wide at the other. The edges are turned up all around except at the narrow end. The dust is poured into the blower from the sack. By shaking the pan gently and blowing upon the dust, such sand as accompanies the dust is separated from it, and the weigher gets nothing but gold for his pay.

blow in

To spend money. To arrive.

blowing

A logger's word meaning *going to town to celebrate.*

blow in with the tumbleweeds

To arrive unexpectedly.

blown up

In mining, said of a manager of a mine who has skipped out without paying the men.

blow out

A cowboy's expression meaning *to kill.*

blowout

The cowboy's word for a celebration. In mining, a spreading outcrop.

blow out his lamp

A cowboy's expression meaning *to kill someone.*

blowpipe

A rifle. In logging, a pipe that transports sawdust to the *cyclone, q.v.*

blow the plug

Said of a bucking horse that exhibits all the tricks of the rodeo arena.

blow up

Said of a horse that starts bucking.

blue belly

A southern cowman's name for a Yankee.

blue-jay camp meeting

The westerner's term for a group of chattering blue jays.

blue lightnin'

The cowman's term for a six gun.

blue meat

The flesh of an unweaned calf.

blue whistler

A bullet, so called because of the blue frame of the pistol. A norther.

bluff

In poker, a bet on a hand that the player does not believe is the best, made in such a way that his opponents will think it is a strong hand and retire from the pot.

Bluff

See cold blazer, fourflusher, put the saddle on him, run a blazer.

boardinghouse man

A logger's name for the cook.

boarding with Aunt Polly

Said of the logger who is drawing insurance for sickness or accident.

board tree

In logging, a clear, straight-grained oak, suitable for clapboards or shingles.

boar's nest

A lumber camp. The cowboy's name for a line camp, so called because its single occupant is more interested in his duties as a cowhand than in the art of housekeeping. These camps usually consist of one- or two-room shacks and a small corral and storage shed for horse feed. They are furnished with a minimum amount of equipment so that visiting prowlers will not profit. Single men who do not mind loneliness and who can eat their own cooking are usually assigned to these camps. Because there is too much waste in killing a beef for one man, the principal diet of this cowboy consists of beans, *lick (q.v.)*, coffee, flour, lard, a few cans of food, and a slab of white, salt-covered sowbelly. (John M. Hendrix, "Batchin' Camp," *Cattleman*, Vol. XVI, No. 8 [July, 1934], 5).

boat horn

In river boating, used for signaling.

boat landing

A place on the bank of a river where boats stop to discharge and take on passengers and freight.

BOATS

See alligator, barge, bateau, buck snatcher, buffalo boat, bull boat, canoe, catamaran, flatboat, Indian raft, keelboat, limber hole, Mackinaw, piroque, pole boat, sea mule, skin canoe, snag boat, sounding boat, starboard steamboats and equipment, tow, towboat, wannigan, wharf boat, wood boat, yawl.

boat ways

Wooden structures onto which steamboats were hauled to be repaired.

bobabza

In mining, a mine rich in ore; undoubtedly a play on *bonanza*.

bob sawyer

A tree rooted to the river bottom, its broken top bobbing and sawing with the undulations of the current; a trap for careless boatmen.

bobtail flush

In five-card poker, a worthless three-card flush.

bobtail guard

The first guard at the night herding of cattle.

bobtail straight

In five-card poker, a worthless three-card straight.

body bunches

See *belly bunches*.

body spin

A rope trick accomplished by bringing a wide, spinning loop up and over the head and thence down around the body during the spinning. It can be performed from the ground or from horseback.

bog camp

A camp established close to a boggy area so that men will be handy to pull out cattle that may become mired in it. A logging camp near a swamp.

bog down

Said of a band of sheep that bunch up and refuse to move.

bogged his head

Said of a horse that has put his head between his forelegs in preparation for bucking.

bogged to the saddle skirts

What the cowboy says when he is deeply implicated in some situation.

boggin' 'im in

An expression used in rodeo riding when the rider fails to *scratch (q.v.)* his horse, also called *boggin' time in*.

boggin' time in

See *boggin' 'im in*.

boggy crossing

A stream crossing that is full of quicksand or boggy earth. Something that one does not fully understand.

boggy top

The cowboy's name for a pie with no top crust.

bog hole

An alkali hole, a mud hole, or quicksand which cattle are likely to enter for a little moisture and then become mired too deeply to extricate themselves.

bog rider

A cowboy whose immediate duty is to rope mired cattle and pull them to dry ground. He rides a stout horse and frequently carries a short-handled shovel, which he uses to get the bogged animal's legs clear. Placing one end of his rope about the animal's horns, he wraps the other end around his saddle horn. After cinching up his saddle as tightly as the latigo straps can be drawn, he mounts and starts his horse slowly. Then inch by inch the cow is pulled to dry ground. (Will C. Barnes, "The Bog Rider," *Cattleman*, Vol. XVII, No. 8 [January, 1930], 27–28.)

bohunk

The logger's name for a Bohemian, Czech, Serbian, Pole, Russian, or Slovack. More loosely, any foreigner. Still more loosely, any disliked person.

boiler

A logger's name for the cook, especially an inferior one.

boiler deck

The second deck of a steamboat. Why it is so called is not known; the boiler was on the lower deck, and the second deck was the living quarters for the crew. Boilers have never been placed on the boiler deck, and historians have no idea how this misnomer came about, but it has stuck with tenacity. The term was also used to designate the inside cabin space on the second deck.

boiler feed pump

The pump that replenishes the water supply in the boilers of a steamboat. See *doctor*.

boilermaker and his helper

What the cowboy calls a drink of whisky with a beer chaser.

boil out

A logger's expression meaning to *wash one's clothes*. Also *boil up*.

boil over

Said of a horse that starts bucking.

boil up

See *boil out*.

bois de vache

A trapper's name for buffalo chips; from the French, meaning *cow wood* or *fuel*. Buffalo chips were a common substitute for wood in early days.

bole

The stem or trunk of a tree, usually the lower, usable or merchantable portion of the trunk.

bologna bulls

Animals of inferior quality whose meat is used to make Bologna sausage.

bolt

A short section of tree stem, 2 to 5 feet long; used as primary material by wood turneries and shingle and stave mills. To split trees or timber into such sections.

bolt cutter

A *bucker*, or logger, who saws felled trees into *bolts*. See *bolt*. Also called *bolter*.

bolter

See *bolt cutter*.

bonanza

In mining, a large body of paying ore; a spectacularly rich ore body. Hence, any unusually promising or profitable enterprise.

bone hunter

One who hunted bones of dead animals, especially buffalo bones; also called *bone picker* and *bone pilgrim*. Bone hunting was quite an industry for a time after the buffalo were slaughtered. The bones were sold to fertilizer plants.

bone orchard

A cowboy's name for a cemetery.

bone picker

A *bone hunter*, q.v. A buzzard.

bone pilgrim

See *bone hunter*.

bones

Dice.

bone-seasoned

A cowman's term meaning *experienced*.

bone yard

A cowboy's name for a cemetery. An emaciated horse. In river boating, any location where worn-out steamboats were moored while being scrapped or awaiting disposition.

bonnet

In mining, a brass fulminating cap used as an explosive. The covering of the upper deck of a cage to protect the miners from falling rock.

bonnet strings

Buckskin thongs hanging from each side of the brim of a cowman's hat at its inner edges. The ends are run through a bead or ring, and by pulling these up under the chin, the cowboy has a hat that will stay on during a fast ride or in windy weather. He does not care to ride back several miles to hunt for a hat that has blown off, for he is usually too busy to stop.

bonus

In logging, a term used to describe logs that have fallen in such a way that one *choker*, or short cable, can encircle two or more logs and haul them down together, instead of one at a time, which is normal procedure.

boob

A logger's name for a railroad-tie cutter.

boodle

What the traders and freighters called graft or illegal fees.

booger

To scare. To confuse.

boogered up

A cowboy's expression meaning *crippled*.

book count

An estimate of the number of cattle on the ranch, based on the ranch records. Selling cattle by book count was commonly resorted to in the early days, sometimes much to the profit of the seller.

book miner

What the miners called a geologist.

Books

See beef book, Bible, Bible "Two," black book, book count, books don't freeze, brand book, discharging book, dream book, prayer book, ranch records, shepherd's Bible, tally sheet, wish book.

books won't freeze

A common byword in the northwest cattle country during the boom days when eastern and foreign capital was so eager to buy cattle interests. This saying is credited to a saloonkeeper named Luke Murrin, whose saloon was a meeting place for influential Wyoming cattlemen. One year during a severe blizzard, when his herd-owning customers were wearing long faces, Luke said, "Cheer up, boys; whatever happens, the books won't freeze." In this carefree sentence he summed up the essence of the prevailing custom of selling by *book count* *(q.v.)* and created a saying that has survived through the years.

boom

In logging, logs or timbers fastened together end to end and used to hold floating logs. The term also includes the logs so held. There are many varieties of booms, depending on construction and use, among them the bag, barge, bracket, catch, fender, fin, glancing, holding, lumber, pocket, receiving, round, rudder, shear, sorting, and storage booms. Also, the projecting arm of a log-loading machine that supports the logs during loading. It may be of either the swinging or the rigid type. Also, a barrier of connecting floating timbers placed across a stream or around an area of water to retain floating logs; also called *big-pond boom*.

boomage

A toll charged for the use of a boom in which saw logs are collected.

boom company

A company that collects logs for booms.

boomer

A participant in a land rush; a settler or squatter. A logger's name for an itinerant worker who works a few days and then quits; also (an older meaning), a man in charge of a boom.

boomerang stallion

A stallion unfit for breeding because of a slit in his sheath that permits his sex organ to drop down instead of forward, thus making it impossible for him to reproduce.

boom head

A windlass used in logging.

boom house

In logging, the house where the boom *master (q.v.)* lives.

booming

In logging, the formation of a *boom (q.v.)*; the impounding of logs in a boom.

boom loader

A swinging boom used in loading logs on trucks or flatcars.

boom man

In logging, the man who either operates a boom loader or is in charge of the line of floating timbers, called *boom sticks*, that prevents logs stored in an area of water from floating away. Also, a worker who poles floating logs to a mill.

boom master

In logging, the man in charge of a *boom, q.v.* Also called *boom tender*.

boom rat

A name for one who rafts logs in a boom.

boom stick

One of the logs fastened together to make a boom to hold floating logs.

boom-stick cutter

The logger who trims and prepares boom sticks.

boom tender

See *boom master*.

booshway

The leader of a company of trappers; a corruption of the French *bourgeois*, meaning *citizen* or *member of the middle class*.

booster

A *capper (q.v.)*, or decoy, as for gamblers.

boot

The cowman's footwear. The cowboy's boots are generally the most expensive part of his rigging, and he wants them high-heeled, thin-soled, and made of good leather. The tops are made of lightweight, high-grade leather, and all the stitching on them is not merely for decoration but serves the purpose of stiffening them and keeping them from wrinkling too much at the ankles where they touch the stirrups. (John M. Hendrix, "Boots," *Cattleman*, Vol. XXXIII, No. 11 [April, 1937], 5).

The boots are handmade to order. The cowman has no use for hand-me-down, shop-made footgear, and no respect for a cowhand who will wear them, holding to the opinion that ordinary shoes are made for furrow-flattened feet and are not intended for stirrup work.

The high heels keep the cowman's foot from slipping through the stirrup and hanging, they let him dig in when he is roping on foot, and they give him a sure footing in all other work on the ground. Too, the high heel is a tradition, a mark of distinction, the sign that the one wearing it is a riding man, and a riding man has always held himself above the man on foot.

A cowhand wants the toes of his boots more or less pointed to make it easier to pick up a stirrup on a wheeling horse. He wants a thin sole so that he has the feel of the stirrup. He wants the vamp soft and light and the tops wide and loose to allow the air to circulate and prevent sweating.

When a man is seen wearing old boots "so frazzled he can't strike a match on 'em without burnin' his feet," he is considered worthless and without pride.

In packing, a horseshoe with both heel and toe calked. Also, the end piece of the aparejo. In stagecoaching, a leather-covered, triangular-shaped rack to hold mail, express, and baggage, placed at the rear or front of the coach.

boot bar

A slender stick of wood used in an aparejo to stiffen the boot. When the boot of the aparejo is properly filled with hay by the skilled packer and provided with slots to received the ribs of wood, these conform to the shape of the boot, as formed by the padding of hay. Hay is also packed over the upper portion of the bars where that portion of the boot comes into contact with the body of the mule. The boot bar holds the ribs in place, thus stiffening the aparejo.

bootblack cowpuncher

A man who came from the East to go into the cattle business for the money there was in it; so called by the old-time cowman.

Boot Hill

A name given to the frontier cemetery because most of its early occupants died with their boots on. The name has had an appeal as part of the romantic side of the West and has become familiar as representing the violent end of a reckless life. But to the westerner, Boot Hill was just a graveyard where there "wasn't nobody there to let 'em down easy with their hats off." Like the old saying, "There ain't many tears shed at a Boot Hill buryin'," and it is "full of fellers that pulled their triggers before aimin.'"

bootleg

In mining, a charge of explosive that fails to break rock.

boot-pack

Heavy rubber shoes worn by loggers in winter or during the cutting season. The sides are usually somewhat higher than those of regular shoes. They are usually fastened with buckles or laces and are large enough to allow the wearer room for several pairs of thick woolen socks. *Calked shoes (q.v.)* are usually worn in the drive.

Boots

See boot, boot-pack, California moccasins, calked shoes, corks, custom-mades, Justin's, mule-cars, peewees, shop-mades, stogies.

boot stick

A hard wooden stick used in an aparejo to stiffen the boot. They are 21½ inches long, 2½ inches wide, and ¾ inch thick. The ends must be rounded or tapered on one side. These ends face the inside back piece of the aparejo; they must be exactly the right size so that it is not necessary to force their adjustment to the bottom of the boot.

booze-blind

A cowboy's expression meaning *very drunk*. A man with a full-grown case of booze blindness perhaps "never knowed he had a twin brother till he looked in the mirror behind the bar." Very often he got to the state where he "saw things that wasn't there." Speed Carlow declared that no man "could gargle that brand of hootch without annexin' a few queer animals."

border draw

A cross draw with the gun carried at or near the hip but hanging butt forward, on the opposite side from the hand making the draw. A quick stab of the hand across the body reaches the gun, and the continuation of the movement lifts it clear of the holster. So called because of its popularity with cowmen near the Mexican border. (Eugene Cunningham, *Triggernometry* [New York, Press of Pioneers, 1934], 423.) Also called *cross draw*.

border shift

The throwing of a gun from one hand to the other and catching, cocking, and if need be, firing it without seeming to pause. (Eugene Cunningham, *Triggernometry* [New York, Press of Pioneers, 1934], 423.)

bore and stroke

The logger's estimate of a man's capabilities.

boring

Said of a horse that is constantly leaning the weight of his head and neck on the bit.

bornite

In mining, a combination of copper with sulphur and iron; one of the richest copper minerals, with a beautifully varied peacock color resulting from tarnishing.

borracho

A drunkard; from the Spanish. The word is used near the Mexican border.

borraska

In mining, out of pay; lacking in rich ore; from the Spanish *borrasca*, meaning *barren rock*. The opposite of *bobabza, q.v.*

borreras

Sheep; from the Spanish. In New Mexico *borreras* is used almost as commonly as *sheep*.

borrowed

A cowman's euphemism for *stolen*.

bosal

A leather, rawhide, or metal ring around the horse's head immediately above the mouth; used in place of a bit; from the Spanish *bozal*, meaning *muzzle*.

bosal brand

A brand burned across a horse's nose; so called because it is in the position where a *bosal (q.v.)* would rest.

bosalea

A riding headstall used in breaking a bronc; it is not intended for use in tying up the animal. From the Spanish *bozal*.

bosque

A clump or grove of trees; a thickly wooded area. From the Spanish, meaning *forest*.

boss

A trapper's name for the hump on the neck and shoulders of a buffalo.

Bosses

See augur, big augur, big boss, big bull, big savage, big sugar, bigwig, booshway, boss faller, bourgeois, brains, brass nuts, bucker, buggy boss, bull of the woods, bull-wagon boss, camp boss, capitaine, caporal, Captain Jim Crow, cargador, chef de voyage, cock-a-doodle-doo, collar-and-tie man, conductor, corral boss, enemy, fire boss, foreman, gaffer, governor, grandpa, hay stopper, head taster, high salty, job shark, king pin, king snipe, labor shark, man catcher, man grabber, nigger driver, old man, powders, presidente, push, ramrod, ranchers, range boss, right-hand man, rod, roundup captain, second rigger, segundo, shift boss, shifter, side push, side rod, skipper, slave driver, slave puncher, slave pusher, straw boss, super, supreme being, top screw, trail boss, uncle, wagon boss, wagon master, walker.

boss faller

In logging, the boss of the crew that fells trees.

bossloper

A woods hunter; a trapper.

boss-simple

Afraid of one's employer or superior. Stupid.

Boston dollar

A cowboy's name for a penny.

botch

A bungled worked-over brand. A botched job was an acute mortification to most rustlers.

both ends against the middle

Describing a method of trimming cards for a crooked faro game. A dealer who used such a pack was said to be "playing both ends against the middle," and the saying became common in the West.

bottle-butted

A logger's term for a tree with a great enlargement at its base.

bottle fever

Addiction to liquor.

bottom

Endurance, as, "This horse has plenty of bottom." One of the sayings of the cow country is, "Real bottom in a good horse counts for more than his riggin'." Also, low ground next to a stream.

bottom dealer

In gambling, a card cheat who deals from the bottom of the deck while pretending to deal from the top.

bottom layout

In monte, after the shuffle and cut, the dealer's practice of holding the deck face down and then drawing off two bottom cards and placing them on the table face up.

boudin

A hunters' and trappers' delicacy made from the buffalo intestine containing chyme, cut in lengths, wrapped around a stick, and toasted before a fire until crisp. Also a kind of sausage prepared by stuffing forcement made of selected buffalo tidbits into the large intestine of the animal and cooked by boiling, frying, or roasting on a stick. From the French, meaning *blood pudding* or *sausage*.

boughten bag

The cowboy's name for a traveling bag used by an easterner.

boulder

A large, loose, rounded stone.

bounce

A cattle term meaning *to turn animals*; not commonly used.

bourgeois

The chief trader or trapper, who held a license from the government and was all-powerful.

bowie knife

A heavy sheath knife with a strong single-edged blade 9 to 15 inches long, originally made by frontier blacksmiths from old files, horse rasps, etc. Named for Colonel James Bowie, one of the heroes of the Alamo, who invented it.

bow up

Said of an animal that humps its back in a storm. To show fight. As one cowboy was heard to say, "He bows up like a mule in a hailstorm."

box brand

A cattle brand whose design is framed by lines.

box canyon

A gorge with but a single opening, the inner terminal being against a wall of rock within the mountainous mass; also called *blind canyon*.

boxcars

In dice, the roll of twelve, made up of two sixes.

box pannier

A flat, narrow wooden box, usually covered with green rawhide with the hair left on, lashed to the packsaddle to carry camp equipment.

box up the dough

A logger's expression meaning *to cook*.

Boys

See button, door knob, fryin' size, hen wrangler, pistol, punk, weaner, whistle, yearling, younker.

boy scout

What the loggers call a high school or college student who plants trees or visits in the woods.

brace box

In faro, a dealing box designed to facilitate cheating.

braced

Crooked; said of a faro game or house that maintains very high odds in favor of the house by means of crooked games, dealers, etc.

brace game

A crooked faro game. Many trusting or ignorant cowboys were victims of the crooked gambler.

bradded brand

A cattle brand with a letter or figure having enlarged termini.

Braggarts

See flannelmouth; got calluses from pattin' his own back; half horse, half alligator; talk like a Texan; too much mustard.

Brahma

A breed of cattle imported from India, China, or Africa, popular in the Southwest, especially in the hotter areas. The cattle are highly resistant to flies and ticks and the effects of desert heat. Usually pronounced *bray'mer*.

brail

In logging, a crib of loose logs surrounded by a boom of longer logs fastened at the ends. Three or four brails are fastened together side by side, forming a raft, which is towed by steam tugs. Also, a section of a log raft, usually towed in groups of six.

brains

In logging, a company official; a man from the head office.

brain tablet

A cowboy's term for a cigarette.

brake a load

In packing, to work the packs close together and into their proper relative positions after they have been tied together with a sling rope. Also, *break a pack*.

brake sticks

In stagecoaching, wooden sticks, 3 or 4 inches wide, connected to the brakes, making it possible for the driver to put great resistance on the moving wheels.

brand

The mark of identity burned on the hide of an animal. The origin of brands dates back to antiquity, and there has never been anything to take its place as a permanent mark of ownership. As the cowman says, "A brand is somethin' that won't come off in the wash." To burn such a mark on an animal's hide. Also, the deed to a saddle horse.

brand artist

A rustler; a man expert at changing brands.

brand blotter

A cattle thief who mutilates brands in order to destroy the legitimate owner's claim. Also called *brand blotcher* or *brand burner*.

brand book

An official record of brands of a cattle association.

brand botcher

See *brand blotter*.

brand burner

See *brand blotter*.

brander

The man whose immediate duty is to place a brand upon an animal during branding. When the calf is dragged to him, he jerks the branding iron from the fire, hits the rod on his forearm to jar off the coals, and slaps it on the animal's hide. He may be working away from the fire with an assistant. In that case, when the iron becomes too cold to scar the hide, he yells to his helper, "Hot iron!" and another iron, glowing a cherry red, is brought from the fire at a trot.

BRANDERS AND MARKERS

See butcher, cutter, fireman, floating out-fit, iron man, iron tender, ketch hand, marker, mavericker, outside man, rawhide artist, sooner, tally man.

BRANDING

See blot, branders, branding chute, brand inspector, burn cattle, burn 'em and boot 'em, burnin' and trimmin' up calves, burning rawhide, burnt till he looks like a brand book, Calf on the ground! Calf on the string! chute branding, cookstove, corral branding, cut of cows and calves, dotting iron, gauch iron, herrar, Hook 'em cow! Hot iron! hot stuff, iron, ironing the calf crop, jack a maverick, maverick, More straw! open-range branding, op'ra, picking a sleeper, range-branded, rolling a calf, run a brand, rustling, scorcher, slappin' a brand on, snappin' turtle, tally branding, warting, working brands, work over, wrastling calves.

branding ax

In logging, a tool for marking the ownership of a log.

branding chute

A narrow, boarded passage into which cattle are driven and held so that they can be branded without being thrown.

brand inspector

A man hired by a cattle association to inspect brands at shipping points and cattle markets.

BRANDS

See barbed brand, bench brand, bosal brand, botch, box brand, bradded brand, brand, brand blotter, brand book, brander, brand you could read in the moonlight, butt brand, calling the brands, clip a brand, cold brand, connected brand, counterbrand, county brand, decoy brand, drag brand, fast brand, fire out, fluidy mustard, flying brand, fool brand, forked brand, greaser madhouse, hair brand, hair over, lazy brand, map of Mexico, maverick brand, open brand, picked brand, rafter brand, road brand, rocking brand, running brand, running iron, saddle brand, set brand, skillet of snakes, sleeper brand, slow brand, stamp brand, swinging brand, tumbling brand, vent brand, walking brand, whangdoodle.

brand you could read in the moonlight

A large brand, or one covering a large area of hide.

brasada

Brush country; from the Spanish *brazada*, meaning *armful*. In parts of Texas this term is particularly applied to a region densely covered with thickets and underbrush. (J. Frank Dobie, *Vaquero of the Brush Country* [Dallas, Southwest Press, 1929], 229.)

brass nuts

A logger's name for the superintendent.

brattish

In mining, *brattice*, a partition to improve ventilation.

brave maker

A name the cowboy occasionally gives to whisky. It has been said that "when a man has to go into a barroom to build up his courage, he mighty often has to prove it."

breachy

A cow that jumps over or breaks through fences.

break

Rough land.

break a hamestring

The logger's expression meaning *to do one's best*.

break even

In faro, to be in such a way that each card is played to win and lose an even number of times. To bet against the bank according to the system whereby one card is backed to win twice and lose twice or to win four times and lose four times.

breaking

Conquering, taming, and training a horse by force and fight.

breaking age

The age at which horses are usually broken, between three and one-half and four years.

breaking around

In mining, drilling a hole to blast out rock and make footage in the face of a drift.

breaking brush

Riding in the brush country.

BREAKING IN HORSES

See bittin' ring, blinding, bosalea, breaking, breaking age, breaking patter, breaking pen, broken, bronc saddle, bronc stall, buck the saddle, bust, cavesson, cavvy-broke, choke down, curry the kinks out, ear down, gentling, green-broke, halter-broke, harness broke, hazer, Indian-broke, ironing him out, jerk-away horse, kick the frost out, lady-broke, let the hammer down, makin' shavetails, riding the rough string, rough-break, roughed out, run on the rope, sack, second saddle, set the hair, slicker-broke, smoothin' out the humps, snappin' broncs, soak, stake breaking, start a bronc, Stay with him! three saddles, top off, top out, twist a horse, twisting out, uncorkin' a bronc, unrooster, whip breaking, whipper in, wiping him out, worked, work over.

breaking patter

The soothing yet derisive talk that horse tamers use to distract their mounts while saddling and breaking them.

breaking pen

A small corral used for breaking horses.

breaking the barrier

In rodeo, said when the contestant breaks through the barrier before it is released, an act that is penalized by the addition of ten seconds to his time.

breaking the medicine

Overcoming an enemy's efforts to harm one. Breaking a jinx.

break in two

Said of a horse that starts to buck.

break off

In faro, said of a card that fails to win after winning two or more times. Thus, if the ace has been bet to win three times and wins and then loses on the next play, the players say, "The ace broke off."

break one's pick

In mining, to quit, be discharged, or become discouraged.

break range

Said of horses that run off the home range.

break-through

In mining, a passage cut through the pillar to allow the ventilating current to pass from one room to another.

break up

Said of river ice that begins to melt and crack in the spring.

breast

In mining, the heading of a drift, tunnel, or other horizontal working.

breasting up

In mining, said when lack of space in the mine forces the mule driver to have the mule push the ore car with its breast rather than pull it.

breccia

In mining, an aggregate composed of angular fragments of the same rock or of different rocks united by a matrix or cement.

breed

Short for *half-breed*, a person of mixed Indian and white blood. To mate animals for reproduction.

BREEDING

See cover, good stick, grade, high-grade, line breeding, warm the blood.

breeding range

A range or pasture used for breeding cattle.

briar

A logger's name for a crosscut saw.

bridal chamber

In mining, the chamber at the end of a narrow tunnel in which work is progressing.

bridge monkey

A logger's name for a bridge builder.

bridle

The headgear of a horse, composed of a crownpiece, browband, throatlatch, and, on each side, a cheekpiece. Most cowboys prefer a plain headstall that has no buckles or conchas down the cheeks to interfere with roping. When the cowboy ropes something and holds it, he keeps his horse facing it so that the rope naturally runs out beside the head. In steamboating, an auxiliary rope used with the *cordelle, q.v.*

bridle chain

A short piece of chain fastened to the bit ring on one end and to the reins on the other. Some riders prefer chains to reins because reins may get wet when the horse drinks and because a tied horse will often chew reins. In logging, the skid chains that are wrapped around sled runners for brakes on an icy road. In mining, the safety chains used to support the cage if the shackle should break or to protect a train on a slope if the shackle or drawbar should fail.

bridle head

See *bridle*.

bridle ring

A metal ring at each end of the bit, to which the reins are fastened.

BRIDLES

See biddy bridle, bittin' ring, bosal, bridle, bridle chain, bridle head, bridle ring, browband, bucking rein, California reins, cheekpiece, cricket, crownpiece, ear-head, fiador, freno, hackamore, headstall, horse jewelry, one-eared bridle, open reins, post romal, throatlatch, tied reins, war bridle.

bridle-wise

Said of a horse so well trained that the rider can control and guide him in the direction desired solely by laying the bridle reins on that side of his neck.

brigade

In river boating, a name for the crew of a keelboat.

Brigham

A common name for gravy on Arizona ranches.

Brigham Young cocktail

A strong whisky. Cowboys near the Utah border said of it, "One sip and you're a confirmed polygamist."

brindle

A cow with spots of different colors. To go.

bring-'em-close glasses

A cowboy's name for field glasses.

bringing up the drags

In the rear of a column of cattle; also sometimes used in speaking of a slow or lazy person.

brittle silver

Stephanite, a sulphide of silver and antimony containing 68.5 per cent silver and variable amounts of antimony. It also sometimes contains iron, copper, and arsenic.

broaching

In mining, trimming or straightening a working.

broad

In three-card monte, a playing card.

broadax brigade

In logging, a name for a crew of railroad-tie men; so called because of the heavy axes they use to smooth the ties.

broadhorn

Longhorn cattle. In river boating, a boat similar to a flatboat, whose movements were usually regulated, as far as possible, by two great oars, or sweeps, that projected like horns from each side of the boat. The boats were usually 150 feet long and 25 feet wide, were manned by eight or ten men, and were used for carrying various cargoes. Vessels of the flatboat type rarely proceeded upstream in river-boating days.

broad pitcher

In three-card monte, a dealer, so called because he throws a *broad*, a playing card. This term appeared about the time of the Mexican War. Also called *broad tosser*, *monte tosser*, and *monte thrower*.

broad tosser

See *broad pitcher*.

brockled

Said of an animal covered with splotches of various colors.

Broke

See between a rock and a hard place, cattle-poor, close to the blanket, didn't have a tail feather left, down to his last chip, down to the blanket, palau, sold his saddle, stuck, sweater.

broke down

A logger's description of one too old to work.

broken

Said of a horse that has had the rough edges taken off, though to the tenderfoot he would still seem fairly wild.

broken bit

A bit composed of two pieces of metal joined by a swivel.

broken mouths

Sheep with missing teeth.

broken wind

A lung infection of horses. Broken-winded horses have difficulty breathing, especially after running.

bronc belt

A broad leather belt sometimes worn by a *bronc fighter* (*q.v.*) to support his back and stomach muscles.

bronc breaker

A man who breaks wild horses. Also called *bronc scratcher* and *bronc snapper*.

bronc buster

A man who follows the hazardous trade of horsebreaking as a steady business. Also called *bronc squeezer*, *bronc twister*, and many other names. He has to be good—even better than the man who just breaks horses —and a good bronc buster is hard to find. The best cowhands can ride the "snuffy" ones but won't. This is the buster's job, for which he receives a few extra dollars a month. A good bronc buster never abuses horses. He takes great pride in his work, and it is an honor to be pointed out as the rider of the *rough string* (*q.v.*) for a big outfit. He does his best to make good cow horses out of his charges and not spoil them. No outfit wants spoiled horses, and a man who spoils them lasts only long enough to ride one horse.

The bronc buster's job requires strength and skill, and he has to possess the sixth sense of knowing which way the horse will jump next. Once in the saddle, he does his best to keep the bronc's head up. If he is thrown, he is certain to crawl back on the animal immediately, providing he has not been crippled; to let the horse think he has won the fight would give him bad ideas. Falls have no terrors for the seasoned rider, but the thought of a foot's becoming hung in the stirrup or of finding himself under a man-killer's hoofs worries him plenty. How to fall is one of the first things he learns. He learns how to kick free of the stirrups, go limp, and hit the ground rolling. He always knows he is going a jump or two before he actually goes.

His working years are short, and by thirty he is too old for the game. Then he has to be content to ride horses other men have gentled, the jar and lunge of the rougher ones having torn him up inside.

bronc fighter

Another name for a *bronc buster (q.v.)*, but a name that more properly fits the man who has never learned to control his own temper and who, therefore, usually spoils the horse rather than conquers it.

bronco

A wild or semiwild horse, often shortened to *bronc;* from the Spanish. A horse usually retains this appellation until he has been sufficiently gentled to be considered reliable.

bronco baile

A cowboy dance enlivened by bronc busting; from the Spanish.

bronc peeler

A name for a rider of the *rough string, q.v.*

bronc saddle

A specially built saddle used in breaking horses or riding bad horses, made with a wide, undercut fork, built-in swells and a deep-dished cantle. Also called *bronc tree.*

bronc scratcher

A man who breaks wild horses. Also called *bronc breaker* and *bronc snapper.*

bronc snapper

See *bronc scratcher.*

bronc squeezer

See *bronc buster.*

bronc stall

A narrow enclosure in which a wild horse can be tied with just enough room for him to stand. Once a horse is fastened in the stall, he can do nothing but snort, and a man can place his hand upon him without fear of being bitten or kicked. It is a gentling place for bad horses used at many ranches, especially where a number of horses are broken for work in harness. The cowboy seldom uses such a contrivance but does his gentling in the middle of a bare corral, or wherever he happens to be.

bronc stomper

A name for the rider of the *rough string (q.v.)*, whom the old-timer would describe as a "man with a heavy seat and a light head."

bronc tree

See *bronc saddle.*

bronc twister

See *bronc buster.*

brook stick

In logging, the long pole used in the log pond to *pocket (q.v.)* the logs.

broomtail

A range mare with a long, bushy tail. Usually shortened to *broomie.*

BROTHELS

See hog ranch, hurdy-gurdy house, parlor house.

browband

The front part of the bridle.

brow logs

In logging, the logs on each side of the track at a loading landing.

brown gargle

A cowboy's term for coffee.

brunette vide poche

What the early traders and trappers called a gold digger, as applied to a woman of the suburb of St. Louis nicknamed *Vide Poche;* from the French, meaning *empty pocket.*

brush

A cowboy's term for low-growing bushes. Also, a skirmish. In logging, an area of the woods other than the landing. A logger working in the woods is said to be "in the brush."

brush ape

A logger.

brush buster

A cowboy expert at running cattle in the brush. The cowboy of the plains country has a much easier time working cattle than the brush hand. The brush buster has to be a good rider because he has to ride in every position to dodge the brush. At one time or another during his ride, he is practically all over the horse, first in one position, then in an entirely different one, as he dodges the brush. In order to dodge successfully, he has to keep his eyes open, although thorns and limbs are constantly tearing at his face. When he comes out of the brush, he may have knots on his head and little skin left on his face, but he goes right back in at the first opportunity.

The brush buster dresses differently from the plains cowboy. Compared with the romantic cowboy of fiction, he is a sorry-looking cuss. No big hats or fancy trappings for him. He is not much in the sun, and a big hat would give too much surface for the brush to grab. His chaps are never of the hair variety, and his flapping leather bat-wings are likely to be snagged. He wears a strong, close-fitting canvas jacket without a tail. If he can afford gloves, he wears them; otherwise, his skin has to pay the penalty. Some of the tougher busters claim it is "cheaper to grow skin than buy it" anyway. His saddle is a good one, though smooth and without fancy stamping to invite the hold of thorns. Every saddle is equipped with heavy, bull-nosed *tapaderos* (*q.v.*), and these, together with his duck-covered elbows, fend off most of the whipping brush. (J. Frank Dobie, *Vaquero of the Brush Country* [Dallas, Southwest Press, 1929], 209.)

The brush buster does practically all his work on horseback and is tireless and full of courage. No other cowman is such a glutton for punishment.

brush cat

A sawmill worker's name for a logger.

brush country

A section covered with low-growing trees and brush. The most famous section of such country is in southwest Texas.

Brush country

See brasada, brush buster, brush country, brush hand, brush horse, brush popper, brush roper, brush roundup, brush splitters, brush thumper, brush whacker, limb skinner.

brush hand

A cowboy who works in the brush country. Usually called *brush popper, q.v.*

brush horse

Usually a lightweight horse used in brush country. He has to be agile, although a big horse is better for making an opening. He requires little reining, and once he gets sight of the cow, nothing can stop him. Like his rider, the brush horse is a brute for punishment and game as they come. The number of horses in the brush hand's mount is greater than in other mounts because the work is too hard to keep a horse at it long at a time. Between rides each horse is given a rest to allow the thorns to work out and the wounds to heal. Yet no matter how stove-up he becomes, he is always ready to break into the brush at the first opportunity.

brushing up

Said of cattle that are hiding in the brush.

brush popper

The most popular name for the *brush hand, q.v.* The brush popper knows he will never catch a cow by looking for a soft entrance into the brush; therefore, he hits the thicket center, hits it flat, hits it on the run, and tears a hole in it.

brush rat

A logger.

brush roper

A *brush hand (q.v.)* who specializes in roping. It is said that just two things are required to make a good brush roper—a damned fool and a race horse. Nevertheless, he is without a peer when it comes to roping. He uses a short rope and a small loop, and frequently has nothing but a hind foot to dab his rope on. There is neither space nor time to swing a loop, and to avoid entanglements his cast must be made expertly at just the right moment. The plains cowboy, with his long rope and his wide, swinging loop, would be worthless in the brush country.

brush roundup

A gathering of cattle in the brush. Actually it is more of a drive than a roundup and is done quietly. It takes many workings to scare out a good percentage of the hidden cattle. The drive starts as early in the morning as possible, since cattle in the brush country cannot be worked well in the heat of the day. Often these drives are made on moonlight nights because brush cattle lie in the brush and bottoms during the day and come out to feed at night.

brush snakes

A cowboy's name for brush cattle that stay in the brush all day and come out at night to graze.

brush splitters

Cattle of the brush country.

brush tail

A logger's name for a horse, as contrasted to *hardtail* or *shavetail*, his names for a mule. Also called *bush tail*.

brush thumper

A *brush hand*, q.v.

brush whacker

A *brush hand*, q.v.

buck

In logging, to saw felled trees into log lengths or bolts, see *bolt*. To pile logs. To bring or carry, as *to buck water*. In early-day gambling, to avoid disputes over whose turn it was to deal by passing around a pocketknife, known as a *buck*, which came to rest with the player whose turn it was to chip for the remainder. The buck was usually a knife with a buckhorn handle carried by most westerners in early days. Hence the name—and the modern-day expression *to pass the buck*. See also *bucking*.

buck ague

Nervousness, like that which develops when one is trying to shoot a deer or other animal. Also called *buck fever*.

buckaroo

A cowboy; a name used in the Northwest. The terms *baquero*, *buckhara*, and *buckayro*, corruptions of the Spanish *vaquero* or *boyero* (both meaning *cowherd*), are also used. (Philip A. Rollins, *The Cowboy* [New York, Charles Scribner's Sons, 1936], 39.) In logging, one who rafts logs in a boom.

buckayro

See *buckaroo*.

buckboard

A light, four-wheeled vehicle in which elastic boards, or slats, extending from axle to axle and upon which the seat rests, take the place of ordinary springs. Instead of sides, the body has an iron rail 3 or 4 inches high which holds in luggage or packages carried on the floor.

buckboard driver

A mail carrier; so called because he usually used a *buckboard* (q.v.) for his deliveries. Ranch mail, especially in the early days, was always small, no matter how infrequently it arrived or how large the outfit. The owner's business involved little correspondence, and the cowboys' inspired less. Few men with close home ties would exile themselves on the range. Many were on the dodge from the scene of some shooting scrape and were known by no other than a nickname.

bucker

A horse that pitches. In logging, one who saws felled trees into log lengths. The boss of a timber-cutting crew.

BUCKERS

See beast with a bellyful of bedsprings, blind bucker, bucker, carnival, cinch binder, close-to-the-ground bucker, cloud hunter, day-money horse, ducker and dodger, gut twister, haul hell out of its shuck, high roller, honest pitcher, livin' lightning, pile driver, pioneer bucker, runaway bucker, salty, show bucker, spinner, suicide horse, sulker, sunfisher, weaver.

bucket

In steamboating, one of the thwartship

paddles on the end of a paddle wheel that dip in the river and propel the boat. A plank forming part of the bucket is called a bucket plank. The extreme depth to which the paddles are submerged is called the *dip*.

bucket dogie

A calf purchased in the corn belt or from a farmer and shipped to a ranch to restock the range.

bucket hunter

A calf being fed milk from a bucket rather than from a cow. The striking motion a calf makes when sucking or drinking from a bucket is called *hunting*.

bucket man

A rustler's contemptuous name for a cowboy.

bucket of blood

A tough saloon. The original Bucket of Blood was Shorty Young's notorious dive in Havre, Montana, and when its reputation spread, the name came into use to describe others of similar character.

buck fever

See *buck ague*.

buckhara

See *buckaroo*.

buck herd

In sheep raising, a herd of rams turned together and held away from the ewes.

buck hook

A blunt-nosed, up-curved piece added to the frame of a spur and locked in the cinch or in the side of a plunging horse.

bucking

Said of a horse that is lowering the head and leaping with the back arched. In Texas called *pitching*.

BUCKING

See arching his back, blow the plug, blow up, bogged his head, boil over, break in two, broken, bucking, bucking on a dime, bucking straight away, buck jump, buck the saddle, casueying, cat-back, chinning the moon, circle buck, come apart, come undone, crawfish, crow hop, double shuffle, fallback, fence-

cornering, fence-worming, fold up, frog walk, goat, hard to sit, haul hell out of its shuck, hop for mama, jackknifing, kettling, kick the lid off, laying a rail fence, moan, pinwheel, pitching, pitching fence-cornered, pump handle, pussy-back, rain-bowin', rear-back, riding, riding equipment, sheep-jump, shoots his back, slattin' his sails, straight buck, stuck his bill in the ground, sunfish, swallows his head, swapping ends, take you to church, throw back, throwing the pack, trying to chin the moon, turn a wildcat, turned through himself, unload, unwind, walkin' beamin', warp his backbone, whing-ding, windmilling, wompoo, wrinkled his spine.

bucking on a dime

Said when a horse does his bucking in one spot.

bucking rein

Usually a single rope attached to the hackamore of a bucking horse. Gripping this rope helps the rider keep his balance. In rodeo contests he is not permitted to change hands.

bucking rim

A round-headed projection on the cantle of some saddles.

bucking roll

A roll of blankets tied across the saddle, just behind the fork, to help wedge the rider in the saddle and make it more difficult for the horse to throw him. Sometimes a leather pad, stuffed with hair, 3 or 4 inches high, and tied down on each side of the fork just behind the horn.

bucking season

In sheep raising, the mating season when breeding is done, usually late in December or January so that the lambs will be born in the spring.

bucking straight away

Bucking of a horse that consists of long jumps straight ahead without any twists, whirling, or rearing. A straightaway bucker is an easy horse for some to ride but poison for others. He is usually big and strong and rough in his actions. His chief stock in trade is to jump extremely high and then, as he starts down, to kick high with his hindquarters. At the same time the cantle of the saddle hits the seat of the rider's pants, and the rider hits the dirt. A horse of this type usually hurts his rider when bucking him off, because he generally throws him high and hard. (Bruce Clinton, "Bucking Horses," *Western Horseman*, Vol. III, No. 3 [May–June, 1938], 10.)

bucking the tiger

In gambling, playing faro. During the early days the professional gambler of the frontier carried his faro outfit in a box on which was painted a picture of a Bengal tiger. Tigers were also pictured on his chips and oilcloth layout, and the game became known as the *tiger*.

buck jump

The plunging and leaping of a horse trying to shed his rider. The expression is particularly used when a horse leaps as he bucks.

buck-nun

A recluse; a man who lives alone.

bucko

In logging, a worker who rafts logs in a *boom, q.v.*

buck out

A cowboy's expression meaning *to die*, usually in a tragic way.

buck out in smoke

To die in a gun battle.

buck rake

A large wooden fork pushed ahead of a team or tractor and used to collect cut hay.

buckshot land

The westerner's name for poor clay soil.

buckskin

A soft, yellowish or grayish leather originally made of the skin of a deer. A horse of light-yellow color produced by the breeding of sand and blood bays. In logging, a log from which the bark has been peeled off.

buck snatcher

A river boat used in piratical undertakings.

buck strap

A handhold consisting of a narrow strap riveted to the leather housing of the saddle just below and on the off side of the base of the horn. Top riders have nothing but contempt for this handhold, which is barred in contests.

buck the saddle

Said of a green bronc that, at the first saddling, is allowed to buck with the empty saddle while he is held with a rope.

buck wood

To saw wood.

buddling

In mining, separating ores by washing.

buds

A mark of ownership of cattle made by cutting down a strip of skin on the nose of an animal.

bueno

In open-range days in the Southwest, a "good" cow; from the Spanish. So called because the cow was unclaimed by anyone at the roundup and its brand could not be found in the brand book. Such animals were good pickups because they were supposed to get by brand inspectors at shipping points and market centers. (Jack Potter to R.F.A.)

buffalo boat

A boat made by stretching buffalo hides over a frame, used by Indians and early fur traders.

buffalo chip

Dried buffalo manure, frequently used for fuel on the plains in the early days. Also called *buffalo wood*.

buffalo cider

The liquid in the stomach of a buffalo, which the thirsty hunter drank when he had killed his game at a great distance from water.

buffalo crossing

A place where buffalo herds crossed a stream.

buffalo dance

A dance held by Plains Indians before a

buffalo hunt. It was an important, ritualistic ceremony calling on the gods to aid the hunt.

buffaloed

Mentally confused, bluffed. Also, struck on the head with the barrel of a six gun—Wyatt Earp's favorite method of fighting.

Buffaloes

See boss, buffalo cider, buffalo crossing, buffalo ground, buffalo lick, buffalo pound, buffalo range, buffalo ranger, buffalo run, buffalo wallow, buffler, cíbola, dépouille, prairie beeves.

buffalo gnat

A small insect that tortured the buffaloes in the summer. .

buffalo grass

A perennial low-growing grass common on the former buffalo ranges of the West. Also, a species of grama grass.

buffalo ground

A region where buffaloes abounded.

buffalo gun

A heavy-caliber rifle used by the buffalo hunters, usually a Sharps .50.

buffalo horse

A horse trained for buffalo hunting.

buffalo lick

A region where buffaloes found a saline mineral in the ground and licked it for salt.

buffalo mange

A westerner's name for lice, of which the buffalo hunters usually had a supply.

buffalo pound

A place where buffaloes congregated during the winter.

buffalo range

Buffalo feeding grounds; a section where buffaloes ran in the old days. Also, an uninhabited section; the wide-open spaces.

buffalo ranger

A buffalo that rambled from the herd and lived alone.

buffalo robe

The skin of a buffalo dressed with the hair on for use as a covering, carriage robe, etc.

buffalo run

A plain where buffaloes roamed.

buffalo running

Hunting buffaloes on horseback.

buffalo skinner

A man who made a business of skinning buffaloes for their hides. Usually the hunter did the killing and hired a crew of skinners to do the skinning.

buffalo soldier

An Indian's name for the Negro soldier of the early frontier forts, probably because of his color and hair.

buffalo stamp

Tracks of hard blue soil, said to have been caused by buffaloes crowding each other, stamping, and licking the ground for salt.

buffalo tug

A strap made of buffalo hide.

buffalo wallow

A depression in the earth pawed out by buffaloes to make a smooth, dusty surface in which they could roll to shed ticks and dead hair.

buffalo whooper

A man hired by cattlemen to keep buffaloes off their cattle range.

buffalo wolf

A very large gray wolf that preyed upon buffaloes.

buffalo wood

See *buffalo chip*.

buffler

A trader's name for a buffalo.

buford

In rodeo, a calf or steer that is small, weak, and easily thrown or tied.

bug

In gambling, a device used by crooked gamblers to hold cards under the table.

buggy

In mining, the carriage of an aerial conveying system. A wheelbarrow.

buggy boss

A title given to a ranchowner from the East, who made his inspection tours in a buggy because he did not ride horseback well.

bugheway

An ugly customer; a blackguard. A corruption of the French *bourgeois*, meaning *citizen* or *member of the middle class*.

bug juice

A cowboy's name for whisky.

bug torch

A miner's lamp.

build a high line

A logger's expression meaning *to tell a tall tale*.

build a smoke under his hoofs

To shoot at someone's feet.

building a loop

Shaking a noose out of a rope in preparation for making a throw.

built high above his corns

A cowboy's description of a tall person. Cowboys are strong for exaggeration. I heard one speak of another cowboy as being "so tall it'd take a steeple jack to look 'im in the eye," and again, "so tall he couldn't tell when his feet was cold."

bulge

To appear suddenly, as, "He *bulged* into the road ahead."

bulgine

A logger's name for an engine.

bulkhead

In steamboating, any wall or partition. In mining, a tight partition in a mine for protection against water, fire, or gas. Also, the end of a flume, from which water is carried in iron pipes to hydraulic workings.

bull

In logging, an ox. A boss. A prefix (except in the case of *bull cook, q.v.*) meaning superlative in size, power, or authority.

bull bars

Bars placed across the rear of a branding chute to prevent cattle from backing out.

bullbat

A *bronc buster, q.v.*

bull block

In logging, the main pulley block used in high-lead logging; one of the largest pieces of the block and tackle used in the woods.

bullboat

A lightweight boat used by the fur traders and Indians on the Missouri River and its tributaries. The excessive shallowness of some of the streams precluded the use of any craft drawing more than 9 or 10 inches. The bullboat had probably the lightest draft for its size of any vessel ever constructed, and was admirably suited for its particular use.

It resembled an enormous shallow oval basket and ordinarily was about 25 feet long, 12 or 15 feet wide, and perhaps 2 or 3 feet deep. Its framework was made of willow poles fastened together with rawhide lashings. The frame was covered with buffalo hides that had been sewed together. It was made watertight with a mixture of melted buffalo fat and earth or ashes. The finished boat was very light.

The boat was steered by means of poles used by two men, and therefore shallow water was preferred to deep water. When the poles could not reach bottom, the boat drifted with the current until a shallow stretch was reached, where the polers could regain control. In spite of their lightness, the boats could carry up to 6,000 pounds.

bull bucker

In logging, the man in charge of the gang whose job is to *buck (q.v.)* the fallen trees. He records the daily cut of fallers and buckers, going from log to log, measuring the small end of each with wooden calipers or a "cheat stick," which gives a reading in board feet for a log of known length.

bull chain

The big chain that hoists logs up the chute from millpond to sawmill.

bull cheese

Buffalo meat cut in thin slices and dried in the sun.

bull cook

The flunky in a logging camp who fed the draft animals in the days before tractors took the place of livestock in most logging operations. Today, the camp chore boy, who sweeps the bunkhouse, cuts wood, and fills the wood boxes. If pigs are kept in camp, he feeds them. He is the perennial butt of camp jokes.

bulldog

To trip and throw a steer. The bulldogger throws his right arm over the steer's neck, gripping either the loose bottom skin at the base of the right horn or the animal's nose with his right hand while seizing the tip of the left horn with his left hand. The bulldogger then rises clear of the ground and, by lunging his body downward against his own left elbow, so twists the neck of the animal that the latter loses his balance and falls. The first bulldogger was a Negro named Bill Pickett who astonished the cowboys of his day by dropping off a running horse onto the neck of a steer and throwing the animal by hand. Others began trying it with success, but it was not until a good many years later that enough bulldoggers were present at any one rodeo to make a contest. As far back as 1910 and 1911 at some shows a single steer was bulldogged, purely as an exhibition.

bulldogger

One who bulldogs. See *bulldog*.

BULLDOGGING

See bulldog, bulldogger, dogger, hoolihaning, mug, steer wrestling, twisting down.

bulldogs

A cowboy's name for short tapaderos. See *tapadero*.

bull donkey

The logger's name for a large logging engine.

bulldozer

A standard crawler-type tractor used in latter-day logging. It had a heavy steel blade mounted across the front at a right angle to the tracks. The blade could be raised or lowered by hydraulic or cable devices. The angle of the blade and tractor could not be changed, and all pushing action was straight ahead.

bullet

In gambling, an ace.

bullfrog

In mining, a small truck used to push cars up a slope.

bullhead

A dehorned animal.

bull hides

A common name for heavy leather chaps.

bulling

What a cowboy calls *balking*; said of an animal that is refusing to move.

bulling steer

A steer that, though castrated, has retained some sexual odor and attracts other steers. Such steers are a nuisance when trailing cattle.

bullion

In mining, uncoined gold or silver.

bull-necked

Headstrong.

bull nurse

A cowboy who accompanies cattle on the train to their ultimate destination.

bull of the woods

A logging-camp foreman; the woods boss. A contest staged in logging shows at district fairs. This contest is held on a large log with a number of contestants wearing boxing gloves and calked boots, plus regular gear. The last man to keep his balance and stay on the log is acclaimed the "bull of the woods."

bull outfit

A common name for a freighting outfit using cattle as the motive power.

bull pen

A logger's name for the bunkhouse.

bull-pen boy

A logger's name for the bunkhouse caretaker.

bull planers

Large sawmill planers.

bull prick

In logging, a bar with a tapering end used to pry a hole in a stump so that a shot of powder can be inserted. A marlin spike used in splicing wire rope. A compensating pin that allows for slack between the log trailer and truck.

bull pusher

A freighter's name for a man who drove bull teams.

bull rails

In steamboating, dressed planks, usually of pine or poplar, inserted between the sections spacing the stationaries along the outboard sides of the main deck (along the guards). Usually four or five such rails are placed in each section, creating a rail fence. They are set in slots so that they can easily be removed when necessary. They are found only on packet boats.

bull riding

A rodeo event in which the contestant rides a bull equipped with *bull rigging, q.v.* In the early contests the rider was allowed to hang on with both hands, setting himself well back with his feet well forward and spurring the shoulders and neck only. Later two hands were barred and one hand had to be kept free. Finally a *bull rope q.v.* was substituted for the bull rigging.

bull rigging

In early-day rodeo, a specially made surcingle used in riding wild bulls. It consisted of a heavy leather strap, 3 inches wide and about 2 feet long, with two handholds about 9 inches apart. At each end was a heavy ring to which latigos and cinch were attached as on a saddle. In logging, the connecting equipment which goes between lines used in a cable logging operation and from which chokers are hung.

bull rope

In rodeo, the loose rope used in bull riding. The rope, usually owned by the bull rider, is fastened on the bull in such a manner that it falls off at the end of the ride. There can be no knots or hitches in the rope, and it must have a bell attached that hangs under the bull's belly. The contestant may cling only to this bull rope and must not touch any part of the bull or himself with his free hand.

BULLS

See animal, cattle.

bull shoes

Shoes much like horseshoes, sometimes made of rawhide, sometimes of iron, placed on work oxen to keep their feet from getting sore.

bull's manse

A cowboy's name for the home of the big boss.

bull tailing

A game once popular with the Mexican cowboys of Texas. A bull would be released from a pen of wild bulls, and with much yelling a cowboy would take after him. Seizing the bull by the tail, the rider rushed his horse forward and a little to one side, throwing the bull off balance and "busting" him with terrific force. (J. Frank Dobie, *Vaquero of the Brush Country* [Dallas, Southwest Press, 1929], 16, 19). Bull tailing may be considered the forerunner of *bulldogging (q.v.)*. With the increase in the value of cattle, owners frowned upon the sport, which soon died out.

bull team

A team of oxen.

bull thrower

A name the early trapper often gave his large-bore rifle.

bull train

A wagon train drawn by oxen, such as those used by the early freighters.

bull wagon

A wagon drawn by oxen.

bull-wagon boss

The wagon boss of a bull train. Also called *bull-wagon master*.

bull-wagon master

See *bull-wagon boss*.

bullwhacker

A man who whacked, or drove, ox teams in early freighting days.

bull wheels

Huge wooden wheels used in logging.

bull whip

A long woven whip attached to a handle of hickory or white ash 3 feet long upon which the *bull whacker* (*q.v.*) could firmly plant both hands. At the butt each lash, which was attached to the stick by a soft strip of buckskin, formed a loop and was frequently more than 1 inch thick. The lashes were from 18 inches to more than 10 feet long and graduated in thickness to the tip, which was the thickness of a lead pencil. The number of strands in a bull whip was also graduated. At the butt there were as many strands as the maker—usually the bullwhacker—could weave, often fourteen. At the tip, this number was reduced to six. From the top down to six or eight feet from the end the whip was made of leather, often old boot tops. The rest was made of tough buckskin or elk skin.

bull whipper

In logging, a man who works in the lowlands where the big trees grow and sometimes drives as many as eight yoke of oxen. A driver who pulls logs out of the woods with ox team.

bull-windy

A cowboy's name for a balky horse.

bum

An orphan lamb that lives by robbing others of their mother's milk; a lamb whose mother has deserted it. Also called *bummer*.

bum a lamb

To take a lamb away from its mother and raise it by hand.

bumblebee whisky

What the cowboy calls a strong whisky with a sting.

bummer

See *bum*.

bump

In logging, to replace or remove from a job. In gambling, to raise, to bet an amount greater than that put into the pot by the preceding better.

bums on the plush

What the logger calls the idle rich; people who ride in passenger cars.

bunch

A group of cattle. To herd a group of cattle together. See also *belly bunches*.

bunched hay

Shocks of hay made by running a hayrake the long way down a windrow and sumping the hay into small piles. This is a fast method, but hay collected in this way is tangled and hard to pitch, and the leaves are badly scattered.

bunch grasser

A range horse living upon bunch grass, a dense turf grass of the West. Also, a man who lives in the foothills.

bunch ground

A name occasionally used for the round-up grounds.

bunch her

In logging, to quit work.

bunching

In logging, rolling logs into compact piles for transportation with big wheels or other equipment.

bunch quitter

A horse that has the habit of leaving the remuda and pulling for the home ranch or parts unknown.

bunk

A built-in bed, as in a bunkhouse or steamboat stateroom. To sleep. In logging, a logging car. To pile logs on bunks.

bunker

The logger's name for his bed partner. Also called *bunky*.

bunkhouse

The cowhands' sleeping quarters at the ranch. The logger's living quarters.

bunkhouse gang

The workers who share a bunkhouse.

BUNKHOUSES

See bull pen, bunkhouse, dice house, dive, doghouse, dump, houses, louse cage, ram pasture, shack.

bunk log

The bottom log of a truckload of logs.

bunky

See *bucker.*

bunting

See *bucket bunting.*

Bunyan camp

What the logger calls a camp with poor living accommodations.

buoy

In the old river-boat days, a bench 4 or 5 feet long with one support removed, floating upside down with the other support extending above the water to resist the current and keep the bench afloat. It was anchored in the shoals of a reef by a rope tied to a heavy stone.

burden strap

A tumpline; a strap used by Indians, usually the women, to support loads carried on their shoulders or backs.

burl

A hard, woody growth on a tree trunk or on roots, more or less rounded in form. It is usually the result of the entwined growth of a cluster of buds. In lumber a burl produces a distorted and unusual, but often attractive, grain.

burn

An area in which fire has injured a forest.

burn a card

In gambling, to expose and bury a card or place it on the bottom of the pack. In blackjack, after the cards have been shuffled and cut, the dealer *burns* the top card of the deck by showing it and placing it face up on the bottom of the deck.

burn cattle

To brand cattle.

burned hay

Hay that is stacked wet and turns brown or black when it heats.

burn 'em and boot 'em

To brand calves. After a calf is branded, it is usually booted toward its anxious mother.

burnin' and trimmin' up calves

Branding, earmarking, and castrating calves.

burning rawhide

Branding; used mostly in reference to rustling.

burn powder

A cowman's expression meaning to *shoot a gun.*

burn the breeze

To ride at full speed. One cowhand, in telling of a fast ride he had made, said, "When I pushed on the reins, I had that hoss kickin' the jackrabbits out of the trail."

burn the stick

A logger's expression meaning *to slide down a pole.*

burnt cards

See *burn a card.*

burn the wagon

A cowboy's expression meaning *to get rid of all excess baggage;* also used to mean *to burn one's bridges behind him.*

burnt till he looks like a brand book

Said of a much-branded horse or steer. A horse with many brands shows that he has changed hands often and that he has no friends among his former owners. The brands are a good sign of his untrustworthiness.

burro

A small donkey extensively used in the early West as a carrier of freight; pronounced *boo'r-ro,* not *burrow,* by westerners. Also, a stand shaped like the roof of a house to hold a saddle when it is not in use. Placing the saddle on a burro is much better than laying it down or hanging it by a stirrup. If the cowhand does lay his saddle down, he puts it on its side or stands it on its head; he does not drop it on the skirts. If he hangs it up, it is usually hung by the horn string. In logging, the jenny ass used in setting poles.

burro load

A unit of measure in hauling, as a *burro load of firewood*.

burro milk

A cowboy's expression meaning *nonsense*.

BURY

See plant, put to bed with a pick and shovel.

bury the hatchet

An expression originating in Indian custom, meaning *to cease hostilities*.

buscadero

In the Southwest, a tough, gun-packing officer of the law; later occasionally used to mean any gunman; from the Spanish *buscador*, meaning *searcher*.

buscadero belt

A gun belt 4 to 6 inches wide, with a slotted flap on each hip for carrying a gun.

bushed

Exhausted; worn out. Also, short for *bushwhacked*. See *bushwhack*.

busheling

In logging, paying on a piecework basis for felling and cutting timber.

bush rat

In logging, a woodsman.

bush tail

See *brush tail*.

bushwhack

To ambush. One cowboy friend used to say, "Some men are bad—behind a bush."

bushwhacker

A woodsman. Also, one who ambushes.

business riding

Riding a bucking horse when the rider, unable to spur his mount, hooks his spurs in the cinch and makes it his "business" to stay on—if possible.

bust

To throw an animal violently. To break a horse. In gambling, a worthless hand. Also, to reach too high a count, as in blackjack, when a player's total card count exceeds twenty-one.

busted cinch

A broken cinch; hence an expression meaning *failure*.

busted flush

An incomplete poker hand; hence an expression meaning *plans gone awry*.

buster

Short for *bronc buster*, q.v.

BUSTERS

See bronc breaker, bronc buster, bronc fighter, bronc peeler, bronc scratcher, bronc snapper, bronc squeezer, bronc stomper, bull-bat, buster, contract buster, cowboy, flash rider, jinete, mansador, peeler, rough-string rider, twister.

busting

In rodeo, a contest in which the rider *busts* a steer by turning his horse and riding off at an angle after roping the head or horns and throwing the slack around the far side of the steer. As soon as the slack is taken out of the rope, the steer is pulled to the ground.

BUSTING

See busting, steer busting, rodeo events and stunts.

butcher

During branding, the man who cuts the earmarks, dewlaps, wattles, and other inerasable marks of identification on the animals.

butcher-knife wagon

A wagon with narrow tires that make deep, narrow ruts in the trail.

butt

The base of a tree or the large end of a log. The trunk of a tree denuded of its branches.

butt brand

A brand placed on the rear or buttocks of an animal.

butt chain

The chain at the end of a harness tug to fasten a horse to a singletree. Also, sometimes, any short length of chain.

butt cut

In logging, the first portion of a tree cut off above the stump; also called *butt log*.

butte

A conspicuous hill or mountain left standing in an area leveled by erosion.

butterboard weaner

See *blab*.

butterfly

A rope trick. The performer starts the rope spinning, either in front of himself or around his head. Then the noose is enlarged and rapidly darted from side to side, vertically spinning to the right and then to the left, in a pattern similar to the shape of a butterfly.

buttermilk

A cowboy's name for a motherless calf.

buttermilk cow

A bull.

buttermilk horse

What the cowboys of some sections call a palomino.

butt heads

A name occasionally used for dehorned cattle.

butt hook

In logging, part of the rigging suspended from the skidder carriage that travels on the sky line used in high-line logging. The rigging consists of a line carrying the fixed butt hook and a second or sliding hook. The hook tender grabs the butt hook, a second hooker takes the sliding hook, and each fastens on three choker lines that have been noosed around logs by choke setters. The hook tender highballs the whistle punk, who then signals the skidder lever man to wind up the skidder line and pull the six logs to the place of assembly. First trailing the ground, then rising high in the air, the logs slide and jump, looking alive and dangerous as the whining cables swing them along, to dump them at last in a great heap at the landing.

butt log

See *butt cut*.

butt off

To cut a defective portion from a log, usually from the *butt, q.v.*

button

A cowboy's name for a young boy.

butty

In mining, a fellow workman.

buy a trunk

An expressive western phrase meaning *to leave the country*.

buying chips

In gambling, preparing to enter a game; hence, also said of one who is taking part, unasked, in a dispute or fight.

buying on tick

Buying on credit; an expression used by cowmen and loggers.

buzzard-head

A poor horse; in cowboy parlance, one that "was dead but jes' wouldn't lie down."

buzzard-head

A mean-tempered range horse.

buzzard-wings

See *bat-wings*.

buzz saw

A spur whose rowel has a few long, sharp points.

by the bushel

Contract log work, usually contract felling or bucking. Also called *by the inch* or *by the mile*.

C

"Only a fool argues with a skunk, a mule, or a cook"

caballada

A band of saddle horses; from the Spanish. The word refers to the extra horses not at the time under saddle—the supply of saddle horses maintained by a ranch. It is not used to refer to unbroken horses. See also *cavvy*.

caballero

Horseman; from the Spanish, meaning *cavalier* or *knight*. A hardened but gay cowboy who can jump on his horse at any moment and tell the rest of the world to go to hell.

caballo

Horse; from the Spanish. The word is used in light conversation, but generally the cowboy calls his horse *hoss*.

cabestro

Halter; from the Spanish. The American cowboy uses this word mostly for a horse-hair-rope halter, to distinguish it from a leather one.

cabin

On a river packet boat, the long hallway running the length of the interior of the passenger quarters on the boiler deck, usually fancifully trimmed. On either side of the cabin are rows of doors leading into staterooms. The forward end is usually designated the men's cabin, and the ship's office and a bar are located there. The aft end is the ladies' cabin. On a towboat, the cabin is the space aft of the officers' rooms on the boiler deck; a lounging area. On both packet and towboat, the cabin serves the dual purpose of lounging area and dining hall. On river steamboats the term is not used in connection with such rooms.

cabin fever

Restlessness and hostility among cowboys snowed in at a line camp and forced to spend too much time in each other's company.

cable

The rope the cowboy uses for a *rope corral, q.v.*

cable rig

A saddle rigged with a steel cable under the seat; now obsolete.

caboodle

A cowboy's word for the whole amount, the entire lot.

caboose

See *cuna*.

cabrón

In the Southwest, an outlaw of low breeding and principle; from the Spanish, meaning *cuckold*.

cache

A term used by traders and hunters to designate a hiding place for provisions and effects; from the French. Though it was a point of honor among most trappers never to violate another's cache, the hiding places were sometimes discovered and the provisions "raised" or "lifted" by persons who had no right to them.

cackleberries

A logger's name for eggs.

cackler

A logger's and miner's term for a clerk; a white-collar worker.

cactus

A thorny desert plant of many varieties; also, a term sometimes used to designate the desert country as a whole.

cactus boomers

A name for wild brush cattle.

cage

In mining, an elevator for transporting men and material up and down a shaft; so

49

called because of the iron bars that often enclose the cage. It may have from one to four decks or platforms, and is steadied by guides on the sides of the shaft. In logging, the section of the sawmill in which the *bear fighter (q.v.)* works; also called *nest*.

cage cover

In mining, the iron sheets fixed above a cage to protect its occupants.

cage guides

Vertical pieces of wood, iron, or steel fixed in a mining shaft, between which the cages run to prevent them from striking one another or any portion of the shaft.

cager

In mining, the person who puts the cars on the cages at the bottom of the mine shaft or at intermediate landings and otherwise attends the elevator.

cage seat

Mine-cage scaffolding, sometimes fitted with strong springs, to take the shock when the cage reaches the pit bottom.

cahoots

Partnership. The cowman always *went into cahoots* or *throwed in* with another man when he entered a partnership.

caisson

In mining, a hollow steel cylinder with a cutting edge on the lower end, used for making shafts. The caisson is forced down into the ground by weights and other means, and as the caisson sinks the shaft lining is built higher and higher.

caisson disease

In mining, a disease induced by remaining for some time in a compressed atmosphere followed by too rapid a return to the surface; characterized by bubbles of gas forming in the blood, neuralgic pains, and paralytic symptoms. Also called *the bends*.

cake wagon

A wagon used on modern ranches to carry cottonseed-meal cake to feed the cattle.

calaboose

Jail; from the Spanish *calabozo*.

Calamity Jane

What the gamblers called the queen of spades.

calf crop

Calves born during the calving season.

calf fries

The testicles removed from castrated bull calves and fried; in the Southwest considered as much a delicacy as sweetbreads.

calf horse

A horse used in roping, so trained that he will back away, still facing the thrown calf, to take up the slack.

calf-legs

A horse whose legs are too short in proportion to its body.

Calf on the ground!

The call of the *flanker (q.v.)* to the ropers telling them that the calf to be branded has been thrown.

Calf on the string!

The roper's call that the calf to be branded has been roped.

calf roping

A rodeo event in which a cowboy, astride a horse, must rope a calf, jump from his horse, dash to the calf, and tie the animal by three legs against time. The event had its origin in actual practice, when cowboys on roundup had to rope a calf and drag it to the branding fire in the same way.

calf 'round

To loaf; to idle about. It means, in the language of one cowhand, to "keep 'bout as busy as a hibernatin' bear."

calf roundup

A term for *spring roundup*, which is held to brand the calves born during the winter. It occurs after the grass has come, taking place in March throughout the South and later in the northern regions.

calf slobbers

A cowboy's name for meringue.

calf time

Springtime on the ranch.

calf wagon

A wagon used by some of the old-time trail drivers to haul the calves born on the trail. Also called *blattin' cart*. Some trailers did not use such a wagon and, rather than delay the herd, killed the calves or gave them to settlers who happened to live nearby.

calico

A pinto horse. A cowboy's term for a woman, so called because of the dress material she commonly wore. It was said in the Old West that "calico on the range was as scarce as sunflowers on a Christmas tree."

calico fever

The "ailment" of one who is crazy about girls or lovesick.

calico queen

The frontier name for a honkytonk woman.

California

To throw an animal by tripping it.

California buckskin

A cowboy's name for baling wire.

California collar

A hangman's noose, so called because of its frequent use in California in vigilante days.

California drag rowels

A spur whose rowels drag the ground when its wearer is afoot. It is of the Spanish-California type, with a straight heelband and a small button on the end on which to loop the spur leather, and the heel chains pass under the instep to hold it in position on the boot.

California moccasins

A cowhand's name for sacks bound about the feet to prevent them from freezing.

California pants

A style of pants used on the range, usually of heavy striped or checked wool of excellent double weave.

California prayer book

A gambler's name for a deck of cards.

California reins

Reins made of one piece of leather, not separated as with open reins.

California rig

See *California saddle*.

California saddle

A light, high-horned saddle with one cinch placed near the center of the saddle and covered stirrups. This saddle is not much good in mountainous country, for the cinch will not hold when the horse is going downhill. Also called *California rig, center fire, single-barreled saddle, single fire,* and *single-rigged saddle*.

California skirts

A stock saddle with round skirts, so called because it is a favorite style in that state.

California slingshot

In logging, the name given to crotch-line loading. In this logging system two poles are used with the rigging, which resembles a slingshot in the middle.

California sorrel

A red-gold horse of the palomino type.

California tree

The framework of a *California saddle, q.v.*

California twist

In roping, a cast in which the rope is thrown with a single overhand twist and no twirling.

calked shoes

Shoes or boots with calks, pointed metal studs, on the soles, worn by loggers on the drive to keep them from slipping when working on logs.

calking cement

A logger's expression meaning *going to town*.

call

In poker, to ask for a show of hands after putting into the pot a sum equal to the largest bet made by any preceding player.

callin'

What the cowboy calls courting a girl.

calling the brands

Giving cattle brands a name. Brands have made necessary a language all their own, and though they are an enigma to the tenderfoot, the cowman is very adept at reading them.

calling the turn

In faro, guessing correctly the order in which the last three cards in the faro box appear.

call the landings

In steamboating, to direct the pilot to the boat landings. This was a duty of the steamboat clerk and was accomplished by speaking into a tin trumpet hooked into a speaking tube connecting the office with the pilothouse. Before the boat came to a landing place, the clerk blew his breath into the speaking tube, which produced a shrill whistle in the pilothouse, and when the pilot replied, the clerk directed him to the place where the boat was to be landed.

call the turn both ways

In faro, to name correctly the cards in the last turn. For example, if a player has bet his money on an ace-trey or a trey-ace combination and the last three cards are ace, deuce, and trey, he will be paid two for one on the bet. The expression *from the case card* means the same thing.

CALVES

See acorn calf, bucket dogie, buford, buttermilk, calf crop, churn-dash calf, deacon, dogie, droop-eyed, freemartin, full ear, hairy-Dick, hot foot, leppy, long yearlin', mug, open heifer, orejano, pail-fed, poddy, rusties, sanchos, short yearling, skimmy, sleeper, slick, spike weaner, weaner, windbelly, yearling.

calzoneras

Mexican-style trousers with buttons down the sides, sometimes worn by the early traders.

cama

A name the cowboy sometimes gives his bedroll; from the Spanish, meaning *bed*.

camino real

A main highway; from the Spanish. In the Southwest in early days this term was used to signify a route over which most traffic moved.

camisa

A shirt; from the Spanish.

campanyero

Friend; companion; from the Spanish *compañero*.

camp boss

The man in charge of a camp, especially a lumber camp.

camp dog

In logging, a helper who looks after the camp sleeping quarters and bunks; a flunky.

camp eye

In logging, a camp guard or watchman.

CAMPING

See dry-camp, form camp, make a port, Man at the pot! moving camp, noon, nooning it, running guard, sage-henning, sleepin' out, star-pitch, Tucson bed.

camping on his trail

A cowboy's expression meaning *following someone closely*.

camp inspector

A title given by loggers to a man who drifts from camp to camp, trying out the food and living accommodations but working as little as possible; a vagrant logger.

camp jerker

See *camp tender*.

camp mover

See *camp tender*.

campo santo

A cemetery; from the Spanish, meaning literally *holy field*. Though not commonly used in the Southwest, the term is well understood.

camp outfit

The equipment and provisions used in making camp on the range.

camp robber

A cowboy's name for the Rocky Mountain jay; so called because of the bird's boldness in robbing a camp of anything it can carry off.

CAMPS

See boar's nest, bog camp, bog hole, camp boss, camp outfit, cow camp, dry camp, garbage can, ghost town, grand encampment, Indian deading, Jones' place, line camp, lobby, maniac den, mining camp, placer camp, quartz camp, Rocky Mountain college, roll the cotton, sheep camp, sign camp, silver camp, squaw camp, wannigan, wet camp.

camp staller

A horse that refuses to leave camp in the morning.

camp tender

In sheepherding, the man who brings supplies to camp and moves the camp for the herders. Also called *camp mover*, *camp jerker*, and *wagon boss*. He is more often in town or at headquarters than in camp.

can

To wire a tin can to a cow's neck to prevent it from breaking a fence. To discharge an employee. In faro, the dealer's metal dealing box. Also called *faro box, tell box, q.v.*

cañada

A small canyon; a narrow green valley; from the Spanish.

canal

The main artificial stream from which irrigation water is obtained.

canalón

In placer mining, a ground sluice; a channel; from the Spanish, meaning *gutter*.

candy side

In logging, the crew of a high-lead camp that has the best equipment; the opposite of *haywire outfit, q.v.*

candy wagon

In logging, a station wagon or bus that transports men to and from work in the woods; *crummie* is the more popular term.

canned

Finished; through; fired.

canned cow

The cowboy's name for canned milk.

canoe

One of several kinds of small boats. The canoe used by white men on western rivers was never made of bark but always from the trunk of a tree, mostly commonly a cottonwood tree. The cottonwood was selected for three reasons: it was large, it was readily available, and it had a grain that allowed the makers to transform it into the desired form. The canoes were any size up to 35 feet long and 4 feet wide. It usually took two men about a week to build one. With broadax and adz they hollowed out and shaped the log, leaving the bottom of the hull about 3 or 4 inches thick and the sides about 2 inches thick. Sections of solid wood were left untouched every 5 or 6 feet, forming bulkheads to give added strength to the canoe and prevent dangerous shifting of the cargo through rapid water.

can openers

A cowboy's name for spurs.

cant

In logging, a slab of wood cut from a log. To toss.

cant dog

A peavey, a wooden lever with an iron spike at one end; used by the logger and the riverman. See also *cant hook.*

cant hook

A logging tool similar to the peavey but shorter and lighter, with a toe ring and lip at the end instead of a spike; used in loading sleighs.

cantina

A tavern. One of the pockets of the knapsack used by the pony-express rider. From the Spanish, originally meaning *wine cellar* and later, in Spanish America, *tavern* or *knapsack*.

cantinesses

Saddle pockets; a corruption of the Spanish *cantina, q.v.*

cantle

The raised back of a saddle.

cantle-boarding

Riding loosely so that the lower back hits the *cantle, q.v.*

cantle drop

The outside of the back of the *cantle, q.v.*

can't-be-rode horse

An *outlaw (q.v.)* horse. Any horse that is difficult to ride.

can't cut her

A logger's expression meaning *unable to do something.*

can't hack her

A logger's expression meaning *unable to do something.*

can't hook cattle

Cattle without horns; muleys (mulleys).

can't-whistle

The cowboy's name for a harelipped person.

canvas bungalow

A logger's tent used as living quarters.

canyon

A deep valley with high, steep sides. From the Spanish *cañón*, originally meaning *tube* or *cannon.*

cap

In mining, a narrow or pinched place in a vein of ore. A change from paying to barren ground. A barren section in the *gangue, q.v.*

cap-and-ball layout

A cowboy's term for a shiftless and unprogressive ranch or outfit.

capitaine

What the early traders called their leader; from the French, meaning *captain.*

caponera

A herd of geldings; from the Spanish.

caporal

A cowboy's name for the boss, the manager or assistant manager of the ranch; from the Spanish, meaning *chief.*

capote

Coat; from the Spanish.

capper

A confederate or decoy for a gambler or gambling house. He frequents the gambling houses and is allowed by the dealer to win large sums to lead the unwary cowboy to buck a *brace game, q.v.*

cap rock

The escarpment of the high plains, as the cap rock of the Texas Panhandle.

capstan

A metal spool on a boat deck which may be turned manually or mechanically and upon which ropes are tightly wound to make secure ties. It is used for lifting heavy weights or exerting power. A *capstan bar* is a wooden club inserted in a hole in the capstan and used to wind the rope manually. A capstan is said to be set on *double purchase* when the gearing mechanism is set to produce slow rotation speed and great pulling power.

Captain Jim Crow

In logging, the boss of the railroad-tie makers.

carabo pole

In freighting, a pole similar to a cattle prod, only a little lighter and longer and with a brad in the small end; used by freighters to prod oxen in the early days when wagons were pulled by these animals. From the Spanish *carabao.*

carajo

An ox driver. A mule skinner. Sometimes, any base fellow. Also, an exclamation used by mule skinners, cowboys, and other outdoor workers; from the Spanish *caray*, meaning, like *caramba, confound it!* and *jo*, meaning *whoa!*

caravan

A train of wagons. A string of pack mules, as used in early freighting.

carbonate

The common term in the West for an ore containing a considerable proportion of carbonate of lead. The combination of carbonic acid with various bases; soft carbonates have lead for a base, and hard carbonates have iron for a base. An ore of lead and silver.

carbonite

In mining, a chemical combination of carbon dioxide. Carbonites of the metals are often found in the upper portions of ore bodies.

card mechanic

A card cheat. A person adept at manipulating cards.

card mob

A group of card cheats who work together as a team.

carcage

The Indian's arrow quiver; from the Spanish *carcaj (carcax)*.

cárcel

Jail; from the Spanish.

card man

What the loggers call a union man; often shortened to *card*.

CARE FOR

See ride herd on.

careless with his branding iron

An expression describing a rustler or a person suspected of having designs on other folks' livestock.

carga

In mining, a load of clean ore ready for the furnace, weighing, in the Mexican measure, 300 pounds; from the Spanish.

cargador

In a pack train, the man second in importance to the pack master; he makes up and forms the cargo, equalizes the packs, cares for the mules, repairs the aparejos, etc.; from the Spanish, meaning *freighter*.

cargo

Collectively, the loads carried by a pack train, as *to form cargo*, i.e., to arrange in an orderly and convenient manner an aggregation of loads.

cargo cover

Canvas used to protect the *cargo (q.v.)* in camp or bivouac.

carling

In steamboating, a lightly built exposed joist supporting a deck or roof.

carne seco

Dried beef; from the Spanish.

carnival

To buck in a showy manner.

carnival hand

A cowboy's name for a stunt rider.

Caroline nine

In dice shooting, a throw of nine. Also called *Carolina niner*.

carpieta

A blanket made in Mexico, similar to the Navajo blanket except that it is made in solid colors. It makes a splendid saddle blanket.

carreta

A simple cart with rimless wheels made in one piece, usually cut from an oak log, with a hole cut in the center for the axle. The wooden axles usually squealed like a stuck pig. From the Spanish.

carretero

A wagoner, carter, or driver; from the Spanish.

car rider

In mining, a brakeman or laborer employed to ride on the cars to the dumper, or on cars pushed from the cradle, and to apply the brake to prevent hard bumping.

carrier piece

A fold of leather sewed in between the back and belly pieces of an aparejo at the rear to which, by means of lacing, the crupper is attached and which thus serves to support the crupper and prevent it from hanging too low on the mule's buttocks.

carro

A crude cart; from the Spanish.

CARRY

See pack.

carry the balloon

A logger's expression meaning *to look for*

work. The logger calls his bedroll a *balloon;* hence the expression.

carrying the news to Mary

Said of a horse that is running off with a saddle on his back.

cartwheel

A spur with a rowel having few, but long, points radiating from its axle. A name the cowboy sometimes gives a silver dollar.

carvin' horse

A *cutting horse, q.v.*

carvin' scollops on his gun

Making *credits,* or notches, on a gun to commemorate a killing; done mostly in fiction.

casa grande

To Spanish-American cowboys, a place where all the hands gathered for fun and frolic. The ranch owner's home; used only in the Southwest. From the Spanish, meaning *large house.*

case

In faro, a small counting rack used to keep a record of the cards in the order in which they are pulled out of the box during one deal. Also called *case rack* and *case keeper, q.v.* See *cases.*

case card

In faro, the fourth or last card of any one denomination drawn from the dealer's box; for example, three jacks have been played, the remaining jack is a *case card.*

case keeper

In faro, a device for keeping a record of cards as they are drawn. The houseman or dealer who operates this device and keeps track of the cards that have already been exposed.

case of slow

Said of a loser in a gun fight—a man too slow in getting his gun into action.

case of worms

An infestation of screw worms.

case rack

See *case.*

cases

In faro, the last card of a group still remaining in the card box and yet to be played after three cards of that kind have been played.

cash in

A cowboy's expression meaning *to die.* In poker, faro, etc., to hand in one's checks or chips in exchange for cash.

cash in his six-shooter

An outlaw's phrase meaning *to hold up a bank.*

casing

In mining, a wall or partition between compartments in a shaft. A wall of rock of uniform thickness extending deep into the earth; also called *casing rock.* A zone of rock lying between a vein of ore and barren rock.

cassinette

Cloth made of cotton and wool, used in freighting days.

cast his robe

Said of an Indian who went on the warpath.

casueying

The pitching of a horse (pronounced *kasoo'ying*), a term used primarily in south Texas.

cat

Short for *catamount,* meaning literally *mountain cat;* cougar. In faro, two cards of the same denomination in the last turn. In logging, any tractor, not necessarily a caterpillar, though the name comes from that type. A powerful tractor that hauls logs out of the woods.

catalog woman

What the cowboy called a wife secured through a matrimonial bureau. Usually, as Alkali Allison said, "one of them widders that wants her weeds plowed under."

catamaran

A boat used in western log-storage basins to raise sunken logs.

cat-back

Mild bucking.

catch-as-catch-can

In calf roping, a method by which the roper is entitled to catch a calf in any way as long as he turns loose of the loop before throwing it at the calf; the calf may be caught in any manner that holds it until the roper gets his hands on it.

catching pen

An inner corral.

Catch up!

In freighting, the wagon master's call to the freighting teamster telling him to harness the horses, hitch them to the wagons, collect the blankets and other trappings, and make everything ready for departure. See *All's set!*

cat-eyed

Said of a bad man, who has to be constantly alert to keep from being "downed" by a rival jealous of his reputation. A man of this type makes it his business to sit with his back to the wall, facing the door. If the door is closed, he watches the knob for advance notice of an entrant. In cowboy lingo, "You'd never find 'im settin' on his gun hand."

catface

In logging, a scar on the surface of a log, generally elliptical in shape, resulting from wounds which have not healed over; also, a fire scar at the base of a tree.

catgut

A cowboy's term for a rope, particularly a rawhide one.

cathop

In faro, the last turn if the dealing box contains a pair and a case card.

cat skinner

In logging, the operator of a tractor.

cattalo

A hybrid offspring of buffalo and cattle, the first of which were the results of experiments by Charles Goodnight of Texas.

CATTLE

See anchor cattle, animal, baldface, blackjack steer, bologna bulls, bow up, breachy, brindle, broad horn, brockled, brush snakes, brush splitters, bueno, bulling steer, bulls, bunch, buttermilk cow, butt heads, cactus boomers, can't-hook cattle, cattle breeds, cavaida, cedar braker, coaster, combings, cow, cow poke, cows, critter, cut, decoy herd, double-wintered, downer, droop-horn, dry stock, duke, feeders, good point, grassers, grown stuff, grubber, head, heavy cow, herd, herd-broke, hold the cut, horned jackrabbits, hospital cattle, hunting strays, immigrant cattle, issue cattle, Kansas-wintered, ladino, lead steer, line-back, lobo stripe, long-ear, long twos, lop-horn, marker, maverick, mealy nose, milk pitcher, mixed cattle, mixed herd, mocho, mossy horn, mountain boomers, muley, Nellie, on the hoof, on their heads, open heifer, orejano, otero, outlaw, patrida, pelón, petalta, pony beeves, poverty cattle, rough steer, rusties, sabinas, scalawag, scrub, sea lions, she stuff, shortage, slick-ear, snubbed stock, spoiled herd, springer, stampeder, steer, steers, stockers, stool-and-bucket cow, straight steer herd, strays, stripper, stub-horn, stuff, surly, swimming the herd, tailings, timber cattle, toro, trail herd, twist-horn, vaca, vacada, warmed-up stock, wet herd, wet stock, wet stuff, wild stuff, windies, windsucker, winter kill, wohaw, wrinklehorn, Yaks.

CATTLE BREEDS

See Aberdeen Angus, Brahma, Herefords, hothouse stock, longhorn, magpies, Mexican buckskin, open-faced cattle, shorthorn, Sonora reds, spraddle horns, whitefaces, yellow-bellies, zorillas.

CATTLE BUYERS

See sharpshooter, stock buyer.

CATTLE DISEASES AND AILMENTS

See bearded, bighead, big jaw, case of worms, gotch ear, grass staggers, hollow horn, hoof-and-mouth disease, loco, lump jaw, saged, Spanish fever.

cattle drift

Cattle that are moving with a storm or during a drought. See *drift*.

CATTLE DRIVING

See andale, bend, cattle herding, circle rider, drag, drag rider, drive, dry-drive, following the tongue, haze, head 'em up, keeping up the corners, lay-up, lookout, night drive, pounding 'em on the back, Powder River! Let 'er buck! prod pole, regular, stringing 'em out, trail count, up the trail.

cattle grubs

The larvae of the heel fly.

CATTLE HERDING

See bobtail guard, bunch, can, cattle driving, chouse, close-herd, cocktail guard, cut in, cutter herds, cut the trail, cutting double-barreled, cutting out, cutting the herd, cutting a wagonway, day-herd, dodge out, dropping trailers, eatin' drag dust, feed cover, graveyard shift, greasy-sack ride, herd, hold the cut, hunting strays, killpecker guard, laneing, locate, loose-herd, night guard, night herd, off herd, pasture count, pulling bog, range herding, rawhidin', relief, riding bog, rustle, shipped her, shooting 'em out, shove down, singin' to 'em, squeeze 'em down, standing night guard, starting the swim, swallow dust, throw out, traveling with the grass, trimming the herd, work, working the herd.

CATTLE HERDS

See bunch, decoy herd, herd, mixed herd, spoiled herd, straight steer herd.

cattle issue

A government issue of cattle to reservation Indians in compliance with treaties.

Cattle Kate

Any woman involved in cattle rustling. The original "Cattle Kate Maxwell," whose real name was Ella Watson, was hanged with her paramour, Jim Averill, for cattle stealing, in Wyoming in 1889, during the Rustler's War. Though history has not proved her to be a thief, her name has gone down as such.

cattle lick

A location where blocks of salt are placed for cattle to lick. A region where there is natural salt in the ground at which cattle lick.

cattleman

One who raises cattle.

cattle paper

Notes, mortgages, etc., in which cattle are put up as security.

cattle-poor

Said of one who owns many cattle when they are cheap and money is scarce.

cattle range

An unsettled or sparsely settled region given over to cattle raising.

cattle spread

A cattle ranch, including the animals, buildings, equipment, and employees.

cat wagon

A name given to a wagon that carried women of easy virtue who plied their trade along the cattle trails or on the range.

catwalk

A narrow boardwalk along the top of a shipping chute from which a cowboy helps drive cattle into the shipping cars.

caught in his own loop

A cowboy's expression for one who has failed through some fault of his own.

caught in the bind

A logger's expression for being *in a predicament.*

caught short

A cowboy's expression meaning *unarmed in a crisis.* In the language of one cowhand speaking of an unarmed man, "He was caught short, and now he's deader'n hell in a preacher's back yard."

cavaida

The freighter's name for stray or loose stock; a corruption of the Spanish *caballerango,* meaning *one who cares for horses.*

cave-in

In mining, the collapse of a working.

cavel

In river boating, a big cleat, provided with two prongs, called *horns,* secured to the deck of a boat or a barge, used in securing mooring lines and the like.

caverango

A *wrangler, q.v.;* a corruption of the Spanish *caballerango,* meaning *one who cares for horses.* The cowman further shortened it to *wrangler, q.v.*

cavesson

A headpiece used in horse training, a weighted noseband with three rings, to any of which the lunging rein can be attached; from the French *caveçon*.

cavvy

A remuda, or band of saddle horses; used more commonly on the northern ranges. See *caballada*.

cavvy-broke

Said of a horse broken to run with the saddle horses.

cavvy man

The horse wrangler, who keeps the saddle horses together.

cayuse

The wild horse of Oregon; named for the Cayuse Indians, an equestrian people. A *mustang, q.v.* The name is now commonly used by the northern cowboy to refer to any horse. At first the term was used for the western horse, to set it apart from a horse brought overland from the East. In later years the name came to be applied as a term of contempt to any scrubby, undersized horse. (Francis Haines, "The Cayuse Horse," *Western Horseman*, Vol. II No. 2 [March–April, 1937], 11.)

cayuse wind

A cold east wind, opposite of *chinook, q.v.*

cedar braker

A wild cow that ranges high in the *cedar brakes, q.v.*

cedar brakes

Broken land overgrown with scrub cedars.

CELEBRATIONS

See Basque barbecue, bender, blowing, blowout, fandango, fiesta, high-heeled time, hoolihaning, jamboree, rendezvous, running wild, scalp feast, stay out with the dry cattle.

celerity wagon

A name given a vehicle used extensively on the Butterfield Stagecoach Line. It was a type of "mud wagon" and was especially adapted for use on heavy roads and for rugged mountain country where a coach might be in danger of capsizing. The wagon was comparatively light, having a trim body with a firm duck superstructure provided with roller flaps at the sides.

cement

In mining, gold-bearing gravel united and hardened into a compact mass.

CEMENT

See mustard.

cementation

In mining, the forcing of cement into cracks under great pressure to prevent water from coming into the mine.

CEMETERIES

See bone orchard, bone yard, Boot Hill, campo santo, grave patch, still lot.

center

In steamboating, to center an engine or get it caught center, a calamity that might disable the engine at a critical moment, throwing the steamer out of the channel and hanging her up for hours, or even days, on a sandbar. There might be an even more calamitous sequence: the boat might be on rocks or snags and sunk. The disgrace of centering an engine was so great among rivermen, especially among engineers, that no "cub" ever held his head high again after suffering such a misfortune.

In logging, a rock or other obstacle upon which logs pile up in a drive.

center fire

See *California saddle.*

center stitch line

The stitch line that divides an *aparejo (q.v.)* into two equal parts.

chaff

A fur trapper's word for ridicule.

chaffee work

In mining, manual labor.

chaffer

An early-day trader's word meaning *to haggle over a trade.*

chain

The logger's unit of measure, 66 feet, or 4 rods, long.

chain bit

A horse bit made of a short piece of chain.

chain gang

A cowboy's name for the wagon crew on roundup.

chain hobble

A short chain, about 2 feet long, fastened to the horse's foreleg and left loose at the other end. This method of hobbling is not commonly used, because the loose end strikes the horse's legs if he starts to run and, besides causing pain, often trips and injures him.

chalcocite

In mining, the richest combination of copper with sulphur; in its hard, steely form it is called *glance*.

chalcopyrite

A brass-colored combination of copper with iron and sulphur; not as rich as bornite or chalcocite.

chambermaid to the mules

The logger's title for a stable caretaker.

changing band

In logging, replacing a dull band saw with a newly sharpened one.

changing mounts

Exchanging one horse for another. This is routine practice in a cow outfit during roundup and occurs several times a day. A rider may change his circle horse for a cutting horse or for his rope horse, depending on the duty he is going to perform. Later, if he is going on night herd, he changes to his night horse. There are always a few broncs in his string, and he works them in rotation to give his other horses a rest. When he puts his saddle on one of the broncs, the result is a thrill producer.

Since all the horses of the remuda are kept away from the camp, when the riders are ready to change mounts, the wrangler drives the horses to camp, where they are penned in a rope corral. Then each man ropes the mount he wants. In the early morning he usually selects a gentle horse, though on cold mornings even a gentle horse will have a hump in his back. At noon the cowboy's courage rises with the warmth of the sun, and he catches one of the wilder horses, if he is riding circle.

chaparral

A clump of low evergreen oaks. A clump or thicket of thorny shrubs. From the Spanish.

chaparral bird

A road runner, which commonly lives in chaparral. It has long legs, a slender body, a long tail, and a large, powerful beak. It has wings but seldom uses them; its chief defense is speed in running. It is also called *chaparral cock* and *road runner*, the latter because it often runs down the trail in front of a rider as though challenging him to a race.

chaparral fox

A sly, tricky person; a sneak. One of those fellows who, in the words of Frank Ortega, you "wouldn't trust as far as you could throw an elephant ag'in the wind."

chaparro

An evergreen oak; from the Spanish.

chapo

A short-coupled horse with a chunky build; also called *chupo*.

chapping

The act of whipping someone with a pair of chaps. This is often done in rough horseplay, when a group of cowboys get together for a kangaroo court. When used against someone of vile disposition, it can be severe punishment.

chaps

Leather overalls worn by the American cowboy; an American abbreviation for the Spanish *chaparejos (chaparreras)*, meaning *leather breeches* or *overalls*. The Spanish word was too much of a mouthful for the American cowboy, so he "bit shallow" and said *chaps*, pronouncing it *shaps*.

They are skeleton overalls worn primarily as armor to protect a rider's legs from injury when he is thrown or when a horse falls upon him, pushes him against a fence or another animal, attempts to bite him, or carries him through brush, cacti, or chaparral; they are also protection against rain and cold.

In spite of motion pictures and popular fiction, the cowhand sheds his chaps when he dismounts for ground work, for they are hot and uncomfortable to walk in. Only the brush hand keeps his on, because he never knows when he is going to have to tear a hole in the brush. When the cowboy rides to town, he usually leaves his chaps hanging on a nail in the bunkhouse. If he does wear them to town, he takes them off when he arrives and either hangs them over his saddle horn or throws them behind the bar of some saloon where he is known.

Chaps

See angoras, armitas, bat-wings, bull hides, buzzard wings, chaps, chap string, Cheyenne cut, chigaderos, chinkaderos, chivarras, dude chaps, grizzlies, hair pants, leggin's, open-shop pants, parade chaps, pinto chaps, riding aprons, rodeo chaps, shotgun chaps, twelve-hour leggin's.

chap string

A short string that holds the legs of the chaps together in front at the waist. It is not so strong that it will not break when the cowboy gets hung up in the riding gear.

chaqueta

A jacket sold by the early traders; from the Spanish *jaqueta*.

charco

A pool or puddle of water; used in the Southwest; from the Spanish.

Charlie Taylor

A substitute for butter, a mixture of sirup or sorghum and bacon grease.

chase a cloud

To be thrown high from a horse.

chasers

In logging, those who work along the lines and free the logs when they are stalled by stumps or trees. Those who work on a pile of logs to unfasten cables from logs. In high-lead logging, the men who unhook logs from the *choker, q.v.*

chase the cow

A logger's request for someone to pass the milk at the dining table.

chassé

To go; from the French *chasser*, meaning *to hunt* or *chase*. *Chasséd into* is commonly used as a synonym for *happened upon*.

cheap stick

A rule used by the scaler, who gauges a sawyer's pay.

cheater bar

In logging, a length of pipe used to tighten the binders on a truck load.

cheaters

In gambling, marked cards.

Cheating

See bend, blazing, blown up, boodle, both ends against the middle, bottom dealer, brace box, braced, braced game, bug, card mechanic, card mob, check cop, clip, cold deck, cold game, copper on and copper off, crimp, crimp artist, daub, .deal from the bottom, dealing brace, digger ounce, dildock, dispatchers, doped cards, double odd, edge work, fairbank, false front, gambling, gaper, gig, ginny up the pasteboards, glass work, gouge, humps, ice, jump the cut, load the doctor, make a pass, odd, open a snap, pack the deal, pin work, plumbing the bones, ring in, ring in a cold deck, roping in, shade work, snaking a game, squeeze, stack the cards, sweating a steer.

check

In logging, a small lengthwise separation in the wood, caused by too-rapid evaporation of moisture from the surface.

check cop

In gambling, a device or sticky substance held in the palm of the hand to hide checks.

checkerboard crew

In logging, a mixed crew of white and Negro workers.

checking

In poker, waiving the right to initiate the betting.

check man

Check forger.

check-racked

In gambling, to be refused one's winnings in a gambling house, sometimes because the player has broken the bank, sometimes because the house suspects the player of cheating. Not restricted to faro.

cheek

In mining, the side or wall of a vein.

cheeking

Grasping the cheek strap of the bridle just above the bit and pulling the horse's head as far toward the saddle as possible while mounting to prevent the horse from running or bucking. If a man does not know a horse, he is sure to cheek him the first few times. Cheeking pulls the horse toward the rider if he starts in motion, and this has the advantage of almost swinging the rider into the saddle without effort. Swinging in the opposite direction would make mounting difficult. (John M. Hendrix, "Gittin' Up in the Big Middle," *Cattleman*, Vol. XXI, No. 5 [October, 1934], 5.)

cheekpiece

The side part of the bridle.

cheese block

A block or wedge used to check a log.

chef de voyage

The fur trader's title for the leader of an expedition; from the French.

Cherokee outlet

A strip of land about 57 miles wide extending westward from the 96th to the 100th meridian in the northwestern part of the present state of Oklahoma, granted by the United States in 1828 to the Cherokees as a western outlet from their lands to the buffalo hunting grounds. Sometimes confused with the *Cherokee Strip, q.v.*

Cherokee Strip

A strip of land about 3 miles wide along the northern boundary of the Cherokee Outlet, in what is now the state of Kansas. Sometimes confused wth *Cherokee outlet, q.v.*

chestnut

A horse of brownish hue with neither flax nor black mane or tail; the mane and tail are always approximately the same color as the body.

chew gravel

To be thrown from a horse.

chew it finer

A request to explain in more simple words. One cowhand I know admitted that he'd "never got past the flyleaf of a primer," and words that "showed up as big as a skinned hoss" discouraged him.

chew out

To administer a tongue-lashing, as "He *chewed* that dude *out* proper."

chew the cud

To argue; to carry on a long-winded conversation. Blackie Taylor spoke of two "augurs" with, "Their tongues was so frolicsome their prattle sounded like rain on a tin roof, but it wasn't long till they both run out of smart answers."

Cheyenne cut

A type of wing chaps developed in Wyoming; the wing is narrow and straight and the under part of the leg piece is away at a curve from the knee downward with no snaps below that point. Also called *Cheyenne leg*.

Cheyenne leg

See *Cheyenne cut.*

Cheyenne roll

A saddle devised by Frank Meanea, a saddlemaker of Cheyenne, to create something different from the saddles of his day. The saddle was made with a leather flange extending over, to the rear, of the cantle board. (Bruce Clinton to R.F.A.) The saddle was brought out about 1870 and became very popular throughout the seventies and eighties, especially east of the Rockies.

chicken horse

A small, scrubby horse killed for dog and chicken feed.

chicken saddle

An unusually small saddle.

chickory outfit

A contemptuous term for a logging company.

chigaderos

See *armitas*.

Chihuahua cart

A heavy wooden cart with solid wooden wheels.

Chihuahuas

Large Mexican spurs; named for a state in northern Mexico. Made in one piece with wide heel bands, the genuine Chihuahua spur is often a beautiful piece of workmanship, inlaid with silver in the most intricate designs, even to the spokes of the rowels. (Dick Halliday to R.F.A.)

chileno

A name occasionally given to a ring bit; from the Portuguese.

chili

A favorite dish of the Southwest, made of meat and red peppers. A cowboy's name for a Mexican.

chili chasers

The cowman's name for border patrolmen on the Mexican border.

chili eater

A cowboy's name for a Mexican; commonly used to mean *low-caste* or *low-brow*.

chimney

In mining, a pipe-shaped pocket or ore body found in a generally perpendicular position. Also, sometimes the richer areas in lodes as distinguished from the poorer ones.

chin jaw

The logger's term for small talk; social conversation.

chinkaderos

Often shortened to *chinks*. See *armitas*.

chinning the moon

Said of a horse that is bucking high or standing on his hind feet and pawing the air.

chinook

A warm wind in the Northwest from the Japan Current, which melts the snow even in midwinter. Also (capitalized), the term used for the common Indian language understood by all tribes of the Northwest.

Chinook jargon

A trade language used in the Pacific Northwest, composed of elements from *Chinook (q.v.)*, Nootka, English, French, and other languages.

chin spot

The white snip on a horse's face which increases in size to include part of the lower lip.

chip box

A place where dried dung fuel is kept; also called *chip pile*.

chip on one's shoulder

A logger's challenge to a fight. A contentious attitude; a quarrelsome mood.

chipper

A poor rancher who is forced to use cow chips for fuel; used mostly in the Sand Hill country of Nebraska. In logging, a machine in which wood waste is cut into chips for by-products.

chipping station

A place where Indians made stone arrowheads, axes, etc.

chippy

A miner's name for his excavating drill. Also, the word most outdoor men call a whore.

chips

Counters used in gambling. Ordinarily white chips are worth $1.00; red, $5.00; blue, $10.00; and yellow, $100.00.

chip sack

A sack used by the freighters; it was hung on the side of the wagon and filled with dried buffalo or cow chips during the day to provide fuel for the evening fires.

chip wagon

A two-wheeled cart used in the early days on the range to carry cow chips when wood was scarce.

chiseler

A gambler who tries to pick up another's

bet in a banking game. A gambler who borrows money in a private game and does not repay it.

chivarras

Leggings or chaps, generally those made of goatskin; from the Spanish *chiva*, meaning *female goat*.

chlorides

In mining, ore compounds of chloride and other elements, usually halogens of silver.

choc

A logger's name for a low-grade beer originally made by the Choctaw Indians.

choke

To hang.

choke-bored pants

A cowboy's name for the flare-hipped, tight-kneed riding breeches of the easterner.

chokedamp

Mine gas that causes choking or suffocation when there is insufficient oxygen.

choke down

To subdue a horse by choking it with a rope.

choker

In high-lead logging, a loop of wire rope used to noose a log. A logger's word for cheese.

choker holes

A logger's name for doughnuts.

choke rope

A rope placed around the horse's neck, used by many old-time Wild West–show riders. When the horse lowers his head to buck, the rope slips down near his jaws. With a firm grip on the rope, the rider rears back against it, thus more or less choking the horse down, as well as steadying himself in the saddle and therefore making the ride much easier.

choker setter

In logging, the man who places the *choker (q.v.)* around a log that is to be placed on a landing. Also called *chokerman*.

choke strap

A cowboy's name for a necktie, something for which he has little need. The name is also used by loggers.

choke the horn

To catch hold of the saddle horn while riding a bucking horse. If a rider concentrates on holding to the horn instead of trying to ride with his whole body, the horse will soon have him "knockin' a hole in his vest with his chin." George Phillips, the old "foothill filosopher," once described such a rider with, "His head got to poppin' back and forth, lookin' like every jump it would pop plumb off, back and forth, forth and back, jes' like he was sayin', 'How-de-doo, how-de-doo.'"

choke the stump

In river boating, to tie up to the bank for any reason.

cholla

A particularly spiny species of cactus. It grows to a height of 6 or 8 feet and has many stumpy branches which are easily detached, and on this account has a most vicious reputation for embedding itself in passers-by. From the Spanish.

choosin' match

The selection of mounts on a ranch. The choice rotates according to seniority with the firm, and each puncher chooses his string from the remuda of the ranch. His choice is final, and even the foreman respects it.

chopper

A man employed in cutting out cattle on a roundup. In sheep raising, an old ewe in medium flesh. In logging, formerly one who chopped down trees; *feller* is now more common.

chopping

A tract upon which the trees have been or are being felled.

chopping horse

A cutting horse.

chops

In faro, a system of progressive betting in which the player adds a check when he wins and removes one when he loses. The system is barred in many gambling houses.

chore boy

A logger's term for one who cleans the sleeping quarters, cuts firewood, builds fires, and carries wood. Also called *barroom man, buck, bull cook,* and *flunky.*

chouse

To handle cattle roughly, to make them nervous, or to annoy them and stir them up unnecessarily.

chow time

What the logger calls mealtime.

Christmas

What the logger calls payday.

chuck

The cowboy's name for *food, q.v.*

chuck-a-luck

A gambling game of English origin brought to this country about 1800 and now the most popular dice game in the West. It is played with three dice tumbled in a bottle-shaped wire cage called a *chuck cage* and a board with squares numbered from one to six. In placing stakes on any square, the player bets the bank even money that one of the dice will show the number chosen. The game offers opportunity for the highest kind of play, for one may bet on any of the possible combinations of numbers, at odds running as high as 180 to 1. The chuck cage looks something like a tin horn; hence the expression *tinhorn gambler,* for the game is rather looked down upon, and chuck-a-luck gamblers are never admitted within the aristocratic circles of faro dealers. See also *tinhorn gambler.*

chuck box

A box bolted to the rear of the chuck wagon. It has a hinged lid that, when let down and supported by a stout leg, forms a wide shelf or table. This is the cook's private property, and woe unto the nervy puncher who tries to use it for a dining table. Occasionally this privilege is granted to the wrangler, who generally eats after all the others have finished and are changing horses, but never to a rider.

The box contains shelves and convenient drawers to hold plates, cups, knives, and forks. Others are stored with coffee, bacon, beans, and other chuck. Also in every chuck box the cook has a drawer for a few simple remedies, such as liniment, pills, salts, quinine, and calomel; and he might sneak in a bottle of whisky for his personal use in case of "snake bites." See *chuck wagon.*

chuck eater

An easterner who came west to learn ranch work. The cowboy contends that all the help he rendered was to make the chuck disappear.

Chuck houses

See houses.

chucking the Rio

Said of a cowman of the Northwest who was affecting the dress and manners of the southwesterner.

chuckle-headed as a prairie dog

The cowboy's expression for contrary; undiscerning.

chuck-line rider

A name applied to anyone out of a job and riding through the country. Any worthy cowboy may be forced to ride chuck line at certain seasons, but the professional chuck-line rider is just a plain range bum, despised by all cowboys. He takes advantage of the country's hospitality and stays as long as he dares wherever there is no work for him to do and the meals are free and regular. Also called *grub-line rider.*

chuck wagon

The mess wagon of the cow country; usually an ordinary farm wagon fitted at the back end with a large *chuck box, q.v.*

In the open-range days the chuck wagon was the most widely known and most talked of institution in the cattle country. Nothing added more to the harmony of the cowboy's life than a well-appointed chuck wagon. It furnished a complete index to the good or bad management of the ranch.

Once a hand has thrown his bedroll into the wagon, he has pledged allegiance to the brand for which it stands, and he will fight for it until he leaves it. He may cuss the cook, the company, and everybody connected with it, but he had better not hear an outsider say anything against it.

The life of the cowboy away from headquarters has always centered around the chuck wagon. It is his home, bed, and board; it is where he gets his fresh horses, and it means fire, dry clothes, and companionship; it is hospital and office, his playground and social center. At night it is his place of relaxation, where he spins his yarns, sings his songs, smokes his cigarettes at leisure, and spends the happiest years of his life.

chuck-wagon chicken

A cowboy's name for fried bacon.

chuckwaller

A chuckwalla, a large plant-eating lizard found in the desert regions of the Southwest.

chunk

A trader's word meaning *to keep up* and also *to put wood on a fire.*

chunk out

In logging, to clean skid roads, especially to remove chunks of wood.

church key

A logger's term for a can opener.

churn-butted

In logging, said of a tree with a great enlargement at the base.

churn-dash calf

A calf whose mother is wild and will not let it nurse regularly.

churn-head

A cowboy's name for a hard-headed horse or one with no intelligence.

churn-twister

A cowboy's contemptuous name for a farmer.

chute

A narrow, fenced lane, usually connecting one corral with another. A narrow passage designed for loading cattle into cattle cars or passing them to dipping vats. The enclosure from which horses and bulls are freed into the rodeo arena. In mining, a flume of sliding ore. A chimney of ore. In steamboating, one of two narrow channels split off from a main channel and separated by a narrow rift.

chute branding

A method of branding a cow by running it into a narrow chute and dropping a bar in front of the animal and another one behind it so that it cannot move forward or backward. The cow is then branded through the side railings.

chute-crazy

Said of a horse which rears, backs, and otherwise shows extreme nervousness when placed in a rodeo chute.

chute fighter

A horse which rears and then sulks while in a rodeo chute. See *chute-crazy.*

chute freeze

The state of a horse that "freezes" in a chute and refuses to move no matter how much he is prodded.

CHUTES

See Arizona trigger, branding chute, bull bars, catwalk, chute, crush pen, loading chute, pinch chute, snappin' turtle, squeezer, timber shoot.

cíbola

Buffalo; a term used in the Southwest; from the Spanish.

cibolero

A buffalo hunter; from the Spanish.

ciénaga

A wet, swampy place with many springs; from the Spanish.

CIGARETTES AND TOBACCO

See Bible, brain tablet, dream book, fill a blanket, heifer dust, hoja, killickinnic, kinnikinnick, makin's, paper-collar stiffs, pimp stick, ponche, prayer book, punche, quirly, rest powder, rollin's, salve eater, Scandihoovian dynamite, shuck, Single Twist, snoose, Swedish condition powder.

cimarrón

A Mexican cowboy's term for an animal which, deserted by all its friends, runs alone and has little to do with the rest of its kind.

Also, one who flees from civilization and becomes a fugitive or a wild person. From the Spanish, meaning *wild* or *unruly*.

cinch

A broad, short band made of coarsely woven horsehair or sometimes of canvas or cordage, and terminating at each end with a metal ring. (Philip A. Rollins, *The Cowboy* [New York, Charles Scribner's Sons, 1936], 126.) Together with the latigo, it is used to fasten a saddle upon a horse's back. From the Spanish *cincha*.

cincha

In packing, a broad canvas band used to secure an aparejo to a mule's back. It is 6 inches wide and not more than 30 inches long. At one end it has a facing of leather on both sides, and is provided with five holes to carry lacing, by means of which it is attached to the loop or eye of the lash rope; the other end is faced with leather in a similar manner, and is supplied with a strong hook of metal or wood. Also called *cinch*. From the Spanish.

cinch binder

A horse which rears on its hind legs, loses its balance, and falls backward.

Cinches

See billet, busted cinch, cinch, cinch ring, cinch sores, cinch up, D ring, flank girth, flank rigging, girth, hair cinch, latigo, rear cinch, riding equipment, saddles and equipment, tack-berry buckle, tarrabee, trunk strap.

cinch ring

A metal ring at the end of the *cinch* (*q.v.*), used to fasten the cinch, by means of the latigo, to the saddle ring.

cinch sores

Sores caused by a badly fitting *cincha*, *q.v.* If the aparejo is improperly ribbed and is too weak in front, the cinch will work forward, causing such sores, which are painful and retard travel as well as throw the load forward. If the aparejo is ribbed too weak in the rear, the load will be thrown over the animal's kidneys, causing much discomfort.

cinch up

To fasten a saddle upon a horse's back by drawing the cinch up tight with the latigo straps; never expressed as merely "cinch."

cinnabar

In mining, sulphide of mercury.

circle buck

The bucking of a horse in long, rapid, and evenly timed leaps in a circle of 30 or 40 feet, the horse leaning inward toward the center of the circle.

circle horse

A horse used *on circle* (*q.v.*) during the roundup. The wilder horses are used for this task. They do not have to be specially trained, but they must be tough and have endurance.

circle rider

One of the horsemen who, on roundup, widely separate into small parties, start miles from a chosen holding spot, and then ride toward it, driving slowly before them all the cattle they encounter.

circular story

A long story a cowboy tells for the benefit of a tenderfoot, rambling on until he has seemingly reached the end, but then starting at the beginning again and continuing in a circle. There is a "sell" at the bottom of every tale the cowboy tells the tenderfoot. If the "pilgrim" does not "bite," the cowboy keeps talking, but sooner or later the greener usually pulls the cork under, and then there's "a heap of hilarity in camp."

I remember a puncher who told one for the benefit of an old man from the East, and after this taleteller had talked "till his tongue hung out like a calf rope," the old man asked, "Would you mind talking a little louder? I'm hard of hearing." In a case of this kind the teller of the yarn feels "as helpless as a dummy with his hands cut off" and "might as well been talkin' Chinese to a pack mule."

claim

A piece of land claimed by a settler or a miner in accordance with the law.

claim jumper

One who unfairly and unlawfully appropriates a homestead or mine claim from the prior and rightful owner.

Claims

See mining claims.

claim stake

A stake used in marking out the boundaries of a *claim*, *q.v.*

clam gun

What the logger calls a shovel.

claw leather

To catch hold of the saddle horn while riding a bucking horse. See also *choke the horn*.

claybank

A horse of yellowish color, produced from breeding a sorrel and a dun.

clean-boled

In logging, free and cleared of branches; used to designate timber with a satisfactory length of clear bole.

clean his plow

To thrash a man. One puncher, in telling of a fight he heard in the bunkhouse when passing it, said, "It sounded like they was shoein' a bronc inside." When he went to see what the trouble was, he found both fighters so skinned up "their own folks wouldn't know 'em from a fresh hide."

clean setter

A skilled rider who rides "straight up" without showing daylight.

clean straw

What the cowboy calls clean sheets.

cleanup

In mining, the process of periodically separating the valuable mineral from the gravel and rock which have collected in the sluices or at the stamping mill.

clear cutting

In logging, a method of cutting that removes all merchantable trees in the area in one cutting.

clear-footed

Said of a horse which is able to dodge successfully gopher holes, obstructions, etc.

clear ground

In logging, an open place which is easy to work in.

clear heart

The best grade of lumber, so called because it is cut from the heart of the log.

clears

A logger's name for full-fledged members of the I.W.W. At one time many of the loggers joined the I.W.W.

Clerks

See cackler, call the landings, collar-and-tie men, commis, counterjumper, inkslinger, mining recorder, mud clerk, pay cheater, pencil pusher, shark, tally hand, tally man, underclerk.

cleavage

In mining, the property of splitting more or less readily in certain definite directions, as, for example, in slate.

clip

In gambling, a device for holding cards up a sleeve.

clip a brand

To cut the long winter hair away from an animal in order to read a brand correctly.

clip his horns

To place someone in a disadvantageous position; to make him harmless.

clippers

In sheep ranching, the shearing tool. Also, a name for the men who shear the sheep or for the shorn sheep themselves.

clogs

A hobble for a horse made by using forked sticks about $1\frac{1}{2}$ or 2 inches in diameter and about 2 feet long and lashing them with rawhide thongs to the front legs of a horse; used principally in the brush country.

close-coupled

Said of a horse having a short body.

closed event

An event at an approved rodeo that is not open to all members in good standing of the Rodeo Cowboy's Association. In order for an approved rodeo to hold a local closed event, it must hold the same event for members of the R.C.A.

close-herd

To herd cattle in a compact group. To dance cheek to cheek.

close range

A range enclosed with a wire fence.

close seat

A steady and firm seat in the saddle.

close to the belly

In stud poker, cautious play in which the player bets only on a wired pair or when he has the best hand showing. Also called *close to the vest*.

close together

In freighting, to close up the space between animals.

close to the blanket

In gambling, almost broke, or having lost nearly all one's money.

close-to-the-ground bucker

A hard-bucking horse which is very quick in his actions but never gets very high off the ground. He kicks sideways with his hindquarters and seems to be trying to explode and disintegrate. He shakes his head from side to side and with quick-changing movements hurls his body through the air, doing everything possible to confuse his rider. With his fast and violent actions it seems no task for him to befuddle the rider and cause him to lose his sense of timing and direction. Very frequently the rider loses track of his mount entirely and finds himself gathering a handful of something he does not want. (Bruce Clinton, "Bucking Horses," *Western Horseman*, Vol. III, No. 3 [May–June, 1938], 28.)

CLOTH

See cassinette, jerga, Osnaberg sheets, tarp.

CLOTHES

See advertising a leather shop, armitas, baldface, boil out, barboquejo, boots, buffalo robe, California moccasins, California pants, calzoneras, camisa, capote, chaps, chaqueta, choke-bored pants, choke strap, row rigging, dashboard running jeans, desperado flag, doll rags, dress, dressed up like a sore toe, fish, flag at half mast, flap, flasharity, fried shirt, full war paint, fumadiddle, G-string, hats, Herefords, highwater pants, Levi's, low-neck clothes, mantilla, Mormon shirttail, peal, poncho, rebozo, serape, shoes, sourdough pants, Sunday-go-to-meetin' clothes, tin coat, tin pants, visiting harness, wipes.

clothesline

A cowboy's term for his rope.

cloud hunter

A horse which rears wildly, vaults upward, and paws frantically with his forefeet.

clouding the trail

Hindering someone in his endeavor to accomplish something; deceiving.

cloud watcher

A horse which travels with his head too high to watch his cattle work.

coarse gold

In mining, gold that occurs in large grains, in contrast to gold dust.

coarse vein

In mining, the horizontal line on which an ore-bearing vein cuts the *country rock*, *q.v.*

coaster

One of the longhorn cattle from the coast country of Texas; also called *coaster horn*. In mining, one who "picks a dump," or gleans ore in abandoned mines.

coaster horn

see *coaster*.

coasting on his spurs

Riding with the spurs locked in the cinch or under the horse's shoulders.

cobbing

In mining, ore sorting.

cocinero

See *coosie*.

cock-a-doodle-doo

The foreman of a ranch.

cocklebur outfit

A small ranch; a "one-hoss" outfit; a "seedy" outfit.

cock shop

In logging, the camp office.

cocktail guard

The last watch before daylight. It is the one despised by all herders because it is at a time when men most want to sleep. Before the watch is over, it is morning, the cattle are beginning to move, and the other cowboys are eating their breakfast and getting hot coffee.

Use of this term varies from one region to another. In some regions the period of the first guard, from six to eight o'clock in the morning, is called the *cocktail guard*.

cod-wad

In river boating, a triangular block of wood built inside the stem of a boat, used as a seat for the bitts to heel on.

COFFEE

See Arbuckle's, belly-wash, blackjack, black water, brown coffee, Indian coffee, jamoka, six-shooter coffee.

coffee cooler

A prospector. A loafer.

coffee grinding

In roping, taking a *dally (q.v.)* the incorrect way, by winding the rope clockwise on the saddle horn instead of counterclockwise.

coffin

A cowboy's term for a trunk.

coffin varnish

A cowboy's term for whisky.

coil

A cowboy's term for rope.

cold blazer

A cowboy's term meaning *to bluff*.

cold-blooded stock

Cattle or horses without pure, or hot, blood; not thoroughbreds.

cold brand

See *hair brand*.

cold collar

In freighting, a freshly harnessed horse.

cold deck

In logging, a pile of logs left for later loading and hauling. In gambling, a stacked deck of cards. To introduce a stacked deck into play. In faro, the term is used when the game is played with the pack held in the dealer's hand, in which case the dealer also uses all the other tricks of card manipulation. In the old days faro dealers depended largely upon their skill in stacking and dealing from the hand. Other expressions with the same meaning are *put the ice in, put the chill in,* and *put the cooler in*. Also, a general term meaning *to take unfair advantage*.

cold-footed

Cowardly. One cowhand of the desert country, with the westerner's contempt for cowardice, informed a group of natives who had proved their meekness that they "shore had cold feet for such a hot country."

cold game

In gambling, a game that is so thoroughly dishonest that the player has no chance of winning.

cold hands

Poker hands dealt face up.

cold-jawed

Said of a hard-mouthed horse.

cold-meat wagon

A cowboy's name for a hearse.

cold player

In gambling, a player with a losing streak.

cold shake

A logger's term for a dismissal.

cold shoeing

Shoeing a horse without the aid of fire, forge, or anvil; the shoes are simply nailed on.

cold shot

A logger's name for a link used in joining pieces of chain.

cold trail

Cowboy vernacular for old trail markings. Also, a trail so old that a tracker could not follow it.

colear

To tail an animal, or throw it by the tail; from the Spanish.

collar

In mining, the top of a shaft or winze; the timbering of a shaft when carried above the surrounding surface. In packing, the portion of the aparejo which lies over the mule's withers, shaped to relieve the mule of all pressure on the withers.

collar and hames

The shoulder fitting and curved wooden or metal pieces to which the traces are fastened in draft harness. A stiff collar and a necktie.

collar-and-shoulder style

The help-yourself system of food serving used in some lumber camps and loggers' boardinghouses; similar to cafeteria style.

collar-and-tie men

A logger's term for the company office men, store clerks, etc.

color

In mining, a particle of gold, visible in the pan.

Colorado mockingbird

A burro.

colors

In faro, a system of betting by which the player bets all black cards to win and all red cards to lose, or vice versa, the player either following one color combination throughout the entire deal or reversing one or more times.

COLTS

See horses, portranka, potros, potrillo.

Comanchero

A trader, usually a Mexican, who traded goods with the Comanche Indians for furs, etc., in the early days.

comb

To spur a horse to make him pitch.

comb his hair

To hit someone over the head with the barrel of a pistol. After a person had his "hair parted" in this manner, he was, in the language of one cowman, apt to "sleep as gentle as a dead calf."

combings

The last cattle driven from the circle on roundup.

come a dodge

A trader's expression meaning *to play a trick*.

come-along

A rope halter made so that it will tighten when a horse refuses to follow and loosen when the animal obeys.

Come an' get it!

A common call of the cow-camp cook to signify that a meal is ready. Many variations are added, according to the talent and disposition of the caller.

come apart

Said of a horse that has started to buck.

come a-smoking

To come shooting.

comeback

A ready retort; many cowmen have a genius for repartee. In mining, a term for renewed mining in an area where activity has been slight.

come out a-stooping

Said of a cow that comes out of a corral in a crouching run.

comet split

An earmark similar to the *key split (q.v.)* except that the tail end is curved. Also called *tail split*.

come undone

Said of a horse that has started to buck.

COME UPON

See jump.

coming grass

Approaching spring. A philosophy of the range is, "No matter how hard the winter, spring always comes."

commis

A clerk in training for the position of *bourgeois (q.v.)* with the early fur traders; from the French.

Commissary Jimmy

A logger's name for a storekeeper.

Committee saddle

See *Association saddle*.

community loop

An extra-large loop or noose thrown by a roper.

compadre

A southwestern cowboy's term for a close friend, partner, companion, or protector; from the Spanish.

compañero

Friend, companion; from the Spanish.

company buster

In mining, a contemptuous term for an employee who works aboveground.

company work

See *daywork*.

complex spin

In roping, the spinning of two separate nooses, one in each hand, one loop spinning horizontally and the other vertically, or both alike.

COMPLAIN

See beef, beefing, freak, kick like a bay steer, pumpkin roller.

compound cradle

In mining, an apparatus composed of three tiers of *blanket tables (q.v.)* and mounted on two rockers; used for washing gold-bearing earths. To wash gold-bearing material in such a cradle.

compressed hay

A cowboy's name for dried cow chips used for fuel.

Comstock Lode

A fabulously rich lode of silver and gold discovered in 1859 at Virginia City, Nevada; the name came to be used to mean any rich mineral lode.

concentrate

See *concentration*.

concentration

An intermediate process in the recovery of metals from ore by which part of the worthless material is cheaply eliminated, leaving the metals in a comparatively small amount of richer materials called *concentrate*. The concentrate is then treated by some more expensive final process, such as smelting.

concentration table

A concentration device that makes use of the fact that metal-bearing minerals are usually heavier than the worthless minerals with which they occur. The finely ground ore is mixed with water and passed in a thin stream over a sloping table that is shaken with a bumping motion that forces the heavy metallic particles toward one end.

concha

A shell-shaped metal ornament; from the Spanish, meaning *shell*. In the language of the cowboy it means a small, semiflat, circular metal disk, usually made of silver. It is used for decorative purposes, attached to chaps, belt, or hatband or to the saddle skirt or the browband of the bridle.

Concord

A common name for the coach used on the Overland Mail, made by Abbott-Downing Company, of Concord, New Hampshire. The coach had an arching roof with a railing around the outer edge. In front was the boot where the driver sat with his feet braced against the footboard. Behind his feet were a sack of tools, a treasure box, a water bucket, a buffalo robe, and perhaps some mail. At the rear was another boot, a sort of projecting platform covered with a leather curtain. This was used to carry the baggage, express, and mail. Any overflow of packages or mail was carried on top of the coach. Waterproof canvas curtained the doors of the coach and also protected the passengers from rain and cold wind. This coach was the best of its type and when new cost from $1,000 to $1,500.

conductor

A traveling official of a stagecoach line, usually a former driver, who was responsible for the welfare of both the passengers and the cargo.

Conestoga wagon

A large, very heavily built wagon, with broad wheels, a bed higher at each end than in the middle and a dull-white cloth cover which had a similar curve of still more pronounced degree. The broad wheels were designed for travel over prairies. The wagon bed was constructed in concave shape so that the wagon's contents would not spill out when it was going up and down hills. Another distinguishing characteristic of the conveyance was its colors: the underbody was always painted blue, and the upper woodwork was invariably bright red. This color scheme was as inevitable for every Conestoga wagon as though it had been prescribed by law. This early wagon was named for Conestoga, Pennsylvania, where it was built. Also called *scoop wagon*.

CONFERENCES

See big talk, Indian powwow, junta, make medicine, miner's meeting, powwow.

CONFUSED

See buffaloed, got his spurs tangled up, haywire, jackpot.

conglomerate

A sedimentary rock consisting of water-worn, rounded pebbles or boulders of older rocks cemented with a fine-grained ground mass. Commonly called *pudding stone*.

conk cover

The cowboy's name for a hat.

conk wood

A destructive tree fungus which is visible on the affected tree.

conky

A log or tree affected with *conk wood*, *q.v.*

connected brand

A brand consisting of two or more letters or figures run together.

consumos

A term used by the early freighters and traders for interstate duties; from the Spanish, meaning *excise tax*.

contact

In mining, the junction of two different formations.

contact vein

In mining, a vein along the plane of contact of two dissimilar formations and separating the formations.

contest saddle

See *Association saddle*.

contract act

In rodeo, an act that is retained on a contract by the rodeo committee to perform in the arena. A contract act does not compete for prize money.

contract buster

A man who makes his living from his ability to sit a bucking horse. He does most of his work at so much per head and finds employment on the smaller ranches which are unable to maintain a first-class rider throughout the year. He travels through the country from ranch to ranch, breaking horses as he goes, and will ride anything that wears hair.

conversation fluid

A cowboy's name for whisky. Some westerners drink only enough to "gather a talkin' load," but there are others who can't stop "till they get floored or frenzied."

converter

A cowboy's name for a preacher.

CONVICTS

See tiger.

cook camp

In logging, the building in which food is prepared.

cookhouse

The ranch building where food is prepared, also including the dining room.

cookie

A cowboy's name for the range cook. If ever there was an uncrowned king, it was the old-time range cook. He had to be good to qualify as a wagon cook because he had to be both versatile and resourceful. He was the most important individual in camp, and even the boss paid him homage. He was conscious of his autocratic powers, and his crankiness is still traditional.

The present-day range cook follows this tradition. He can absolutely be depended upon to have three hot meals a day, rain or shine, cold or hot, that are good to eat and in sufficient quantity that, no matter how much company drops in, there will be plenty to go round. Through necessity his equipment is limited; yet this does not seem to hinder his speed. On one day he may be trying to cook in the rain with a scant supply of wet wood; on another he may have difficulty keeping the wind from scattering his fire, blowing the heat away from his pots or sand into his food, and yet he works without discouragement. The outfit must be fed on time.

He has many duties to perform. He is stakeholder when bets are made, arbiter to settle quarrels, and doctor for both man and beast, concocting some sort of dosage from his assortment of bottles. He acts as father-confessor and listens to complaints. He is banker for those who have loose change that might slip out of their pockets during rough cow work. He may do a little laundry so that one of "his boys" can call on a nearby "nester gal," or help another mend a torn garment. As long as he keeps the coffee on a bed of hot coals so that any hand can help himself at all hours, his shortcomings, if any, are overlooked. He has to be a good packer in order to stow things in his wagon so that they stay tied down; he has to be able to repair his wagon to keep it rolling; and he is the first to grab a shovel in case of a tragedy.

Though the boys kid him and cuss his crankiness, they certainly will not concede this privilege to an outsider. If he is clean, they will tolerate the poor quality of his bread.

Almost any cook likes to talk, and while the boys eat, he squats against the rear wheel of the wagon and entertains himself and them by discussing everything from the weather and women to politics and poker. If he is a good cook, the boys do not interrupt him. (John M. Hendrix, Editorial, *Cattleman*, Vol. XX, No. 12 [May, 1934], 5.)

cookie pusher

A cowboy's name for a waitress in a restaurant.

Cooking

See box up the dough, food, meals.

cooking mutton

Setting a sheep range afire to destroy sheep, as was occasionally done in range wars between sheepmen and cowmen.

Cooks

See bean master, belly cheater, belly robber, biscuit roller, biscuit shooter, boardinghouse man, boiler, cocinero, cookie, cook's louse, coosie, dinero, dough-belly, dough boxer, dough-puncher, dough roller, dough wrangler, flunky, grease ball, grease burner, grease belly, grub spoiler, grubworm, gut burglar, gut robber, hash burner, hasher, hash slinger, kitchen mechanic, lizard scorcher, mess boiler, mess moll, mulligan mixer, old woman, pothooks, pot rustler, pot walloper, Sallie, sheffi, sizzler, sop and 'taters, sourdough, star chief, stew builder, stomach robber, swamper.

cook shack

A cowboy's name for the kitchen, especially when it is a separate building.

Cooks' Implements

See Dutch oven, gouch hook, lizard scorcher, pothook, round pan, sourdough keg, squirrel can, wagons, wreck pan.

cook's louse

A cowboy's name for the cook's helper.

cookstove

A branding iron.

cooler

In gambling, a holder for a prepared deck of cards for a crooked game.

cool your saddle

To dismount and rest from riding.

coon

A favorite name for an early-day trapper. "I'd like to meet the old coon," one would say, or, when he was in distress, "I'm a gone coon."

coona

A New Mexico dance which starts out like a country dance but turns into an Indian swing, in which the dancers copy the manner in which an Indian dancer swings his body.

coon-footed

Said of a horse with long and very low pasterns.

coon pen

In steamboating, the after section of the texas where the Negro cabin help were quartered.

coosie

A cowboy's name for the cook, short for the Spanish *cocinero*. A cowhide stretched under a wagon for carrying wood or other fuel. See *cuna*.

cooster

A cowboy's word for a valise or suitcase.

cootie cage

What the logger called a bunk or berth in camp quarters.

copper

In mining, a metallic element, ductile and malleable and of pale-red color tinged with yellow. In faro, a small disk resembling a checker, which is placed on a stack of faro checks to bet them to lose; hence, to bet against or nullify an opponent's plan by instituting an opposing action. Also *copper bet*.

copper bet

See *copper*.

copper glance

In mining, the hard steely form of chalcocite, the richest copper sulphide.

copper on and copper off

In faro, a dishonest system of beating the bank from the outside, probably invented by Kid Stevens and Jerry Daley. It is worked by a gang of four, one of whom keeps cases while the others play. The lookout always shifts his eyes off the layout just as the card is being pulled by the dealer, and at this instant one of the players, also watching the dealer, sees whether that card is going to win; if so, he pulls the copper off a stack of checks previously bet to lose and takes the bet; if not, he leaves the copper on the stack and collects. The player moves

the copper with a looped hair, which he controls with his right hand.

copper the odds

In gambling, to bet all odd cards to lose. A player may also *copper the deal*, thus betting every odd card to lose and playing the even cards, or odd-even.

cordelle

In steamboating, a towline used to pull a boat from shore. Also, to tow a boat with such a line. A cordelle was nearly 1,000 feet long and was fastened to the top of a mast which rose from the center of the boat to a height of nearly 30 feet. The line was connected to the bow of the boat by means of a *bridle*, a short auxiliary line fastened to a loop in the bow, and a ring through which the cordelle was passed. The bridle prevented the boat from swinging around the mast under force of wind or current when the boat's speed was not great enough for the rudder to hold it steady. The line was long to lessen the tendency to pull the boat toward shore, and it was fastened to the top of the mast to keep it from dragging and to enable it to clear the brush along the bank. It took from twenty to forty men, walking in single file, to cordelle a boat along average stretches of river, and the work was always very difficult. A boat could also be towed by using a line fastened upstream to an anchor or *deadman*, a beam or log buried in the sand. In this case the line was wound up by a steam capstan on the boat.

corduroy road

A road built of logs or poles placed side by side across low or swampy places in a roadway.

corks

A logger's name for *calks*, the short, sharp spikes in the soles of a logger's boots. See *calked shoes*.

corn

What the logger calls a poor grade of whisky.

corn freight

Goods shipped by mule team; so called because corn had to be carried to feed the mules, reducing the amount of space available for freight and thus increasing cost. However, mule-team freight was much speedier than bull-team freight (*grass freight, q.v.*), and customers requiring speed demanded that goods be shipped by *corn freight*.

corona

A cowman's name for a shaped pad placed under the skirt of a saddle. In packing, a pad placed upon the mule's back before the blanket and aparejo are put on; a numeral is placed on one side of the pad to indicate the owner. From the Spanish, meaning *crown*.

corpse-and-cartridge occasion

What the cowboy called a gun battle. The aftermath of some of the early western gun battles, as one cowman said, "looked like beef day at an Injun agency."

corral

An enclosure or pen for animals; commonly pronounced *kr-rall'* by cowmen; from the Spanish. It is usually a circular pen built of stout, horizontal wooden rails which are supported by posts set firmly in the ground. The rails are lashed to the posts with green rawhide, which contracts when dry and makes the entire structure as strong as iron. The corral is circular so that the animals cannot injure themselves by crowding into corners. Also, to drive stock into such an enclosure.

In freighting, to form a circle, perhaps 100 yards across, with the wagons of the train connected strongly with each other, each wagon being fastened at the rear to the wagon in front by its tongue and ox chains. The circle formed a strong barrier that the most vicious ox could not break and made a strong entrenchment in case of Indian attack. The pilot led the train in the circle which he had previously measured and marked out to form the fortification for the night. The wagons followed him so closely around the circle that but a wagon length separated them. Each succeeding wagon followed in the tracks of the preceding one until its tongue and ox chains would reach the wagon in front. So accurate was the measure and so nearly perfect was the practice that the last wagon of the train always precisely closed the gateway. As each wagon was brought into position, it

was dropped from its team (the teams being inside the circle), the team was unyoked, and the yoke and chains were fastened to the wagon in front. Within ten minutes from the time the lead wagon halted, the barricade was formed and the teams were unyoked and driven to pasture.

corral boss

The man in charge of the stock and corrals on a dude ranch. It is his duty to assign horses to dudes.

corral branding

Branding calves in a corral. This method of branding may not be so picturesque as branding in the open, but it is easier on men, cattle, and horses. Having no herd to hold, every man can take part in the branding. The actual work is done in the same manner as branding in the open, but the steers and dry cows are worked out before they reach the pens. The mother cows are cut back outside the pens, where they bawl until the calves are turned out to relieve their anxiety and receive their sympathy.

corral dust

What the cowboy calls lies and windies.

corral pup

A young man who saddles the horses for guests on a dude ranch.

Corrals

See Arizona trigger, belly-buster, blind trap, breaking pen, catching pen, corral, crowding pen, feed bag, fighting corral, op'ra house, roadhouse, rope corral, round pen, sheep corral, snorting pen, snubbin' post, squeezer, trap corral, water trap, wing fence.

corregidor

The chief magistrate of a town formerly in Mexican territory; from the Spanish.

corrida

An outfit of cowhands; from the Spanish, meaning *race*.

corriente

A word used by the Southwestern cowboy to signify inferiority when referring to the quality of cattle; from the Spanish, meaning *running* or *ordinary*. (Harold W.

Bentley, *Dictionary of Spanish Terms in English* [New York, Columbia University Press, 1932], 129.)

corrugate

To make small irrigation ditches in a field.

corus

The covering of a saddle, at first made of two pieces of leather stitched together through the middle, with a hole cut for the fork and a slit for the cantle. It was worked and shaped to fit the tree and, after the rigging was in place, was slipped down over the saddle and buckled or laced in front of the horn.

cotton-patch loop

In roping, an extra-large loop; also called *community loop*.

cottonwood blossom

A cowboy's term for a man hanged from the limb of a tree.

couldn't drive nails in a snowbank

A cowboy's phrase for an ignorant person.

couldn't find his saddle seat with a forked stick

A cowboy's phrase for a man riding in extremely rough country.

couldn't ride a pack horse

A cowboy's phrase for a man who cannot ride a mildly bucking horse.

couldn't ride nothin' wilder'n a wheel chair

A cowboy's phrase for a man with no riding ability.

couldn't teach a settin' hen to cluck

A cowboy's phrase for an ignorant person.

could outhold a warehouse

A cowboy's phrase for a lucky person, especially a winner at cards.

coulee

A dry creek; a deep cut in the earth's surface, its sloping sides covered with brush; a ravine; used in the Northwest as a syn-onym for the Southwest's *arroyo*; from the French *coulée*, meaning *flow*.

count coup

To be the first to strike an enemy with an object held in the hand. To recount one's exploits. From the Plains Indian's custom of establishing bravery by striking an enemy at close quarters.

counterbrand

A brand placed on an animal to supersede an earlier one. In early days when a brand was superseded by purchase or by discovery that the wrong brand had been placed upon an animal or that the brand had been put in the wrong place, it was customary for the brander to burn a bar through the original brand and put the new brand above or below it and also on that part of the animal where it properly belonged, if the old brand was differently situated. Later in the cattle industry, counterbranding was done by re-peating the undesired brand and placing the new one upon the animal where it belonged, and the use of the bar through the discarded brand was discontinued. (Philip A. Rollins, *The Cowboy* [New York, Charles Scribner's Sons, 1936], 240.) See also *vent brand*.

counterjumper

The logger's name for a commissary clerk.

country rock

In mining, the rock beyond the sides of the lode; the strata between or across which the lode is found.

county brand

A brand used only in Texas in the early days, consisting of a letter or group of let-ters for each Texas county and, unlike other brands, always placed upon the animal's neck. This brand was intended to make stealing more difficult, since the rustler would have to see that his doctored brand was recorded in the county of the county brand or alter the recorded brand.

county hotel

What the logger calls the county jail.

coup

See *count coup*.

coup stick

A stick or other object with which an Indian struck an enemy. See *count coup*.

COURAGE

See gravel in his gizzard, grit, gritty as fish eggs rolled in sand, he'll do to ride the river with, knows how to die standin' up, more guts than you could hang on a fence, sand, square.

coureur de boise

A French or half-blood hunter, trader, or boatman of the northern and western United States and Canada; from the French, meaning *forest hunter* or *woodsman*.

courier

A trader's name for a special messenger; from the French *courrier*.

court cards

In gambling, the face cards of all suits.

COURTING

See cut a rusty, dropped his rope on her, gallin', ride herd on a woman, rotten loggin', sage-henning, settin' the bag.

COURTS

See miner's court, mustang court, prairie-dog court.

court skin

In gambling, a *court card (q.v.)*, as contrasted to a *spot card*. Also called *redskin* and *paint skin*.

Cousin Anne

A miner's name for the wife of a Welsh miner.

Cousin Jack

A miner's name for a Cornish miner.

Cousin Jack Lantern

A lamp made from a can and a candle and used by miners on occasion.

Cousin Jenny

A miner's name for a Cornish girl or woman.

cover

To copulate, as a stallion *covers* a mare.

covered his back with his belly

A cowboy's phrase for a man forced to sleep in the open without blankets. Such a situation is also spoken of as "usin' his back for a mattress and his belly for a blanket."

cover his dog

To gather all the cattle in a given region, the job of the roundup captain.

covering

Getting the drop on someone.

cow

The cowboy's generic term for everything from a sucking calf to a ten-year-old bull.

COWARDLY

See booger, buck fever, cold-footed, down in his boots, gun-shy, his tail is dragging, rustler's pneumonia.

cowboy

A man who tends cattle. This word seems to have originated in Revolutionary days, when a group of Tory guerrillas roamed the region between the lines in Westchester County, New York, and called themselves by this name. I have never been able to discover why they gave themselves this name, since they had nothing to do with cows except for stealing a few.

The next men who called themselves *cowboys* were a bunch of wild-riding, reckless Texans under the leadership of Ewen Cameron, who spent their time chasing longhorns and Mexicans soon after Texas became a republic. To the Mexicans they became the symbol of calamity.

Then came the real cowboy as we know him today—a man who follows the cows. A generation ago the East knew him as a bloody demon of disaster, reckless and rowdy, weighted down with weapons, and ever ready to use them. Today he is known as the hero of a wild West story, as the eternally hard-riding movie star, as the "guitar-pickin'" yodeler or the gayly bedecked rodeo follower.

The West, who knows him best, knows that he has always been "just a plain, everyday, bow-legged human," carefree and courageous, fun-loving and loyal, uncomplaining and doing his best to live up to a tradition of which he is proud. He has been called everything from a *cow poke* to a *dude wrangler*, but never a coward. He is still with us today and will always be as long as the West raises cows—changing, perhaps, with the times, but always witty, friendly, and fearless.

cowboy change

Gun cartridges of various sizes used for small change. In the early West paper money was unknown, gold and silver coins being the only money used. A silver fifty-cent piece was the smallest coin in circulation, but it was sometimes necessary to make change to the value of quarters and dimes. For this the standard sizes of cartridges were used, and they became known as *cowboy change*.

cowboy cocktail

Straight whisky, because that is the way the cowboy wanted it.

cowboy of the Pecos

A true cowboy. In the old days the saying, "He's a cowboy of the Pecos," had a broad meaning. The Pecos River drained a wild empire. There was no law west of it. Its brackish waters were shunned by the buffaloes and even the coyotes. The country was hot, birdless, and infested with snakes. The Lincoln County War was fought in the territory drained by it, and its name became a symbol of toughness.

In one sense *cowboy of the Pecos* might mean that the one so described was exceptionally expert as a cowboy and rider; in another, it might mean that he was a rustler. But in either sense, he was sure to be salty and efficient. There is an old saying that "when a badman dies, he either goes to hell or to the Pecos." Another saying is, "Once a cowboy has watered on the Pecos, he'll always return."

Cowboys

See baquero, Bill-show cowboy, blazer, bootblack cowpuncher, brander, bronc breaker, bronc buster, bronc fighter, bronc peeler, bronc scratcher, buckaroo, bucketman, buffalo whooper, bull nurse, chain gang, chucking the Rio, corral pup, corrida, cowboy, cowboy of the Pecos, cow crowd, cowhand, cow milker, cow nurse, cow-pen herd, cow poke, cow prod, cowpuncher, dabster hand, dogieman, gate horse, greasy-sack outfit, gunny sacker, hacendado, hand, hard-winter bunch, haywire outfit, heel squatter, hillbilly cowhand, hood, lead drive men, lead man, leather pounder, limb skinner, night herder, phildoodle, pilot, pliers man, puncher, ranahan, ranches, rawhider, rep, roustabout, saddle slicker, saddle stiff, saddle warmer, saint, salt, sheep dipper, shove-down crew, three-up screw, top hand, trail crew, trail hand, turtle, twister, vaquero, waddy, wrangler.

cow bunny

An affectionate name for the wife or sweetheart of a ranchman.

cow camp

A cowboy's headquarters on a roundup; a place where a group of cowmen have gathered for cow work.

cow chips

Dried cow droppings, a popular fuel in the early days on the plains, where timber was scarce. Also called *cow wood*. It was hard to get a fire started with them, but when dry, this "prairie coal" made a hot one. However, it soon burned out and required replenishing. It also made as much bulk in ashes as there was in fuel, and the ashes had to be carried out as often as the fuel was put in the stove. It was claimed that in cold weather the constant exercise of carrying in fuel and carrying out ashes was what kept the fire tender warm, rather than the heat of the fire.

Many of the old-time cooks in the early days had nothing else to cook with, and though this fuel gave off a peculiar odor when burning, it did not affect the food. When cow chips were damp, it was very hard to make a fire with them, and a certain old range cook claimed that in one season he "wore out three good hats tryin' to get the damned things to burn."

cow crowd

An outfit or unit of cowboys.

cowcumbers

What the logger calls pickles.

cow folks

Old-timers in the cow business, or persons who have been raised in it.

cow geography

Drawing a rough map or route in the sand with a stick to give directions for reaching a certain destination such as sections of the range.

When two friendly riders meet on the trail, they stop and sooner or later swing off their horses to loosen the cinches and give their bronc's backs a chance to air. Then, squatting on their boot heels, they will fish around for a cowboy pen and paper, which are a broomweed stalk and plenty of loose dirt to draw in. Jesse Evans used to say, "A cowhand kin jes' talk better when he's a-scratchin' in the sand like a hen in a dung heap." They can draw a picture of a brand and show how one brand can be worked into another. Perhaps some nester with a pretty daughter has squatted in a certain valley, and directions will be drawn for getting there. Then with a swipe of the hand the cowboy can have a clean slate and start another lesson in cow geography.

cow grease

A cowboy's name for butter.

cowhand

One who works with cattle. On the range this is the most common term used by the cowhand himself when referring to one of his profession. Usually shortened to *hand*.

cow-hocked

Said of a horse whose hind legs almost touch at the hocks and then spread at the pastern joints, like those of a cow.

cow horse

A horse the cowhand rides while working cattle. A good cow horse has to possess strength and intelligence, both qualities well trained. He has a natural instinct for sensing direction and detecting danger, day and night. He is game and brave and will drop dead in the performance of his work if need be. He is well adapted to his place, tough and inured to the hardships of his life. His lightness of foot and quickness of motion fit him for the work better than any other type of horse.

He soon learns his rider, and they work together. Of necessity he is sure-footed and always has an eye for the trail. He must have good feet, limbs, heart, and lungs, so that he will have endurance; above all, he must have good sense.

cow hunt

The primitive forerunner of the round-up; also called *cow drive, cow work*, and *work*.

cowman

One who raises cattle.

cow milker

A term of contempt for the roustabout on a ranch.

cow nurse

One whose duty it is to look after sick or crippled cattle, which are kept in a separate herd.

cow outfit

See *spread*.

cowpen herd

The cowboy's name for the small herd of the "little feller."

cow poke

A device to prevent fence crawling, made of a green sapling about 4 feet long and with a forked prong. This was put on top of the animal's neck and lashed with a piece of rope well up on the neck. Also, a name for the cowboy himself.

cow pony

A *cow horse q.v.* Occasionally a westerner uses this term in speaking of his horse, but it is used mostly by easterners and writers who have never lived in the West. The cowman usually calls him a *hoss*, and *cow hoss* is the almost universal term for him.

cow prod

A cowboy.

cowpuncher

A more recent name for a cowboy, derived from the metal-pointed prod employed to drive cattle into stock cars. While *punching* is now the accepted term for herding livestock, it is ordinarily restricted to cattle, the term *herding* being used in connection with horses. A cowpuncher might punch or herd cattle, but colloquial English makes him *herd* horses and will not let him *punch* them. *Cowpuncher* is usually shortened to *puncher*.

cow ranch

A ranch where cattle are raised.

cow range

The plains over which cattle range.

cow rigging

Clothes, or the costume, worn by the cowman when he is working. As one cowhand said, "You'd have to be some persuader to get a puncher to shed his cow riggin' for any of that gearin' of the shorthorn."

Cows

See buttermilk cow, cattle, cow, dry stock, heavy cow, milk pitcher, open heifer, she stuff, stool-and-bucket cow, wet herd, wet stuff.

cow salve

A cowboy's term for butter.

cow savvy

Knowledge of cattle and the cattle business.

cow sense

Such sense as is needed for success in cattle raising. Common sense.

cow skinner

A severe winter storm which kills cattle and from which all the owner can salvage is the hides.

cow's mouth

What the logger calls the falling notch in a tree.

cow spread

See *cow*.

cow talk

The conversation between two or more cowmen when they get together and talk about cattle. Jack Potter once started a letter to me on a certain date but did not finish it for quite a while. When I finally received it, his excuse for the delay was that a friend came by his house and "started talkin' cow, and I followed him off."

cow town

In the early days, a town at the end of the trail, from which cattle were shipped. Later, any town in the cattle country which depended upon the cowman and his trade for its existence. Many an old-time cowboy had to leave one of these trail towns in a hurry, as one said, "without waitin' to kiss the mayor good-by."

cow whip

A long whip used more often to pop than to lash cattle.

cow wood

Dried *cow chips, q.v.*

coyote

A prairie wolf; pronounced *ki'yote* by the westerner; from the Spanish. It is much smaller than the timber wolf. It is very shy and has never been known to attack man unless mad, cornered, or rabid. Also, a man who has the sneaking and skulking characteristics of the animal. In mining, an excavation suggestive of those made by coyotes; see also *coyoting*.

coyote dun

A dun horse with a dark stripe running down its back, sometimes into the tail, and often marking the legs.

coyote hole

In mining, a small tunnel driven into the rock horizontally at right angles to the face of the mine.

coyoting

Irregular surface mining in which holes resembling those made by coyotes are dug.

coyotin' round

Sneaking; drifting aimlessly from one place to another.

coyotin' round the rim

Touching a subject on the edges, as in a conversation or speech; hinting.

crack-a-loo

A game played by cowboys in which coins are pitched against the ceiling of a room and then fall to the floor. The person whose coin comes to rest on or nearest a predetermined crack in the floor wins the game.

cracker

A strip of rawhide at the end of a bull whip.

Crack! Whip the saw!

In logging, a cry shouted when two men were sawing a tree and heard a cracking noise within the trunk. The saw was then swung quickly around to one side or the other and the sawing continued. Sawing on the side, if executed in time, stopped the splitting.

cradle

In mining, a *rocker*, a wooden box, longer than it is wide, provided with a movable slide and hopper, and mounted on two rockers. It is used for washing gold-bearing earths. To wash gold-bearing material in a rocker. See also *compound cradle*.

cramp

To force a steamboat to a desired direction.

craps

A gambling game played with two dice. The player wins if he throws a seven or eleven, but loses if he throws a *crap*, a two, three, or twelve, or if he throws a seven after he has made a *point* by throwing a four, five, six, eight, nine, or ten.

crawfish

Said of a horse that pitches backward. To back away.

crawl his hump

To start a bodily attack upon someone.

Crazy

See *loco, sent for supplies, short of hat size*.

crazy dray

See *crotch*.

crazy weed

Locoweed.

crease

A method once used to capture wild horses. It consisted of shooting a horse with a rifle so that the bullet grazed only the cords in the top of the animal's neck just in front of the withers, about an inch or so deep, close to the spinal column. This caused a wound which temporarily paralyzed a nerve center connected with the spinal cord and the brain and knocked the horse down. He was thus stunned long enough for the hunter to tie him down before he recovered. Success with this method called for expert marksmanship and an abundance of luck. From talks with old horse hunters and from other records, I find that this method was very rarely successful and that for every horse captured in this way fifty were killed.

credit

A notch carved upon a gun to commemorate the killing of a victim. Outlaws and gunmen of the wild bunch who killed for the sake of brag followed this custom, but no man of principle wanted to remember the men he had killed.

Credit

See buying on tick, cattle paper, jawbone, on tick.

cremello

A type of albino horse with cream-colored coat, pink skin, and blue, "china," eyes.

crevice

In mining, to work or explore rock crevices for gold.

crevicing

In mining, picking out gold with a knife from cracks in rocks.

crib

A miner's term for his lunch. In logging, a crate made of 2-by-12-inch grub planks, the sides and ends held solidly together top and bottom by heavy 2-inch hickory or oak pins. When completed, the platform was tipped up, allowing the crib to slide gently into the water. There were usually three of these platforms to allow the lumber to be separated into three grades. A number of cribs were fastened into regular strings by strong plank couplings at the front and rear and crosswise.

cribber

A horse that has the habit of gnawing on wood, as on hitch racks or stall partitions.

cribbing

In mining, the timber lining of a shaft or winze. The term is applied to rough or light timbering, as distinguished from solid setwork.

cricket

A little roller inserted in the bit to make a chirping noise, giving the horse something with which to amuse himself with his tongue and creating a music the cowboy loves to hear.

crimp

One who cheats by bending cards or marking their backs, as with the fingernails. See also *crimp artist, crimper.* To bend the end of a card, or cards, in a deck in such a way that the cheat or his confederate can cut the deck at a certain place, or so that a player will unknowingly cut at the place desired by the cheat. Also, the bend itself.

crimp artist

A *crimp (q.v.)* who is good at that form of cheating; also called *crimper.*

crimper

See *crimp artist.*

critter

A word used by the cowboy to mean *cow.* The word *cow* stands for cattle in general. Female cattle are designated as *she stuff,* and the sex of an individual animal is noted by such expressions as "that two-year-old heifer" or "that line-backed steer."

crockhead

A cowboy's name for an unintelligent horse.

crook

A logger's term for a defect consisting of an abrupt bend that occurs in logs and poles.

crooked river

What the riverman called that part of a river filled with reefs and sand bars, or containing a series of bends.

crop

An earmark made by cutting off one-half of the cow's ear smoothly, straight from the upper side.

crop-eared

Said of any animal with ears shortened by freezing or sunburn.

cropping

In mining, exposed metal in the earth. Also called *outcrop.* See also *cropping out.*

cropping out

The natural exposure of bedrock at the surface, in distinction from that part of a vein which appears at the surface, which is called the *cropping* or *outcrop.*

croppy

An outlaw horse with his ears cropped to identify him as such.

crossboard

In steamboating, a large wooden *X* painted white and usually nailed to a tree close to the river's edge where it could be readily seen by steamboat pilots; used to warn of shallow channels, dangerous curves, and various channel conditions. Also called *day mark.*

cross-buck saddle

A packsaddle,. so called because of its similarity to the woodcutter's cross-buck sawhorse. It consists of two short, parallel planks connected at each end by a short wooden cross. Of necessity it has two cinches and is used to carry equipment or freight.

cross canyon

A canyon bisecting another canyon.

cross colors

In faro, a variation of the color system in which the player reverses his color system at will throughout the deal. See *colors.*

cross course

In mining, an intersecting vein of metal.

crosscut

In mining, a passageway in a mine extending through the rock to link the main shaft with the ore body where the actual mining is taking place. See also *crosscut tunnel.* In logging, to cut a board, timber, or log at right angles to the general direction of the fibers; also called *buck.*

crosscut tunnel

In mining, a tunnel driven at approximately right angles to a main tunnel, or from the bottom of a shaft or other opening, across the formation. The term *crosscut* would seem more appropriate, since *tunnel* implies a passageway open to the surface at both ends, like a railroad tunnel.

cross draw

See *border draw*.

cross haul

A method of loading log-transportation vehicles in which one end of a line is passed over the load and around the log to be loaded and is made fast to the load. Power applied to the other end of the line imparts a rolling motion to the log.

cross-hobble

To hobble one front foot of a horse to the hind one on the opposite side. This method is dangerous to a nervous horse because he may panic, fight the hobbles, throw himself, and be injured.

crossing

A place to ford or cross a river.

crossings

In steamboating, places where the main channel, after following one side of the river bed for a distance, crossed to the other side. In these places the channel generally split into two *chutes*, narrow channels separated by a shallow rift, neither of which might have the required depth of water. The pilot first selected the most promising channel. If it proved too shallow, he backed up and tried another.

cross member

Either hewed or sawed timber supporting railroad rails.

crosstree

In packing, two saddle boards, shaped somewhat like the McClellan saddle tree, connected at front and rear (at pommel and cantle) by crosspieces shaped like the letter X, termed the *cruz (cross)*, or *forks* of the saddle, supplied with a breast strap, breeching, and quarter straps, holding cincha and latigo, or tightening straps, accompanied by a saddle pad or blanket.

cross vein

In mining, an intersecting vein. A vein which crosses the bedding planes of the strata. This usage appears to conflict with the same term applied to two veins which actually cross each other.

crotch

In logging, the fork of a tree or branch. A small sled, without a tongue, often made from the natural fork of a tree, with a crosspiece nailed midway through the V and pulled by horses as an aid in skidding logs on stony or bare ground; also called *crazy dray*, *go-devil*, and *lizard*.

crotch line

A device for loading logs on railroad cars.

crotch tongue

Two pieces of wood in the form of a V joining the front and rear skids of a logging sled.

crow bait

A cowboy's term for a poor horse or for anything of poor quality.

crowding pen

A small corral used for branding grown cattle.

crow hobble

The name used in Montana for the *Scotch hobble*, *q.v.*

crow hop

The antics of a horse making a pretense at bucking by jumping about with arched back and stiffened knees.

crown

The upper part of a tree, including the branches and their foliage.

crown fire

A fire which runs through the tops of living trees, brush, or chaparral.

crownpiece

The top part of the bridle, a strap passing over the top of the horse's head.

cruise

In logging, a survey of forest lands to

locate and estimate volume and grades of standing timber; also, the estimate obtained in such a survey.

cruiser

In logging, a man who estimates standing timber and maps its terrain for logging; also called *land-looker*.

crumb

A logger's name for a louse. Also sometimes used by the cowboy.

crumb boss

A logger's name for the bunkhouse janitor.

crumb castle

A cowboy's name for the chuck wagon.

crumb incubator

A cowboy's name for his bed. See *crumb*.

crumb roll

A logger's name for his bedroll; also called *balloon*.

crumb up

To get rid of body lice.

crummie

In logging, the man who takes care of the logger's bunkhouse. Also, a bed in the bunkhouse. A bus which transports workers to and from the woods.

crupper

A leather band attached to the front lacing and carrier pieces of an aparejo and fitting under the mule's tail, its purpose being to steady the aparejo and to prevent it from slipping to the front. In rodeo, a similar band used in riding tricks performed from the hips of a trick riding horse; there are numerous variations of crupper tricks.

crush pen

A name for the narrow branding chute. See *chute branding*.

crying room

The headquarters of a rodeo; the office where alibis are offered and disappointments aired.

cub engineer

In steamboating, a young man just learning the trade.

cub pilot

In steamboating, an apprentice pilot; also called *striker pilot*.

Cuidado!

A warning shout, meaning *Look out!* or *Take care!* From the Spanish.

cuitan

An Indian pony; pronounced *coo-ee-tan'*. The first coastal Indian tribe to see a horse called him *e-cu-i-ton*; in the later trade jargon or Chinook it became *qui-tan*; hence the present word.

cull

A scrubby cow or other animal. In logging, a tree or log of merchantable size rendered unmerchantable because of poor form, an excess of limbs, rot, etc. To reject a tree, log, or board in scaling and grading. A logger's word for hash.

cultus

Mean, worthless; from the Chinook Indian.

cuna

A green cowhide stretched to the running gear of a chuck wagon. The head and forelegs are lashed toward the front of the wagon, the sides to the sides of the bed, and the hind legs to the rear axle. It is tied lower at the back to make it easier of access, and while it is drying is filled with rocks or something heavy to make it bag down, thus increasing its carrying capacity. It is used to carry wood or other fuel. From the Spanish, meaning *cradle*. Also called *bitch*, *caboose*, *coosie*, and *possum belly*.

cunt splice

In logging, a makeshift splice for temporary use.

cup

In logging, a cut or notch made in the base of a tree or stump with an ax to hold ammate or other such chemical.

Cupid's cramp

The ailment of a cowboy in love.

curb bit

A bit with an upward curve, or *port*, in the center of the mouthpiece; one of the most widely used bits in the cattle country.

curb strap

A piece of adjustable leather under the horse's chin. Sometimes a curb chain is used on a hard-mouthed horse.

curl him up

A cowboy expression meaning *to kill someone*.

curl his tail

A cowboy's expression meaning *to get a man or an animal on the run*.

Curly Bill spin

A gun spin, the reverse of the *single roll*, *q.v.*; more commonly known as *road agent's spin*, *q.v.* In some localities it takes this name because Curly Bill Brocius was said to have used it to kill Marshal Fred White when the latter attempted to arrest him in Tombstone, Arizona.

curly wolf

A tough character.

curry him out

To rake a horse across his sides with spurs when riding.

curry the kinks out

To break a horse; to take the meanness out of him.

Cussing

See airin' the lungs, private cuss words.

custom-mades

What the cowboy calls his made-to-order boots.

cut

A group of cattle separated from the main herd for any definite purpose, as for shipping or for branding. To castrate an animal. In lumbering, the yield, during a specified period, of products that are cut. In mining, to intersect a vein of metal.

cut a big gut

A cowboy's expression meaning to make oneself ridiculous.

cut a rusty

A cowboy's expression meaning *to do one's best*, to do something clever, or to court a girl. A logger's expression for cutting a shine.

cut a shine

A cowboy's expression meaning *to perform an antic*.

cut-back

A cow or steer rejected on roundup for any reason; a *cull*, *q.v.*

cut-bank

A precipitous hillside or jump-off. Cut-banks constituted one of the dangers in the path of herders trailing longhorns up from Texas. They are caused by the wind's whipping around some point and eroding the soil until precipitous banks, sometimes yards high, have been formed. There is no way of detecting them in the dark, and more than once the mangled bodies of a man and a horse have been found at the bottom of one after a stampede.

Cut 'er loose!

A bronc rider's signal to release his mount, given when he is ready to start his ride at a rodeo contest.

cut for sign

To examine the ground for tracks or droppings, the two *signs*.

cut his picket pin and drifted

Said of a cowboy who left for parts unknown of his own free will and not under compulsion.

cut his suspenders

Said of a cowboy who left one place for another. To leave the country.

cut his wolf loose

Said of a cowboy drinking, shooting, or on any other kind of "tear." One of the favorite stunts of the old-time cowboy was to ride his horse into a saloon. A story used to be told in New Mexico about the time three or four young punchers rode their horses into a saloon where one of those overdressed eastern drummers happened to be partaking of his after-dinner refreshment at the bar. Being considerably jostled by one of the horses, he complained bitterly to the bartender.

This bar-dog, an old stove-up former cowpuncher, glared at the drummer a moment and came back in characteristic style with, "What the hell you doin' in here afoot anyhow?" Perhaps he didn't appreciate all that livestock in the saloon, but he appreciated even less complaints coming from an outsider.

cut horse

Short for *cutting horse, q.v.*

cut in

To drive stragglers or wandering cattle back into the herd from which they have strayed.

cut of cows and calves

A cut made on roundup by segregating all cows with calves into a separate group preparatory to branding.

cutoff battery

In lumbering, a particular set of saws in a sawmill.

cut straw and molasses

A cowboy's term for poor food.

cutter

A pistol. One engaged in cutting out cattle. A good *cutting horse, q.v.* The man who cuts earmarks during branding.

cutter herds

Bunches of cattle held about a hundred miles apart along the trail by cowboys hired, as in roundup season, to cut trail herds for several different ranches.

cut the bed

A cowboy's expression meaning *to share one's bed with another.*

cut the deck deeper

A request to explain something more fully or more clearly.

Cut the rope!

What the miner tells the hoisting engineer when he wants to descend the shaft.

cut the trail

To halt a herd of cattle for an inspec-

tion. A trail cutter has the herd driven past him in a thin line so that he may identify any animal which does not properly belong to the particular herd.

cutting area

In logging, a section of woodland upon which timber is being cut or is to be cut.

cutting a wagonway

Digging the earth from a steep river embankment for a more gradual approach where the chuck wagon could cross. Some such wagonways, dug when adequate tools were lacking, "looked like beaver slides."

cutting double-barreled

Cutting out animals from a herd by two men; usually only one man works a single animal.

cutting gate

A wide, swinging gate so arranged that it can be operated with a long extension by a man sitting on top of the fence; used, like a switch on a railroad track, to shunt cattle into one of several pens which it serves.

cutting horse

A horse especially trained for cutting out cattle from a herd. A good cutting horse is the top-ranking and most talked of horse in cattle work. This coveted title comes only after years of training and experience, and the rider who can boast of such a horse is the envy of his comrades and the pride of the entire outfit.

When a good cutting horse begins his work, he is made to understand which animal is to be cut. He works quietly until the animal is urged to the edge of the herd. Naturally the cow tries to remain with her companions, and here is where the cutting horse proves his worth. A good cutter is both mentally and physically alert, possesses speed and action, and knows how to use them. He must spin and turn faster than the cow; and it takes an expert rider to stay on, for he must anticipate the horse's turns to keep from getting spilled. All the work must be done in such a manner as to excite the herd as little as possible.

While the horse needs no assistance from his rider, an unskilled rider will certainly hinder the work of the horse. The work of a good cutter under an equally good rider is a joy to watch.

cutting out

Riding into a herd of cattle, selecting the animal to be cut, and keeping it on the move away from the herd and toward the cut being formed. It it hard and exciting work, but it gives both horse and rider the opportunity to prove their worth.

cutting the herd

Inspecting a trail herd for cattle which do not properly belong in it.

cyclone

In lumbering, the funnel-shaped cone in a sawmill that causes sawdust, under air pressure, to be forced to the outside edges of the cone, where it slides to the bottom of the cone and onto a conveyer.

cyclone shot

In mining, a very powerful charge of explosives.

D

"You never know the luck of a lousy calf"

dab

A word used in roping, as "dabbed his rope on."

dabble in gore

To become entangled in a shooting scrape.

dabster hand

A cowboy expert at his work; used in eastern Washington.

dads

In lumbering, to cut a hole or slot in a piece of lumber.

dally

To take a half hitch around the saddle horn with a rope after a catch is made, the loose end being held in the roper's hand so he can let it slip in case of an emergency or shorten it. The expressions *daled, vuelted, dale vuented,* and *dolly welter* are also used, all from the Spanish phrase *dar la vuelta,* meaning *to take a turn* or *twist with a rope.*

The early American cowboy gave the expression the nearest English pronunciation, *dolly welter,* which brings to mind a story told by S. Omar Barker of a tenderfoot roper who made a lucky catch and was immediately advised from all sides to "take your dolly welter," whereupon he retorted that he "didn't even know the gal." Later the expression was shortened to *dally,* which is now the most common term.

dally man

A rider who uses a *dally (q.v.)* in roping. He makes his catch with a free rope and takes his turns around the saddle horn. He needs a longer rope than the *tie man,* who ties his rope to the saddle horn, because he cannot throw it all out but has to have some left for his turns.

dally steer roping

In rodeo, steer roping in which the roper dallies the rope around the saddle horn and brings the steer to a stop, with the rope tight and the steer facing the horse.

dally team roping

In rodeo, team roping in which the ropers must not tie the ropes to the saddle horn but must take several turns around the horn with the rope to hold the roped steer. Each roper keeps the rest of the coiled rope in the same hand with which he reins his horse. See *team roping.*

dally your tongue

A cowman's command to someone to stop talking.

dan

A logger's and miner's word for dynamite. Also called *Dinah* and *dine*.

DANCES

See antelope dance, baile, bronco baile, coona, doin's, fandango, heifer brand, hoe dig, jamboree, makin' the calico crack, scalp dance, shakin' a hoof, shindig, stomp, storming the puncheons, struggle, war dance, wrastle.

dancing devil

A name used on the desert for a whirling sandstorm.

danglers

Little, one-inch-long, pear-shaped pendants hanging loosely from the end of the axle of the spur rowel; their sole function is to make music that the cowboy loves to hear. Also called *jinglebobs*.

Daniel Boones

A cowman's contemptuous title given to long-haired pseudo scouts and would-be bad men.

dashboard running jeans

What the logger calls bibless overalls.

dashboards

What the cowboy sometimes derisively calls another's feet. Most cowboys take great pride in the smallness of their feet. If you want to get a rise out of one, just tell him that his feet "look like loadin' chutes" or accuse him of carrying most of his weight "on the spur end."

daub

In gambling, a color compound used to mark cards while playing.

daunsy

A cowman's word for moody or downcast. One of the West's philosophies is, "The man who wears his chin on his instep never sees the horizon."

day-herd

To stand guard over cattle in the daytime while they graze.

day hole

In mining, any heading or level in a mine communicating with the surface.

daylightin'

Riding so that daylight can be seen between the rider's seat and the saddle.

day mark

See *crossboard*.

day money

In rodeo, the amount of prize money paid to the winners of each go-round.

day-money horse

In rodeo, a bronc considered a consistently good bucker, tough enough to earn a high score but not good enough to buck off his rider.

day's drop

In sheepherding, the total number of lambs born during a given day.

day shift

A group of miners, or other laborers, who work during the day.

daywork

All work other than that done by the piece or on contract, such as repairing roads, handling cars, etc.; it does not include work for which the men are paid by the month. Also called *company work*.

deacon

A cowboy's name for a runty calf.

deacon seat

In logging, the one classic piece of camp furniture, a bench made of halved logs, flat side up, usually running from one end of a room to the other.

dead air

A miner's term for mine air containing carbonic acid (producing blackdamp); also, air in a poorly ventilated mine. See also *chokedamp*.

dead card

In faro, a card when none of its denomination remains in the dealer's box.

deadfall

What the cowman calls a drinking or gambling establishment of bad repute. In logging, an area in a forest encumbered with trees that have been blown down or have fallen from age or decay. In mining, a dumping platform at the mouth of a mine.

deadhead

In steamboating, a person traveling aboard a passenger vessel who did not pay fare—perhaps a friend of the owner or the captain's wife. Also, freight that was shipped without charge was said to *go deadhead*. In logging, a sunken or partly sunken log.

deadline

The dividing line between a neutral and a hostile or prohibited area; a line drawn by early-day cattlemen beyond which sheep were not allowed to go; otherwise, there might be some dry-gulching or a range war. In the early days in Texas the Nueces River was called *Sheriff's Deadline* because outlaws in the region would not let a sheriff cross west of it. In rodeo, an elastic or leather strip, usually about 6 feet long, stretched out and fastened to the ground several feet in front of the chute at the end from which the stock come out. The distance between the chute opening and the deadline varies according to the arena conditions and the stock. In mining, a row of marked powder kegs or other danger signal placed by the *fire boss (q.v.)* to warn miners not to enter workings containing gas.

dead lode

In mining, a lode that does not contain valuable minerals in paying quantity.

dead log

In logging, a log that will float.

deadman

In the cattle country, a cable made by twisting a half-dozen strands of barbed wire and passing them around the top of a fence post and then around a large rock sunk deep in the ground. In logging, a short log buried securely in the ground and used as an anchor for guy lines. A fallen tree. A piece of timber to which the hawser of a boom is attached. In mining, a wooden block used to guard the mouth of a mine against runaway cars. In steamboating, an anchorage consisting of a trench 4 feet long and 2 to 3 feet deep dug on shore perpendicular to the line of torsion, in the bottom of which a log of wood is securely fastened; to this

log the towing line is fastened, and a small trench is dug in the direction of the boat to accommodate the rope and prevent lifting strain. From this deadman a line is taken to the capstan.

dead man's hand

In gambling, a term used throughout the West to describe a hand made up of aces and eights, considered to be bad luck. This superstition was handed down from the time Jack McCall killed Wild Bill Hickok in Deadwood, South Dakota, in 1876, while he sat in a poker game holding such a hand.

dead meat

What the early trappers called carrion.

dead-mouthed

Said of a horse whose mouth has become insensitive to the bit.

dead riches

What the miner calls uncoined gold or silver.

dead rock

In mining, the material removed at the time a mine is opened, which is of no value for milling purposes.

deadwood

Control, as, to "have the *deadwood*" on someone. To get the drop on an enemy; to gain an advantage over someone.

dead work

In mining, the developing of a mine preparatory to stoping.

deal card

In faro, any card on the layout which no longer has action either because the dealer has already drawn the four cards corresponding to it in the various suits or because it happens to be the first or last card drawn.

dealer's choice

In poker, the privilege of the dealer to choose the game to be played—draw poker, stud poker, or any form of either game; the dealer also designates which card or cards are to be wild.

deal from the bottom

To cheat at cards by dealing from the bottom of the deck.

dealing brace

Using crooked faro boxes or manipulating cards so that the dealer is sure to win; these sure-shot games are practiced by the lowest class of gamblers.

Dearborn

A type of wagon made in Dearborn, Michigan, and popular in the West.

DEATH

See belly up, big jump, bite the dust, bite the ground, buck out, buck out in smoke, cash in, die-up, finished his circle, gone over the range, go under, grass is waving over him, hung up his saddle, journada del muerto, last roundup, long trail, misty beyond, pass in his chips, passed in his checks, rubbed out, sacked his saddle, shakin' hands with St. Peter, stretch, take the big jump, turned his toes to the daisies, turn on his back, went under.

DECEIVE

See clouding the trail, throw dust.

deckhand

In river boating, on a packet that carries a Negro deck crew, the Negro boss on the watch; he is the go-between for the mate and the roustabouts. On a towboat, a man employed to do deck work and handle lines.

deck log

In logging, the platform in a sawmill upon which logs are held before sawing. Also called *mill deck.*

decorate a cottonwood

An early-day cowman's expression meaning *to hang someone from a tree.*

decoy brand

A small brand placed on an animal's belly or other out-of-the-way place; used by some ranchers to trap rustlers. Choice animals would be otherwise unbranded to tempt the thieves, but the ruse was rarely successful since the rustlers were suspicious and as smart as the ranchers.

decoy herd

A small herd of cattle used in snaring wilder animals or in starting a cut of cattle on roundup.

deep

In mining, the lower portion of the vein.

deep-dished

See *dish.*

DEFEAT

See holler calf rope, horns sawed off.

defect

In logging, any irregularity or imperfection in a tree, log, or piece of lumber that reduces the volume of sound wood or lowers its durability, strength, or utility value.

dehorn

To remove horns from cattle. A hard drinker, especially one inclined to fight when drunk. A logger's word for any kind of drinking liquor; also used by old-time Wobblies to denote anything that took the mind of the worker off the class struggle; anything in opposition to I.W.W. teachings.

democrat pasture

A pasture formed by closing a gap across a rimrock or a canyon.

democrat wagon

A light spring wagon used on a great many ranches.

den tree

A hollow tree used as a home by an animal.

deposit

In mining, a mass of ore or metal in the ground.

dépouille

A buffalo hunter's term for the broad fat portion of buffalo flesh extending from the shoulders to the tail; from the French, meaning *skin stripped from an animal.*

derrick

A wooden crane used on ranches to stack hay.

derringer

A small, .41-caliber, short-barreled pistol with a large bore, using a blunt-nosed bullet, capable of delivering a heavy blow at short range. This weapon was popular, especially among gamblers and bunko men, as a *hide-out gun (q.v.)* from the early 1870's to the close of the century.

desert canary

A westerner's name for a burro.

desert rat

A veteran prospector of the desert country, usually one without a mine or any other property.

desperado flag

The red sash some early-day cowboys wore around their waists. This was one of the favorite adornments of Charles M. Russell, the famous cowboy artist.

DETERMINED

See hell in his neck.

devil

A trader's term meaning *to harness*.

devil's bedposts

What the gambler calls the four of clubs.

dewclaw

In animals, a vestigial toe that does not reach the ground. A small horny projection just above the back side of the hoof of a cloven-footed animal.

dewey

A cowboy's name for a six-shooter.

dewlap

A mark of ownership made on the underside of the neck or brisket of an animal by pinching up a quantity of skin and cutting it loose but not off. When the wound heals, it leaves a hanging flap of skin. Some marks are slashed up and are called *dewlaps up;* others are slashed down and are called *dewlaps down.*

dew wrangler

A wrangler who herds horses early in the morning.

diameter limit

In logging, under a diameter-limit cutting agreement, a specified diameter at breast height (4½ feet above the ground) above which all trees are cut.

diamond hitch

In packing, a common method of roping a pack on a pack animal; when completed, the rope is interlaced on top of the pack in the figure of a diamond. An ordinary knot is "tied," but a diamond hitch is always "throwed," because a rope of 40 or 50 feet long is thrown back and forth across the animal as the hitch is made.

diapper

What the logger calls a man who works on the pond at a sawmill and sends logs up to the saws.

diarrhea of the jawbone

A cowboy's expression for talkativeness; running off at the mouth.

DICE

See gambling.

dice house

A cowboy's name for the bunkhouse.

dickey

In stagecoaching, a special seat attached to the body of the stagecoach just above the boot.

didn't have a tail feather left

Said of a cowboy cleaned at the gambling table or otherwise completely broke.

didn't keep his twine on his tree

Said of a rustler who did not keep his rope on the saddle horn where it belonged.

die in a horse's nightcap

To be hanged.

diesel cold deckers

In logging, log-hauling machines which drag themselves along by winding in cables that are anchored to stumps along the path ahead.

die-up

The wholesale death of cattle during blizzards and droughts over a wide range of territory. Die-ups are dreaded by all cattle-men but welcomed by skinners who own no cattle. During the now-famous die-up in Texas, ambitious skinners, not satisfied with the natural death of cattle, began killing them for their hides, and this led to "skin-ning wars." (J. Frank Dobie, *Vaquero of the Brush Country*, [Dallas, Southwest Press, 1929], 24.)

digger ounce
A lead weight, sometimes weighing as much as 5 or 6 ounces, used by early Cali-fornia traders to cheat Digger Indians who brought in gold to trade for goods.

diggers
A cowboy's name for spurs. A name occa-sionally given to old stove-up horses around the ranch.

diggin' for his blue lightnin'
Drawing a gun.

DIGGING
See gophering, mining.

diggings
A mine.

Dig out the bedroll and drift!
A command which informs a cowhand that he has been fired.

dig up the hatchet
A trapper's expression meaning *to go on the warpath*.

dig up the tomahawk
To declare war; to start trouble. When a cowboy "pulls his hat to a fightin' angle," it is a warning of dire things to come.

dike
In mining, a fissure made and filled with igneous rock, most commonly porphyry. It is often barren, but in some cases it is min-eralized or carries a mineralized selvage and so appears as the wall of a lode.

dildock
In gambling, one who uses a marked or stacked deck of cards.

diligencia
What the early traders called legal steal-ing.

dilly road
What a miner calls the mine railroad.

dilsey
A name sometimes used for a saddle mare; on most ranges mares are not used as riding horses.

Dinah
A logger's and miner's name for dyna-mite. Also called *dine*.

dine
See *Dinah*.

dinero
A cowman's word for money. Also, a name for the cook. From the Spanish.

ding-dong
In logging, the steel triangle struck to notify the loggers that a meal is ready.

dingle
In an old-style logging camp, the roofed-over space or alley between the kitchen and the sleeping quarters commonly used as a storeroom. In a newer-style camp the shed-like structure for storing food supplies.

dink
In rodeo, a roping or steer-wrestling horse that is poorly trained or does not perform well.

dinkey
A small logging locomotive. Also called *dinkey-donkey*.

dinkey-donkey
See *dinkey*.

dinner plate
A name for the old broad-horned Spanish saddle, which, in the cowboy's language, had a horn "big 'nough to play a game of seven-up on."

dip
Strong antiseptic used to kill ticks, lice, or scab on cattle or sheep. Also, the cow-boy's name for pudding sauce. In mining, the inclination of a vein or other structure below the horizontal in a mine.

dipping needle
In mining, a compass needle which is

pivoted in such a way that it can swing vertically—that is, up and down—as well as horizontally to the earth's surface. As is commonly known, a compass needle is affected by a magnetic field, being pulled away from its normal north-south direction. Thus, when such a needle is carried near a deposit of some magnetic ore, it will tend to point downward toward the ore.

dipping vat

A vat or tank in which cattle are dipped for ticks, etc. A cowboy's name for a bathtub.

DIRECTION

See anti-godlin, beeline.

dirt dobbers

A logger's name for the men who build grades for new railroads.

dirt hider

In logging, a road grader.

dirtied his shirt

Thrown from a horse.

DISADVANTAGE

See caught in the bind, caught short, grabbin' the brandin' iron by the hot end, his leg tied up, shorten his stake rope, take the slack out of his rope.

discharging book

In river boating, a long, slim book used on packet boats to record the items of freight to be unloaded at each landing place. As the articles came off the boat, the clerk checked them off his list and thereby kept track of the shipments. Also called *discharge book*.

discovery

In mining, the first finding of a claim. A discovery is necessary before the location can be held by a valid title. The first opening is called the *discovery shaft* or *discovery tunnel*.

discovery claim

In mining, the first claim in which a mineral deposit is found. When the deposit is found in a gulch or a stream, the claims are simply marked and numbered from the discovery claim either by letters or by figures up or down the gulch or stream.

DISGRACED

See sold his saddle.

DISGUSTED

See auger, lookin' for a dog to kick, looking for trouble.

dish

A cowboy's name for the seat of the saddle; depending on its depth, the seat is spoken of as either *shallow-dished* or *deep-dished*.

DISHES

See baldface dishes, eatin' irons.

DISHWASHERS

See pearl diver, pot rastler.

dish-wheeled

Knock-kneed; said of a man or an animal.

DISMOUNTING

See cool your saddle, light.

dispatchers

In gambling, loaded dice. Also called *dispatches*.

disseminated ore

In mining, ore in which the metal-bearing particles are sparsely scattered through the rock mass. An example is one common type of copper ore body containing scattered copper sulphides that form only a small percentage of the whole mass; such ore bodies are called *disseminated deposits*. Since the rock in which ore bodies of this sort are found is porphyry, such deposits are often called *porphyry coppers*.

DISTANCE

See two whoops and a holler.

district attorney

Son-of-a-bitch stew, q.v. When the law began its westward march and started to question and clamp down on the cowboy government of the happy, carefree days, the blame for this cramping of liberties was placed upon lawyers. The natural resentment felt by the riders of the range toward the law was reflected in this name they gave the dish. The implication is obvious.

ditch

In mining, an artificial water course, flume, or canal, with or without natural channels.

ditch rider

An irrigation patrolman who turns water into laterals and watches for breaks in ditch banks.

ditty

A cowboy's name for a new tool or contrivance, or for practically anything unfamiliar to him.

dive

A cowboy's name for the bunkhouse. Also, a low saloon. I think it was Charles M. Russell who said of such a saloon that it "would make all the other dives in the West look like a ladies' finishing school." I heard another cowman describe a dive as a place "where a rattlesnake would be ashamed to meet his mother."

divining rod

In mining, a witch-hazel rod used in prospecting for ore. It is claimed that when one adept at the art carries such a rod slowly in suspension, it dips and points downward when brought over a spot where treasure is to be found. Also called *doodlebug*.

division

In stagecoaching, the number of "drives," usually several hundred miles, supervised by an agent or superintendent.

'dobe wall

A wall made of *adobe, q.v.* To stand someone against an adobe wall and execute him by shooting him. Llano Pierce once spoke of a friend in Mexico being " 'dobewalled into kingdom come."

dockers

In sheep raising, the men who clip off the tails of the lambs.

dock piece

The portion of the crupper that fits under the animal's tail; also, that portion of the animal's tail under which the dock of the crupper rests.

doctor

To cut the knee tendon of a wild longhorn so that he can walk but cannot run. In steamboating, a type of feed boiler used to a great extent on the Mississippi River steamers, invented shortly after the Civil War. It was used to feed water to the boilers or to pump out the steamer. Operated on the walking-beam principle, it proved one of the most efficient and reliable pumps of its kind.

Doctor C. C.

The logger's camp doctor; short for *compound cathartic*.

doctor gate

A gate in a corral, usually in a lane down which animals are driven and then "dodged" (separated) by swinging the gate back and forth to shunt them into various classifying pens.

DOCTORS

See Doctor C. C., Epsom salts, Genuine Jimmy, Indian doctor, jaw cracker, old pills, pill roller, Quinine Jimmy, saddlebag doctor, sawbones.

dodge out

To cut out calves from a herd.

dodge-post fence

A wire fence built with posts set 6 feet apart, alternating first on one side of the wire and then on the other.

dodgers

In logging, the men who pry the dogs out of the logs. See *dog*.

dofunnies

A cowboy's name for the useless little trinkets he carries in his war bag.

dog

In logging, a large spiked steel arm that holds the log in position while being sawed.

dog chain

In logging, a chain used to hold the logs together in a log pond or boom.

dog-fall

To throw an animal with its feet under it.

dog fight

A cowboy's name for a fist fight. The early cowman felt that such fights were beneath his dignity. As one said, "If the Lord had intended me to fight like a dog, He'd a-give me longer teeth and claws."

dogger

One who bulldogs. See *bulldog*.

dog holes

Holes in a piece of lumber caused by the dogs on the carriage that are used to hold the log or cant in place. See *dog*.

doghouse

A cowboy's name for the bunkhouse.

doghouse stirrups

A name for the old wide wooden stirrups of the early range; so called because it was claimed that they had enough lumber in them to build a doghouse.

dogie

A scrubby calf that has not wintered well and is anemic from the scant food of the cold months; also *dogy* or *dobie*. It is, in the language of the cowboy, "a calf who has lost his mammy and whose daddy has run off with another cow." Although the word is used commonly in the West and is understood by all cattlemen, there has been some controversy over its origin. One version is that during trail days, when it was discovered that the northern range was good cow country, especially for fattening beef, there arose a demand for young animals. It became the usage to call them *dogies*, especially yearling steers, to distinguish them from the steers that were fat enough for market.

Another, more likely, version is that the term originated in the eighties after a very severe winter had killed off a number of orphan calves. The bellies of the survivors very much resembled a batch of sour dough carried in a sack. Having no mothers whose brand would establish ownership, and carrying no brand themselves by which they might be identified, these orphans were put into the maverick class. The first to claim them was recognized as the owner, no matter where they were found.

One day on roundup a certain cowman who was trying to build up a herd drove in a bunch from along the river.

"Boys, there's five of them dough-guts in that drive, and I claim every damn one of 'em!" he yelled.

During that roundup all orphan calves became known as *dough-guts*; later the term was shortened to *dogie*, which has been used ever since throughout cattle land to refer to a pot-gutted orphan calf. The term became popular through western songs, though a great percentage of the singers pronounce it *doggie*, as if they were singing of a pup.

The word is also sometimes used by the cowboy to mean laced shoes.

dogie lamb

An orphan lamb.

dogieman

A small rancher or nester who gets his cattle from outside farm districts.

dog loop

A small loop used in calf roping.

dogtown

An area occupied by a community of prairie dogs.

dog warp

In logging, a rope with a strong loop on the end, used in breaking dangerous jams on falls and rapids and in moving logs from one position to another.

dogwatch

In steamboating, a two-hour watch designed to change the hours of the watches kept by the crew. The first dogwatch was from 4:00 to 6:00 P.M.; the second, from 6:00 to 8:00 P.M.

dogwood

A cowboy's name for sagebrush because its odor when wet is like wet dog's fur.

dogwood switch

A westerner's term for an arrow.

doin's

A trapper's and trader's term for food. A fandango. A fight. Any special activity.

dollar hole

In steamboating, a large tin funnel leading overboard from the pantry for the disposal of garbage; so called because much wasted food was dumped into it.

doll-babies

A cowman's name for the wooden pegs used in making hair ropes.

doll baby

A two-wheeled cart used for short-distance hauling.

doll buggy

In logging, a small, two-wheeled cart used to haul big timbers short distances to avoid loading them on a wagon.

doll rags

What the trader called the cloth or clothes he sold.

dolly

In steamboating, a wooden block on rollers used in moving heavy objects. In logging, a two-wheeled iron support on which lumber is placed so that it can be moved; also, a type of trailer for a logging truck.

donkey

In steamboating, a hoisting engine on the boat. In logging, a portable steam engine equipped with drum and cable and used in cable logging.

donkey doctor

In logging, a mechanic who maintains and repairs *donkeys*. See *donkey*.

donkey logging

Logging with a *donkey, q.v.*

donkeyman

The engineer or operator of a *donkey, q.v.* Also called *donkey puncher* and *donkey skinner*.

donkey puncher

See *donkeyman*.

donkey's breakfast

A logger's name for a straw bed.

Donkeys

See burro, Colorado mockingbird, desert canary, mountain canary, Rocky Mountain canary, Washoe canary.

donkey skinner

See *donkeyman*.

Don't drag your feet!

In logging, an admonishment to a workman not to "ride the saw" or neglect his end of the job.

don't know sic 'em

A cowboy's expression meaning *ignorant*. I have heard many unique references to ignorance, such as, "He don't know 'nough to pack guts to a bear," "He don't know dung from wild honey," and many others. Ted Logan referred to a man with, "His head's so hollow he's got to talk with his hands to get away from the echo."

don't travel like a colt no more

A cowboy expression meaning that one is getting old and stove-up.

doodlebug

See *divining rod*.

Do one's best

See break a hamstring, cut a rusty.

door knob

A cowboy's term for a small boy—one who, in cowboy lingo, still "has the growin' itch."

doped cards

In gambling, marked cards.

doping

In stagecoaching, greasing the wheels of a coach. It was a part of the stagecoach driver's work to grease the coach at each home station. If the driver forgot to dope the wheels, a hotbox resulted.

dotting iron

A branding iron, primitive forerunner of the stamp branding iron. Unlike the stamp iron, which brands with one application, the dotting iron was made in three separate parts, a bar, a small half circle, and a large half circle; by using various combinations, a number of different brands could be made. (J. Evetts Haley, *Charles Goodnight, Cowman and Plainsman,* [Bos-

ton, Houghton Mifflin Company, 1936],
18.)

double-barreled

Said of a two-cinch saddle; also called
double fire and *double-rigged*.

double fire

See *double-barreled*.

double hitch

A packer's crosstree hitch in which the
loop of the running rope was brought under the boot of the aparejo instead of around
the side pack on each side.

double hobble

A short strap with leather cuffs at each
end, fitted so that the cuffs can be buckled
about the forelegs to keep a horse from
straying.

double-jacker

In mining, one who uses both hands on
a large hammer and strikes the jack or
wedge used to separate rocks for blasting.

double odd

In faro, a method of cheating for the
house in which the dealer surreptitiously
introduces two extra cards which he can
control. See also *odd*.

double out

To cut grass to bridge and fill in so that
a mired wagon can be pulled out of the
mud. To pull a wagon out of the mud by
hitching additional teams to it. In gambling, a betting system in which the case
card is played to fall the same way that the
third card falls; also applied to cards other
than the case card.

double overbit

An earmark made by cutting two triangular pieces from the upper part of the
animal's ear. See *double underbit*.

double-rigged

See *double-barreled*.

double roll

A gun spin accomplished by spinning two
guns forward, one on each trigger finger,
cocking and releasing the hammer as it
comes under the web or lower part of the
thumb. It is more of a stunt than a practice.

double shuffle

A sudden shift in the gait of a pitching
horse.

double stringer

In sheep raising, a fleece large enough
to require two strings to tie it.

double tripping

In steamboating, a method of loading
freight by placing half the freight on the
bank, steaming over the bar, unloading the
other half, returning for the first half,
passing over the bar again, and then loading
the second half.

double underbit

An earmark made by cutting two triangular pieces from the lower side of the animal's ear. See *double overbit*.

double-wintered

Said of cattle held in the North for two
winters to mature them into prime beef.

dough-belly

A cowboy's name for the cook.

dough boxer

A cowboy's and logger's name for the
cook.

doughgods

A cowboy's name for biscuits; a logger's
name for camp bread.

dough puncher

A cowboy's and logger's name for the
cook.

dough roller

A cowboy's and logger's name for the
cook.

dough wrangler

A cowboy's and logger's name for the
cook.

downcast

In mining, a ventilating shaft with a
descending current of air.

downdraft

A downward draft, as in a flue, chimney,
or shaft of a mine.

downed

A cowboy's word meaning *killed*.

downer

A cow which, after a drought or a hard winter, is weak from undernourishment; every time she attempts to move faster than a walk she falls and has to be tailed up again.

The late John Hendrix, an old-timer friend of mine, told this story concerning downers:

"There was an old cowman down in the Brady country a good many years ago, who got all his 'downers' up one frosty morning and, while they were steadying down, rode over the hill to skin one he felt pretty sure had died during the night. Just as he rode over the hill, he heard gunshots back in the direction of the cattle he had just left. Loping back, he saw three friends from town hunting quail around his stack-yards.

" 'For God's sake don't shoot around here, fellers,' he cried, riding up to them.

" 'Why, Lige, you told us last fall we were welcome to hunt out here whenever we wanted to. Besides, we're not goin' to shoot any of your cattle.'

" 'I know you're not, fellers,' replied the cowman. 'That's not the idea. When you shot awhile ago, fifty-five head of my old "Nellies" tried to run and fell down, and I'm too danged weak in the back to tail 'em any more times today.' " (John M. Hendrix, "Feedin,' " *West Texas Today* [March, 1937], 7.)

down in his boots

Frightened; cowardly, said of a person, in cowboy parlance, "as yeller as mustard without the bite."

down in the skillet

The Texas Panhandle country.

down steer

An animal off its feet in a loaded stock-car.

down to his last chip

Out of money; broke.

down to the blanket

Almost out of money; almost cleaned.

dowser

In mining, one who searches for subterranean supplies of water, ore, etc., with the aid of a *divining rod*, q.v.

drag

The rear of a column of cattle on the trail. It is made up of the footsore, the weak, the young calves, the weary, and the lazy; also called *tail*. The cattle themselves are called *drags*, and this term is also sometimes applied to lazy humans. The average cowhand has little use for a lazy person, and his descriptions of one are rather highly flavored. I heard Hunk Bouden speak of one with, "The hardest work he ever done was take a long squint at the sun and a quick squat in the shade." Wishbone Wilson spoke of a man being so lazy "he had to lean ag'in a buildin' to spit," and Curly Hicks said of another that he "didn't do nothin' but set 'round all day on his one-spot."

drag brand

A cattle brand with a bottom projection which angles downward to some degree.

drag day

In logging, the day of the month on which a logger can draw his pay in advance of payday.

drag down

In gambling, after winning, to reduce the size of the next bet.

dragging her rope

What the cowboy says of a woman who is trying to catch a husband. Jack Davis used to say that such a woman "might have a short rope, but she shore throwed a wide loop."

dragging his navel in the sand

Leaving in a hurry. Bill Keith, in describing to me a friend running on foot, said, "He was hobbled with a pair of hairy chaps, but he couldn't have made better time if he'd been stripped to the buff."

drag her

A logger's expression meaning *to quit a job and go on one's way.*

drag it

A cowboy's expression meaning *to leave,* usually under compulsion.

drag one's feet

In logging, to "ride a saw" and fail to do one's share on a two-man saw.

drag rider

A cowboy whose duty it is to follow the drags. See *drag.* This is the most disagreeable job in cattle driving because the man has to ride in the dust kicked up by the entire herd and contend with the weak and lazy critters until his patience is sorely tried. While the other riders may be singing in the pure air up ahead, there is no music in the soul of the drag rider, and he is using his vocal powers to cuss beneath the neckerchief he keeps tied over his nose and mouth. Also often called *tail rider.*

drag split

An earmark in which the inner end of the split runs at an angle to that of the outer end.

drag-tails

In packing, mules that were farthest away from the *bell (q.v.)* when traveling; also, a lazy packer.

draw

A shallow natural drain for rainfall. The withdrawal of a gun from a holster, as in the phrase "quick on the *draw.*"

DRAWING A GUN

See border draw, border shift, diggin' for his blue lightnin', draw, fill your hand, flip-cock, fumble, hip draw, leather slapping, pinwheel, reach, shoulder draw, skins his gun, throw down, unshucked.

draws dead

In rodeo, said of a cowboy who draws stock in a rodeo that is nearly impossible to win on, such as a saddle bronc that runs off without bucking or a steer that stops and turns back.

dream book

A cowboy's term for his book of cigarette papers.

dream sack

A cowboy's sleeping bag.

DRESS

See boots, clothes, feathered out, hats, rag-out, rig up, rubbed up, shoes, slick up, some deck is shy a joker, spraddled out, swallow forkin', totin' stars on his duds.

dressed in a hemp four-in-hand

Said of someone being hanged.

dressed up like a sore toe

A cowboy's expression meaning *dressed in fancy togs.*

drift

The marching of cattle in large numbers away from a particular locality, either to avoid the local conditions or to seek better conditions elsewhere. The term is more commonly used when the cattle wander aimlessly before a winter storm, though a drift might occur in summer as the consequence of a stampede or the result of a lack of water or grass because of a drought. Drifts usually happen only with cattle, for horses have enough sense to avoid them and to find shelter for themselves. (Philip A. Rollins, *The Cowboy* [New York, Charles Scribner's Sons, 1936], 209.)

In mining, a horizontal passageway, usually one that follows the vein or other formation. In river boating, debris floating in the river or lodged along the shore in a drift pile. The motion of a boat floating with no mechanical aid. A synonym for *current,* as in the expression, "How does the *drift* set around this bridge pier?"

DRIFT

See cattle drift, drift fence, winter drift.

drift bolt

In river boating, an extremely long bolt used in fastening barge timbers together.

drift fence

A fence built by ranchmen to keep cattle from drifting too far away from their home range. See *drift.* These fences ran east and west for indefinite distances to turn the drift when cattle moved south by the thousands trying to escape the blizzards coming from the north.

On the open range the drift fence was

unlawful because the land was government land and therefore public, but the cowmen felt that such a fence was a matter of necessity. Yet in severe winters it often proved to be a deathtrap for cattle.

drift mining

A method of mining gold-bearing gravel by means of drifts and shafts. Also called *placer mining, q.v.* See also *hydraulic mining.*

drilled her deep enough

What the Cornish miner says when he quits.

drilling uppers

In mining, drilling upward into a hanging wall.

D ring

One of the two iron or steel rings on a cinch, usually with one flat side but sometimes perfectly round.

DRINKING

See belly up, bender, bendin' an elbow, dehorn, freighting his crop, hear the owl hoot, high lonesome, h'ist one, horrors, lay the dust, lookin' down the neck of a bottle, paintin' his nose, paint his tonsils, put on the sideboards, putting on the rollers, rust the boiler, using his rope arm to hoist a glass, wearin' callouses on his elbows.

drive

The moving of cattle on foot from one location to another. To move cattle in such a way. In logging, logs or timbers that are being floated on a stream from the forest to a mill or shipping point. A mass of logs floated in a boom. In stagecoaching, the distance between the points where the drivers and their vehicles were changed, usually about 60 miles.

drive a fair business

A trader's expression meaning *to make a profit.*

driver

In logging, a railroad engineer. Also, a lumberman who floats logs downstream, especially in time of high water.

DRIVERS

See buckboard driver, carajo, carretero, four-up driver, holdup man, Jehu, knight of the ribbons, lasher, little Mary, long-line skinner, mulero, mule skinner, nursey, two-up driver, whip, whipster.

drive the hearse

In faro, to keep a record of the cards played, by means of a *case, q.v.* Also, *to keep cases.*

driving pitch

In logging, high water suitable for driving logs downstream.

droop-eyed

Said of a calf whose eyelid muscles had been cut by a rustler so that it could not see to follow its mother.

droop-horn

An animal with drooping horns.

drop

In logging, a sudden downward angle of a cut or mark.

drop band

In sheep raising, a flock of ewes who are about to drop their lambs.

drop-band herder

A sheepherder who is in charge of the *drop band, q.v.* It is his duty to see that expectant mothers are at the tail of the band to keep them from being disturbed by the others.

drop gap

In cattle raising, a place in a wire fence where nails rather than staples are driven into posts, from which the wires can be lifted and fastened down until they are passed over and then replaced on the nails.

dropped his rope on her

Said of a cowman who has married.

dropping trailers

In cattle herding, letting off men at various intervals to trail loose cattle and drive them to a central roundup ground.

drop stirrup

A heavy leather strap below the stirrup to enable the rider to mount more easily. Used by women riders.

drum

In logging, a power unit on which a cable is wrapped.

DRUNKENNESS

See bed him down, booze-blind, borracho, bottle fever, jag, roostered, Somebody stole his rudder, talking load, walking whisky vat.

dry

What the old-time trapper always said when he was thirsty.

dry band

A band of ewes which did not drop lambs during the season.

dry-camp

To camp without water.

dry-drive

To drive without water for the cattle.

dry-gulch

To kill; to ambush.

dry-ki

In logging, trees killed by flooding; often found in areas flooded by beaver dams.

dry-lander

What the cowboy called a farmer of irrigated land.

dry route

A route on which there is no water.

dry shooting

Practicing fanning or shooting with an unloaded gun.

dry stock

Cattle, regardless of age or sex, that are giving no milk.

dry storm

A cowboy's name for a sandstorm.

dry wash

The dry bed of a stream.

dubber

A trader's name for an adz-shaped piece of iron used as a hammer.

duck

What the logger calls a bed urinal.

ducker and dodger

A horse that bucks by jerking his head down on one side, then down on the other, at the same time swapping ends with his hindquarters.

dude

What the cowboy calls a person who comes west for enjoyment, thrills, and rest.

dude chaps

Fancy chaps, such as those worn by dudes and actors, in which a real cowboy would not be seen.

dude ranch

A ranch which has been converted into a place of recreation for easterners.

DUDES

See dude, dudette, dudolo, S. A. cowboy, swivel dude.

dudette

A female dude; described by the cowboy as a young lady who comes west to marry a cowboy; also called *dudine*.

dude wrangler

A man who serves as a guide to the guests at a dude ranch, usually a former cowboy out of a riding job.

dudine

See *dudette*.

dudolo

A rare type of westerner who lives by sponging off dudes and dudettes. A play on the word *gigolo*.

duff

In logging, forest litter and other organic debris in various stages of decomposition on top of the mineral soil; typical of conifer forests, where the rate of decomposition is slow and litter accumulation exceeds decay.

duffer

A cowboy's name for a codger or for a useless fellow.

dugout

A rectangular pit dug into the ground, usually on a hillside, covered with a framework of timber and turf elevated 3 or 4 feet above the ground. Dugouts were very common in the early West as first and temporary residences. As the old saying goes, "It's a dwelling whose front yard took in considerable territory." Also, a canoe made from a log of cottonwood. The log was cut to the desired length, the branches trimmed off, and the log hollowed out. The ends were given a canoe shape, the top hewed off so as to leave about two-thirds of the log. To support the sides and give strength to the craft, the timber was left in place at points from 4 to 6 feet apart, making solid partitions. These canoes were strong, light, and easily managed and were propelled with a paddle, though some carried a sail which was used when the wind was favorable.

dugway

A place on the steep bank of a stream graded down to let cattle and wagons enter or leave a stream.

duke

A bull.

dulce

In the Southwest, a young man's word for his sweetheart, girl, or lady friend; from the Spanish, meaning *sweet*.

dump

In logging, a name for the bunkhouse. In mining, a deposit, or place of deposit, of waste rock, or tailings.

dumped

Thrown from a horse.

dunnage

In logging, lumber of a grade below that recognized in standard lumber grades; cull lumber usable for certain purposes.

duplex

In logging, a *donkey (q.v.)* which both yards and loads logs.

Dupont

A trapper's name for gunpowder; named for its manufacturer, E. I. du Pont de Nemours and Company, founded in 1802.

dust

To throw dust into the eyes of a charging steer or cow. To go. Also, short for *gold dust*, a popular term for money.

dust a horse

To fan a horse with the rider's hat when riding.

dust cutter

A name stagecoach travelers gave a drink of whisky secured at some stations after a long, dusty ride.

dusted

Thrown from a horse.

duster

A dust storm. In mining, a machine used to drill holes for blasting when run without water; also called *widow-maker*.

dust his ears

To fan a horse with the rider's hat when riding.

Dutchman

In logging, a prop placed under a log to keep it from pinching a saw during bucking. A prop used for any similar purpose, such as supporting the hitch of an arch while it is being hooked onto a tractor. A certain kind of block that is put around a tree to haul up the rigging; thus the rigger will say, "We hung up the Dutchman." In mining, a ridge in the center of a drill hole that causes the steel to stick—sometimes the steel is released when the men "shoot the rounds."

Dutch oven

A very thick, three-footed skillet with a heavy lid, used for cooking much of the cowboy's food, but especially biscuits. It is placed over hot coals, and more coals are placed on the lid to brown the food on both sides.

dying on their backs

In sheep raising, said of sheep dying helplessly. When other animals roll over, they are able to make a complete turn and get back on their feet. But when a sheep rolls over, because of its short legs it is not always able to regain its feet, especially if it has a heavy coat of wool, as in the spring. If it is not helped to its feet, it will lie on its back until it dies.

dying with throat trouble

Being hanged. It was hard to get a range man to talk of a hanging, nor would he admit having had anything to do with one. It was a stern and solemn matter and not the subject of jests nor casual conversation.

dynamite

A cowboy's name for cheap whisky.

dyno

In mining, a rock worker who handles explosives.

E

"Man's the only animal that can be skinned more'n once"

eagle bill

A slang name for a tapadero, a leather stirrup covering, so called because of its shape.

eagle's nest

In sawmills, the cage from which saws are controlled. A man works on the *nest*, which is placed above a series of endless chains on which the lumber is transplanted to the *cutoff battery* of saws. The worker operates more than twenty levers, each one controlling a saw. It is highly specialized work.

ear down

To distract a horse's attention by holding his head down by the ears while the rider mounts. Sometimes the man doing the earing will catch the tip of the horse's ear with his teeth. This action causes the horse to stand very still to avoid pain.

ear head

A headstall made in two pieces, with a loop for the right ear, one buckle on the left cheek, and no noseband, throatlatch, or browband. The bit ties in with buckskin strings. This type of headstall is used only on broken horses.

early boughten

A cowboy's term occasionally used for a greenhorn.

earmark

A mark of ownership cut in the ears of cattle. To make such cuts.

EARMARKS

See barbs, bits, comet split, crop, double overbit, double underbit, drag split, earmark, fanned split, flickers, full split, grub, hack, hole earmark, hooks jinglebob, J split, key split, long-ear, mark, overbit, overhack, over-half-crop, overround, overslope, oversplit, rocker split, saw-set earmark, sawtooth earmark, seven overbit, seven underbit, sharp, slash, slope, split, steeple fork, stick ears, swallow-fork, swallowtail, tip, underbit, underhack, under-half-crop, under round, underslope, undersplit.

EASTERNERS

See blue belly, bootblack cowpuncher, buggy boss, chuck eater.

easy on the trigger

A cowboy's expression meaning *excitable* or *quick to anger*.

easy water

What the riverman called a stretch of water easy to navigate.

eatin' drag dust

Riding in the *drag (q.v.)* of a trail herd, Thus, humiliated.

EATING

See fall to, fed, Fire and fall back! freighting his crop, lining his flue, padding out his belly, put on the sideboards, put on the nose bag, walking the table, yard the grub.

eatin' gravel

Thrown from a horse. The rider is said to be "eatin' gravel without stoopin'."

EATING IMPLEMENTS

See eatin' irons, tools.

eatin' irons

What the cowboy calls the knives, forks, and spoons with which he eats.

edge work

In gambling, markings on the edges of cards.

educated thirst

A cowboy's phrase describing a man who drinks champagne and fancy mixed drinks. Very few of the early western saloons carried stocks of fancy liquors. In his drinking the cowman did not belong to the "garden variety." When he got drunk, he wanted everybody to know it, and all usually did if they were in the same town. The liquor served in the average frontier bar would, in the words of one cowman, "draw a blood blister on a rawhide boot"; and Zeb Fisher declared that the bartender of a certain saloon "served a free snake with ever' drink."

eighter from Decatur

In dice, eight as a point; also called *Ada from Decatur.*

eight-string saddle

A saddle with eight sets of strings used to fasten the different pieces of leather in place. The work saddle is usually an eight-string one.

eighty-niner

A person who settled in Oklahoma in 1889.

elbow room

The wide-open spaces. The old-time open-range cowman felt that he was being crowded if a neighbor settled within fifty miles of him, and he complained of not having *elbow room.*

El Dorado

The West, or a place in the West, thought to offer fortune to the adventurous immigrant; applied specifically to localities where gold had been found or was reputed to have been found.

Elk River

A gambler's term for three tens in a poker hand.

emigrant ticket

A ticket for transportation, as on a railroad, sold to an emigrant at a reduced price.

emigrant train

A line of wagons, cattle, etc., on the way to a new settlement. A railroad train carrying emigrants.

emigrant wagon

A large, heavy wagon used by emigrants; a prairie schooner.

empty saddle

A danger signal on a ranch. A horse showing up at the ranch carrying an empty saddle has a great significance in the cattle country. There is much anxiety concerning the rider because he may be dead or hurt or maybe afoot, perhaps far from home, which in itself might mean tragedy. As Will James said, "To range folks, such a sight [a horse coming home with an empty saddle] hints to a serious happening." (Will James, *All in a Day's Riding* [New York, Charles Scribner's Sons, 1933], 216.)

ENDURANCE

See bottom.

enemy

A miner's name for the shift boss, but not used in his presence.

engagement

In trapping, an agreement by which a trapper signed on for a three-year hitch with a fur company.

engagés

In trapping, the regularly employed

hunters—that is, hired hunters as distinguished from *free trappers*—who were furnished with an outfit by a company and so bound to sell their furs to that company; from the French.

ENGLISHMEN

See remittance man.

enriched ore

In mining, ore in which the original metal content has been increased by the addition of metal brought down by slowly descending surface water. This water dissolves the metal from the upper portion of the ore bodies, where there has been oxidation, and deposits it again lower down as a result of chemical reaction with sulphides that have not yet been oxidized.

entitled to a warm corner

A cowboy's expression for a cowman who has faithfully performed his duties and grown old in the service.

entry fee

In rodeo, the money paid by a contestant to the rodeo secretary before he can enter an event or rodeo. The size of the fee varies with the amount of the rodeo purse, ranging from $10.00 at the smallest rodeos to a maximum of $100.00. A contestant must pay a separate entry fee for every event in which he competes.

epizootic

A cowboy's name for distemper or strangles, a catarrhal disease of horses.

eppus outfit

A contemptuous name for a logging company.

Epsom salts

A logger's name for the camp doctor.

equalizer

A cowboy's name for a pistol. It is a common saying in the West that "a Colt makes all men equal."

ESCAPE

See leg bail, lick it, Mexican standoff, slope.

esposa

A trader's term for a wife; from the Spanish.

estanco

A trader's word for a government trading post; from the Spanish.

event

In rodeo, one of the five standard events —saddle bronc riding, bareback riding, calf roping, steer wrestling, and bull riding— held at rodeos approved by the Rodeo Cowboy's Association. Other events such as team roping, steer roping, and team tying may also be seen in many parts of the country.

ewe-necked

A cowboy's term for a horse with a long, thin neck resembling that of a ewe.

exalted

Hanged. Almost any cowman is, in the words of one, "too proud of his Adam's apple to want to be exalted."

excuse-me-ma'am

A cowboy's term for a bump in the road.

EXPERIENCE

See bone-seasoned, hair off the dog, hear the owl hoot.

EXPLAIN

See chew it finer, cut the deck deeper, ride over that trail again.

exploitation

The active working of a mine, as distinguished from prospecting.

EXPLOSIVES

See bang juice, bootleg, cyclone shot, dan, Dinah, grease, high explosives, Let loose the powder! noise, powder, puff, sawdust, spit, squip, stew, string, torch a squib, Vaseline.

express box

A box used by Wells, Fargo and Company to carry money and other valuables. It meant ready cash to holdup men.

express rider

A rider who carried mail for the pony express.

extra tackling

What the trader called his personal accessories.

eye

In packing, the center stitch line of the *aparejo, q.v.* In mining, the top of a mine shaft.

eyeballer

What the cowboy calls a meddler.

eyeballing

The cutting off of the upper eyelids of cattle, a practice that was resorted to occasionally in the brush country to prevent cattle from going back into the brush. Not being able to protect their eyes from the brush, the animals were glad to stay in the open country.

eye openers

Small sticks used to prop open the eyes of cattle. Eye openers had the same purpose as the practice of *eyeballing, q.v.*

F

"The man that always straddles the fence usually has a sore crotch"

face

In mining, the heading of a drift, tunnel, or other horizontal working. Also called *breast.*

face cards

In gambling, any king, queen, or jack in a deck of cards. (The ace is not a face card.)

facings

In packing, the additional pieces or strips of leather applied to certain parts of the *aparejo (q.v.)* to strengthen them.

factor

The head of a trading post. An agent stationed among the Indians as a representative of the federal government or of a fur company.

fade

In dice, to cover part or all of the shooter's center bet.

fag

A cowboy's word meaning *to leave in a hurry.*

Failure

See barkin' at a knot, busted cinch, busted flush, caught in his own loop.

fairbank

A cheating method used by crooked gamblers which lets a player win or favors him temporarily, thus enticing him to increase the size of his bet or continue to play.

fairground

To rope an animal by throwing the rope over its back while it is still running and then throwing the animal violently to the ground, where it usually lies long enough to be hog-tied.

fair lead

In logging, a unit used to guide a line onto a drum from any angle.

fall

To fell a tree.

fallback

A fall in which a bucking horse attempts to stand erect on his hind feet, loses his balance, and falls backward; also called *rear-back.*

fall clip

The growth of wool shorn from sheep in the fall of the year.

fallen hide

The hide of a cow or steer who has died from natural causes.

faller

In logging, a more modern name for *chopper*, one who cuts down trees. *Fallers* work in pairs; *buckers* work alone. Both are called *sawyers* on the West Coast.

Fall in!

The freighter captain's command for the wagons to fall into line for the start.

falling ax

A logger's ax with a long handle or a long, narrow bit, designed especially for felling trees.

fall roundup

See *beef roundup*.

falls out of bed

Said of a horse that pulls back on the halter rope.

Fall to!

A westerner's expression inviting someone to eat; also to begin eating.

false cut

In gambling, a cut of the cards in which the deck remains in its original position.

false front

A building front so constructed as to extend above or beyond the building itself. Business buildings of early cow towns and other frontier towns were constructed in this way.

false pond

A trader's term for a mirage.

fancy fluff-duff

Anything fancy, from food to finery. For some of the ranch dances the ranchwomen would make doughnuts, bake pies, and cook other *fluff-duffs* "just to let the boys know they wasn't eatin' at the wagon."

fandango

A dance of Spanish origin. The word was used by freighters and trappers to mean any kind of dance, and sometimes a boisterous gathering or a fight.

fanega

A freighter's unit of measure, about 1.6 bushels.

fanned split

An earmark in which pieces of the ear have been formed by splitting so that the outside ends are wider than the ends attached to the ear.

fanning

Waving or slapping a hat against a horse's sides while riding a bucker. Using the hat in this manner serves as a balance. When a rider loses his hat, he usually soon follows it to the ground. Gripping a gun with one hand and with rapid passes with the other hand knocking back and releasing the hammer. Fanning is mostly done in western fiction, although there are men who can use this method of shooting. Ordinarily a man might fan for practice and pastime, but he seldom resorted to it when his life was at stake. The trick is interesting in theory but is of doubtful practical value. When a large-caliber gun is fired, the recoil causes the gun to buck up into the air. Though it is possible to work an unloaded gun very rapidly in this manner, in actual shooting the gun will not stay still to be slapped, at least not long enough for accuracy.

fanning on her fat

Fanning (a horse), *q.v.*

fanning the hammer

Fanning (a gun), *q.v.*

fantail

A wild horse. A horse with a long, bushy tail. In steamboating, a walkway, a continuation of the engine-room guard on a stern-wheel boat, built with a deep upward curve to join the cylinder timber at the end. The engineer stood on the fantail to lubricate various paddle-wheel bearings and cams.

faradiddle

See *fumadiddle*.

farewell man

What a logger calls a camp welfare man.

FARMERS

See settlers and farmers.

farmer splice

In logging, a rough splice at the end of a cable forming a temporary loop.

FARMING TOOLS

See foot burners, grasshopper plow, prairie breaker.

FARMS

See Hoosier belt, hundred-and-sixty, jay country.

faro

A gambling game. Faro requires a more elaborate layout than other games. It requires, first, a large board with thirteen squares representing the respective values of the cards. Every dealer has a *case*, a small, folding box about 4 inches high, usually silver-plated, in which the deck is placed, face up. Across the top of the case is the *cage*—thirteen wires, on each of which four buttons are strung, forming an abacus. A tally of every card played is kept on this abacus—for example, one wire with its four buttons represents the four kings and four aces. The cage is carefully kept to determine the odds and protect both players and dealer. The dealer usually keeps the case himself, but in more elaborate establishments a second dealer is hired as casekeeper. Such houses also employ a lookout, who sits upon a high stool overlooking the board to watch for errors by the dealer, particularly when they go against the house. The dealer frequently asks the lookout to exchange places with him when luck is running consistently against him.

The card on top of the deck as play begins is the *soda card* and pays nothing. The next card is the *loser*, the next the *winner*, and so throughout the deck to the last card, the *hock* card, which also pays nothing. When the dealer had proceeded *from soda to hock*, he reshuffles the deck. Cards can be bet either way—to win, by simply placing chips upon any square on the board; to lose, by *coppering* the pile of chips with some token such as a Chinese coin or a checker. Workers and businessmen are known as *producers* and usually play *straight up*, betting on a single card to win or lose. But professionals *copper the heel* by betting on several cards at once. Although not easily done, faro is sometimes *braced*; tiny holes are punched in the cards so that the dealer may see what is coming and to the bank's advantage pull two cards instead of one, giving the wink to the casekeeper to arrange his part of the swindle.

faro bank

A gambling house in which a faro game is set up. The bank for the game of faro—the capital with which the proprietor backs the game; also, the game of faro itself.

faro box

See *tell box*.

fartknocker

What the cowboy calls any kind of hard fall, especially when thrown from a horse.

fast brand

A brand deep enough to be permanent; the opposite of *slow brand*, *q.v.*

FAT

See beef plumb to the hocks, gras, put on tallow, seal fat, shore had tallow, tallow.

father the herd

To bed down for the night.

Father of Waters

An Indian's name for the Mississippi River.

fathom

In mining, a space 6 feet forward of and 6 feet vertical to the width of the vein. In river boating, a depth of 6 feet.

fat pine

A common name for pitch pine.

fatten the kitty

In gambling, to add chips to an unopened jackpot.

fault

In mining, the natural displacement of rock on one side of a plane.

fawche

A trader's word meaning *angry*; from the French *fâcher*.

feather-headed

A cowboy's term meaning *lightheaded*; brainless.

feathered out

A cowboy's expression meaning *dressed up*.

fed

A trader's word meaning *ate*.

fee-bee

In dice, five as a point.

FEED

See bunched hay, burned hay, feed lot, feed rack, hay bottom, hay crib, lodged, overgraze, overshot stackers, put to grass, shelled hay, sled dog, stackyard, standing feed.

feed bag

A *morral (q.v.)*, or nose bag. A cowboy's name for the mess house. A logger's name for his lunch pail.

feed cover

A canvas laid on the ground at a picket line, upon which grain is placed to feed animals.

feeder

In mining, a small vein starting from some distant point and running into a main lode.

feeders

Cattle which are shipped or driven to the corn belt for fattening before marketing; also, men who feed such cattle.

feedin' off his range

Meddling in another person's affairs. According to the western code, no one questions a stranger. If he rides through for the aimless pleasure of going places and seeing things, that is his own business. If he chooses to explain his reason for traveling, the cowman will listen, but if his reason is one which he dares not tell, that is still his business.

feed lot

A small enclosure in which cattle are fed.

feed rack

A rack built for hay or other feed. A cowboy's name for the mess house.

feed trough

A cowboy's name for the mess house.

feel like chawin'

A cowman's expression meaning *hungry*.

FEES AND TOLLS

See boomage, consumos, entry fee, fixin', grass fee, grass money, guía, pass goods, royalty.

FEET

See dashboards, mud hook.

feller

A faller, one who fells trees.

fence cornering

A style of bucking in which the horse zigzags in a manner resembling the zigzags of the frontier rail fence. Also called *fence-worming*.

fence crawler

An animal that cannot be kept in a fenced pasture.

fence cutter

One of the men who cut fences during the fence-cutting wars of the cattle country in the 1880's. Most of these men were farmers and cattlemen fighting the larger ranchowners who had begun fencing in the open range.

fence lifter

A cowboy's term for a very heavy rain, when as Peewee Deewees used to say, "the weather gets plumb wholesale."

fence rider

A latter-day cowboy who keeps barbed-wire fences in repair; also called *fencer*. He rides leisurely along the fence, following a narrow, ever deepening trail that has been cut by many earlier trips. During his journey he watches for broken or loose wires, fallen posts, missing staples, water gaps that may have washed deep enough to allow cattle to get under the fence, open or tampered-with gates, and anything else that lessens the security of the fence.

He carries a pouch, usually a boot top sewed at the bottom, containing staples, a hammer or hatchet, a pair of wire cutters, and a coil of stay wire. With these tools he can repair any damage he finds. (John M. Hendrix, "The Fence Rider," *Cattleman*, Vol. XX, No. 11 [April, 1934], 5.)

FENCES

See barbed wire, deadman, dodge-post fence, drift fence, drop gap, furrow fence, gates, wing fence.

fence stretcher

A tool for pulling the fence wire tightly from post to post. A roll of wire may be attached to a truck or wagon which stretches the wire as it moves forward.

fence wagon

A wagon used to haul tools and material for building and repairing fences.

fence war

A feud among cattlemen who protested the action of certain ranchowners in fencing off parts of what had formerly been open cattle range. See *fence cutter*.

fence-worming

See *fence-cornering*.

fender

One of the heavy leather shields sewed to the stirrup leathers. In logging, a log or heavy pole placed at the side of a skidding trail to prevent the skidding load from rolling off the truck.

fiador

A looped cord ordinarily made of braided horsehair, passing from the front of the bosal upward and over the top of the horse's head; sometimes corrupted to *theodore*. From the Spanish.

fiddle

A horse's head. The rider strives to keep a bronc from putting "his fiddle between his feet."

fiddle-foot

Said of a horse that prances around and of a person who drifts, or has "itching feet."

fiddle-headed

Said of a horse with an ugly-shaped head.

FIELD GLASSES

See bring-'em-close glasses.

fiesta

A festival or celebration; now used to designate any party where Spanish food, decorations, or costumes are featured.

fifth quarter

The hide and entrails of a slaughtered animal.

fifty years' gathering

A logger's personal belongings.

FIGHT

See beef, brush, buffaloed, buying chips, cast his robe, clean his plow, comb his hair, corpse-and-cartridge occasion, count coup, crawl his hump, dabble in gore, dig up the hatchet, dig up the tomahawk, dog fight, doin's, fandango, free-for-all, gouging, knock his ears down, lock horns, pat him on the lip, put the calk to him, range war, sharpen his hoe, shove his nose down.

fighting claim

In mining, a piece of property in litigation.

fighting corral

In early days, the forming of the wagons of a wagon train in a close circle for protection from Indian attack and to prevent cattle from stampeding.

fighting the bear

Separating strips from boards in a sawmill. This is the job of the *bear fighter*, the man who works back the "edges" and separates all strips from the boards and directs them below to an endless chain that runs under the cage in which he works. These strips come rapidly, and the worker must be fast.

fighting the bits

Said of a horse that throws its head around when reined. Also said of an impatient or restless person.

fighting wages

Money drawn for work where there was fighting to be done, such as in range wars or against organized rustling. Under such conditions the pay was much higher than ordinary cowboy wages.

figure eight

A loop thrown so as to catch the forelegs of an animal in the lower part of the *8* while his head is caught in the upper part. This is done by throwing the straight overhead loop at an animal passing to the left, so that the honda will hit him just behind the left ear, the loop going out in front and dropping over his head. The sudden stopping of the loop when it hits the animal at the honda causes the loop to fold across, and it is then up to the animal to get his forefeet into the lower part of the loop. (W. M. French, "Ropes and Roping," *Cattleman*, Vol. XXVI, No. 12 [May, 1940], 17–30.)

fill

A low place filled in with dirt in the construction of an irrigation ditch.

fill a blanket

A cowboy's expression meaning *to roll a cigarette*.

filling the yoke

A freighter's expression meaning that the wheelers were pulling well.

filly

A young female horse. An unmarried woman.

fill your hand

To draw a gun.

fimps

In dice, a pair of fives.

final head

In rodeo, an additional short, final go-round occasionally held, open only to the top men of the event. An extra share of prize money is put up for the event.

final horse

In rodeo, one of the most difficult horses to ride, used for the final decision on championships.

finger loop

In packing, a cinch loop. About 15 inches from the end of the cinch a round piece of leather 3 inches in diameter is sewed on, and two holes are punched through it. A leather thong is attached to it, leaving a 3-inch loop. The loop is used to secure the end of the latigo strap after cinching.

finished his circle

Said of a cowman who has died.

fink

What the union logger calls a strikebreaker. The word is also applied to a strike guard, a plain-clothes officer, an informer, or a stool pigeon.

Fire and fall back!

A command often shouted at some diner at the chuck wagon who dallied too long over the pots and pans while selecting his food, thus holding up the others and slowing the meal.

fire assay

The assaying of metallic ores, usually gold and silver, by methods requiring furnace heat.

fire board

In mining, a blackboard on which the *fire boss (q.v.)* indicates every morning the amount of gas present in different parts of the mine.

fire boss

In mining, an underground official who examines the mine for firedamp and has charge of its removal.

firebox

In stagecoaching, a name given by the Indians to a stagecoach accompanied by military escort. The Indians had great respect for such a coach. In steamboating, the area immediately forward of the steamboat furnace, where the fireman held sway; also called *furnace room*.

firebreak

A natural or man-made barrier from which all or most of the inflammable materials have been removed, designed to stop or check creeping or running fires or to serve as a line from which to work and to move men and equipment in putting out fires.

fire canoe

An Indian's term for a steamboat.

FIRED

See break one's pick, bump, can, canned, cold shake, Dig out the bedroll and drift! get the pink slip, put his saddle in the wagon, Roll your bed! walking papers.

fire door

A door or opening through which fuel is supplied to a furnace or stove. In mining, a fireproof door, such as a door sealing off an area of the mine in which there is a fire.

fire escape

A cowboy's term for a preacher, so called because through him one could escape the fires of hell.

fireguard

A firebreak made by plowing two parallel sets of furrows about 50 yards apart with four furrows in each set. The grass between the sets is burned by men trailed by water-laden wagons. To a cowman a burned-out range is a sad sight and truly, as one said, "looks like hell with the folks moved out."

fireman

The man who tends the branding fires and keeps the irons hot.

FIREMEN

See grease burner.

fire out

To alter a brand to indicate change in ownership. See *counterbrand, vent brand.*

FIRES

See backfire, cooking mutton, crown fire, firebreak, fireguard, gob fire, ground fire, head, hot spot, logging operation, prairie fire, surface fire, wildfire.

fire scar

In logging, a scar resulting from a healed-over injury caused by fire in the trunk or other woody part of a tree.

fire season

A period of the year during which fires are likely to occur, spread, and do sufficient damage to warrant organized fire control.

fire viewer

In mining, a person who examines the workings of a mine with a safety lamp.

fire wall

In mining, a fireproof wall used as a fire stop.

firewater

An Indian's name for whisky, derived from the custom of traders to demonstrate the alcoholic content by throwing a little of the liquid on the fire to let it burn. Unless this was done, the Indian would not trade, fearing to be cheated.

first rattle out of the box

A cowboy's expression meaning *prompt action.*

fish

The yellow oilskin slicker that all old-time cowboys kept neatly rolled and tied behind the cantle of their saddles, so called because of the slicker's trade-mark, a fish. The cowboy might carry it until he wore it out and never need it, but let him leave it at the wagon for half a day and he was certain to get soaked to the hide. According to cowman philosophy, "A wise cowhand'll have somethin' besides a slicker for a rainy day," but few of them did.

If the cowboy was riding a bronc that might pile him and he was riding a slick-fork saddle, he would tie the slicker behind the fork of his saddle for a bucking roll to help wedge him in. Some riders, when riding a spooky horse which they were interested in training, would tie the slicker behind the cantle so that it nearly touched the ground on the left side. Of course, the horse tried to kick it to ribbons, but he soon got used to it and quit trying to stampede. Through this training the horse also learned not to spook at other harmless articles. (Will James, *All in a Day's Riding* [New York, Charles Scribner's Sons, 1933], 14.)

The cowboy also used his slicker for a pack cover. If he had something he wanted to keep dry when swimming a river, he rolled it up in the slicker and tied it on his saddle. It was also a handy place to carry food or a bottle when he was traveling a distance and ranches were far apart.

The fish was made to turn water, but was not good for keeping out the cold. I know one rider who was caught in a sudden norther without a coat. He came back to the ranch wearing his slicker as an emergency covering, but by the time he had put up his horse and reached the house, he was as "blue as a whetstone." Loud in his condemnation of slickers as overcoats, he finished by saying, "If I'd had *two* of the damned things on, I'd a-froze plumb to death."

fishback

In gambling, a marked deck of cards.

fishhook card

In faro, the seven of the faro layout. The term has other meanings in other games.

fishing

In rodeo, roping in such a way as to sweat a near miss into a fair catch; for example, throwing a wide loop that settles flat on a calf's neck and then falls clear around his neck.

fishlaid

Split veneer used for filling in the manufacture of plywood.

fissure vein

In mining, a crack in the earth across its strata, filled with mineralized matter.

five-eighths rig

A saddle with the cinch between the three-quarter and the center fire. Neither the five-eighths nor the seventh-eighths is commonly used.

five beans in the wheel

A westerner's expression meaning *five cartridges in the cylinder.* No westerner carried more than five cartridges in his gun. The hammer was always down on an empty chamber. He did this for safety, because of the hair-trigger adjustment. Men who knew guns had too much respect for them to take unnecessary chances, and a man who carried six cartridges in his gun was looked upon as a rank pilgrim. As the cowman said, "If you can't do the job in five shots, it's time to git to hell out o' there and hunt a place to hole up."

fix

To castrate cattle. A trader's term for a situation.

fixin'

A trader's term for getting through customs; also, his name for his equipment and personal belongings.

fixin' for high ridin'

A cowboy's expression for preparing to leave in a hurry. A man in this situation "don't stop for no kissin'." Also said of a man doing something that will get him into trouble.

fizzy

See *fuzz-tail.*

flag at half-mast

Said of a cowboy whose shirttail is out—and he wouldn't be a cowboy if he didn't work with it out half the time.

flagging

In sheepherding, staking white flags around the flocks at night to frighten off coyotes. Lighted lanterns are also used. This practice is followed when there are too few herders to maintain a sufficient night guard.

flaggin's

What the logger calls dinner in the woods.

flag his kite

A cowboy's expression meaning *to leave in a hurry.*

flagman

In rodeo, a man who stands on foot at the barrier and signals the start of time in a roping or steer-wrestling event. A second flagman, mounted in the arena, signals the end of time and passes on the legality of the catch, tie, or throw.

flag's up

A logger's reference to mealtime.

flame thrower

A cowboy's term for a six gun.

flank

In roping, to catch the rope with the left hand just against the neck of the calf or against the ear on the opposite side and then slap the right hand into the flank on the corresponding side. By a jerk upward and a pressure of the knees against the calf's side when it makes the next jump, the roper sends the calf's feet outward and throws it on its side. This method of roping is used in branding smaller calves and in calf-roping contests.

flanker

One engaged in flanking; see *flank*. Flankers usually work in pairs.

flank girth

What the Texan calls his hind cinch; always pronounced *girt*.

flank rider

In cattle driving, a rider who stays about one-third of the distance of the length of the column of cattle behind the swing riders, and two-thirds of the distance behind the point riders.

flank rigging

In rodeo, a flank strap from the rear of the saddle that fastens far back around the flanks of the horse. Also called *scratcher cinch*. Though most horses used in bucking contests will buck without it, flank rigging makes them "turn the works loose."

flannelmouth

A cowboy's name for a person who talks too much, a person who talks nonsense, or a braggart. Doc Strawn used to tell of a braggart who "had more lip than a muley cow" and invariably "bragged himself out of a place to lean ag'in a bar."

flap

A westerner's word for an Indian's breechcloth or similar piece of clothing.

flapboard

The back of the chuck wagon, hinged at the bottom so that it can be let down to serve as a table.

flasharity

A cowboy's term for a fancy riding outfit or fancy clothes.

flash in the pan

Said of a gun that failed to fire. The expression came to be applied to a man who talked big but did nothing.

flash rider

A bronc buster who takes the rough edges off unbroken horses.

flat

In mining, a horizontal deposit of metal.

flatboat

In the early West, the standard water vehicle for traveling families, first built in the Ohio River Valley. Flatboats varied greatly in size, each craft being built according to the needs of the purchaser. The purchaser considered such factors as the nature of the stream to be navigated, the boat's capacity to withstand Indian attack, and the length of the trip. The boat was rarely less than 20 feet long and 10 feet wide; at times it was a regular floating home, 60 feet long and 20 feet wide.

Its hull was usually made of square timbers of hardwood, and when fully loaded would draw from 1 to $2\frac{1}{2}$ feet of water. Upright timbers 4 feet high and about 5 inches thick were set on top of the hull, the whole being enclosed like a house with heavy planks. When completed, the boat had a roof, a window or two in the cabin, and a trap door in the roof. It floated at the mercy of the current, and was steered by a sweep as long as the boat itself.

flathead

A logger's name for a sawyer.

flat-heeled puncher

An amateur cowboy; a farmer turned cowboy.

flats

A logger's name for griddlecakes.

flatter

A flatboat man.

fleabag

A cowboy's name for his sleeping bag.

flea-bitten

A white horse covered with small brown freckles.

flea trap

A cowboy's name for his bedroll.

fleece

The wool of a sheep. A trapper's term for the flesh of a buffalo lying over the ribs. A trader's term for a scalp, and also for the layer of flesh covering the ribs.

fleece tiers

Men who tie sheared wool into bundles,

place the bundles in large sacks, and tramp them down tightly.

FLESH

See baby beef, beef, blue meat, bologna bulls, bull cheese, fleece.

flickers

An earmark in which small, narrow strips are formed on the outer edge of the ear by cutting the ear parallel to the outer edge for a distance of about 2 inches.

fling line

A rope used as a lasso.

flip-cock

To fan a gun. *See* fanning.

flipper

A device for moving lumber, consisting of a lever powered by a donkey engine.

float

In mining, bits of ore or metal that have been dispersed or washed away from an outcropping deposit, carried down a slope or hill, and deposited at varying distances from the original body of ore. The term is not usually applied to stream gravel.

floater

A logger's name for an itinerant worker; a hobo. A riverman's term for the body of a drowned man.

float gold

In mining, flour gold; particles of gold so small and thin that they float on water. Gold brought down from a vein or lode by the action of the water.

floating coffin

What the press called the early paddle-wheel steamboat because many of the boats hit snags and sank, burned, or exploded.

floating island

A detached mass of floating trees, logs, and accumulated debris formerly found in western rivers.

floating outfit

An outfit of five or six men and a cook kept by the larger ranches to ride the range in the winter months and brand late calves and cattle that had escaped the roundup.

floating palace

A large, richly outfitted steamboat.

floating wagon

A chuck wagon used by a *floating outfit* (*q.v.*) or by cowboys rounding up scattered cattle.

float-my-stick

In trapping, a stick attached to a beaver trap with a string. If the beaver ran away with the trap, the stick, floating on the surface of the water, indicated the whereabouts of the animal and enabled the trapper to recover his property. Also called *float pole* and *float stick*.

float ore

In mining, particles of ore detached from the vein and found below it. Water-worn particles of ore. Fragments of vein material found on the surface some distance from the vein outcrop.

float pole

See *float-my-stick*.

float stick

See *float-my-stick*.

flookan

In mining, flucan, a soft clay found between a vein and a wall.

floor

In mining, the rock underlying a horizontal vein or deposit.

flop

What the sheepherder calls his morning and afternoon periods of rest and napping. A logger's term for his bed and for going to bed.

flop gate

In placer mining, an automatic gate used when there is a shortage of water. The gate closes a reservoir until it is filled with water, when the gate automatically opens and allows the water to flow into the sluices. When the reservoir is empty, the gate closes again.

flotation

In mining, a process of concentration in which the metallic particles in ore that has been ground and mixed with water are thinly coated with oil and subjected to a stream of rising air bubbles that carries them to the surface of a tank. There they are skimmed off as rich *concentrate*. See *concentration*.

flower rowel

A rowel of a spur shaped like the petals of a daisy.

flow sheet

In mining, a diagram that shows the various processes used in the treatment of an ore.

flue

In steamboating, a pipe which runs through the boiler and through which flame and hot gases are piped from the furnace. The western-river boiler used on nearly all steamboats is designed on the return-flue principle; that is, the flame is passed under the boilers from the flame bed and into the flues at the rear end, returning forward through the flues and into the smokestacks immediately over the top of the furnace doors.

fluidy mustard

The enigmatical name given by the cowboy to an odd-looking brand brought into the district from the outside, having no numerals, letters, or familiar figures by which it may be called.

flume

In placer mining, an inclined channel, usually of wood and often supported on a trestle, for conveying water from a distance, to be utilized for power, transportation, etc. To divert the waters of a stream with such a channel in order to lay bare the auriferous sand and gravel forming the stream bed.

fluming

Using or making a *flume, q.v.*

flung him away

Thrown from a horse. One cowhand described how a friend was thrown with, "He went sailin' off, his hind legs kickin' 'round in the air like a migratin' bullfrog in full flight."

flunky

A cook's helper, a word used by cowboys, loggers, and rivermen.

flush

Having plenty of money. In gambling, a hand composed of cards all of the same suit.

fly

A sheet of canvas stretched from the end of the chuck wagon to provide shade and shelter for the cook.

flying brand

A brand whose letter or figure has wings.

flying Dutchman

In logging, a wire rope with a block on one end. Attached to a tree, the rope is used to divert the course of a log in yarding.

flying mount

Leaping from the ground into the saddle without using the stirrups.

fodder forker

What the cowboy calls a hay hand or farmer.

fofarraw

A trapper's and scout's word for anything fancy, such as fancy dress; also called *fufurraw*; probably from the French *fanfaron* meaning *bragging* or *boasting*.

fogging

A cowboy's word for traveling at high speed.

fold up

Said of a horse that starts bucking.

Folks on his mother's side wore moccasins.

A phrase meaning that the person referred to is a half-blood; often said of the offspring of a squaw man.

FOLLOWING

See camping on his trail, riding into his dust.

following the tongue

A method drovers used during trail days

to set their direction. At night the North Star was located and the wagon tongue was pointed in the direction to be traveled the next day.

FOOD

See air-tights, appalos, atol, aux ailments du pays, axle grease, baby beef, bait, bait can, bear sign, beef issue, big antelope, black Mike, blackstrap, boggy top, boudin, Brigham, bull cheese, cackleberries, calf fries, calf slobbers, canned cow, carne seco, Charlie Taylor, chili, choker, choker holes, chuck, chuck-wagon chicken, coffee, cowcumbers, cow grease, cow salve, cut straw and molasses, dip, district attorney, doin's, doughgods, eating, fancy fluff-duff, flats, forbidden fruit, found, fried chicken, frijoles, fritos, goat meat, goozlum, gordos, green meat, grub, grunt, gun-wadding bread, hen fruit, hen-fruit stir, horse thief's special, hot rock, hound ears and whirlups, huckydummy, immigrant butter, Indian bread, jerking, jerky, John Chinaman, Kansas City fish, larripy dope, larrup, lick, long sweetenin', looseners, machinery belting, meals, Mexican strawberries, Mormon dip, muck-a-muck, music roots, Ned, nigger-in-a-blanket, open-face pie, pemmican, pig's vest with buttons, piloncillo, pinole, piñon, pooch, poor bull, poor doe, potluck, prairie butter, prairie oyster, prairie strawberries, punk, rib stickers, sea plum, shakers, sinker, skid grease, skunk eggs, soft grub, son-of-a-bitch-in-a-sack, son-of-a-bitch stew, sop, sourdough bullet, sourdoughs, sow bosom, splatter dabs, spotted pup, spuds with the bark on, state doin's, states' eggs, strawberries, string of flats, swamp seed, terrapin, Texas butter, throat-ticklin' grub, trapper's butter, wasp nest, whistle berries, wool with the handle on.

fool brand

A brand too complicated to be described with a brief name.

fool hoe man

A cowboy's term for a farmer.

fool's gold

In mining, pyrite, a sulphide of iron.

foot-and-walker line

In stagecoaching, a name given to a stagecoach line when passengers were forced to get out and help push the vehicle through a mudhole, across a bad place in the road, or up a steep hill.

foot burners

What the cowboy called a walking plow, or a single-bottom plow, used by the nester.

footermans

A term sometimes used by Wyoming cowboys for men afoot.

footwall

In mining, the under wall of a vein, a wall of rock bounding the vein's lower surface.

forbidden fruit

A logger's name for pork.

forced nursing

The hand nursing of a lamb whose mother refuses to accept it.

forced production

In mining, the working of a mine so as to produce greater output than can be maintained.

force piece

In mining, timber placed diagonally across a mine shaft or drift to secure the ground.

fore-and-aft road

In logging, a skid road in steep country over which logs are skidded into water. So named by early-day Maine loggers who alternated logging jobs with voyages at sea.

forecastle

In steamboating, the forward end of the main deck extending to the cabin structure and hence usually exposed to the weather.

forecastle deck

In steamboating, the first deck above the water, the deck covering the hold.

forefooting

Roping an animal by the forefeet. The roper approaches the animal from the left side, and a medium-sized loop is thrown over the animal's right shoulder and a little ahead, in a position to receive one or both feet as they reach the ground. The noose is given an inward twist as it is thrown, which causes the upper side of the noose to flip backward against the animal's knees, ready for the catch. The method is generally used on horses.

foreman

A man hired by a ranch owner to manage the detailed affairs of the ranch. The boss of a logging gang. The boss of a shift of miners.

forepole

In mining, to keep the working face of a mine closely timbered to prevent rocks, debris, etc., from falling. To secure drifts in progress through quicksand by driving ahead poles, laths, boards, slabs, etc., to prevent the inflow of quicksand on the sides or top, the face being protected by breast boards.

forfeiture

In mining, the loss of possessory title as the result of abandonment or failure to comply with the conditions under which the title is held.

Forgers

See check man.

forging

Said when a traveling horse strikes his front shoes with the toes of his hind shoes. See *anvil*.

fork

The front part of the saddletree which supports the horn. To mount a horse.

forked brand

A brand with a V-shaped prong attached to any part of a letter or figure.

forked end down

An expression the cowboy uses to mean that a man is still on his feet or in the saddle and therefore that everything is all right; the opposite of *forked end up, q.v.*

forked end up

An expression meaning that a rider has been thrown from a horse with the feet above his head or thrown on his head.

form

In freighting, to arrange the wagons in a hollow square or circle. See *fighting corral*.

form camp

See *form*.

form fitter

A saddle with a high horn and a cantle made to fit a man's form.

Forts

See presidio.

fort up

To barricade oneself for a siege.

forty

In logging, 40 acres of timber, the smallest unit in which timber usually changes ownership or is logged on contract. In the unregenerate days, when a camp foreman went into leased woods with orders to cut "around forty" he cut "a round forty"— a "forty" north, a "forty" south, a "forty" east, and a "forty" west—and then filled out his compass.

forty-five

A .45-caliber six gun.

forty-four

A .44-caliber six gun.

forty-niner

A name given a man who joined in the California gold rush of 1849.

forty rod

A miner's name for cheap whisky.

found

A westerner's word for food.

founder shaft

In mining, the first shaft sunk into a mine.

four flush

In stud poker, four cards of the same suit. A bluffer. Someone or something pretentious. To bluff, as with a four-flush hand, by making a claim of some kind.

fourflusher

A bluffer. An incompetent person posing as a competent one.

four-up

What the logger calls a four-mule team.

four-up driver

A cowman's and logger's term for a driver of four teams or spans of horses or mules.

fox fire

A phosphorus light seen on the horns and ears of cattle during electrical storms.

fraid hole

A cowboy's name for a cave or storm cellar.

fraid strap

A strap buckled around the fork of the saddle which a rider holds while riding a bucking horse. A good rider considers it a disgrace to use a fraid strap.

frame a hole

In logging, to bevel the top of a log and make a mortice for a crossarm.

frame a pole

See frame a hole.

freak

A cowboy's name for a grumbler or an unwilling worker. A saddle of unusual pattern.

freedmen's bureau

In steamboating, a section of the *texas* (*q.v.*) reserved for Negro passengers traveling first-class. It was found on boats in southern trades from about 1870 to 1890, and was sometimes quite elaborate.

free-for-all

A winter evening's diversion in a lumber camp that sometimes gets pretty rough.

free grass

The open range of the early days; also called *free range*.

freemartin

A sexually imperfect, usually sterile, female calf born as a twin to a male.

free milling

A method of separating ores containing free gold or silver by crushing and amalgamation, without roasting or other chemical treatment.

free-milling ores

Ores that will separate by simple methods. See *free milling*.

free ranger

During the early days of the barbed-wire fence, a man who opposed the wire barriers. Such opposition started wire-cutting wars on many ranges.

free trader

A trader who outfitted himself and worked on his own, buying, selling, and trapping where he chose; also called *free trapper*.

free trapper

See *free trader*.

freeze onto

A trader's expression meaning *to take something*.

freeze-out

In gambling, a variety of poker in which each player drops out of the game, when his money is gone and all the stakes go to the last player left.

freeze to it

A westerner's term meaning *to hold fast to something*.

freight

The merchandise the freighters and traders hauled in their wagons.

FREIGHTERS

See assistant wagon boss, bull outfit, bull pusher, bullwhacker, cargador, master wagoner, pack outfit, runners, shotgun freighter, silver freighter, wagon train.

FREIGHTING AND EQUIPMENT

See All's set! carabo pole, cargo, cargo cover, Catch up! chip sack, close together, collar and hames, corn freight, corral, Fall in! form, goad stick, grass freight, hair pounder, hatajo, head-and-heel string, jack train, jerk line, jerk-line string, jerk-neck team, jockey stick, Knock up stakes! leaders, lead span, lead team, on the lock, pointers, pole team, quick freighting, rough lock, runner, shackling, staking ground, Stretch out! trailer, trail wagon, wagons, Wo-ha-a-a! Yoke up!

freighting his crop

A cowboy expression describing a man eating or drinking heavily.

freight outfit

A wagon train engaged in hauling freight across the plains.

freight wagons

A gigantic wagon, like the Conestoga, with wheels 4 inches wide and 1½ inches thick. It carried 5,000 to 6,000 pounds of freight and was pulled by five or six yoke of steady oxen.

Frenchmen

See pork eater.

freno

A bit; also the entire bridle, including the bit; from the Spanish.

fresh horse

A horse that has had a few months' rest and has gained a good amount of flesh and sometimes developed a very "bad heart" since last ridden.

fried chicken

A cowboy's name for bacon that has been rolled in flour and fried.

fried gent

A man caught in a prairie fire.

fried shirt

A cowboy's name for a stiff-bosomed shirt.

Friend

See amigo, campanyero, compadre, compañero, old coon, old hoss, old socks, running mate, tillicums.

frijoles

Dried Mexican beans, a staple diet in the range country; from the Spanish.

fritos

Fried beans; from the Spanish.

frog

The triangular pad in the sole of a horse's hoof. It has an elastic action and expands laterally when pressed upon.

frog walk

A form of mild pitching indulged in by most horses on cold mornings when first mounted; said of a horse making short, easy hops.

from the case card

See call the turn both ways.

from soda to hock

In faro, soda is the first card exposed face up before bets are made. The last card in the box is said to be in hock. In the West the expression from soda to hock became common as meaning from beginning to end or the whole thing, like the expression from soup to nuts used in the East.

from who laid the chunk

Action or quality of a superior degree. A common description of great speed is, "He burned the breeze from who laid the chunk."

front-door puncher

A cowboy who spends too much of his time in town.

front jockey

The leather on the top of the skirt of the saddle, fitting closely around the horn.

frothy

A cowboy's expression meaning angry.

frozen walls

In mining, a condition existing when the vein is stuck to the granite wall and devoid of slickensides.

fryin' size

A cowboy's term for a youth; also, a man of short stature. I once asked a "shorty" of the range why he was so continuously in a good humor and why nothing seemed to anger him. His answer was, "I can't afford to get mad. My size won't let me whip nobody."

Fuel

See bois de vache, buffalo chip, chip box, compressed hay, cow chip, cow wood, lump oil, miner's oil, prairie coal, prairie pancake, round browns, squaw wood, surface coal.

full ear

An unbranded calf or yearling with no earmark.

full-grown in body only

A cowboy's expression for a simple-minded or foolish person.

full house

In poker, a hand consisting of three of a kind and a pair.

full-rigged

A saddle whose tree is entirely covered with leather. A packsaddle or aparejo, supplied with sling straps and cargo cinch and no sling or lash ropes.

full seat

A saddle whose seat is entirely covered with leather.

full sixteen hands high

A cowman's appraisal of another man's worth, a tribute to his ability and honesty.

full split

An earmark consisting of a split extending three-quarters of the length or width of the ear, or even further.

full stamp

A saddle covered with fancy stamped designs. The purpose of these hand-tooled saddles is not merely to satisfy a rider's ego. The rough indentations cause friction between the leather and the rider's smooth trouser legs, allowing him to sit tight in the saddle without the tiresome leg cramps that would result from riding a fractious horse in a smooth saddle.

full war paint

What the cowboy calls his best Sunday-go-to-meetin' clothes.

fumadiddle

A western term for fancy dress; also called *faradiddle*; perhaps corruptions of *fofarraw*, *q.v.*

fumble

To bungle an attempt at drawing a gun.

As one cowhand said, "He reached and fumbled, and it was a fatal weakness."

fur country

A region where fur-bearing animals abound.

fur hunter

One who hunts fur-bearing animals for their pelts.

FURNACES

See adobe furnace, fire assay, firebox, fire door, grate bar.

furrow fence

A furrow plowed around one's holdings. Kansas recognized this furrow as constituting a fence and passed trespass laws to prosecute anyone crossing it. During the late trail days furrows were plowed on each side of the cattle trails to keep drovers within certain bounds.

fur trader

A trader among the Indians who traded beads and other gewgaws for furs.

fusil

A Hudson Bay Company trade gun; from the French.

fuste

A saddletree; a Mexican saddle; a packsaddle; from the Spanish. American cowboys frequently use the word to mean a Mexican saddle to distinguish it from the American cowboy's saddle. The Mexican saddle has less leather than the American. It has a flat horn and a low cantle and is noted for making a horse's back sore; therefore it is not tolerated by the American cowboys.

fuzz-tail

A range horse with a bushy tail; also called *fuzzy* and *fizzy*.

fuzz-tail running

Mustanging; hunting wild horses.

fuzzy

See *fuzz-tail*.

G

"Polishin' your pants on saddle leather don't make you a rider"

gaberel
A tin horn used in some logging camps to call the men to a meal.

gabezo
A logger's name for an ordinary hand.

gaboon
A spittoon in a western saloon, made of a plug-tobacco box filled with sand or sawdust.

gad
A cowboy's name for a spur. A small, pointed wedge used by the miner. A trader's word meaning *to goad*.

gad hunter
A miner's lamp used in searching for lost gads or drills. See *gad*.

gaff
To spur a horse. In logging, the steel point of the pike pole, consisting of a screw point and a spur.

gaffer
A logger's name for the general superintendent. A miner's name for the shift boss.

galena
In mining, a sulphide of lead that contains silver in greatly varying quantities. A trapper's name for the lead from which he made his bullets.

galena pills
What the trapper and trader called bullets.

gal-leg
A spur with a shank in the shape of a girl's leg.

gallery
In mining, a level or drift; applied chiefly to collieries.

gallin'
What the cowboy called courting a girl. It is told of one cowhand on the Pitchfork Ranch that when he went *gallin'*, the girl's "old man had to pour water on the porch steps to keep him from settin' there all night."

gallows frame
In mining, the head frame, the support for the hoisting machinery; also called *gallows*.

galves
A cowboy's name for spurs.

gambler's ghost
A white mule.

gambler's gun
A *derringer, q.v.*; so called because of its popularity among early-day gamblers.

GAMBLERS
See anchor man, booster, broad pitcher, capper, card mechanic, card mob, chiseler, cold player, gut puller, hearse driver, heel, heeler, leg, mechanic, monte dealer, monte sharp, opener, pigeon, piker, rounder, saddleblanket gambler, second dealer, square decker, stool pigeon, tinhorn.

GAMBLING
See Ada from Decatur, Ada Ross the stable hoss, ante, back in, beat the board, bet the limit, bet the top, big Dick, big Joe from Boston, big natural, blackjack, blind opening, bluff, bottom layout, box cars, brace game, break even, break off, bucking the tiger, bump, burn a card, bust, buying chips, call, calling the turn, call the turn both ways, Carolina nine, cathop, cheating, check-racked, checking, chops, chuck-a-luck, close to the belly, cold deck, cold game, colors, copper on and copper off, copper the odds, craps, cross colors, dealer's choice, double out, drag down,

drive the hearse, eighter from Decatur, fade, faro, faro bank, fatten the kitty, fee-bee, fimps, fishhook card, freeze-out, from soda to hock, gate, give a square deal, gun turn, hangman's turn, hard seventeen, have action, heel bet, heel a string, hit me, Indian poker, inside, inside corner, jackpot, Johnny Hicks, kangaroo card, keeping cases, keeping tabs, keno, kitty, last turn, lay 'em down, layin' down his character, layout, little Dick, little natural, little Phoebe, lose out, make a brush, misdeal, monte, Nina from Carolina, no-dice, old thing, one on the layout and three in the hand, one side against the other, open bet, open the pot, outside, paddle wheel, paroli, pass, pass the buck, Phoebe, piking, playing on a shoestring, playing on velvet, play the bank, play the evens, poker, pot, roller, rolling faro, second button, set his hoss, shade, short faro, showdown, single out, sixie from Dixie, skin faro, skin game, skin the deck, sleeper, snake-eyes, snap, snowball the layout, soft seventeen, Spanish monte, square deal, stand off, stay, steal a pot, string bet, stringing along, stronger than (the) nuts, Sunday school, sure-thing bet, sweater, sweeten the pot, switch, table stakes, tapping the bank, There's a one-eyed man in the game, three-card monte, three-one, throwing the game, tiger, top layout, turn, twenty-one, twist the tiger, under the gun, viggerish, vingt-et-un, whipsawed, winning out, win out.

GAMBLING CARDS AND HANDS

See ace-high, ace-kicker, aces up, back to back, big cat, big digger, big dog, big tiger, blaze, bobtail flush, bobtail straight, broad, bullet, bust, busted flush, Calamity Jane, California prayer book, case card, cases, cat, cheaters, cold hands, court cards, court skin, dead card, dead man's hand, deal card, devil's bedposts, Elk River, face cards, fishback, flush, four flush, full house, high-belly strippers, hock, hock card, holdout, hole card, jack stripper, little cat, little dog, little tiger, looloo, lotto cards, low-belly strippers, medicine turn, monte layout, paint skin, paper, pat hand, readers, reflectors, royal flush, second, sight, soda, splits, spot card, strippers, trey-deucer, wedges, whiteskin.

GAMBLING EQUIPMENT

See behind the six, bird cage, bones, brace box, bug, can, case, case keeper, chips, cooler, daub, dispatchers, harness, high layout, ivories, keno goose, marker, monte bank, monte table, poker chip, rigging, sand tell box, sand tell liquid, shears, shiner, snake tell box, tab, tell box, velvet.

GAMBLING HOUSES

See hell, mitt joint.

GAMES AND CONTESTS

See birling, bull of the woods, bull tailing, crack-a-loo, gambling, hand game, hot back, hot bottom, log birling, rolleo, shuffle the brogue, thimblerig.

gancho

In sheepherding, a shepherd's crook.

gandy dancer

A logger's term for a section hand on a railroad in the woods; also, a pick-and-shovel man.

gang mill

A sawmill in which gang saws are used.

gangplank

A board or set of boards used as a temporary boardwalk from a steamboat to shore, or from one boat to another. The act of laying the boards was called *building a gangway*.

gangue

In mining, crevice material, worthless minerals that accompany a metal bearing mineral in an ore. Ore mixed with other rock material.

gangway

A ship-to-shore passageway for passengers or for the conveyance of freight.

ganted

A cowboy's word meaning *thin* or *poor*.

gaper

In gambling, a small mirror held in the palm of the hand, used for cheating in card games.

garbage can

A logger's name for a logging camp with poor living accommodations.

gash vein

In mining, a vein which continues for

practical purposes only a short distance below the sod, generally narrowing as it descends.

gas skinner

The engineer of a gasoline boat.

gate

In monte, the top card when play starts. The monte dealer shuffles and cuts the cards, places them face downward, draws off the two bottom cards, and places them face upward on the table. This is the *bottom layout*. Then from the top he draws two cards, forming the *top layout*. The pack is then turned face upward, and the card exposed is the *gate*.

gate horse

A cowboy stationed at the corral gate for any purpose.

GATES AND EQUIPMENT

See belly buster, cutting gate, doctor gate, fences, Texas gate.

gate saw

A mill saw which is strained in the gate or sash to prevent buckling.

gather

Cattle brought together in a roundup.

gauch iron

An iron bar with a hook on it, used in branding. Also, the *running iron, q.v.*

gauge stick

In steamboating, a broom handle which, pushed against one of the three gauges in the end of the boiler, opened the valve and permitted the steam and water to escape into a short trough below. If a stream of water ran from the first and second gauges but not from the third when so opened, there was a normal supply of water in the boilers. If water came from the first but not from the second gauge, the *doctor (q.v.)* was started and the supply increased. When water reached the third gauge, the supply was cut off.

gear

What the freighter called the harness for the horses and other equipment. What the logger calls his blanket roll.

geed-up

A cowman's term for lame or out of commission.

gee string

See *G-string*.

gelding

A castrated horse.

gelding smacker

A cowboy's name for a saddle.

general cache

A number of caches in the same general locality. See *cache*.

general work

A term sometimes used in referring to a roundup.

gentler

An animal used to *neck (q.v.)* to a wilder one to subdue the latter until he becomes more tractable. A horsebreaker.

gentling

Breaking and taming unbroken horses.

Genuine Jimmy

A logger's name for the camp doctor; probably a corruption of *Quinine Jimmy*.

GEOLOGISTS

See book miner.

gerga

See *jerga*.

get a rise from

A cowboy's expression meaning *to make a person angry*.

Get a saddle!

One logger's admonishment to another logger not to "ride the saw," or neglect his end of the job.

getaway money

The money a rodeo contestant has left after a show to make his way to the next one.

get down to cases

In the West, to confine one's efforts to the matter in hand.

get hard-nosed

A logger's expression meaning *to get angry.*

get his back up

In cowboy parlance, to get into a fighting mood.

get his bristles up

To get into a fighting mood.

get his hog back

A cowboy's expression for recovering something that has been taken from him. (William MacLeod Raine to R.F.A.)

get rid of his leaf lard

To lose weight.

get the bacon

To succeed in one's efforts.

get the bulge on

To get the drop or advantage with a gun.

get the drop

To get someone at a disadvantage before he can draw his own weapon.

get the pink slip

A logger's expression for being fired.

getting long in the tooth

A cowboy's expression for ageing.

GETTING THE DROP

See get the bulge on.

getting up the horses

Driving the saddle horses from the range or pasture to camp or headquarters in preparation for the roundup.

ghost cord

A thin string tied about the horse's tongue and gums, and thence passed below the lower jaw and up to the rider's hand. (Philip A. Rollins, *The Cowboy* [New York, Charles Scribner's Sons, 1936], 152.) It is used by some busters as punishment for bucking and can be an instrument of extreme torture. Ghost cords are of many kinds. Some men have a secret style all their own and guard its nature jealously. Most ranchers frown upon the breaker who uses a ghost cord, since it has a tendency to make an outlaw of the horse.

ghost town

An abandoned town; usually one that came into being near a mine and was abandoned when the mine played out.

ghost walks

The logger's payday.

giant

A large nozzle used in hydraulic mining.

gig

To cheat; to swindle. To spur a horse.

giggle talk

What the cowboy calls foolish speech.

Gila monster

A large lizard found in Arizona and New Mexico, named for the Gila River. It belongs to the only species of lizards known to be venomous.

gimlet

To ride a horse in such a way that its back becomes sore.

gimlet-ended

A cowboy's description of someone with small hips.

gin

See *gin pole.*

gin around

To chase around; to chase cattle unnecessarily.

ginny line

In logging, a light cable used to string the *haulback (q.v.)* through the woods.

ginny up the pasteboards

To mark or identify playing cards for purposes of cheating.

gin pole

In logging, a pole used to load logs; also called *gin.*

giraffe

In mining, a car higher at one end than at the other, for use on inclines.

girdle

In logging, to kill a tree by cutting a circular ring around its trunk.

GIRLS

See muchacha, mujer, women.

girth

A Texan's name for a cinch; always pronounced girt.

git-up end

What the cowboy humorously calls the rear end of a horse. It is this end upon which he lays the quirt when he wants the horse to go.

give a square deal

In gambling, to deal the cards fairly.

give her snoose

A logger's expression meaning to increase power; a tribute to the potency of the snuff, or snoose, used by loggers.

Give him air!

A cry given by the rider of a bad horse to his helpers when he is ready to start his ride.

glad hand

In mining, an air-hose coupling.

glance

In mining, any of the various ores having a luster which indicates their metallic nature.

glass work

In gambling, cheating with a mirror. See gaper.

glory hole

In mining, an open excavation formed by drawing off ore through an underground passage. An open pit produced by surface mining. To carry on surface mining.

glory rider

A rider who rides an outlaw horse, simply for the satisfaction of trying to conquer the beast.

go

A term used by the near packer to the off packer, meaning that a hitch is formed and ready to be tightened.

Go

See amble, anti-godlin, ballin' the jack, buy a trunk, calking cement, cut his picket pin and drifted, cut his suspenders, dragging his navel in the sand, drag it, dust, fag, fixin' for high ridin', flag his kite, high-tail, hit the breeze, hit the trail, hive off, hua, humped his tail at the shore end, hurry, jump up dust, leavin' Cheyenne, light a shuck, made a nine in his tail, pasear, pull stakes, put out, quit the flats, Roll your wheels! shake a bush, tail out, vamoose, wagon west.

goad stick

A sharpened pole or stick used by early freighters to prod their oxen.

goat

A bucking term for half-hearted pitching. A trapper's name for an antelope.

goat meat

A cowboy's euphemism for deer meat killed out of season.

gob fire

In mining, a fire in the collieries produced by spontaneous combustion.

go-devil

In the early West, a taut wire which stretched from the top of the bank of a stream to an anchorage in midstream and carried a traveling bucket for the water supply. In logging, a crotch, q.v. In mining, a gravity plane.

godown

A cut in the bank of a stream to enable animals to cross or get to the water.

go-easter

A cowboy's name for a carpetbag bought at a store for a trip.

goin' down the rope

In roping, approaching the catch holding the rope taut.

goin' like the heel flies are after him

Traveling with great and sudden speed.

The expression originated from the way cattle run frantically to get into a bog or water when attacked by heel flies.

goin' over the withers

A roping term. The roper, rope tied to saddle horn, rides up close abreast of the animal to be caught, leans over the animal's back, and throws the loop about the forefeet. The catch being made, he spurs his horse square away from the victim, tripping it and completely turning it on its back.

gold-braid trade

In steamboating, a packet trade catered to by large steamers whose officers were outfitted in uniform.

gold colic

A desire to find gold or to make money. See *gold fever*.

gold digger

In mining, one who digs or mines for gold. The term is used almost exclusively to designate a miner engaged in placer mining; a miner engaged in mining in solid rock is called a *quartz miner*. More recently, a female who goes with some man for all the money she can play him for.

gold diggings

A region where gold is found mixed with sand or gravel.

gold dust

Fine particles of gold, such as those obtained in placer mining.

gold fever

A mania for seeking gold, an expression applied particularly to the excitement caused by the discovery of gold in California in 1848–49. Also called *gold colic*.

gold field

A region where gold is found.

gold mine

A mine containing or yielding gold. It may be either in solid rock (a quartz mine) or in alluvial deposits (a placer mine).

gold wash

A place where gold is washed; used chiefly in the plural.

gold washer

One who mines gold by washing auriferous earth.

gone beaver

A trapper's expression meaning that a beaver had been caught in a trap.

gone over the range

A cowman's reference to death.

gone to Texas

At outs with the law; an old expression dating back to the days when Texas developed the reputation for producing and harboring outlaws.

Many men left their real names behind when they crossed the Red River. Names were not important in the early West, and most cowboys were known only by a nickname. As one cowman said, "The West don't care by what you call yourself. It's what you call others that lets you stay healthy."

In the early days many cowboys, seeing a stranger approaching the ranch, would ride up a draw out of sight until they made sure that the rider did not stop for a visit. The more "sheriff-looking" the visitor, the more stimulating the effect on the cowboy's rate of speed.

While attending a rodeo in Las Vegas, New Mexico, I heard an old former sheriff telling one of his cronies about a certain man who had "been out of Texas long 'nough to tell his right name."

good comeback

A cowboy's term for a quick and efficient retort.

good-enoughs

Horseshoes purchased by the keg in various sizes, ready to put on a horse's feet cold. Such shoes are used where there is no blacksmith to make a perfect fit for the individual horse.

good Indian

In the frontier days, a dead Indian. Frontiersmen held every live Indian to be a bad one.

good lay

A well-managed ranch.

Goodnighting

A definition of this term can best be given in the words of my friend J. Evetts Haley: "One of his [Goodnight's] most talked-of discoveries was made on the Goodnight Trail in 1867. When being trailed or worked, stock cattle have a tendency to get in heat, and upon starting with a herd of cows, Goodnight always put in a number of bulls. The trail is doubly hard on them, and after their testicles had been banged and bruised between their legs for several hundred miles, they sometimes died. He lost two on the Pecos drive, and another, a big dun bull from South Texas, had swelled and was about to die. Goodnight roped and threw him and got down to cut him, thinking he might recover. As he got out his knife, and thought how he could hardly spare another bull, an idea struck him.

"He called to a hand to bring him a piece of grass rope, then quite rare, from the wagon. He pushed the dun's seeds up against his belly, and cut off the entire bag. He unraveled a piece of the rope, and having no needle, took his knife, punched holes in the skin, and sewed up the wound like an old tow sack. Within a week, instead of being dead, that bull was in the lead of the herd giving everything trouble, and his voice was as coarse as ever. Thereafter Goodnight practiced the operation generally upon his old bulls on the range, almost doubling, he believed, their period of usefulness. Of course, as he said: 'It does not make a young bull of an old one, but it does enable the old one to do a great deal of work.'"

Throughout the southwestern range country this operation is known as *Goodnighting*. (J. Evetts Haley, *Charles Goodnight, Cowman and Plainsman* [Boston, Houghton Mifflin Company, 1936], 446.)

good point

Cattle in a fat or good condition.

good scald

A cowman's expression for a good job; the opposite of *poor scald*. The term comes from hog slaughtering.

good stab

A cowman's expression for a good, workmanlike job.

good stick

A cowman's expression for a successful breeding.

good trader

A trader who was successful in trading with the Indians.

goose

To spur a horse.

goose drowner

A cowboy's term for a cloudburst, a very heavy rain.

goose hair

A cowboy's name for a feather-stuffed pillow.

gooseneck

A spur with a long shank shaped like a goose's neck, the rowels fitting in its mouth.

goose pen

A hole in the base of a large tree caused by fire that has burned out the rotted center.

goose-pen butt

The base end of a log, part of which has been hollowed out by fire.

goosey

Nervous; touchy; said of man or horse.

goosing

In hydraulic mining, driving the gravel forward with the stream from the *giant, q.v.*

goozlum

A logger's name for gravy.

gopher

A logger whose job is to dig holes under logs to be hauled to the landing. Many logs in the northwestern forests are so huge that a hole has to be dug under them to allow a choker to be slipped around them. When the ground is frozen, the *gopher* is a *powder monkey*, because then his job is done with gunpowder.

gopher hole

In mining, a *coyote hole, q.v.* The term is sometimes used to designate any horizontally drilled hole, usually on a level with the mine.

gopher-hole blasting

In mining, a term applied in the Middle West and West to a method of blasting rock by means of charges placed in small tunnels driven into the face of the floor level.

gophering

Digging for something. I once heard a cowman characterize a certain old prospector by saying that he'd "been gopherin' in them hills as far back as an Injun could remember." In mining, prospecting work confined to digging shallow pits or starting adits; so called because of the similarity in appearance to the crooked little holes dug in the soil by gophers. A primitive method of extracting ore by digging out rich pockets or streams, leaving irregular holes like gopher holes.

gordos

What the trapper called wheat pancakes.

go-round

In rodeo, a round required to allow each contestant to compete on one head of stock. The number of go-rounds in a rodeo varies from one in a small, one-day contest to as many as seven or more in a larger rodeo.

gossan

In mining, the outcrop of a lode, usually colored by the decomposition of iron. Picture ore of a very rich grade.

got a halo gratis

A cowboy's expression meaning *killed*.

got busted

Thrown from a horse.

got calluses from pattin' his own back

A cowboy's description of a braggart.

gotch ear

A drooping ear, caused by an infestation of ticks that have undermined the supporting cartilages of the animal's ear.

got her made

A logger's expression used when quitting the job, signifying that the boomer has made enough stake to move on.

got his spurs tangled up

Said of one who is confused or mixed up.

gouch hook

A pothook used by the cook on roundup for lifting the heavy lids of his cooking utensils.

gouge

To cheat; to swindle. In mining, a layer of soft material along the wall of a vein, favoring the miner by enabling him, after "gouging" it out with a pick, to attack the solid veins from the side.

gouging

Squeezing or punching out a person's eye, a method of fighting which reached its highest development among the boatmen of the western rivers.

go under

A trapper's expression meaning *to die*.

government job

A logger's euphemism for a personal job that is done on company time.

government light

In river boating, a beacon maintained by the government for aiding pilots at night. Each light is provided with a number and has an official name.

GOVERNMENT MEN

See alcalde, corregidor, factor, officers, steamboat inspector.

governor

What the logger calls an employer, a superintendent, a manager, or a director.

Go 'way 'round 'em, Shep!

A sheepherder's phrase used as a warning of danger or of something to be avoided. If the danger is great, the sheepman often adds the phrase, "There's seven black ones and a coulee!" The sheepman judges the size of his flock by the number of black sheep in it. Seven black sheep indicates a large flock, and any westerner knows the danger of riding off the rim of a coulee.

go with the woolies

A cowboy expression meaning *to herd sheep*.

go wolfing

A trader's expression for leaving the bodies of persons or animals on the prairie for wolves to devour.

grab

A logger's name for a company store. Skidding tongs.

grabbin' the apple

Catching the saddle horn while riding a bucking horse.

grabbin' the brandin' iron by the hot end

A cowboy's expression for taking a chance or getting the worst of something.

grabbin' the nubbin'

Catching the saddle horn while riding a bucking horse.

grabbin' the post

Catching the saddle horn while riding a bucking horse.

grade

In cattle raising, the breeding up of cattle; see *grade up*. In logging, the classification of logs or lumber according to quality. In mining, the percentage of metal or other desired material in an ore.

grade up

In cattle raising, to improve the breed.

grained

A trapper's expression for a treated beaver skin. The skin was stretched over a hoop or framework of osier twigs and was allowed to dry, the flesh and fatty substance being carefully scraped off, or *grained*.

grain-fed

Said of a horse regularly fed on grain. Grain feeding makes for harder muscles and greater endurance than grass feeding; consequently, work horses doing heavy work are usually grain-fed.

grain gold

In mining, gold that has become granular in the process of heating.

grand encampment

A place where trappers met at the end of the season to sell pelts and buy supplies; also called *rendezvous, q.v.*

grandpa

What the logger calls the general superintendent.

granger

A cowboy's name for a farmer. This term is used principally in the Northwest, the Southwest's term being *nester*.

granny bar

A logger's and miner's name for an enormous crowbar.

grapevine telegraph

The mysterious way news traveled on the frontier.

grapplin' irons

Spurs.

gras

A trader's term meaning *fat;* from the French.

grass

What the miner calls the surface of the ground.

GRASS

See vegetation.

grass-bellied

A cowboy's term for bloated cattle; also called *pot-gutted*.

grass-bellied with spot cash

Rich; having plenty of money.

grassed him

Thrown from a horse.

grassers

Grass-fed cattle.

grass fee

A fee for grazing privileges, especially money paid to Indians for grazing rights on their lands; also called *grass money*.

grass freight

Goods shipped by ox teams, so called because the motive power could eat off the land on the way to the destination. Grass freight was much slower but much cheaper than freight hauled by mule teams (*corn freight*, *q.v.*).

grasshopper
To jump a steamboat over a sand bar.

grasshopper plow
Originally a plow that could be drawn—though often only by fits and starts through prairie sod—by inadequate, poorly-trained teams when available.

grass hunting
Thrown from a horse.

grass is getting short
In mining, an expression meaning that operations are endangered because of diminishing funds.

grass is waving over him
A cowboy's reference to a dead person.

grass line
In steamboating, a Manila or other fiber rope, as distinguished from a wire cable.

grass money
See *grass fee*.

grass-root mining
Mining in soil immediately below the surface of the ground.

grass roots
A miner's term for the surface of the earth. *From the grass roots down* means *from the grass roots to the bedrock*.

grass rope
A cowman's name for a rope of any fiber other than cotton; originally one made of bear grass, but now usually one made of sisal or Manila hemp.

grass staggers
A condition of cattle produced by eating locoweed.

grass train
In early freighting, an ox train; so called because oxen could live on grass, while horses and mules had to have grain. See *grass freight*.

grate bar
One of the series of cast-iron slats spaced in the base of a coal furnace or stove upon which the fire is laid.

gravel in his gizzard
A cowboy's expression for courage; said of a brave man.

grave patch
A cowboy's name for a cemetery.

graveyard shift
In cattle herding, the night-guard shift from midnight to 2:00 A.M. Also called *graveyard stretch*. In mining, the night shift, usually beginning at 11:00 P.M.

graveyard stretch
See *graveyard shift*.

gravy run
In rodeo, a lucky draw, an animal that makes it easy to win, such as a bronc that bucks well every time or a consistent steer that is easy to catch and throw.

grazing bit
A small bit with a curb in the mouthpiece. It is a good all-round lightweight bit, does not punish a horse, and is used now in most states east of the Rockies.

grazing permit
A permit issued by the government to stockmen, allowing them to graze an allotted number of cattle or sheep on a specified area at a fixed price per head.

grease
A miner's name for nitroglycerin.

grease ball
A logger's name for a cook.

grease burner
A logger's name for a fireman or for a cook.

grease-hungry
A trapper's expression meaning that he had been without meat for some time.

grease joint
What the cowboy calls an eating house in town.

greaser

A cowboy's name for a Mexican, particularly one of low caste; a term of disrespect or insult.

greaser madhouse

A cowboy's name for the intricate Mexican cattle brands.

greasewood

A low-growing western bush that burns easily; a shrub of the spinach family, abundant in the regions of alkaline soil in the western United States.

greasy belly

A cowboy's name for the cook.

greasy-sack outfit

A small ranch outfit that carried its commissary pack in a cotton bag on a mule in lieu of a chuck wagon.

greasy-sack ride

A ride on which a group of cowboys were sent, without a chuck wagon, to scour rough country for cattle; on these rides they carried their food in small cotton bags, called *greasy sacks.*

great seizer

A cowboy's name for a sheriff.

Great White Father

An Indian's name for the President of the United States.

green-broke

Said of a horse ridden only a time or two and then turned out for the winter.

green chain

A long platform where fresh-cut lumber is graded and sorted as it comes from the mill on chains.

greener

See *greenhorn.*

green hand

A trader's term for an inexperienced person.

greenhorn

A cowboy's name for a tenderfoot; also called *greener.*

green lambs

Newborn lambs.

green meat

Meat that has not been hung for aging.

green pea

A cowboy's name for a tenderfoot.

green planer

A planing mill in which green lumber is surfaced.

Green River

A trapper's hunting knife made at Green River, Wyoming, and bearing that trademark; also, to kill someone by thrusting the knife into him all the way to the trademark, far up the blade.

green up

Said when the grass begins to turn green.

GREETINGS AND FAREWELLS

See adiós, hasta la vista, Which way's the wagon?

gringo

A Mexican's name for an American.

grissel heel

An old-timer, especially one "sot" in his ways. Chuck Evans spoke of a certain grissel-heel as being "so obstinate he wouldn't move camp for a prairie fire."

grit

A westerner's term for bravery.

gritty as fish eggs rolled in sand

A cowboy's description of a brave person.

grizzlies

A name sometimes given to chaps made of bearskin with the hair left on.

grizzly

In mining, an iron grating that catches the larger stones passing through the sluices and throws them aside.

groanin' cart

A cowboy's term for a heavily supplied chuck wagon.

ground apples

A logger's term for rocks found in the "sawing woods."

ground fire

A fire that not only consumes all the organic material of the forest floor but also burns into the underlying soil itself; for example, a peat fire.

ground hog

In logging, a tie man who camps far from the main camp; also, a logger who works on the ground. In mining, a small truck used to push cars up a slope.

ground hogging

Ground-lead logging.

grounding

A cowboy's term for letting the bridle rein touch the ground; the horse then stands without being tied.

ground lead

In logging, a system of donkey logging in which logs are dragged through the woods, smashing and bruising young trees.

ground money

In rodeo, the purse and entry fees, split equally among all the entrants in an event in which no one qualifies and thus no one wins.

grout

In mining, a solid wall of mortar and gravel.

growler

A name for the chuck wagon.

grown stuff

A cowman's name for full-grown cattle.

grub

A cruel earmark, made by cutting off the entire ear smooth with the head, sometimes resorted to by rustlers to destroy the original earmark. A term used throughout the West for food.

grubber

An animal that noses about the roots of the locoweed and eats them; such an animal is said to be *grubbin' loco*.

grub house

A cook shack.

grub-line rider

A *chuck-line rider, q.v.*; sometimes shortened to *grub-liner*. Visiting from one ranch to another was one way for a man to live through the winter. Some cowboys chose to spend the winter months this way for the sake of variety, and if such riders were not too plentiful, they were welcome. People who had been shut in all winter were glad to see new faces, and these riders brought news from the outside.

grub pile

A cowboy's name for a meal; also, often the cook's summons to a meal.

grub spoiler

A cowboy's name for the cook.

grubstake

Provisions; also, to furnish provisions. When one *grubstakes* another, it is usually with the understanding that the provider is to share in the profits of whatever enterprise is embarked upon. In mining, the supplies needed by a prospector, supplied him by a patron who shares in his findings.

grubstaker

One who provides a *grubstake, q.v.*

grubworm

A cowboy's name for the cook.

grulla

A mouse-colored or bluish-gray horse. From the Spanish, meaning *crane*. Such horses are produced from mixtures of liver chestnuts, mahogany bays, and some blacks. Also called *smoky* and *mouse dun*.

grunt

A logger's term for pork or bacon. A ground man who acts as helper to a lineman. An electrician's helper in a sawmill.

grupera

A packer's term for the crupper, which goes under the mule's tail; from the Spanish.

G-string

An Indian's breechcloth.

guard-deep

A riverman's expression meaning *loaded*; *guard-deep with freight* meant that a boat was heavily loaded.

guardrail

An outside railing around a steamboat. The rails around the main deck (lower deck) of a packet were usually called *bull rails*; those around the boiler deck were called *boiler-deck rails*; those around the roof were called *roof rails*; and those around the top edge of the texas were the *texas rails*. These rails were forms of fencing to keep persons and articles from going over the edge or the side of the boat.

guards

That portion of the steamboat's deck located outboard on the sides. The main-deck guard was found on the sides of the main deck, usually extending from the forecastle back to the kitchen or the toilet rooms, commonly about three-fifths the length of the vessel. In width the main-deck guard extended from the nosing in to the deck-room bulkhead, making an avenue down the side about 6 to 10 feet wide on a stern-wheeler and frequently double that on a side-wheeler. The term *loaded to the guards* meant that freight had been heaped about until the main guards were flush with the surface of the river. The main-deck guards protected the hull against collision.

guest of honor at a string party

A man who had been hanged. Chick Coleman spoke of one whose "neck was too damned short, and they took 'im out to stretch it."

guía

A freighter's term for a paper which certified that the merchandise being transported had been cleared through a customhouse. A permit, passport, or certificate of safe conduct.

guides

In mining, strips of wood or steel rope used to hold the cage in position in the shaft during its rush to the surface.

guinnie

A logger's name for an Italian.

gulch

A ravine, canyon, or gully; the deep and narrow bed of an intermittent stream.

gullet

The curved portion of the underside of the fork of a saddle.

gully-washer

What the cowman calls a very hard rain. After such a rain, in cowboy parlance, it is usually "wet 'nough to bog a snipe."

gummers

Old sheep that have lost their teeth.

gun

A pistol. The rifle, with the exception of the buffalo gun, was never called a *gun*, but rather *Winchester*, *rifle*, *.30–.30* (from the caliber of the gun), or the slang name *Worchestershire*. (Philip A. Rollins, *The Cowboy* [New York, Charles Scribner's Sons, 1936], 57.) In logging, a log that has slipped up endwise in a boom.

gun fanner

One who fans his gun when shooting; see *fanning*. The real fighter has nothing but contempt for the gun fanner, and the fanner has small chance to live when pitted against the man who takes his time and pulls the trigger once. By *taking his time* is meant pausing only that fraction of a second that makes the difference between deadly accuracy and a miss. The muscles are fast, but there is a mental deliberation.

gunman

A man specially trained in the use of the pistol and ever ready to demonstrate this skill in blazing gunplay. The word soon came to take into account the character of the man and became synonymous with *killer*.

gunman's sidewalk

The middle of the street, so called because there the gunman could see on all sides and avoid an ambush.

GUNMEN

See buscadero, gunman, gunny, gun shark, gun-wise, hired killer, keener, leather slapper, notcher, pronto bug, quick-draw artist, short-trigger man, thumber, tie-down man, two-gun man, wore 'em low.

gunnel
See *gunwale*.

gunnin' for someone
Looking for an enemy to shoot.

gunning stick
In logging, two sticks attached by a hinge, used to determine the direction of the fall of a tree. Also called *gun stick*.

gunny
A cowman's name for a gunman who is for hire as a killer.

gunny sacker
During some sheep wars the sheepman's name for the cowman; so called because he raided the sheep camps wearing a gunny sack over his head.

gunsel
A tenderfoot. The creation of this now popular word is credited to John Bowman at a Livermore, California, rodeo in 1938. When he saw a duded-up imitation westerner walking along wearing an extremely baggy-seated pair of pants, it created quite a sensation, and Bowman called them *gunsel drawers*. The term was soon shortened to *gunsel* and was used to mean a modern version of the old-time greenhorn, or a glorified dumbbell. It gradually came to mean anyone who did things the wrong way, and so was not an enviable title.

GUNS
See weapons and ammunition.

gun shark
One expert in the use of a gun.

gun-shy
A cowboy's word meaning *cowardly*. I heard one cowboy say, "When I see a coward with a gun I get plumb scared." Charlie Russell, in *Trails Plowed Under*, spoke of another's being "as gunshy as a female institute."

gun slinging
Shooting a gun.

guns on the table
A cowboy's expression for fair play; something aboveboard.

GUN SPIN
See Curly Bill spin, double roll, road agent's spin, single roll.

gun stick
See *gunning stick*.

gun tipper
One who shoots through the end of an open holster without drawing his weapon. The holster works on a swivel.

gun turn
In faro, two fives drawn from the box in a single turn. So called from an old pickpocket saw: "Two fives together, what the mark had in his leather." Also called *pickpocket turn*.

gun-wadding bread
A cowboy's term for light bread.

gunwale
In river boating, usually the top edge of the side of a barge.

gun-wise
Said of one with a thorough knowledge of guns.

gurglin' on a rope
Said of one hanged.

gut burglar
A logger's name for the cook.

gut-eaters
A name the cowboy sometimes had for an Indian because of his taste for beef entrails.

gut hammer
A logger's term for a triangular piece of iron upon which a camp cook beats the signal for mealtime.

gut hooks
A cowboy's name for spurs.

gut lancers
A cowboy's name for spurs.

gut line
What the cowboy calls a rope of rawhide.

gut puller
A faro dealer, probably so called because

pulling cards from the dealer's box suggested the act of gutting a crayfish or other crustacean by selecting the middle fin of the tail and pulling out the large intestine with it.

gut robber
A cowboy's name for the cook.

gut-shot
Said of one wounded in the stomach or intestines.

gut-shrunk
A cowboy's expression for having been without food for a considerable length of time.

gutter board
In logging, a path followed in skidding logs; also called *runway*.

gut twister
A bucking horse of ability.

gut warmer
A cowboy's name for whisky.

gut wrapper
In logging, a piece of chain or cable within a load of logs, used to hold an individual tier together.

gut wrenches
A cowboy's name for his spurs.

guy line
In logging, a supporting line on a pole.

gypped
Affected by gypsum water. To the cowboy this word has an entirely different meaning from *swindled*. Many of the creeks and rivers running through the country in which he works are heavily saturated with gypsum or other alkaline salts. Drunk in moderate quantities, if it is fairly cool, such water causes no ill effects, but drunk in large quantities during branding or a dusty roundup, the water produces an effect similar to that suffered by the small boy who has eaten freely of green apples—only much worse. No matter how old the old-timer, or how much of the water he has consumed in the past, he is never immune to *gypping*. He knows it, but if he is thirsty enough, he will drink water wherever it is found regardless of mineral or other content, even though it has the same effect as the famed croton oil. (John M. Hendrix, "Cow Camp Sanitation," *Cattleman*, Vol. XXI, No. 11 [April, 1935], 5–6.)

gyppo
In logging, a small outfit that works on a contract basis. The term is ordinarily explained as reflecting a belief that such small outfits often "gyp" employees out of their wages. Also, a pieceworker.

gyppo contractor
In logging, a contractor who subcontracts by piecework. Also, a contemptuous term for one who furnishes poor accommodations.

gypsy
In logging, a winding drum on a donkey engine.

H

"It's the man that's the cowhand, not the outfit he wears"

hacendado
A ranch owner; from the Spanish.

hacienda
The homestead of a ranch owner who raises stock; from the Spanish, meaning *landed estate*. In mining, a smelter.

hack
An earmark made with a short split about half the length of the split or slash.

hackamore
A halter; a corruption of the Spanish, *jáquima*, meaning *headstall*. The American

cowboy pronounces his Spanish "by ear." When he first heard the word *jáquima*, he pronounced it *hackamer*, which gradually became *hackamore*, as it is found in the dictionary today. (S. Omar Barker, "Sagebrush Spanish," *New Mexico Magazine*, Vol. XX, No. 12 [December, 1942], 19.)

It is usually an ordinary halter having reins instead of a leading rope, with a headpiece something like a bridle, a bosal in place of a bit, and a browband about 3 inches wide that can be slid down the cheeks to cover the horse's eyes, but without a throat latch.

had a bilious look

A cowboy's description of anything not in first-class condition.

had his hair raised

Said of a man scalped by Indians.

had his pony plated

A cowboy's expression meaning that he had his horse shod.

Haggle

See chaffer.

hail

In steamboating, a signal given from shore to an approaching boat by a prospective shipper or passenger; in daylight, the wave of a handkerchief or newspaper in slow, deliberate arcs; at night, the wave of a lantern. The pilot of the boat, seeing the hail, responded by giving a short toot on the boat's whistle. Packets frequently hailed one another to transact business in midstream by blowing four blasts on the whistle immediately after the passing signals had been completed.

hair brand

A dishonest brand made by holding the branding iron against the animal just long enough to burn the hair but not the hide. The hair grows out, effacing the sign of the brand, and the rustler can then put his own brand on the animal. Also called *cold brand*. To brand in the manner described above.

hair case

A cowboy's term for a hat.

hair cinch

A saddle cinch made of horsehair.

hair in the butter

A cowboy's expression for a delicate situation.

hair lifter

A frontier name for an Indian on the warpath; also, a dangerous and exciting incident.

hair off the dog

A cowboy's expression for one who has gained experience.

hair over

Said of a brand when the hair grows back over it.

hair pants

Chaps with the hair on.

hairpin

To mount a horse.

hair pounder

A cowboy's and logger's term for a teamster.

hair rope

A rope made of horsehair. This rope is never used as a reata; it kinks too easily and is too light to throw. A hair rope is used for a hackamore tie rope, called a *mecate*, q.v.

hairy Dick

A cowboy's name for an unbranded animal, especially a calf.

half-breed

A half-blood, especially the offspring of a white father and an Indian mother. In logging, a type of donkey engine.

half-breed bit

A bit that has a narrow, wicket-shaped hump in the middle of the mouth bar, within which a "roller," or vertical wheel with a broad and corrugated rim, is fixed. (Philip A. Rollins, *The Cowboy* [New York, Charles Scribner's Sons, 1936], 148.)

half hamming

A manner of riding in which the rider

sits on one side, on one thigh, one spur being hooked solidly in the cinch; similar to riding *monkey style, q.v.*

half horse, half alligator

A name for a boasting frontiersman or river boatman of the early West.

half-pint size

A cowboy's term for something small.

half-rigged saddle

A saddle with a triangle of leather tacked on for a seat.

halter-broke

Said of a horse trained to run with the remuda; a horse broken to lead.

halter puller

A horse with the habit of pulling back on the halter rope.

halter-shy

Said of a horse afraid of the halter.

hame-headed

Stupid; applied mostly to horses.

hamstring

To sever the Achilles tendon of an animal thereby rendering it unable to control its legs. Wolves often brought down their victims by hamstringing them. Also used figuratively to mean *to foil someone's plans* or *to place him at a disadvantage.*

hamstrung

Said of a horse that has strained a ligament in one of its quarters.

hand

A measurement used in describing the height of a horse. A hand equals 4 inches; thus a 15-hand horse is 60 inches high, the measurement being taken from the ground to the top of the horse's withers. Also, short for *cowhand,* the most common term in the cow country for a cowboy.

hand-and-spit laundry

What the cowboy called a laundry run by a Chinese, who, the legend goes, "sprayed a feller's best Sunday shirt with his mouth for a sprinklin' can."

handbill roundup

A roundup announced by handbills. So called by cowboys because in the early eighties the Wyoming Stock Growers' Association covered such a vast territory that it resorted to sending out handbills announcing dates for the start of roundups.

handcarter

An early traveler who went West with his supplies and possessions in a handcart which he pushed across the plains and mountains to his destination. This practice was mostly followed by the early Mormons traveling to Utah with Brigham Young.

hand game

An Indian gambling game in which one player guessed in which hand another had concealed a stone or other small object.

handhold

A hole made in the belly piece of the aparejo, in the center of each side, to enable the packer to insert the hay or grass that forms the padding. Also called *handhole.*

handle

A saddle horn; so called because it provides something to hold to.

handling

In steamboating, any activity on board which requires communication between the engine room and the pilothouse. The term very evidently came from the system of bell pulls used on western-river steamboats; they had to be *handled* from the pilothouse.

hand milking

In sheep raising, milking a mother ewe by hand to secure food for her lamb when the mother refuses to nurse it.

handy with the running iron

Said of a cattle rustler.

hang an ax

A logger's term meaning *to fit a handle to an ax.*

hang and rattle

A cowboy's term meaning *to stick to the finish.*

Hanging

See California collar, choke, cottonwood blossom, decorate a cottonwood, die in a horse's nightcap, dressed in a hemp four-in-hand, dying with throat trouble, exalted, guest of honor at a string party, gurglin' on a rope, hemp fever, human fruit, hung up to dry, lookin' through cottonwood leaves, lookin' up a limb, lynching bee, mid-air dance, necktie frolic, necktie party, necktie social, playing cat's cradle with his neck, riding under a cottonwood limb, rope croup, rope meat, stiff rope and a short drop, strangulation jig, stretch hemp, string up, telegraph him home, Texas cakewalk, use him to trim a tree.

hanging bolts

In mining, one of the long bolts used to fix shaft timbers in their hanging position until a support can be fastened into the wall to hold them up.

hanging wall

In mining, the upper wall of a vein; a wall of rock binding the vein's upper surface.

hangman's turn

In faro, a jack and king showing in one turn.

hang-up

In logging, a fouling of the line on the log being hauled. To get a line caught behind trees or stumps.

hang up his hide

A cowboy's expression meaning *to put someone out of commission*.

hang up his rope

A cowboy's expression meaning *to quit one's job* or *to quit the calling*. Also said of someone too old to work with cattle any longer.

hankerin' to sniff Gulf breeze

Said of a wanted man "rollin' his tail south" and making for the Mexican border.

happy hunting ground

A white man's term for the Indian's hereafter.

Happy

See singin' with his tail up, tail over the dashboard.

happy jack

A cowman's term for a crude lamp made from a tin can in which a candle burns.

hard-boiled hat

A cowboy's name for a derby, something he could not always resist using for a target.

hard chink

A trader's term for coins, such as silver and gold; also called *hard money*.

harder than the hubs of hell

An expression used when miners strike hard rock when breasting or drilling.

hard hat

A logger's name for a safety engineer, so called because of this official's attempts to get loggers to wear helmets while on the job as protection from falling branches.

hard money

Coin money, the only kind seen in the early West.

hard-mouthed

Said of a horse whose mouth has become insensitive to the bit.

hard land

A miner's term for hard rock.

hard-rock miner

A miner who does his mining in hard rock; usually shortened to *rocker*.

hard seventeen

In faro, a total of seventeen without an ace, or with an ace counted as one.

hardtack outfit

A lumbering firm which provides its camp with a poor table. The name comes from a hard, cheap bread.

hardtail

A cowboy's and logger's name for a mule.

hard to sit

Said of a good bucking horse.

hardware

A common name for a gun. I heard one cowhand speak of a heavily armed man with, "He's packin' 'nough hardware to give 'im kidney sores."

hard-winter bunch

A group of cowmen whose favorite pastime is talking of the particularly hard winters through which they had passed.

hard-wintered

A range man's term for anyone who seems to be in hard circumstances, as, "He musta hard-wintered some by the looks of his outfit."

harness

What the logger calls his tool belt. In gambling, a device for holding out cards in reserve.

HARNESS

See devil, freighting and equipment, hook up.

harness-broke

Said of work horses broken to a wagon or other vehicle.

harp

What the logger calls an Irishman.

hash burner

A logger's name for the cook.

hasher

A logger's name for the cook.

hash slinger

A cowboy's name for the cook or for a waitress in town.

hasler

A logger's name for a woman who waits tables in a cookshack.

hassayampa

A liar, or someone incapable of telling the truth. The name is derived from the old legend that anyone who drank from Hassayampa Creek in Arizona could never again tell the truth.

hasta la vista

A Spanish farewell, frequently used as a friendly parting in regions of the cattle country where Spanish is spoken; equivalent to *I'll see you later*.

hatajo

A train of pack animals, commonly mules, used in transporting merchandise, especially in mountainous regions where other modes of transportation were impossible. From the Spanish, meaning *small herd* or *flock*.

HATS

See bonnet strings, conk cover, hair case, hard-boiled hat, John B., lid, louse cage, pot, sombrero, Stetson, tin hat, war bonnet, woolsey.

haulback

In logging, the light cable that carries the main line from the donkey back to the timber; the line that returns the choker to the woods after a turn of logs has been yarded.

haul hell out of its shuck

Said of a good bucking horse, and also of a person raising a disturbance.

haul in one's horns

To withdraw from a position; to back down.

Haul in your neck!

A command to someone to cease his aggressiveness.

have action

In faro, said of any card that wins or loses. All cards in the dealer's box except the *soda* and the *hock* have the power to win or lose, according to the order in which they are drawn from the box.

hay baler

A cowboy's name for a horse.

hay bottom

A place where hay has been or is customarily stacked. The bottom couple of feet of a haystack. Also called *straw bottom*.

hay burner

A cowboy's name for a horse, usually one kept and fed hay and grain instead of being turned out to pasture. Also, a horse of little value.

hay crib

A log wall without a roof enclosing hay-stacks.

hay hill

In logging, any icy pitch of road on which hay, earth, or light debris has been scattered to act as a brake on sleigh runners.

hay knife

A cowboy's term for a long, wavy-edged knife used to cut through a stack of hay. By using the hay knife, one may remove the end of a stack without disturbing the water-shedding contour of the rest of the stack. Sometimes hay cut with a hay knife is moved with a *Jackson fork, q.v.*

hayrack

A wagon with one high rack and one low rack, used for loading and hauling hay. A heavy rack with stanchions into which hay is piled in a feed lot.

hay shaker

A cowboy's term for a farmer.

hay shoveler

One who feeds cattle from haystacks in winter. A farmer.

hay slayer

A hay hand.

hay sled

A large sled used to collect hay from the shocks for hauling to the stack; used in conjunction with a derrick or stacker.

hay sling

A rope or chain, doubled and laid on a hay sled before loading, used with a derrick to pick up the entire sled load at one time.

hay stopper

What the miner calls the shift boss.

hay waddy

A worker in the hayfields and feed lots.

haywire

Crazy, muddled, twisted up. When a westerner removes baling wire from hay, he twists it into crazy shapes before throwing it away, thus keeping stock from be-coming entangled in it. The expression originated from this practice.

The logger uses this word to describe anything broken, crazy, foolish, flimsy, or otherwise not as it should be—anything and everything poorly operated or poorly put together.

haywire outfit

An inefficient outfit or ranch. In logging, a contemptuous name for loggers with poor equipment; the opposite of *candy side, q.v.*

haze

To drive cattle slowly.

hazer

A man who assists the buster in breaking horses. His duty, especially when the horse is broken outside the corral, is to keep the animal turned so that his bucking will not take him too far away.

haze the talk

A cowman's expression meaning *to change the subject of the conversation.*

head

A word used in referring to a number of animals, as, "He had a thousand head of steers on the lower range." A large body of water coming through irrigation ditches when the head gates are raised; see *head gate.* The hottest, most active forepart of a blaze in a forest.

Headache!

A logger's warning to duck or to beware a heavy load overhead.

head-and-heel

In rodeo, an event in which one roper catches a steer by the head and another ropes the hind feet, both putting down the animal against time. See *header* and *heeler.*

head-and-heel string

In packing, a practice of tying the halter rope of each mule to the tail of the animal preceding it to keep the train in single file.

head catch

The act of roping an animal by the head instead of by the feet.

head dam

A storage dam for holding water for log driving.

head 'em up

To put a *leader*, a steer which leads the others, in the direction the drover wishes the herd to go.

header

In roping, a member of a two-man roping team who ropes the steer by the head. The header has two loops; if he misses with both, the team retires with no time. See *heeler*.

head faller

In logging, the senior partner of a two-man falling team.

head for the settin' sun

On the dodge. In early days every lawbreaker headed west for the unsettled frontier, where there was a greater distance between sheriffs.

head frame

In mining, a hollow structure, built of wood, concrete, or steel, erected over the shaft workings.

head gate

An upstream gate on an irrigation ditch.

heading

In mining, the breast or face of a working.

headings

In mining, the mass of gravel and pay dirt above the head of a sluice.

headlight

What the miner calls his lamp.

headquarters

The house of a ranch owner; the business office of a ranch.

head rigger

In logging, the man next in authority to the *hooker*, *q.v.*

headright

A right to a portion of public land granted by the government to the head of a family settling upon it; also, the land so granted.

head saw

The saw in the mill which cuts the logs into lumber.

head-shy horse

A horse which has developed the habit of jerking away from any attempt to bridle him, especially when a bit is used instead of a hackamore.

headstall

The headgear of a horse, that part of the bridle which encompasses the head.

HEADSTRONG

See bull-necked.

head taster

A cowboy's name for the ranch manager.

head tree

In logging, the spar at the donkey engine in sky-line yarding.

heap big chief

The head chief of a tribe of Indians.

hearse driver

In faro, a name for the case keeper.

heart-and-hand woman

A wife obtained through a matrimonial agency. The name originated from the old magazine *The Heart and Hand*, published by a matrimonial bureau. The cowboy's simple soul believed all the descriptions. Hell, wasn't it printed?

Often a bachelor cowboy started his "letter courtship" out of curiosity, through desire to receive news from the outside, or just for a joke. In time he very often discovered that he had committed himself and found himself driving a buckboard 50 miles to meet a ladylove whom he had never really intended to see in his home corral. When she stepped off the train, he sometimes discovered that his little joke had backfired because "the photograph she'd sent didn't show up all the blemishes." Many a woman of this kind was a widow of the grass variety, but, as the cowboy would say, "She didn't let none of it grow under her feet."

hear the owl hoot

To have many and varied experiences. To get drunk.

heartwood

In logging, the central portion of the trunks of trees, entirely dead and without function; usually darker and more durable in service than the outer portion, or sapwood.

heating his axles

A cowboy's description of someone running swiftly on foot. Ranicky Reynolds described such a runner as "shore heatin' his axles and doin' his best to keep step with a rabbit."

heave

In mining, the horizontal dislocation of one lode by another.

HEAVEN

See happy hunting ground.

heavy cow

A cow carrying an unborn calf.

heel

To rope an animal by the hind feet; the method is never used on horses. In gambling, a name given a cheap gambler.

heel a string

In faro, to place a copper on the bottom of the checks when a string bet is made, thus coppering the first card and automatically playing it to lose while the last card included in the string bet is played to win.

heel bet

In faro, a type of string bet whereby the player bets one card to win and one to lose, or two to win and two to lose.

heeled

A cowboy's word meaning *armed with a gun.*

heeler

In rodeo, a member of a two-man roping team who ropes second and tries to catch one or both feet of a steer after his partner has already roped the head. The heeler has two loops, and if he misses both, the team receives no time. See *header.* A miner's name for the shift boss. In faro, a player who consistently makes *heel bets;* see *heel bet.*

heel fly

A small fly which stings cattle in the tender part of the heel, driving them frantically to water or bog holes to escape the torment.

heel-fly time

A dreaded season in the cattle country, from the middle of February to the middle of April, when heel flies are at their worst.

heel squatter

A common name for a cowboy; so called because it is a common practice for him to rest by squatting upon his heels. This is not a comfortable seat for the layman, but the cowboy will squat comfortably on his boot heels to eat his meals when out on the range or to spin his yarns. In fact, he is always ready "to take comfort in a frog squat."

heft

A freighter's word, meaning *weight.*

hefty

Large or heavy. I heard one cowboy say, in describing a large man, "For weight and size he'd take first prize at a bull show." Another conveyed the same thought with, "He's as wide as a barn door and long as a wagon track."

heifer brand

A handkerchief tied around a man's arm to designate that he is to play the part of a female at a dance where there are not enough ladies to go around. He is then said to dance "lady fashion," and his reward is to be allowed to "set with the ladies" between dances. This privilege, however, quite often makes him feel "as out of place as a cow on a front porch."

Sometimes a playful puncher ignores this emblem of womanhood and gets pretty rough, but these volunteer "females" can take it and pay back with interest.

heifer dust

A logger's name for snuff.

hell

A gambling house, especially a low dive.

hell bender

A logger's term for a log.

hell-bent for trouble

Seeking fights or making oneself otherwise obnoxious.

He'll do to ride the river with.

The highest compliment that can be paid a cowman. It originated back in the old trail days when brave men had to swim herds across swollen, treacherous rivers. The act required levelheaded courage. As time passed, the phrase came to mean that the one spoken of was loyal, dependable, and trustworthy and had plenty of sand.

hell-for-leather

A cowboy's expression for great haste.

hell in his neck

Said of a determined man.

hellin' 'round town

Said of a cowboy going from place to place in town seeking trouble. This was done mostly by the younger men. Older and more settled cowboys held the theory that "pullin' up the town to look at its roots don't help its growth none" and that "only a fool spends his time makin' the town smoky."

hell on wheels

An expression that originated during the building of the Union Pacific Railroad in 1867. As the rails were laid westward, the honky-tonks, gambling hells, and harlots were loaded on flatcars and moved to the next terminal. All the hell of the deserted town was then put on wheels to "pull their freight." The expression was also sometimes used in speaking of the old-time gun fighters. Clee Taggart described them as "them longhairs who done their damndest to fertilize the cow country's reputation for bein' wild and woolly."

hell rousers

A cowboy's name for his spurs.

hell stick

What the cowman sometimes called the sulphur match so common on the range in the early days; when struck it really gave him a "whiff of hell."

hell wind

What the cowman called a tornado.

hell with the hide off

Said of someone extremely troublesome.

hemp

A cowboy's term for his rope.

hemp committee

A name sometimes given to vigilantes, a group of self-appointed law enforcers bent upon a hanging.

hemp fever

A hanging. The victim was sometimes spoken of as being "given a chance to look at the sky."

hen fruit

A logger's name for eggs.

hen-fruit stir

A cowboy's name for pancakes.

Henry

A breech-loading, lever-action repeating rifle first used by the Union Army in the Civil War. This type of rifle never became popular as a military weapon, but was used to some extent upon the frontier.

hen skin

What the cowboy called a comforter stuffed with feathers.

hen wrangler

A name given a chore boy employed on a ranch.

herbe salée

A trapper's name for salt grass; from the French.

herd

A bunch of cattle. To bunch cattle and keep them bunched.

herd-broke

Said of cattle that have become accustomed to traveling in a herd.

herder

A common name for a sheepherder.

herd ground

See bed ground.

herd law

A law concerning the ranging and grazing of cattle.

Herefords

A breed of white-faced cattle common on present-day ranches. A cowman's name for a full-dress suit, so called because of its white front.

herrar

To brand; from the Spanish.

hickory

A cowman's term for sagebrush.

hickory Mormon

A halfhearted Mormon, sometimes the son of Mormon parents, but not a thoroughgoing saint himself.

hidalgo

A Spanish nobleman or landed proprietor in the West.

hide-and-tallow factory

A name given the slaughter pens of the early days when there was no market for cattle and they were slaughtered for their hides and tallow.

hide buyer

A man who buys buffalo and cattle hides.

hide-out

What the cowman calls a shoulder holster.

hide-out gun

An auxiliary weapon, usually short-barreled so that it could be hidden upon one's person. A *derringer (q.v.)* was especially popular as a hide-out gun.

HIDES

See hide with a stovepipe hole, kip pile, parflèche, plew, rawhide, robe hide, slunk skin.

hide with a stovepipe hole

A hide with the brand cut out, much resembling a tent canvas with a stovepipe hole cut through it. This ruse was resorted to by rustlers and meat thieves to hinder identification of the animal by its owner.

There was a certain outfit whom old man Barnes, of the Booger F, suspected of beefing his cattle. He was always complaining about their "half-solin' their insides with his beef." I happened to be with him one day when we rode into their camp just after supper.

"See there," said Barnes to me, "ever' damned one of 'em is settin' there pickin' Booger F gristle out of his teeth right now."

HIDING

See among the willows, belly through the brush, brushing up, cow folks, gone to Texas, hankerin' to sniff Gulf breeze, head for the settin' sun, hole up, in the brush, lookin' over his shoulder, on the cuicado, on the dodge, on the lookout, on the scout, pull for the Rio Grande, riding the coulees, riding the high lines, riding the owl-hoot trail, running wild, stampede to the wild bunch, sundowner, take to the tall timbers, take to the tules, travels the lonesome places, two jumps ahead of the sheriff, watering at night, whipping a tired pony out of Texas.

HIDING PLACE

See cache, general cache, hiding.

highball

In logging, a signal sent from the woods to the logging-engine operator to go ahead. A signal to start, to go on, to hurry.

highball outfit

A large or first-class business, especially in lumbering; an enterprising camp, one in which the men are worked at top speed.

high banker

A logger's term for a pretentious person.

high-belly strippers

A deck of cards doctored so that cards with high values can be controlled.

high climber

In logging, the man who tops and prepares a *high-lead tree, q.v.* Since his is the most dangerous job in the industry, he is permitted to be the only prima donna in the woods. A person who tops and rigs spar trees or poles.

high explosives

In mining, explosives of greater detonating force than black powder.

high-grade

In cattle raising, to breed up cattle to a pure breed. In mining, to steal ore from a mine; also, to mine only the rich ore.

high-grade ore

In mining, rich ore.

high grader

In mining, one who steals and sells, or otherwise disposes of, high-grade or specimen ores. A common practice in the early days of gold mining. The term is also applied in a literal sense to one who works in rich veins.

high grading

The stealing of small particles of ore or gold by employees in a mine.

high-grass constable

A cowboy's name for a rural law officer.

high-heel

A cowboy expression meaning *forced to walk*.

high-heeled time

A common description of the cowboy's idea of a good time with fun and frolic.

high layout

In faro, a dishonest layout which is approximately an inch higher than the square layout. It is used with a tell box which is held flush with the layout. By manipulating his box, the dealer can make the cards move out of the box and into the layout or back, thus controlling the turn. This layout is largely used with youngsters or suckers who are not familiar with the standard layout.

high-lead logging

See *sky-line logging*.

high-lead tree

A tree that has been transformed into a rooted mast or spar for use in *sky-line logging, q.v.* After the tree has been limbed and topped, the high climber swarms up the tree, perhaps 200 feet from the ground, and then attaches blocks and tackles for yarding logs.

high line

In logging, 1-inch steel rope extending often a half mile to either end of the "set."

high-line rider

What the cowboy called an outlaw. He usually rode the high country to keep a lookout for sheriffs or posses.

high-line sky rigger

In logging, a high-line cable.

high lonesome

A cowboy's definition of a big drunk.

high-low

In trick roping, a body spin which repeatedly raises and lowers the noose from the ground to the limit of the operator's reach above his head.

high rigger

In logging, the brave man who "tops the spars," that is, climbs the tall trees and saws off the tops.

high roller

In rodeo, a horse which leaps high into the air when bucking; also called *high poler*. This horse, while not quite so fast as others, is extremely rough and goes after his rider with a cool and deliberate aim that seldom fails to disqualify him. This type of horse pleases the spectators, for he puts on a great show, and his actions are easily followed.

high salty

A name for the foreman of a ranch.

high-tail

A cowboy expression meaning *to depart suddenly and unceremoniously*.

high-water pants

Logging trousers rolled up halfway to the knees.

hike

A logger's term meaning *to climb a pole*; possibly derived from the Chinook *hyak*, meaning *to hurry*.

hillbilly cowboy

A cowboy working for an outfit which ranges pretty well into the sticks.

hill diggings

Placer mining in the hills.

hill rat
A prospector of the hill country.

hinny
The offspring of a stallion and a female ass.

hip draw
A method of drawing a gun, worn on the hip, usually slanting forward with the butt turned to the rear, and unlimbered with a swift downward and upward motion.

hippin's
A cowboy's name for underbedding.

hippodrome stand
A rodeo stunt in which the rider stands upright with his feet in straps and leans forward while the horse runs at full speed; the rider generally uses two or more horses in the stunt.

hip shooting
Firing a gun without raising it above the level of the waist. When firing at close range, accuracy is not needed, sights are unnecessary, and the gun is shot by instinctively pointing it at an adversary and firing as soon as it clears the holster.

hired killer
A gunman who leased his services to a less courageous man to remove an enemy.

his calves don't suck the right cows
A cowman's reference to a rustler.

his cinch is gettin' frayed
Said of one who has worn out his welcome. An unwanted person might be described as being "welcome as a polecat at a picnic," "welcome as a rattler in a dog town," or "pop'lar as a tax collector." Of such a person it is said that "folks go 'round 'im like he was a swamp."

his cows have twins
Said of someone suspected of stealing cattle.

his leg tied up
Said of someone at a disadvantage. The expression originated from the custom of tying up the leg of a green bronc to shoe or saddle him. Shoeing some of the western horses is ticklish business. After completing such a job, Jake Wheeler, of the Horse-collar, declared that he "tacked iron on ever'thing that flew past." I remember one cowhand, kidding another from way back in the hill country, telling us that they "had to tie his leg up to give 'im a haircut" when he came to town.

his saddle is slipping
Said of someone losing his efficiency. Said of someone telling a tall tale.

his tail is dragging
Said of someone who is discouraged. Said of a coward.

his thinker is puny
Said of a weak-minded person. Such a person is said to be "off his mental reservation."

h'ist one
A cowboy's expression meaning *to take a drink*.

hitchin' bar
A hitch rack.

hitching rein drop
A rein or strap used to hitch a buggy horse.

hitchin' grounds
An area near a frontier store where customers usually hitched their teams and horses.

hitching weight
A weight which, placed on the ground and attached by a strap to the horse's bit, keeps the animal from going away. Used on buggy horses or wagon teams only.

hit me
In blackjack, a request for another card.

hit the breeze
To travel; to depart.

hit the clock
A logger's term for ringing in or out on a time clock or signing a time card.

hit the daylight

In rodeo, said when a horse ridden in a contest comes out of the chute.

hit the flats for home

Said of someone who leaves town or a neighboring ranch and starts across the prairie for home.

hit the knots

Said of a logger who snores in his sleep.

hit the timber line

Said when the sheepshearing is completed and the sheep make for the summer range in the mountains.

hit the trail

A cowman's expression meaning *to leave* or *to travel*.

hive off

A cowman's expression meaning *to leave*. (William MacLeod Raine to R.F.A.)

hiveranno

A trapper's name for someone who had passed several winters in the Indian country. From the French *hiver*, meaning *winter*, and *année*, meaning *year*. Also called *hiverant*.

hiverant

See *hiveranno*.

hobbled stirrups

Stirrups connected by a strap or rope passing under the horse's belly. They have the advantage of furnishing a form of anchorage during bucking, but are held in contempt by the skilled rider and are barred from rodeos. Though hobbled stirrups practically tie a rider into the saddle, they are extremely dangerous, for if the horse falls, the rider has no chance to free himself quickly. In the cow country a man who rides with hobbled stirrups is considered "plumb loco," and is certainly not a top hand.

hobble out

To hobble horses to keep them from running loose.

hobble

One of two leather cuffs buckled about the forelegs of a horse above the pastern joints, the two cuffs being connected with a short swivel chain. Most men get the same result with a wide band of cowhide or a diagonally cut half of a gunny sack. Hobbles are applied only at a camp; at the ranch, if the horse is not placed in a corral, he is turned loose. When a rider camps at night, he wants to be able to find his horse in the morning. With hobbles on, the horse can move about and graze with a certain amount of freedom, but he will be unable to go far because he can travel at only a slow walk.

HOBBLES

See chain hobble, clogs, cross-hobble, crow hobble, double hobble, hobble, hopple, running W, Scotch hobble, sideline.

hobble-tongued

Said of one who stutters.

hobble your lip

A cowboy's advice to someone to quit talking so much.

hock card

In faro, the last card in the box which is said to be *in hock*. Like the *soda card*, the hock card does not have any action. Originally it was known as the *hockelty card*, and in the early days of faro, when it counted for the bank, a player who had bet on it was said to have been *caught in hock*. Also, a gambler who had been trimmed by another sharper was said to be *in hock to his conqueror*. As late as the middle 1880's in the underworld a man was *in hock* when he was in jail. The phrase is now used principally in reference to pawnshop pledges, a meaning it seems to have acquired in recent years.

hoe dig

A cowboy's name for a dance; also called *hoedown*. Any old-timer will tell you that "dancin' in them days wasn't jes' wigglin' 'round and shakin' your rump."

hog

A sawmill machine that reduces waste pieces of lumber and slabs to chip form for fuel or other uses.

hogan
A lodge made of earth used by the Navaho Indians.

hogback
A horse with a roached back; the opposite of *swayback*. A narrow ridge with steep sides leading from a higher to a lower level.

hog chains
In steamboating, iron rods supported on wooden timbers, forming a truss system which held the ends of a boat up and the middle down. The flimsy hull construction of the western steamboat tended to warp up in the middle and sag at the extremities; the hog-chain system overcame this tendency. The hog-chain posts were usually built at angles and extended through the hurricane roof and were thus a conspicuous part of the boat's superstructure.

hog fuel
A logger's term for leftover pieces of wood on the ground.

hogger
A logger's name for the engineer of a logging locomotive.

hogging
In steamboating, a technical term for bending or breaking the hull out of shape.

hoggin' rope
A short rope used in hog-tying; also called *hoggin' string* and *piggin' string*.

hog head
A logger's name for a railroad engine; taken from railroaders' talk.

hog leg
Originally a popular name for the Bisley model single-action Colt, but later applied to any big pistol.

hog ranch
A cowboy's term for a place of kept women, usually situated near some fort and patronized by soldiers and cowboys. The term was used principally in the Northwest.

hogskin
What the cowboy sometimes calls the small eastern riding saddle.

hog-tie
To render an animal helpless after it is thrown by tying its two hind legs and a front one together with a short piece of rope. The ties are made with half hitches, and the rope used is a small, soft one about 3 feet long. On one end is a loop which the man doing the tying slips on the foreleg of the downed animal. Standing behind the animal, with one knee on it to help hold it down, he then sticks his foot under and behind the hocks and boosts the hind legs forward, at the same time drawing the hoggin' rope under and around both hind feet. This action puts the two hind feet on top, pointing forward, and the forefoot below, pointing back. With two or three turns and two half hitches the animal is thoroughly tied. Horses are never hog-tied.

hoist
In mining, the engine that pulls ore, men, or materials out of a mine.

hoja
What the early trader called the corn-husk he used for cigarette wrappers; from the Spanish, meaning *leaf*.

hokey-pokey
To put carbon disulphide ("high life") on an animal. It puts the animal into a frenzy, and was a popular joke with cowboys, especially when in town.

hold
The signal by the *near* to the *off* packer to hold his pack in position while the near packer brakes the load.

holding spot
The location selected for stopping and working a herd on roundup.

hold of the jerk line
A cowman's expression meaning *to be in control*.

holdout
In gambling, an extra card held out, as up the sleeve.

hold the cut
To hold a herd of cattle cut out from the main herd for any purpose.

hold the high card

A cowman's expression meaning *to have an advantage over someone*.

holdup man

A robber. In cattle driving, a man stationed at crossroads, on a hill, or at a critical point to keep a herd of cattle from leaving the trail.

hole card

In stud poker, the first card received by a player, which is dealt face down.

hole earmark

An earmark made by punching a hole in the animal's ear.

hole up

To stay indoors in bad weather. Also said of an outlaw hiding out, yet prepared to defend his liberty.

holiday

What the logger calls an open area in the timber.

holler calf rope

To give up; to surrender; to acknowledge defeat; to declare that one has had enough.

hollow horn

A run-down condition of cattle, popularly ascribed to hollowness of their horns.

Holsters

See ace in the hole, hide-out, open-toed holster, shoulder holster, tied holster.

hombre

A southwestern cowboy's name for a man. Generally used by Americans to mean a man of low character, or used in conjunction with such adjectives as *bad* and *tough*.

home guard

A logger's term for a local worker who has been on the job for many years, as compared to the *boomer*, *q.v.* A permanent or long-time employee of the company.

homeless as a poker chip

Said of a restless person, one with a wanderlust who never remains long in one locality.

home range

The territory with which a herd of cattle is acquainted or where it belongs.

home station

In stagecoaching, a station every 50 miles or so along the stagecoach line. Small communities grew up around these stations. Scattered between the home stations were the isolated swing stations where the livestock was kept. The home stations were larger than the swing stations and were built of rough lumber. Here meals were served to the stage passengers.

Life at the home station was less monotonous than at the swing stations. In addition to the daily arrival and departure of coaches there was the social life of the people who made it their home. When a dance was held at a home station, men and women would come from as far away as 50 miles, by stagecoach or wagon and often on horseback.

homestead

A tract of land taken up from the public domain by a settler under the homestead laws. To live on and prove up such land.

homesteader

A person who took up *a homestead, q.v.*

home sucker

A cowman's name for a homeseeker who came west to farm.

honda

A knotted or spliced eyelet at the business end of a rope for making a loop. Sometimes a metal ring is used, though some men claim that metal objects might blind an animal and will not "set" to keep the struggling brute from freeing itself. Hondas tied in the rope should be protected with a piece of slick leather sewn about the upper end of the loop so that the rope will not burn through it. (W. M. French, "Ropes and Roping," *Cattleman*, Vol. XXVI, No. 12 [May, 1940], 17-30.)

honest pitcher

A horse which starts pitching as soon as mounted and tries by every device to unseat its rider. Some horses will make no effort to pitch until they get their riders off guard; then, before the riders are aware of the horse's evil intentions, they find themselves on the ground. The latter horses are not classed as *honest pitchers*.

honeycomb

In logging, an expanded, or "opened-up," section of a piece of lumber caused by high temperatures in a dry kiln. The outside of a piece becomes dry and hard, and the inside dries very slowly. Part of the piece shrinks and thus opens, or *honeycombs*.

honeydew

A logger's name for whisky.

honky-tonk

A low saloon, dance hall, or other place of amusement.

honky-tonk town

One of the towns at the end of the old cattle trails, so called because its business district was composed largely of saloons and honky-tonks. Such a town was tough and, as the cowman would say, "a bad place to have your gun stick."

hood

The man who drives the *hoodlum wagon* (*q.v.*) on trail or roundup, most generally the *nighthawk*, *q.v.*

hooden

A cabin where bachelor cowboys sometimes sleep during bad weather.

hoodlum wagon

A cowboy's name for the bed wagon.

hooey

The half hitch that completes the tie of a calf's legs by the calf roper. The tie usually consists of two wraps around three legs and the *hooey* around two of them to hold it secure.

hoof-and-mouth disease

A disease of cattle. The "disease" of one who talks too much.

hoofed locusts

A cowboy's name for sheep, so called, because, it is claimed, their sharp hoofs killed the grass down to the roots.

hoof shaper

A slang name for a blacksmith, or horseshoer.

hook-a-day

A trader's expression meaning, *You are welcome*.

Hook 'em cow!

The war cry of the branding corral and a phrase of encouragement at every rodeo.

hooker

In rodeo, a bull that uses his horns, throwing his head back and around to rid himself of his rider. In logging, short for *hook tender*, *q.v.* The bull of a yarding crew in a high-lead operation. One employed as a straw boss of the logging crew to tend the hook attached to the main cable, which carries the chokers. His small crew is composed of a rigging slinger and two chokermen.

hooks

A common name for spurs. An earmark made by cuts that are curved at one end like fishhooks.

hook tender

A logger's name for the straw boss.

hook up

To harness horses to a wagon or buggy; the verb *harness* is never used in the cow country.

hooley-ann

In roping, a throw made either from the ground or on horseback. The roper carries the loop in his hand, and when the chance presents itself, he swings one quick whirl around in front of him toward the right and up over his head and releases the loop and rope in the direction of the target. As it comes over, it is turned in a way to flatten out before it reaches the head of the animal to be roped. It lands straight down and so has a fair-sized opening.

It is a fast loop and is strictly a head catch, being especially used to catch horses in a corral. It is thrown with a rather small loop and has the additional virtue of landing with the honda sliding down the rope, taking up the slack as it goes. (W. M. French, "Ropes and Roping," *Cattleman*,

Vol. XXVI, No. 12 [May, 1940], 17–30.)
(Dugg Green to R.F.A.)

The rope is not slung over the horse's head, for to sling it so would cause even the steadiest old horse to become excited. By using the hooley-ann, a half-dozen men can rope mounts at the same time without exciting the horses. (John M. Hendrix, "Roping," *Cattleman*, Vol. XXII, No. 1 [June, 1935], 16, 17.)

hooligan wagon

A wagon used on short cattle drives to carry fuel and water in a country where these commodities are scarce.

hoolihan

A cowboy's term meaning *foul* or *dirty play*.

hoolihaning

In rodeo, the act of leaping forward and alighting on the horns of a steer in bulldogging in such a manner as to knock the steer down, without having to resort to twisting him down with a wrestling hold. This practice is barred at practically all recognized rodeos. Also, to throw a big time in town—to paint the town red.

hoosegow

A cowboy's name for jail, now used throughout the country. From the Spanish *juzgado*, meaning *tribunal* or *court of justice*.

Hoosier

A logger's term for a greenhorn. The term originated when a Pacific Coast lumber company recruited Indiana farm boys to come west as apprentice loggers. Thus *Hoosier* meant first a logger who did not know his trade, then one who could never master the necessary skills, and finally one who regularly slights his job.

Hoosier belt

A cowboy's term for farming country and for a region of range country where farmers became numerous.

Hoosier up

To frame up a plot for slowing down work. To gang up on someone or against something. To malign.

hooter

A cowboy's name for a hoot owl.

hoot-nanny

In logging, a small device used to hold a crosscut saw while sawing a log from underneath.

hoot-owl hollow

A cowboy's name for a very remote and isolated place of residence.

hop for mama

A cowboy expression for the bucking of a horse.

hoppin' dog holes

Said of a cowhand riding in prairie-dog country.

hopple

Another word for *hobble, q.v.*

hop-skip

A rope trick in which the roper hops into and out of a vertical noose while keeping the rope spinning.

horn

The part of the saddle above the fork. Its technical term, *pommel*, is never used by a cowman. In mining, a spoon or scoop of horn in which washings are tested in prospecting.

horned jackrabbit

A name sometimes given the longhorn by the old-time cowman because it was all horns and speed.

horning a prospect

Selling someone mine stocks of questionable value.

horning the brush

Said of a very angry or aggressive person.

hornin' in

A cowboy's term for meddling or intruding. One of the cowman's codes was, "Never interfere with nothin' that don't bother you."

horn spoon

In mining, a longitudinal section cut from the underside of an ox horn and scraped thin; used for washing auriferous gravel and pulp where delicate tests are required.

horns sawed off

Said of one rendered harmless, with the fight taken out of him.

horn string

A leather or buckskin string fastened to the horn of the saddle and used for securing a rope to it.

hornswoggling

The dodging and wriggling movement of a roped steer, by means of which he throws off the rope. The steer thus *horn-swoggles* the cowboy from whom he escapes.

horn-tossin' mood

Said of an angry person.

horrors

What the trapper called delirium tremens.

horse

To man, probably the most important animal of the equine family. A male horse, as distinguished from the female, called a *mare*. In mining, a mass of country rock between the enclosing wall of a vein; a fault in the strata formation.

horsebreaker

A man who breaks horses as a profession.

HORSEBREAKERS

See bronc breaker, bronc buster, bronc fighter, bronc peeler, bronc scratcher, bronc stomper, bullbat, buster, contract buster, flash rider, gentler, hazer, horsebreaker.

HORSE BREEDS

See appaloosa, buttermilk horse, horse colors, horses, Oregon puddin' foot, palouse horse, Percheron, quarter horse.

HORSE BUYERS

See stock buyer.

HORSE COLORS

See albino, bay, bayo coyote, blood bay, brockled, buckskin, calico, California sorrel, chestnut, claybank, coyote dun, cremello, flea-bitten, grulla, horse breeds, horse markings, horses, Indian pony, moros, nigger horse, overo, paint, palomilla, palomino, piebald, pinto, pumpkin skin, roan, sabino, sorrel, stocking, straight-colored horses, tobiano, trigueño, zebra dun.

HORSE DISEASES AND AILMENTS

See bighead, broken wind, epizootic, hamstrung, kack biscuit, nigger brand, set fast, wind-broken.

HORSE HERDERS

See nighthawk, wrangler.

HORSE HERDING

See wrangle.

HORSE HERDS

See band, scalawag bunch, seraglio, stud bunch.

horse jewelry

Fancy riding paraphernalia.

horse man

One who raises horses.

horseman

A mounted person, or one skilled in horsemanship.

HORSE MARKINGS

See apron-faced horse, blaze, chin spot, moon-eyed, race, skewbald, snip, socks, star, star strip, stew ball, walleyed, willow-tail.

HORSEMEN

See riders.

horse pestler

A herder of saddle horses; a wrangler.

horseplay

The tricks, pranks, and practical jokes by which the cowboy displays his peculiar and rough sense of humor.

horse ranch

A ranch upon which horses are raised.

horse rustler

A *wrangler, q.v.*

HORSES

See all-around cow horse, bangtail, barefoot, bell, bell horse, buckers, boomerang stallion, breaking a horse, bridle-wise, bronco, broomtail, brush horse, brush-tail, buffalo horse, bunch, grasser, bunch quitter, buzzard-bait, buzzard-head, caballada, caballo, calf horse, calf legs, camp staller, can't-be-rode horse, caponera, cayuse, chapo, chicken horse, choosin' match, chopping horse, churn-head, chute-crazy, chute fighter, chute freeze, cinch binder, circle horse, clear-footed, close-coupled, cloud watcher, cold-blooded stock, cold collar, cold-jawed, colts, coon-footed, cow-hocked, cow horse, cow pony, crease, cribber, crockhead, croppy, cuitan, cut horse, cutter, cutting horse, dead-mouthed, dilsey, dink, ewe-necked, falls out of bed, fantail, fiddle-foot, fiddle-headed, filly, fresh horse, fuzz-tail, gelding, gentler, grain-fed, halter puller, halter-shy, hard-mouthed, hay baler, hay burner, head-shy horse, hogback, hotblood, individual, jay-bird stallion, jennet, jughead, ketch colt, killer, kitchen string, last year's bronc, long horse, manada, man-killer, mesteño, mockey, montura, mount, mule-footed, mule-hipped horse, mustang, nag, Navvy, neck-reiner, nigger-heeled, night horse, notch in his tail, off-wheeler, oily bronc, one-man horse, outlaw, owlhead, parada, parrot-mouth horse, pecker neck, peg pony, pestle-tail, pie biter, plug, puddin' foot, puller, range horse, rat-tailed horse, raw one, remudera, ridge runner, ridgling, rim rocker, rocking-chair horse, rope horse, rough string, saddle band, saddler, salado, salty bronc, set down, shavetail, short horse, skate, slick, smooth, smooth-mouth, snake-eyes, snipe-gutted, snorter, snorty, snub horse, sour-mouth, Sunday horse, swimming horse, tender, tender-mouth, tongue horses, walking stick, wassup, wheeler, wheel horse, whey-belly, whistler, whittler, widow-maker, winter horses, work horse, wrangle horse, wring-tail, Yakima, yegua.

HORSESHOEING

See blinding, cold shoeing, had his pony plated, hoof shaper, Indian-shod, iron burner.

HORSESHOES

See bar shoe, boot, bull shoes, good-enoughs, shoe, slipper.

HORSE TEAMS AND STRINGS

See band, cavvy, remuda, rough string, saddle band, scalawag bunch, shotgun cavvy, snaking team, swing team, tongue horses, winter horses.

horse thief

One who steals horses, a dangerous business in the old days, because when the thief was captured, there was no wait for the courts, but the thief was hanged to the nearest tree.

horse thief's special

A cowboy's name for a dish made of boiled rice and raisins.

horse wood

In steamboating, wood gathered and piled along the riverbank; generally logs from which the bark had been stripped in the winter and fed to horses to keep them from starving.

horse wrangler

See *wrangler*.

hospital cattle

Weak stock that have not wintered well.

hostler

A logger's name for a locomotive mechanic.

hot back

A game played by loggers in which a man stooped over blindfolded with his head in a hat and one hand on the small of his back, while the others formed a circle around him. One of the men in the circle would hit the victim's hand, and he would try to guess who had hit him. If he guessed right, he traded places with the striker.

hotblood

What the cowman called a thoroughbred.

hot bottom

The same game as *hot back (q.v.)*, except that the logger gave his victim a resounding whack on the seat of the pants.

hot-foot

To burn a calf between the toes with a hot iron, a practice followed by some rustlers to keep the calf from following its mother.

hothead
A person with *gold fever, q.v.*

hothouse stock
A contemptuous name given by old-timers to the newly introduced Hereford cattle.

Hot iron!
The call of the brander when he wants a freshly heated iron.

hot lead
Bullets fired from a gun.

hot logging
A logging operation in which logs go from the stump to the mill without pause.

hot rock
A cowboy's name for a biscuit.

hot roll
A cowboy's name for his bedroll.

hot rope
A rope that slips through one's hands so quickly that it burns the flesh.

hot shot
An electrical charge used to make the tamest horse buck when ridden by an amateur. The points of the charge are supposed to hit the horse on the shoulders. Hot shots are also used in rodeo chutes.

hot spot
A region of frequent forest fires.

hot stick
A charged rod used in stockyards to prod cattle.

hot stuff
Heated branding irons. An expression for something good or extraordinary.

hound ears and whirlups
A cow-camp dessert originated by Lum Pagrum, a wagon cook of New Mexico. *Hound ears* were made from sour dough which was dropped from a spoon into hot grease and fried brown. The dough usually spread out in the shape of a dog's ears. *Whirlup* was a sauce made with water and sugar beaten up with flavoring and spices. When available dried fruit was chopped or mashed and added to the whirlup, which was poured over the hound ears.

HOUSES AND SHELTERS
See adobe, azotea, big house, boom house, bull's manse, bunkhouse, canvas bungalow, casa grande, cookhouse, cook shack, dugout, feed bag, feed trough, grub house, headquarters, hogan, hooden, jacal, line camp, lodge, medicine lodge, mess house, rag bungalow, rag house, ranches, shebang, timber shanty, white house, wickiup, wigwam.

hovel
A stable for logging teams.

Hua!
A word used by the traders, meaning *Get along!* From the Spanish *Gua!* meaning *Gracious!*

hubbing
Driving a wagon so that the hubs strike gateposts or other objects.

huckydummy
A cowboy's name for baking-powder biscuits with raisins.

hudge
A miner's iron bucket used for hoisting.

huggin' rawhide
Sticking to the saddle while riding a bucking horse.

hull
A cowboy's term for his saddle.

hull inspector
In steamboating, a term used for a bad snag in or near the steamboat channel.

human fruit
The body of a man hanging from a tree after a lynching.

humboldt
In logging, a wedge-shaped piece of wood which, when cut or sawed out of a tree, leaves an undercut.

humpback
A logger's name for a sawyer.

humping freight

In steamboating, loading and unloading freight from a steamboat.

humped his tail at the shore end

Said of a man or an animal leaving in a hurry.

humps

In faro, cards which have been trimmed so that the dealer can locate and manipulate them at will. The trimming is done with special shears and may follow any number of patterns—all the cards stripped except the aces or other desired cards, certain cards with rounded edges, etc. The term is no longer restricted to faro. Also called *strippers* and *wedges*.

hundred-and-elevens

Spur marks on a horse's sides.

hundred-and-sixty

A westerner's name for a homestead, commonly 160 acres.

HUNGER

See feel like chawin', grease-hungry, gut-shrunk, I'm wolfish, lank inside, narrow at the equator, Spanish supper.

hungry loop

Said of a rope thrown by a roper intent on a catch.

hung up

Said when a rider's foot is caught in a stirrup and he is being dragged by the horse; one of the most dreaded accidents in the cow country.

hung up his saddle

Said of one who has retired from the cattle business, or one too old to ride. A reference to death.

hung up to dry

Said of one hanged.

hunk

What the American miner calls any foreign-born miner; also called *hunky*.

hunker

To sit or squat upon one's heels. The cowboy rarely uses a chair; he saves it "for company."

HUNTERS

See bone hunter, bossloper, cibolero, coureur de bois, mesteñero, skin hunter, wolfer.

HUNTING

See buffalo running, chassé, fuzz-tail running, keep your moccasins greased, make meat, running meat, stand.

hunting a horse

A common excuse given by a cowboy for a presence or absence not easily explained; also, a common alibi for being on another cattleman's range. (Agnes Morley Cleaveland, *No Life for a Lady* [Boston, Houghton Mifflin Company, 1941], 67.)

Old man Johnson had a pretty daughter, and a certain Mill Iron puncher used to drop by when he thought the old man was not at home. One day he was surprised to find the old man sitting on the front porch. "Have you seen a little sorrel mare with our brand 'round here?" stammered the surprised cowhand, giving this threadbare excuse.

"Go right on into the parlor; you'll find 'er a-sittin' on the sofa," grinned the old man, jerking his head toward the front door. That horse hunter didn't fool him. He had been young once himself.

hunting leather

Catching hold of the saddle while riding a horse.

hunting strays

Looking for cattle or horses that have strayed away from the home ranch or the rest of the herd. The expression is also used as a favorite excuse of cowboys who want to make an unannounced visit to some girl on a neighboring ranch. Also used as a cover-up by anyone who wants to ride over his neighbor's range for any legitimate or illegitimate purpose. See *hunting a horse*.

hunting water

Said of a sheepherder who has become a little "tetched" from his long periods of isolation.

hurdy-gurdy

In mining, a water wheel operated by the impact of a stream of water on its radially placed paddle; sometimes called *hurdy-gurdy wheel*.

hurdy-gurdy house

A place of low resort featuring cheap liquor, noisy music, lascivious dancing, and prostitution.

hurricane

A logger's term for a path of fallen timber made by a hurricane.

hurricane deck

What the cowboy calls the saddle of a bucking horse. In steamboating, on the usual packet, the third deck (in order upward: the main deck, the boiler deck, and the hurricane deck); also called *upward deck* or *roof*. Some rivermen confine the term *hurricane deck* to the forward end of the roof.

hurries

In mining, the landing place on which ore cars stand.

hurry

To bully someone. In mining, a slang name for an ore chute. To convey or drive cars filled with ore.

Hurry

See escape, go, make beaver, make tracks, makin' dust, on the high lope, punch the breeze, railroad without steam, rattle his hocks, ride like a deputy sheriff, roll his tail, run like a Nueces steer.

hydraulic mining

A method of placer mining in which the gravel is washed by a stream operated under hydraulic pressure. Invented in California and first used by a miner named Matterson on American Hill near Nevada City, the method was ideally suited to the needs of the time.

hymns

What the cowboy calls the songs he sings to cattle. They are usually religious tunes accompanied by profane words and as "hymns" would surely shock the clergy.

Not all cowboys are good singers. There are many who "couldn't pack a tune in a corked jug" and sound as though they are "garglin' their throats with axle grease, or givin' the death rattle." An old cowhand I knew only as Cutbank used to say, "They lost their voices explainin' to so many different judges how they'd come to have their brands on somebody else's cows."

I

"Success is the size of the hole a man leaves after he dies"

I broke my pick.

A miner's saying meaning that he is discouraged.

ice

A gambler's term for a stacked deck; see *cold deck*.

Idaho brain storm

A cowboy's name for a tornado. A whirling sandstorm.

idiot stick

What the miner calls his shovel; sometimes shortened to *idiot*.

if that's the way your stick floats

An expression used by the beaver trapper meaning *if that's what you're driving at*. See *float my stick*.

Ignorance

See couldn't drive nails in a snowbank, couldn't teach a settin' hen to cluck, don't know sic 'em, needs a wet nurse, ought to be playing with a string of spools, pelado.

Illnesses and diseases

See airin' the paunch, Arizona tenor, bends, boarding with Aunt Polly, caisson disease, hunting water, Job's comforter, leaded, lunger, mal de vache, miner's elbow, off his feed, riding the bed wagon, shake, stone on his chest, week on the bed wagon.

I'll shoot through the barrel and drown you!

A gunman's threat. During the old Kansas cow-town days full water barrels were placed at convenient locations along the street for use in case of fire. In those wild times gun battles were plentiful, and gun fighters and innocent bystanders alike ducked behind these water barrels for safety. More than one man got a good wetting from a bullet coming through the barrel he was hiding behind. The phrase became a common threat in the West.

immigrant butter

A cowboy's name for bacon grease, flour, and water.

immigrant cattle

Cattle brought onto a range from a distance.

impregnation

In mining, a metallic deposit having undetermined limits or limits in no way sharply defined.

I'm wolfish.

What the trapper said when he was hungry.

incline

A passageway into a mine or between mine workings that is neither horizontal nor vertical.

incline drift

In mining, a drift run at an incline to subserve the drainage. A misnomer applied to a slope sunk upon a deposit having a slight departure from the horizontal.

Indian affairs

Matters relating to Indians; the phrase occurs in the names of governmental bodies or the titles of officials dealing with Indian matters, as the Bureau of Indian Affairs, the Commissioner of Indian Affairs.

Indian agency

The office of an Indian agent or the headquarters of such an agent.

Indian annuity

An annual payment made to Indians by the United States government.

Indian bread

A tasty strip of fatty matter extending from the shoulder blade backward along the backbone of a buffalo. When seared in hot grease and then smoked, it became a tidbit the buffalo hunter used for bread. When eaten with lean or dried meat, it made an excellent sandwich. Also, bread made of Indian corn meal.

Indian-broke

Said of a horse trained to allow the rider to mount from the right, or off, side, instead of the left, or near, side.

Indian Bureau

One of several names given to the Bureau of Indian Affairs.

Indian claim

A claim of ownership made by Indians to a piece of land. The right to a piece of land acquired or alleged to have been acquired from Indians.

Indian coffee

Coffee served to an Indian who came to a cow camp begging for food. Some water was added to the old grounds in the coffee-pot, and the pot was set on the fire to boil. Such coffee was resented by the cowman but was held to be good enough for an Indian.

Indian council

A council or legislative assembly of Indians.

Indian deading

A steamboatman's term for a deserted Indian camp containing cottonwood trees the Indians had cut down for the smaller branches, which they fed to their horses during heavy snow in winter. The dead trees made excellent fuel for the steamboats because they were dry and seasoned.

Indian Department

The Bureau of Indian Affairs, the department or office of the federal government having to do with Indians.

Indian doctor

An Indian medicine man. A white man who followed the Indian's methods of healing.

Indian factor system

A system of government-owned and operated stores set up among the Indians where they could buy and sell goods at advantageous prices. The system was intended to protect the Indians from exploitation and secure their friendship.

Indian file

Single file, the manner in which Indians traveled through the woods.

Indian goods

Goods used in trading with the Indians, often merely beads and other trinkets.

Indian haircut

A scalping. One haircut the white man tried to avoid.

Indian hatchet

A tomahawk.

Indian list

A cowman's term for a blacklist.

Indian medicine

A plant or plants such as Indians used in their medications. *To make medicine* meant *to hold a meeting.*

Indian moccasin

Soft shoes, usually made of softened buckskin and decorated with beads, worn by Indians.

Indian nation

A group of related Indian tribes, such as the Sioux.

Indian office

A federal office through which transactions with the Indians were carried out.

Indian payment

Payment in money or goods made by the federal government to Indians.

Indian poker

An informal game of poker played on a blanket spread upon the ground, around which gather all the hands who want to take out a small stake.

Indian pony

A name the old-timers of the Southwest gave a paint or pinto horse, which was a favorite among the Indians.

Indian powwow

A noisy frolic. A conference.

Indian razor

Originally a pair of clam shells with which Indians pulled out their beards, later a metal device for this purpose was supplied by traders.

Indian reservation

An area of land set apart by the federal government for the occupancy of Indians.

Indian ring

A group of politicians, contractors, etc., who connived to rob Indians of annuities paid them by the government.

INDIANS

See bad Indian, gut eater, hair lifter, half-breed, heap big chief, mansito, 'Pache, redskin, scalping party, scalp lifter, siwash.

Indian saddle

A somewhat crude form of saddle used by the Plains Indian.

Indian scout

An Indian serving as a scout for the American Army. A white man who served as a scout against the Indians.

Indian service

Missionary service among the Indians. Agents or soldiers in the service of the Bureau of Indian Affairs.

Indian shoeing

A method of horseshoeing in which the entire hoof was covered with a piece of rawhide fastened with thongs. When dry, the rawhide formed to the foot and made a tough, lasting foot protection.

Indian side of a horse

The right side of a horse; so called because the Indian mounted from that side, whereas the white man mounts from the left.

Indian sign

Tracks or other indications that Indians had been in the neighborhood. A curse or hex, as *to put the Indian sign* on someone.

Indian signboard

The bleached shoulder bone of a buffalo commonly seen on the plains in the early days. Indians often painted messages upon the bones.

Indian trade

Trade or dealings with Indians.

Indian up

To approach without noise; to sneak up.

Indian whisky

A cheap whisky sold to the Indians by early traders. Teddy Blue Abbott, who claims the whisky was invented by Missouri River traders, gives the following recipe for making it: "Take one barrel of Missouri River water, and two gallons of alcohol. Then you add two ounces of strychnine to make them crazy—because strychnine is the greatest stimulant in the world—three bars of tobacco to make them sick—because an Indian wouldn't figure it was whisky unless it made him sick—five bars of soap to give it a bead, and half-pound of red pepper, and then you put some sage brush and boil it until it's brown. Strain this into a barrel and you've got your Indian whisky." (E. C. Abbott and Helena Huntington Smith, *We Pointed Them North* [New York, Farrar & Rinehart, 1939], 145.)

indications

In mining, signs of the presence of gold or other metals.

individual

What the cowboy calls his privately owned horse.

in hock

See *hock*.

ink

A cowboy's term for a Negro.

inkslinger

A logger's name for the bookkeeper.

inner circle

The shorter, or inside, circle on roundup, usually ridden by men whose horses had not yet become hardened to cow work.

INNS

See posada.

in place

In mining, a vein or lode enclosed on both sides by fixed and immovable rock.

INSECTS

See buffalo gnat, buffalo mange, cattle grubs, heel fly, no-see-ums, pants rats, seam squirrels, vinegaroon, warbles, wolf.

inside

In steamboating, to go between a snag and the shore. In gambling, participation in a game as a member of the staff of a gambling house, as distinguished from participation as an independent player.

inside corner

In faro, a type of bet taking in three cards; so called because the check is placed on the "inside corner" of any card, thus indicating the other two cards in the layout to be included.

intake

In mining, the passage through which the ventilating current enters a mine.

integrated logging

A method of logging designed to make the best use of all timber products. It removes in one cutting all timber that should be cut and distributes the various timber products to the industries that can use them to the best advantage.

in the brush

On the dodge. Early lawbreakers kept many a sheriff "ridin' the hocks off his horse." Frequently pursuer and pursued got close enough together to "swap lead and then have another hoss race." A logger's phrase meaning *in the woods*; working in the timber.

in the chips

To have a lot of money, a reference to gambling chips.

in the shade of the wagon
A cowboy's expression for taking life easy.

Irish baby buggy
A logger's and miner's name for a wheelbarrow.

IRISHMEN
See harp.

iron
Short for *branding iron*. A six gun.

iron burner
A logger's name for a blacksmith.

ironed by a blacksmith
Shackled with leg irons. In frontier days criminals were shackled with leg irons by a blacksmith.

iron hat
In mining, the outcrop of a lode, usually colored by the decomposition of the iron.

ironing him out
See *ironing out the humps*.

ironing out the humps
Taking the rough edges off a bucking horse. Also called *ironing him out*. This duty became routine on roundup when fresh horses were saddled, especially in cool weather. On one particular roundup when the horses were unusually snuffy and the riders were being thrown in all directions, one cowboy quietly observed that these riders were "fallin' off like wormy apples in a high wind." My observations of the cowboy are that, no matter what the circumstances, he always has a comparison both witty and fitting.

ironing the calf crop
Branding the season's calves.

iron man
The man handling the branding irons at branding time.

iron mule
A logger's name for the donkey engine. In mining, a small dump cart with caterpillar drive.

iron tender
The man who heats and tends the branding irons.

IRRIGATION
See acequia, canal, corrugate, ditch rider, fill, head, laterals, pothole, riding the ditch, zanja, zanjero.

island
In freighting, a spot of ground where the freighter would unhitch and go back for his trailer when he was doubling over a hill or other hard place.

issue cattle
Cattle issued by the government to reservation Indians.

ITALIANS
See quinnie.

ivories
A cowboy's name for poker chips. A gambler's name for dice.

J

"The wilder the colt, the better the hoss"

jacal
A hut; a rude habitation; a hovel; pronounced hah-cal'; from the Spanish, meaning *Indian hut*.

jack
A male ass; a logger, or any man of the woods.

jack a maverick

To brand a maverick. The owner of a large herd of cattle considers it his privilege to brand any maverick he finds with his cattle or near his ranch.

jackass

A logger's name for a donkey engine.

jackass mail

A name given the early mail lines which used mules to carry mail over the rough mountains. Also a name given the San Antonio and San Diego Mail Line because of its irregularity and its uselessness to Californians anxiously awaiting their mail. In their opinion it took a jackass to conceive such a route.

jacketing

Skinning a dead lamb and placing its pelt upon the body of an orphan so that the mother of the dead lamb will nurse it. Ewes recognize their offspring by smell and refuse to nurse lambs not their own.

jackhammer

A type of rock drill used by miners.

jack-head pit

A small shaft sunk within a mine.

jackknifing

Said of a horse that is clipping his front and hind legs together, sometimes as part of a straight buck. In mining, a collapsing of square-set timbers from wall pressure or because of imperfect erection.

Jack Mormon

A man who lived among the Mormons, followed their ways of life, but never joined their church.

jack-pine savage

A cowboy's name for a man from the timber country.

jackpot

A cowboy expression signifying either a general smashup or a perplexing situation. In logging, an unskilled piece of logging work; a bad slash. To pile trees or logs crisscross without regard for orderliness. In rodeo, an event for which no purse is put up by the rodeo and winners split all or part of the entry fee. In poker, a pool when some player has a hand containing a pair of jacks or better. A game in which such a pot is used. A deal in which everybody antes.

jack-roll

A logger's term for robbing a man who is helplessly drunk.

Jackson fork

A large steel fork operated by horses or by pulleys and used to move quantities of loose hay; used on latter-day ranches.

jack staff

In steamboating, the staff on the bowsprit or fore part of a vessel on which the union jack is flown.

jack stripper

In gambling, a jack trimmed for the purpose of cheating.

jack train

A name occasionally given to a pack train of mules.

jag

A small load, usually of hay. *To get on a jag* means *to get drunk*.

jaggers

What the logger calls the frayed, ragged strands that break in a wire rope. The strands are especially troublesome to the choker setter.

Jail

See prison.

jakoma

A cowboy's name for a *hackamore, q.v.*

jam

An immovable mass of logs blockading a stream.

jamb

In mining, a vein or bed of earth or stone which prevents the miners from following a vein of ore.

jamboree

A word for anything from a dance or a drinking party to a gun fight or a stampede. (Philip A. Rollins, *The Cowboy* [New York, Charles Scribner's Sons, 1936], 77.)

jamb pike
A pike used by loggers in driving logs down a stream; also called *driving pike*.

jammer
In logging, a steam engine for loading logs on cars; a western pine-country term.

jamming the breeze
A cowboy expression meaning *going at full speed*.

jamoka
A cowboy's name for coffee; formed by combining *java* and *mocha*.

jap
A miner's name for an excavating drill.

javelina
A musk hog, native to the brush country, said to "look like a ball of hair with a butcher knife run through it."

jawbone
What the cowman calls credit. A cowhand who lives on his credit until next payday is said to *live on his jawbone*.

jaw cracker
What the cowboy called a traveling dentist who went through the country to relieve cowboys of their pain, teeth, and money.

jaw crusher
In mining, an ore-crushing machine.

jay-bird stallion
A scrub stallion.

jay country
What the cowboy calls a farming region.

Jehu
A common name for the driver of a stagecoach.

jennet
In the cowman's language, a small Spanish mare.

jenny
A female ass.

jerga
A heavy woolen fabric woven in varying degrees of thickness and used for floor covering; sometimes carried by the early traders.

jerk
What the logger calls a punk.

jerk-away horse
A horse that has acquired the habit of jerking away from his handler. This is a bad trait, and the trainer usually rigs up an outfit of rope and ring to break the horse of it.

jerked down
Said of a horse that has been pulled to the ground by a roped steer.

jerking
A method of curing meat accomplished by stripping the hams of the animal in a manner that left a thin membrane covering each piece and cutting other parts into slices about an inch thick, dipping them for a moment in strong boiling brine, smoking them briefly, and completing the curing process by exposure to the sun. Those who have never enjoyed a well-cured piece of jerked venison can have little conception of how palatable it is. With a pocketful of this food, a hunter could travel all day without becoming hungry. It was very sustaining against fatigue.

jerk line
"A single, continuous rein, starting from its fastening at the top of the brake handle, extending to and through the hand of the driver, who either was astride the wheel horse (the near one, if two) or was seated on the wagon's front. The line continued thence along the long file of horses' backs and to the left side of the lead animal's bit, without touching the bit of any intermediate brute. A single, steady pull on the line guided this lead animal to the left. Two or more short jerks turned it to the right." (Philip A. Rollins, *The Cowboy* [New York, Charles Scribner's Sons, 1936], 195.)

jerk-line string

A string of horses or mules harnessed in single file or in a series of spans, following a well-trained leader controlled by a *jerk line, q.v.*

jerk-neck team

In freighting, a team of horses or mules pulling a wagon and leading a second team and wagon from the tail of the first. The rear endgate of the first wagon was protected from the tongue of the following one by a bump board. When oxen were used, they were hitched to the leading wagon, and short-tongued wagons were hooked behind it.

jerk wire

In logging, a wire attached to the whistle on a yarding donkey, by which the whistle punk or jerk blows starting and stopping signals.

jerky

Dried beef (see *jerking*). The Spanish and the Indians first dried buffalo meat by cutting it thin and drying it in the sun. When dry, it could be ground up like meal. When cooked in a soup, it swelled to considerable proportions and served as a nourishing food. Later the white man followed their example, and jerky became a staple food. From the Spanish *charqui* (charque). Also, a wagon with boards for seats or a wagon without springs.

jerry gang

A logger's name for a crew of railroad tracklayers.

jewelry chest

An outside box on the front of the chuck wagon in which were stored hobbles, extra cartridges, and anything else that might be needed in a hurry in an emergency.

jig

A miner's name for a machine that concentrates ore by means of sieves.

jigger

To overrun a horse.

jiggle

The ordinary gait of a cow horse, averaging about five miles an hour. To ride at such a gait.

jig juice

A freighter's name for whisky. Also called *jig water*.

jig water

See *jig juice*.

jill poke

In logging, a lever used to dump logs from flatcars into a mill pond.

Jim Crow

What the logger calls a small, unusable crosstie.

Jim Hill

A railroad spike used in the woods to hold heavy lines in place while spiking, named for the builder of the Great Northern Railway.

Jim Hill mustard

Wild mustard, discovered in the early nineties, when Jim Hill built the Great Northern Railroad to Seattle. It dries and blows, forming a tumbleweed as common as the Russian thistle. The term is used exclusively in the Northwest.

jinete

In the cattle country, a bronc buster, or a man who is an excellent rider; from the Spanish.

jinglebob

An earmark formed by cutting a deep slit that leaves the lower half of the ear flapping down, one of the most hideous earmarks ever devised. It was made famous by John Chisum, a pioneer rancher of Lincoln County, New Mexico. Also, *danglers, q.v.*

jingler

A horse wrangler.

Jingle your spurs!

A cowboy's command to someone to get a move on, or hurry up.

jingling

A wrangler's term for rounding up the horse band.

jobber

A logging contractor or subcontractor.

job hog

In logging, a man who takes another man's job away from him; a man who is overly eager to get work.

Job's comforter

A cowman's name for a boil.

job shark

A logger's name for an employment agent.

job-simple

A logger's term for a worker who fears losing his job and also for a stupid person.

jockey

A name occasionally given to a sheepherder.

jockey-box

A box beneath the driver's seat in a wagon in which small articles were carried. The driver often picked up small rocks and threw them into his jockey box for ammunition with which to pelt his charges over a hard pull.

jockey stick

In freighting, a hickory stick, about five feet long, somewhat like a rake handle, stretched between a pilot mule or horse and its mate.

John B.

A cowboy's hat, named for its maker, John B. Stetson. The cowman takes pride in the age of his Stetson. As one writer said, "A Stetson will take on weight with age and get to the point where you can smell it across the room, but you can't wear it out." The big Stetson is just as much a part of the cowboy as his hands and feet. See also *Stetson*.

John Chinaman

What a cowboy calls boiled rice.

John Henry

What a cowboy calls his signature. He never "signs" a document, but "puts his *John Henry* to it."

John Law

A frontier name for a law officer.

Johnny-come-lately

A tenderfoot; someone new to the country.

Johnny Hicks

In dice, to throw a six.

Johnny Newcomer

A logger's title for someone new on the job.

Jones' place

A cowboy's name for a line camp. A privy. A name sometimes given to a honky-tonk.

jornada

What the trapper and the freighter called a day's journey or march; from the Spanish.

jornada del muerto

A section of country without water; from the Spanish, meaning *journey of death*.

Joshua tree

A yucca of the southwestern desert region.

J split

An earmark formed of cuts made with the bottom generally curved to the left.

Judas steer

A steer used at slaughterhouses, trained to lead other cattle to slaughter.

judge

In mining, a type of measuring instrument. In rodeo, an official, usually a cowman, who scores the riding events and flags roping events. In roping events he signals the completion of the tie to the timekeepers and passes on the legality and firmness of the tie before the roper's time is recorded. In the steer-wrestling event he determines if and when the steer has been properly thrown and signals the timekeepers. In the riding events he scores both the animal and the contestant.

juggling

In trick roping, a body spin in which the roper repeatedly raises and lowers the noose from the ground to the limit of his reach above his head.

jug handle

A mark of ownership made by cutting a long slash in the skin of the brisket of cattle, not cutting out either end; when healed, the mark looks like the handle of a jug.

jughead

A horse which lacks intelligence and has to be pulled around considerably before he is made to understand what is wanted of him.

jump

To come upon suddenly, as, "He *jumped* a brand burner at the edge of the range." To take possession unlawfully, as, to *jump* a claim. To relocate abandoned property.

jumper

One who appropriates a claim (see *jump*). A laborer who rides on a company ticket and leaves the train before reaching the job for which he was hired; also called *jumper toter*.

jumper toter

See *jumper*.

jump the cut

In gambling, to manipulate the cut of the cards to the advantage of the dealer.

jump up dust

A cowboy's expression meaning *to leave in a hurry*.

juniper

The western equivalent of *hayseed*.

junin' 'round

A cowboy's expression meaning *restless*.

junta

A cowman's term for a business meeting; from the Spanish.

jusgado

See *hoosegow*.

just a ball of hair

A very thin cow or calf.

Justins

As any cowman knows, a name synonymous with good cowboy boots. From the day in 1879 when Joe Justin settled at Old Spanish Fort on the Texas side of Red River and made his first pair of boots, down through the years to the present modern factory in Ft. Worth, Texas, Justins have set the style in cowboy boots. A few men have left their names to enrich permanently the vocabulary of the westerner through the excellence and popularity of a necessary product. Among these are Colt, Stetson, Levi, and Justin.

K

"Kickin' never gets you nowhere, 'less'n you're a mule"

kack

A saddle.

kack biscuit

A cowboy's name for a saddle sore.

kafir-corner

A settler who raised kafir; hence a farmer, settler, or nester.

kangaroo card

In faro, a system of betting the first card. The player bets his money on the card which, added to the *soda card (q.v.)* will total eleven. Thus if the soda card is four, the player *bets the kangaroo card*, or bets that the card will be seven.

KANSANS

See sand cutter.

Kansas City fish

What the cowboy calls fried side pork.

Kansas neck blister

A bowie knife.

Kansas-wintered

Said of cattle that were driven from Texas or Oklahoma and kept in Kansas over the winter before being sold.

keelboat

A western river boat used by explorers, military commanders, and other river travelers before the days of the steamboat; so called because on the bottom of the boat was a heavy timber, or keel, about 4 inches wide and equally thick which extended from bow to stern. The timber was so placed to take the shock of a collision with any submerged obstruction. The boat was 60 to 70 feet long; it had a 15- to 18-foot breadth of beam and a 3- to 4-foot depth of hold.

The boat carried sweeps, or oars and had a mast and sail and poles. One steersman and two men at the sweeps could navigate the boat downstream. Progress against the current was effected by wind or poling.

The keelboat also carried a heavy rope, often more than 1,000 feet long, one end of which was fastened high up on the mast. The other end of the cable extended to the shore and was used to pull, or cordell, the boat when necessary. Cordelling a keelboat along average stretches of the river was very difficult work. Often there was no established towpath, and the changing conditions of the river prevented the development of one except along a few stable stretches. In places where it was impossible to walk and work at the same time, a few men would carry the end of the line beyond the obstruction and make it fast, while the other crewmen would get on board and pull the boat by drawing in the line. This operation was called *warping*.

When the boat was being cordelled, a crewman, called in French a *bosseman* (boatswain's mate), stood at the bow, near where the bridle was attached; it was his duty to watch for snags and other obstructions and to help steer the boat by holding it off the bank with a pole. He had to have great strength, the ability to make prompt decisions, and a thorough knowledge of the river. The master of the boat stood at the rudder, which was manipulated by means of a long lever from the rear end of the cargo box. From this elevated position he could see everything.

In propelling a keelboat by pole, eight or ten men ranged themselves along each side, near the bow, facing aft, each one grasping the pole, one in front of the other, as close together as they could walk. At the captain's command "Down with the poles," the men would thrust the lower ends into the water close to the boat and place the ball ends against their shoulders, so that the poles would be well inclined downstream. All the men would push together, forcing the boat ahead, as they walked along the cleated boards toward the stern, until the foremost man had gone as far as he could. The captain then ordered them to raise the poles, and they walked quickly back to the bow to repeat the operation. The steering was done while the poles were up.

keelboatman

A keelboat operator or crewman.

keener

A trapper's and trader's name for a man who was a good shot.

keep cases

In faro, to keep a record of the cards as they are drawn from the faro box. The expression became synonymous with the word *watch*; therefore, *to keep cases* on someone is to watch him.

keeping up the corners

In the old trail days, keeping the stronger cattle in the herd moving in such a way as not to impede the progress of the others, seeing that the rear of the column was no wider than the *swing*—that part of the column between the leaders and the drags—to prevent the cattle from becoming overheated, and seeing that the herd did not become spaced out so that the marching column became too long.

keep tabs

In gambling, to make a record of cards as they won or lost.

keep your eyes skinned

An expression used by most western men meaning *to watch carefully*.

keep your moccasins greased

Originally, a trapper's and hunter's expression meaning *to step softly when stalking game*; later adopted by the cowman and used to mean *to go easy*.

Kelley's

Hand-forged bits and spurs made by P. M. Kelley and Sons, of El Paso, Texas. As a school boy in Childress, Texas, the elder Kelley spent his spare time at ranch headquarters listening to the cowboy's criticisms of the bits and spurs then in vogue, and determined to make some which would be "just right."

With limited tools and the aid of a younger sister, he began making these riding tools by hand, selling them direct to the cowboys as fast as he could make them. From this start his business grew until his name became synonymous with good bits and spurs throughout the cattle country.

kennebecker

A logger's name for any kind of knapsack.

keno

A cowman's word meaning that everything is all right. The satisfactory conclusion of any act might evoke the exclamation, "Keno!" From the gambling game.

An old English gambling game, called *lotto*, which became known as *keno* in the United States. It is a percentage game with little betting. It is played with a large globe, called the *keno goose*, ninety small ivory balls numbered from one to ninety, and lotto cards, which are sold to the players at a price fixed by the operator of the game.

After the lotto cards have been distributed, the roller releases the ivory balls one by one from the neck of the keno goose. The number on each ball is called off as it appears, and any player finding such a number on his card covers it with a button. The first player to cover a row of five numbers calls, "Keno!" and wins all the money that has been paid for the cards, minus the operator's take of 10 to 15 per cent. It is an easy matter to cheat at this game, for the roller can palm the balls as they come from the goose and substitute others which match cards already handed out to cappers.

keno goose

In keno, the large globe from which the numbered balls are taken. See *keno*.

kept his brandin' iron smooth

Said of a rustler who worked overtime. The expression originated from the fact that a branding iron must be smooth and free of rust and scale to give satisfaction.

kept the double doors swingin'

Said of a habitué of the saloons.

ketch colt

An offspring obviously not of the herd sire.

ketch dog

A dog trained to catch cattle by the nose and hold or throw them until they could be tied, or to worry a steer until a puncher could get to the steer with his rope.

ketch hand

A cowhand whose duty it is to rope calves for branding.

Ketch my saddle!

The sure cry of a cowboy who has been thrown and whose mount is running away with his saddle. The horse may belong to the company, but the saddle is his private and highly prized property.

ketch rope

What a cowboy calls his lariat, to distinguish it from other ropes.

kettle-bellied

A cowboy's expression for a pot-gutted person or animal.

kettling

Bucking.

key split

One of several earmarks resembling cotter keys of different shapes.

kibble

A miner's hoisting bucket.

kick-back rider

A rider who while riding a bucking horse spurs high behind. He often comes to grief, because in spurring too high he loses his knee grip.

kicked into a funeral procession

Said of one killed by a kicking horse.

KICKING

See bucking, let out, running.

kick like a bay steer

A common Texas saying meaning *to kick vigorously* or *to complain bitterly*. The cowhand rarely complains, for it is his philosophy that "kickin' never gets you nowhere, 'less'n you're a mule."

kick the frost out

To unlimber a horse.

kick the lid off

To start bucking. To start any violent action.

kidney pad

A contemptuous name the cowboy gave the little riding saddle used by an easterner; also called *kidney plaster*.

kidney shot

A shot that strikes an animal in the region of the kidneys.

KILL

See bed him down, blow out his lamp, curl him up, curl his tail, 'dobe wall, downed, dry-gulch, got a halo gratis, Green River, kicked into a funeral procession, land in a shallow grave, made wolf meat, man for breakfast, Pecos, salivate, sarve up brown, sawdust in his beard, strapped on his horse toes down, wipe out.

killer

A vicious horse. A bad man; most of the professional gunmen were looked upon as killers because their guns were for hire.

killickinnic

See *kinnikinnick*.

killpecker guard

In many sections of the cattle country, the period of cattle herding from sundown until 8:00 P.M.

king pin

A logger's name for any kind of boss, the name being derived from the heavy bolt that holds the front gear of a wagon together.

king snipe

In logging, a name for the boss of the bridgebuilders, the boss of a track-laying crew, or the foreman in charge of logging-railroad maintenance.

kinnikinnick

A mixture of dried sumac leaves, the inner bark of red osier dogwood, and sometimes tobacco which the Indians smoked. It emits a delightful odor. Also called *killickinnic*.

kip pile

A buffalo skinner's term for a pile of buffalo hides. The skinners sorted and graded hides into different piles, the bulls in one pile, the cows in another, and the younger animals in the *kip pile*.

kissed the ground

Thrown from a horse.

kitchen bitch

A logger's name for a lamp made by placing a wick and tallow in a tin can.

kitchen mechanic

A logger's name for the camp cook.

kitchen mule

The mule upon which the commissary was packed when the packers were ready to move out.

kitchen strap

The flank strap on a saddle.

kitchen string

The work horses used for the chuck wagon.

kitchen wagon

A name sometimes used by freighters for the chuck wagon.

kitty

In gambling, a certain part of a pool set apart for the payment of the expenses of the game.

kiva

The central building of the pueblo where

Pueblo Indian ceremonies were held and the tribal council met.

KNAPSACKS

See cantina, kennebecker, sack, traveling bag.

knee grip

The clamping of a rider's knees against a horse when riding. This practice is important in riding a bad horse, but the rider cannot maintain his balance by knee grip alone. The feet should be braced forward and out against the stirrups, to catch the rider's weight when the horse lands, thus enabling the rider to balance for the next jump.

kneeing

Splitting the hide of a wild steer about an inch and a half between the knee and ankle on one foreleg and cutting a small tendon or leader. When the steer is turned loose, he can walk, but his running days are over.

knees

In logging, devices used to move a log into place on a saw carriage.

knight of the ribbons

A stagecoach driver.

KNIVES

See Arkansas toothpick, bowie knife, Green River, hay knife, Kansas neck blister, weapons and ammunition.

knobhead

A mule.

knock his ears down

A logger's expression meaning *to thrash a person.*

Knock up stakes!

A freighter's command to pull up hitching stakes at a camp and get ready to move on.

knothead

A cowboy who never attains skill in his work. An unintelligent horse.

knowledge box

A logger's name for a schoolhouse.

knows how to die standin' up

Said of a courageous man, one unafraid in a fight.

kyack

A packsaddle. Kyacks are hollow containers, one on each side of the horse, each of sufficient capacity to hold the equivalent of two 5-gallon cans placed side by side.

L

"A loose hoss is always lookin' for new pastures"

labor

In steamboating, to vibrate excessively as a result of running in shallow water; particularly characteristic of stern-wheelers.

labor shark

A logger's name for an employment agent.

laced his tree up

A cowboy's expression meaning that he has saddled his horse. I remember Octillo Crane's telling me of his trying to ride a particularly vicious horse. He described the attempt in this manner: "I had trouble gettin' my wood on 'im, and when I did get my tree laced up, it didn't do me much good, 'cause I didn't get settled 'fore I goes sailin' off, flyin' low and usin' my face for a rough lock till I'd lost 'nough hide to make a pair of leggin's."

ladino

An outlaw cow of the brush country. The

term is often applied to any vicious animal. From the Spanish, meaning *crafty* or *sagacious*.

lady-broke

Said of a horse that has been thoroughly gentled.

lagging

In mining, poles or boards used for spans from one stud piece to another, designed not to carry the main weight but to form a ceiling or a wall to prevent fragments of rocks from falling through.

lair

In packing, the rope used in securing pack covers, or mantas, around the pack. The rope was about 30 feet long and ⅜ inch thick, of the best handlaid Manila. At one end an eye or loop was tied; the free end, well sized, or wrapped, was passed through the eye and tied fast. Also called *lair rope*. To *lair* or *lair up* was to secure the pack cover to the pack by means of the lair.

lair rope

See *lair*.

lamber

In sheep raising, a man who tends ewes and lambs during lambing season; also called *nursemaids*.

lambing season

The spring of the year, when the ewes begin to drop their lambs.

lamb licker

A cowboy's name for a sheepherder, so called from the ewe's habit of licking her newborn lamb.

lame pen

A pasture on a ranch where crippled animals are kept.

lamp oil

A cowboy's term for whisky.

Lamps

See bitch, bug torch, Cousin Jack Lantern, gad hunter, happy jack, headlight, kitchen bitch, mine rescue lamp, miner's friend, miner's lamp, pit lamp.

landed

Thrown from a horse.

landed forked end up

Thrown from a horse headfirst.

landed on his sombrero

Thrown from a horse headfirst.

land in a shallow grave

To be killed and buried without ceremony, as out on the plains far from any settlement where graves could be dug properly. Many cowboys whose deaths were caused by stampedes, lightning, drowning, gun fights, or falling horses were buried thus.

landing

In logging, a place where logs are assembled to be loaded or to be rolled into a river. In steamboating, a place where steamboats stopped to be loaded or unloaded.

land looker

See *cruiser*.

laneing

Herding cattle in such a way that they cannot be turned. An untrained helper gets on the side of the cattle opposite another hand to assist him in turning them. The two men thus form a lane which keeps the animals from turning. A man of experience comes up from behind and on the same side as the person he is assisting. (Duff Green to R.F.A.)

lank inside

A logger's expression meaning that he is hungry.

lap

In logging, the tops of trees left on the ground after the woods have been logged.

lap and tap

In rodeo, a start that occurs when the calf or steer is released from the chute without a head start on the roper or steer wrestler. Lap-and-tap starts are most frequently seen in indoor arenas where there is not room to give the stock a long score.

lariat

A rope used in picketing or lassoing animals, especially one made of horsehair, though it may also be made of hemp or rawhide. From the Spanish *la reata*, meaning *rope to tie horses in single file*. The word is often used in the Southwest, where *reata* or *riata* may also be heard. The word *rope* is used in the Northwest. *To lariat* means *to fasten* or *to catch* with a lariat. *Reata* is never used as a verb. Californians do not like the word *lariat*—they use either *reata* or *lass rope*.

larripy dope

A cowboy's name for any kind of sirup.

larrup

A cowboy's name for molasses. To strike; to thrash.

larrupin' truck

A cowboy's term for anything he considers "great stuff."

larry

A miner's name for a small truck used to push cars up a slope.

lasher

A man who assisted the driver of a string team by using the whip, handling the brakes, and helping with the swearing.

lash rope

A rope used to fasten packs on a pack-saddle.

lash rope with cincha and hook

A rope about 50 feet long, 9/16 or 1/2-inch thick, of the best handlaid Manila. At one end it had an eye or loop to receive the lacing of the cinch. The other end was well sized, or wrapped, to prevent unraveling.

lasso

A long rope, usually made of hide, with a running noose. Though Mexicans introduced this name to the cow range, the word comes from the Portuguese *laco*, meaning *snare*. To rope by means of a lasso. Stockmen of the Pacific Coast are the only ones using *lasso* to any extent; the southwestern cowmen prefer *rope*.

lass rope

A rope; used especially in the Northwest.

last roundup

A cowboy's reference to death.

last turn

In faro, the last three cards in the dealer's box, the two having action and the *hock card*, which is dead. Also, a confidence game based on faro.

last year's bronc

A horse in his second season of work.

laterals

The network of smaller ditches in an irrigation system.

latigo

A long leather strap used to fasten a saddle on a horse. The strap is passed successively through the cinch ring and the rigging ring and tied much in the manner of a four-in-hand tie.

Lave ho! Lave!

A command used by mountain men to wake others from sleep; apparently a corruption of the Spanish *levantor*, meaning *to rouse*.

lawdog

A cowman's name for a sheriff or a deputy sheriff.

law wrangler

A name frequently used by the cowman for a lawyer. The average cowman has little use for lawyers, although he admires their learning. One cowhand referred to a certain attorney as "the smartest lawgiver since Moses."

LAWYERS

See law wrangler.

lax

A logger's term meaning *to loosen*; to have the effect of a laxative.

lay

A chance throw with a rope. A cowboy's bed. A cattle ranch or outfit.

lay 'em down

Said when a cowman dies. Said when a gambler lays his cards on the table in a poker game.

lay for

To lie in wait for; to ambush.

layin' down his character

Said of one playing a deuce in a card game. I heard one cowhand telling another about a game in which he quit loser, and he finished by saying, "I tried all night to get somethin' higher than a two-spot." Another loser said that when he started the game he had " 'nough money to be called 'mister,' but the trouble was I was jes' called—too many times."

laying a rail fence

Said when a horse is pitching *fence-cornered,* or jumps first in one direction and then in another.

laying the trip

A phrase describing a method of roping in which the rider ropes a steer by the horns, flips the rope around the steer's rump, and angles his horse to the left, the rope thus becoming taut around his right hipbone. In this manner the steer is *busted,* or *bedded down.* The rider's weight is in the left stirrup to counterbalance the impact of the steer, and his right foot is out of the stirrup so that he is ready to dismount and tie the steer down.

layout

A ranch, its employees, and equipment. A cowboy's personal equipment. In faro, a suit of thirteen spades, pasted or painted on a board, cloth, or table top. Other suits are rarely used.

layover

In cattle driving, a voluntary halt at a ranch or a town. See *lay-up.*

lay the dust

A cowboy's expression meaning *to take a drink.* An expression used in describing a light sprinkle of rain.

lay-up

In cattle driving, a compulsory halt. See *layover.*

Lazy

See loafing.

lazy brand

A brand in which a letter or figure is lying on its side.

lazy pen

A pasture in which weak cattle are kept.

leaching

In mining, the slow dissolving of the soluble constituents of an ore by water or solutions that percolate through it. Natural leaching often takes place in the upper portions of ore bodies. Artificial leaching in tanks, by solutions of sulphuric acid and various sulphates, is used in the recovery of copper from certain ores.

lead chucker

A cowboy's name for his six gun.

lead drive men

Men who because of their knowledge of of the country are chosen to make the circle drive on roundup. While other riders drop off at intervals to comb a given territory for cattle, the lead men ride on to complete the circle and drive in the cattle from the farthest edges.

leaded

A cowboy's word meaning *shot.* Said of a miner who has lead poisoning.

leaders

In freighting, animals placed in the lead of the other teams. The leaders were always the lighter-weight animals and the best broken to respond to the spoken commands of the driver.

lead line

In river boating, a piece of sash cord about 30 feet long to which a lead weight was attached and which was used to determine the depth of the water; pronounced *led.* The lead line was used mostly on the Mississippi River (a *sounding pole* was generally used on the Ohio River). The cord was marked off into fathoms and fractions thereof; 1 fathom (6 feet) was termed *mark one;* 2 fathoms was *mark twain;* 3 fathoms was *mark three.* Any measure beyond *mark four* was *no bottom.* The person who took the sounding with a lead line and called them to the pilot was called the *leadsman.*

lead man

A *point rider (q.v.)* of a trail herd. At the extreme forward tip of the moving column, called the *point*, rode the two lead men, one on each side. This was the honored post of the cattle drive and the station of greatest responsibility, since it was these men who must determine the exact direction to be taken.

lead plum

A cowboy's name for a bullet.

lead-poisoned

A cowboy's term meaning *shot*.

lead pusher

A cowboy's name for his gun.

lead rope

A short rope used to lead a horse.

lead span

The lead team of a vehicle drawn by more than one team.

lead steer

In cattle driving, a steer which, by his aggressiveness and stamina, took his place at the head of the trail herd and retained his leadership to the end of the trail. He was invaluable to the drover and, as an individual, was always honored with a name. There have been many stories written about famous lead steers; for example, those written by J. Frank Dobie, J. Evetts Haley, Jack Potter, and others. These stories always move the heart of a real cowman. To him these steers were more than mere bovines.

lead team

In freighting, the team at the front when more than one team was used.

lead wagon

In freighting, the wagon to which the teams were hitched. Other wagons were hooked on behind the lead wagon. A lead wagon carried an average of 6,500 pounds.

leaky mouth

A phrase describing someone who talks too much. When two such men get together, Dick Blocker said they "jes' jabber at each other like a couple of honkers on a new feed ground."

leaned against a bullet goin' past

Said of someone who had been shot.

Lean forward and shove!

A cowboy's order to someone to get out of the way in a hurry.

leaser

A miner who works in a mine on shares instead of for wages, paying part of the proceeds from the ore he digs out to the owner of the mine as "royalty"; more properly called *lessee*.

leather pounder

A name for a cowboy.

leather pusher

A name occasionally used for a saddle maker.

leather slapper

A gunman.

leather slapping

The act of drawing a gun and shooting.

leavin' Cheyenne

A cowboy expression meaning *going away*. The expression was taken from the cowboy song "Goodbye, Old Paint, I'm Leavin' Cheyenne," a song usually used as a finale at a cowboy dance, much in the way that "Home, Sweet Home" was used in other sections of the country.

leavings

In cattle driving, a place where a trail leaves a river.

ledge

In mining, a term used on the Pacific slope for *lode, q.v.*

left side

See *near*.

leg

A professional gambler; probably a shortened form of *blackleg*. In earlier times a professional gambler was also known as a *Greek*.

leg bail

Said of a prisoner who has escaped from jail.

leggin' case

A punishment imposed by a cowboys' kangaroo court, consisting of a lashing with a pair of leggin's, or chaps.

legging

In sheep raising, a method of separating sheep, when brands have become mixed and there are no chute corrals. Each animal must be caught by the leg and separated from the other brands. This is a painful process and is cordially despised by every herder.

leggin's

What the cowboy of southwest Texas calls chaps; he rarely uses *chaps*.

leg jockey

The flat leather plate or flap overlying the stirrup leather where the stirrup leather issues from the side of the saddle; also called *seat jockey*.

leg piece

In mining, the upright timber that supports the cap piece in a mine.

length

In mining, a portion of a vein taken on a horizontal line on its course.

lenses

In mining, deposits of ore that have well-defined edges or contacts but occur in irregular lens-shaped forms instead of in tabular veins.

lent

What a cowboy calls a green hand.

lépero

An early trader's word for a thief; from the Spanish, meaning *one of the rabble*.

leppy

A cowboy's name for an orphan calf.

Let loose the powder!

A miner's order to set off an explosion.

let out

A cowboy's expression meaning *to kick*, as, a horse *lets out*.

let the hammer down

To take the rough edges off a horse.

levee

In river boating, any sloping or graded wharf. On the Mississippi River, an embankment constructed to prevent overflow during times of high water.

levee rats

A man or boy who hung around a levee.

level

In mining, a drift along a vein. All the mine workings at a certain horizontal elevation. One of the stations on the shaft from which the crosscuts are driven. These stations are numbered from top down, as, *first level, second level, third level, bottom level*. Sometimes they are indicated by the distance from the surface.

Levis

Cowboy overalls. This is perhaps the best-known first name in the West. Only a "greener" would have to be told that Levis are overalls, for Levi Strauss, of San Francisco, the pioneer overall manufacturer of the West. Since their introduction in 1850, practically all cowboys have worn them because they are stout and comfortable. They are not to be confused with the bib overalls that farmers wear. A cowboy would not be caught in a pair of those. Levis are made just like a pair of pants except that they have many copper rivets to reinforce seams and pockets. The cowboy wears them with turned-up cuffs; when he is shoeing his horse, these cuffs serve as a handy repository for extra horseshoe nails.

LIARS

See Pecos Bill, tall tales.

lick

A cowboy's name for molasses. A shortened form of *salt lick, q.v.*

lick block

A block of hard salt put out for cattle to lick.

lick it

A trader's expression meaning *to run* or *to get away*.

lick log

A tree which has been chopped down and in whose bark notches or small troughs have been cut and filled with salt so that animals can lick it. Also called *salt log*.

lick salt

A block of hard salt; also called *lick block*, *q.v.* An expression meaning *to loaf*. The expression *lick salt together* refers to close friendship or to cronies.

lid

A name a cowboy occasionally gives to his hat.

Lidgerwood

In logging, one of the three most commonly used high-line installations, the others being the North Bend and the Tyler.

lift

In mining, the space separating one *level (q.v.)* from another.

light

A cowboy's term meaning *to dismount from a horse*.

light a shuck

A cowboy's expression meaning *to leave in a hurry*. "In the early days, corn was carried as the principal food for man and beast. It was carried unshucked in the wagon beds. Selected shucks were placed at convenient places by all fires. On leaving one campfire to go to another, a man was usually blinded by the light of the fire he was just leaving. On turning his back to the fire, he found the surrounding woods pitch dark. To penetrate this blackness and give his eyes a chance to accustom themselves to it, so as not to fall over dead limbs, brush and briars, the departing guest would light the tip of one of the whole corn shucks in the fire and lift it high above his head. The bright blaze would last for a matter of only a minute or so, just enough time to get well beyond the blinding light of the fire. Consequently, when a departing guest lit his shuck, he had to leave instantly or its light would be wasted. So, 'he lit a shuck and left.'" (Frank Ryan, "On the Jefferson Road," *Texian Stomping Ground* [Austin, Texas, Folklore Publications, No. XVII, 1941], 9–10.)

lightning

A miner's name for cheap whisky.

lightning flash

A cowboy's name for cheap whisky.

lightning pilot

In steamboating, an expert pilot; this title was the highest encomium known on the river.

lightnin' stock

A trader's name for his rifle.

light rider

A rider who keeps in balance upon and with the horse and who, no matter how great his weight, can ride long distances without retightening the cinches or galling the horse's back.

lightwood

What the steamboatmen called southern pine full of resinous sap used in the *torch basket, q.v.*

Like a steer, I can try.

A cowboy saying applicable to many forms of conduct. It originated from the fact that a steer never loses his interest in the female and that when steers are brought together they will try to mount, or "ride," each other, no matter that their efforts are fruitless. (J. Frank Dobie, *The Longhorns* [Boston, Little, Brown and Company, 1941], 181.)

limber

In logging, a man who trims the limbs from trees.

limber hole

In river boating, a small notch provided in the bottom hull timbers of a wooden boat to allow drainage of water.

limb skinner

An appropriate name for a *brush hand (q.v.)*, though his limbs are the ones that get skinned.

Lincoln skins

A name given to greenbacks during stage-coaching days.

line

A cowboy's slang name for his rope. In steamboating, a rope of any type; the word *rope* is seldom used on the rivers. A mooring line is *taut* when it is tight, *slack* when it is relaxed, *stiff* when it is new and unpliable, and *limp* when it is pliable.

line-back

A cow with a stripe down its back that is of a different color from the rest of its body. See *lobo stripe*.

line breeding

The breeding of animals of the same strain. The breeding of animals with the purpose of securing descent from a particular family, especially in the female line.

line camp

An outpost cabin or dugout on a large ranch in which line riders are housed; also called *boar's nest, sign camp*.

liner

In logging, a tree exactly on the logging boundary line.

line rider

A cowhand who patrols a prescribed boundary to look after the interests of his employer. It is a hard, monotonous job, yet more interesting than riding fence, for he can ride a new route each day. While the fence rider looks primarily for breaks in the fence, the line rider looks for everything, including the condition of the watering places and the grazing lands. He pushes strays of his brand back on the range and drives off those which do not belong there. The worse the weather the more he has to ride. Drifting cattle have to be thrown back into the brakes, holes have to be chopped in frozen watering places, and weak stock have to be tended.

It is a lonely job, and the line rider works long hours. He does his own cooking and has no one to talk to except his horses. He has no cheerful campfire to get up by on cold mornings, and he will smell no appetizing odors of fried meat and coffee until he builds a fire on the cold ashes of his little cookstove and cooks for himself. Sometimes two men are placed in the *line camp (q.v.)*, and although they spend the day riding in opposite directions, the job is not so lonely because they can keep each other company at night.

Perhaps the thing uppermost in the thoughts of this rider is the day when he can return to headquarters and hear a real cook yell, "Come an' get it!" (J. Frank Dobie, *Vaquero of the Brush Country* [Dallas, Southwest Press, 1929], 149–50; John M. Hendrix, "Batchin' Camp," *Cattleman*, Vol. XX, No. 2 [July 1934], 5.)

liner machine

In mining, the large rock drill mounted on columns which can be raised or lowered along a wall and thus placed in position to drive drifts.

lines

What the logger calls cables.

lining his flue

A cowboy's expression meaning *eating*.

line up

In packing, to lead the pack mules to position at the rear of the rigging on the proper flank of the *bell horse, q.v.*

linked vein

In mining, a steplike vein in which the ore follows one fissure for a short distance, then passes by a cross fissure to another nearly parallel, and so on.

lint-back

A cowboy's name for a cotton picker.

Liquor

See aqua ardiente, aguardiente, awerdenty, base burner, boilermaker and his helper, brave maker, Brigham Young cocktail, bug juice, bumblebee whisky, choc, coffin varnish, conversation fluid, corn, cowboy cocktail, dehorn, dust cutter, dynamite, educated thirst, firewater, forty rod, gut warmer, honeydew, Indian whisky, jig juice, lamp oil, lightning, lightning flash, mescal, mountain dew, neck oil, nose paint, pair of overalls, Pass brandy, Pass whisky, pine top, pop skull, prairie dew, red disturbance, redeye, red ink, salteur liquor, scamper juice, scorpion Bible, sheepherder's delight, shinny, snake-head whisky, snake poison, stagger soup, station drink, strong water, strychnine, tanglefoot,

Taos lightning, tarantula juice, tequila, tiswin, tonsil paint, tonsil varnish, tornado juice, trade whisky, valley ten, white mule, wild mare's milk.

little cat

In poker, a hand with an eight high, a three low and no pair.

little Dick

In dice, four as a point; also called *little Joe, little Joe from Baltimore*, and *little Joe from Kokomo*.

little dog

In poker, a hand with a seven high, a deuce low, and no pair.

little feller

A cattleman with small holdings.

little giant

In placer mining, a miner's term for a jointed iron pipe and a nozzle which decreases in diameter with the increase of hydraulic pressure.

little Joe

See *little Dick*.

Little Mary

A name the old-time trail man frequently gave to the driver of the *calf wagon, q.v.*

little natural

In dice, a throw of seven when the player is "coming out."

little Phoebe

In dice, five as a point.

little red wagon

What a miner called his portable toilet.

little tiger

In faro, a hand with the eight high, the trey low, and no pair.

live dictionary

A cowboy's name for a schoolteacher and also for a talkative woman—one who, as Jug Jeter would say, "was shore in the lead when tongues was give out." Jug did not have much use for women, and said he got his name because it was said he "never went to town till his jug needed fillin'."

live log

A log that will float.

live rolls

Metal rollways which carry lumber through a sawmill.

livin' lightning

A name for a bucking horse of ability.

lizard

See *crotch*. Also, to drag timber; to skid logs.

lizard scorcher

A cowboy's name for a camp stove. A logger's name for the cook.

lizzy

A cowboy's name for the saddle horn.

llano

Prairie; a flat, open plain without trees; from the Spanish.

Llano Estacado

The Staked Plain, a high and arid plateau of 40,000 square miles situated in Texas, New Mexico, and Oklahoma; from the Spanish.

load

A pack or packs forming the burden for one pack mule. Hence, *to load up* was to place the loads, as formed in cargo, on the pack mules. A cowboy's word meaning *to lie* or *tell tall tales*.

loader

In logging, the man who swings logs to the *top loader* or *second loader* on the railroad cars; also, a man who supervises the loading of logs.

loading chute

A corral with a chute used in loading cattle in stock cars.

loading jack

In logging, a platformed framework upon which logs are hoisted from the water before they are loaded into railroad cars.

loading leverman

In logging, the man who operates a loading boom and its log tongs, the first with a swing line and the second with a loading line.

load of hay on his skull

A cowboy's description of a long-haired man.

load the doctor

To load dice for crooked playing.

loafer

A timber wolf; a corruption of the Spanish *lobo*.

LOAFING

See bringing up the drags, calf 'round, coffee cooler, Don't drag your feet! drag one's feet, freak, in the shade of the wagon, pirooting, porch percher, pressing brick, red flagger, riding the saw, soakin', stackwad.

lobby

A logger's name for the place in a logging camp where the men wash and wait for mealtime.

lobo

A timber wolf; also called *loafer*; from the Spanish.

lob of gold

In mining, a small but rich deposit of gold.

lobo stripe

The white, yellow, or brown stripe running from neck to tail down the back of a *line-back (q.v.)*, a characteristic of many Spanish cattle.

locate

To herd cattle on new range until they feel at home. In mining, to enter a claim to a quantity of public land granted in a land-warrant scrip. To make and file a claim of ownership to the mineral rights of a defined piece of land.

location

In mining, those successive acts by which a claim is appropriated. Also, such a claim itself.

locked spurs

Spurs whose rowels have been fastened with a string or horsehair so that they will not move. When these spurs are held firmly in the cinch, it is next to impossible for a horse to unseat his rider, and their use is barred at all rodeos. When not locked, spurs do not assist the rider in staying on; on the contrary, they act in the manner of ball bearings to throw him.

lock horns

To engage in combat. To engage in an argument or fight with someone. Very commonly during fights male animals of the plains get their horns locked together and, being unable to free themselves, remain in this state until they starve to death.

loco

A condition of cattle resulting from feeding on locoweed. Applied to human beings, foolish, absurd, or crazy. From the Spanish.

lode

In mining, an aggregation of mineral matter containing ores in fissures; strictly speaking a fissure in the country rock filled with mineral; usually applied to metaliferous lodes. In general miner's usage, a tabular deposit of valuable mineral between definite boundaries. Whether or not it is a fissure formation is not always known, but it must not be a placer; that is, it must consist of quartz or other rock in place and bearing valuable mineral.

LODES AND VEINS

See blanket veins, coarse vein, contact vein, cross vein, dead lode, fissure vein, gash vein, linked vein, lode, mother lode, quartz lead, quartz reef, quartz vein, slide, spur, strike, vein, veta.

lodge

An Indian's living quarters; also, a family of Indians living in such quarters.

lodged

A term applied to a crop of hay or grain not standing erect, usually because of wind or rain. If badly lodged, the crop may be worthless.

lodge mound

The site of a former Indian *lodge, q.v.*

lodgepole
A pole used by Indians in erecting a *lodge, q.v.*

lodgepole pine
A western pine of lodgepole size.

lodgepole vehicle
A *travois, q.v.*

lodgepoling
Among Indians, a sound thrashing or drubbing, as with a lodgepole.

log
A length of a felled tree. To work at logging.

log beam
The traveling beam in which a log travels in a sawmill.

log birling
See *birling*.

log-butt
To cutt a piece from the end of a log to remove a defect.

log car
A railway car upon which logs are hauled.

log carriage
The carriage which takes the logs to the saws in a sawmill.

log chute
In logging, a chute made of two split logs laid close together lengthwise with the smooth sides up; down this chute logs are sent skidding into the river.

log drive
The moving of a log crop down the river to the mills.

log dump
A place to which logs are hauled and skidded preparatory to transportation by water or rail.

logged-off land
In logging, a section of forest in which all the trees have been cut down.

logged-over land
In logging, a section of forest in which only a part of the trees have been cut down.

logger
The name the lumberjack of the Northwest prefers to be called; he never calls himself a *lumberjack*.

loggerin'
In rodeo, riding out of the chute at a rodeo with one or both hands gripping the saddle horn.

logger's smallpox
The calk marks on the body of a logger, scars of his many fights.

LOGGERS
See Arkie, ball hooter, B. B.'s, bear fighter, bell man, bindle stiff, blazer, boltcutter, boob, boomer, boom man, boom master, boom rat, boom-stick cutter, boy scout, bridge monkey, brush ape, brush cat, brush rat, bucker, bucko, bull bucker, bull cook, bull of the woods, bull-pen boy, bull whipper, bush rat, camp dog, camp eye, card man, cat skinner, chambermaid to the mules, chasers, chickory outfit, choker setter, chopper, chore boy, clears, cruiser, crumb boss, crummie, dirt daubers, dodgers, donkey doctor, donkeyman, driver, eppus outfit, faller, farewell man, feller, flathead, gabezo, gandy dancer, gopher, ground hog, grunt, gyppo, gyppo contractor, hard hat, hardtack outfit, head faller, head rigger, highball outfit, high climber, high rigger, hooker, hook tender, humpback, jack, jobber, Johnny Newcomer, limber, loader, loading leverman, logger, log jockey, log maker, logman, log watch, lokey man, long logger, lumberer, lumberjack, lumber rustler, lumber stiff, master chopper, master swamper, monk, monkey, mud hen, old safety first, Paul, Paul Bunyan's boy, peeler, polecat, pole maker, pond monkey, puncher, punk, pussy pusher, rigger, rigging slinger, river driver, road monkey, roustabout, savage, saw gang, saw whetter, sawyer, scaler, scorer, Sears Roebuck guy, second faller, set, shanty, shanty boy, shanty gang, shanty man, shanty team, short staker, shotgun outfit, side, single jack, skidder, skidder crew, skidder-crew fellow, skid greaser, skidding lever man, skidway men,

sky hooker, sky rigger, slasher, slave, sled tender, slough pig, sluicer, sniper, stable dog, stakey, stump detective, swamp angel, swamper, tail crew, tame ape, third loader, third rigger, tie peeler, tie whacker, timber beast, timber camp, timber cruiser, timber head, timber inspector, timberjack, timber pirate, timber savage, timber wolf, top loader, tree looker, unit, whipsawyer, whistle punk, white-water bucko, windfall bucker, wood butcher, wood head, wood hick, woods crew, works, yarder.

loggin'

Tying a horse to a log. Since a log will move, this method of staking allows the horse more freedom and eliminates the danger of entanglements from more rigid staking.

Logging

See ball hooting, bank, banking ground, bedding, birling, boom company, booming, buck, bunching, burn the stick, busheling, butt off, by the bushel, California slingshot, changing band, chopping, chunk out, clear cutting, clear ground, cold deck, Crack! Whip the saw! crosscut, cross haul, cruise, cup, dads, diameter limit, donkey logging, driving pitch, drop, fall, forty, frame a hole, Get a saddle! girdle, grade, granny bar, ground hogging, ground lead, gun, gutter board, hang up, head dam, hike, hot logging, integrated logging, jackpot, jam, lax, lizard, log, log-butt, log drive, log dump, logging show, logging side, log banding, log off, log rolling, log running, lop, lumbering, lumber a tract, misery whip, nose, pick, play the woods, pullboat logging, release cutting, riding her out, ring up, river drive, diver driving, route, run, run a juggle factory, Russian coupling, sack, sack the rear, sack the slide, sawmills and machinery, scale, selective logging, shake the lines over the iron mule, shelterwood, shoot a jam, show, skidder system, sky-line logging, sled dogging, sluiced, snake, snipe, snipe-nose, spar, swamp, tail down, tail tree, thinning, timber cruise, timber hunting, timber pirate, topping, top the spars, tow through, wood down, work by the mile, yard.

logging berries

A logger's name for prunes.

logging bob

A bobsled used in logging.

logging boom

In logging, usually two logs suspended above the ground; the projecting arm of a log-loading machine which supports the logs during loading. It may be of either the swinging or the rigid type.

Logging camps

See Bunyan camp, cock shop, cook camp, dingle, timber camp.

logging chain

A levered chain grab hook attached to the evener to which a beam is hitched in loading logs.

Logging crews

See broadax brigade, candy side, checkerboard crew, loggers.

Logging machinery and equipment

See arch, asshole, baloney, barker, bicycle, big hole, big-wheel rigs, binder, bitch chain, blowpipe, boom head, boom loader, branding ax, briar, brook stick, bulgine, bull block, bull chain, bulldozer, bull prick, bull wheels, butt hook, cant dog, cat, cheater bar, cheese block, chipper, choker, clam gun, cold shit, crib, crotch line, cunt splice, cutoff battery, diesel cold deckers, dinkey, dirt hider, dog, dog chain, dog warp, dolly, donkey, drum, duplex, Dutchman, fair lead, falling ax, fender, flipper, flying Dutchman, gaff, gin pole, ginny line, grab, gunning stick, gut wrapper, guy line, gypsy, harness, haul back, high line, high-line sky rigger, hog head, hoot-nanny, Irish baby buggy, iron mule, jackass, jamp pike, jammer, Jim Hill, knees, Lidgerwood, lines, loading jack, logging bob, logging boom, logging chain, logging wheels, log measurer, log rule, log way, log wrench, McLean boom, main line, marking hammer, Molly, Molly Hogan, mule, muley cow, North Bend, Oregon block, pack rat, painter leg, pass line, peavey, peeling bar, picaroon, pig, pigtail, pike pole, pot, Pulaski, rat lines, rig, river donkey, road donkey, saw gummer, scoot, siwash tree, skidder, skidding line, skirt, sky hook, spider, springboard, spud, squaw ax, squirrel lines, stamp ax, stinger, straw line, Swede fiddle, swing, swing-dingle, swing donkey, swing line, trail tree, Tyler, unit, wedge, wood harp, yarder.

logging protection

Practices followed to provide protection from forest fires during and after logging; forest-fire patrols and shutdowns during days of high wind and low humidity save millions of seedlings from fire.

Logging railroads

See hoghead, log car, logging machinery and equipment, takeaway.

Logging-railroad workers

See driver, gandy dancer, hogger, hostler, jerry gang, lokey man, shag, steel gang.

logging shirt

A coarse overgarment of hemp cloth worn by loggers.

logging show

A logging operation.

logging side

That part of a logging operation in which the logs are brought from the woods to the place to be loaded.

logging wheels

A pair of wheels, usually about 10 feet in diameter, used in transporting logs.

log jam

A number of logs which, impeded in passing down a stream, have formed a compact, entangled mass.

log jockey

A logger who rafts logs in a boom.

log kicker

A steam-operated, armlike machine that throws or rolls logs upon the deck after they have been elevated into the mill by an endless chain.

log landing

A place to which logs are hauled and skidded preparatory to transportation by water or rail; also called *banking ground, log dump,* and *rollway yard.*

log maker

A logger whose job it is to saw the felled trees into specified log lengths.

logman

A logger engaged in getting out logs.

log measurer

A device for gauging logs which takes the round measure of the ascertained square running feet of the log.

log off

To fell trees, prepare logs, and transport them to market.

log pond

A pond near a sawmill in which logs are kept until ready for sawing.

log rolling

In logging, rolling logs or allowing logs to roll to a desired spot, as into a river.

log rule

In logging, a tabular statement of the amount of lumber which can be sawed from logs of given lengths and diameters.

log running

Floating or guiding logs down a stream.

Logs and lumber

See backbreakers, barber chair, bark mark, big blue, big-pond boom, bird's eye, black diamonds, board tree, bole, bolt, bonus, boom, boom stick, brail, brow logs, bunk log, burl, butt, butt cut, cant, catface, checks, churn-butted, clean-boled, clear heart, cow's mouth, crook, cross member, crotch, cut, deadhead, dead log, deadman, defect, dog holes, dunnage, fishlaid, goose-pen butt, ground apples, heartwood, hell bender, high-lead tree, honeycomb, horse wood, humboldt, Jim Crow, lap, live log, log, log jam, log trap, mill log, nigger holes, paling board, peavey log, pecker pole, peeler log, piece, rawhide lumber, rollaway, saw log, schoolmarm, shake, sinkers, skid, slab, sleeping sawyer, string, stub, stump shot, sweep, timber break, top load, trees and forests, turn, upper, wire edges.

log scale

The lumber content expressed in board feet, of a log or a number of logs.

log scaler

A man who measures a log as it enters the mill with a scale stick and records the volume of board feet. The log is then kicked onto a sloping deck where it rests until it is sawed.

log trap

A deadfall made of heavy logs.

log watch

In logging, the head driver; an expert river driver who during the drive is stationed at a point where a jam is feared. His duty is called a *log watch*.

log way

A sloping chute, trough, slide, or enclosed passage for logs; also called *gangway*.

log wrench

A logger's name for a cant hook or peavey.

lokey man

A man who works on a locomotive that pulls logs from the woods to the mill.

loma

A trader's name for a hill; from the Spanish.

lone ranger

A cowboy's name for an unmarried man.

lone-wolfing

A cowboy's expression for living alone or for avoiding the companionship of others.

long-ear

To place a silk handkerchief on hard ground and listen by putting an ear to it. Old plainsmen often followed this practice, which somehow magnifies sounds otherwise inaudible. From this practice originated the saying, "Keep your ear to the ground," that is, use caution, go slowly, and listen frequently. An animal which has been earmarked. Thus, more loosely, an unbranded animal.

long-eared chuck wagon

A cowboy's name for the mules which packed the provisions when these animals were used instead of wagons in rough country.

long-haired partner

What the cowman sometimes calls his wife.

long hairs

A name for the men of the early West who wore their hair long.

longhorn

A name given to the early cattle of Texas, descended from Spanish cattle imported to the region; so called because of the enormous spread of their horns. The saga of the longhorn is an interesting one. For a valuable study of this historic bovine, I recommend *The Longhorns,* by an able recorder of the West, J. Frank Dobie (Boston, Little, Brown and Company, 1941). Also, a native Texan.

long horse

A horse which can travel great distances at high speed.

long knife

An Indian's name for the white soldier because of the sword he carried.

long-line skinner

A driver of two or more teams.

long logger

A logger in the West Coast forests; so called because the standard lengths of the Douglas fir and redwood logs are as long as 40 feet.

long rider

A western outlaw; so called because he often had to ride long distances or spend long hours in the saddle to escape capture.

long rope

A cowboy's name for a cattle thief.

long route

An employee who must work a long time for one outfit to garner a grubstake; the opposite of *boomer, q.v.*

long sweetenin'

A cowboy's name for molasses.

Long Tom

What the buffalo hunter frequently called his long rifle. What many early westerners called a large-caliber rifle. In mining, a type of trough used for washing gold-bearing dirt. It is placed on an incline, and a stream of water is introduced into the upper end. It is essentially an immobilized rocker 10 to 30 feet long. The lower end, called the *riddle*, replaces the hopper; here a heavily perforated sheet-iron botton allows the mass of earth and water to drop through to a *riffle box*, which is similar to but longer than the bottom of a rocker, where the riffles catch the gold particles.

long trail

A cowman's reference to death.

long twos

Cattle nearer three years old than two.

long yearlin'

A calf eighteen months old or older.

look at the river

In steamboating, said of pilots who went down the river in a boat not under their command to see the conditions of the river. A good many of them ran up and down the river at every opportunity, not because they really hoped to get a berth but because, being guests of the boat, they found it cheaper to *look at the river* than stay ashore and pay board.

lookin' at a mule's tail

What the cowboy called plowing. The old-time cowboy despised any work that could not be done on horseback. The sentiment of the whole tribe was expressed by the one who said that he "wouldn't be caught on the blister end of *no* damned shovel."

lookin' down the neck of a bottle

Drinking whisky from a bottle.

lookin' for a dog to kick

A cowboy expression for disgust.

lookin' for someone

A cowboy expression for seeking an enemy to down.

LOOKING FOR TROUBLE

See hell-bent for trouble, hellin' 'round town, lookin' for someone, pawin' 'round for turmoil.

lookin' over his shoulder

On the dodge. One cowman expressed his philosophy to me with, "A man that looks over his shoulder at every piece of straight road ain't leadin' a straight life." To look over one's shoulder is also to break a strict code of range etiquette followed by honest men. When two riders meet on the trail, speak, and pass on, it is a violation of this code for either to look back. Such an act is interpreted as an expression of distrust, as though one feared a shot in the back.

lookin' through cottonwood leaves

Said of someone hanged.

lookin' up a limb

Said of someone hanged.

lookout

In cattle driving, a man who went ahead of the herd to find grazing land. In gambling, the dealer's assistant who watches for cheating and sees that the dealer does not overlook any bets, a task which, when several players are playing various systems simultaneously, may become quite complicated.

Look out, cowboy!

A warning shout likely to be heard in a corral during branding. When this cry goes up, it is no disgrace to run.

look-see

A cowman's term for an inspection tour or an investigation of some sort; the word *look* is rarely used by itself.

looloo

In gambling, a winning hand, particularly one claimed to be unbeatable in a particular section of the country. A looloo was often invented by natives of a region to win a game from a stranger. The first looloo is said to have been invented in the 1870's by a miner at a saloon in Butte, Montana, in a game with a stranger in the region.

loose-herd
To let cattle scatter somewhat while herding them.

looseners
A logger's name for prunes.

lop
In logging, to chop branches, tops, or small trees after felling so that the slash will lie close to the ground. To cut limbs from a felled tree.

lope
In the West, a long, swinging stride of a horse; a gallop.

lop-horn
A steer or cow with a horn that grows downward.

lose out
In gambling, said of card that loses on the fourth play after having lost three times in one deal. To bet on a card which loses four times in one deal.

lost his hair
Scalped by Indians.

lost his hat and got off to look for it
Said of a rider who has been thrown from a bucking horse, an alibi which, of course, no one believes.

lost his horse
Thrown from a horse.

lost his topknot
Scalped by Indians.

lotto cards
Cards sold to a player in *keno, q.v.*

louse cage
A logger's name for his hat. A logger's name for the bunkhouse.

low-belly strippers
In gambling, high cards of a deck which have been shaved along the belly, thereby making it possible for the card sharp to cut to a high or low card at will.

low-neck clothes
What the cowboy calls his very best clothes, which he wears on special occasions. Tonto Sutton described a cowboy who attended a dance as "all spraddled out in his low-necked clothes," and added, "He showed up public as a zebra, wearin' a b'iled shirt and smellin' of bear grease and lavender-flavored soap, lookin' as miserable as a razorback hog stroppin' hisself on a fencepost."

LOVE
See calico fever, callin', cupid's cramp.

LOYAL
See pure, stand by.

lumber a tract
To cut the trees in a particular area and send the logs to market.

lumberer
A lumberjack, or logger; one who fells forest trees and takes them to market.

lumbering
The business or action of cutting down forest trees and marketing them.

lumberjack
A term loosely applied to any worker in the woods. More strictly, a *logger*, the latter being the name used by the workers themselves. The loggers of the Pacific Northwest use the term *lumberjack* contemptuously in referring to the workers in the small timber of other regions.

lumber rustler
A logger. In some sections, a common laborer.

lumber stiff
A logger.

lumber tally
A record of lumber giving the number of boards or pieces by size, grade, and species; also called *mill tally.*

lump jaw
Actinomycosis, a disease of cattle causing suppurating tumors about the jaw; also called *big jaw, lump jaw,* and *wooden tongue.*

lump oil

A cowboy's name for coal oil or kerosene.

lunch in

A logger's expression for eating a noon meal served in the dining quarters of the logging camp.

lunger

A person suffering from tuberculosis who came west in search of health. Smoky Saddler described one with, "His lungs wasn't stronger than a hummin'bird's, and he didn't have 'nough wind to blow out a lamp."

lynching bee

A hanging without recourse to law. A gathering of people for the purpose of lynching someone.

M

"A cow outfit's never better than its hosses"

Mac

A male parasite who made his living procuring for some woman of the red-light district of a cow town.

macaroni

A logger's term for sawdust.

McCarty

See *mecate*.

McLean boom

A type of loading boom used in West Coast logging.

machine burn

In logging, a burn on a piece of wood when it stops in a sawmill machine, the burn resulting from the action of the knives on one spot.

machinery belting

A cowboy's name for tough beef.

Mackinaw

A river boat used on the Missouri River. It resembled the flatboats used on the Ohio and Mississippi rivers principally in that it was suitable only for downstream navigation and its career was limited to one voyage. When it reached St. Louis, it was sold as lumber for a few dollars.

The Mackinaw was a flat-bottomed boat with a pointed prow and a square stern. It was usually about four times as long as it was wide. A large Mackinaw was as much as 50 or 60 feet long. From the edge of the raftlike structure which constituted the bottom of the Mackinaw rose a gunwale several feet high; thus the hold of a large boat was 4 or 5 feet deep. The oarsmen sat on benches near the forward end of the craft, and in the stern a seat eight or ten feet high in the air, reached by a ladder, was provided for the helmsman. From this elevated position the helmsman kept watch for trouble, manipulated his rudder, and shouted orders to the crew in the bow. The central section of the Mackinaw was used for cargo and was separated from the rest of the boat, both fore and aft, by strong, watertight partitions. The hold was elevated a foot or so above the actual bottom of the hull, so that water would not damage the cargo. The crew worked from dawn to nightfall, and sometimes moved the boat more than 100 miles a day; however, the average speed was 4 or 5 miles an hour.

made a nine in his tail

A cowboy's expression meaning that a man or beast has left in a hurry. When a cow runs from fright, she often lifts her tail in the shape of a figure nine, or at least in the shape of the figure the cowman uses in most "nine" brands; hence the saying.

made of the same leather

A cowboy's description of men having

the same dispositions, ideas, and tastes. According to one cowhand, they are "close 'nough to use the same toothpick."

made wolf meat

An expression used by the early trappers, meaning that a man had been killed and left on the prairie for the wolves to eat. The expression was later adopted by the cowman.

mad scramble

In rodeo, a finale in which fifteen or more Brahma bulls and steers and mules straddled by cowboys rush into the arena in all directions from the chutes.

maggot

A cowboy's name for a sheep.

magpie

A species of bird found on the range. A name for a Holstein cow.

maguey

The century plant. A cowman's term for a four-strand rope a scant ⅜-inch in diameter made from the fiber of this plant. It is a hard rope that throws easily and holds a wide loop. It is the rope used by trick ropers in making their fancy catches. In cow work it has its disadvantages; it becomes very stiff in wet weather and breaks easily when tied hard and fast.

MAIL

See jackass mail, moccasin mail, moccasin telegraph, overland mail, pony express, pony stamps, way pocket, way pouch.

mail-order catalog on foot

A tenderfoot dressed in range clothes of an exaggerated style.

mail-order cowboy

A tenderfoot, devoid of range experience, dressed in custom-made cowboy regalia. The average mail-order cowboy "looks like he was raised on the Brooklyn Bridge."

main line

In logging, the cable that handles the log. The hauling line on a cable logging operation. Legal tender in sawmills where checks or coupons are used instead of cash.

make a brush

In gambling, to build a small initial bet into a considerable sum.

make a hat

A logger's term meaning *to take up a collection.*

make a pass

In gambling, to cut a pack of cards in such a way as to put the two parts of the pack as they were before the cut; a form of cheating.

make a port

A freighter's term meaning *to find a camping place.*

make beaver

A trapper's expression meaning *to hurry.*

make her out

What the logger tells the timekeeper when he wants his pay check; an expression meaning that he is quitting.

make keno

In keno, to secure five numbers in a row. See *keno.*

make meat

A trapper's and trader's term for laying in a store of provisions by hunting buffalo, deer, or other meat; to kill for food.

make medicine

To hold a conference; to plan some action; an expression taken from the Indian custom.

make tracks

A trapper's expression meaning *to hurry.*

makin' a hand

A cowboy's expression meaning that someone is living up to the exacting code of the calling—a high compliment. This code calls for courage and loyalty, uncomplaining cheerfulness and laughter at dangers and hardships, lack of curiosity about another's past, and respect for womanhood. These qualities, together with others, constitute a code that the cowboy must live up to if he *makes a hand.*

makin' dust

A cowboy's expression for going somewhere in a hurry.

makin' far-apart tracks

A cowboy's expression for running at high speed on foot.

makin' hair bridles

A cowboy's expression for serving time in the penitentiary. Most cowboys who were sent to prison spent their time making horsehair bridles because the work seemed to bring them closer to a horse. Some of the bridles they turned out were masterpieces.

In typical cowboy language, Charlie Russell wrote a letter to a friend concerning a mutual acquaintance, saying; "Charley Cugar quit punchin' and went into the cow business for himself. His start was a couple o' cows and a work bull. Each cow had six to eight calves a year. People didn't say much till the bull got to havin' calves, and then they made it so disagreeable that Charley quit the business and is now makin' hoss-hair bridles. They say he hasn't changed much, but wears his hair very short and dresses awfully loud." (Charles M. Russell, *Good Medicine* [Garden City, Doubleday, Doran, 1930], 107.)

makin's

Materials needed for making cigarettes. The old-time cowboy never smoked any cigarettes other than the ones he rolled himself from his makin's. If he ran out of makin's when he was situated where he could not buy more, he asked another rider for them, and they were never refused, unless the refusal was an intentional insult.

makin' shavetails

An expression used by cowboys of the Northwest for breaking horses. See *shavetails* and *tail pulling*.

makin' the calico crack

A cowboy's expression for swinging a girl off the floor in an old fashioned square dance.

makin' the town smoky

A cowboy's expression for shooting up a town or generally raising hell.

malachite

In mining, the bright-green carbonate of copper.

mal de vache

A trapper's illness caused by eating too much fat meat without other food; from the French.

maleta

A bag made of rawhide. A satchel. From the Spanish.

mal pais

The region of lava mesas in the Southwest; from the Spanish, meaning *bad country*.

manada

A herd of mares, more especially brood mares; from the Spanish. (Don, "Vaquero Lingo," *Western Horseman*, Vol. II, No. 5 [September–October, 1937], 11.)

mañana

A word used freely by Americans along the Mexican border to mean *tomorrow, sometime, perhaps never*, a leisurely postponement. (Harold W. Bentley, *Dictionary of Spanish Terms in English* [New York, Columbia University Press, 1932], 161.)

Man at the pot!

A shout heard in a cowboy camp at mealtime. If a man gets up to refill his coffee cup and hears this yell, he is duty-bound by camp etiquette to go around with the pot and fill all the cups held out to him.

man cage

A miner's name for a cage used to raise and lower men in a mine shaft.

man catcher

A logger's name for an employment agent.

man for breakfast

A killing. This expression originated in frontier days when there were so many killings at night in the tough cow towns and mining camps that when the good citizens awoke the next morning they could see the body or bodies laid out before breakfast.

mangana

In roping, a throw which catches the animal by the forefeet. The throw is made by pointing the hand downward, dragging the loop forward, and swinging it out so that it practically stands on edge. The throw stands a big loop in front of the animal, and all he has to do is step into it. It is a loop which must be perfectly timed to be successful, since the animal will stop rather than hit it if the loop is stood too far ahead of him. The throw is reserved for horses and is seldom used on cattle. Also called *forefooting*, q.v. From the Spanish, meaning *lasso*.

mangana de pie

In roping, a throw with the foot. A fancy throw, it is rarely used in actual cow work. It is made by putting a well-opened loop on the ground with the toe beneath the honda and, as the animal to be roped goes by, pitching the loop straight forward with the foot. From the Spanish.

mangeur de lard

A trapper's term for one of the beginners or new recruits brought from Canada to do common labor; so called because on the way he was fed pork rather than game.

man grabber

A logger's term for an employment agent.

man hole

In mining, an opening large enough to permit access between two workings.

maniac den

A cowboy's name for a sheep wagon or camp. The cowman felt that a sheepherder was more or less crazy or he would not be herding sheep and that for the disorderly arrangement of his camp *den* was a fitting word.

manifesto

A trader's term for bill of merchandise.

Manila

A rope of Manila. Most of the ropes sold and used in the ranch country are made of Manila fiber, of three-strand construction, and laid extrahard for strength and smoothness.

man-killer

A cowboy's term for a vicious horse.

mansador

A bronc buster or horse breaker; from the Spanish *manso*, meaning *tame*.

mansion

A cowboy's name for a sheepherder's wagon.

mansito

What the traders called a Christianized Indian; from the Spanish meaning *very tame* or *gentle*.

manstopper

A cowboy's term for a gun.

manta

A packer's pack cover, made of 72-inch No. 4 cotton duck. Each pack was ordinarily wrapped in a manta, particularly one containing goods likely to suffer damage or deterioration during transportation. From the Spanish.

mantanza

A place where cattle were slaughtered for the hide and tallow; also called *tallow factory*. From the Spanish.

mantilla

A shawl, one of the early trader's items of trade; from the Spanish.

man trip

In mining, a trip of the lift up the shaft with a load of men.

map of Mexico

An American cowboy's term for one of the intricate Mexican brands, which are usually large and give no clue to a name by which they can be called.

mark

A cut on an animal's ear or other part of the skin as an indication of ownership. Each kind of mark has a name and is registered along with the owner's brand. To make such a cut. See *earmarks*.

marker

In cattle raising, a cow with distinctive coloration or other marks easily distinguished and remembered by the owner and his riders. Such an animal has frequently been the downfall of a rustler. A man who cuts earmarks on cattle at branding time. In sheep raising, one of the black or spotted members of the flock by which the herder checks his band. In faro, a square token, usually of ivory or a synthetic material, provided by the house and used by the player as a substitute for money, provided his credit is good. The player announces the value of each marker as he bets and must settle in cash after each deal, returning the markers to the bank.

marking hammer

In logging, a hammer bearing a raised device which is stamped on logs to indicate ownership; also called *marking iron.*

MARKS OF OWNERSHIP

See brands, dewlap, carmarks, jug handle, wattle.

marm school

A cow-country school, so called by the cowboy because the teacher was invariably a woman.

MARRIAGE

See dropped his rope on her, trap a squaw.

martingale

A strap passing between the horse's forelegs from bridle to girth. It is intended to hold the horse's head down and thus keep him from rearing.

massive deposit

In mining, a deposit deep underground. It is well described by its name, for it is just that—a large mass of ore sometimes as thick as it is wide and deep—a great clump of heavily mineralized rock that would leave behind it a huge, irregular underground cavern if it could be mined completely.

master chopper

A logger's name for a man in charge of a logging gang.

master swamper

A logger's name for a man in charge of swampers, or road makers, in logging operations.

master wagoner

The man in charge of a wagon train.

MATCHES

See hell stick.

matrix

In mining, the country rock in which the vein is found; the rock or earthy material enclosing the ore.

matte

A rich artificial sulphide of copper formed as an intermediate product in smelting, between ore and metallic copper.

maverick

An unbranded animal, usually a motherless calf, of unknown ownership. To brand such an animal with one's own brand. Many and varied stories are told concerning the origin of this word. Some of the stories have even gone so far as to brand as a thief the man from whose name the term originated. Nothing could be further from the truth. He was a useful, prominent, and honorable citizen, a lawyer, and one of the signers of the Texas Declaration of Independence. He never made any claims to being a cattleman. In fact, his ignorance regarding cattle was responsible for his leaving such a colorful addition to our language. Here is the apparently true story:

Samuel A. Maverick, a lawyer, took over a bunch of cattle for a debt before the Civil War and placed them in charge of a Negro on the San Antonio River about 50 miles south of San Antonio, Texas. The Negro, ignorant about cattle, failed to brand the offspring of the herd and let them wander far and wide. In 1855 Maverick sold his entire outfit—brand, range, and all—to Toutant de Beauregard, a neighboring stockman. According to the terms of the deal, in addition to the number of cattle present and actually transferred in the trade, Beauregard was to have all the others that he could find on Maverick's range, both branded and unbranded. Beauregard, being a thrifty man, instituted a systematic roundup, and wherever his riders found an unbranded animal, they claimed it to be a *Maverick*, put Beauregard's brand on it, and drove it in. At a time when the prairies were full of unbranded cattle, these riders took in so much territory that the news began to spread. The term *maverick* soon came to be applied to all unbranded range cattle. The term spread over the entire cattle country and gained such common usage that it found its way into the dictionary. (*Prose and Poetry of the Live Stock Industry* [Denver, 1905]; George M. Maverick [son of Samuel A. Maverick], *St. Louis Republic*, November 16, 1889.)

maverick brand

An unrecorded brand. A thief could easily hold an animal on the range with one of these unrecorded brands until he was able to drive it off. In case suspicion was aroused, there were no records to connect him with the theft.

mavericker

A man who rode the ranges in the early days to hunt and brand mavericks. In the beginning the practice of roping and branding any calf which was not at the time following its mother was not considered stealing but was counted legitimate thriftiness. Calves of this kind were considered anyone's cattle. Many ranchers who would not condone theft in any form sent their cowboys out "to do a little mavericking" at so much per head.

When the cowboy saw how easy it was to build up a herd for his boss, he began wondering why it would not be just as legitimate and a lot more profitable to himself to maverick on his own hook. Not until then did the ranch owners decide that it was stealing and caused laws to be passed against it. After this *mavericker* was but another name for a cow thief.

maverick factory

A term for a rustler's practice of making mavericks by killing the mother with her telltale brand.

maw bell

A logger's name for a telephone.

MEALS

See Basque barbecue, chase the cow, chow time, collar-and-shoulder style, Come an' get it! crib, ding-dong, flaggin's, flag's up, food, grub pile, lunch in, mulligan car, nose-bag show, Roll out! Breakfast on the boards! staked to a fill.

mealy nose

A cow or steer of the longhorn type with lines and dots around the eyes, face, and nose of a lighter color than the rest of its body.

MEAN

See bad men, cultus, oily, plum cultus, snake blood, snaky.

measured a full sixteen hands high

A cowboy's appraisal of a man's worth, a high compliment to his ability and honesty.

meat- and hide-hungry

A description double-rigged riders give to the center-fire saddle because it is difficult to keep in place on the horse's back and thus rubs sores on its back.

meat bag

A trapper's term for the stomach. Trappers of early times lived almost entirely on meat.

meat in the pot

A cowboy's term for a rifle, so called because this weapon was used by the hunter to secure meat for the camp.

mecate

A hair or maguey rope used as saddle reins with a hackamore, or as a tie or lead rope; Americanized to *McCarty*. Because a hair rope has long been traditional for this purpose, there has developed a tendency to call any hair rope a *mecate*. A hair rope is never used as a reata. It kinks too easily and is too light to throw. From the Spanish.

mechanic

In faro, a dealer capable of operating a faro box as the occasion demands; one adept at making the cards come as he pleases.

MEDDLERS

See eyeballer, feedin' off his range, hornin' in, Paul Pry, wedger in.

medicine

A westerner's term for power; taken from the Indian. A trapper's term for an oily substance obtained from the gland in the scrotum of the beaver, used for baiting a beaver trap. The beaver, attracted by the smell and wishing a closer inspection, would very foolishly put his leg into the trap.

medicine bag

A bag of herbs used by the Indian for religious purposes.

medicine iron

An Indian's name for a white man's gun.

medicine lodge

An Indian sweat lodge.

medicine man

Among North American Indians, one who practiced healing; a priest; a prophet.

medicine tongue

What the cowboy calls fluent talk or wordiness.

medicine turn

In gambling, a combination of the queen and nine, falling together in that order in a single turn; probably so called from a play on the word *quinine*.

medicine wolf

A cowboy's name for a coyote.

meeting

In mining, the place at middle depth of a shaft, slope, or plane where ascending and descending cars pass each other. A siding or bypass on underground mining roads.

MEETINGS

See conferences.

MEN

See badlander, bad men, bastonero, batch, breed, buck-nun, can't whistle, chaparral fox, curly wolf, gunmen, hombre, jackpine savage, long hair.

merry-go-round

In trick roping, a spin with an independent noose around and clear of the body, the roper using first one hand and then the other.

merry-go-round in high water

The *milling (q.v.)* of cattle in a stream.

Although it is highly desirable to get stampeding cattle to mill on land, when they do so in water, the result is anything but desirable. When they begin swimming around in an ever tightening circle in water, they become hopelessly massed, and the loss from drowning is enormous unless the herders are fortunate in breaking up the mass in its early stages. To stop them is a difficult and dangerous task, since the rider cannot enter the center of the mass to break it up, and pushing from the outside causes it to become tighter.

mesa

A flat-topped hill; an elevated plateau; a mountain shaped like a table; from the Spanish.

mescal

A colorless liquor made from the juice or baked heads of plants belonging to some species of agave; from the Spanish *mezcal*.

mesquital

A region covered with *mesquite, q.v.*; a clump of mesquite shrubs; from the Spanish *mezquital*.

mesquite

A tree or shrub found in the Southwest, especially in the flat country. The wood is exceedingly hard and durable underground. The plant is covered with thorns, and its fruit is a pulpy bean full of grape sugar, upon which cattle feed when they can get nothing better. From the Spanish *mezquite*.

mesquite grass

A rich pasture grass growing in western Texas among the mesquite trees; also called *buffalo grass* and *grama grass*.

mess boiler

A logger's name for the camp cook.

messenger

In stagecoaching, a man who, armed with a sawed-off shotgun, rode beside the driver to defend the company's or shipper's property from outlaws and road agents; also called *shotgun messenger*. He had charge of the treasure and other valuables, checking on a waybill every item as it passed out of or came into his hands. He rode the entire length of his run, working approximately six days and nights without sleep except such as he could catch while riding along. His place was on the box with the driver; armed to the teeth and warmly dressed, he was expected to keep that place all the time. Although not so spectacular as the driver, he was fully as important an employee of the stage line. His was a responsible position. Acting as a stage conductor, he worked in a division of 200 to 250 miles and was paid $61.50 a month and board. For nine days out of every three weeks he rested to be alert for his run.

As mining operations increased in the West, the value of the stage's cargo increased, and so did the desperadoes. Some of these were disgruntled former employees of the stage company. Under these circumstances it was extremely necessary to hire levelheaded messengers who could be trusted. It became a further responsibility to guard the heavily armed express coaches on the line. As the hauling of express grew in importance, it was decided to send out a special coach on Mondays which would carry no passengers.

mess house

The cook shack on a ranch or at a logging camp.

mess moll

What the logger calls a female cook.

mess wagon

A cowboy's name for the chuck wagon. In freighting, the wagon carrying the provisions, cooking utensils, levers for raising loads of 4 or 5 tons, the iron jacks, extra tires, coils of rope, pulleys, wheels, extra spokes, bars of iron, and almost always a small forge—a regular wrecking outfit. It usually traveled at the end of the moving column.

mesteñero

A hunter of wild horses; more commonly called *mustanger*; from the Spanish *mesteño*, meaning homeless.

mesteño

A horse; a mustang; from the Spanish.

METALS AND ORES

See amalgam, amalgamate, apex, argentiferous, auriferous, azurite, bastard quartz, bed, sphalerite, blanket veins, blende, blossom, blossom rock, bonanza, bornite, brittle silver, bullion, carbonate, carbonite, carga, cement, chalcocite, chalcopyrite, chlorides, cinnabar, coarse gold, color, Comstock Lode, copper, copper glance, dead riches, disseminated ore, enriched ore, float, float gold, float ore, fool's gold, free milling, free-milling ores, galena, gangue, glance, gold dust, grade, grain gold, impregnation, indications, lenses, lob of gold, lodes and veins, malachite, matte, mill run, mines, nigger, pay dirt, pay gravel, pay ore, pay rock, pay shoot, pay streak, picture ore, placer deposits, placer gold, porphyry, probable ore, prospect, quartz gold, quicksilver, ruby copper, scad, scale gold, shotty gold, silver glance, stamp-mill recovery, sulphide wash gold, wedge rock.

metate

A corn-grinding stone used on the frontier; from the Spanish.

met his shadow on the ground

Said of a rider thrown from a bucking horse.

Mexican buckskin

What the northern cowboy sometimes called a longhorn driven up the trail from Texas.

Mexican iron

Rawhide; so called because it was extensively used by the Mexicans and wore like iron.

Mexicano

A common name for a Mexican.

Mexican oats

Nonsense; an expression equivalent to *baloney*.

MEXICANS

See bean eater, chili, chili eater, greaser, Mexicano, never-sweat, oiler, pelados, pepper gut, shuck, spick, sun grinner, vaquero.

Mexicans don't count.

A boast of the gunman of the Southwest who felt it beneath his dignity to *count coup* on the Mexicans (and Indians) he killed. Some gunmen kept a careful record of the white men they killed by filing notches on their guns for their victims, but more often such gun notching was left to the writers of romantic fiction.

Mexican standoff

A cowboy's expression for an escape from a serious difficulty. Early-day cowboys claimed that if a Mexican did not win quickly in a gun fight, or if he found much opposition, he left in a hurry.

Mexican strawberries

A cowboy's name for dried beans.

mica

In mining, one of the constituents of granite. When separately crystallized, it occurs in clear laminated plates. It is found in the lode as well as in the matrix of the lode.

mid-air dance

A cowboy's term for a hanging.

Mike

A miner's name for a heavy hammer.

MILKING

See pailing cows.

milk pitcher

A cowboy's name for a cow that is giving milk.

mill

In mining, a plant for the concentration of ore by means of concentrating tables, flotation cells or other devices.

mill boom

A sawmill boom in which logs are impounded.

mill carriage

In a sawmill, a carlike conveyer upon which the logs are brought up to and past the saw.

mill chain

At a sawmill, a chain which draws saw logs from the pond into the mill.

mill creek

A creek upon which a sawmill is located.

mill cut

A specified amount of lumber cut by a sawmill.

mill deck

See *deck log*.

miller

A hand who tends the windmills on a ranch.

mill hole

In mining, a passage left in the stope through which rock and ore are thrown.

milling

The marching of cattle in a compact circle. This formation is resorted to in stopping stampedes. As the cattle mill in a circle, they wind themselves up into a narrowing mass which becomes tighter and tighter until finally it is so tight they can no longer move. The term is reserved strictly for cattle. When the same action is carried out with horses, it is called *rounding up*.

mill log

A log suitable for sawing in a sawmill.

mill rider

A hand whose duty it is to keep the windmills on the ranch in repair.

mill run

In mining, the returns of a given lot of ore; the assay of ore in quantity, as distinguished from a specimen assay.

mine

Any excavation made for minerals. An open, as distinguished from an untouched, deposit. An underground working, as distinguished from a surface working or quarry.

mine bank

In mining, an area of deposits that can be worked by excavation above the water level. The ground at the top of a mining shaft.

MINE RAILROAD WORKERS

See car rider, mucker, swamper.

mineral claim

See *mining claim*.

mineral entry

The filing of a claim for public land to obtain the right to any minerals it may contain.

mineral land

Land rich in mineral deposits.

mineral rod

A miner's term for a divining rod.

MINERALS

See metals and ores, mica, mouse-eaten quartz, pyrite, quartz.

mine rescue apparatus

In mining, apparatus permitting workers to carry out rescue operations in noxious atmosphere, such as that in mines during fires or following explosions. Such equipment includes oxygen tanks and breathing apparatus, including a regenerating substance to purify the breathed air and a closed circulation system.

mine rescue car

A mine railway car especially equipped with rescue apparatus, safety lamps, first-aid supplies, and other materials. These cars serve as movable stations for the training of miners in using rescue apparatus and giving first aid to the injured; as centers for the promotion of mine safety; and as emergency stations for assisting at mine fires, explosions, or other disasters.

mine rescue crew

A crew usually consisting of five men thoroughly trained in the wearing and use of *mine rescue apparatus, q.v.*

mine rescue lamp

An electric safety hand lamp used in rescue work. It is equipped with a lens that concentrates or diffuses the light beam as required.

miner's box

A wooden or iron box, located in or near the working place of the miner, in which he keeps his tools, supplies, etc.

miner's court

An independent court of justice set up by miners remote from settled regions.

miner's dial

An instrument used in surveying underground workings.

miner's elbow

A swelling on the back of the elbow caused by inflammation of the bursa over the olecranon; so called because the condition is common in miners.

miner's friend

A common name for the Davy lamp, a common type of safety lamp.

miner's inch

In mining, a water-inch; an opening 1 inch through a 2-inch plank, with a head of water 6 inches above the opening; such an opening will pass 93 pounds, or about 9 gallons, of water per minute.

miner's lamp

Any one of a variety of lamps used by a miner.

miner's law

Law such as that prevailing among the early miners of the West.

miner's meeting

A meeting of gold and silver miners in the West in connection with a *miner's court, q.v.*

miner's oil

An oil producing little smoke, used in a miner's wick-fed open lamp.

MINERS

See abajador, arreador, assistant pit boss, banksman, butty, cager, coaster, company buster, Cousin Jack, day shift, double-jacker, dyno, fire viewer, gold digger, gold washer, hard-rock miner, high grader, leaser, mine railroad workers, mine rescue crew, muckman, nipper, pithead man, pitman, powder hand, powder man, prospectors, quartz miner, quartz reefer, river sniper, rust eater, shack, short faker, short-stage man, shovel stiff, sluicer, staker, tar baby, ten-day miner, tool nipper, tributer, wife.

MINES

See adit, advance workings, air hole, air

shaft, attle, back, bank, blind lead, blind level, blind stope, blind vein, block heads, blowout, bobabza, bonanza, borraska, brattish, break-through, breast, bridal chamber, bulkhead, cap, casing, cave-in, cheek, choke-damp, collar, contact, coyote hole, cribbing, crosscut, crosscut tunnel, day hole, dead air, deadfall, dead rock, deep, diggings, dip, ditch, downcast, downdraft, drift, dump, eye, face, feeder, fire door, fire wall, flat, flookan, floor, footwall, force piece, founder shaft, frozen walls, gallery, glory hole, gold diggings, gold field, gold mine, gold wash, gopher hole, gossan, gouge, grass, grass roots, grout, hanging wall, harder than the hubs of hell, hand land, head frame, heading, headings, heave, horse, hurries, hurry, incline, incline drift, in place, intake, iron hat, jack-head pit, jamb, lagging, ledge, leg piece, length, level, lift, location, lode, lodes and veins, man hole, massive deposits, matrix, meeting, metals and ores, mill hole, mine, mine bank, minerals, mining, mining debris, open cut, operator, ore channel, ore chute, ore dump, ore pocket, ore reserves, outcrop, pack wall, patch, patio, peg, penthouse, pillar, pilot tunnel, pinch, pipe, pit, pitch, pitcher, pit head, pit mouth, placer, placer diggings, placer mine, plat, pocket diggings, pockety, post, prospect, prospectant rock, prospect hole, prospect tunnel, puck, quarry, quartz mine, runaround, scale, selvage, set, shaft, shaft house, shoofly, skin diggings, slickensides, snake hole, snatch, sole, sollar, stope, tailings, tail race, tick hole, trouble, tunnel, upcast, upraise, vug, wash place, wintz.

MINING

See Are you ready? assessment work, breasting up, broaching, chaffee work, coyoting, crevice, crevicing, cropping, cropping out, cross course, cut, Cut the rope! dead work, dike, drilling uppers, Dutchman, exploitation, forced production, forepole, goosing, gopher-hole blasting, grass is getting short, grass-root mining, grizzly, high-grade, hill diggings, hydraulic mining, jackknifing, leaching, man trip, Mud! open up a vein, overhand stoping, pack mustard, peg, placer diggings, plant, prospect, quartz mining, river mining, river sluicing, rob, rocking, salt, stoping, strike, strike a lead, turn, twist her tail, underhand stoping, winnowing.

mining camp

A place where miners live and work; a colony of miners settled temporarily near a mine.

mining claim

That portion of the public mineral lands which a miner takes and holds for mining purposes in accordance with mining laws. A parcel of land containing precious metal in the soil or rock. An area of mining land held by a claimant by virtue of location and entry. Also called *mineral claim*.

MINING CLAIMS

See discovery, discovery claim, fighting claim, forfeiture, mining claim, mining recorder, placer claim, pocket claim, quartz claim, sluicing claim, stake notice.

mining debris

The tailings from hydraulic mines.

mining district

In the early years of mining in the West, an organized self-governing settlement of miners independent of all other authority. A section of country, usually designated by name and described or understood as being confined within certain natural boundaries, in which gold and silver or other minerals may be found in paying quantities.

mining ditch

A ditch for conducting water; a sluice.

mining for lead

A cowboy's expression for probing for a bullet in the body of someone who has been shot.

MINING MACHINERY AND EQUIPMENT

See air hoist, anchor, arrastrar, arrastre, banjo, barney, bitches, blanket tables, blast furnace, blower, bonnet, buggy, bullfrog, cage, cage cover, cage guides, cage seat, caisson, chippy, concentration table, cradle, deadman, dipping needle, fire board, flop gate, flume, gallow frame, gallows, giant, glad hand, granny bar, ground hog, guides, hacienda, hanging bolt, hoist, horn spoon, hudge, hurdy-gurdy, idiot-stick, Irish baby buggy, iron mule, jackhammer, jap, jaw crusher, jig, jill poke, judge, kibble, larry, liner machine, little giant, long tom, man cage, Mike, mineral rod, mine rescue apparatus, mine rescue car, miner's box, miner's dial, mining ditch, mining railroads, motor bed, moyle, muck stick, mule, ore car, ore mill, ore separator, pickety-poke, pit prop, pit pumps, placer dredge, pounder, quartz battery, quartz crusher, quartz mill, quartz fuse, ram, riffle, riffle box, rocker, roundhouse, scraper, self-feeder, shield, ship, sill, single jack, skip, sluice, snore holes, spiling, spoon, stamp hammer, stamp mill, stoping machine, stopperboards, stull, sweat board, tom, undercurrent, warrior, wash pan, whim, whip, widow-maker, wiggle-tail, witch stick, wooden piston.

MINING PROCESSES

See amalgamation, assay, assay balance, assayer, assay master, assay value, bar diggings, buddling, canalón, carga, cementation, cleanup, cobbing, compound cradle, concentration, drift mining, fire assay, flotation, flow sheet, flume, mill, pan, patio process, placer mining, roast, sampling works, smelting, stamping, Washoe process.

MINING RAILROADS

See dilly road, giraffe, mule, ore car, slag buggy, trams.

mining recorder

In a mining camp, a person selected to keep a record of all mining claims and properties.

MIRAGES

See *false pond*.

mired down

What a freighter said when he was stuck in the mud.

misdeal

In gambling, any departure from the rules of correct dealing procedure.

misery whip

A logger's term for a cant hook.

Missouri feather bed

A cowboy's name for a bed made of straw ticks.

misty beyond

A cowboy's reference to death, something he does not fully understand.

mitt joint

A gambling place where marked cards are used.

mixed cattle

Cattle of various grades, ages, and sexes.

mixed herd

A herd of cattle of mixed sexes.

mixing brands

In sheep raising, the mixing of two or more brands or herds. This always entails a lot of hard work and is about the worst thing that can happen in lambing season. See *legging*.

Mix me a walk.

What the logger says when he is quitting and asking for his time.

mix the medicine

A cowboy's expression for the ability to cope with any situation.

moan

To buck. As a rider mounts a bronc, another cowboy may give some such useless warning as, "Look out, he's goin' to *moan* with you!"

moccasin

A shoe made of deerskin or other soft leather, worn by the American Indian.

moccasin mail

Trail messages left by trappers. When one trapping party preceded another, the leading party left messages of warning or reassurance in moccasins tied in trees. Later, cowmen on the trail left similar messages in the sand or in trees and referred to them by this name.

moccasin telegraph

The grapevine system of conveying news on the plains.

mochila

In the days of the pony express, a name for one of the mail pouches built into the skirt of the saddle. Later, a large piece of leather covering the saddle and put on after the saddle was cinched on the horse. It had a hole for the horn and a narrow slit to allow the cantle to slip through. The contraption is virtually obsolete now, but was frequently used in the early days, especially in California. From the Spanish, meaning *knapsack*.

mocho

An animal which has lost part of an ear or tail; also, a gotched or droop-horned animal. From the Spanish, meaning *cropped*.

mockey

A wild mare.

Modoc

The early California cattleman's name for a squatter; probably named for the Modoc Indians, whom he despised with equal vigor.

Molly

A logger's name for a strand of cable.

Molly Hogan

A logger's name for a reinforced eye on the end of a logging cable.

MONEY

See adobe, beaver, big pay, blow in, Boston dollar, cartwheel, cowboy change, dinero, fighting wages, flush, getaway money, ground money, hard chink, hard money, Lincoln skins, main line, mount money, overalls and snoose, pot, prize money, real, road stake, short bit, stake money, velvet, wampum.

monk

A logger's term for a lumberyard worker.

monkey

A logger's name for a bridge builder.

monkey nose

A cowboy's term for a *tapadero (q.v.)*; so called because of its shape—a short, turned-up front.

monkey style

A style of riding in which the rider seizes the horn of the saddle with one or both hands, pushes himself sideways out of the saddle, and stands on one stirrup with the knee rigid, his other leg resting midway between hip and knee across the seat of the saddle. His flexed knee joint and both hip joints absorb the shock.

Monkey Ward cowboy

A cowboy wearing a mail-order outfit and having little or no range experience.

monte

A card game, of Spanish and Mexican origin, in which three players bet on a bottom and top layout of two cards each. A Spanish pack of forty cards is generally used with no eights, nines, or tens, although sometimes only the nines and tens are discarded, and a forty-four-card pack is used. After the shuffle and cut the dealer holds the pack face downward, draws the two bottom cards, and places them on the table face upward. This is called the *bottom layout*. The pack is then turned face upward; the card thus exposed is the *gate*. If it matches in denomination a card in either layout, the dealer pays all bets which have been made on that layout.

monte bank

A table for monte, or a place where the game is played; also the game monte itself.

monte dealer

A dealer in a monte game; also called *monte banker*.

monte layout

The layout of monte cards.

monte sharp

A gambler who cheats at monte.

monte table

A table used in monte.

monte thrower

See *broad pitcher*.

monte tosser

See *broad pitcher*.

Montgomery Ward woman sent west on approval

A homely woman. The cowman has his own unique expressions for homeliness. Roarin' Edens spoke of a woman he considered shy of beauty by saying, "She had a face built for a hackamore." Dutch Roeder spoke of a certain lady whose beauty he did not admire with the statement that "she ain't nothin' for a drinkin' man to look at." Another puncher, speaking of a woman of considerable heftiness, said that she "only needed four more pounds o' lard to git into a sideshow," while Rowdy Bibbs spoke of another as being "uglier'n a Mexican sheep."

montura

A cowboy's term for a riding horse. A term occasionally used for a saddle. From the Spanish.

moon

One month, the Indian's measurement of time.

mooner

A logger's name for a mythical creature of the logging woods.

moon-eyed

Said of a horse with white, glassy eyes.

moonlight roping

Roping of brush cattle. Such cattle hide out in the brush in daytime and come out to little clearings to feed at night. On moonlight nights the cowman takes advantage of this habit.

moonshining

Working on roundup in country so rough that packs had to be used in place of chuck wagons. Also, night driving and dry camping.

more guts than you could hang on a fence

A cowboy's expression for someone with unusual courage.

more lip than a muley cow

A cowboy's expression for someone who talks too much.

More straw!

The call the branders send up when they want more calves brought to the branding fire.

more wrinkles on his horns

A cowboy's expression for someone who has become older and wiser. This expression came from the fact that the wild cattle of the brush and brakes were horn-wrinkled from old age reached through the freedom bought by wisdom.

Mormon blanket

A cowboy's term for a quilt made from scraps of faded overalls and jumpers.

Mormon brakes

A tree tied behind a wagon to retard its downhill speed. This device is said to have been first used by Mormon pioneers who crossed the San Bernardino Mountains in 1850.

Mormon buckskin

A cowboy's term for baling wire.

Mormon dip

A cowboy's term for milk gravy.

Mormon dog

A tin can filled with pebbles, used in place of dogs in some sections of the Northwest to scare cattle from their hiding places in rough country.

Mormon iron

Rawhide; perhaps so called because the Mormons used rawhide instead of nails in the construction of their tabernacle as well as other structures. Also called *Mormon nails*.

MORMONS

See hickory Mormon, Jack Mormon.

Mormon shirttail

A shirt with a short tail; so called because the early Mormons usually lacked sufficient material to make long-tailed shirts.

Mormon tangle

A packer's name for a *squaw hitch*, or packer's knot.

moros

A horse of a bluish color.

morphidite

A logger's name for any vehicle that is different from a standard truck, such as a lift truck or a straddle truck; a corruption of *hermaphrodite*.

morral

A term widely used in the cattle country for a horse's feed bag. It is a fiber bag carried on the saddle horn when the rider is going on a trip and is riding a grain-fed horse. Also called *nose bag*. From the Spanish.

mossy horn
A Texas longhorn steer, six or more years old, whose horns have become wrinkled and scaly; also called *moss horn*. The term is sometimes applied to an old cowman.

Mother Hubbard loop
An extra-large loop on a rope.

Mother Hubbard saddle
An early-day saddle, the first improvement upon the Mexican saddle, which consisted of little more than a tree and stirrup leathers. The Mother Hubbard had a housing like a mochila, an almost square piece of leather with a hole for the horn and a slit for the cantle, the whole being detachable. Later this leather was made a permanent part of the saddle, and was designed to give more comfort to both horse and rider.

mother lode
In mining, the principal lode or vein passing through a particular district or section of country.

mother up
Said of female stock when they claim their young.

motor bed
In mining, the inclined bottom of a stamp used in crushing ores. One of a series of inclined terraces; the pulp passes through the screens of one battery and is discharged into the next, where it is crushed still finer.

motte
A western term for a clump of trees.

mount
The horses assigned to a rider for his personal use during his employment at a ranch. The number of horses assigned a rider depends largely upon the size of the ranch and the kind of country to be worked. Seven to ten horses make an average mount, including one or two broncs which the cowboy rides on circle to get them used to cow work. The word *mount* is usually used in sections which employ the term *remuda* in speaking of the band of saddle horses. In the northern, or *cavvy*, country personal horses are called the *string*.

mountain boomer
A cowboy's name for a cow of the hilly country. A species of large mountain lizard.

mountain canary
A westerner's name for a burro.

mountain dew
A trader's name for the liquor made in Taos, New Mexico.

mountain lamb
A westerner's euphemism for a deer killed out of season.

mountain meal
A miner's name for infusorial earth, or diatomite, used in making explosives.

mountain oyster
The testicle of a bull. Some find it a choice delicacy when roasted or fried.

MOUNTING
See cheeking, ear down, flying mount, fork, hairpin, Indian-broke, Indian side of a horse, near, pony-express mount, running mount, settin' on his arm, step across, take a run.

mount money
In rodeo, money paid to a performer riding, roping, or bulldogging in an exhibition and not in competition.

mouse-eaten quartz
A miner's term for porous quartz.

mouthy
A cowboy's word for someone inclined to talk a great deal. Such a person is not usually held in high repute by the cowman, whose philosophy is "The bigger the mouth the better it looks when shut."

move a peg
A trader's expression meaning *to move a step* or *to move a leg*.

mover
An emigrant moving west to settle; a person who participated in the tide of western migration. A person habitually moving

from one range to another in a covered wagon, usually a squatter. As one cowboy said, many squatters "had 'nough offspring to start a public school." Another cowman of my acquaintance once referred to such an outfit with, "By the number of descendants he's got he musta been a bishop in Utah."

moving camp

Transferring a roundup camp. In earlier days, when a roundup camp was to be moved, the wagon boss gave instructions which no one but a cowhand familiar with the country could understand. The night-hawk drove up the remuda early. Saddle horses were caught and saddled, and the rest of the horses were left to graze nearby. The rope corral was coiled and put into the wagon, and beds were rolled and piled into it, too. Every cowhand found something to do, or he would not be a cowboy. Some harnessed the cook's teams while others helped him pack and stow his pots and utensils.

When everything was ready, the cook crawled upon his wagon seat and was handed the lines by a thoughtful cowhand, who, before he realized the lines were out of his hands, saw the cook herding his half-raw broncs across the rough, roadless country. The mess wagon was rattling and swaying so wildly behind that running team that the cowboy wondered how the outfit held together. By the time the cowboys reached the new camp at noon, the cook had camp set up and a hot meal waiting for them.

movin' sheep

Running sheep over a cliff or off the range, a common occurrence during the war between sheep and cattle factions.

moyle

In mining, a drill or short bar sharpened to a point, used in cutting hitches and in broaching.

mozo

In packing, the assistant on a pack train; from the Spanish, meaning *young man*.

muchacha

In the Southwest, a common term for a girl; from the Spanish.

muck

In mining, earth, including dirt, gravel, hardpan, or rock, to be or being excavated. To excavate or remove dirt.

muck-a-muck

A term for food sometimes used by cowboys of the Northwest, borrowed from the Cayuse Indian.

mucker

In mining, a workman who removes gravel, hardpan, etc., from a mine; he loads mine cars and in most mines is also a *trammer*, pushing the cars to the mouth of the shaft, tunnel, or adit.

muckman

A common name for a miner. A miner's term for his long-handled shovel.

muck stick

A miner's term for his shovel.

Mud!

In mining, the call of a driller indicating that the water poured into the drill hole has formed mud and that the hammering on the drill is to stop.

mud clerk

In steamboating, the second clerk, whose duty it was to go out on the unpaved levees in any weather and deliver and receive freight. Since the levees were usually muddy in rainy weather, the name was fitting.

mud drum

In steamboating, a long tube of boiler steel set thwartships under a battery of boilers and connected to each boiler by a *mud-drum leg*. The sediment in raw river water settled in this drum and periodically was discharged by opening a valve at its base which was piped overboard. The sound emitted when the valve was opened was a peculiar, hoarse, sullen roar, quite disturbing to passengers not acquainted with steamboats, who frequently suspected that the boilers were about to blow up. This operation was called *blowing out the mud drums*. Thus when a riverman felt the daily urge, he excused himself by saying, "Well, I've got to go below and blow out my mud drums."

mud hen

A member of a logging crew that works in the swamps.

mud hook

A trapper's term for a foot.

mud wagon

A type of vehicle used extensively during stagecoaching days and much more simply constructed than a coach. It weighed less than the Concord and was built much lower to the ground to reduce the danger of overturning. The mud wagon was slung on thorough braces rather than on mainsprings. Largely because of its light weight and its low center of gravity, this vehicle was employed in mountain travel and over heavy roads. It was usually pulled by mules. Nine passengers were accommodated inside, and another rode on the outside seat with the driver. Also called *stage wagon*.

mug

A cowboy's term meaning *to bulldog* (a calf).

mujer

A girl or young lady. The cowboy uses this word for color and variety when speaking of his girl. From the Spanish, meaning *woman* or *wife*.

mula

What the early trapper called a mule. The inexperienced merchants of Santa Fe were likely to have a large supply of this stubborn merchandise on hand. About the only chance they had of getting rid of them was when the trappers came to town to get full of Taos lightning and could be persuaded to buy them for an Indian or Mexican sweetheart. From the Spanish.

mulada

A drove or herd of mules. The word was occasionally used by Americans as a convenience, being shorter than *mule herd*, or *herd of mules*.

mulatto

A packer's name for a drove of mules.

mule

A miner's and logger's name for a *donkey*, *q.v.*

mule-ears

A cowboy's name for boots with pull-on straps at the top. Also, a name for *tapaderos* (*q.v.*), so called because of their shape.

mule-footed

A cowboy's term for a horse with round hoofs, a characteristic usually found in mountain horses.

mule-hipped horse

A horse with hips that slope too much.

mulero

A mule driver; also called *mule skinner* (*q.v.*)—mules are always *skinned*, never *driven*. From the Spanish.

mule's breakfast

A cowboy's name for a straw bed.

MULES

See Arizona nightingale, bell sharp, dragtail, four-up, gambler's ghost, hardtail, kitchen mule, knobhead, long-eared chuck wagon, mulada, mula, mulatto, pack mule.

mule skinner

A mule driver. A miner's name for the man who drives the ore cars in a mine. A logger's name for the engineer of the *donkey*, *q.v.*

mule train

In packing, a train of pack mules. Occasionally, a train of wagons drawn by mules.

muley

A hornless cow. Such a cow, handicapped in defending herself from other cattle, beds down at night on the outside edge of the herd, away from the horned stuff. Coming thus under the cowboy's personal observation as he circles the herd, she is either cussed or called something endearing by him. The cowboy does not like to drive muley cattle because they jamb together, suffer from the heat, and lose more weight than horned cattle. Then, too, they force him to use the greatest patience. (J. Evetts Haley, *The XIT Ranch* [Chicago, Lakeside Press, 1929], 192.)

muley cow

A logger's term for his cant hook.

muley saddle

A saddle without a horn.

mulligan car

A logger's name for a railroad car from which lunch is served in the woods so that the men need not return to the cookhouse.

mulligan mixer

A logger's name for the cook.

Murphy wagon

A wagon used by the early freighters; named for its maker, the Murphy Company of St. Louis.

music roots

A cowboy's name for sweet potatoes.

mustang

A wild horse, a term restricted to the un-mixed variety. To catch wild horses. From the Spanish *mesteño*, meaning *strays from the mesta*. A *mesta* was a group of cattle and horse raisers; thus the early mustangs were horses that escaped from the *mestas* and ran wild.

mustang court

A cowboy's kangaroo court.

mustanger

A man engaged in catching mustangs for a livelihood; from the Spanish *mesteñero*.

mustangler

A herder of mustangs.

mustard

A miner's name for cement.

mustard the cattle

To stir up cattle and get them heated or excited.

mutton puncher

A cowboy's term for a sheepherder.

muzzle

A wooden or metal hood with projecting spikes, fitted over a calf's nose to wean it. This term seems to be peculiar to the Northwest; in other sections the same contraption is called *blab*.

muzzle-loaders

What a logger called old-fashioned bunks into which men had to crawl over the foot of the bed.

N

"You can judge a man by the hoss he rides"

nag

A cowboy's term for a horse of poor quality.

narrow at the equator

A cowboy's expression meaning *hungry*. I heard one puncher say that his "stomach was so shrunk it wouldn't chamber a liver pill," and another that his "tapeworm was hollerin' for fodder."

Navy

A westerner's term for the Navy Colt revolver.

Navvy

A Navajo Indian pony, which the cowboy held to be about the poorest specimen of horseflesh on earth.

near

A western horseman's term meaning *left*. A cowboy mounts from the *near*, or left, side of the horse. To the driver of horses the *near-wheeler* is the left-wheeler. See *off*.

neck

To subdue an unruly cow or one with a roving disposition by tying it to a more tractable cow. This practice was frequently resorted to in the days of the longhorn. After the two animals had worn themselves down trying to go in different directions at the same time, the wilder one was enough subdued to move along in company with its fellows. A good neck animal was valued highly by its owner.

neck meat or nothin'

A cowboy's expression meaning *all or nothing*.

neck oil

A cowboy's term for whisky.

neck-rein

To guide a horse by pressure of the reins against its neck rather than pressure against the bit.

neck-reiner

A horse trained to turn at the slightest pressure of the reins on his neck.

necktie frolic

A hanging.

necktie party

A hanging.

necktie social

A hanging.

neck yoke

In freighting, a bar, usually of wood, connecting two draft animals working abreast and supporting the end of the pole or tongue of the vehicle which they drew.

Ned

A trader's name for a United States soldier. A westerner's name for bacon or salt pork.

needle

A long stick of timber between wickets at a movable dam to stop the flow or leakage of water. A *needle flat* was a small barge used in transporting such timber.

needle gun

A rifle used on the frontier, so called because of its long firing pin, which detonated the powder by plunging through the paper cartridge to strike the primer at the base of the bullet.

needs a wet nurse

A cowboy's expression describing an irresponsible or ignorant person.

Nellie

A cowman's name for an old, skinny cow or steer.

NERVOUSNESS

See buck ague, goosey, walking the fence, wire-edged, wobbly horrors.

nester

A squatter who settles on state or government land. The term was applied with contempt by the cattleman of the Southwest to any early homesteader who began tilling the soil in the range country. Viewed from a ridge, the early nester's home, with its little patch of brush cleared and stacked in a circular form to protect his first feed patch from range cattle, looked like a gigantic bird's nest. The cowboy, ever quick to notice resemblances, mentioned it to the next man he met, and the name spread and stuck to every man that settled on the plains to till the soil. (John M. Hendrix, "Feedin'," *West Texas Today* [March, 1936], 6.)

nesting

Homesteading. See *nester*.

never-sweat

A cowboy's name for a Mexican.

new ground

What a cowboy sometimes calls a tenderfoot.

NEWS

See grapevine telegraph, stern-line telegraph.

nice kitty

A cowboy's term for a skunk.

nickel-plated

A cowboy's term for the best in anything, from the nickel-plated decorations on his clothing and riding gear to a well-dressed woman.

nicking

See *creasing*.

nigger

In steamboating, an engine used to hoist freight and to warp the boat over sand bars. In mining, a dark-colored ore. In logging, an air-activated arm with a hook, operated by a sawyer, used to turn a log for selective cutting.

nigger brand

A cowboy's term for a galled sore on a horse's back caused by careless riding. To ride so as to cause such sores.

nigger catcher

A small, slotted leather flap on one or both sides of a saddle, usually at the base of the fork or cantle of a two-cinched saddle. Its purpose is to hold the long, free end of the latigo through the slit when the saddle is cinched up.

nigger day

A logger's name for Saturday.

nigger driver

A logger's term for a foreman, especially a strict one.

nigger engine

A steam ram or plunger used in a sawmill to turn and adjust a log on the carriage.

nigger-heeled

Said of a horse whose front toes turn out with the heels in.

nigger holes

In logging, holes in a piece of lumber caused by the *nigger, q.v.*

nigger horse

A black horse.

nigger-in-a-blanket

A cowboy dessert, usually made of raisins in dough.

night drive

The trailing of cattle at night.

night guard

The night watch of a cattle herd. Each man in camp, except the cook and the wrangler, must serve his turn. Usually there were two men to each guard for the average herd. Upon reaching the bed ground,

they rode in opposite directions as they circled the herd. This practice served the double purpose of keeping the men separated and having a man looking each way so that no animal could slip away unnoticed in the dark. Two punchers riding side by side and talking would be bound to neglect their job. If things went smoothly, they kept up this riding until they were relieved.

This was truly a job for a man "with fur on his brisket" on stormy nights when it was so dark "he couldn't find his nose with both hands." He had no stars to comfort him and could not even strike a match. If the cattle were unusually nervous, he had to be extremely cautious; as one cowhand put it, "You had to ride a mile to spit." On pleasant nights the work was not so hard; but even then the cowboy must stay in the saddle all the time, and the hours seemed long and lonesome.

When working with the roundup or with a trail herd, the cowhand did not get much sleep, and what he did get was interrupted by having to take his turn at night guard. But after he was on the job a while, he rarely needed to be waked. Sleeping with his ear to the ground, he could hear the rider coming off the herd when he was still a great distance away, and by the time he reached camp, the new guard was ready to take his place.

nighthawk

A man who herded the saddle horses at night—one of those fellows who was said to have "swapped his bed for a lantern." Though his duty—keeping the saddle horses from straying too far away—was identical with that of the day wrangler, colloquial usages caused the day man to *wrangle* horses and the nighthawk to *herd* them. (Philip A. Rollins, *The Cowboy* [New York, Charles Scribner's Sons, 1936], 220.) Some outfits used only one wrangler and had no nighthawk.

The job of the nighthawk was a lonely one, and it was hard for him to keep from dozing in the saddle; the sleep he got in the daytime at a noisy camp made him long for a softer job. If the horses were quiet, and he stood in well with the cook, he might sneak in and get a cup of coffee from the pot which was kept on the coals for the night herders when they changed shifts.

If the night was dark, he was apt to

lose a few horses and would be late bringing up the remuda at daylight. Then he caught it from the boss, for, no matter how good his excuse, it carried no weight with the man in charge.

night-herd
To take charge of cattle on the bed ground.

night herder
A cowhand whose immediate duty was to herd cattle at night.

night horse
A horse picketed so that he can be instantly caught for night use. A good night horse is of a special type, and in the days of the open range was one of the most essential horses. He was selected for his sure-footedness, good eyesight, and sense of direction. He must not be high-strung, but must be gentle, unexcitable, and intelligent. He was never used except for night work, and during stampedes much depended upon him. His rider's life depended on his ability to see, run, dodge, and keep his footing. He could see an animal straying from the herd and turn it back without guidance, and he could find his way back to camp on the darkest night. Every cowman loved his night horse and valued him beyond price.

night mare
A humorous name for the *night horse* (*q.v.*), though it is never a mare.

nimble-blooded
A cowboy's expression for anyone or anything active.

Nina from Carolina
In dice, nine as a point.

nipper
A miner's name for the flunky who collects and distributes tools in a mine.

nipple
In an early-day gun, a metal cap containing an explosive set on the end of a tube. When the cap was struck by the hammer, fire flashed from the tube and ignited the main powder charge in the barrel.

no beans in the wheel
A cowboy's expression meaning that

there were no cartridges in the cylinder of a gun.

no breakfast forever
A cowboy's expression for someone caught in a prairie fire and burned to death.

no-dice
In dice, a throw that does not count in the game and must therefore be repeated by the thrower. No-dice occurs when neither die hits the board, wall, or table, or when one or both dice fall off the playing surface. If only one die hits the board, the throw counts. The same applies when one or both dice hit a person or object after hitting the wall. Authorities differ about whether a cocked die counts as no-dice.

noise
A miner's term for dynamite.

no medicine
A cowboy's expression meaning *no information* (upon a subject).

NONSENSE
See burro milk, Mexican oats.

noon
A trader's and freighter's term for making a noon stop for camp, with all the activities that would be concerned in such a stop, such as unharnessing teams, building fires, cooking the noon meal, and then starting on again. Also called *nooning it*.

nooning it
See *noon*.

North Bend
In logging, one of the three most commonly used high-line systems, the others being the Lidgerwood and the Tyler.

norther
A driving gale from the north that hurtles over the Southwest and, coming into collision with warm, moist breezes from the Gulf of Mexico, causes a sudden and extreme drop in temperature. What is called a *blizzard* in the rest of the West is called a *norther* in Texas and the Southwest. As one cowhand at Amarillo, Texas, said of such storms, "They jes' pour off the North Pole

with nothin' to stop 'em but a bob-wire fence, and it's full of knotholes." A particularly violent gale is called a *blue norther* because it is usually accompanied by blue-black clouds.

Northwest

A name the American trappers gave to Hudson's Bay Company.

nose

In logging, to trim or round the end of a log. In steamboating, the stem, forward end of the hull, or forecastle. Steamboats have many "human" trimmings: *noses, eyes, knuckles, bellies, ribs, knees.*

nose bag

A *morral, q.v.* A cowboy's name for an eating house. A logger's name for his lunch pail.

nose-bag show

In logging, a camp where the midday meal is carried to the woods in lunch buckets; not highly thought of by loggers of these later days.

no-see-ums

What an Indian called the buffalo gnats, because they were so small; the cowboy adopted the name.

nose paint

A cowboy's name for whisky. One cow-hand spoke of another at a bar "paintin' his nose with cow swallows of that stuff that cures snake bites."

nosing

In steamboating, the planking around the outer edge of a deck, usually backed upon a second layer of planking called *skirting*.

notcher

A gunman who placed a notch on his gun for each man he killed; a man who apparently killed to gain a reputation as a desperado.

notch in his tail

A cowboy's expression for a horse that has killed a man.

no time

In rodeo, a ruling signifying that a contestant in a calf-roping or bulldogging contest has failed within the allotted time. These sad words have wrecked many a contestant's hopes for a chance at final money.

Now you're logging!

A logger's expression of commendation.

nubbin'

A cowboy's term for the saddle horn.

nursey

A cowboy's name for the driver of the old-time calf wagon used on trail drives. What the driver answered when he was called this was salty and unprintable.

nutcrackers

A cowboy's name for teeth.

nutria

A trapper's name for a beaver or a beaver skin; actually, the skin of a coypu.

nutter

In sheep raising, a man who castrates the young males of the lamb crop.

nutting

Castrating young male lambs.

O

"Another man's life don't make no soft pillow at night"

ocean wave
A rope trick that consists of flipping a noose backward and forward in an undulating movement.

odd
In faro, a method of cheating for the house in which the dealer surreptitiously introduces an extra card that he can control. See also *double odd*.

odd-even
See *copper the odds*.

off
To a westerner, the right side. The horseman mounts from the left side. To a stagecoach driver or teamster, the right-hand leader.

off herd
In cattle herding, off duty.

off his feed
A cowboy's expression for someone who looks or feels bad.

off his mental reservation
A cowboy's expression for a weak-minded person.

OFFICERS
See buscadero, chili chaser, great seizer, high-grass constable, John Law, lawdog, redcoat, star toter, stock detective, town clown.

off the reservation
A phrase referring to Indians who had left their reservation. Also, said of anyone speaking or acting out of turn.

off-wheeler
In freighting, the horse on the right of the team nearest the vehicle.

oiler
A cowboy's name for a Mexican.

oily
A cowboy's term meaning *tough* or *mean*.

oily bronc
A bad horse.

Okie
A logger's term of disparagement.

Oklahoma rain
A cowboy's name for a dust storm.

OLD
See broke down, digger, don't travel like a colt no more, getting long in the tooth.

old cedar
A six gun. A gun with a cedar stock.

old coon
A trapper's and trader's form of address for a friend; a term of camaraderie.

old hard-eye
The saw filer in a sawmill; so named because he closes one eye while filing a fine edge on the saw teeth. Also called *old squint-eye*.

old hoss
A trapper's and trader's form of address for a friend; a term of camaraderie.

old man
A cowboy's name for the owner or boss of the outfit. A steamboatman's name for the captain. A logger's name for the boss or superintendent. In each case, the name is used in speaking of the man, not to him. The *old man* may not be half as old as the speaker. The term is used in no disrespectful sense; indeed, it is rather a term of endearment.

old-man him
A cowboy's expression for throwing a looped rope over the neck or back of a wild bronc in a corner or crowded enclosure,

moving him over, and passing the free end of the rope through the loop; in this fashion the animal is roped wherever the roper sees fit, for greater control and security.

old pills

A logger's name for the camp doctor.

old reliable

A cowman's name for his Sharps rifle; so called because it could always be depended upon.

old safety first

What a logger calls the welfare man.

old socks

A logger's affectionate name for a friend.

old squint-eye

A logger's name for a saw filer in a sawmill.

old thing

A faro bank. The game of faro. The implication is that the game is braced. In argot, syphilis.

old-timer

A man who had lived in the country a long time. Most old-timers had to fight many battles before the country became settled, and it could be said of such a one that "his scars was a regular war map." It was said of all good old-time Texans that they were "raised to vote the Democratic ticket, love good whisky, and hate Mexicans."

OLD-TIMERS

See alkalied, blond Swede, duffer, entitled to a warm corner, grissel heel, home guard, hung up his saddle, more wrinkles on his horns, mossy horn, old-timer, silver tip.

old woman

A cowboy's affectionate name for the cook, but used behind his back.

on circle

In roundup, a term applied when cowboys leave camp in a bunch, with the foreman turning off the riders at intervals to gather cattle and drive them to a designated point, called the *roundup ground*. The point will change each day until the range is completely covered.

one-eared bridle

A bridle composed of a single broad strap with a slit in it which fits over one ear to keep it in place.

one-eyed scribe

A cowboy's name for his six gun.

one foot in the stirrup

A cowboy's expression meaning, according to context, *to do something halfheartedly* or *to be ready for an emergency*.

one-horse outfit

A small ranch or outfit.

one-man horse

A horse broken in such a way that he will let no one ride him except the man who has broken him.

one on the layout and three in the hand

In faro, the three-seven system used by cheap gamblers. See *three-one*.

one side against the other

In faro, a system in which the player bets the ace, deuce, trey, four, five, and six to lose and the king, queen, jack, ten, nine, and eight to win, or vice versa. The seven is usually barred.

on his own hook

A trapper's expression describing a free trapper, one who did not work for a fur company.

on the Black Hills

An early expression which referred to driving a man from his chosen range and pushing him so far north that his final destination was the Badlands of the Dakotas, to the cowman, a place synonymous with hell.

on the cuidado

On the dodge; from the Spanish meaning *on the lookout*.

on the dodge

Running and hiding from the law. As Dewlap Burdick said, a man on the dodge was usually "one of them fellers that keeps his hoss wonderin' at the hurry they're in, and he don't leave 'nough tracks to trip an ant."

on the drift
Said of a cowboy who is looking for a job or aimlessly riding through the country.

on the high lope
Said of a cowboy who is going somewhere in a hurry, generally ahead of a sheriff.

on the hoof
Live cattle. Also, cattle traveling by trail under their own power, as distinguished from cattle being shipped by rail.

on their heads
An expression describing cattle that are grazing.

on the lift
An expression describing an animal that is down and cannot get up without help.

on the lock
A freighter's term used when the movement of the front wheel of a wagon was stopped or blocked.

on the lookout
On the dodge.

on the loose
A phrase describing a trapper who had desided to leave the employ of a fur company and trap on his own.

on the peck
A cowboy's expression meaning *fighting mad*. Jim Houston, in telling a yarn about being charged by a cow on the peck when he was afoot in a branding corral, said: "There wasn't no love light in that cow's eyes as she makes for me. I fogs it across the corral like I'm goin' to a dance and she's scratchin' the grease off my pants at ever' jump. Seein' I can't make the fence in time, Brazos Gowdy jumps down and throws his hat in the old gal's face. Seein' a cowboy come apart in pieces like that makes her hesitate till I climb the fence without losin' anything more'n some confidence, a lot a wind, and a little dignity.

You can take it from me that a cow with a fresh-branded calf might be a mother, but she shore ain't no *lady*."

on the prairie
An Indian expression meaning *free whiskey*. In opening a trading session with the Indians, it was a custom for a trader to give them a quantity of liquor *on the prairie*. The expression was soon adopted by both trappers and traders to describe anything free or given away.

on the prod
Another phrase meaning *on the peck, q.v.*

on the scout
On the dodge.

on the warpath
A cowboy's expression meaning *fighting mad*—as one cowman said, "mad as a bear with two cubs and a sore tail."

on tick
A cowboy's and logger's expression meaning *on credit*.

open a snap
To start a crooked gambling layout.

open bet
In faro, a wager playing a given card to win; so called because there is no copper placed upon it.

open brand
A cattle brand that is not boxed with framing lines.

open cut
In mining, a longitudinal surface working not entering cover.

opener
In poker, the person who begins the betting. The cards—a pair of jacks or better—with which a person may open the jackpot.

open-faced cattle
What the cowman calls white-faced Herefords.

open-face pie
A cowboy's and logger's name for a custard pie.

open heifer

A heifer that has not been spayed.

open range

Range that is not under fence.

open-range branding

The branding of calves or cattle on the open range away from corrals, a practice followed by the larger outfits in the early days. Open-range branding was also sometimes done by an owner when he came across a calf that had been overlooked during the roundup. It was more difficult to drive one or two head of cattle than a large herd, and a good cowman avoided driving his stock as much as possible. To avoid a long drive back to headquarters, the cowboy would rope the calf, tie it down, build a fire, and brand it where he found it. Open-range branding was also frequently practiced by the rustler, especially if he was where he was not likely to be seen by some range rider. For this reason the practice came to be looked upon with suspicion unless it was carried out in the presence of a regular roundup crew.

open reins

Reins not fastened together; reins independent of each other. Most cowhands prefer open reins because if the horse falls or the rider is thrown, the reins will fall to the ground and the horse will step on them, giving the rider a chance to catch him.

open roundup

A roundup in which the final bunching of cattle is in the open, not within a corral.

open-shop pants.

A cowboy's term for chaps.

open stirrups

Stirrups without tapaderos, or toe fenders.

open the pot

In gambling, to place money in the jackpot, thereby opening it for play.

open-toed holster

A holster with an open end, usually swung on a rivet.

open up a vein

In mining, to begin extracting ore.

open winter

A cowboy's term for a mild winter with no blizzards or storms.

operator

In mining, a person who works a mine either as an owner or as a lessee.

op'ra

The riding of a wild horse. A branding.

op'ra house

The top rail of the corral fence, from which one can watch a cowboy riding a bucking horse. It is also a time-honored conference place for all true range men where they talk over things in true range style—with laconic phrases that state their meaning without frills or mental reservations and silences that carry their thoughts forward to the next utterance.

opposition

A trapper's term for a competitive establishment operated near "his" river.

ORDERS

See powders, read the Scriptures, telling off the riders.

ore

In mining, mechanical or chemical compounds of metals with baser substances; a mineral consisting of a metal and some other substance, such as oxygen, sulphur, or carbon, in combination, being the source from which metals are usually obtained by smelting. A mineral serving as a commercial source of the metal it contains.

ore car

In mining, a car used to carry ore or waste rock from the mine.

ore channel

In mining, the space between the walls or boundaries of a lode which is occupied by ore and veinstone.

ore chute

In mining, an opening in ore or rock through which ore is dropped downward. An ore bin or pockets underground. A trough or lip at the bottom of a bin for moving ore to a car or conveyer. A channel shaft or trough in which ore is conveyed from a higher to a lower level.

ore dump

In mining, a heap or pile of ore at the tunnel or adit mouth, at the top of the shaft, or at some other place near the mine.

Oregon block

A temporary device, usually a chain or cable, passed around a stump and used to change the direction of the logging cable.

Oregon diamond hitch

A packer's knot formed by not bringing a loop of the running rope under and forward of the standing rope; so called because it was widely used in Oregon Territory.

OREGONIANS

See webfoots.

Oregon puddin' foot

A type of horse produced by crossing a riding horse with a draft horse, such as a Percheron or Clydesdale. This type was developed to some extent in Oregon for mountain work. Also called *Oregon bigfoot*.

Oregon short line

A name used in the Northwest for *fraid strap, q.v.*

orejano

A long-eared—that is, not earmarked—animal; thus unbranded and unmarked animal, a term used principally in California, Oregon, and Nevada. From the Spanish.

ore mill

In mining, a stamp mill; a concentrator.

ore pocket

In mining, an isolated and limited deposit of rich ore.

ore reserves

In mining, an ore body exposed and ready for stoping. The amount of ore than can be estimated in a mine.

ORES

See metals and ores.

ore separator

In mining, a cradle, frame, jiggling machine, washer, or other device or machine used in separating metal from broken ore, or ore from worthless rock.

original

A cowman's name for an imperfectly castrated horse.

ORNAMENTS

See concha, danglers, fofarraw.

Osnaburg sheets

Heavy duck sheets used by traders; named for Osnaburg, Germany, where a similar fabric was made.

otero

A cowboy's term for an unusually large steer, one "big as a mountain." From the Spanish, meaning *hill*.

otie

A cowboy's shortened form of *coyote*.

ought to be bored for the hollow horn

A cowboy's expression describing someone who seems to be feeble-minded. The expression originated in the early days; if a cow became ill and the sickness was pronounced a case of *hollow horn (q.v.)*, as a cure a small hole was bored in the horn. (J. Frank Dobie, *The Longhorns* [Boston, Little, Brown and Company, 1941], 211.) One cowhand spoke of a feeble-minded person with, "The Lord poured in his brains with a teaspoon, and somebody jiggled His arm."

ought to be playing with a string of spools

A cowboy's expression describing someone young and foolish, and also an ignorant or crazy person.

out-coyote

A cowboy's expression meaning *to outsmart*.

outcrop

In mining, a stratum that emerges on the surface of the ground, a term used in connection with a vein or lode. To crop out or appear above the surface of the ground.

outer circle

A cowboy's term for the longer, outside circle on roundup, which reaches the outside limits of the territory to be "worked." The tougher horses are used on the outer circle.

outfit

A term used by westerners in several references, depending on context: All the people engaged in any one enterprise or living in any one establishment, as a trader's organization or a ranch. A party of people traveling together. The physical belongings of any person or group of persons. In logging, the company and equipment engaged in the removal of a section of timber.

outfox

A westerner's word meaning *to outsmart* or *outguess*.

outlaw

A horse which is particularly vicious and untamable. A wild cow or steer. A man who has committed deeds that have placed him on the wrong side of the law; a man who follows the western philosophy that "the best health resorts are the places unknown." As Charlie Russell said, in his *Trails Plowed Under*, some of the early outlaws lived a life "that'd make some o' them scary yellow-backed novels look like a primer."

OUTLAWS

See bad men.

out of the money

In rodeo, a phrase describing a riding contestant who loses by being thrown, drawing an inferior horse, or breaking some rule.

output

In mining, the gross produce of a mine.

outraker

In steamboating, one of the joists supporting the main deck from the hull outboard to the *nosing, q.v.*; invariably pronounced by rivermen as though it were spelled *outrigger*. The portion of the main deck over the hull is supported by similar joists called *deck beams* or *floor timbers*.

outrider

A cowboy who rides about the range to keep a sharp lookout for anything that might happen to the detriment of his employer; also called *range rider*. While his duties are similar to the line rider's, unlike the line rider, who patrols a prescribed boundary, the outrider is commissioned to ride anywhere.

outriding

Performing the duties of an *outrider, q.v.*; also called *range riding*.

outside

In gambling, participation in a gambling game as a patron; the opposite of *inside, q.v.* A professional who is beating the game from *outside* is posing as a sucker in order to fleece the house.

outside man

A cowboy who represents his brand at outside ranches during a general roundup. He is usually at the top of the cowboy profession and is a riding encyclopedia on brands and earmarks. His work is to follow the roundups of other ranges and turn back strays of his brand. His eye is so well trained that he can discover cattle belonging to his outfit in a vast, milling herd raising a fog of dust that an ordinary man could not see through. See *rep.*

overalls and snoose

A logger's term for what he works for—his pay.

overbit

An earmark made by doubling the ear in and cutting a small piece out of the upper part of the ear; the cut is 1 inch long and about 1/3 inch deep.

overgraze

To graze land to excess.

overhack

An earmark made by simply cutting down about 1 inch on the upper side of the ear.

over-half-crop

An earmark made by splitting the ear from the top, midway, about halfway back to the head and cutting off the upper half.

overhand stoping

In mining, work started from the bottom of a block of ore, the ore being removed from below. In this way the work of drilling and blasting is done over the miner's head.

overhand toss

In roping, a favorite method of catching horses in a corral. The only difference between this method and the hooley-ann is that the hooley-ann turns over as the whirl is started and the overhand toss turns over as it leaves the hand. The loop is fairly small, and while it is held at shoulder height, the bottom part of it is kept swinging back and forth. When the throw is made, the loop is swung backward around the head and released toward the target. The loop is turned over as it is swung upward before it is let go, so that at the final moment the back of the hand is facing the left, thumbs down. In this way, when the loop comes down, the honda is on the right instead of on the left (W.M. French, "Ropes and Roping," *Cattleman*, Vol. XXVI, No. 12 [May, 1940], 17–30.)

overhead loop

In roping, a throw made by starting the whirl across the front of the roper to the left, with two or three whirls around the head for momentum, and then casting at the target by whirling the loop out in front as it comes across the right shoulder. (W. M. French, "Ropes and Roping," *Cattleman*, Vol. XXVI, No. 12 [May, 1940], 17–30.)

overland coach

A stagecoach operating across the western plains, especially one used on the Overland Mail Route.

overland mail

Mail that was carried overland by stagecoach; an overland mail system or service.

overo

A word of Argentine origin used by horse breeders to describe a pinto horse with distinctive color characteristics in which the white spots always begin at the belly and extend upward. The dark spots are usually smaller and more plentiful. From the Spanish, meaning *blossom-colored horse*. See *tobiano*. (George M. Glendenning, "Overos and Tobianos," *Western Horseman*, Vol. VII, No. 2 [January–February, 1941], 12.)

overround

An earmark made by cutting a half-circle from the top of the ear.

overshot stacker

On cattle ranches, a forklike arrangement, used with a buck rake, which throws hay backward onto a stack. Both devices shell the hay badly and leave it tangled and hard to remove from the stack.

overslope

An earmark made by cutting the ear about two-thirds of the way back from the tip, straight to the center of the ear at its upper side.

oversplit

An earmark made by a simple split of the ear downward on the upper side.

over the hump

A logger's term meaning *over the mountains*.

over the willows

A cowboy's expression meaning *high water*. If the trail boss rode back to the herd after he had viewed the turbulent river ahead and announced that the river was *over the willows*, he meant that it was at flood stage and that there would be several hundred yards of swimming water.

owlhead

A cowboy's term for a horse that cannot be trained to be ridden or to work.

own hook

A westerner's expression meaning *alone*. When he declares that he will do something *on his own hook*, he means to do it alone.

oxbows

The old-style large wooden stirrups. Also called *ox-yokes*.

Oxen

See bull, bull team, wohaw.

ox-yokes

See *oxbows*.

P

"A change of pasture sometimes makes the calf fatter"

'Pache

A shortened form of *Apache* commonly used by southwesterners in early days.

pack

A cowboy's term for a bundle or bale. A packer's term for that portion of the load carried on one side of the mule's back. A load might consist of a single pack or of several packs, depending on the nature of the articles to be packed or the exigencies of the service. A cowboy's term meaning *to carry*. A cowman never *carries* anything, but *packs* it, as *packs a gun, packs his saddle*, etc.

pack a balloon

A logger's expression meaning *to carry one's bedroll*.

pack a card

A logger's expression meaning *to carry a union card*—that is, to be a union man.

pack cover

A section of heavy canvas used to wrap articles that might deteriorate from exposure to rain and dampness.

packer

A man who transported goods by means of pack animals.

packer first class

A packer skilled in the art of preparing cargo, including loading a pack mule and adjusting a load so that it balanced evenly on the mule's back. Such a packer was familiar with the *diamond hitch (q.v.)* and other hitches used in securing loads and was versed in the customs of the pack service.

packer second class

A novice in the art of packing.

PACKERS

See arriero, freighters, mozo, packer, packer first class, packer second class, pack-master, pack-mule express, pack outfit, pack rat, padrone.

packet

A river steamboat designed to carry freight on its decks and provided with quarters for passengers.

PACKING AND EQUIPMENT

See atajo, basket hitch, bell, blind, brake a load, diamond hitch, freighting, go, hold, line-up, load, manta, Mormon tangle, mule train, Oregon diamond hitch, packs, pack train, pack up, petata, settle, slinging and lashing, Tie! Tied! turned the pack.

packing the rigging

In logging, a term used by wobblies to describe a man who was carrying I.W.W. organizing supplies—literature, dues, books, etc.

packmaster

A master in the art of packing. A man who had charge of a pack train.

pack mule

A mule trained and used to carry loads of freight.

pack-mule express

A name given to packers who delivered mail, gold, and other articles. Their service was similar to that of an express company.

pack mustard

A miner's expression meaning to *carry a hod*.

pack outfit

Such supplies or equipment as one could pack or carry. A pack-mule freighting outfit. A company of outfitters who supply and guide campers.

pack rat

A rodent of the Rocky Mountains; so called because of his practice of leaving something in exchange when he carries anything off; also called *trade rat* and *wood rat*. Thus, a westerner's term for a petty thief. A name for a packer or guide. In logging, a lumber carrier.

packs

A trader's term for pack animals or a pack train.

packsaddle

A saddle used to carry freight, camp equipment, and other materials on the back of a pack animal; an *aparejo, q.v.*

PACKSADDLES AND EQUIPMENT

See alforja, aparejo, aparejo cover, aparejo hay, bag pannier, boot, boot bar, boot stick, box pannier, carrier piece, center stitch line, cincha, collar, corona, cross-buck saddle, crosstree, crupper, double hitch, eye, facings, finger loop, fuste, grupera, handhold, hyack, lair, lash rope, packsaddle, panniers, pole hitch, protecting sticks, rendering ring, ribbing up, rigging, rigging cover, saddle bar, salea, sawbuck, set up, shoe, sombre-jalma, tamping sticks, xerga.

packs a long rope

A cowboy's expression describing a cattle rustler.

packs his gun loose

A cowboy's expression describing someone who was always ready for a gun fight.

pack the deal

In gambling, to deal cards dishonestly.

pack the mail

A cowboy's expression meaning *to ride fast.*

pack train

A group of animals carrying packs of freight. An organization comprising perhaps fifty pack animals, a proper complement of men, and a complete equipment for carrying freight. It was one of the West's principal means of freighting in the early days, especially in rough country.

pack up

In packing, to load up; to place the loads, as formed in cargo, on the mules.

pack wall

In mining, a natural wall of rock left standing to support the roof.

pack way

In packing, a narrow path used by pack animals.

padding out his belly

A cowboy's expression describing someone who is given to eating at every opportunity.

paddle

An oarlike implement, used without an oarlock or other means of attachment to the boat. A horse's gait in which the horse wings out with his front feet.

paddle board

In steamboating, one of the broad, flat boards, or floats, attached radially to the circumference of a paddle wheel.

paddle box

In steamboating, the semicircular structure covering the upper portion of the paddle wheel.

paddle wheel

In steamboating, a water wheel used in propelling the boat. Paddle boards were attached radially to the circumference of the wheel, which revolved on a horizontal rotating shaft. The wheel was parallel to the length of the ship and half-submerged in the water. When a single wheel was used on the boat, it was placed at the stern; when two wheels were used, they were placed one on each side of the vessel near the stern.

In gambling, an early-day game requiring a large board with squares numbered from 1 to 100 and an upright wheel bearing the same numbers. "Choose your square! Your money down in time, and the wheel goes round!" cried the operator, as he spun the wheel. With astonishing regularity the wheel stopped short of or passed slowly over the number upon which the largest stakes were piled.

pad plate

In saddlery, an iron bow, either malleable or wrought, upon which the pad is formed, giving stiffness to the pad and serving as a means of attaching the mountings.

padre

In the Southwest; a priest; from the Spanish.

padrone

In packing, a title used on the Pacific Coast for the owner of a pack train.

paggamoggon

An Indian weapon consisting of a wooden handle 22 inches long, about the size of a whip handle, covered with dressed leather. At one end was a thong 2 inches long, which was tied to a round stone weighing 2 pounds and covered with leather. At the other end was a loop of the same material, which was fastened around the wrist. Armed with this weapon, the Indian could strike a very severe blow.

pail-fed

A calf raised on skimmed milk.

pailing cows

What the cowboy calls the chore of milking, the one he most detests.

paint

A horse with irregular patterns of white and colored areas. It is a favorite with fiction writers but fails to meet with much favor as a cow horse. Not being good for close, quick work, it does not develop into a cutting horse and is inclined to acquire the habit of fighting the bits.

Paint horses are very showy, and for this reason the cowboy does not object to having one in his string to use as his "gallin' horse"; but when it comes to real cow work, he prefers a solid-colored horse. Because of their colors, these horses were popular among the Indians. But an adage of the cow country is, "Color don't count if the colt don't trot."

paint dauber

In sheepshearing, a man who paints the owner's brand on newly sheared sheep.

painted cat

A name frequently given by the cowboy to a woman of the frontier dance hall or bawdy house.

painter

The westerner's name for a panther, or mountain lion. In steamboating, the rope at the bow of a rowboat, yawl, or skiff used for mooring purposes; sometimes a *stern painter* was used as well. A man employed to paint a steamboat was called a *painterman*.

painter leg

In logging, a root or grub used to tie up log rafts.

paint for war

A cowboy's expression meaning *to prepare to do battle* or *to lose one's temper*.

paint his tonsils

A cowboy's expression meaning *to drink whisky*. I once heard a cowboy speak of another's drinking by saying, "He's takin' the first layer off his tonsils."

paintin' his nose

A cowboy's expression for getting drunk.

paint skin

A gambler's name for any court card, as distinguished from a *spot card*; also called *court skin* and *redskin*.

pair of overalls

A cowboy's term for two drinks. When a cowboy customer says to the bartender, "Give me a pair of overalls," the latter knows he wants two fast drinks and sets out two glasses with the bottle.

Palacio

What the early freighters called the Palace of Governors in Santa Fe.

palau

A trader's term meaning *broke*, or *penniless*.

paleface

An Indian's name for a white man.

paling board

In logging, the outside part of a tree, taken from the sides to square the tree so that it can be sawed into boards.

palomilla

A milk-white or cream-colored horse with a white mane and tail; from the Spanish.

palomino

A dun-colored or golden horse with a white, silver, or ivory mane and tail; from the Spanish *palomilla*.

Palouse horse

A shortened form of *Appaloosa horse*; see *Appaloosa*.

pan

To separate gold from earth or gravel by means of a pan; also, *pan out*. The pan is made of sheet steel and is about 4 inches deep and 18 inches wide, with a long flare from bottom to top. The gravel is shoveled into the pan, which is immersed in water and agitated to wash off the lighter particles; larger pebbles are removed by hand. Because of its greater gravity, any gold in the pan settles to the bottom. An expert panner can separate the gold from the gravel and sand without any loss of gold.

pancake

A cowboy's name for the small English riding saddle.

panel crupper

A name occasionally given to a crupper, a loop of leather passing under the horse's tail and fastened to the saddle to hold it in place; so called because it is made in two sections.

panniers

In packing, pouches made of canvas or leather fitting over the forks of a packsaddle and strapped to the pack animal with cinch and tightening strap, or latigo. From the French *panier*, meaning *basket*.

panning

See *pan*.

pan out

See *pan*. The expression is now also used to mean *give results*, especially as compared with expectations.

panther tracks

What the cowboy calls spur marks across the saddle.

pantry

In steamboating, a room just off the main cabin on a packet containing sinks, shelves, tables, coffee urn, iceboxes, tableware, etc., and usually connected by stairs to the kitchen.

pants rats

What the cowboy calls body lice. When one of the hands of a certain Montana ranch came home after spending a week in an Indian camp, the boys decided that his clothes needed delousing. They made him strip and throw his clothes to them to be put into a pot of boiling water. When he quit throwing garments through the door, one of the boys yelled to find out if that was all, and the naked cowboy yelled back, "I can't go no deeper without a skinnin' knife."

Charlie Russell tells an amusing story about these insects. "It's one spring round-up, back in the early '80s," he wrote. "We're out on circle, and me an' Pete's ridin' together. Mine's a center-fire saddle, and I drop back to straighten the blanket and set it. I ain't but a few minutes behind him, but the next I see Pete is on the bank of this creek, which didn't have no name then. He's off his hoss and stripped his shirt off. With one boulder on the ground and another about the same size in his hand, he's poundin' the seams of his shirt. He's so busy he don't hear me when I ride up, and he's cussin' and swearin' to himself. I hear him mutter, 'I'm damned if this don't get some of the big ones!'

"Well, from this day on, this stream is known as Louse Creek." (Charles M. Russell, *Trails Plowed Under* [Garden City, Doubleday, Doran & Company, 1935], 77.)

paper

In early-day poker, a gambler's name for marked cards prepared beforehand by a sharper.

paper-backed

A cowboy's expression meaning *weak*. Ben Langford spoke of one cowboy as being "so weak he couldn't lick his upper lip," and I heard a cowhand of the Three T refer to another as being "so puny he couldn't pull my hat off."

paper-collar stiffs

A logger's name for cigarettes.

paper wagon
What the Indians called a stagecoach, because it carried the mail.

papoose
An Indian baby or young child.

papoose basket
A basketlike cradle for a papoose.

papoose board
A board to which a papoose was strapped so that he could be carried about.

papoose coat
A garment worn by a papoose.

parada
A term used principally in California, Oregon, and Nevada for the main herd of cattle. The term is also sometimes used in referring to a band of broken horses. From the Spanish, meaning *stop*, *halt*, or *relay of horses*.

parada grounds
A location selected to work a herd of cattle. See *parada*.

parade chaps
Chaps made for show only. As the cowhand would say, "Shake a thorny bush at one of 'em and they'd fall apart."

parflèche
A word used in the Northwest for the prepared hide of an animal, such as a buffalo, dried on a frame after the hair had been removed; from the French-Canadian. The cowboy adopted the word to refer to his poke, or warbag, and changed it to *parflesh*. The word is rarely used in the Southwest.

parker
What the cowboy occasionally calls a bed comforter.

parlor gun
What the cowman calls a Derringer or small gun; by this name he expresses his contempt for anything but a "man-sized gun."

parlor house
A cowboy's name for a house of the red-light district, one of the better houses which has a parlor for entertainment. Cheaper, parlorless houses are *cribs*.

paroli
In faro, a bet made up of the original stake plus the accumulated winnings; from this word comes the modern-day *parlay*. From the Italian and French.

parrot-bill
A cowman's name for a pistol with a semiround butt.

parrot-mouth horse
A horse with protruding front teeth, a condition sometimes, but not always, caused by old age.

partida
A herd of cattle; from the Spanish, meaning *group* or *band*.

partisan
A name for the chief of a party of trappers.

partner
In steamboating, a common name for a co-worker.

PARTNERSHIP
See cahoots, compadre, made of the same leather, partner, throw in.

pasear
A southwesterner's word meaning *to go leisurely* or *to go on an inspection tour*; from the Spanish.

paso
A southwesterner's word for a pass or a ford. A double-step, six feet.

pass
A passage; a road; a narrow entrance; a narrow and difficult place of entrance or exit, as a *pass* through the mountains. In gambling, to give the next player an option; to refuse to bet.

Pass brandy
A trader's name for brandy made in El Paso, Texas, in the early days.

pass goods

An expression the early freighters used meaning *to get merchandise through customs*.

pass in his chips

A cowboy's expression meaning *to die*.

pass line

In logging, the line by which a high rigger moves up and down at his work after he has topped a tree.

pass the buck

A common saying that originated in the West in the late 1860's. In early-day poker it was customary for the players to cut for deal, and the winner of the opening pot continued to deal until he lost, when the privilege went to his conqueror. With the introduction of draw poker, it became the custom to pass the deal to the left after each hand.

On the western frontier this practice led to the custom of using a *buck*. It could be any object, but was usually a knife, and since most western men in those days carried knives with buckhorn handles, this name was adopted. The buck was placed in front of the dealer to mark the deal and was passed along at the conclusion of each pot. In some sections a player who did not wish to deal was permitted to ante and pass the buck. Thus the term became a slang expression for letting someone else perform a task originally imposed upon one or for letting someone else take the blame for an act. (Herbert Asbury, *Sucker's Progress* [New York, Dodd, Mead & Company, 1938], 28.)

Pass whisky

A trader's name for aguardiente distilled from grapes; the drink was made in El Paso, Texas, in the early days.

pass in his chips

A common early western expression meaning *to die*; later changed to *pass in his checks*.

pastern

The part of a horse's leg between the joint next to the foot and the coronet of the hoof.

pastor

Among Spanish-speaking people, a term for a sheepherder.

pasture

Grazing ground; ground covered with grass to be eaten by cattle or horses. Land appropriated for grazing. To feed on grass. To place cattle on grazing ground.

pasture count

A count of cattle made on the range or in a pasture without herding them together for that purpose; also called *range count*. The counters ride through the pasture, counting each bunch of grazing cattle and drifting it back so that it does not get mixed with the uncounted cattle ahead. This method of counting is usually done at the request and in the presence of a representative of the bank that holds the papers against the herd.

pasture man

A cattleman who leases grazing land.

pasture range

An expanse of open country suitable for grazing stock.

Pastures

See democrat pasture, lame pen, lazy pen, parada grounds, pasture, pasture range, pony pasture, shipping trap, shotgun pasture, starve-out, weak pen.

patch

In mining, a small placer claim outside the main gulch.

pat hand

In draw poker, a hand that is played without drawing more cards. A hand that falls complete, as a flush, a full house, a straight, or four of a kind.

pat him on the lip

A logger's expression meaning *to thrash* or *whip a person*.

patio

An enclosed courtyard. In early-day mining, a place where ores were mixed and amalgamated by the tread of horses. See *patio process*. From the Spanish.

patio process

In mining, a process of amalgamating silver ore by spreading it on an open floor for treatment; the early Mexican miners used this method with silver ores. A yard where ores are cleaned and sorted.

patron

A trader's name for the head of a barge engaged in the Missouri River fur trade. In river boating, a rudder man on a *mackinaw, q.v.*

Paul

A logger; a shortened form of *Paul Bunyan,* the mythical hero of the loggers.

Paul Bunyan's boy

A logger.

Paul Pry

A cowboy's name for a meddler.

paunched

Said of one shot in the stomach. One cowhand spoke of another's being paunched with, "He got a pill in his stomach he couldn't digest."

pawin' 'round for turmoil

Said of a cowboy looking for trouble (and usually finding it).

pay cheater

A logger's name for the timekeeper.

PAYDAY

See Christmas, drag day, ghost walks.

pay dirt

In mining, soil containing ores, such as gold, in sufficient quantities to justify mining.

pay gravel

In placer mining, a rich strip or lead of auriferous gravel.

pay ore

In mining, those parts of an ore body which are both rich enough and large enough to work with profit.

pay pole

What the logger calls a marketable log.

pay rock

In mining, the lode material in which the *pay,* or mineral is found.

pay shoot

In mining, that portion of a deposit composed of pay ore.

pay streak

In mining, the ore body proper, or the thin seam of decomposed material which takes its place and preserves the continuity of the ore body; that portion of a vein which carries the profitable or pay ore.

PEACE

See bury the hatchet, smoke the peace pipe, wash off the war paint.

peacemaker

The 1873-model Colt revolver, which became the most famous in the world and was the favorite of many noted gunmen. It was originally chambered for the .45-caliber, center-fire, black-powder cartridge, but almost immediately after its introduction was chambered for the .44 Winchester (.44-40) center-fire cartridge, and was used as a companion arm to the equally famous Winchester 1873-model rifle.

peal

A cowboy's term for a sock, foot, or stocking, and also for a worthless person; pronounced *pay-ahl'*; from the Spanish. To rope an animal by the hind foot. This throw is commonly used in "stretching out" a cow or steer—never a horse—that has been roped by the head or neck. When adroitly cast, the loop turns so as to form a figure eight, and one hind foot is caught in each loop of the figure.

pea picker

A logger's name for a farmer who works in some seasons in a sawmill.

pearl diver

A cowboy's and logger's name for a dishwasher in a restaurant or in a logging camp.

peavey

In logging, a stout lever 5 to 7 feet long, fitted at the larger end with a metal socket and pike and a curved steel hook that works on a bolt; used especially in driving logs. A peavey differs from a cant hook in having a pike instead of a toe ring and lip at the end. It is said to have been devised by John Peavey, a blacksmith at Bolivar, New York. Also called *peavey log wrench*.

peavey log

In logging, the top log on a load.

peavey log wrench

See *peavey*.

pecker neck

A saddle horse untrained for cow work.

pecker pole

A logger's name for a long, thin pole.

peckerwood mill

A small, portable sawmill.

Pecos

A cowboy's term for shooting a man and rolling his body into a river; from the Pecos River.

Pecos Bill

A cowboy's name for a liar; from the mythical character of the West.

Pecos swap

A trade made without the consent or knowledge of the other interested party; a theft.

peddler of loads

A cowboy's name for a teller of tall tales. It did not take much persuading to start a cowman on a "campaign against truth," and he "could color up a story redder than a Navajo blanket."

peeler

A cowboy's term for a man who skins the hides off cattle; also called *stripper*. A shortened form of *bronc peeler*, q.v. In logging, usually a logger who removes bark from timber cut in the spring months when bark "slips." A log used in the manufacture of rotary-cut veneer; also called *peeler log*.

peeler log

See *peeler*.

peeling

A cowboy's term for skinning the hide off cattle. A cowboy's term for riding a rough horse.

peeling bar

In logging, a bar used to pry bark from logs.

peewees

A cowboy's name for boots with short tops, the most popular style of boot found upon the range today.

Carl B. Livingston, of Santa Fe, New Mexico, tells the following story of the origin of the short-top boot: "A group of the best ropers and riders of the plains went on a roping expedition to South America in 1905. Among these were some of the champions of the world. . . . The American cowboy by far excelled the *gaucho* of the Pampas in roping. They took in a great deal of money at their roping exhibitions, but always, unfortunately, there was some law which they had violated, and would have to pay out immediately all they had taken in.

"The papers in the states were full of the exploits of the North Americans, as they were called. Among the events exhibited was the American cowboy's method of throwing a yearling, plunging at the end of a lariat. The orthodox American cowboy method was to grab the yearling by an ear with one hand, while the yearling was bouncing in the air, catch him on the bounce, and then bust him on the ground. These yearlings were wild and strong and the boys did not always throw them on the first bounce. Sometimes the bawling yearlings, in pitching, would run a hoof down a cowboy's high-top bootleg, thus the legs of the boots became ripped and torn. The boys, whom the papers had made over so much, were at least returning home a great success in their adventures, but sadly low in finances.

"Heroes could not come home with ragged boots. They simply whacked off the tops, and laced the edges together with string. When the crowd came stomping into Old Sol's Lone Wolf Saloon, in Carlsbad, they were shockingly asked by their comrades who had stayed at home, 'Where'd you git such funny boots?' The adventurers reared back their shoulders, indignantly stuck out their chests, and replied simply, 'Them's the style!' And so they have become the customary height of boot from that day to this, for these boys who had roped all over North and South America were princes of the cowboy profession, and set the styles." (Carl B. Livingston, "Development of the Cattle Industry in New Mexico," *Cattleman*, Vol. XXIV, No. 12 [May, 1938], 21–31.)

peg

In mining, a prop of timber supporting the end of a stull, or cap of a set of timber. To mark out a mining claim.

pegging

A cowboy's term for ramming one horn of a downed steer into the ground to hold him down, a practice not allowed in contests.

peg pony

A saddle horse which, while galloping in one direction, can stop short in his tracks, change direction, and instantly bound off on a new course. He is highly valued by the cowman, especially for cutting work. Also called *peg horse* or *pegger*.

pelado

An ignorant person. A person of low social cast. A border American's term of contempt for a Mexican, by whom the term was greatly resented. An idle fellow hanging about a Mexican town. From the Spanish, meaning *penniless person*. (Harold W. Bentley, *Dictionary of Spanish Terms in English* [New York, Columbia University Press, 1932], 178.)

pelón

A name the cowboy sometimes gives a muley, or hornless, cow; from the Spanish, meaning *bald*.

pelter

A cowboy's name for a saddle.

pemina buggy

A wooden cart similar to the *carreta* (*q.v.*) but more French in design; probably introduced by the French trappers.

pemmican

Originally a North American Indian food made of buffalo meat or venison which was dried, mixed with tallow, pounded, and pressed tightly into cakes, sometimes with a few serviceberries added to improve the flavor. It was also composed of beef cured, shredded, and mixed with fat. It contained much nutriment in a small compass and was of great value on long journeys. It was later adopted by the trappers and traders of the early days.

pencil pusher

A logger's name for a bookkeeper.

penny dog

In mining and logging, an assistant foreman.

penthouse

In mining, a shed or horizontal barricade across one end of a shaft, made of strong timbers loaded with rock to protect against an accidental fall from above.

peon

A term used in the Southwest for a common worker or a person held in serfdom by a landlord or creditor; from the Spanish *peón*, meaning *day laborer*.

pepper-and-salt rope

A hair rope made with alternating strands of black and white horsehair.

pepperbox

A revolver of an early type having five or six barrels revolving upon a central axis; also called *coffee mill*.

pepper gut

What a cowboy sometimes called a Mexican, because he ate so much pepper.

Percheron

A large horse, originally from Le Perche, France, used to some extent in the Northwest for breeding with the native horse to obtain a larger animal for mountain use.

permit

A logger's short timecard used as a substitute for regular membership in a union.

Personal belongings

See extra tackling, fifty years' gathering,

fixin', parflèche, plunder, possibles, thirty years' gathering.

persuader

A six gun. A spur. The "cracker" on a bull whacker's whip.

pestle-tail

A wild horse with a brush or burr tail.

petalta

A herd of cattle rounded up for cutting out.

petata

In packing, a square piece of matting made of palm leaves placed over packs to protect them from rain.

petmakers

A cowboy's name for his spurs.

phildoodle

What the cowboy calls a drugstore, or imitation, cowboy.

Phoebe

In dice, a throw of five.

picaroon

A logger's tool similar to a hammer, but with a tapered point and no claw.

pick

In logging, a pick handspike; a pick pole. To free a log jam by releasing the key logs.

picket

A cowboy's word meaning *to stake* (a horse).

picket pin

A wooden or iron stake, driven into the ground, to which an animal is picketed. When it was the practice to stake night horses, picket pins were carried as part of the chuck-wagon equipment. If the horseman had no picket pin, he dug a hole in the ground, tied a knot in the end of his rope, buried it and then tamped the dirt closely around it. It is surprising how well it would hold.

pick-pocket turn

See gun turn.

picket rope

A rope used for picketing horses. The cowboy would not use his lariat for staking if he could help it, for he had to tie an extra knot to make a slip noose to keep from choking the horse, and this caused a kink in the rope that made it unfit for any other use.

pickety-poke

What the miner calls a drilling machine used in soft rock.

Pick him up!

In rodeo, a judges' cry to attendants meaning that they are to pick up a rider after his time is up or the horse has bucked himself out. They are to catch the animal so that the rider can dismount and the saddle can be removed. The expressions *Take him up!* and *Cage him up!* are also used. See *pick-up man.*

pickin' daisies

A phrase describing a rider thrown from a horse.

picking a sleeper

A cowboy's expression for plucking the hair around a brand. Frequently an animal was found on the range whose brand was difficult to decipher. This was especially likely to occur in winter when the animal's hair was long and rough. When an animal of this sort was found, it was caught and held down while someone plucked the hair from around the brand. Frequently a brand would be identifiable to the touch but had not been burned deep enough to be legible. Or some rustler might have hair-branded the animal and might not have been able to return to pick it up before the hair grew out again. The operation of picking such a brand was known as *picking a sleeper.*

pick up his hind feet

A cowboy's expression for roping an animal by the hind feet.

pick up his toes

A cowboy's expression for roping an animal by the front feet.

pick-up man

In rodeo, a horseman who stands ready to take up a horse ridden by a contestant when the ride is over.

piebald

Spotted; painted. A horse with patches of white and black.

pie biter

A horse that secretly forages in the camp kitchen to indulge his acquired tastes.

pie box

A cowboy's name for the chuck wagon, perhaps in wishful thinking.

pie buggy

A cowboy's name for a ranch wagon sent to town for supplies.

pie card

What the logger calls a union card used as a means of getting food or lodging; a workman's daily record sheet.

piece

A logger's term for a log.

pie in the sky

A wobbly's reference to the bourgeois heaven.

pie wagon

A cowboy's name for a trailer used behind the chuck wagon.

pig

A cowboy's name for the saddle horn. A logger's name for a pressure vessel used to force oil through an engine after the engine has been overhauled and before it is used.

pigeon

In gambling, the victim of a professional gambler; the term has been used from about 1600 to the present time.

piggin' string

A short rope used for hog-tying; see *hoggin' rope.*

pig's vest with buttons

A cowboy's name for salt pork or sowbelly.

pigtail

In logging, a device made of iron driven into a tree or a stump to support a wire or small rope.

pike pole

In logging, a long pole with a sharp spike in one end but no dog; used as a lever in raising weights or in driving and floating logs.

piker

In faro, one who makes small bets all over the layout; hence, a term for a cheap sport or a man without courage.

Pike's Peaker

A gold seeker who went to the Pikes Peak area during the gold rush in 1858–59.

Pikes Peak fever

The excitement caused by the discovery of gold in the Pikes Peak region in 1858–59.

piket

A cowboy's name for a skunk; pronounced pee-kay'.

piking

In faro, making small bets all over the layout; see *piker.*

piled

Thrown from a horse. After making a very hard ride, one cowhand of the TU Ranch said, "After that ride all I needed to make me a cripple was a handful o' lead pencils."

pile driver

A horse that humps its back and comes down with all four legs as stiff as ramrods when it bucks.

pile it on

A cowboy's expression for throwing a rope on something.

pile up

In sheepherding, a dreaded calamity that occurs when the lead sheep stumbles over some object or falls off a cliff and the following sheep, pushed by the pressure from those behind, pile up until many are killed.

pilgrim

Originally, a cowman's name for imported hot-blooded cattle; later, his name for a tenderfoot.

piling

In logging, logs to be driven into the ground to support other structures.

pillar

In mining, part of an ore body left in place to help support the rock when the rest of the ore is mined out.

pill roller

A cowboy's term for a doctor.

piloncillo

A small loaf of unrefined sugar; from the Spanish *pilón*.

pilot

In cattle work, a man whose duty it was to guide the roundup wagons over the roadless plains and brakes to the next camping place. He had to be well acquainted with the country and to use good judgment concerning the location of the next camp with regard to water and suitable surroundings for working cattle.

In steamboating, the man who guided the boat. In no other kind of navigation were the qualities of quick perception, intuitive grasp of a situation, nerve to act boldly and promptly, and coolness and judgment in times of danger so important and so consistently in demand. He had to be a skilled riverman and thoroughly familiar not only with the particular river on which he was navigating but also with rivers in general and their ways.

pilothouse

In steamboating, the structure above the texas from which the pilot guided the ship. It was placed thus to be high enough that the pilot could see every part of the river. It was glassed in on all sides so that he could see in every direction.

pilot tunnel

In mining, a small tunnel driven ahead of the main tunnel to determine its grade and direction.

pimple

A cowboy's term for the small eastern riding saddle.

pimp stick

A logger's name for a cigarette.

pinch

In mining, the place at which a mineral vein or bed becomes markedly thin; a narrow section where the walls of the vein come close together.

pinch chute

A cowboy's name for a branding chute.

pinched

In mining, a word describing a section where a vein narrows as though the walls had been squeezed in.

pin crape on the kid

Said of a rustler that killed a mother cow to steal her calf.

pineapple

In a sawmill, a pineapple-shaped roller on a planer which presses down and forces lumber to the straight edge on the roller platform as the lumber moves on its way to be planed.

pine straw

A logger's name for dried pine needles.

pine top

A logger's name for cheap whisky.

ping-pong

A logger's term meaning *to curry mules*.

pink pretties

A logger's name for gentle socialites.

pinole

A Mexican flour prepared from the seeds of various plants, roasted, ground, and mixed with other ingredients; it was also made by parching Indian corn, grinding it, and mixing it with cinnamon and sugar.

piñon

A species of pine tree found in North America, in the West usually of the dwarf variety; also, the edible seed of this tree.

pinto

A piebald, or spotted, horse; from the Spanish *pintar*, meaning to *paint*. See *paint*.

pinto chaps

Spotted hair chaps made by sewing in pieces of hair of another color.

pinwheel

A manner of bucking of a horse in which the horse leaps forward in an upward jump, turns with his feet in the air, and lands on his back; a horse that will do this is very rare. Also, a method of tossing a gun so that the gun comes to rest in a virtual firing position except that the forefinger is not in the trigger guard. The movement is started by throwing the butt down with a jerk of the wrist, with the muzzle up. The gun is filliped into the air so that it revolves and the butt drops naturally into the palm of the hand.

pin work

In gambling, the marking of playing cards for the purpose of cheating.

pioneer bucker

A horse that bucks in circles and figure eights; so called because he is always seeking "new territory."

pipe

A miner's term for a pipelike body of ore.

pirooting

A cowboy's term for meandering or for "foolin' 'round."

piroque

On the Missouri River, a trapper's and trader's boat whose hull consisted of two log canoes about 6 feet apart, which were fastened together and covered with a rough wooden flooring. Propelling a piroque upstream was much heavier work than propelling a canoe, although a rather large sail could be used on such a boat, provided the wind was favorable, without any danger of an upset. The cargo, which was placed on the flooring, was protected from the weather by skins. Oars were provided in the bow for rowing, and a single oar was placed in the stern between the boats for steering.

piss fir

A logger's name for white fir or lowland white fir; so called because of its strong odor.

pistol

A cowboy's name for a young, inexperienced rider. A cowboy never called his gun a *pistol*.

pistol-whip

To whip someone with the barrel of a six gun. Sug Morgan, speaking of such an incident, said, "I let 'im feel my gun where the hair was thinnest and put a knot on his head that'd sweat a rat to run around." Some writers of westerns have their heroes grasping their guns by the barrel and clubbing with the butt. No one but a greener would pull this stunt. What do they think the villain is doing all the time it takes the hero to get hold of the barrel?

pit

In mining, a shallow shaft.

pitch

In mining, the dip of a lode.

pitcher

In mining, a sloping dip or inclination in a bed of ore.

pitchfork gladiator

What the cowboy sometimes calls the hay hand.

pitching

A Texan's word for *bucking, q.v.*

pitching Betsy

A name for the *Concord, q.v.*; so called because of its pitching motion.

pitching fence-cornered

Said of a bucking horse that leaves the ground while headed in one direction and lands in another at approximately a forty-five-degree angle.

pit head

In mining, the landing at the top of a shaft.

pit-head man

In mining, the man in charge of unloading the cages and the mineral at the pit head.

pit lamp

An open lamp worn on a miner's cap, as distinguished from a safety lamp.

pitman

In mining, a man employed to examine the lifts and pumps and the drainage of a mine. In steamboating, a connecting rod similar to the rod on a locomotive—the beam connecting the wrist pin on the crank to the crosshead of the engine.

pit mouth
In mining, the opening of a shaft at the surface of the ground.

pit prop
In mining, a piece of timber used as a temporary support for the mine roof.

pit pumps
In mining, pumps used in a shaft.

pitted
A cowboy's word describing cattle caught in a corner or draw during a snowstorm.

placer
In mining, a place where gold is obtained by washing; an alluvial or glacial deposit, as of sand or gravel, containing particles of gold or other valuable mineral.

placer camp
A camp of placer miners.

placer claim
A mining claim located upon gravel or ground whose mineral contents are extracted by the use of water, as by sluicing or hydraulicking.

placer deposits
In mining, surface deposits of gold. Gold ore formed when an outcropping vein is worn away by weathering and the particles are caught up by streams, carried away, and deposited in some lower place into which the water naturally flows. A mass of gravel, sand, or similar material resulting from the crumbling and erosion of solid rocks and containing particles or nuggets of gold or other minerals.

placer diggings
A region in which placer mining is or may be carried on. Mining by placer methods.

placer district
A region where placers occur; see *placer*.

placer dredge
A dredge used in placer mining.

placer field
An area where placers occur; see *placer*.

placer gold
In mining, gold occurring in more or less coarse grains or flakes and obtainable by washing the sand, gravel, etc., in which it is found.

placer ground
Ground where gold can be obtained by placer mining.

placer mine
A mine from which *placer gold (q.v.)* may be obtained.

placer mining
The separating of particles of gold from the deposits or formations in which they occur by means of washing, either in a gold pan or by hydraulic means.

placer prospect
An indication that placer mining will be profitable.

plain trail
What the cowboy calls clearly visible *sign' (q.v.)* in trailing.

plant
A cowman's word meaning *to bury*. A moving custom was practiced at many early-day burials. The dead man's horse, fully saddled, was led to the graveside. There the horse was silently unsaddled from the off, or wrong, side—a solemn announcement that none of the mourners were the dead man's equal in equestrian skill. In mining, to salt a mine or place minerals in a worthless mine.

planter
In steamboating, a river snag similar to a *sawyer (q.v.)* except that it was firmly set and did not move.

plat
In mining, a small chamber on the side, or sole, of a level where it intersects a shaft, used to facilitate dumping. When it is cut in the sole, it is called a *trip plate*.

play a lone hand
A cowboy's expression meaning *to do something alone* or *live alone*.

playing a hand with his eyes shut

A cowboy's expression describing someone who is taking a chance.

playing cat's cradle with his neck

A cowboy's expression describing someone who has been hanged.

playing checkers with his nose

A cowboy's expression describing a man who is in jail, or one who is not to be trusted.

playing on a shoestring

In gambling, starting with a small sum and running it into a large amount by making lucky bets.

playing on velvet

In gambling, playing with money won from the bank; the term is not restricted to faro.

play the bank

To play faro.

play the evens

In faro, a system by which the gambler plays the even case cards to win.

play the woods

A logger's expression meaning *to work at logging*.

plaza

A square in the center of town; so called in most western towns.

plew

A trapper's name for a prime beaver skin; also *plus*. At one time such a skin was worth about six dollars and was the basis of exchange among mountain men and traders. Since mountain prices for trappers' equipment and luxuries at the rendezvous were very high, the trapper rarely had any cash left when he returned to the hunt. From the Canadian French *pélu*, meaning *hairy*.

pliers man

A rustler's derisive name for a loyal cowboy who worked for a fenced ranch.

plow-boying

A cowboy's expression for riding with a rein in each hand and pulling the horse's head around with one rein while pulling the other rein against his neck.

plow chaser

A cowboy's name for a farmer.

plow handle

A cowboy's name for a six gun; so called because of the shape of the stock of the Colt single-action army revolver which was made from a single piece of walnut or other hardwood and polished smooth. The gun was designed so that it recoiled freely in the hand, thus making a smooth stock preferable, for the gun was muzzle-heavy, and its almost perfect balance allowed it to slip back to shooting position after the recoil.

PLOWING

See lookin' at a mule's tail, turning the grass upside down.

plug

A broken-down horse. To shoot someone with a gun.

plumb cultus

A westerner's expression meaning *as bad as they make them*; cussed. See *cultus*.

plumbing the bones

What the gambler calls loading dice.

plunder

A cowboy's term for his personal belongings of odds and ends. In steamboating, a collection of articles belonging to a particular shipment of freight, particularly a moving shipment; sometimes termed *moving plunder*.

plute

A logger's shortened form of *plutocrat*; his term for a wealthy person.

pocket

In mining, a small body of ore. An enlargement of a lode or vein. An irregular cavity containing ore. In logging, to shove the logs to a sawmill.

pocket claim

In mining, a place where gold occurs in pockets or small cavities; also called *pocket diggings*.

pocket diggings

See *pocket claim*.

pocket hunter

In mining, a prospector who searches for pockets of gold. In California, a term for a prospector who searches for small gold deposits that occur on the surface in the mother lode and other districts of the state.

pockety

In mining, a word describing a region containing only occasional deposits of ore. A word applied to a mine in which the pay ore occurs in small, detached bodies with intervals of poor or barren material; the word implies a slur on the mine.

poco

Little; scanty; a small amount; a word used by cowboys in combination with such words as *tiempo (time)* and *malo (bad)*; from the Spanish.

poddy

A name a cowboy occasionally gives to an orphan calf, usually a big-bellied and undernourished one.

pogonip

A frozen winter mist of Nevada to which Indians and whites ascribed all bodily ills, especially pneumonia. From the Shoshonean Indian, said to mean *white death*.

point-award system

In rodeo, a method by which champion cowboys are selected for each event of the year. Each cowboy is awarded one point for every dollar he wins at R.C.A.-approved rodeos during the year. At the end of the year the cowboy who has accumulated the most points in each event is awarded the championship.

pointers

In freighting, the animals placed between the wheelers and the leaders.

point rider

In cattle driving, one of the men who rode at the head of a column of cattle on the trail and acted as pilots. They usually worked in pairs, and when they wanted to change the course of the herd, they rode abreast the foremost cattle, one on each side of the column, and then quietly veered in the desired direction. The leading cattle would swerve away from the horseman approaching them and toward the one going away from them. This was the honored post of the drive, and also the most dangerous and responsible. These men were the first to swim the rivers and the first to meet attacks by Indians. See *lead man*.

poke

A sack in which a cowboy carries his *plunder, q.v.* The term is rarely used except in the Northwest; in other sections such a sack is called *war bag* or *war sack*. Also, a wooden collar used to restrain a *fence crawler, q.v.*

poker

Any of several varieties of card game in which each player, at a single stage or at successive stages in the dealing, meets or calls the highest bet or raise at the table, raises the bet, or withdraws from the betting. The game is played by two or more persons, each of whom, if not bluffed into declaring his hand, bets on the value of it, the player with the highest value winning the pool.

There are hundreds of forms of poker, but they differ only in details, and all follow the same basic principles. The two most popular poker games are *draw* and *stud*. In draw poker, each player is dealt five cards, face down. The undealt cards are set aside for later use, and there is a betting interval. Each active player in turn may discard one or more cards, if he so wishes, and the dealer gives him replacement cards from the top of the deck. There is another betting interval, followed by a *showdown*, in which the highest hand among the active players wins the pot.

Stud poker is the principal form of open poker, in which each player has some of his cards face up. In *five-card stud* the dealer gives each player a face-down card, called the *hole card*, and then a face-up card. Each player looks at the face of his hole card but does not show it. Here the deal is interrupted for a betting interval; from this point on, all cards are dealt face up.

poker chip

A chip or counter used in poker to represent money.

poker face

A face or facial expression that reveals nothing of what is on its owner's mind nor what is in his hand.

poker shark

An expert poker player.

pole boat

A river boat; so called because of the means by which it was propelled upstream. The boat, usually made of pine planks, was 20 to 30 feet long, 3 to 5 feet wide, 2 to 3 feet deep. It was pointed at both ends and had a flat bottom. Even when heavily loaded, it could be moved in water less than a foot deep. It was easily navigated downstream by means of ores or poles, but going upstream, especially against a rapid current, was a far different matter. The crew consisted of four, six, or eight men, depending on the size of the craft. Each man was armed with a long, stout pole made of ash or hickory, with a heavy, wrought-iron spike at one end. There were two methods of propulsion. By the first method an equal number of men stood on each side of the boat, planted their spikes in the bottom of the stream at an angle, and, with the upper end of the poles against their shoulders, walked as far toward the stern as possible, moving back and forth on narrow wooden runways, about 10 inches wide, built on each side of the boat. In this manner they pushed the boat upstream nearly a boat's length. Two men would then hold the boat until the others hurried back to the bow and planted their poles in the bottom again. By the second method two groups of men, one near the bow and the other near the stern, stood facing the bow and took turns pushing their poles while a helmsman corrected the boat's tendency to zigzag. Both methods were widely used for many years.

polecat

A logger's name for a tie man who camps far away from headquarters.

pole hitch

In packing, the formation of a half hitch over each side pack. It was distinguished from other hitches in that the rope did not pass under the belly of the animal. The hitch compressed the load to extreme tightness so that the aparejo itself need not be fitted tightly to the body of the animal; in other words, the load could be compressed while the aparejo could be loose on the animal, a necessary condition when the animal must climb mountains. It was not used when a lash rope was available. It could also be used for packing odds and ends after the cargo was loaded and a loose animal was available, or when the packers were pressed for time. It was also used to secure a travois or an improvised litter to an aparejo.

pole maker

A logger whose specialty is harvesting and trimming piling and cedar poles for telephone and telegraph lines. Pole makers usually work in advance of the major log harvest.

pole team

In freighting, the animals next to the wagon. These animals were always the heavyweights, old, well trained, and able to hold back the load or their unruly teammates.

POLING

See steamboating, walking the boat.

ponche

A trader's name for tobacco; from the Spanish.

poncho

A covering made by cutting a hole for the head through the middle of a blanket; used by Mexicans and cowboys as a protection against the weather; from the Spanish.

pond monkey

A logger's name for a worker on the mill ponds.

pony

A small model of heavy sawmill machinery; used in light work.

pony beeves

Young cattle about two years old, the right age for fattening for market.

pony express

A rapid (for those days) postal system employing relays of ponies, especially the system which operated in 1860–62 from St. Joseph, Missouri, to Sacramento, California.

pony-express mount

A cowboy's term for a running mount made by leaping into the saddle without touching the feet to the stirrups.

pony pasture

A small pasture used for saddle horses.

pony stamps

The stamps attached to pony-express mail.

pooch

A cowboy's name for a dish made of tomatoes, sugar, and bread cooked by the chuck-wagon cook.

pool boat

In steamboating, a boat on which the pilothouse was built forward of the cabin on the second deck, and not on top of it.

pool camp

The roundup camp of several outfits which have thrown in together.

pool roundup

A roundup in which cattlemen over a wide range of territory pool their resources and men.

poontang

A logger's word for sexual intercourse.

Poor

See buzzard-bait, corriente, crow bait, cull, cut-back, ganted, just a ball of hair, slab-sided.

poor box

An early-day logger's name for a box kept at a logging camp to receive the penalties imposed on players participating in contests the loggers held at night, such as singing, storytelling, reciting, and whistling. If a player was unable to perform, he had to put a pound of tobacco in the poor box.

poor bull

What the traders called meat from buffalo bulls, which was very poor eating.

poor doe

A cowboy's name for lean, tough venison of any kind.

popgun

A trader's name for any worthless gun.

popper

The very tip, or "business end," of the whip used by freighters and stage drivers. It was made of buckskin cut in the shape of a long V, the bottom end of the V running into a strand which was braided into the tip. When the driver cracked the whip, the popper made a loud report like a gun going off.

popping salute

A trapper's expression for a greeting of bullets.

pop raise

A riverman's term for a sudden rise in the river, usually not a very great one; rivermen invariably speak of a *raise*, not a *rise*.

pop skull

A cowboy's term for whisky.

porch percher

What a cowboy calls a town loafer.

porcupine

A miner's term for a drill stuck in a hole; see *Dutchman*.

pork eater

An American trapper's name for a Frenchman.

porphyry

In mining, an igneous rock (rock that has solidified from a molten state) in which some of the minerals are well crystallized, floating in a finer-grained ground mass like raisins in a cake. Since the first disseminated copper deposits were found in porphyry, they are often called *porphyry coppers*.

port

The raised portion of a bridle bit. In steamboating, one of the principal cities on the route of a packet. The left-hand side of a boat, looking forward; the right-hand side is *starboard*. An opening in a steam cylinder through which steam was admitted or exhausted.

portage

The carrying or transporting of canoes, goods, etc., overland from one stretch or body of navigable water to another; portage was resorted to around rapids, falls, etc. To carry equipment in this fashion.

portage book

In river boating, a record book in which were kept the names of the crew, time served, and wages paid; a time book.

portage collar

A leather harness used in carrying loads over a *portage, q.v.*

portage path

A path along which boats and goods were portaged; see *portage*.

portranka

What a cowboy sometimes calls a filly colt.

posada

A trader's term for an inn or roadhouse; from the Spanish.

pose

A rest, especially one on a *portage, q.v.* A portage was measured not in feet but in *poses*. These usually occurred every one-third to one-half mile, and *pose* came to mean that distance. From the French *poser*, meaning *to deposit*.

posse

A band of men organized to run down lawbreakers. One reformed outlaw told of a posse keeping on his trail until he "got saddle sores."

possibles

What the trapper called his personal property, such as ammunition and tobacco, often carried in a *possible sack*, a wallet of dressed buffalo skin, which was also used for clothing and cooking utensils.

possum belly

See *cuna*.

post

In mining, a single vertical piece of tim-ber wedged between the top and bottom of a crosscut for support in a mine. Also called *prop*.

postage stamp

A cowboy's name for the little riding saddle used by easterners.

post hay

A cowboy's expression for tying a horse to a post and failing to obtain food for the animal.

pot

A logger's name for a transformer; also, his name for a donkey engine. A cowboy's name for a derby hat. In faro, a bet taking in four cards. In poker, the money in the pot.

pot-bellied

A cowboy's expression for bloated, or big-bellied; pot-gutted.

pothole

A bog hole. A small basin occasionally used to catch excess irrigation water.

pothole rider

A *bog rider, q.v.*

pothook

A hook used by the chuck-wagon cook to hold pots over a fire.

pothooks

A cowboy's name for the cook.

potluck

A word used by the cowman and other frontiersmen, for food contributed by a guest. *To bring potluck* means *to bring food with one.*

pot-rack outfit

A ranch crew that uses no tents on round-up in country where it was the custom to do so.

pot rastler

A logger's name for a dishwasher.

potrillo

A cowboy term for a male colt.

potro

A young horse, so called until he sheds

his milk teeth, at about four and one-half years of age; a colt or filly.

pot rustler

A cowboy's name for the cook.

pot walloper

A logger's name for the cook.

pounder

A miner's name for an ore stamp mill.

pounding 'em on the back

A cowboy's expression for riding drag. See *drag, drag rider*.

pour the bud into

To whip a horse.

poverty cattle

A cowman's name for feeder cattle.

powder

A logger's and miner's term for dynamite.

powder-burnin' contest

What the cowboy called a gun battle. After participating in such a fight, Carey Nelms said, "After that powder-burnin' contest my gun was emptier'n a banker's heart." He was not hit, but said one bullet came so close "it raised a blister."

powder hand

In mining, a rock worker who handles explosives.

powder man

A man in charge of explosives in any operation requiring their use. Also called *powder monkey*.

Powder River! Let 'er buck!

A cowboy's shout of encouragement. A password. A cry of derision. This is a very familiar cry throughout the northwest cattle country. In the Argonne during World War I it was the battle cry of the Ninety-first Division, and it might be said that it has been heard around the world.

While in Cheyenne, Wyoming, many years ago, I met Agnes Wright Spring, at that time a member of the editorial staff of the *Wyoming Stockman-Farmer*, who gave me a story of the origin of this famous

phrase, originally told by E. J. Farlow, a former cowman mayor of Lander. According to Mr. Farlow, the saying originated after a roundup in the fall of 1893, when a herd of cattle was being driven to Caspar:

"The night we camped on the divide between the head of Poison Creek, near where the town of Hiland now stands, and the headwaters of 'Dry Powder' River, I told the boys we would water the herd in the Powder River at about 10 o'clock the next morning.

"None of them had ever seen Powder River and they were all excited. In the morning when they were catching horses for the day, I called out to them to get their swimming horses as we were going to cross Powder River several times before night. Missouri Bill Shultz, who had already roped his horse, turned him loose, muttering that 'this damned buckskin couldn't even wade a river.'

"About 10 o'clock the lead of the herd reached the river and it was almost dry, the water standing in holes and barely running from one hole to the other. The herd followed down stream for a distance of about two miles before they were watered, and we crossed it many times.

"When Missouri Bill saw it he looked at it very seriously for some time and then said, 'So this is Powder River,' and that night in camp he told us he had heard of Powder River and now he had seen Powder River, and he kept referring to Powder River nearly every day until we reached Caspar which we did in twenty-eight days' trailing.

"In the evening before we were going to load for shipping, and the cattle were all bedded down near the stockyards, the boys all adjourned to the saloon for a social drink, and Missouri Bill said, 'Boys, come and have a drink on me. I've crossed Powder River.' They had the drinks, then a few more and were getting pretty sociable.

"When Missouri Bill again ordered he said to the boys, 'Have another drink on me, I've swum Powder River,' this time with a distinct emphasis on the words *Powder River*. 'Yes, sir, by God, Powder River' with a little stronger emphasis. When the drinks were all set up he said, 'Well, here's to Powder River, let 'er buck!'

"Soon he grew louder and was heard to say, 'Powder River is comin' up—

eeyeeeep!—Yes sir, Powder River is risin',' and soon after with a yip and a yell, he pulls out his old six-gun and throwed a few shots through the ceiling and yelled, 'Powder River is up, come an' have 'nother drink.' Bang! Bang! 'Yeow, I'm a wolf and it's my night to howl. Powder River is out of 'er banks. I'm wild and woolly and full o' fleas and never been curried below the knees!'

"Bill was loaded for bear, and that is the first time I ever heard the slogan, and from there it went around the world."

Many a cowboy, exuberant with whisky, brought to light his own version, such as: "Powder River, let 'er buck—she's a mile wide—an inch deep—full o' dust and flat fish—swimmin' holes for grasshoppers—cross 'er anywhere—yeou—uhh—yippee—she rolls uphill from Texas!"

powders

A cowboy term for orders from the boss.

powwow

An Indian's word for conjuration performed for the cure of diseases, accompanied by noise and confusion and often by dancing. Also any meeting, such as a conference, accompanied by confusion. The cowman also uses the word to refer to a get-together for a conference, though not accompanied by noise and confusion.

prairie

An extensive tract of land, mostly level, destitute of trees and covered with grass.

prairie beeves

What the trader and trapper called buffaloes.

prairie belt

A cartridge belt, introduced by the Army in 1870, provided with loops that held about fifty cartridges.

prairie bitters

A beverage common among the early hunters of the West; it was made of water and buffalo gall and was considered an excellent medicine.

prairie breaker

A very heavy and strong plow used in breaking prairie land.

prairie butter

A cowman's name for the grease left from fried meat or bacon which he sometimes poured over his bread.

prairie coal

A cowman's name for dried cow chips used for fuel.

prairie dew

A cowboy's term for whisky.

prairie dog

A small burrowing rodent, related to the marmot and the squirrel, found on the prairies west of the Mississippi. Prairie dogs are characterized by a sharp bark like that of a small dog; hence their name. They are about 1 foot long, exclusive of the tail. Their burrows are quite close together, and each burrow has a mound of excavated earth near the entrance to protect it from high water.

prairie-dog court

A cowboy's name for a kangaroo court.

prairie-dog village

A group of prairie-dog burrows.

prairie feathers

What the cowboy calls a bed stuffed with hay.

prairie fire

A fire that sweeps over a grassy prairie, destroying everything before it, a catastrophe much dreaded by a stockman because it often destroys not only his buildings and hay stacks but also the grass upon which his cattle feed.

prairie lawyer

A common name for the coyote because it makes so much chatter.

prairie oyster

What the cowman calls the roasted or fried testicles of a bull, considered by some to be a delicacy.

prairie pancakes

A cowboy's name for dried cow chips.

prairie schooner

A strong, heavy wagon of the early days,

with a long, high bed and a canvas cover that suggested a schooner under full sail.

prairie strawberries
A cowboy's name for beans.

prairie tenor
A cowboy's name for a coyote.

prairie wood
A cowboy's name for dried cow chips.

prairie wool
A cowboy's name for grass.

PRAISE
See Now you're logging!

PRANKS
See tricks.

prayer book
What the cowboy calls his book of cigarette papers.

prayin' cow
A cow rising from the ground. A cow rises rear end first. By the time her hindquarters are in a standing position, her knees are on the ground in a praying attitude.

PREACHERS
See converter, fire escape, sin buster, sin twister, sky pilot.

presidente
What the southwestern cowboy occasionally calls the big boss of the ranch; from the Spanish.

presidio
A Spanish fort or post where soldiers, usually fewer than fifty, lived with their families and cultivated the land about them. Such posts were garrisons designed to protect the frontiers and safeguard the missions.

pressing brick
A logger's expression for standing around in town.

PRIESTS
See black robe, padre.

PRISON
See big pasture, calaboose, cárcel, county

hotel, hoosegow, jusgado, makin' hair bridles, skookum house.

private cuss words
A cowboy's self-coined profanity for which the public awards a sort of copyright to the inventor. The words may not even be profane, but the public soon learns that the user only releases them when he's "madder'n a drunk squaw," and they can be effective enough to "take the frost out of a zero mornin'."

prize money
In rodeo, money paid to the winners of the various events. It includes the purse put up by the rodeo committee and the entry fees paid by all the contestants.

probable ore
In mining, any blocked ore not certain enough to be "in sight," and all ore that is exposed for sampling but whose limits and continuity have not been proved by blocking. Also, any undiscovered ore of whose existence there is a strong probability. Ore that is exposed on either two or three sides, depending on the character of the deposit.

pro belle cutem
"Skin for skin," the motto from the seal of the Hudson's Bay Company, somewhat humorously suggesting the danger of loss of life involved in the fur trade. The words are found in Job.

prod pole
A pole about 6 feet long with a steel spike on one end and a heavy handle on the other, used to prod cattle into stockcars. Near the spiked end and extending out a short distance at right angles from the pole is a flat-headed screw. This screw is twisted into the matted end of a steer's tail when he is down and refuses to get up, and this method usually gets a "rise" out of him.

producer
In rodeo, the name of the individual who runs or produces a rodeo. The role and responsibilities of the producer vary from rodeo to rodeo. In some cases the rodeo committee acts as the producer, hiring the stock contractor and the contract acts and supervising all the other work to be done. In other cases the stock contractor is

also the producer. In cases where there is no sponsoring organization, the rodeo producer acts as the promoter, renting the arena, paying the expenses, and collecting the gate receipts.

pronto

A cowboy's expression meaning *quickly, soon,* or *hurry*; from the Spanish. The word is no longer restricted to the part of the country under Spanish influence but is commonly used throughout the United States.

pronto bug

A gunman who spent his time practicing to perfect a fast draw.

prospect

In mining, the name given to any mine workings whose value has not yet been made manifest. A mineral deposit or excavation, more or less superficial, indicating a deposit. To examine land for possible occurrence of valuable minerals by drilling holes, ditching, or other work. The gold or other mineral obtained by working a sample of ore.

prospectant rock

What the miner calls waste rock.

prospect hole

In mining, any shaft, pit, drift, or drill hole made for the purpose of prospecting the mineral-bearing ground.

prospecting

In mining, searching for places where gold or silver may be profitably mined; also, making preliminary explorations to test the value of lodes or placers already known to exist.

PROSPECTING

See speck.

prospecting claim

A large mining claim, larger than those usually granted, given to the first prospector who discovers gold in the district.

prospector

In mining, a person engaged in exploring for valuable minerals or in testing supposed discoveries of the same. Rarely did the old-time prospectors develop a mine; they were always seeking a better one.

prospector's compass

What the westerner calls a burro's tail.

PROSPECTORS

See Argonaut, coffee cooler, desert rat, dowser, forty-niner, gold colic, gold fever, hill rat, hothead, miners, Pike's Peaker, pocket hunter, prospector, quartz on the brain, sage rat, silver hunter.

prospect tunnel

In mining, a tunnel or entry driven through a barren region or a fault to ascertain the character of the strata beyond. Also called *prospect entry*.

protection forest

A forest whose chief value is in regulating stream flow, preventing erosion, holding shifting sand, or exerting other indirect beneficial effects.

protecting sticks

In packing, sticks used on the aparejo cover to stiffen the ends; sometimes called *shoes*.

PROVISIONS

See grubstake.

prowl

In cattle herding, to go back over a territory after a roundup in search of cattle that may have been overlooked.

puck

In mining, a wall or pillar built of waste rock to support the roof.

puddin' foot

What the cowboy calls a big-footed or awkward horse.

pueblo

A Pueblo Indian village made up either of separate adobe or stone buildings or of one large, many-storied, terraced building that served to house the whole community.

puff

A miner's term for dynamite.

Pulaski

In logging, a light, single-bit ax with a straight handle and a narrow, adzlike trenching blade attached to its head; named for its designer, E. C. Pulaski, a forest ranger.

pullboat logging

In logging, a system of moving logs by means of a hauling engine mounted on a boat.

puller

A cowboy's term for a horse that is always leaning on the bits and wanting to go.

pull for the Rio Grande

To hit for that border line which has, for so many men on both sides, meant life or death; *on the dodge.*

pulling bog

Pulling cattle from bog holes.

pull in his horns

A cowboy's term meaning *to back down from a fight.*

pull leather

To grab the saddle horn while riding an unruly horse.

pull stakes

A cowboy's expression meaning *to leave;* to move, bag and baggage.

pull the trip

In roping, after roping a cow, to drop the rope under the animal's right hipbone and around its buttocks for the busting. See *steer busting.*

pump-handle

Said of a horse that bucks with a seesaw effect, landing alternately on his front and rear feet. He is an easy horse to ride; as one cowboy said, "A baby couldn't fall off him." A man who draws such a horse at a riding contest feels himself cheated, and the sarcastic remarks from the side lines do not improve his temper.

pumpkin piler

A westerner's name for an immigrant farmer, especially one from Missouri.

pumpkin roller

A cowboy's name for a grumbler or agitator. Such persons are not tolerated in a cow camp. They are also called *freaks,* be-

cause the cowboy, being an uncomplaining and loyal soul by nature, feels that such people do not belong to the calling. Also, a name for a green hand.

pumpkin-seed saddle

A cowboy's name for the small eastern riding saddle.

pumpkin skin

What cowmen in some localities call a palomino horse.

punche

A poor grade of tobacco used and traded by Indians of the Southwest.

puncheon

A trader's name for a wooden stake.

puncher

A shortened form of *cowpuncher,* a man who works cattle. In logging, the operator of a *donkey,* a logging engine.

punch the breeze

A cowboy's expression meaning *to go in a hurry.*

puncture lady

A cowboy's term for a woman who preferred to sit on the side lines at a dance and gossip; according to the cowboy, she usually made a good job of puncturing someone's reputation.

punk

An early pioneer's term for tinder made from a fungus and used with flint and steel to start his fires. A cowboy's term for an inexperienced hand. A logger's term for a boy or for any young man not yet professionally dry behind the ears. A signalman for a logging crew. A logger's name for bread.

pup's nest

A cowboy's name for a prairie dog's burrow.

pure

A cowboy's word for a thoroughbred animal. His word for someone who is loyal.

push

A miner's name for the shift boss. A logger's name for the camp boss, the assistant superintendent, the man in charge of a side of woods, or the man in the field who directs the logging operations; also called *pusher*.

push on the reins

A cowboy's expression for urging one's mount to full speed.

pussy-back

A mild bucking with the back arched; also called *cat-back*.

pussy pusher

A logger's name for a *cat skinner*, the engineer of a donkey engine.

put a kid on a horse

A common practice in the ranch country when errands are to be run or messages are to be sent. It does not take a man from his work.

put a spoke in his wheel

In cowboy parlance, to hinder or stop someone from carrying out some action or intention.

Put 'em east and west, boy!

In rodeo, a judge's call to a cowboy in a riding contest who is spur-buttoning, telling him to spur the horse's shoulders with the toes pointed outward.

put his saddle in the wagon

A cowboy's expression signifying that the one spoken of had been fired and was no longer riding for the ranch.

put on the sideboards

A cowboy's expression for encircling the rim of a whisky glass with thumb and forefinger so that it can be filled to the brim without spilling the contents. Logger's expression for loading one's plate with all the food it will hold.

put leather on his horse

A cowboy's expression for saddling a horse.

put on tallow

A cowboy's expression for gaining weight or fattening.

put on the nose bag

A cowboy's expression meaning *to eat a meal*.

put out

A trapper's term meaning *to travel*. A trader's term meaning *to leave* or *to start*.

put the calk to him

A logger's expression for thrashing someone.

put the loop on

A cowboy's expression meaning *to lasso*.

put the saddle on him

To saddle a horse. A cowboy's expression for trying to bluff or "ride" someone.

putting on the rollers

A cowboy's expression for drinking and having a high old time.

puttin' the leggin's

A cowboy's expression for whipping someone with *leggings*, or chaps.

putto

A wooden stake which is driven into the ground and to which one end of the picket rope is attached; from the French *poteau*, meaning *post*.

put to bed with a pick and shovel

A cowboy's expression for a burial.

put to grass

To turn cattle onto a range or into a pasture.

put windows in his skull

A cowboy's expression meaning *to shoot someone through the head*.

pyrite

In mining, fool's gold; iron disulphide; a pale, brass-colored mineral.

Q

"Any hoss's tail kin ketch cockleburs"

quaker
What the cowman calls a quaking aspen tree.

QUALITY
See bore and stroke, from who laid the chunk, good stab, makin' a hand, measured a full sixteen hands high, salty dog, shine, skookum, square, wildcat's ankle.

QUANTITY
See units of measure.

QUARRELING
See chip on one's shoulder, whittle whanging.

quarry
In mining, any open work in rock; excavation of the entire mass, as distinguished from work on a seam or vein by means of shafts or approaches under cover.

quarter horse
A saddle horse of the range country with great endurance; so called because of its ability to run a short distance (a quarter of a mile) at high speed; formerly called *short horse.*

quartz
In mining, a quartz vein, or ore obtained from such a vein, containing deposits of gold or silver. A natural silica, one of the commonest of minerals, both in ore bodies and in barren rock. The most laborious and expensive of all kinds of mining is that where gold occurs in a solid, continuous vein of rock, enclosed between distinct walls of some other kind of stone.

quartz battery
In mining, a stamp or series of stamps used in crushing quartz ore.

quartz camp
A camp of quartz miners.

quartz claim
In mining, a claim on which valuable mineral-bearing quartz occurs or is believed to occur.

quartz crusher
In mining, a machine for crushing or pulverizing quartz.

quartz fuse
In mining, an inferior fuse that burns too quickly.

quartz gold
A miner's term for gold that is not rounded and water worn but irregular and frequently twisted in form. Such gold is usually very bright and is always of fine quality.

quartz lead
In mining, a lode or vein of mineral-bearing quartz.

quartz mill
In mining, a machine for pulverizing quartz; a stamp mill.

quartz mine
A mine from which gold or silver is obtained by quartz mining.

quartz miner
A miner who does quartz mining.

quartz mining
Mining on veins or ore bodies in place, as distinguished from surface digging or washing (alluvial or placer mining). Underground mining in rock; so called because quartz is the chief mineral associated with gold in such deposits. See *quartz* and *quartz vein.*

quartz on the brain
An expression describing someone with gold fever.

quartz reef

In mining, a lode or vein of quartz.

quartz reefer

A miner engaged in mining for gold in a *quartz reef* or *quartz vein, q.v.*

quartz vein

In mining, a deposit of quartz in the form of a vein. Auriferous veins are also often called *quartz veins*, and mining for gold in the rock is called *quartz mining*.

quick-draw artist

A cowboy's term for an expert in the art of drawing a gun rapidly.

quick freighting

Freighting carried on with horses and mules the year round. Grain was stored at stations here and there along the way for feed.

QUICKNESS

See pronto.

quicksand

A deep mass of loose or moving sand mixed with water which forms in many western rivers. It is dangerous to persons or animals that get into it for it will not support their weight, and when they sink into it, it is very difficult to get them out.

quicksilver

In mining, mercury, a metal that is liquid at all ordinary temperatures, used in the amalgamation process of extracting gold and silver from ores.

Quién sabe?

An expression commonly used by all ranchmen to mean that they have no information upon a subject; pronounced *kin savvy*. From the Spanish, meaning *Who knows?*

Quinine Jimmy

A logger's name for the camp doctor.

quirly

A cowboy's name for a cigarette.

quirt

A flexible, woven-leather riding whip with a short stock about 1 foot long and a lash of three or four heavy, loose thongs. Its stock is usually filled with lead to strike down a rearing horse that threatens to fall backward, and it can also be effective as a blackjack. A loop extends from the head so that it may be carried on the rider's wrist or the saddle horn. From the Mexican-Spanish *cuarta.*

quista

A *quirt, q.v.*

QUIT

See break one's pick, bunch her, drag her, drilled her deep enough, got her made, hang up his rope, make her out, Mix me a walk, throwed in his hand.

quit the flats

A cowboy's expression meaning *to leave the country.*

QUIVERS

See carcage.

R

*"Montana for bronc riders and hoss thieves,
Texas for ropers and rustlers"*

race

A crooked blaze on a horse's forehead.

rack

A gait or pace of a horse, especially an amble or a single-foot. A cowboy's word meaning *to ride.*

rafter brand

A brand with semicone-shaped lines above

the letter or figure, similar to the roof of a house.

raftering

What the cowboy calls lying under a blanket or tarp with his knees up. A practice sometimes followed by a cowboy sleeping in the open during a rain to form a watershed.

rag bungalow

A logger's term for a tent used as living quarters; also called *rag house*.

rag house

See *rag bungalow*.

rag-out

A cowboy's expression meaning *to dress in one's best*.

railing

A westerner's term for gathering sagebrush by means of an iron rail dragged along the ground by two horses, one hitched at each end of the rail; this process breaks off the brush at ground level.

RAILROADS

See hell on wheels, logging railroads, mining railroads, stock train.

railroad without steam

A logger's expression meaning *to travel fast*.

RAIN

See weather.

rainbowin'

Said of a bucking horse that is bowing his back and shaking his head.

raise

A cowboy's term meaning *to see someone or something in the distance*, as, "He *raised* a posse comin' over the hill." A trapper's term meaning *to steal from another's cache*; also, *to lift*. In mining, a shaft or winze that has been worked from below; an underground mine opening that leads upward, either vertically or on an incline; a connection excavated upward from one crosscut to another.

raised on prunes and proverbs

A cowboy's expression describing a fastidious and religiously inclined person.

raised on sour milk

A cowboy's expression describing a cranky or disagreeable person.

raise hair

A trapper's term meaning *to scalp*. Like the Indian, the trapper also enjoyed *counting coup* after a battle—that is, telling how many of the enemy he had approached closely enough to strike.

raking

Another word for *scratching, q.v.* Raking generally applies when a rider gives his legs a free swing, rolling the rowels of his spurs along the horse's sides from shoulder to rump. It is one of the highest accomplishments aspired to by bronc riders.

ram

In mining, a small truck used to push cars up a slope.

ram pasture

What the cowboy sometimes calls the bunkhouse.

ramrod

A logger's name for the superintendent or manager.

ran a butcher shop and got his cattle mixed

Said of a cattle rustler who had been caught.

ranahan

A top cowhand; an efficient cowboy; often shortened to *ranny*.

ranch

An entire cattle- or sheep-raising establishment, including buildings, lands, and animals. The principal building of a ranching establishment, which is usually the owner's dwelling, together with other structures adjacent to it. The collective personnel of a ranching establishment. To operate a cattle- or sheep-raising establishment. From the Spanish *rancho*.

Ranch equipment

See buck rake, derrick, fence stretcher, hay sled, hay sling, Jackson fork, stacker, stack pole.

rancher

A man who operates a *ranch*, a title restricted to a member of the proprietor class.

ranchero

A Mexican rancher; from the Spanish.

Ranchers

See big sugar, rancher, ranchero, ranchman, rawhider, suitcase rancher, white-collar rancher.

Ranches

See big house, cap-and-ball layout, cattle spread, cocklebur outfit, cow ranch, dude ranch, good lay, hacienda, houses, layout, one-horse outfit, ranch, range line, sheep ranch, shirttail outfit, siwash outfit, spread, three-up outfit, tough lay, wild willow west.

Ranch hands

See alfalfa desperado, Arbuckle, cowboys, fodder forker, hay shoveler, hay slayer, hay waddy, hen wrangler, miller, mill rider, pitchfork gladiator, stacker, stiff man, windmiller, windmill monkey, wood monkey, wood sheller.

ranchman

Anyone connected with the running of a ranch, either an employee or an employer.

Ranch records

See beef book, book count, books won't freeze, tally sheet.

range

Open country where cattle graze.

Range

See breeding range, cattle range, close range, cow range, free grass, home range, open range, range, sheep range.

range boss

A man who works mostly for company-owned outfits. His work is to secure and protect the company's range, run its business, keep the men at work, and see that the cattle are bred up. He sees that fences are kept in repair and that the water supply functions and does everything within his ability to better the interests of his employers. To be successful, he has to be a leader of men and know horses, cattle, and the range. (John M. Hendrix, "Bosses," *Cattleman*, Vol. XXIII, No. 10 [March, 1937], 65–75.)

range-branded

Said of cattle branded upon the range away from corrals.

range bum

A cowboy's term for a professional *chuck-line rider, q.v.*

range count

See *pasture count.*

range cradle

A sheepherder's name for a sheep wagon.

range delivery

Delivery of cattle in which the buyer, after examining the seller's records and considering his reputation for truthfulness, paid for what the seller claimed to own and then rode out and tried to find it. (Philip A. Rollins, *The Cowboy* [New York, Charles Scribner's Sons, 1936], 225.)

range herding

Herding cattle upon a particular range.

range horse

A horse born and bred on the range. Except for being branded, such a horse is never handled until he is old enough to break.

range lambing

Lambing of late lambs occurring on the range when the weather is warmer.

range line

The boundary line of a cattle ranch.

range pirate

In the open-range days, a man who turned stock loose on the range without owning open water and range in proportion to the cattle he turned loose.

range riding

Performing the duties of an *outrider, q.v.*

range rights

Rights to the use of a certain range in consequence of priority of occupation and continuous possession.

range war

In early days, disturbances, often involving armed encounters, that arose from conflicting claims to the cattle range.

range word

A cowman's word of honor. When he gives his *range word*, it can be safely taken as law and gospel. When trying to protect a friend or telling a windy to a tenderfoot, he can lie bigger and better than anyone else. To him, as one cowman said, "Ananias was jes' an ambitious amateur." But when he prefaces his remarks with, "Speakin' for the ranch," or, "I'm givin' my *range word* for it," you can expect to hear the truth.

rank

A westerner's word for an animal that is tough and hard to handle.

ranny

A shortened form of *ranahan, q.v.*

rat

A logger's name for a workman who informs against a fellow worker.

rat lines

In logging, short sections of small lines that are used to transfer the position of the heavier lines.

rat-tailed horse

A horse with a tail that has but little hair.

rattle his hocks

A cowboy's expression meaning *to travel fast.*

rawhide

The hide of a steer or cow. It was one of the most useful products of the pioneer cattleman. From it he made ropes, hobbles, clotheslines, bedsprings, seats for chairs, overcoats, trousers, brogans, and shirts. He patched saddles and shoes with it. He used strips of it to bind loose wagon tires or lash together pieces of broken wagon tongue. It also served as a substitute for nails and many other things. Also, a cowman's term for a weak cow. A cowboy's word for gathering cattle alone on the range with an individual camp outfit; also, his word for teasing. A logger's word for rolling logs down a skidway.

RAWHIDE

See Mexican iron, Mormon iron, straps.

rawhide artist

A name given to a hand skilled in the use of the branding iron.

rawhide lumber

A logger's term for unfinished slabs of lumber with the bark left on.

rawhider

A name given to one of the early-day movers who traveled from one section of the West to another; see *mover.* His outstanding characteristic was that he always had a wagon full of cowhides, which he cut into strips and used for every known purpose. Also, a name sometimes given to the operator of a small cattle ranch. A name a northern cowboy sometimes gave to a Texan.

raw one

A cowboy's term for a green bronc.

reach

To make a motion as if to draw a gun; also, to draw a gun. When a man went after his gun, he did so with a single, serious purpose. There was no such thing as bluff. Every action was aimed toward shooting as speedily and as accurately as possible and making his first shot the last of the fight. In steamboating, a piece of straight river; the current drives through such a place in a pretty lively way.

Reach for the sky!

A gunman's command to raise the hands in the air.

reaching for the apple

Catching hold of the saddle horn while riding.

readers

In gambling, marked cards.

readin' sign

In tracking, interpreting the markings

found on the trail. One cowhand spoke of a good tracker as being able to "follow a wood tick on solid rock in the dark o' the moon." Another referred to a tracker who "had a nose so keen he could track a bear through runnin' water." On one occasion Pima Norton spoke of a friend who "could track bees in a blizzard."

read the Scriptures

A cowboy's expression meaning *to lay down the law* or *to give orders*.

real

A Spanish coin valued at about 12½ cents.

rear-back

See *fallback*.

rear cinch

The hind cinch; see *rear girth*.

rear girth

A Texan's term for the hind cinch.

rear jockey

The leather on top of the skirt of a saddle, fitting closely around the cantle.

reata

A rope, particularly one made of braided leather or rawhide; from the Spanish, meaning *rope to tie horses in single file*. See *lariat*.

rebozo

A term used by the early traders for a shawl, a shoulder sash, or a muffler; from the Spanish.

red card

What the logger calls a card of membership in the I.W.W.

redcoats

What a cowboy of the Northwest calls a member of the Royal Canadian Mounted Police.

red disturbance

A cowboy's term for whisky. Some of it, in the words of John West, "would make a muley cow grow horns."

redeye

A cowboy's term for whisky.

red-eyed

A cowboy's word meaning *angry*.

red flagger

A cowboy's term for a man said to spend his time looking for sundown and payday.

red ink

A cowboy's term for whisky.

Red River cart

A two-wheeled cart made entirely of wood and rawhide, even to the wheels and linchpins; named for the Red River of the North. The wheels were about 5 feet in diameter, and the rims were about 3 inches wide. There were four spokes in each wheel, set at right angles to one another at the hub, which was well built. The rims were joined by tongues of wood, and a crude form of rawhide known as *shaganappi* was used for tires. On some such carts even cruder wheels, made of solid sections sawed from the ends of trees, were used. The whole cart was made with an ax and an auger.

redskin

A white man's name for an Indian. A gambler's term for a court card, as distinguished from spot cards. See *court skin* and *paint skin*.

reef

To slide the legs back and forth along the horse's sides as one spurs.

reguarda

A rawhide shield made to fit in front of a horse's breast for protection when working in the brush country; from the Spanish.

regular

What the old-time trail driver called a drive that went "as fine as silk" to the Wichita Mountains and "hell broke loose" from there to the end of the drive.

reflectors

In gambling, cards prepared for cheating by means of indentations on the back.

release cutting

In logging, the cutting of larger trees that are overtopping young trees to permit the young trees to make a good growth.

relief

In cattle herding, what the cowboy called the change of guard.

RELIGION

See anxious seat, medicine bag.

remittance man

An early-day westerner's term for a socially outcast member of the English aristocracy who came West to relieve his family of further embarrassment; so called because he depended for existence upon the remittance of money from his family overseas.

remuda

A cowman's word for the extra mounts of each cowboy herded together and not at the time under saddle; from the Spanish, meaning *replacement*. Also occasionally called *remotha*, a corruption of the Spanish *remonta*, meaning *remount*; in the Southwest the word is pronounced *remootha*. Most Texas cowmen merely say *the hosses*. The *remuda* is to the Southwest what the *cavvy* is to the Northwest, though the northwestern cowboy usually calls these horses the *saddle band*.

A horse usually goes into the remuda when he is four years old. By the time he is six, he is fairly well trained for cow work, but he does not reach his period of full usefulness until he is about ten years old. Each year the remuda is culled of horses too old for the best work. An old cow horse is pensioned for a life of ease and grass if he has been good and faithful; otherwise, he is sold for farm work.

A good cowman knows that his outfit is no better than its horses, and he watches them closely. Every day he checks the horses and counts them out to the wrangler. Each cowboy is responsible for the condition of his string, and the man who abuses his horses doesn't last long with the outfit. No horse is overworked, no horse is overlooked. Each man realizes that his work is handicapped unless these horses are in top condition.

A rule of all remudas is that all horses must be geldings. Mares are never a part of the remuda, because they are bunch quitters and failures as saddle horses. As Charlie Russell said, "Lady hosses are like their human sisters. They get notions of goin' home, and no gentleman cayuse would think of lettin' a lady go alone." Stallions, on the other hand, fight and otherwise disturb a peaceful remuda.

When the work is over in the fall, the horses of the remuda are turned out to run the range, rest, and heal their scars. A small portion of the horses are kept up to be grain-fed and used by the men who remain to do what winter riding there is to be done. The average remuda holds from ninety to one hundred horses, a number necessary to mount a cow outfit of eight or ten men.

remudera

A Mexican's name for a bell mare.

rendering ring

A packer's term for a ring in the cinch through which the latigo was passed to tighten the aparejo on the animal's back.

rendezvous

The annual meeting in the mountains between trappers with their packs of furs and fur-company representatives with their caravans of goods to be sold or exchanged for furs to provide the necessities and the luxuries of wilderness life. Held during the summer and attended by various Indian tribes, it was the occasion for feasting and dissipation. These great frontier fairs flourished from the early 1820's to 1840.

renegade rider

A cowboy employed to visit ranches, sometimes as far as fifty or more miles away, and pick up any stock branded with his employer's brand, taking it on with him to the next ranch or range. He took his gather to the home ranch as often as he could, changed horses, and went out again.

rep

A cowboy who represented his brand at other ranches; also called *outside man* or *stray man*. Also to represent a brand at other ranches. This job grew out of efforts of ranch owners to recover their stray cattle. It became a regular part of the open-range system to have one man of each ranch work with the roundup to look out for and carry along cattle in his employer's brand until he could return them to their home range, branding their calves at the roundup. He assisted in the work of the roundup, but his first duty was to look after the cattle of his brand.

As a rule, the top hand of an outfit was given this enviable position, and he was considered a notch higher than the common puncher and got more pay. He had to know brands, and the job was a responsible one. He liked the work because he could travel around, mingle with friends, and make new ones in other outfits.

When he reached the outside limit of the drift from his company's range, he cut from the day herd the cattle of his brand (the *rep cut*), took his mount from the remuda, packed a horse with his bedroll, and "dragged it for home," driving his gather before him.

REPRIMAND
See chew out, orders.

rep's cut
During the roundup the bunch of cattle designated by a *rep (q.v.)* of an outside ranch as belonging to his brand.

re-ride
In rodeo, a second ride allowed a bronc rider or bull rider in the same go-round when the first ride is unsatisfactory for any of several reasons.

rerun
In rodeo, a steer or calf that is used for the second time in a steer-wrestling or roping event in the same rodeo in the same go-round. Generally, rerun stock is easier to wrestle or tie, although if bulldogging steers are rerun too frequently, they get wise to the methods of the bulldogger and are sometimes hard to catch.

REST
See flop, pose, shadin', snapping time, take five.

RESTAURANTS
See grease joint, nose bag.

RESTLESS
See cabin fever, fiddle-foot, fighting the bits, homeless as a poker chip, Junin' 'round.

rest powder
A logger's term for *snoose*, or snuff.

ribbing up
In packing, placing in an aparejo the sticks or other devices used to give stiffness to the sides of the aparejo.

ribbons
What the early westerner called the lines of a harnessed team or teams.

rib stickers
A cowboy's name for beans.

rib up
A cowboy expression meaning *to persuade*.

rib wrenches
A cowboy's name for spurs.

RICH
See bums on the plush, grass-bellied with spot cash, in the chips, plute, wallow in velvet.

ride herd on
A cowboy's expression meaning *to take care of*.

ride herd on a woman
A cowboy's expression meaning *to court a woman*.

ride like a deputy sheriff
A cowboy expression meaning *to ride recklessly*.

ride over that trail again
A cowboy's request to explain something more simply or more fully.

RIDERS
See bog rider, brush buster, brush hand, brush popper, brush roper, caballero, carnival hand, chuck-line rider, circle rider, clean setter, drag rider, fence rider, flank rider, glory rider, grub-line rider, jinete, kick-back rider, light rider, line rider, outrider, pistol, rep, point rider, renegade rider, salty rider, shadow rider, side riders, swing kicker, swing rider, tail rider.

ridge runner
A wild stallion that keeps to ridges and high points to watch for danger and warn his harem.

ridgling
A male horse one or both of whose testicles have not descended within sight.

ride Polly

A logger's expression for drawing pay as the result of an accident or sickness.

ride shank's mare

A logger's term meaning *to walk*.

RIDICULE

See chaff.

RIDING

See à la Comanche, bake, bareback riding, bedrock 'im, beefsteak, bicycling, blow a stirrup, boggin' 'im in, breaking brush, bucking, burn the breeze, business rider, cantle boarding, choke the horn, claw leather, close seat, coasting on his spurs, couldn't find his saddle seat with a forked stick, couldn't ride a pack horse, couldn't ride nothin' wilder'n a wheel chair, daylightin', dismounting, dust a horse, dust his ears, fanning, fanning on her fat, fighting the bits, fogging, forging, gimlet, Give him air! grabbin' the apple, grabbin' the nubbin', grabbin' the post, half hamming, hell-for-leather, hit the flats for home, hoppin' dog holes, huggin' rawhide, hunting leather, ironing out the humps, jamming the breeze, jigger, jiggle, kick the frost out, knee grip, loggerin', monkey style, mounting, neck-rein, nigger brand, op'ra, pack the mail, peeling, plow-boying, pull leather, push on the reins, rack, reaching for the apple, riding it out, riding out, riding on his spurs, riding safe, riding sign, riding slick, riding straight up, Roman riding, safety first, savin' saddle leather, scratching, scratching gravel, seeing daylight, set back, settin' the buck, sloppy riding, sounding the horn, spiked his horse's tail, spurring, squeeze the biscuit, squeezin' Lizzie, standing up to save saddle leather, stay in one's tree, stickin' like a postage stamp, taking leather, three-legged riding, three-quartering, thrown from a horse, thumbing, tight-legging, toe riding, trimming his ears with a hat, Waltz with the lady!

riding aprons

See *armitas*.

riding bog

A cowboy's expression for riding the low range in the spring while cattle are in a poor condition and extracting any animal that has become bogged or mired in a bog hole.

riding circle

During roundup, searching out and driving all the cattle found over a wide range of territory to a designated holding spot.

riding 'em down

In cattle driving, the gradual urging of the point and drag cattle closer together to put them on the bed ground.

RIDING EQUIPMENT

See bits, barboquejo, biddy bridle, bits, blind bridle, bosal, breaking, bridle, bridle chain, bridle ring, bridles, browband, buck hook, bucking rein, bucking roll, cabestro, California reins, ear head, fiador, ghost cord, hackamore, horse jewelry, martingale, open reins, Oregon short line, reguarda, saddles and equipment, spur, spurs, surcingle, tapaojos, tree ring.

riding fence

A cowhand's expression for keeping the fences in repair. See *fence rider*.

riding for a blind bridle

A cowman's expression describing a native who was working for a homesteader; the homesteader used bridles with blinders, which were held in great contempt by the cowman. The expression was considered an insult.

riding for the brand

A cowboy's expression for working for a particular ranch. The cowboy never *worked*; the word *work* was suggestive of the day laborer. He *rode* for a certain outfit. In early days, *riding for the brand* had a deep significance on the range. It meant that the cowboy was loyal, tireless in looking after the interests of the brand, and willing to fight for it and even lay down his life for it, as long as he was riding for it.

riding her out

In logging, said of a river driver who is caught in a log jam that gives way so that he has to stick to a moving log and navigate through tossing timbers in rushing waters.

riding into his dust

A cowboy's expression for following someone or following someone's lead.

riding it out

A cowboy's expression for staying with a bucking horse until he is conquered.

riding on his spurs

Said of a rider that hooks his spurs in the cinch, keeping them there during the ride.

riding out

A cowboy's expression for patrolling a prescribed boundary to look after the interests of the employer. See *line riding*.

riding out of town with nothing but a head

Said of a cowboy the morning after a big drunk. As one cowhand remarked, he "had a headache built for a hoss." Another declared that he "had a taste in my mouth like I'd had supper with a coyote."

riding safe

Said of a rider that is sitting close to the saddle, legs tightly clinched against the horse's sides, the spurs set firmly in the cinch.

riding sign

A cowboy's expression for riding the range to follow animals that have strayed too far and turning them back, pulling cattle from bog holes, turning cows away from loco patches, and doing anything else in the interest of an employer.

riding slick

A cowboy's expression for riding without locked spurs or hobbled stirrups and without a saddle roll.

riding straight up

A cowboy's expression for riding sitting straight up in the saddle and holding the reins in one hand, with the other in the air.

riding the bag line

See *riding the grub line*.

riding the bed wagon

A cowboy's expression for laying off on account of sickness or accident.

riding the coulees

Said of a man on the dodge from the law.

riding the chuck line

See *riding the grub line*.

riding the grub line

A cowboy's expression for going from ranch to ranch accepting meals without paying for them, a practice among jobless cowboys. Also called *riding the chuck line* and *riding the bag line*.

riding the high lines

Said of an outlaw on the dodge. Many bad men were forced to ride trails "that'd make a mountain goat nervous."

riding the owl-hoot trail

Said of an outlaw, who did much of his riding at night.

riding the rough string

An expression describing a man whose job it is to break horses. Such a job, as he says, "ain't like attendin' a knittin' bee."

riding the saw

A logger's expression for loafing, said when a partner on a crosscut saw does not do his share of the work.

riding the shows

Competing for prize money at rodeos; said of a professional buster who follows rodeos.

riding under a cottonwood limb

Said of a hanging, and also of a man committing an act for which he deserved to be hanged.

riding with an extra cinch ring

Said of a rustler or of a man suspected of rustling.

riffle bar

In mining, one of a series of bars, slats, or other obstructions placed across the bottom of a sluice box or other gold-washing apparatus to catch particles of gold. Also called *riffle*, *riffle block*.

riffle box

In mining, a cradle or boxlike contrivance with riffles, or obstructions, along the bottom for catching particles of gold.

RIFLES

See weapons and ammunition.

rig

A cowboy's term for his saddle. A logger's term for any outfit, apparatus, or machine.

rigger

In logging, a tree trimmer.

rigging

The middle leathers attached to the tree of a saddle connecting with and supporting the cinch by latigos through the rigging ring. In packing, a collective term for the aparejos of the train. In logging, the cable, blocks, and hoops used in cable logging. In gambling, a harness for holding out cards in reserve.

rigging cover

In packing, covers used to protect the aparejos in camp or bivouac.

rigging pecker

A logger's name for an organizer for the I.W.W.

rigging ring

The iron ring attached to a saddle for fastening the cinch; also called *tree ring* and *saddle ring*.

rigging slinger

In logging, one of the men who splice broken wire ropes and secure blocks and lines; also, one of the men who attach the chokers to the main yarding line.

right-hand man

A ranch foreman.

right side

See *off*.

rig up

A logger's expression meaning *to dress up in one's best*.

rildy

A cowboy's name for a comforter or a blanket.

riled

A cowboy's word meaning *angry* or *stirred up*.

rim-fire

A saddle with one cinch that is placed far to the front; also called *Spanish rig* and *rimmy*.

rim firing a horse

A cowboy's expression for putting a bur under the saddle blanket to make a horse pitch, one of the many pranks of the cowboy.

rim rocker

A cowboy's name for a horse agile enough to climb steep hills and travel over rocks and rough country.

rim-rocking sheep

Running sheep over a cliff to destruction, something cattlemen often did during the early-day wars between the cattle and the sheep factions.

rincon

A southwesterner's word for a nook, a secluded place, or a bend in a river; from the Spanish.

ring bit

A bit with a metal circle slipped over the lower jaw of the horse. A cruel bit devised by the Spanish, it is not looked upon with favor by American cowmen. It can be extremely severe unless handled carefully and is hardly a bit for a man who loses his temper.

ringbolt

In river boating, a large iron ring fastened in rock or concrete by means of a pin and used to attach mooring lines; generally found on wharves and docks and sometimes on bridge piers.

ringer

In gambling, a harness for holding out cards in reserve; see *rigging*.

ringey

A cowboy's term meaning *angry* or *riled*.

ring in

In gambling, to substitute cards.

ring in a cold deck

In gambling, to substitute a marked deck of cards.

ring toter

An early-day name for a man who, with two green sticks and a cinch ring, branded mavericks on the range, trying to build a herd of calves that did not rightly belong to him; another name for a rustler.

ring up

In logging, to tally the number of pieces of lumber of a particular size, length, and grade and then enter the total beside the item on a record sheet and draw a ring around it.

riñón

A species of conifer.

RIVER-BOAT CREWS

See brigade, flatter, gas skinner, keelboatman, patron.

river donkey

A logger's name for a logging engine on a raft.

river drive

In logging, the action of floating or guiding logs down a river.

river driver

A logger who drives logs down the river in the spring; also called *river hog*.

RIVER HAZARDS

See bob sawyer, buoy, crossboard, floating island, hull inspector, planter, sawyer, towhead, wooden island.

river hog

See *river driver*.

river horn

In river boating, an early-day wooden trumpet used as a signaling device by navigators of western-river keelboats and flatboats.

RIVER LANDINGS

See boat landing, choke the stump, landing, levee, port, wharf, wooding station.

riverman's Bible

The Waterways Journal, the weekly trade paper founded in St. Louis in 1887 and devoted to steamboating affairs.

river mining

An early-day method of mining by diverting a stream temporarily and securing the gold from the dry, exposed bed. Such a project, undertaken only in the summer during the low-water season, allowed a maximum working period of five months.

RIVERS

See Big Muddy, big swimmin', break up, crooked river, crossings, drift, easy water, Father of Waters, over the willows, pop rise, reach, slough, snaggy, swimming water.

river sluicing

Hydraulic mining along a river.

river sniper

In mining, a gold panner.

river talk

In river boating, the colorful speech of the professional flatboat man. Like other frontiersmen, he spoke in an incessant series of metaphors, similes, and comparisons. He described everything, whether an inanimate object or some human action, by likening it to something else. And, like frontier people, he colored his discourse with references to his own occupation.

roach

To trim the hair of the mane or tail of a horse.

road agent

A robber, usually a robber of stagecoaches.

road agent's spin

A gun spin, the reverse of the *single roll*, q.v.; also called *Curly Bill spin*, q.v.

road brand

A special brand of any design for trail herds as a sign of ownership en route. Such a brand helped the herders keep from mingling their herd with outside cattle and spiriting off their home range those animals of disinterested ownership. (Philip A. Rollins, *The Cowboy* [New York, Charles Scribner's Sons, 1936], 240.)

This type of brand originated in Texas during the trail days when a law was passed that all cattle being driven beyond the northern limits of the state were to be branded by the drover with "a large and plain mark, composed of any mark or device he may choose, which mark shall be branded on the left side of the stock behind the shoulder." With the passing of trail driving, this brand was no longer used.

road donkey

In logging, a donkey engine that drags logs along the skid road.

roadhouse

A cowboy's term for a corral in an out-of-the-way place used by rustlers to hold stolen stock temporarily.

road monkey

In logging, a man who works on a forest road gang; a man who keeps skid roads in good shape.

road run

A logger's term for a narrow, washed-out hole in the skid road.

road runner

See *chaparral bird*.

ROADS

See access road, camino real, corduroy road, fore-and-aft road, portage path, runway, skid road, spur, stage, stage road, wire road.

road stake

A logger's term for money he had earned and saved to carry him to the next job.

roan

A horse with a more or less uniform mixture of white and colored hairs over the entire body. If the darker color is sorrel, the horse is a *strawberry roan*; if bay, the horse is a *red-roan*; and if mahogany bay or black, the horse is a *blue-roan* or *black-roan*.

roast

In mining, to burn or oxidize an ore in order to eliminate the sulphur that is combined with the minerals.

rob

In mining, to gut a mine; to work for the ore in sight without regard to supports, reserves, or any other considerations. See *stood up*.

ROB

See cash in his six-shooter, rolled, stood up.

robbersary

A logger's name for the company commissary.

robber stick

In logging, a measuring stick carried by the scaler. Also, a club carried by the logging foreman.

robe hide

A robe made of buffalo hide. Such robes were made from buffaloes killed in the winter when their hair was heavy. They brought much better prices than those made from animals killed in other seasons.

rocker

In mining, a short trough for separating gold; designed so that water and gravel could be rocked or shaken in it until the lighter, coarser material had been separated from the gold. Looking somewhat like a child's cradle, with similar rockers and a perpendicular handle to set it in motion, it was basically a wooden box or trough about 20 inches square, whose bottom sieve had holes 1 inch in diameter. Under this a canvas or wooden apron sloped from the lower end of the hopper back to the upper end of the cradle. Sometimes a second piece of canvas was stretched underneath the first piece down to the hopper's lower end. Two or three *riffle bars* were attached to the bottom of the lower half of the rocker. Also called *rocker cradle*. See *riffle bar*.

rocker cradle

See *rocker*.

rocker split

An earmark; a long curved undersplit starting at the top end of the ear.

rocking

In mining, the process of separating ores by washing in a *rocker, q.v.*

rocking brand

A brand resting upon and connected with a quarter-circle.

rocking-chair horse

A horse with an easy gait.

rock out

In mining, to separate gold from auriferous gravel by means of a *rocker*, *q.v.*

Rocky Mountain canary

A cowboy's name for a burro.

Rocky Mountain college

What the trappers called a winter camp in which they sat up in one lodge until midnight and spun yarns or debated.

rod

What a cowboy sometimes calls the boss.

rodding the spread

A cowboy's expression for bossing the outfit.

rodeo

A cowboy contest; in colloquial Mexican, a cattle roundup; from the Spanish *rodea*, meaning *to surround* or *encircle*. The cowboy contest is commonly called *ro'de-o*, while the Mexican roundup is called *ro-day'o*; in the latter sense the word is rapidly becoming obsolete.

Some rules of rodeo bronc riding are as follows: Only one rein is allowed, and it must be free from knots or tape and must not be wrapped around the hand. While making a ride, the rider must not change hands on the reins, and his rein hand must be held above the horse's neck. The rider must leave the chute with both feet in the stirrups and both spurs against the horse's shoulders. He must "scratch" ahead for the first five jumps, then behind. He has to stay on the horse and ride clean for 10 seconds. If he loses a stirrup or touches leather with either hand, hits the horse with his hat, or looks cross-eyed at the judges, he is disqualified.

Fanning a horse with the hat used to be considered spectacular, but modern rodeos forbid quirting, fanning or even touching the animal with the hand.

RODEO

See added money, arena director, average, bareback rigging, breaking the barrier, chute- crazy, chute fighter, chute freeze, crying room, day-money horse, dink, entry fee, no time, out of the money, point-award system, producer, rerun, riding the shows, rodeo events and stunts, splitting.

RODEO ARENA

See barrier, score.

RODEO EQUIPMENT

See bareback rigging, bull rigging, riding equipment, ropes, saddles.

rodeo chaps

In rodeo, chaps strong enough to protect a rider's legs against chute fences and Brahma hoofs and horns; most of them are slicked up with a lot of fancy inlay and monogram doodads to satisfy the owner's idea of showmanship.

RODEO EVENTS AND STUNTS

See bareback riding, bite-'em lip, buford, bull riding, bull rope, busting, calf roping, closed event, contract acts, Cut 'er loose! dally steer roping, dally team roping, day money, draws dead, event, final head, final horse, fishing, flank, flank rigging, go-round, gravy run, ground money, head-and-heeler, hippodrome stand, hit the daylight, hooker, jackpot, judge, lap and tap, loggerin', mad scramble, mount money, Pick him up! prize money, Put 'em east and west, boy! re-ride, Russian drag, saddle bronc riding, scratching, screwing down, single steer tying, standard event, steer decorating, steer wrestling, team roping, trading out, tying down, wild-cow milking, wild-horse race.

RODEO MEN

See arena director, flagman, pick-up man, producer, snubber, stock contractor, timer, time judge, untie man, whistle judge.

roll

In roping, a corkscrew, wavelike motion of a rope that travels along its end and lands on the object roped with a jar. Many ropers use the *roll* to release their nooses from roped animals when they want to recover their ropes from grown cattle that have been heeled. See also *saddle roll*.

rollaway

In logging, piled logs waiting the spring drive on a high river.

rolled

A logger's term for being robbed while drunk.

roll 'em

A logger's expression meaning *to go to bed*.

rolleo

A logger's name for a *birling (q.v.)* contest.

roller

A gambler's name for a game of *keno, q.v.*

roll his tail

A cowboy's expression for leaving in a hurry.

rolling a calf

A method of throwing a calf for branding. This is a spectacular stunt requiring considerable strength and skill. It is a somewhat dangerous and very tiring method of getting a calf down, accomplished by reaching over the back of the calf, catching it with one hand at the same time jamming a leg in front of the calf. The cowboy does not resort to this method unless he wants to show off or a girl happens to be visiting the branding for the day.

rolling faro

An early variety of faro played with an ordinary faro layout and a wheel, somewhat similar to that used at roulette, on which a suit of cards had been painted. Instead of drawing cards from a box, the dealer spun the wheel, and the winners and losers were determined by the position of the pointer. This game was never popular, principally because most of the wheels were crooked, being worked by body pressure or by mechanical devices, and it vanished from the gambling scene before the Civil War.

rollin's

A logger's name for cigarette tobacco.

roll one for a job

A logger's expression for taking a job away from an incumbent.

Roll out!

A logger's call to get out of bed; the morning call in the bunkhouse; also, *Roll up!* In roping; a loop made by jerking the noose forward over the hand and wrist and releasing it so that it will roll out on edge, leaning somewhat to the right. It is usually only effective when thrown at an animal passing in front of the roper toward his right. It can be used to forefoot horses, but is better as a heel loop for cattle, a rather small loop being rolled under the belly of the animal in position to catch both hind feet. (W. M. French, "Ropes and Roping," *Cattleman*, Vol. XXVI, No. 12 [May, 1940], 17–30.)

Roll out! Breakfast on the boards!

A cook's call for breakfast in a logging camp.

rollovers

In trick roping, spins started either vertically or horizontally in which the noose is made to roll over the roper's shoulders or one or both arms.

rolls

In a sawmill, metal rollways that carry lumber through the mill.

rolls his gun

A cowboy's expression for someone who starts shooting.

rolls his own hoop

A cowboy's expression for someone who attends to his own business.

rolls in

A logger's expression for going to bed.

rolls it

A roper's expression for throwing a rope.

roll the cotton

A cowboy's expression for rolling his bed and moving camp or for taking a trip.

roll the guff

A logger's expression meaning *to converse*.

rollway yard

A log landing or log dump.

Roll your bed!

A cowman's command meaning *You're fired!*

Roll your wheels!

In freighting, a command used in the early days by freighters, bullwhackers, and mule skinners to start a team. By the time the cowman seized the expression for his own, it was a command to get going in any sense.

romal

A flexible whip made on the bridle reins when they are fastened together; from the Spanish *ramal,* meaning *branch* or *ramification.* Thus, attached as it is by the loop of the bridle reins, the romal becomes but a "ramification" of the rein, a handy addition that may be used as a quirt and dropped from the hand without fear of its getting lost.

Roman riding

In rodeo, a contract stunt in which a rider stands on a horse's back with the reins in his hands. Roman riding can also be done on two horses, and there are some Roman riders who can handle teams of as many as five horses running abreast.

roof

In steamboating, the roof of the boiler deck; also called the *upper deck.* The expression "The captain is on the *roof*" meant that he was stationed at the forward end of the upper deck, his station on a packet when the boat was being maneuvered at a lock or landing. The term did not include the covering over the skylight, which was referred to as the *skylight roof.* The forward end of the roof was commonly called the *hurricane deck.*

room crosscut

See *crosscut.*

roostered

A cowboy's word meaning *drunk.*

rooter

A cowboy's name for a hog.

rope

The most important tool of the cowman, made of many different materials and serving many purposes. It catches his horse, throws his cattle, drags his wood to camp, and pulls cattle from bog holes. It ties up his bed, helps in fighting prairie fires, secures his packs, stakes his horses, serves as a corral, is useful as a cow whip, and is a weapon for killing snakes. It also serves as a guide in snowstorms when it is tied from his bunkhouse door to the stable or the woodpile. In early times it helped pull his wagons across rivers and rough places, and it was frequently used to mete out frontier justice. Without it the cowboy would be practically useless. It is said that he does everything with a rope except eat with it. There are truly many men who can do anything with a rope except throw it straight up and climb it.

rope-and-ring man

A cowboy's name for a rustler; so called because he used a rope and a cinch ring to run his illegal brands. I once heard a reformed rustler admit that he "quit rustlin' cows for the good of my gullet."

rope corral

A temporary corral at the cow camp, made by three or four cowhands holding ropes between them to form an obtuse U and used to pen saddle horses until they could be caught for saddling.

The corral was formed by using a heavy rope called a cable, held about three feet off the ground either by men or sometimes by forked sticks. This made a seemingly frail prison for a bunch of horses, but early in his life the range horse learned to respect the rope. He remembered the burns and falls he received when he was first thrown and branded. If a horse had not learned his lesson and broke out of the corral a time or two, the top roper of the outfit was given the nod to "pick up his toes" the next time he broke out. It might break the horse's neck, but the boss would rather have him dead than spoiling the other horses. Frequently the rope cable was shaken vigorously to remind the horses that it was a rope.

As soon as the desired horses were caught, the rope was dropped and the remaining horses allowed to go back to grazing. This was done quietly, and any rushing or jamming was carefully avoided. Having performed its duty, the cable was coiled up and placed in the wagon to be ready for the next saddling.

rope croup

A cowboy's term for a hanging.

rope horse

A horse especially fitted for and trained in the work of roping. A man can learn to ride and do ordinary cow work in a short time, but to become a proficient roper requires years of practice; yet no matter how expert a roper may become, he will have small success without a good rope horse.

The rope horse must have strength and intelligence, both qualities well trained. Of all cow work, roping requires the most skill and is the hardest and most dangerous. When the roped animal is "tied onto," the slightest pull on the reins causes the well-trained horse to sit back, hind feet well under him, forefeet braced well out in front to receive the shock. The slightest pressure on the side of the neck with the reins causes him to whirl instantly to face the catch.

A good rope horse never allows a cow to get a side run on him, nor does he allow an inch of slack to let the rope wind him up. Experience has taught him the consequences of such blunders. The instant the roped animal falls, the horse will pull against the rope, dragging the dead weight along the ground.

When running an animal to be roped, the educated rope horse knows when the cowboy takes down his rope and what is expected of him. He runs like the wind to the left side of the cow but never past her. There he sticks until his rider casts his rope; then he "does his stuff." If the roper misses, he knows that, too. At a roundup where a large crew is working, the top ropers and the top roping horses stand out above the rest. Any successful contest roper gives his horse most of the credit. As Will Rogers once said, "Contest ropin' is just like a marriage. It's a partnership affair between the roper and his mount."

rope meat

A cowboy's term for the victim of a hanging.

ROPERS

See brush roper, dally man, header, heeler, rope tosser, small-loop man, smooth roper, tie-hard, tie man.

ROPES

See belly rope, big loop, bird cage, blocker loop, bull rope, cable, catgut, choker, choke rope, clothesline, coil, come-along, cordelle, doll-babies, fiador, fling line, grass line, grass rope, gut line, hair rope, hemp, hoggin' rope, honda, hot rope, jakoma, ketch rope, lair, lariat, lair rope, lash rope, lash rope with cincha and hook, lasso, lass rope, lead rope, line, maguey, manila, mecate, pepper-and-salt rope, piggin' string, reata, riding equipment, rope, seago, skin string, sling rope, stake rope, string, tie rope, tom horn, trip, twitch, W, whale line.

rope-shy

A cowboy's term for a horse that jumps away from the rope when its rider is roping, and also for an animal with a fear of ropes.

rope tosser

A roper who, instead of swinging the rope around his head before throwing, spreads it out behind and to one side of him and with a quick, graceful throw, or toss, launches it with unerring aim over the head of the animal. This method is used almost entirely in catching a calf out of a herd, since it is done so quietly and easily that the animal is snared before he has a chance to dodge or move.

ROPE TRICKS

See body spin, butterfly, high-low, hop-skip, juggling, merry-go-round, ocean wave, rollovers, roping, skipping, stargazing, wedding ring.

ROPING

See blocker loop, building a loop, calf horse, California twist, catch-as-catch-can, coffee grinding, community loop, complex spin, cotton-patch loop, dab, dally, dog loop, fair-ground, figure eight, flank, fore-footing, goin' over the withers, head catch, heel, hooey, hooley-ann, hornswoggling, hungry loop, jerked down, lay, laying the trip, mangana, mangana de pie, moonlight roping, Mother Hubbard loop, old-man him, overhand toss, overhead loop, peal, pegging, pick up his hind feet, pick up his toes, pile it on, pull the trip, put the loop on, rodeo events and stunts, roll, rolling a calf, Roll out! rolls it, rope tricks, roping out, rosebud, shakin' out, sing, smear, snail, snake, snare, spread, stack it on, steer busting, steer roping, stretchin' out, Texas tie, tie on, tying fast, underhand pitch, washerwoman loop, waste a loop, whirling.

roping in

A cowboy's expression for cheating in gambling.

roping out

A cowboy's expression for roping the hands' mounts in a corral, catching them for saddling.

rosadero

A vertical wide leather shield sewed to the back of the stirrup leathers; from the Spanish.

rosebud

A roper's term for a knot tied in the dally end of a rope.

rosin-belly

A logger's name for a common laborer in a sawmill.

rotten loggin'

A cowboy's expression for the comparatively rare practice by romantic couples of sitting on a log in the moonlight and "sparking."

rough-break

To rope, choke down, blindfold, and saddle a green bronc and then mount, strip off the blindfold, dig in with the spurs, slam the horse with the quirt, and proceed to fight it out. Many early-day ranchers followed this method of breaking horses, and three such rides by the buster were considered sufficient to turn the horse over to a cowboy.

roughed out

A cowboy's expression describing a horse ridden a time or two but still likely to buck when mounted.

rough lock

In freighting, a method of locking one wheel of a wagon with a chain passed through the spokes and around the rim and made fast to the wagon; such a device was used as a brake to hold a load, usually on a grade. To brake a wagon by means of such a device.

rough steer

A cowboy's term for a steer of poor breeding and scrawny development.

rough string

A string of wild and semiwild horses that fight every time they are saddled. Every ranch that raises its own horses has some that have never felt the saddle.

rough-string rider

A professional bronc buster. Of necessity all cowboys are good riders, but the men who handle the rough strings have to be bronc busters, and they draw a few extra dollars a month for this perilous work. However, it is not so much the money that most of them care about as it is the honor. It is a sign of ability to ride the rough string for a large outfit. As one cowboy said, "The rider of the rough string maybe ain't strong on brains, but he ain't short on guts."

Each man has his own way of breaking a horse, but all good busters strive to break so that the horse's spirit remains unbroken, for a spiritless horse is worthless. The buster strives to break quickly to save the boss time and money. He is more interested in staying on the horse than in the manner of his performance. His very calling demands that he stay on, as a matter of pride and because horses become outlaws when they can throw their riders.

round browns

A cowman's name for solid cow chips.

rounder

In faro, a gambler who plays largely with stake money. Faro etiquette requires a rounder who wins to give the other rounders ten to twenty-five dollars to bank for him.

roundhouse

What the miner calls his chisel.

round pan

The large pan, or tub, that received the dirty dishes after a meal at a cow camp. For a cowboy to fail to throw his dishes in this pan was a breach of range etiquette, and he would certainly be called names by the cook that would "burn the grass to cinders for yards around."

round pen

A name the cowboy occasionally gives the corral.

round turn

In early-day logging, the circular track where teamsters turned around at the end of the haul.

roundup

The gathering of cattle, the cattleman's harvest. In early days the roundup was the most important function in cattle land. There were two a year, the spring roundup for the branding of the calf crop, and the fall roundup for the gathering of the beeves for shipment and the branding of the late calves and those overlooked in the spring.

Unlike most customs of the cattle country, the roundup is neither Spanish-Mexican nor western American in origin. It originated in the mountain country of Kentucky, Tennessee, the Carolinas, and the Virginias. The people of those states let their cattle run loose and annually held roundups to gather them, but they performed the work in a haphazard sort of way. The western cowman perfected the system and brought it to the attention of the public as an important and colorful phase of the cattle industry.

The early western attempts, called *cow hunts* or *cow drives*, were crude; but as the industry grew and spread over the West, they became extremely efficient and effective. After fences came, the practice became an unnecessary pageant, but in the open-range days the roundup sometimes covered thousands of miles. Stockmen found it necessary for their mutual protection to take some co-operative action; therefore, the roundup system was adopted and perfected.

Roundups varied in detail in different sections, but in the main they were essentially the same throughout the cattle country. Each ranchman of the district being worked furnished men and bore his share of the general expense, this share proportioned according to the number of cattle owned. Each ranch furnished a sufficient number of horses for its riders, but only the larger outfits sent chuck wagons. Each district was worked successively by ranges until each was cleaned up in regular rotation. At the end of the drive every owner knew by the carefully kept tally the increase of his herd and the number of older cattle he owned that had been gathered in by this raking of the range.

The open-roundup system lasted only a comparatively few years, but during its existence it was the event every cowman looked forward to with interest and eagerness. Not only was it his harvest time, but also it served as a reunion with old friends and a means of cultivating new acquaintances.

ROUNDUP

See bedding out, beef cut, beef roundup, blackballed outfit, brush roundup, bunch ground, calf roundup, chain gang, changing mounts, chopper, combings, cover his dog, cow camp, cow hunt, cutter herds, fall roundup, gather, general work, getting up the horses, handbill roundup, herding cattle, holding spot, inner circle, moonshining, on circle, open roundup, outer circle, outside man, pool camp, pool roundup, potrack outfit, prowl, rep's cut, riding circle, roundup, running cattle, rustle the pasture, scattering the riders, smoking out the cattle, spring roundup, tally man, telling off the riders, throwing over, wagon boss, working ahead of the roundup.

roundup captain

The man chosen to act as boss of the roundup. He was boss over all, and his word was law, no matter if he did not own a hoof. The owners of the cattle were as much under his orders as any common puncher or horse wrangler. He knew all the brands of the country and had to be a diplomat to keep peace between warring factions. He had to know men and cattle and select the right man for the right job, as well as the proper roundup grounds. Certain men knew certain ranges better than others; accordingly the captain sent them out to scour these ranges for cattle. He selected from among the cowboys he knew to have good judgment as many "lieutenants" as he needed. These he put in charge of small units to run the cattle out of the brakes, arroyos, and other parts of the range. One cowboy's description of a roundup boss was, "He's the feller that never seems to need sleep, and it makes 'im mad to see somebody that does."

roustabout

A man of all work around a cow camp. A laborer in a logging camp who does rough work, picking up jobs where he can. A man, usually a Negro, employed in the deck department of a steamboat who worked under the mate and did any task assigned to him.

route

In logging, the total time of operation by any given logging camp. A *long route* is a logger's term for a long stretch of employment on one job.

ROUTE

See dry route, stage route, trade.

rowel

The wheel of a spur. There are many different kinds and shapes of rowels.

royal flush

In poker, an ace-high straight flush, the highest possible hand, barring wild cards.

royalty

In mining, the lessor's share of the proceeds.

rubbed out

A common expression among the early traders and trappers meaning *dead;* an English version of the Indian's figurative language.

rubbed up

A trader's expression meaning that he had stopped to slick up and dress in his best before going into town.

ruby copper

In mining, cuprite, a beautiful natural red copper oxide.

rudder

In steamboating, the broad blade attached to the stern of a boat which, when moved from side to side, steered the boat. Stern-wheel river steamers were invariably equipped with more than one rudder, some-times as many as four or five, and rivermen referred to them as the *rudders*. Side-wheel vessels usually had a single rudder, but some were equipped with *double rudders*. A *monkey rudder* was a rudder aft of the wheel stream of a paddle-wheel boat.

rudderstock

In steamboating, an upright timber (or set of timbers built into a member) fastened into the rudder at its base, to the top of which the tiller was fastened. Later such stocks were built of steel. The rudderstock of a stern-wheel river steamer was usually set vertically, but sometimes it was placed at a 90-degree angle to the stern rake.

run

A rush to new territory by settlers. A stampede of cattle. In logging, to float, drive, or conduct logs down a stream.

run a blazer

A cowman's expression for attempting to deceive or to bluff.

run a brand

To give or use a brand. To burn a brand on an animal with a *running iron, q.v.*

run a juggle factory

In logging, to make wood chips from ties.

runaround

In mining, a passage driven in the shaft pillar to enable men and animals to pass safely from one side of the shaft to the other.

runaway bucker

In rodeo, a type of bucking horse. When the chute gate is opened, this bucker will leave at a fast run and after traveling about 50 yards will "break in two" and start bucking. Generally his first leap will be high and mighty, and if the rider is caught unprepared, he does not have much chance of collecting prize money. When a horse is running his best and then leaps four or five feet into the air and comes down stiff-legged, he lights heavy. The fast forward motion stops so abruptly that the horse appears to shove himself backward as he hits the ground. This trick has caused many riders to meet their Waterloo. (Bruce Clinton, "Buckin' Horses," *Western Horseman*, Vol. III, No. 3 [May–June, 1938], 10.)

run down his mainspring

A cowboy's expression for a runaway horse that is allowed to run until he quits of his own accord.

run like a Nueces steer

A common Texas expression meaning *to run fast*. It originated from the fact that the wild cattle of the Nueces River country were exceptionally speedy for cattle and endowed with an utter disregard for obstacles in their path.

runner

In freighting, a man who was dispatched by the captain of a wagon train to go ahead of the caravan and procure and send back provisions, rent store space, prospect for sales, and make any other necessary arrangements.

RUNNING

See anvil, boring, break range, carrying the news to Mary, heating his axles, lope, makin' far-apart tracks, paddle, sobre paso.

running brand

A brand with flowing curves at the ends.

running cattle

Working cattle; rounding up cattle.

running guard

In freighting, taking turns at guard duty in camp.

running iron

A branding iron made in the form of a straight poker or a rod curved at the end and used much as one would write upon a blackboard with chalk. In the 1870's a law was passed in Texas forbidding the use of this iron in branding. This was a blow aimed at the brand blotter, whose innocent single iron would tell no tales if he was caught riding across the range. The law made the man found with the single running iron an object of suspicion, and he was sometimes obliged to explain to a very urgent jury.

running mate

A cowboy's term for his pal or his wife.

running meat

A trapper's expression for hunting buffalo or other game for food. Trappers in winter quarters designated certain men to run meat for the group. Commanders of frontier forts followed the same practice.

running mount

A method of mounting a horse on the run without using the stirrups.

running the outfit

Fulfilling the duties of the foreman of a ranch.

running W

A method of tying a horse by means of a rope running from the hobbles to a ring in the cinch, forming the shape of a W. This method is generally used on horses that would run away.

running wild

A cowboy's expression for dodging the law and also for being on a tear, or whooping it up.

run on the rope

A cowboy's expression for an animal, especially a horse, that is snubbed up violently when he starts away after being roped. It is part of the education of a range horse.

run-over

A cattle guard built on a highway, in earlier days made of green poles and sometimes covered with rawhide.

runway

In logging, a path followed in skidding logs; also called *gutter board*.

rush

A gold rush; a stampede of miners seeking a claim in a new field.

rusher

One who participates in a rush to a newly discovered mining area.

Russian coupling

In logging, a narrow unsawed connecting piece of wood that holds together two nearly sawed logs, when the original whole log is not completely bucked.

Russian drag

In rodeo, a method of riding a horse with one foot in a strap and the rider's head hanging off the side of the horse.

rust eater

A miner's name for an ironworker in a mine.

rusties

A cowboy's name for culled, wild, or lean cattle.

rustle

To wrangle or herd horses. To steal cattle. See *rustler*.

rustler

At first, a synonym for *hustle*, an established term for any person who was active and pushing in any enterprise. Later, a name for a wrangler. Still later, a word almost exclusively applied to a cattle thief, beginning in the days of the maverick when cowboys were paid by their employers to "get out and *rustle* a few mavericks." These same cowboys soon became more interested in putting their own brands upon motherless calves to get a start in the cattle business, and this practice was looked upon by the ranchmen as thievery. Thus the word came to connote a thief. Texans preferred the blunter term *cow thief*.

Winter was open season on the rustler, for he was busiest then. Dodging range riders, he rode through the grazing cattle, picking up big calves that had been missed during the summer and fall branding.

RUSTLERS

See brand artist, brand blotter, careless with his branding iron, Cattle Kate, handy with the running iron, his calves don't suck the right cows, his cows have twins, long rope, mavericker, ring toter, rope-and-ring man, rustler, sticky rope, tongue splitter, too handy with the rope.

rustler's pneumonia

A cowboy's term for cold feet; cowardice.

rustle the pasture

A cowboy's expression for bringing in the saddle horses in preparation for the roundup.

RUSTLING

See big loop, burning rawhide, didn't keep his twine on his tree, hot-foot, kept his brandin' iron smooth, maverick factory, mavericking, packs a long rope, pin crape on the kid, ran a butcher shop and got his cattle mixed, riding with an extra cinch ring, rustle, rustling, sleepering, steal a start, swing a wide loop.

rust the boiler

A cowboy's expression meaning *to drink alkaline water*.

rusty

In mining, oxidized; ore coated with oxide; a term applied to gold that will not easily amalgamate.

S

"If the saddle creaks, it's not paid for"

sab-cat

A logger's name for an expert at sabotage; named for the black cat pictured on an I.W.W. emblem.

sabe

See *savvy*.

sabinas

Cattle with red-and-white peppered and splotched coloring; from the Spanish, meaning *female roan horse*.

sabino

A horse with a light-red, almost pink,

roan-colored body and a pure-white belly; from the Spanish.

sachet kitten

A cowboy's name for a skunk.

sack

To flip a blanket or sack at a horse to get him used to it. In logging, to follow a log drive and roll into deep water those logs that have grounded or lodged; to clear a stream of lodged logs; also, *sack the rear*.

sacked his saddle

An expression for a cowman who has died. The saying arose from the cowman's custom, when returning home by train from a trail trip, of placing his saddle in a grain sack and checking it to his destination. This figure of speech was used to convey the thought that he was now on the return journey to his eternal home.

sacking

A cowboy's term for a blanket.

sacking out

A cowboy's expression for tying up the hind leg of a horse and waving a saddle blanket about him to gentle him for saddling.

Sacks

See poke, trap sack, tucker bag, turkey, war bag, way pocket, way pouch, yannigan.

S. A. cowboy

A cowboy's name for a dude wrangler, short for *show about cowboy*.

sack the rear

See *sack*.

sack the slide

In logging, to return to a slide logs that have jumped out.

Sad

See his tail is dragging, I broke my pick, tear squeezer.

saddle

A seat for a rider on horseback. Stock saddles are built to fulfill the cowboys' requirements in cattle work, and the slight variations in the shape of their trees have inspired special names for them. Many changes and improvements have been made in saddles through the years. In logging, a transverse log with a depression cut in it to guide logs on a skid road. In mining, a gold-bearing quartz vein of anticlinal form.

saddle a dead horse on him

A cowboy's expression for burdening someone with an unwelcome obligation.

saddle-bag doctor

The doctor of the early frontier who carried his medicine and implements in saddlebags when he rode over the range calling upon his patients.

saddle band

A northwestern cowboy's term for a *remuda, q.v.* See also *cavvy*.

saddle bar

In packing, part of the aparejo framework that holds the ribs in place and stiffens the aparejo.

saddle blanket

A blanket placed upon a horse's back beneath the saddle. One good blanket is all that is necessary for a horse. Too much padding under the saddle makes him sweat unduly, and an overheated back becomes tender. After the saddle is thrown on and before it is cinched up, a couple of fingers should be inserted under the blanket where it comes over the withers to work up a little slack. Also, a cowboy's term for a griddle cake. A modern-day cowboy's term for a one-dollar bill.

saddle-blanket gambler

A cowboy addicted to gambling around the campfire on a saddle blanket; also, a small-time gambler. Charlie Russell, in his *Trails Plowed Under*, wrote: "You can tell a saddle-blanket gambler's luck by the rig he's ridin'." Rowdy McCloud, a friend of mine with a weakness for cards, told me of his "settin' up all night tryin' to find somethin' better than some very young clubs," in a game where the dealer "seemed to know both sides of the cards the way luck set on his shirttail." His opponents, said Rowdy, "kept showin' me hands that looked as big as a log house, and after that session I could count my coin without takin' it from my pocket."

saddle brand

A brand made by burning a bar or bars across the back of an animal that extend to both sides.

saddle bronc riding

In rodeo, one of the five standard events, in which the rider must ride a regulation saddle, may use only one rein attached to the simple halter, and must not touch the saddle, the horse, or himself with his free hand.

saddle bum

A drifter of the cattle country; a shiftless person who is too lazy to work but rides about the country seeking free meals.

saddle gun

A rifle or Winchester carried in a *saddle scabbard, q.v.*

SADDLE MAKERS

See leather pusher, saddler.

saddler

A man who makes saddles. Also, an easy-gaited horse.

saddle ring

The metal ring fastened to the tree of a saddle from which the latigo straps hang.

saddle roll

A roll of blankets tied across a saddle just behind the fork to help wedge the rider in the saddle.

SADDLES AND EQUIPMENT

See anquera, apishamore, apple, apple-horn, arch irons, Association saddle, back jockey, basto, bear trap, billet, biscuit, bronc saddle, bucking rim, bucking roll, buck strap, cable rig, California saddle, California skirts, California tree, cantinesses, cantle, cantle drop, carpieta, Cheyenne roll, chicken saddle, Committee saddle, corona, corus, dinner plate, dish, dock piece, double-barreled, eight-string saddle, empty saddle, five-eighths rig, flank rigging, fork, form fitter, fraid strap, freak, front jockey, full-rigged, full seat, full stamp, fuste, gelding smacker, gullet, half-rigged saddle, handle, hogskin, horn, horn string, hull, hurricane deck, Indian saddles, kack, kidney pad, kitchen strap, latigo, Lizzy, meat-and-hide hungry, mochila, montura, Mother Hubbard saddle, muley saddle, nigger catcher, nubbin', packsaddles, pad plate, pancake, panel crupper, pelter, pig, pimple, postage stamp, pumpkin-seed saddle, rear jockey, rig, rigging ring, rimfire, sacking, saddle, saddle-blanket, saddle ring, saddle roll, saddle scabbard, saddle strings, seat, seat jockey, seven-eighths rig, side jockey, six-string saddle, skeleton rig, skirt, slick fork, slick saddle, strainer, suadero, swell fork, teeth in the saddle, terrapin, Texas saddle, Texas skirt, Texas tree, three-quarter rig, three-quarter seat, trap, tree, visa, way pocket, way pouch, whang strings, wood.

saddle scabbard

A heavy saddle-leather case in which to carry a rifle or Winchester when riding. The gun fits in as far as the hammer, leaving the stock exposed. The favorite way of carrying the gun is to loop the front strap at the very end of the scabbard over the saddle horn, while the other end, or barrel section, is merely slipped through a loop formed by a second strap from the back rigging ring on the saddle. To take off both rifle and scabbard, all that is necessary is to slip the front strap off the horn and slide the whole thing out of the back loop. The height of the scabbard must be adjusted to come at the bend of the knee. Most riders carry the gun on the left side, butt to the front. This arrangement allows them to have the gun on the same side when they get off to shoot.

saddle slicker

A cowboy.

saddle stiff

A cowboy.

saddle strings

Little rawhide strings that hold the saddle leathers together. The ends are tied and left hanging, allowing packages to be tied on as well as serving as a decoration.

saddle tramp

A professional *chuck-line rider, q.v.*

saddle warmer

A man riding horseback; a cowboy.

SADDLING

See blinder, laced his tree up, put leather on his horse, sacking out, slappin' his tree on.

safety first

Holding to the saddle horn while riding a bucking horse.

safety shoes

A logger's shoes with iron-reinforced toes.

sag

A cowman's term for a slope.

sagebrusher

A cowboy's name for a person living in a remote place; also, his name for a tourist or a traveling camper.

sagebrush philosopher

A loquacious westerner.

saged

A cowboy's word for an animal sick from eating sagebrush.

sage hen

A cowboy's term for a woman.

sage-henning

A cowboy's term for being forced to stay overnight in the desert without blankets. A cowboy's term for courting.

sage rat

A cowman's name for a resident of arid lands or for a man especially susceptible to the charms of the desert. A cowman's name for a prospector.

saguaro

A columnar cactus of immense size found in the Southwest.

saint

A rustler's name for a loyal cowboy.

sala

What a cowman sometimes calls a dance hall; from the Spanish, meaning *parlor* or *large room*.

salado

A wind-broken horse; pronounced *sal-owed* by Americans; from the Mexican Spanish, meaning *vained*.

salea

In packing, a raw, softened sheepskin placed on the back of a pack animal for padding beneath the packsaddle; from the Spanish *zalea*.

salivate

A cowboy's word meaning *to liquidate* or to shoot full of holes.

Sallie

A cowboy's name for the cook.

SALOONS AND TAVERNS

See bucket of blood, cantina, dive, honky-tonk, hurdy-gurdy house, Jones's place, sala, whisky mill, whoop-up.

salt

In mining, to make a worthless mine or claim appear valuable by secretly placing in it a small amount of gold dust or high-grade ore.

SALT

See cattle lick, lick block, lick log, lick salt, salting mutton, salt lick.

salteur liquor

What the early trappers called diluted alcohol or other spirits given to Indians; the more they drank the more it was diluted.

salting mutton

A sheep raiser's expression for placing salt in salt troughs for sheep. A band of 1,500 sheep will eat about 100 pounds of salt every two or three days.

salt lick

A region of natural salt where buffaloes and, later, cattle obtained salt. Also, a man-made block of salt for cattle and sheep; see *lick log*.

salt log

See *lick log*.

salty

A cowboy's word for a good hand. The word is also used in the sense of showing fight or aggressiveness. I heard one cowhand speak of another as being "salty as Lot's wife"; and another spoke of a man as being "salty as Utah." Also, a cowboy's word for a hard-bucking horse.

salty bronc

A cowboy's term for a mean horse.

salty dog

A cowboy's term for anyone especially good at his work or a master in his line of endeavor.

salty rider

A cowboy's term for a rider with guts; an exceptionally good rider.

salve eater

A logger's name for a snuff dipper.

sampling works

In mining, a place where ores are sampled and their values determined and where they are sometimes bought and sold.

sancho

A Mexican's name for a dogie, a scrubby calf.

sand

A cowboy's word for courage. Skeets Moore characterized a friend with, "His craw was plumb full o' sand and fightin' tallow"; and a Wyoming cowhand spoke of another as having " 'nough sand for a lake front." Also, a logger's word for sugar.

sand auger

A cowman's name for a little sand whirlwind.

sandbox

In stagecoaching, one of the boxes filled with sand and placed around the wheel axles of the coach from which sand could be dropped on the brake when necessary. In logging, a box used for a cuspidor in camp.

sand cutter

A cowboy's name for a Kansan.

sand eel

What a cowboy sometimes calls a snake. Spade Kruger used to tell of a section of the country so full of snakes that "you

have to parade 'round on stilts to keep from gettin' bit." Cactus Price concluded another tale by saying, "That's the biggest snake I ever seen without the aid o' likker."

sand liner

A name for a stagecoach of the desert country.

sand tell box

In faro, a dealer's box constructed to manipulate cards which have been slightly sanded on the backs; see *tell box*.

sand tell liquid

In faro, a liquid dressing used by dealers to prepare ordinary poker cards for use in a *sand tell box, q.v.* The dressing simulates sanding the backs of the cards, thus permitting manipulation in the box.

sand wagon

A wagon used by some stagecoach companies on routes where it was necessary to cross rivers filled with quicksand. It was built to stand high out of the water and had unusually wide tires. The driver would leave the stagecoach on the bank, put the mail, baggage, and passengers on this wagon, and take them across the river to a coach waiting on the other side.

Santa Fe Trail

The trail between Independence, Missouri, and Santa Fe, New Mexico, over which trade was conducted from about 1822 to about 1880.

santo

A saint or a picture or statue of a saint; from the Spanish.

sapling

In logging, a young tree, usually one with a trunk between 2 and 4 inches thick.

sarve up brown

A trader's expression meaning *to kill*.

savage

A cowboy's name for a hitchhiking tourist. A logger's name for another logger.

savanna

A trader's name for a grassy plain with trees.

savin' money for the bartender

A cowboy's expression for riding a freight train to save fare.

savin' saddle leather

Standing up in the stirrups and riding so that the rider's seat does not touch the seat of the saddle. Tenderfoot riders sometimes ride this way to ease their saddle sores.

savvy

A cowboy's term for knowledge or understanding. A man with plenty of *savvy* is said to be as "smart as a bunkhouse rat," "wise as a tree full of owls," or "full of information as a mail-order catalog." Used as a query it means *do you understand?* From the Spanish *Sabe?* meaning *Don't you know?*

sawbones

A cowboy's name for a doctor. Most of the frontier doctors were "right there with a parin' knife when it came to minin' out lead." A logger's name for the hospital surgeon.

sawbuck

A packer's name for a packsaddle whose ends resembled those of a sawbuck, or sawhorse.

sawdust

A miner's name for dynamite. See also *macaroni.*

sawdust country

In logging, a region in which most of the timber has been cut off and sawed into lumber.

sawdust crew

A logger's term for a sawmill crew.

sawdust eater

A logger's name for a common laborer in a sawmill.

sawdust factory

A logger's name for a sawmill.

sawdust in his beard

Said of a man shot down in a saloon.

sawdust savage

A logger's name for a man who works in a sawmill.

sawed-off shotgun

A shotgun with the barrels cut off short. It was first used by express messengers.

saw gang

In logging, a group of workmen engaged in getting out saw logs.

saw gummer

In logging, a device for deepening and enlarging the spaces between the teeth of a worn saw.

SAWING LOGS

See buck, buck wood, logging.

sawing woods

In logging, the part of the woods where sawing is to be done.

saw log

In logging, a log of size and length suitable for sawing into lumber. A logger's name for a toothpick.

sawmill

A mill at which logs are sawed into salable products. The term includes all the machinery and buildings necessary for the operation of the plant.

SAWMILLS AND MACHINERY

See bull planers, cage, cyclone, deck log, eagle's nest, fighting the bear, gang mill, gate saw, green chain, green planer, head saw, hog, live rolls, log beam, log carriage, log kicker, log pond, lumber tally, machine burn, mill burn, mill carriage, mill chain, mill cut, mill right, nigger, nigger engine, peckerwood mill, pineapple, pony, rolls, sawdust factory, sawmill, steam nigger, Swede, tail off, teakettle outfit.

SAWMILL WORKERS

See bear fighter, diapper, log scaler, old hard-eye, old squint-eye, rosin-belly, sawdust crew, sawdust eater, sawdust savage, shaving crew, shingle weaver, splinter picker, trimmer.

saw-set earmark

An earmark made by cropping the ear and then cutting out the center in the shape of a rectangle; sometimes called *crop and mortice.*

saw timber

In logging, trees of a size and quality that will make logs suitable for sawing into lumber. See *saw log*.

saw-tooth earmark

An earmark made by cutting the end of the ear in and out in the shape of the teeth of a saw.

saw whetter

A logger's name for the man who sharpens saws.

sawyer

In logging, a man who fells trees and cuts them into logs. In river boating, a sunken tree moving slowly up and down in the river under the influence of the current. The moving end might extend either upstream or downstream, and its successive brief appearances above the surface were usually separated by an interval of only a few minutes. But sometimes a log of this sort remained under water for twenty minutes before heaving upward again, and in that time a boat might easily approach the place where it lay hidden and run full tilt into it. There was no way to avoid such a danger, and many a boat suffered catastrophe or grave damage in an accident of this nature.

scab

What a logger calls a workman who will not join a labor union.

scab herder

A cowboy's name for a sheepherder, especially a Mexican herder.

scad

In mining, a fleck of gold remaining in the gold pan after a washing. Also, all the gold in the pan that has been washed.

scalawag

A worthless cutback cow, generally wild and old. The term is also applied to human beings, but not with reference to their age.

scalawag bunch

A cowboy's term for a group of horses that are mean and hard to handle; the *rough string*, q.v.

scale

In logging, the estimated sound content of a given log or group of logs. To estimate the sound content of a log or group of logs. To produce, measure, or work out a given amount of lumber. To measure logs or estimate the yield of lumber. In mining, a loosened fragment of rock that is about to break off and fall.

scale gold

In mining, gold that occurs in small scales, or flecks.

scaler

In logging, the man who does scaling; see *scale*.

SCALP

See bark, fleece, had his hair raised, Indian haircut, lost his hair, lost his topknot, raise hair, scalping, scalp lifting, scalp lock, scalp pole, tickle fleece, topknot, voucher.

scalp chant

An Indian chant indicating that an enemy's scalp had been secured.

scalp dance

An Indian dance to celebrate the scalping of an enemy. Scalps were placed upon lances, and with song and dance both men and women would participate.

scalp feast

An Indian feast of rejoicing over securing scalps.

scalp halloo

A shout given by an Indian to announce the taking of an enemy's scalp.

scalp hunter

A man who hunted to secure enemy scalps, often to obtain the bounty on them.

scalping

Taking an enemy's scalp. In logging, removing turf or other vegetation in an area where a tree has been planted.

scalping party

A party or group of Indians out to secure enemy scalps.

scalp lifter

A white man's name for an Indian.

scalp lifting

The taking of scalps.

scalp lock

A long lock of hair left on the crown of the head by the warriors of some American Indian tribes as a challenge to their enemies.

scalp pole

A pole upon which Indians displayed the scalps of their enemies.

scalp taker

A trader's name for a long knife.

scamper juice

A cowboy's name for whisky.

scape

In western-river steamboating, a contraction of *escape*; the rhythmic and period of emission of exhaust steam from the engines. The term *scapes out on the roof* means that the steam exhausted from the main cylinders was piped upward above the roof and released into the atmosphere from steam pipes referred to as *scape pipes*. These were usually located toward the aft end of the roof, over the engines. On side-wheelers where the engines were placed toward the center of the vessel, the scape pipes came up alongside or just aft of the pilothouse. Boats equipped with condensing apparatus did not have scape pipes.

Scandihoovian dynamite

A logger's name for *snoose*, or snuff.

SCARE

See booger, boss-simple, down in his boots, job-simple, spook.

scatter-gun

A cowboy's name for a shotgun. Every westerner has a deep respect for the scatter-gun, especially if it is loaded with buckshot. In western parlance, "Buckshot means buryin' ever' time," "Buckshot leaves a mean and oozy corpse," and "Absorb a load of buckshot, and they'll have to pick you up with a blotter."

scattering the riders

In roundup, the job of the roundup captain; giving directions to the men starting on circle to drive cattle in from the surrounding country, designating which section each man or group of men was to cover. When the riders stopped to receive their orders, they dismounted to reset their saddles and air their horses' backs a little before recinching for the hard ride ahead. The men were sent in pairs. A man unfamiliar with the country would be paired with one who knew that particular range; a man riding an unreliable horse would be accompanied by one riding a more trustworthy one.

SCHOOL

See knowledge box, marm school.

schoolmarm

A logger's name for an inverted crotch, usually at the base of a tree trunk, commonly caused by two tree trunks growing together.

SCHOOLTEACHERS

See wisdom bringer.

scissorbill

A cowboy's name for one who did not do his work well. A logger's name for a worker lacking in class consciousness—a name that invites violence. Also, a logger who is on strike.

scoop wagon

A freighter's name for the Conestoga wagon; so called because its body resembled a huge scoop.

scoot

A logger's name for a single logging sled.

scorcher

A cowboy's name for a branding iron.

score

In rodeo, the distance between the chute opening and the score line, or the amount of head start given to a steer or calf in a roping or steer-wrestling event. The length of the score is usually determined by the size of the arena or other local conditions.

score line

See *barrier*.

scorer

In logging, an axman who scores or slabs off the outer portion of a tree trunk in preparation for the work of the hewer.

scorpion Bible

A logger's name for inferior whisky.

Scotch hobble

A hobble made with a large loop that will not slip, placed around a horse's neck and arranged so that a bowline knot lies back on one shoulder. The long end of the rope is then placed around a hind leg just below the ankle joint, and the end is run back into the neck loop and tied, just short enough that, when the animal is standing, the foot will be 3 or 4 inches off the ground. To keep the horse from kicking out of the rope, it is usually necessary to take an extra turn about the ankle or twist the rope back on itself. A half-hitch on the ankle will stay on, but, as the cowboy says, "You'll play hell gettin' it off."

SCOUTS

See avant-courier, Daniel Boones, Indian scout, runner.

scraper

In mining, a large, hoelike blade dragged by a cable attached to a hoist and used to take the place of shovelers.

scratch

To spur a horse backward and forward while riding.

scratcher cinch

See *flank rigging.*

scratching

In rodeo, keeping the feet moving in a kicking motion while riding a bucking horse, one of the acts necessary to win in a real bucking contest; using the spurs in a raking motion along the horse's sides.

Stan Adler, in *Hoofs and Horns,* told this amusing little story: "Every year some of them platinum haided leedle gals from Hollywood movie studios come to the Old Pueblo to take in the rodeo an' they shore get bronc idees about what it's all about. Like the time the bareback rider come out on one of them big Brahma bulls an' rode him right purty and slick.

"'Dang, he's a-scratchin' that critter a-plenty,' says one of them old waddies in the stands.

"'Ain't that plumb kind of him?' pipes up one of them leedle blond movie gals. 'The way that old cow is wrigglin' she must be itchin' somethin' scandalous.'"

scratching gravel

A cowboy's expression for climbing a steep bank on horseback.

screwing down

In rodeo, sinking the spurs into the cinch while riding a bucking horse and failing to move the feet in a kicking motion as provided by rodeo rules.

scrub

A cowman's term for an animal that does not grade high in breeding and flesh, also, anything stunted. A logger's term for stunted trees or brush, often in a dense stand.

scupper

In steamboating, a hole, tube, or gutter at the side of a boat to carry off water from the deck.

seago

A rope, particularly a loosely twisted hemp rope used in lassoing; from the Spanish *soga.*

seal fat

A trapper's expression meaning *very fat.*

sea lions

A name given the early-day wild long-horned cattle "that came right out of the Gulf of Mexico"; so called because they could swim like ducks.

seam squirrels

A cowboy's name for body lice. When one cowhand I knew spoke of another "a-settin' on the side of his bunk readin' his shirt by lamplight," we knew what he was talking about.

sea mule

In logging, a boat in the log pond used to push logs.

sea plum

A cowboy's name for an oyster.

Sears Roebuck guy

A logger's name for a novice.

season

In logging, to dry or cure lumber or other forms of wood, either in the open or in a dry kiln.

SEASONS

See between hay and grass, bucking season, calf time, coming grass, fire season, green up, heel-fly time, lambing season, open winter, turnout time.

season's drop

In sheep raising, the total number of lambs born during the season.

seat

The part of a saddle upon which the rider sits; it is said to be the easiest to find but the hardest to keep.

seat jockey

See *leg jockey*.

second

In gambling, the second card from the top of the deck.

second button

In faro, a system whereby the player bets the *case card (q.v.)* to fall as the second card fell; the case keeper records and gives out this information.

second dealer

In gambling, a cheat who deals the second card from the top of the deck, reserving the desired top card for himself or for a confederate.

second faller

In logging, the subordinate in a two-man crew of fallers.

second-growth forest

In logging, the smaller trees left after lumbering, or the trees available for a second logging; trees that have grown since the virgin stand of timber was removed.

second hooker

See *hooker*.

second rigger

In logging, the boss at the outer end of a sky-line operation, in charge of the rigging of the tail tree.

second saddle

A bronc rider's term for a horse that has been ridden a second time.

SEE

See look-see, raise.

seeing daylight

An expression used when a rider leaves his seat with each jump of the horse and the spectators can see between rider and saddle.

segundo

In cattle driving, the assistant trail boss, or second in command; from the Spanish, meaning *second*.

selective logging

In logging, the removal of selected mature, large, or diseased trees as single, scattered trees or in small groups of trees. Young trees start in the openings thus made, and the result is an uneven-aged forest.

self-feeder

In mining, a device that automatically supplies ore to the stamp motors or stamp mill.

selvage

In mining, a lining, a gouge, or a thin band of clay often found in the vein upon a wall.

sendero

A word commonly used in the Southwest for a trail, path, or clearing; from the Spanish.

send up in smoke

To give a warning or make a signal; from Indian smoke signals, a method of long-distance communication.

sent for supplies

A sheepherder's euphemism for *crazy*. The expression originated from the fact that the loneliness of a sheepherder's life often undermined his sanity; such a one was "sent to town for supplies" to give him a chance to be among people.

seraglio

A wild stallion's herd of mares.

serape

A blanket or shawl worn as an outer garment by Mexicans; from the Spanish.

set

A cowboy's shortened form of *settler*, commonly used for a homesteader. A logger's word for a pair of fallers. A miner's term for a portion of the ground taken by a *tributer*, *q.v.*

set afoot

An expression used about a cowboy who, from any cause, lost his horse and had to walk.

set back

A cowboy's expression for a horse that pulls back.

set brand

A brand with a design made in one piece.

set down

A cowboy's expression for being fired from a job without having a horse to ride away. In the early days this manner of firing often ended in gun smoke. Most ranches recognized the seriousness of "settin' a man afoot" and loaned him a company horse to ride to town. There he could leave the horse at a livery stable or turn him loose to find his way back to the home ranch.

set fast

A cowboy's term for a saddle sore.

set his gun goin'

A cowboy's expression for someone who started shooting.

set his hoss

A trader's term for a gambling stake.

set the hair

To ride a horse long enough to take the meanness out of him.

settin' close to the plaster

Keeping a firm and close seat in the saddle when riding.

settin' deep in his tree

A cowboy's expression for a good dependable, and trustworthy hand.

settin' on his arm

A cowboy's expression for a tenderfoot who is trying to mount a horse with one hand on the horn and the other on the cantle of the saddle. One should never attempt to mount a horse in this manner. Not only does it brand him a novice, but it is the most awkward and ungraceful way to climb aboard a horse. If the horse starts off as soon as the rider swings off the ground— and most western horses do—the rider will land behind the saddle and not in it, and that will mean that he will be bucked off.

settin' spin

In trick roping, a spin in which the roper jumps in and out of the spinning noose from a sitting position.

settin' the bag

Courting; also, *settin' 'er*. Bud Taylor used to say, "That naked little runt with the Injun's shootin' iron can shore booger up a good peeler."

settin' the buck

Riding a bucking horse successfully.

set tires

A trader's expression meaning *to tighten the wagon tires*.

settle

In packing, to adjust packs in their places on the aparejo, as in the case of simple box loads. In such a case it was not necessary to brake the load, i.e., to work the near pack up and down until it was in place, since the two packs could readily be settled on the aparejo so that they would ride evenly.

SETTLERS AND FARMERS

See boomer, churn-twister, dry-lander, flat-heeled puncher, fodder forker, fool hoe man, granger, hay shaker, hay shoveler, home sucker, kaffir-corner, mover, pea picker, plow chaser, pumpkin piler, set, sky farmer, sodbuster, soddy, sooner, squatter, stubble jumper, stump rancher, sun-pecked jay, two-buckle boy.

set up

In packing, to prepare an aparejo for use by inserting the ribs and then padding it with hay so as to adjust it properly to the shape of the mule's back. A logger's term for his plate, cup, and saucer.

seven-eighths rig

A saddle with the cinch placed between the Spanish, or rim-fire, and the three-quarter rig.

seven overbit

An earmark made by cutting the ear straight down near the tip for about an inch on the top side and then from near the upper base of the ear, making the cut slope to meet the straight-down first cut.

seven underbit

An earmark made like the seven overbit except that it is cut on the lower side.

sewer hog

A logger's name for a ditch digger.

shack

A cowboy's name for the bunkhouse. A miner's name for a mine guard.

shackling

A freighter's word describing loose wheels; rattling, wobbling.

shad-bellied

A cowboy's expression meaning *lean-flanked*.

shade

To conceal a movement, especially the manipulation of cards on gambling devices.

shade work

In gambling, the marking of the backs of cards for cheating.

shadin'

A cowboy's term for resting. When a cowboy is riding the range and finds a shady spot, he will often dismount and loosen his cinches to give his horse's back some air. If the horse is reliable, he takes the bits from its mouth to allow it a few mouthfuls of grass. Perhaps he takes this opportunity to remove his own boots and straighten the wrinkles in his socks, smoke a cigarette or two, and dream of the future. (John M. Hendrix, Editorial, *Cattleman*, Vol. XXI, No. 12 [May, 1935], 5.)

shadow rider

A cowboy who rides along gazing at his own shadow with admiration; also called *sunshine rider*. Mirrors were sometimes scarce on the range, and some fellows must admire themselves, even though only by watching their shadows. Cloudy days had no silver linings for this type of cowboy. Speaking of a fancy cowboy whom the other riders called Pretty Shadow, Charlie Russell said, "When the sun hit him with all his silver on, he blazes up like some big piece of jewelry. You could see him for miles when he's ridin' the high country." (Charlie M. Russell, *Trails Plowed Under* [Garden City, Doubleday, Doran, & Company, 1935], 5.)

shaft

In mining, a pit sunk from the surface; an opening that leads downward to the vein, either vertically or at an incline.

shaft house

In mining, housing for hoisting machinery at the entrance to a mine shaft.

shag

A logger's name for the brakeman on a logging train.

shake

A trader's word meaning *to have an ague*; also, *ague*. In logging, a wooden shingle made by splitting flat strips from a bolt. Also, a crack or fissure in the stem of a tree, usually caused by frost or excessive bending in a strong wind; a *shake* usually follows the annual rings, while a *check* is radial, that is, extends across the annual rings.

shake a bush

A cowboy's expression meaning *to go away* or *to get busy*.

shakedown

What the cowboy calls his bed.

shakers

What the logger calls salt and pepper.

shake the lines over the iron mule

In logging, to run the donkey engine that is used to load logs onto freight cars.

shakin' a hoof

What the cowboy calls dancing. At many early-day dances there were some religious fellows who could not stand the temptation and were soon "dancin' themselves right out o' the church." There were others, too, scattered through the crowd, who were "cussin'" the blisters on their feet and the new boots that made 'em, but they wasn't missin' a dance, even if their feet was on fire."

shakin' hands with grandma

Grabbing the saddle horn while riding a bucking horse.

shakin' hands with St. Peter

A cowboy's expression for dying.

shakin' out

In roping, preparing to make a cast by opening the noose of a rope with a few quick jerks toward the front while grasping the rope at the honda with the right hand.

shallow-dished

See *dish*.

shank

The part of the spur to which the rowel is fastened.

shank of the afternoon

A cowboy's expression for late afternoon, near the close of day.

shanty

A logger's name for a logging camp; probably from the French *chantier*, meaning woodyard.

shanty boy

A logger who lives in a *shanty, q.v.*

shanty gang

A gang of loggers.

shanty queen

The wife of a *shanty boy, q.v.*

shanty man

A logger.

shanty team

A logging team that works in the timber.

shape up

A cowman's term meaning *to put into an orderly condition.*

shark

A logger's name for an employment agent.

sharp

An earmark made by cutting an overslope and an underslope on the same ear, giving it a sharp or pointed appearance. One of the sayings of the West was, "When you see a man grubbin' and sharpin' the ears of his cows, you can bet he's a thief."

sharpen his hoe

A cowboy's expression meaning *to thrash someone.*

sharpens his horns

A cowboy's expression for someone who works himself into a fit of anger or a fighting mood.

Sharps

A hunting rifle with a lever breechblock action; named for its inventor, Christian Sharps. Early models of the Sharps were made with a percussion cap, and all were breechloaders. It was a favorite rifle until the repeater took its place.

sharpshooter

A cattle buyer who is neither a feeder nor a commission man but buys up small bunches of cattle for a profit.

shaved behind the skin

A cowman's expression describing prairie on which the grass is too short for grazing.

shavetail

A horse with a short-haired tail. In the Northwest it is the custom to "pull" the tails of broken horses. Then, when they are turned loose to run the range and mix with the unbroken horses, the riders who want to gather them for the next season's work can tell them from the wild ones at a distance. These horses are called *shavetails* to distinguish them from the *broomtails*, or bushy-tailed horses. When a rider of Montana or Wyoming says he is "makin' *shave-tails*," a fellow cowhand knows that he is breaking horses, for when a buster has given a horse its last ride, he pulls its tail as a sign that it is broken. (Bud Cowan, *Range Rider* [Garden City, Doubleday, Doran & Company, 1930], 224.)

shaving crew

A logger's name for the crew of planers in a sawmill.

shearer

A man whose specialty is shearing sheep.

shearing band

A band of sheep ready for shearing.

shearing camp

A camp in which sheep are sheared.

shearing pen

An enclosure at a sheep ranch in which the grown sheep are sheared.

shears

An instrument used in shearing sheep. In faro, an instrument used for cutting cards for dishonest dealing and for squaring up the cards after they had been used. Faro cards cost money, and dealers like to conserve them.

shebang

A miner's word for any structure, from a palace to a shanty.

She blows!

What the logger says when the quitting whistle blows.

shed lambing

Lambing that takes place under a shed, especially for early lambs when the weather is bad.

SHEEP

See baa-a-ah, bellweather, biddy, blackface, borreras, broken mouths, bum, chopper, day's drop, dogie lamb, drop band, dry band, gummers, hoofed locusts, maggot, marker, season's drop, shearing brand, stinkers, stubble jumper, underwears, wethers, wool-blind, wooled sheep, woollies, yo.

sheep camp

The migratory home of the early-day

sheepherder, consisting of a canvas-covered wagon which contained a stove and a bunk for his housekeeping.

sheep corral

A corral used for sheep.

sheep dipper

A rustler's name for a loyal cowboy. A man who *dips* sheep, or treats them with a liquid disinfectant.

sheep eater

A sheep dog that bites or tears the sheep. Such a dog is immediately sent back to the home ranch.

sheeped out

A cowman's expression meaning that he had been forced to move on account of the influx of sheep. Steve Gates told of one ranch that was "so ag'in sheep I wouldn't ride through it with a wool shirt on."

sheep feeder

A man who receives sheep from the ranges and places them in feed lots, where they are fattened for market; distinguished from the *breeder*, who grows his sheep on the range.

sheep fever

An intense desire to go into the sheep business.

sheep grower

A man who breeds and raises sheep on a large scale.

sheepherder

A cowman's name for a man who herds and tends sheep. The cowman never called him a *shepherd*. Since Christ was a shepherd, that word sounded too pastoral and honored, and the cowman had anything but Christlike feelings toward the sheepman. As one cowboy said, "There ain't nothin' dumber than a sheep except the man who herds 'em."

SHEEPHERDERS

See camp tender, docker, drop-band herder, jockey, lamber, lamb licker, mutton puncher, nutter, pastor, scab herder, sheep dipper, sheep feeder, sheepherder, sheep puncher, snoozer, social herder, wagon herder, sheepman.

sheepherder's delight

A cowboy's name for rotgut whisky.

sheepherding

The occupation of herding sheep.

SHEEPHERDING

See bog down, buck herd, flagging, gancho, go with the woollies, hit the timber line, pile up, range lambing, sheepherding, sheep hook, tin dogs, trying to find the long end of a square quilt, walking sheep, working the bed ground.

sheep hook

A long pole with a steel hook on one end, used by the sheepherder to catch sheep by the leg.

sheep-jump

A cowboy's expression for a horse that makes short, stiff-legged jumps.

sheep-killing dog

A dog that makes a practice of killing sheep.

sheepman

A sheep breeder; a man who owns large herds of sheep.

Sheep out!

A sheepshearer's shout signaling that he has just run out of sheep to shear.

sheep puncher

A cowboy's term for a sheepherder.

SHEEP RAISING

See bucking season, bum a lamb, dying on their backs, forced nursing, green lambs, hand milking, jacketing, logging, mixing brands, shed lambing, sheep grower.

sheep ranch

A ranch devoted to the breeding and raising of sheep.

sheep range

Range on which sheep are raised or which is suitable for raising sheep.

SHEEPSHEARERS

See barber, blade man, fleece tier, paint dauber, shearer, tallier, tromper, wool tier, wool tramper.

SHEEPSHEARING AND EQUIPMENT

See clippers, double stringer, fall clip, shearing camp, shearing pen, shears, Sheep out! sheepshearing machine.

sheep wagon

In sheepherding, the wagon used by the camp tender to bring in supplies and to move camp. He also cooked in it, and he and the herder slept in it. Also, a *sheep camp, q.v.*

sheet

What the cowman called the canvas used as a wagon sheet.

sheffi

A cowboy's nickname for the cook.

shell

A cowboy's term for an old or skinny animal.

shelled hay

Hay that has lost most of its leaves through handling.

shelterwood

In logging, a system of cutting in which the trees are removed in two or more cuts, the young trees coming under the shelter of the remaining large trees.

shepherd's Bible

A cowboy's name for a mail-order catalog. There is a story about one cowboy who fell for the picture of a girl in a catalog. Thinking that everything he saw pictured was for sale, he sat down and ordered her for a wife, fluffy dress and all, "if she wasn't already took." Then he bragged of how "it won't cost nothin' to have her delivered 'cause the company sends ever'thing *postpaid*."

she stuff

A cowman's term for female cattle.

shield

In mining, a framework or screen of wood or iron used in tunneling to protect the workers; it is pushed forward as the work progresses.

shift

In mining, the length of time a miner or a gang of miners works in one day; the crew working for a given period, as the *day shift*, the *night shift*.

shift boss

The foreman in charge of a *shift*, *q.v.*; also called *shifter*.

shifter

See *shift boss*.

shindig

A cowboy dance. An early-day cowboy dance usually lasted all night. When it broke up at daylight, the ladies retired to "freshen up their spit curls and chalk their noses" and "sort out the weaners that's beginnin' to stir off the bed ground" in the next room. The old bowlegs on the dance floor passed around the last bottle saving a big drink to get the fiddler to play a final tune. Then they threw a stag dance "that's apt to be kinda rough and end up in a wrastlin' match." Like a horse with plenty of bottom, those old saddle slickers just wouldn't tire down. But finally, having no more wet goods to bribe the fiddler with, they called the dance a success and limped to the kitchen for a final cup of coffee, their feet feeling "like they'd wintered on a hard pasture."

shine

A trader's term for something showing superiority.

shiner

In gambling, a sharper's reflector or mirror that shows the face of the top card of the deck as it is dealt, usually being concealed in a ring, a pipe, a coin, a matchbox, etc. Also, a silver dollar with a concave mirror; when the dollar is placed upon a pile of notes or coin, the mirror reveals all the cards dealt over it; also called *glimmer*. In mining, a slaty flake of hard rock.

shingle weaver

A logger's name for a shingle shaver in a shingle mill.

shinny

A logger's name for liquor.

ship

In mining, a box in which ore is hoisted out of a mine through a shaft.

shipped her

An expression a cowboy used when he ran after a cow and came back without her. When he admitted his defeat, the foreman did not hold it against him. He knew the puncher had done his best.

SHIPPING

See boats, freighting, packing, shipping close, shipping point, steamboating.

shipping close

A cowman's expression for shipping every head of cattle fit for market that could be gathered from the range.

shipping point

A railroad station from which cattle are shipped to market.

shipping trap

A small pasture located near a shipping chute and used to hold cattle until they are shipped.

ship tender

A man who loads ore into a ship and, by means of a bell or other signal, notifies the engineer when to hoist the load.

shirttail outfit

A small ranch that employs only one or two men.

shock

A small pile of hay forked from the windrow for drying and for ease in loading; also called *stook*.

shoe

A horseshoe with a calked heel; so called to distinguish it from a *slipper* or a *boot*, *q.v.* A packer's word for the protecting sticks of the aparejo cover.

SHOES

See boots, calked shoes, Indian moccasins, moccasin, safety shoes, teguas, zapato.

shoofly

A miner's term for a passage in a mine.

shook a rope at him

A cowboy's expression meaning that someone had been warned about his misconduct and that his fate would rest upon his future behavior.

shoot a jam

A logger's expression for breaking up a log jam with dynamite.

SHOOTING

See blaze, build a smoke under his hoofs, burn powder, come a-smoking, dry shooting, fanning, fan the hammer, fight, flash in the pan, gun fanner, gunnin' for someone, gun slinging, gun tipper, hip shooting, kill, leaded, lead-poisoned, leaned against a bullet goin' past, makin' the town smoky, paunched, plug, popping salute, powder burnin' contest, put windows in his skull, rolls his gun, set his gun goin', slip shooting, smoke him out, smoke up, swap lead, throw down, throw gravel in his boots, throw lead, throw smoke in his face, thumb whipping, unravel some cartridges.

shooting 'em out

A cowboy's expression for moving cattle out of a corral and onto the range.

shooting iron

A cowboy's name for his six gun.

shoots his back

A cowboy's expression for a bucking horse.

shop-mades

A cowman's term for boots made to order. Cowmen scorn ready-made boots.

shore had tallow

A cowboy's expression meaning that someone was plenty fat—as one cowboy said, "beef plumb to the hocks."

short age

A term for cattle that are less than three years old.

short bit

A cowboy's term for a dime.

shorten his stake rope

A cowboy's expression for placing someone at a disadvantage or cramping his style.

short faker

An itinerant miner.

short faro

A simplified form of faro, much faster than straight faro and operating with a higher percentage in favor of the bank.

short-handled pup

A cowboy's name for a dog with a short or bobbed tail.

shorthorn

Stock not native to the cattle country. A breed of cattle with short horns, such as the Hereford. A tenderfoot.

short horse

An early name for the quarter-mile race horse; now commonly called *quarter horse*, *q.v.*

short of hat size

A cowboy's expression for a sheepherder who was a little crazy.

short-stage man

An itinerant miner.

short staker

A logger's name for a migratory worker; also called *boomer*, *q.v.*

short-trigger man

A cowboy's name for a bad man; a gunman.

short watch

In steamboating, the watch from 4:00 A.M. to 7:00 A.M.

short yearling

A calf just under one year old.

shotgun cavvy

A band of saddle horses made up of the mounts from many different ranches used on the same roundup.

shotgun chaps

Chaps with the outside seams sewed together all the way down the leg; so called because they look like the twin barrels of a shotgun with a choke at the muzzle. They proved more comfortable on windy northern ranges than *bat-wings*, *q.v.*

shotgun freighter

A man who purchased goods and carried them to the gold fields or other trading places. Many farmers and small freighters hauled butter, eggs, dressed hogs, sausages, and other supplies.

shotgun messenger

In stagecoaching, a man who rode with the driver and carried a shotgun; his job was to protect the stage's shipment, especially the treasure chest.

shotgun outfit

A logger's name for a camp at which the men are worked at top speed.

shotgun pasture

A small, fenced pasture such as that of the nester, who was always ready with a shotgun to keep trail herds from passing through.

shotgun wagon

A roundup wagon sent out by a few ranchers who worked independently and did not join the larger outfits.

shotty gold

A miner's term for small granular pieces of gold resembling shot.

shoulder

A freighter's word for putting one's shoulder to the wheel.

shoulder draw

A gun draw from a shoulder holster under the armpit. It is essentially a cross draw.

shoulder holster

A holster worn under the armpit and used for a *hide-out gun, q.v.*

shove down

On mountainous ranges, a cattle herder's expression for rounding up cattle in the higher country in the fall and moving them down into the valleys or lower country for the winter.

shove-down crew

A crew of men employed to *shove down (q.v.)* cattle.

shove his nose down

A logger's expression meaning *to thrash someone.*

shove in the steel

A cowboy's expression meaning *to spur a horse.*

shovel stiff

A miner's name for a shovel worker.

show

A logger's word for any logging operation or adventure. The word has many applications; thus the logger speaks of the *whole show,* a *poor show,* or a *haywire show.*

show bucker

A horse that bucks hard, straight away, and with his nose between his front legs, but is not difficult to ride. In rodeos he looks good from the grandstand, but he is never used in the semifinals.

showdown

In poker, the play in which a bet is called and the hands of the players are shown.

show up on the skyline

A cowboy's expression meaning *to come into view;* to appear.

shuck

A westerner's term for a cigarette made with a cornhusk wrapping. A cowboy's name for a Mexican. A cowboy's term meaning *to discard,* as, "He *shucked* his chaps."

shuffle the broque

An early-day loggers' game. The men sat in a circle on the floor; each man raised his knees, and a rubber ball or other suitable article, known as the *broque,* was passed around under the archway of the knees. A man stationed in the center was "it" until he discovered who had the broque.

sí

A common word for *yes* in the Southwest; from the Spanish.

side

In logging, one complete yarding and

loading crew in a high-line operation, usually consisting of twenty-two men equipped with a spar tree and a donkey engine. One side is called the *haywire*, and the other is called the *candy side*.

side jockey

The leather side extensions of the seat of a saddle.

sideline

To hobble the front and the hind foot on the same side of an animal to prevent it from traveling at speed.

side push

A logger's name for the foreman of a *side*, q.v.

side riders

In stagecoaching, men on horseback who rode with the coach through sections infested with road agents.

side rod

A logger's name for the boss of a yarding crew in the woods.

side-wheeler

A steamboat with paddles on the side. The engines operated independently, one to each wheel, and a man was required to operate each engine. The engineer took the starboard engine and supervised the running of the machinery and the feeding of the boilers; the *striker*, or apprentice engineer, took the port engine and worked under the direction of his superior on watch. In logging, a low-geared engine used for heavy pulling.

sidewinder

A rattlesnake, usually found in the desert, that strikes by swinging its head and part of its body to the left and the right. A cowman's term for a person of little principle. Also, a cowman's name for a pacing horse. A logger's term for a falling tree that strikes another tree and is thus deflected from the line of fall selected by the fallers. Such a tree is extremely dangerous to men near it, for it may bounce back and kill the fallers.

siesta

A southwesterner's term for a noon nap; from the Spanish.

sight

In poker, a show of hands.

sign

A westerner's term for tracks, broken undergrowth, and other evidence of the presence or passage of men (usually Indians) or animals.

Signals

See gaberel, government light, gut hammer, hail, highball, jerk wire, river horn, sign language, smoke signal, steamboat bell, telltale, triangle, warnings, wave 'round, whistling at point.

sign camp

See *line camp*.

sign language

The cowman's means of communication by gestures, adapted from Indian sign language. It was quite often a convenient method of communication in cattle driving. The trail boss who had ridden ahead to look for water need not ride all the way back to the herd but could ride to a high point on the horizon and signal directions to the men with his hat or his hands. The wagon boss of a roundup could also give signs that saved him much riding.

silk

A cowboy's name for barbed wire.

silk popper

A stagecoach driver.

sill

In mining, a windlass frame.

silver camp

A camp or temporary quarters for silver miners.

silver freighter

A wagoner who hauled silver ore.

silver glance

In mining, argentite, a valuable ore containing 87 per cent silver and 13 per cent sulphur.

silver hunter

A man who prospects for silver.

silver thaw

A cowman's name for rain that freezes as it hits the ground.

silver tip

A logger's name for an elderly or graying man.

simp tramp

A logger's name for the camp commissary.

sin buster

A cowboy's name for a preacher. Old man Hobbs used to say, "A heap o' folks would do more prayin' if they could find a soft spot for their knees."

sing

A cowboy's word for the hissing sound made by a rope when it is thrown.

singed

A cowboy's word for someone who had received a flesh wound from a bullet.

singin' to 'em

A cowboy's expression for standing night guard. This was the time when he did most of his singing, and night herding came to be referred to nearly always as *singin' to 'em*.

One day while I was discussing cowboy songs with a group of punchers, one of them offered the following disillusioning comment: "A heap of folks make the mistake of thinkin' a puncher sings his cows to sleep. He's not tryin' to amuse nobody but himself. In the first place, he don't have any brotherly love for them bovines. All he's tryin' to do is to keep 'em from jumpin' the bed ground and runnin' off a lot of tallow. In the second place, these brutes don't have no ear for music, which is maybe a good thing because the average puncher's voice and the songs he sings ain't soothin'. Mostly he has a voice like a burro with a bad cold, and the noise he calls singin'd drive all the coyotes out of the country."

Another puncher offered this opinion: "Mostly the songs he sings are mighty shy on melody and a heap strong on noise, but a man don't have to be a born vocalist to sing when he's alone in the dark if he's got a clear conscience and ain't hidin' out."

Still another explained that at the change of guard, the new man had to sing as he approached the herd so that he "wouldn't bulge up on 'em unawares 'cause the confidence a steer's got in the dark's mighty frail, and once spooked he'll leave a bed ground quicker'n you can spit and holler howdy."

singin' with his tail up

A cowboy's expression for a happy and carefree person.

single-barreled saddle

See *California saddle*.

single dally steer roping

See *dally steer roping*.

single-fire

See *California saddle*.

single jack

A logger's name for a man working alone in the woods. In mining, a heavy, short-handled hammer used in hand drilling.

single out

In faro, a system whereby the gambler plays a card to fall in exactly the reverse of the order in which it previously appeared.

single-rigged saddle

See *California saddle*.

single roll

A gun roll accomplished by spinning the gun forward on the trigger finger, cocking and releasing the hammer as it comes under the web, or lower part, of the thumb.

single steer tying

In rodeo, a recognized event for which a world's champion is named, although it is not one of the five standard events. The event is offered at relatively few rodeos. Similar to calf roping, it differs in that the steer must be thrown by the horse, which runs off at an angle hard enough to pull the steer off its feet. The roper must then dismount, run down the rope, and tie the steer's feet with a pigging string, as in calf roping.

Single Twist

The name of a brand of tobacco used by traders.

sinker

A cowboy's word for a biscuit. A logger's term for a saw log too heavy to float in a pond.

sin twister

A cowboy's name for a preacher.

siphon

In western-river steamboating, a device for sucking water from hulls and dumping it back into the river. The common variety of siphon was operated by steam: a jet of steam under high pressure was introduced at the top of a suction tube whose base was placed in the water to be removed. The steam created a vacuum, lifting the water and forcing it out of a discharge pipe.

SIT

See hunker, rest.

siwash

A cowboy's word for an Indian, used in the sense of one inferior to the white man's standard. Also, to cook with a stick over an open fire.

siwashed

A cowboy's word meaning *blackballed*.

siwash outfit

A cowboy's term for an unenterprising ranch.

siwash side

An expression used by a cowboy of the Northwest for the right side of a horse or the left side of a cow; thus, an expression for anything done backward or ineptly.

siwash tree

A logger's term for a tree used in place of a block to deflect cable.

sixie from Dixie

In dice, six as a point.

six gun

A westerner's name for a pistol; a six-shooter.

six-shooter coffee

A cowboy's term for the strong coffee of the cow camp—said to be strong enough to float a six-shooter.

six-shooter law

The early law of the West when there was no law by statute and every man was a law unto himself.

six-string saddle

A saddle using six sets of saddle strings to hold the various leathers in place. Bronc saddles were usually so constructed.

sizzler

A logger's name for a cook—a better cook than the one he called a *boiler*.

skate

A cowboy's term for a horse of poor quality.

skeleton rig

An early-day saddle consisting of merely a tree, the rigging for a cinch, and the straps reaching to the wide, oxbow stirrups; a saddle without skirts or fenders.

skewbald

A horse with patterns of white on any basic color except black; also called *stew ball*.

skid

In logging, a pair of logs or poles upon which logs are handled or piled. To haul logs by snaking them over the surface of the ground.

skidder

In logging, one who skids logs. A foreman of a crew of men who construct skid roads. A steam engine, usually operating from a railroad track, that skids logs by means of a cable; also called *steam skidder*. A yarding and loading engine that has a steel tower in place of a spar tree.

skidder crew

In logging, a crew of men who work with the steam skidder. See *skidder*.

skidder-crew fellows

In logging, the engineers who operate the steam skidder. See *skidder*. Their work is perhaps the most dangerous in logging.

skidder system

In logging, a method of high-line yarding.

skidding lever man

In logging, the man who winds and unwinds cables on the drums of the donkey engine that operates as a skidding machine in a high-lead logging assembly. In front of him is an array of air valves operated by small levers. To set a free-riding drum in motion, he throws a valve that builds up enough air pressure within a cylinder at one end of the drum to force it firmly against a friction carrier on the donkey's moving bull wheel.

skidding line

In logging, the line that runs from the donkey engine to the sky-line carriage in a high-lead assembly rig.

skidding machine

See *skidding lever man.*

skid grease

A cowboy's and logger's name for butter.

skid greaser

In logging, the man who keeps the skids greased so that the logs will move easily.

skid road

In logging, a road or way along which logs are skidded or dragged to a desired place. In early days these roads were made of small logs, or *skids*, peeled and embedded in the earth to form a trough along a selected route. Down these troughs ox teams pulled the logs. After donkey engines and other machinery took the place of oxen, the loggers began to use the term to mean a place where they gathered in town; in time it was corrupted to *skid row* and the meaning altered to a district frequented by idle workers and prostitutes.

skidway

In logging, two skids laid parallel at right angles to a road, usually raised above the ground at the end near the road. Logs are usually piled on the skidway as they are brought from the stump for loading upon sleds, wagons, or cars.

skidway men

In logging, men who bank, or pile, logs along the railroad.

skillet of snakes

A cowboy's name for an intricate Mexican brand.

skim-milk cowboy

A cowboy's term for a tenderfoot duded up in range regalia.

skimmy

A cowman's name for a calf raised on skim milk.

skin canoe

A Plains Indian canoe made of skins stretched over a frame; also called *bullboat.*

skin diggings

A miner's term for a very thin deposit of placer gold.

skin faro

A dishonest faro.

skin game

A dishonest game in which the players have little or no chance of winning against the bank or table.

skin hunter

A man who hunts animals for their pelts.

skinning his gun

Drawing a gun from a holster.

skinner

In early days, a man employed in skinning buffaloes. A man employed in skinning cattle after a wholesale die-up. A teamster or freighter who used mules; a driver of an ox team was called a *bullwhacker.* In range English, one did not *drive* a jerk-line string, but *skinned* it.

SKINNERS

See buffalo skinner, drivers, skinner.

skin lodge

A Plains Indian lodge made of animal skins stretched over a framework of poles; a tepee.

skinning knife

A long curve-bladed knife designed for removing skins from animals.

skin string

A cowboy's name for a rawhide rope.

skin the deck

In gambling, to palm cards from the deck.

skin trade

A trapper's name for the fur trade.

skin trapper

A man who trapped animals for their skins.

skip

In mining, a square hoisting bucket running on guides or in grooves.

skipper

A logger's name for the foreman or boss.

skipping

In trick roping, jumping into and out of a spinning vertical noose.

skirt

A cowman's name for the broad leathers of a saddle that go next to the horse. A logger's name for a guard used to cover the chains and sprockets on a lumber carrier.

skookum

An Indian word meaning *good* or *great*.

skookum house

A jail on an Indian reservation.

skull cracker

A cowboy's name for an Indian tomahawk.

skunk

An animal common in the West. A logger's name for an informer, a cheater, or any despicable person.

skunk boat

A cowboy's term for a heavy canvas shaped like a narrow scow with sides about a foot high, which, when propped up at each corner with a small stick, forms a barrier about the sleeper's bed, over which he believes no skunk can make its way to bite him. (Will C. Barnes, "The Hydrophobia Skunk," *Cattleman*, Vol. XVII, No. 12 [May, 1931], 17–19.)

skunk eggs

A cowboy's name for onions.

SKUNKS

See nice kitty, piket, sachet kitten, wood pussy.

skunk wagon

In parts of Wyoming and Montana, a cowboy's name for an automobile. It is said to have originated when the first automobile was driven into Landers, Wyoming. An old Indian named Black Coal smelled its smoke while standing in front of Lanagan's saloon and grunted, "Heap skunk wagon," and many of the cowmen in that vicinity have used the name ever since.

sky farmer

A farmer of unirrigated land who was dependent upon natural rainfall. It was said that such farmers spent their time "lookin' at the sky" for signs of rain.

sky hook

In logging, a self-propelled cable-logging device consisting of a powered carriage suspended from a pair of taut skyline cables. The operator rides the carriage, which hoists logs from the ground and carries them to either end of the sky line. See *sky-line logging*. Also, a logger's expression used whenever difficulty arises.

sky hooker

In logging, the top man of a sleigh-loading crew; the man who arranges the logs on top of a load.

skylight roof

In steamboating, the roof or deck covering the skylights on a steamboat, usually 4 to 8 feet higher than the surrounding roof, or hurricane deck.

skylight

In steamboating, glass placed in the roof of a steamboat cabin. In steamboats constructed during the period from 1850 to 1920 the cabin roofs were usually elevated from 3 to 8 feet, and window glass was inserted along the upper sides, thus admitting daylight the entire length of the cabin. Frequently the glass was stained, etched, or otherwise decorated. Only cheaply constructed boats lacked this architectural feature.

sky-line
To transport logs by means of a high line. See *sky-line logging*.

sky-line logging
A method of logging in which a taut cable is stretched between two spar trees. A carriage weighing about a ton rides the two-inch steel cable, and to it and the spars are attached hook lines, skidding lines, slack lines, and other equipment. The most efficient span is about 1,800 feet from head spar to tail tree, though it may be as long as 2,400 feet. Also called *high-line logging*. See *sky hook*.

sky pilot
A cowboy's name for a preacher.

sky rigger
In logging, the man who cuts the tops from trees and later attaches the *high line*. Because of the swaying of the tree when the top falls and because of the danger that the cut may slide down the side of the tree on which he is working, his job is extremely dangerous.

slab
In logging, the exterior portion of a log removed in sawing timber.

slab-sided
A cowboy's term meaning *flat-ribbed* or *poor*.

slack in the jaw
A cowboy's expression for a talkative person.

slack puller
A logger's term for a woman of easy virtue.

slag
In mining, the residue after metals have been removed by a smelter.

slag buggy
In mining, the carriage or pot that conveys slag from a smelter.

slappin' a brand on
A cowboy's expression for branding an animal.

slappin' his tree on
A cowboy's phrase for saddling a horse.

slash
An earmark consisting of a diagonal split. In logging, the branches, bark, tops, chunks, cull logs, uprooted stumps, and broken or uprooted trees left on the ground after logging. Also, a large accumulation of debris after a high wind or a fire.

slasher
A logger's name for a wood chopper.

slattin' his sails
An expression for a bucking horse.

SLAUGHTERING
See beefing, fifth quarter, good scald, hide-and-tallow factory, Judas steer, mantanza, tallow factory.

slave
A logger's term for a worker; a wage earner.

slave driver
A logger's term for a foreman, especially a strict one; also called *slave pusher*.

slave market
A logger's name for an employment office.

slave puncher
A logger's term for a foreman or boss.

sled
A westerner's word for a sleigh.

sled dog
A hay sled used by the cowman in winter.

sled logging
In logging, hauling logs by sled over iced roads to a river landing.

sled tender
In logging, a member of the hauling crew who accompanies the load of logs to the landing, unhooks the grabs, and sees that they are returned to the yarding engine.

sleeper

A calf earmarked by a cattle thief who intended to come back later and steal the animal. The earmark was used by the cattleman as a quick means of identification. Thus, during roundup, when the ranch hands came upon such an animal, they were likely to take it for granted that it had been branded when it was earmarked and leave it to roam, and the thief could return later, put his own brand upon it, and drive it away. To mark an animal in such a way; see *sleepering*. Originally, in faro, a bet placed on a dead card. In many houses it belonged to the first man who grabbed it. In later gambling, money or a bet left on the table or gambling layout that belongs to a player who has forgotten about it.

sleeper brand

An unrecorded and unknown brand found on cattle on a particular range.

sleepering

A rustler's practice of earmarking an unbranded calf that did not belong to him and turning it loose unbranded. Since the earmark was that of the outfit to which the calf belonged, it attracted no undue attention. If the calf passed the notice of the riders of that ranch, the rustler would return when the calf was about 6 months old, wean it from its mother, and slap his own brand on it. Then he would change the earmark to go with his brand, and the new mark usually destroyed the earlier earmark. See *sleeper*.

Sleeping

See camping, covered his back with his belly, raftering, sleeping out.

sleeping out

Sleeping in the open; a common expression in speaking of the roundup, when the cowboy did his sleeping in the open.

sleeping sawyer

In steamboating, a *sawyer* (*q.v.*) that did not reach within 2 or 3 feet of the surface of the water, even when periodically heaving upward. Such sawyers were the most dangerous to boats because they could not be seen.

sleeve gun

A derringer a gambler carried up his sleeve.

slew

A cowboy's term meaning *large amount*.

slick

A cowboy's name for an unbranded animal, particularly a horse.

slick-ear

A cowboy's term for a cow that has not been earmarked or branded.

slickensides

In mining, smooth, polished portions of the wall or of some vertical plane in the lode, caused by friction. They may occur on the ore itself.

slicker-broke

A cowboy's expression for a horse that has been broken to a slicker. This is done by tying a slicker behind the cantle of the saddle so that it nearly touches the ground on the left side. At first the horse may try to kick it to ribbons, but he soon gets used to it and quits trying to stampede. By this training the horse becomes less afraid of other boogers just as harmless and is a much safer horse than one not so trained.

slick fork

A saddle with little bulge or roll at the fork.

slick-heeled

A cowboy's expression for someone without spurs.

slick saddle

A saddle without a saddle roll.

slick up

A cowboy's expression meaning to *dress up in one's best*. When a group of boys at a ranch started slicking up for a shindig, it was, as Dave Hall once said, "shore hard on the soap supply and stock water." An old-time trail driver gave me this description of a cowboy cleaning up after a trail drive: "The first thing he does when he hits the town at the end of the trail is to rattle his hocks for a barbershop where he can take a civilized soakin' in hot water with a big woolly towel and plenty of sweet-smellin' soap. After he comes out of that dippin' vat, he buys ever'thing the barber's got. When he comes out from under them operations, he's so clean and brown he looks like he's been scrubbed with saddle soap, and his own folks wouldn't know 'im either by sight or smell."

At the ranch his everyday cleanliness consisted mostly of "hoofin' it to a wash basin in the mornin' to snort in it a couple of times to get the sleep from his eyes, after which he paws over a towel, which, judgin' from its complexion, has been plumb pop'lar."

slide

A smooth spot on a stream bank formed by beavers or otters sliding up and down the banks. In mining, a type of fault—a vertical dislocation of a lode or a mass of loose rock overlying either lode or country rock.

sliding hook

See *butt hook*.

sliding the groove

A tracker's expression for following a trail so clearly blazoned that it could not be lost.

sling

A packer's term for a ⅜-inch rope of the best handlaid Manila, about 30 feet long and well sized at each end, used in tying the packs together on a mule's back before it was lashed; also called *sling rope*. To tie the packs together with such a rope, as *to sling the load*, *to cross-sling*, *to double-sling*, and *to double-cross-sling*.

slinging and lashing

An early trapper's and prospector's method of securing a load on a mule's back by ropes. Since no padding was used under the load, the animal's back was not protected.

sling joint

A logger's expression meaning *to do manual labor*.

slip

In logging, an incline on which a bull chain and logs are carried from pond to sawmill.

slip gun

A pistol altered so that it could be fired by slipping the thumb off the hammer. Generally the hammer spur was lowered, the trigger removed or tied down, and the barrel cut short so that the weapon could be carried in a pants pocket. (Foster-Harris to R.F.A.)

slipped his hobbles

An expression used for a horse that has escaped from his hobbles, and also for a person who has fallen from grace.

slipper

A type of horseshoe that is smooth and without calks.

slip shooting

A method of shooting a gun accomplished by thumbing the hammer with a wiping motion. It is slower than fanning, but the shots are placed more accurately. Even then accuracy is limited to close range. Also called *slip hammering*.

slope

A cowboy's word meaning *to run* or *to run away*. In the days when Texas was a haven for outlaws, when someone had committed a crime or wouldn't pay a debt, it was said that he had *sloped to Texas*. Also, an earmark made by cutting a diagonal split on the outside edge.

sloper

A westerner's name for a resident of the Pacific Coast.

sloppy riding

A cowboy's expression for sitting loosely in the saddle and allowing the body to flop about in response to the pitching of the horse.

slough

In river boating, a body of water behind an island and separate from the main channel; called a *chute* on the lower river.

slough pig

A logger's name for a man who rafts logs in a boom.

slow brand

An unrecorded brand employed in one

form of cattle stealing. It is unlawful for anyone to mutilate a brand, and the law also requires that every brand must be recorded in the county of its origin. A rustler who blotted out one brand and put another in its place naturally hesitated to record the new brand. He simply used it, trusting that he could get the cattle out of the country before discovery. (J. Frank Dobie, *Vaquero of the Brush Country* [Dallas, Southwest Press, 1929], 121.)

slow country

A cowboy's term for a rocky, steep trail over which he had to ride slowly.

slow elk

A cowman's term for beef butchered without the owner's knowledge. To kill for food an animal belonging to someone else. Some cowmen followed the philosophy that "one's own beef don't taste as good as the other fellow's because fat, tender yearlings are what you kill when they're other folk's stuff." See *big antelope*.

slugging committee

A logger's name for an I.W.W. membership committee.

sluice

In mining, a gold-separation trough made of three boards about 10 to 12 feet long through which water was run rapidly. Cleats were nailed across the bottom to hold the gold when it settled. The gold-bearing gravel was shoveled in at the top, and at the lower end a man shoveled out the material that was too large to go through the sieve located there. In logging, an inclined trough or artificial waterway on which logs are floated down to a pond or river; also called *sluiceway*.

sluiced

A logger's word for being caught in a rush of logs that have broken away from confinement.

sluice head

In mining, a *head*, or the amount of water sufficient for flushing out a *sluice*, q.v.

sluicer

A miner who washed down earth by means of a *sluice*, q.v. A logger who guides logs through a *sluice*, q.v.

sluiceway

In logging, *a sluice*, q.v.

sluicing

In mining, using ground sluices.

sluicing claim

In mining, a claim upon which *sluicing* (q.v.) was carried on.

slunk skin

A cowman's term for the skin of an unborn calf.

SMALL

See fryin' size, half-pint size, poco.

small-loop man

A roper who uses a small loop in roping. A cowboy of the brush country came under this classification.

smear

A cowboy's term meaning *to rope*, as "He *smeared* a rope on it."

smelting

In mining, a metal-recovery process by which the ore is melted in a furnace and the heavy metallic components are allowed to sink to the bottom while the lighter, worthless materials, called *slag*, are poured or skimmed off the top.

smoke eater

A logger's name for a forest fireman.

smoke him out

To shoot at someone to make him come out of hiding, surrender, or divulge a secret.

smoke pole

A cowboy's name for his six gun.

smokes his pipe

A cowboy's expression for a horse whose lip is torn where the bridle bit rests.

smoke signal

A cowboy's term for any kind of warning sign or signal; taken from the Indian means of long-distance communication.

smoke the peace pipe

A cowboy's expression for forgiving and becoming friends after a quarrel; taken from the Indian custom of smoking the pipe of peace at councils.

smoke up

A cowboy's expression meaning *to shoot at someone*. One time a cowboy had his hat shot off his head. Having no enemies, he supposed some rough joker had shot at him. As he picked up the hat and looked at the top where the crown had been shot away, he said, "That's a helluva joke. How'd he know how much of my head was in that hat?"

smoke wagon

A cowboy's name for his six gun.

smoking out the cattle

On roundup, shooting to scare cattle from their hiding places in rough or brushy country when riding circle.

smooth

A cowboy's term for an unshod horse.

smoothin' out the humps

A cowboy's expression for taking the rough edges off a horse. Some horses are inclined to pitch when saddled regardless of their years in service, especially in the spring when the grass is green and they are putting on flesh and feeling good. If there is anything that will cause broken horses to pitch, it is grass fat. After a winter of idleness the cowboy has to do some tall riding before he succeeds in smoothing the humps out of such a horse. Also, usually there are one or two last year's broncs in his string that are starting their careers as cow horses, and they are also likely to pitch for some time.

smooth-mouth

An aged horse.

smooth roper

A man expert in the use of a rope; one who goes about his task without flourish.

snaffle bit

A bit similar to the *bar bit (q.v.)* except that it is made in two pieces connected by two interlocking eyes at the middle.

snag

In logging, a dead tree with falling bark or limbs. A rough branch that has broken off. A rampike; a tree whose top has broken off; especially a tall tree that is a fire hazard.

In river boating, a tree or branch embedded in the river bottom. Every year trees that lined the riverbanks were undermined and fell into the stream. They were borne along by the current until they became anchored in the bottom, where they remained with one end sticking up and pointing downstream, sometimes above and sometimes below the surface. Snags have always been formidable dangers to river navigation. They were also called *sawyers*, and *breaks*, from the ripple or break they made on the surface of the water. Only by the appearance of these breaks could a pilot discover a submerged snag. See *sawyer*, *bob sawyer*.

snag boat

A powerful steamboat, often double-bottomed, used in removing snags and other obstructions from waterways.

snag chamber

In steamboating, a watertight compartment built at the bottom of the hull to prevent the boat from sinking if caught on a snag.

snagged

In river boating, pierced or caught by a snag.

snaggy

Said of a river abounding in snags.

snail

A cowboy's word meaning *to drag with a rope*.

snake

A westerner's name for a low-principled man. A cowboy's word meaning *to drag with a rope*. A logger's word meaning *to drag a log along the ground*. A miner's word for a line drawn through a statement of an employee's earnings when the full amount was owed the company in return.

snake blood

A cowboy's term for meanness. One cowhand was heard to say of another, "He's got snake blood, and he's so tough he has to sneak up on a dipper to get a drink o' water."

snake-eyes

A mean horse. In dice, a cast of two one spots.

snake-head whisky

A cowboy's name for cheap whisky of which it was said that the maker put snake heads in the barrel to give it potency. One cowhand used to say that he "wondered how they kept such stuff corked."

snake hole

In mining, a bore hole.

snake on stilts

A cowboy's expression for a thin person.

snake poison

A cowboy's name for whisky; also called *snake water*.

snake's alarm clock

A cowboy's term for a rattlesnake's rattles.

SNAKES AND LIZARDS

See bell on his tail, belled snake, chuck-waller, Gila monster, mountain boomer, sand eel, sidewinder.

snake tell-box

In faro, a dishonest dealer's box; see *tell box*.

snaking a game

In faro, stealing, marking, and returning a dealer's cards, a trick often practiced in the days when the pack was dealt face down from the dealer's hand. This was usually done when a box was not used; old-timers sometime beat the bank by this method in bygone days. Also, setting up a dishonest game to fleece suckers.

snaking team

In logging, a team of horses used in dragging logs along the ground.

snaky

A cowboy's word meaning *treacherous* or *mean*.

snap

In faro, a temporary game set up in a gambling room or elsewhere, usually with a small amount of capital.

snappin' broncs

Breaking wild horses.

snapping time

A miner's term for a short period of rest.

snappin' turtle

A cowboy's term for a branding chute.

snap up

In packing, to tie animals together by their halter shanks while standing at the rigging.

snare

To catch with a rope.

snatch

A miner's term for a small ventilation chimney.

snatch team

A cowboy's term for a strong team used to supplement another team on a hard pull.

SNEAKING

See coyotin' round, Indian up.

snip

White color on a horse's forehead that extends to the nose as company for the *star* or *star strip*, *q.v.*

snipe

In logging, to trim or round the edge of a log.

snipe-gutted

A cowboy's expression for an animal, especially a horse, that has a slim barrel.

snipe-nose

In logging, to round off the end of a log in order to facilitate skidding.

sniper

A logger's name for a section man.

snooper

One of those cowboys who watched where some of the boys hid their bottles at a dance and then helped themselves.

snoose

A strong, peppery, moist snuff used by loggers instead of chewing tobacco, introduced into the woods by Scandinavian loggers. It is unlike the popular dry snuffs used in the South. The term is also used by sheepherders.

snoozer

A cowboy's name for a sheepherder, who, in the cowboy's opinion, does nothing but sleep.

snore holes

A miner's name for the suction holes that admit water into a washing pump.

SNORING

See hit the knots.

snorter

An excitable horse.

snorting pen

A small circular corral inside a larger one, usually with a post firmly planted in the middle. Also, a breeding pen.

snortin' post

A cowboy's name for a hitching post or rack.

snorty

A cowboy's word for a high-spirited horse and also for a man easy to anger.

snow

What a miner calls a sprinkle of fine dirt preceding a cave-in.

snowball the layout

In gambling, to distribute white checks all over the layout, the mark of a cheap gambler.

snowbird

A frontier soldier who enlisted for the winter to get clothing and food and deserted in the spring.

snub

To tie a horse's head to some fixed object. To dehorn cattle. In logging, to anchor.

snubbed

Dehorned.

snubbed stock

Dehorned cattle.

snubber

A man who snubs a bad horse while the rider mounts. He usually performs this function at rodeos at which there is no chute. On the range the cowboy is mostly on his own and has no help. Also a name the logger gives any mechanical device, other than bridle chains, used for braking a sleigh on a hill.

snubbing post

A vertical, round timber about 5 feet tall, set firmly in the ground at the center of the corral and stout enough to stand the strains to which it is subjected when a bucker is tied to it.

snub horse

In rodeo, a horse used to snub a bucker.

snuffy

A cowboy's word for a wild or spirited horse.

soak

A cowboy's term meaning *to rest* or *loaf*. Often the cowboy lets his horse soak for a few minutes after saddling to allow it to get over the notion of pitching.

sober side of the bar

Obviously, the bartender's side.

sobre paso

A horse's gait—a slow trot; from the Spanish.

social herders

A group of sheepherders who get together for a visit and neglect their charges. The visit usually has an unfortunate outcome, for the herds will invariably mix.

socks

White color on a horse's hoofs that extends only to his fetlocks.

soda card

In faro, the first card that shows face up in the dealer's box; also called *soda*. Like the *hock card* (*q.v.*), it has no action, but is shown before any bets are made. The word *soda* may be a corruption of *zodiac.* The expression *from soda to hock,* meaning *the first to the last card,* came to mean *the whole thing,* as "from soup to nuts."

sodbuster

A cowboy's name for a farmer. A miner's name for a recruit from a farm.

soddy

A cowboy's name for a nester, because the early ones usually lived in sod houses.

sod-pawin' mood

A cowboy's expression meaning *very angry;* from the example of a bull pawing the ground when angry.

soft

A cowboy's word for a horse that tires easily.

soft grub

A cowboy's name for hotel food or fancy victuals.

soft-mouth

A cowboy's name for a horse that is very sensitive to the bit.

soft seventeen

In blackjack, a total of seventeen, which includes an ace when counted as eleven.

Soils and deposits

See alluvium, amygdaloid, bedrock, breccia, buckshot land, chimney, conglomerate, country rock, duff, metals and ores, minerals, mines, mountain meal, muck, quicksand, stratum, topdirt, washing stuff.

sold his saddle

The last word for a cowman disgraced. This cow-country phrase is also used to refer to a person who is utterly broke and has many other interpretations. If a man has betrayed his trust or has done something else to earn the contempt of his fellows, he's *sold his saddle.* Sometimes the expression is used in pity rather than in scorn. If a man has lost his business and become destitute, he's *sold his saddle.* If his mind is deranged, he's *sold his saddle.* The words imply the ultimate in the abandonment of fate.

Even the children of the raw range land had their conception of this phrase. In his excellent book *The Cowboy,* Philip A. Rollins tells this fitting story: "Years ago in a little school at Gardiner, Montana, a small, tow-headed youth, when asked by the teacher as to who Benedict Arnold was and what he had done, replied: 'He was one of our generals and he sold his saddle.'" (Philip A. Rollins, *The Cowboy* [New York, Charles Scribner's Sons, 1936], 133–34.)

Soldiers

See buffalo soldier, long knife, Ned, snowbird, walk-a-heap, yellow legs.

sole

In mining, the floor of a horizontal working.

sollar

In mining, any platform floor or covering in a working.

sombraro

In mining, a solidified mass of metal. Also, the channel that conducts molten metal to the molds.

sombre-jalma

In packing, an aparejo cover made of No. 4 cotton ducking. It was faced at sides and ends with leather to give it sufficient width to cover the aparejo. The ends were protected by wooden sticks, or *shoes,* held in place by caps of leather sewed over either end. The shoes served to stiffen the ends of the aparejo cover and keep it from wrinkling and gathering. The cover was secured to the aparejo by thongs at the ends of its middle or center line. The word, erroneously translated *sovereign hammer,* or *soldier hammer,* is of Arabic and Spanish origin used by the Moroccans of Spain, meaning *overcover.*

sombrero

A broad-brimmed hat used in the Southwest, especially among Spanish-speaking people; from the Spanish *sombra,* meaning shade.

Somebody stole his rudder.

A comment overheard about a drunken man weaving his way up the sidewalk. Watching a drunken cowboy try to walk in high heels under a load of liquor, another cowboy said that he "looked like walkin' was a lost art." Any cowboy walking under this condition looked as if "his legs was a burden."

Some deck is shy a joker!

A cowboy's description of an outlandishly dressed person, usually a tenderfoot.

Songs

See hymns, scalp chant, singin' to 'em.

son-of-a-bitch-in-a-sack

A cowboy dish made of dried fruit rolled in dough, sewed in a sack, and steamed. It takes plenty of patience and cussin' to make it, for it has to be hung in a big hot-water bucket over a pot rack to steam. After seeing one of them made, you would agree that the cook gave it a fitting name.

son-of-a-bitch stew

A favorite cowboy dish made of the brains, sweetbreads, and other choice pieces of a freshly killed calf. If the cowhand wishes to be polite he calls it *son-of-a-gun stew*, but if no delicate ears are present, he calls it by its true fighting name.

When a calf is killed, the tongue, liver, heart, kidneys, sweetbreads, and brains are carried to the cook; and he knows what is expected of him. He chops all these ingredients into small bits with his butcher knife and prepares to stew them slowly in an iron kettle. There are many different ways to make this dish—as many ways as there are cooks. Some may throw in some potatoes, a can of tomatoes, and anything else that is handy. If the eater can tell what is in it, it is not a first-class stew. As the cowboy says. "You throw ever'thing in the pot but the hair, horns, and holler." The longer it is cooked the better it tastes.

Sonora reds

A northern cowboy's name for the red Mexican cattle that came up the trail in trail-driving days.

sooners

A cowboy's name for men who went out on the range and branded cattle before the official date set by the roundup association. This date gave every man an equal opportunity as well as avoiding the necessity of working the cattle more than once, but there were always some dishonest men who worked only to their own selfish advantage. By working ahead of the regular roundup, they could pick up many *mavericks*—calves whose mothers had been killed by wolves or had died from natural causes—and calves missed in the last branding.

This name was also given to persons who entered upon public lands to secure choice areas before the official date on which it was thrown open for settlement, such as the opening of land in Oklahoma.

sop

A cowboy's and logger's name for gravy.

sop and 'taters

A cowboy's name for the cow-camp cook, and also for a horse that paces.

sorrel

A horse of the chestnut type but lighter, of a yellowish or reddish-golden color.

sougan

See *sugan.*

sounding

In steamboating, measuring the depth of a river with a lead, or sounding, line to find the best water. Also, the measurement so taken. Soundings were usually taken from the steamboat. When available, a yawl or a specially designed sounding boat, commanded by the off-duty pilot and provided with a steersman and a crew, proceeded ahead of the steamboat, while the pilot on duty on the steamboat watched through a spyglass.

On a shallow river a *sounding pole (q.v.)* was used instead of a lead line. A deck hand thrust the pole into the water every 5 seconds, calling out the depths in a drawling, singsong voice. Soundings were not always taken just for the immediate purpose of working the boat over a particular bar or shallow area. During the season of low water, the leads were kept going in all difficult places for the purpose of comparison.

sounding boat

A boat used in *sounding, q.v.*

sounding pole

A pole, 12 to 18 feet long, used in shallow-water streams for gauging the depth of the stream. Marked off in 1-foot sections, each section was painted a different color, the first one red, the second white, the third blue, and so on.

sounding the horn

A cowboy's expression for taking hold of the saddle horn while riding a bucking horse.

sourdough

A cowboy's title for a cook and also for a bachelor.

sourdough bullet

A cowboy's name for a biscuit, but not used when the cook was within hearing distance.

sourdough keg

A small wooden keg, usually holding about 5 gallons, in which the cook kept his sourdough. When getting ready for the coming roundup, the cook put 3 or 4 quarts of flour into this keg and added a dash of salt and just enough water to make a medium-thick batter. The keg was then placed in the sun to let the heat ferment the contents for several days. Sometimes a little vinegar or molasses was added to hasten the fermentation.

The purpose of the first batch of batter was merely to season the keg. After the fermentation was well started, the batter was poured out, and enough new batter was mixed to fill the keg. Each day it was put into the sun to hasten fermentation, and each night it was wrapped in blankets to keep the batter warm and working. Some cooks even slept with their kegs.

After several days of this treatment, the dough was ready to use. From then to the end of the season the keg was never cleaned out. Every time the cook took out enough dough for a meal, he put back enough flour, salt, and water to replace it. In this way he always had plenty of dough working.

When making up his bread, he simply added enough flour and water to this batter to make a medium-stiff dough. Every wagon cook thought his sourdough the best ever, and he took great pride in his product. An outfit that let anything happen to its sourdough keg was in a bad shape, and most cooks would just about defend their kegs with their lives.

sourdough pants

A northwestern cowboy's name for blanket-lined overalls favored by riders in the winter.

sourdoughs

Sourdough biscuits; see *sourdough*.

sour-mouth

A cowboy's expression for a horse that frets and fights the bits, finally becoming hard-mouthed.

souse myself

A logger's expression for washing his hands and face.

sow bosom

A cowboy's name for salt pork.

spade bit

A horse's bit with a piece on the mouth bar shaped like a broad screwdriver 3 or 4 inches long and bent backward at the top. When using a spade bit, a good rider never forgets that it can do damage, and he handles his reins lightly.

spaghetti

In steamboating, a steam pipe of standard length used to couple steam pipes to siphons over a fleet of barges.

Spanish bit

A very severe bit with a port about 2¼ inches high and a curb ring instead of a curb strap.

Spanish fever

A splenic fever caused by ticks and spread by the immune but tick-infested, cattle of the southern country to cattle of more northern latitudes. The prevalence of this fever was greatly responsible for ending the trail drives. Also called *Texas fever*.

Spanish monte

A simplified version of faro played by Americans of Spanish origin. It is a bank game, supervised by a houseman or croupier called a *cutter*. The bank collects a percentage of the winnings. The game is played with a standard pack of fifty-two cards, and, unlike other varieties of faro, there is no dealer's box.

The game is played by betting that one designated card of four placed face up on the table will be matched by the dealer before another one of the three remaining cards is matched. Also called *monte bank*.

Spanish supper

What the cowboy calls tightening his belt a notch or two as a substitute for food.

spar

In steamboating, a stout pole like a mast with sharp iron points, used to fend the vessel away from the shore so that the boat would not be grounded in shallow water. In early days steamboats carried two spars lashed upright on their forecastles. Alongside the spars was a similar pole, called a *derrick*, used as a boom pole to handle the spar. See *sparring*. In logging, to cut off the top of a tall tree, the logger sometimes working 70 feet above the ground. In mining, a general term applied to rock with distinct cleavage and luster.

sparring

Dislodging a steamboat that was resting on the river bottom or on a sand bar by spars (see *spar*). Also called *sparring off*. When the boat struck, the ends of the spars were lowered to the river bed. Then, with a block and tackle operated by a small donkey engine, the front end of the boat was raised a foot or more off the bottom. The paddles were then put at full speed, and with luck the vessel was jumped over the bar.

Sparring was a science. Just as soon as reports were received from the pilot who had been sent out in a yawl to sound the bar, the steamboat pilot had to decide how to place the spars and what direction to shove the bow of the boat. Sometimes in sparring advantage was taken of the instability of the sand bars. The forward part of the boat was lifted upon the bar, pushed forward by the engines, and allowed to settle down upon the sand again, the current rapidly washing underneath the hull. The operation was repeated as fast as the spars could be taken up and reset. This method, called *walking her over*, was tedious, and its success depended on the height of the bar, the velocity of the current, and the skill of the pilot in directing the operation.

sparring off

See *sparring*.

spar tree

In logging, a standing tree denuded of all limbs and used for leverage. A tree at the landing to which one end of the skyline cable is attached in cableway logging.

speck

A miner's shortened form of *prospect*; to hunt for gold.

spick

A southwesterner's name for a Mexican.

spider

In logging, a small metal tool used for testing the set in the cutting teeth of a saw.

spikes his horse's tail

A cowboy's expression for a rider going at full speed who pulls his horse to such a sudden stop that the horse literally sits on his tail.

spike team

In stagecoaching, a team of five animals (usually mules) hitched so that the two heaviest animals were the wheelers, two lighter animals were placed in front of them, and the lightest one was hitched single in the lead.

spike weaner

A circle of wire spikes fitted around a calf's nose to wean it.

spiling

In mining, timber used in quicksand or loose ground where lathes are driven behind timbers and kept flush with the headings.

spilled

A cowboy's term meaning *thrown from a horse*.

spinner

A cowboy's name for a horse that bucks in a tight circle, spinning either to right or to left. This type of horse usually does his bucking in a small space, but his actions are so violent, as he whirls and bucks with a backward motion as he hits the ground, that the average rider quickly becomes dizzy, loses his sense of balance, and is soon "eating gravel." This type of bucker seldom hurts his rider when he throws him, because he doesn't throw him high. He merely whirls and turns out from under him, letting him down comparatively easily. (Bruce Clinton, "Buckin' Horses" *Western Horseman*, Vol. III, No.3 [May–June, 1938], 10.)

spit

What the miner calls a light fuse.

spitting around

In mining, lighting the fuses to blast the rounds of explosives.

splatter dabs

A cowboy's name for hot cakes.

splinter belly

A logger's name for a migratory carpenter.

splinter picker

A logger's name for a millworker.

split

An earmark made by splitting the ear midway from the tip about halfway toward the head.

split

In logging, a lengthwise separation of the wood, which usually occurs at the ends of the piece. In gambling, a pair of cards falling together in a single turn; in honest faro this is the only advantage the dealer maintains over the players, for the bank takes half of all money bet on that turn; hence the term, indicating that the bank *splits* the money with the players.

split the blankets

A cowboy's expression meaning *to share one's bed with another*.

splitting

In rodeo, an agreement between two contestants, usually in the same event, to pool and then divide equally all their winnings.

splitting the tail

Cutting a cow's tail lengthwise. It was believed by old-time cowmen that splitting a cow's tail would prevent blackleg.

spoiled herd

A cowman's term for a herd that has acquired the habit of stampeding at every opportunity.

spoiled horse

A horse that is abused at the breaking period until his character is ruined—a man-made outlaw.

spook

A cowboy's word meaning *to scare*.

spooky

A cowboy's word for a horse with a nervous temperament.

spool your bed

A cowboy's expression for rolling up one's bed for packing or moving.

spoon

In mining, a rod used to clean out drill holes.

Spoon!

A logger's shout to a fellow sleeper. When two loggers slept together in narrow quarters, they slept "spoon-fashion," lying on their sides facing the same direction. When one logger yelled, "Spoon!" he meant that he wanted to turn over and his bedmate must also turn.

spot card

In gambling, a playing card bearing a number, as distinguished from a *court card*, or face card.

spotted pup

A cowboy's dish made of rice and raisins cooked together.

spotter

A logger's name for a spy or informer hired by an employer.

spraddle horns

A cowboy's name for the old-time longhorn cattle.

spraddled out

A cowboy's term meaning *dressed up in his best*. It is one of his philosophies that "it's the man that's the cowhand, not the outfit he wears."

spread

A ranch, together with its buildings, cattle, and employees; also called *cow outfit* and *cow spread*. In roping, a throw of the rope.

spread-eagle

To be thrown from a horse with arms and legs outstretched.

spread the mustard

A cowboy's expression meaning *to put on airs*.

springboard

In logging, a narrow platform attached to the tree bole on which loggers stand while felling a big tree.

springer

A cowman's name for a cow about to calve in the spring.

springing

A cowman's word for a cow about to calve. *Springing heavy* means *nearing the time of delivery*. A *springing heifer* is a heifer carrying her first calf.

spring roundup

The roundup of calves in the spring; also called *calf roundup*.

spud

A logger's name for a hand tool used in stripping bark from felled trees.

spuds with the bark on

What the logger calls unpeeled potatoes.

spur

In logging, a branch logging road. In mining, a branch or offshoot of a larger vein.

spur-buttoning

A cowboy's term for sliding the button of the spur along the sides of a bucking horse when scratching instead of turning the rowels against his flesh, a practice of some rodeo riders.

spur leather

A broad, crescent-shaped shield of leather fitting over the instep to hold the spur on the boot.

Spurring

See comb, curry him out, gaff, gig, goose, hundred-and-elevens, raking, reef, scratch, screwing down, shove in the steel, spur-buttoning, throwing the steel.

spurs

The metal necessities worn upon the cowboy's heels. They are one of the essential implements of the cowboy's equipment for controlling his horse. He does not wear them to punish a horse, as many people think, nor does he wear them for ornament. He uses them more than he does the reins, but mostly as reminders. They are necessary in helping a horse over rough places he does not not want to cross, or in signaling him for turnings and quick stops and starts.

If a cowhand used his spurs to cut up a horse, he would not last long at most ranches, and if the outfit was so short-handed that it was forced to keep him on, he would likely be given such a rough string that he would be kept so busy trying to hang on that he wouldn't have time to use his spurs.

The real cowboy loves his horse, and being cruel to him is farthest from his mind. When he buys a new pair of spurs, the first thing he does is to file the points of the rowels until they are blunt. Sharp rowels keep the horse fighting and nervous and shrinking from their touch. When he uses them, a mere touch is as far as he goes, and sometimes a slight motion of the leg is all that is necessary.

He buys a big spur not because it looks scary but because the big one is less cruel. The bigger the rowel and the more points it has the less damage it does. It is the little spur with few points that sinks in. (Will James, *All in a Day's Riding* [New York, Charles Scribner's Sons, 1933], 54.)

The jingle of the spurs is sweet music to any cowhand. It keeps him from getting lonesome when he is riding the range, and as long as he hears the music of his spurs everything is rosy. He rarely takes them off when he is working, and in some sections he loses his social standing when he is caught without them. Many pairs of boots have been worn out without ever having had the spurs removed from them. Spurs are helpful at night, too, as a bootjack for removing the boots.

SPURS

See buck hook, buzz saw, California drag rowels, can openers, cartwheel, Chihuahuas, danglers, diggers, flower rowel, gad, galleg, galves, gooseneck, grapplin' irons, gut hooks, gut lancers, gut wrenches, hell rousers, hooks, Kelley's, locked spurs, petmakers, rib wrenches, rowel, shank, spur leather, spurs, star rowel, steel, sunset rowel, tin-belly, wagon-spoke rowel.

square

A cowboy's word of high praise. This word had a broad meaning on the early-day range. A man entitled to such a testimonial to his worth had to possess qualities of unflinching courage, daring, and self-reliance; and in addition to these he had to be ready and willing to stand by a brother cowman and do his duty efficiently in anything that happened to come up in the work of the day. Moreover, whatever he might have been and have done elsewhere, he must be truthful, honest, and honorable in all his relations to the outfit as a whole and to each of the men with whom he was associated in taking care of its property. Lying, crookedness, and double-dealing were intolerable offenses in this close-bound life. To say of a man that he was *square* was to pay him the highest compliment. (*Prose and Poetry of the Live Stock Industry* [Denver, 1905].)

square deal

In gambling, a deal of twenty-five turns in which the dealer used a pack of cards with square edges. With these cards the chances of a crooked deal were minimized. The expression has since come to mean a *fair deal* in any aspect of life.

square decker

In faro, a dealer who wins for the house by stacking the deck according to the system which he has observed various players using. He is, of course, a skilled manipulator of cards, and nowadays may be found dealing other games besides faro.

square game

In faro, a bank that used square cards exclusively.

square-set stoping

In mining, a system of timbering in which squares on squares of timber are set upon each other.

squat

A westerner's term for a bit of land or a claim. To settle on a claim or on government land.

squatter

A person who settles on state or government land.

SQUATTERS

See Modoc, mover, settlers and farmers, squatter.

squaw ax

An awkward ax used in splitting and hewing wood.

squaw camp

An Indian camp in which women and children lived while the men were away hunting or fighting.

squaw hitch

In packing, a crosstree hitch in which the loop of the running rope was brought around the side pack on each side of the animal. This hitch was first used by the trappers of the Hudson's Bay Company among the Indians of the Northwest. The same hitch has been given different names by different people who used it. The sheepherder called it the *sheepherder's hitch,* the prospector the *prospector's hitch,* etc. The logger uses this term for the bits of the choker about the corner or corners of a log used in turning or changing the position of the log.

squaw horse

A cowboy's name for a poor specimen of horseflesh.

squaw man

A name given a white man who married an Indian woman.

squaw pony

An Indian pony used to pack burdens, as distinguished from one used for war or hunting.

squaw side of a horse

The right side; so called because Indians preferred to mount from that side while the white man mounts from the left.

squaw talk

A cowman's term for any kind of irrelevant or foolish talk.

squaw wind

A northwesterner's term for a *chinook*, *q.v.*

squaw wood

A cowboy's term for dried cow chips or for small, dry, easily broken sticks used for fuel.

squeeze

In gambling, to arrange cards so as to reveal the indicators marked on the corners for cheating purposes.

squeeze 'em down

In cattle driving, to narrow the width of a trail herd to drive it across a river or for any other purpose.

squeezer

A cowboy's name for a narrow branding chute.

squeeze the biscuit

To catch hold of the saddle horn while riding a horse.

squeezin' Lizzie

Holding the saddle horn while riding a horse. One cowhand spoke of another's "hangin' on like an Injun to a whisky jug" during a ride.

squip

A miner's name for a fuse.

squirrel can

A large can or tub used for scraps by the cook on roundup. Whenever anything, from a saddle blanket to a spur was lost, someone would jokingly suggest looking for it in the squirrel can.

squirrel lines

In logging, short sections of small lines used to transfer the position of a heavier line; also called *ratlines*.

stable dog

A logger's name for the man who cared for the stables in camp.

STABLES

See hovel.

stack

A cowboy's shortened form of *haystack*.

stacker

A ranch hand who works on the top of a stack while putting up hay. A device used to stack hay, consisting of two sets of braced pole shears with a transverse cable between their tops. Its operation is similar to that of an overhead crane.

stacking ground

In logging, a temporary holding place for logs.

stack it on

A cowboy's expression meaning *to throw a rope on an animal*.

stack pole

A pole about which hay or forage is stacked.

stacks

In steamboating, a short name for the *smokestacks*. The term *chimneys* was also sometimes used, usually pronounced *chimleys*. One never says *funnel* to a riverman when speaking of the *stacks*; he would think you wanted something to use to pour vinegar into a barrel.

stack the cards

In gambling, to prearrange the position of the cards.

stackwad

An early-day cowboy's name for a man who was slack in his work, who managed to get the "short rides" in range work, or who otherwise sought the easy tasks.

stackyard

A yard in which hay is stacked for the winter feeding of cattle.

stag

A logger's expression for cutting off pants

or overalls about midway between knee and ankle.

stage

In stagecoaching, a section of road between stations, usually about 10 miles long, depending upon the terrain, the water supply, and other conditions. Relays of animals were kept at the stations. Also, a short form of *stagecoach*, *q.v.*

In steamboating, a *stage plank*, or gangplank; a built-up boardwalk sometimes 40 to 60 feet long, swung out ahead of the boat and lowered at landings with the *heel* of the stage on the forecastle and the other end on shore. The sidepiece was called the *stage gunnel*, and the stick of wood separating the wire lines that suspended the stage was called the *spreader bar*. The stage was manipulated from the deck by means of the *belly block* and the *heel block*. The *stage falls* were connected to the tip of the *boom*. A windlass, called the *stage hoist*, was used to raise the stage block into position. Many great Mississippi River packets carried two such stages, one on either side of the forecastle, each having its own boom, mast, and rigging. The device was invented about 1870.

stagecoach

A sturdy, horse-drawn vehicle that carried passengers and mail in the early days. The coach wheels were heavy, with wide, thick tires. The coach body was made of white oak or hickory, braced with iron bands, and supported by stout leather thorough braces. The coaches of the larger lines were lavishly decorated on the outside and had well-appointed interiors. The windows were covered with adjustable leather or canvas curtains designed to keep out wind, rain, snow, and dust; but early accounts of stage passengers indicated that the curtains were not entirely adequate. Teams of four or six horses pulled the coaches. With the coming of the railroads, the stagecoaches passed out of use.

STAGECOACHES AND EQUIPMENT

See boot, brake sticks, dickey, firebox, mud wagon, overland coach, paper wagon, sand boxes, sand liner, stagecoach, swift wagon, thorough braces, through pouch, treasure coach.

STAGECOACHING

See division, doping, express box, foot-and-walker line, home station, near, spike team, stand station, swing station.

STAGECOACH MEN

See drivers, messenger, shotgun messenger, side rider, silk popper, stock tender.

stage road

A road over which stagecoaches traveled.

stage route

A route along which stagecoaches traveled.

stage station

A stopping place on the stage route; also called *stage stand*.

stage wagon

See *mud wagon*.

stagger soup

A logger's name for whisky.

stag

A cowman's term for a male animal castrated late in life.

stake

A trader's and freighter's word meaning *to tether an animal to a stake*. In mining, a short form of *grubstake*, *q.v.*

stake-bound

A logger's expression for having enough money to quit work at any time.

stake breaking

Getting a horse used to being staked, a commoner practice in the Northwest than in the Southwest. It means more work for the cowboy and causes the horse a lot of rope burns that have to be doctored to keep them from giving the horse a lot of trouble.

stake money

In gambling, money borrowed by a gambler so that he can continue play, or money given him by bystanders who believe that his luck is due to change. If he wins, he repays the loan and divides the profits.

stake notice

A notice of a mining claim made public by being affixed to a stake.

staked to a fill

A cowboy's expression meaning that someone has been given a good meal.

stake out

To picket an animal.

staker

A name for an itinerant miner.

stake rope

A Texan's name for a picket rope used to stake horses.

stakey

A logger who has enough wages due him to make him restless to get to town.

staking ground

In freighting, the space allowed each teamster in front of his wagon, about 100 yards, where he staked his animals so that they might graze and rest. He was ever ready to defend the space when anyone tried to encroach upon it.

stallion

A male horse, especially one used for breeding.

stamp

See *stamp mill.*

stamp ax

A logger's name for his log-branding ax.

stamp brand

A cattle brand made with a set branding iron that burns the complete brand with one impression. Such an iron is practical only for a comparatively small brand. Modern cowmen use smaller brands; the use of the running brand is unlawful, for large brands ruin the animal's hide for the leather buyers.

stampede

The wild running of a herd of cattle or horses from fright. To run in such a way. A loud noise or crash. A rush of people to an area rumored to be rich in gold or silver. From the Spanish *estampida,* meaning *stampede.*

A cattle stampede is dangerous both to the animals and to the men herding them. The cattle will often run until exhausted, and of course this is damaging to their weight and condition. The fact that most stampedes occur on stormy nights makes them more difficult to bring under control and more dangerous for the riders. Many a cowboy has been left in an unmarked grave on the prairie as a result of a stampede.

Nothing can happen so quickly as a stampede. It is difficult to realize how suddenly a herd of cattle can rise to their feet and be gone. As the cowman says, "They jes' buy a through ticket to hell and gone, and try to ketch the first train." A stampede spoils cattle and makes them nervous and hard to hold for many days. Often many of them are killed or crippled, and others are so scattered they are never recovered.

Anything can cause a stampede. Thousands of causes have been listed by the cattlemen, some of them so simple that they sound ridiculous to the uninitiated. In the trail days cattle traveling a country strange to them were naturally nervous and suspicious. Also at this time the country was full of thieves who often stampeded a herd with the hope of retrieving some of the scattered ones.

The old-time cowman called them "stompedes," and his description of one was: "It's jes' one jump to their feet and another jump to hell." (J. Frank Dobie, *The Longhorns* [Boston, Little, Brown & Company, 1941], 88.)

The riders make every effort to gain a position alongside the lead cattle and try to head them into a milling circle. Each rider keeps up his singing or some sort of noise, and if he can hear his partner, he knows he is safe. If he does not hear him, he might be down. Contrary to general belief and popular fiction, guns are rarely fired in front of cattle in an effort to turn them. This would only frighten them more.

stampeder

A horse that is easily frightened and runs away blindly. If there is a horse genuinely hated in an outfit, it is the stampeder. He is more dangerous than a bucker, because he is generally sort of crazy and does not look where he is going. Also, a cow or steer that habitually starts a herd stampeding. A person who rushes into a region in which a discovery of gold or silver is rumored.

STAMPEDES

See blazing star, merry-go-round in high water, run, stampede.

stampede to the wild bunch

To commit a crime and dodge the law; to join an outlaw band. According to old man Kip Bronson, at one time in a certain section of the West the "thieves and killers was so thick you'd a thought they had a bill o' sale on the whole damned country."

stamp hammer

In mining, a power hammer that rises and falls vertically like an ore stamp.

stamping

In mining, reducing ore to the desired fineness in a *stamp mill, q.v.* The grain is usually not so fine as that produced by grinding in pans.

stamp mill

In mining, a device for crushing and grinding ore, consisting of heavy iron weights, or *stamps,* dropped at frequent intervals on a thin layer of ore spread out on iron anvils, or *dies. Amalgamation (q.v.)* is usually combined with the crushing when the metal to be recovered is gold or silver; copper and tin ore are stamped to prepare them for dressing. Also called *stamp.*

stamp-mill recovery

The gold recovered by the stamp-mill process. See *stamp mill.*

stanchion

In steamboating, one of the upright posts along the outboard guard of a packet that held up the roof and braced the railings; also called *boiler-deck stanchion.*

stand

A buffalo hunter's word for bringing a whole herd to a halt by killing the leading bull and then killing animal after animal that attempted to get to the front of the herd. As a rule buffaloes refused to leave after they smelled the blood of the first animal shot, and their slaughter was easy.

standard event

In rodeos, one of the five events recog-

nized by the Rodeo Cowboy's Association: saddle bronc riding, calf roping, bareback riding, steer wrestling (bulldogging), and bull riding. To qualify as an R.C.A.-approved rodeo, the rodeo must feature all five events.

stand by

A cowman's expression meaning *to be loyal.*

standing feed

A cowman's term for grass and uncut hay.

standing night guard

Doing guard duty with the herd at night; see *night guard.*

standing up to save saddle leather

Riding a horse by standing in the stirrups without letting the seat touch the saddle, usually done by the tenderfoot to ease saddle sores.

stand off

In faro, to gamble by letting all one's bets ride until a bet has action and then reversing all remaining bets.

stand station

In stagecoaching, a stage station where relay changes were made.

star

A small patch of white on the forehead of a dark-colored horse.

starboard

In river boating, the right-hand side of a boat looking forward, pronounced variously *stabbard, starb'd* and *starboard.* The left-hand side is *port* side.

star chief

A logger's name for the cook.

stargazer

A horse that carries his head high in the air. This characteristic is usually caused by the trainer's rough handling of the bit in the horse's mouth; he carried his head high to break the leverage on the bit.

stargazing

In trick roping, starting a body spin

and slowly assuming a sitting position and then lying on the back, spinning all the while.

star-pitch

A cowboy's term for sleeping in the open without covering.

star rowel

A spur with a rowel of five or six points; one so cruel that it is rarely used by the cowboy.

star strip

A white star on a horse's forehead that extends below the level of his eyes.

start a bronc

To make the first ride in breaking a horse.

starting the swim

In cattle driving, putting the leaders of a trail herd into the water for a crossing. Getting cattle to take to water often called for a great deal of patience, a knowledge of cow psychology, and a lot of experience. If the sun shone in the eyes of the cattle, they had difficulty seeing the opposite bank and would not swim. Sometimes starting the swim was accomplished by keeping them away from the water a day or two and then gradually working them down to an easy take-off place. Frequently, just as the cattle reached the water's edge, the horse herd would be eased into the river ahead of the lead cattle and started for the opposite bank. Usually the drovers had no difficulty getting the cattle to follow the horses.

star toter

A cowboy's name for a sheriff or deputy.

starve-out

A pasture of very few acres at a permanent camp, usually without water and with the grass used up, into which horses are thrown overnight to avoid having to catch them in the morning.

state doin's

A trapper's term for food.

states' eggs

A cowboy's name for eggs; so called because in the early days eggs were shipped in from the states to the cow country, most of which at that time was in the territories.

station drink

In stagecoaching, liquid refreshment for the driver. It was customary for the stage driver to spear a drink at each station, and history fails to record that any saloonkeeper dared refuse it.

stay

In poker, to remain in a hand by meeting the bet, ante, or raise.

stay in one's tree

A cowboy's expression meaning *to remain in the saddle; stay in one's pine* and *stay in one's ellum fork* are variants. These expressions are also often used as shouts of encouragement or admonition.

stay out with the dry cattle

A cowboy's expression meaning *to make a night of it, to carouse,* or *to get drunk.*

Stay with him!

A familiar cry of the breaking corral and a shout of encouragement heard at every rodeo when a man is riding a bucking horse.

steal a pot

In poker, to win a pot by bluffing or because another player with a higher-ranking hand fails to press his advantage.

steal a start

An expression used about an early-day cowman who stole enough cattle to form a nucleus around which he could later legitimately build a herd.

STEALING

See borrowed, high-grade, high grading, jack-roll, Pecos swap, raise, yamping.

steamboat

A steam-powered river boat, in early days generally propelled by paddle wheels. The boat drew only 3 to 4 feet of water and rode high in the water, thus appearing to be larger than its actual dimensions and tonnage. It had successive decks, surmounted by the texas and the pilothouse. Large, lavishly decorated steamboats were impressive sights as they moved along the river and were often called *floating palaces.* See *side-wheeler, stern-wheeler.*

STEAMBOATING

See back-and-belly, bill of lading, boat landing, call the landings, center, cordelle, cramp, deadhead, dogwatch, double tripping, gold-braid trade, grasshopper, handling, hogging, humping freight, inside, jack staff, labor, look at the river, scape, short watch, sparring, tow through, trade, walking, wooding.

steamboat inspector

In steamboating, a government official empowered to enforce steamboat laws and navigation rules and to grant, suspend, or revoke licenses issued by steamboat officers. Inspection offices were maintained in nearly every large river city. A *hull inspector* was a government official who had charge of the examination of hulls, superstructure, cargo stowage, etc. A *boiler inspector* inspected steam boilers and machinery.

steamboat landing

A place where a steamboat came to shore to discharge and take on freight and passengers.

steamboat line

A fleet of steamboats operating over a particular route under one management.

STEAMBOATMEN

See cub engineer, cub pilot, deckhand, lightning pilot, mud clerk, partner, roustabout, steersman, striker pilot, texas tender, trip pilot.

steamboat runner

A solicitor for a steamboat line.

STEAMBOATS AND EQUIPMENT

See ash well, barricade, bell cord, bell pulls, bell stand, bitts, boat horn, boat ways, boiler deck, boiler feed pump, bucket, bull rails, cabin, capstan, carling, cavel, codwad, coon pen, deadman, doctor, dollar hole, dolly, donkey, fantail, firebox, fire canoe, floating coffin, floating palace, flue, forecastle, freedmen's bureau, gangplank, gangway, gauge stick, go-devil, guardrail, guards, hog chains, horse wood, hurricane deck, lead line, lightwood, mud drum, nigger, nosing, packet, paddle board, paddle box, paddle wheel, pantry, pilot house, pitman, plunder, pool boat, port, roof, rudder, rudderstock, scupper, side-wheeler, siphon, skylight roof, skylights, snag chamber, spaghetti, spar, stacks, stage, stanchion, steamboat, stern rake, stern-wheeler, stroke, texas, tiller line, timberhead, torch basket, transom, upper deck, verge staff, wheelhouse.

steam nigger

A power-propelled lever used to adjust logs on a sawmill carriage.

steel

A cowboy's name for spurs.

steel gang

A track-laying crew on a logging railroad.

steeple fork

An earmark made by cutting two splits into the ear from the end, back one-third or halfway toward the head, and cutting out the middle piece, the splits being about 1 inch apart.

steer

A castrated male bovine animal.

steer busting

Roping and throwing a steer with a rope singlehandedly. The roper rides as close to the animal as possible before casting his loop. When it is settled around the horns or neck and has been given a jerk to hold it there, the slack of the rope is dropped just under the steer's right hipbone and around his buttocks. The rider then reins his horse to the left and braces himself for the shock that is sure to follow. When the slack is taken up, the steer is reversed in mid-air and slammed to the ground with a force that knocks the breath out of him. (John M. Hendrix, "Roping," *Cattleman*, Vol. XXII, No. 1 [June, 1935], 16–17.)

steer decorating

A variation of steer wrestling, most frequently seen in Canada, in which the contestant leaves his saddle, jumps to the steer's head, and instead of twisting him to the ground places a small ribbon around the steer's nose or over one of his horns. This event, the result of the Humane Society's complaints against steer wrestling, is recognized in Canada, but it is not held at R.C.A.-approved rodeos in the United States.

steer horse

A roping horse trained to take up the slack in the rope by facing away and pulling forward from the thrown animal.

steer roping

See *single steer tying*.

STEERS

See blackjack steer, bulling steer, cattle, lead steer, rough steer, steer.

steersman

In steamboating, an apprentice pilot, also called *cub pilot*.

steer wrestling

One of the five standard rodeo events; also called *bulldogging*. The contestant rides alongside a running steer, jumps from his saddle to the steer's head, stops it, and twists it to the ground with its head and all four feet pointing in the same direction.

stem

A name sometimes applied to a halter shank; also called *snap*.

step across

A cowboy's expression meaning *to mount a horse*.

sternline telegraph

The mysterious way news gets around among rivermen.

stern rake

In steamboating, that portion of the hull from the *dead flat* to the rear end; the after upward curve.

stern-wheeler

A cowboy's name for a pacing horse. In steamboating, a boat with the paddle wheel in the rear. It had two engines, but both were coupled to the same shaft by a crank at each end. The throttle wheel was in the center of the boat.

Stetson

A name the cowboy often gives his broad-brimmed hat whether or not it is a "genuwine" Stetson. The big Stetson hat is the earmark of the cow country. It is the first thing the tenderfoot buys when he goes west, but he never seems to wear it at just the right "jack-deuce angle over his off-eye." One cowman can tell what state another is from by the size and shape of his hat.

It is not altogether vanity that makes the cowboy pay a high price for his hat. He knows he has to have one of fine quality to stand the rough usage it receives. He may throw it on the floor and hang his spurs on a nail, for he knows a good hat can be tromped on without hurting it, while tromping on a spur does neither the tromper nor the spur any good.

The cowboy's hat has more different uses than any other garment he wears. Often his life depends upon a good hat, for the limber brim of a cheap hat might flop in his eyes at just the wrong time. When he is riding in the scorching sun, the wide brim is like the shade of a tree, and the high crown furnishes space to keep his head cool. The wide brim also shades his eyes so that he can see long distances without getting sun-blind when a lot depends upon his vision. When the sun is at his back, he tilts his Stetson for neck protection. In the rain it serves as an umbrella and makes a good shelter when he is trying to snatch a little daylight sleep.

The crown makes a handy water bucket if his horse cannot get to water, and the brim serves as his own drinking cup. He starts his campfire with his hat by using it as a bellows to fan a sickly blaze, and he can use it again as a water bucket to put out that same fire when he breaks camp. In the winter he pulls the brim down and ties it over his ears to avoid frostbite.

His hat is the first thing a cowhand puts on when he gets up and the last thing he takes off when he goes to bed. But during the day there are many times when he may have to jerk it off to use as a handy instrument. There are times when its sudden use saves a lot of hard work, a long ride, a nasty fall, or even sudden death. Perhaps he is penning a bunch of snaky critters when the wave of a big hat will turn a bunch quitter and save a long ride. It also comes in handy to turn a stampeding bronc from dangerous ground by fanning its head when reins would be useless. It is useful in splitting a bunch of horses in two when the cowboy is afoot in a horse corral.

Perhaps the cowboy is afoot in a branding pen when some old mother cow hears the bellow of her offspring as he is being branded. She comes on the run and on the prod. (Being afoot in a pen with a cow in this mood is, in the language of the cowhand, "more dangerous than kickin' a loaded polecat.") The big hat now comes in handy to throw into the cow's face when she gets too close, making her hesitate long enough to let the cowboy get to a fence.

A big hat in the hands of a bronc rider can be used like the balancing pole of a tightwire walker. If the rider loses his hat, he loses a lot of his balancing power.

Most riders decorate their hats with bands, both as ornaments and for the purpose of adjusting the fit to the head. What they use is mostly a matter of personal taste. Some like leather bands studded with silver conchas, some use strings of Indian beads, and others are satisfied with bands of rattlesnake skin or woven horsehair. Whatever is used will likely serve as a storage place to keep the wearer's matches dry. See also *John B.*

stew
What the miner calls nitroglycerin.

stew ball
A corruption of *skewbald, q.v.*

stew builder
A logger's name for the camp cook; also called *stew bum.*

stick
A logger's name for a pole.

stick ears
A cowboy's name for earmarked cattle.

stick horse
A cowboy's name for a horse that has to be forced to work.

stickin' like a postage stamp
Making a good ride on a bucking horse.

sticks his bill in the ground
An expression describing a horse that lowers his head between his forelegs as he starts bucking.

sticky rope
A cowboy's name for a rustler, whose rope had a habit of "stickin' to other folks' cows."

stiff
A westerner's word for a corpse; later used in a contemptuous way to suggest worthlessness or "dead ones." (Robert W. Wright, *Dodge City, the Cowboy Capital* [Wichita, Kansas, 1913], 167.)

A logger's name for a white-collar worker.

stiff man
In early days, a man who, with wagon and team and a barrel or two of oil or gasoline drove over the range disposing of carcasses by burning them. It was a job for a man who had lost his sense of smell.

stiff rope and a short drop
A cowboy's expression for a hanging.

still lot
A cowman's name for a cemetery.

stinger
A logger's name for that part of a logging truck which extends behind the trailer's wheels.

stingy gun
A cowboy's term for a derringer or bulldog pistol of light weight.

stinkers
A cowboy's name for sheep.

stirrup leathers
The broad leathers that hang from the bar of the tree of the saddle and from which the stirrups hang.

stirrups
Foot supports for the saddle, usually made of wood bound with iron, brass, or rawhide, but sometimes made entirely of iron or brass. There is nothing the cowboy fears more than having a foot caught in a stirrup and being dragged to death by a horse.

STIRRUPS AND EQUIPMENT
See ación, bulldogs, doghouse stirrups, drop stirrup, eagle bill, fenders, hobbled stirrups, leg jockey, monkey nose, open stirrups, oxbows, rosadero, stirrup leathers, stirrups, tapadera.

stock buyers

In stagecoaching, men hired to buy horses and mules for the stage lines. They selected only the best stock and insisted that they be well cared for. Also, men hired to buy cattle for packers or other buyers.

stock contractor

In rodeo, a person or outfit who provides stock for the events. Normally the stock contractor furnishes the saddle broncs and bareback horses, the bulls used in bull riding, the roping calves and steers, and the bulldogging steers. Some of the larger contractors carry a few roping and dogging horses in their strings, as well as the horses to be used by the judges and some extra horses for use in the grand entry. In some cases the stock contractor also acts as the producer, or arena director.

stock detective

A man, usually employed by a cattle association, engaged in trying to catch cattle thieves and brand burners.

stockers

Cattle acquired to build up a new herd on a previously unoccupied range.

stock horse

A brood mare with colt.

stocking

White color on a horse's leg that extends above the fetlock.

stock inspector

A man placed at shipping points and markets to see that the cattle being handled had the proper brands.

stock run

A train of cattle on the way to market.

stock tenders

In stagecoaching, a man employed at a stage station to attend the needs of the horses, to keep them fed and groomed, and to assist in making the change of horses when the stage arrived. To him every stage driver was a hero, and his greatest ambition was to please his superiors by keeping the animals in excellent condition. He drew a salary of 40 to 50 dollars a month. The life of a tender employed at the swing station was lonely indeed. His only entertainment was reading old magazines and papers.

stock train

A train of railway cars loaded with cattle.

stogies

A cowboy's name for cheap, hand-me-down boots.

stomach pump

A spade bit, so called because of the piece of flat steel with a slight curve that goes into the horse's mouth.

stomach robber

A logger's name for the camp cook.

stomp

A cowboy dance. Most of the boys were timid until the dance warmed up. Cochise Jones once said: "They've run in a straight steer herd so long they're shy as a green bronc to a new waterin' trough. Some of 'em dance like a bear 'round a beehive that's afraid of gettin' stung; others don't seem to know how to handle calico and get as rough as they do handlin' cattle in a brandin' pen. The women would jes' as soon dance with a grizzly as one of them kind, but most peelers go more or less loco when a female's around."

stone Johnny

A monument of piled rocks, usually erected by a sheepherder.

stone on his chest

What the miner calls tuberculosis, the disease he most dreads.

stood up

A cowboy's expression for being robbed.

stook

See *shock*.

stool-and-bucket cow

A cowboy's name for a gentle milch cow.

stool pigeon

Originally, a pigeon used to decoy other birds into a trap. A few years before the turn of the nineteenth century the expression came into general use among American gamblers to designate a capper or hustler for a faro bank, and is still so used. An early mention of the word in this connection may be found in the *New York Herald* of July 31, 1835. The use of *stool pigeon* as a synonym for police spy is apparently of comparatively recent origin; as late as the middle 1880's such an informer was known to the underworld simply as a *pigeon.*

stope
In mining, a working above or below a level where the mass of ore is broken.

stoping
In mining, breaking the ore above or below a level; when done from the back of the drift it is called *overhand* or *back stoping*; when done from the sole it is called *underneath stoping.*

stoping machine
In mining, a machine used to drill holes for blasting.

stopperboards
In mining, boards used to close a chute.

STOREKEEPERS
See Commissary Jimmy, factor.

STORES
See grab, robbersary, simp trap, van, wannigan.

STORIES
See tall tales, tear squeezer.

storming the puncheons
What the cowboy sometimes calls dancing.

straddlin' down the road
A cowboy's description of a bowlegged man walking in high-heeled boots.

straight as a wagon tongue
A cowboy's expression for a trustworthy person.

straight bit
A bit made of a straight piece of metal.

straight buck
A type of bucking in which the horse makes straight jumps, without any twists or turns. See *bucking straight away.*

straight-colored horse
A horse with a solid color, such as a bay, black, brown, white, or sorrel. The cowman prefers solid colors in his horses and has little use for the pinto, appaloosa, etc.

straight steer herd
A herd composed entirely of steers.

strainer
A strip of galvanized iron placed over the middle of the saddletree to cover the open space between the saddle boards. Upon this is laid a piece of soft, thick leather fashioned to the form of the rider.

STRANGERS
See swamp angel.

stranglers
An early-day name for the vigilantes.

strangulation jig
A cowboy's term for a hanging. A man being hanged had his hands tied behind him, but his feet were usually free and kicked about in his death struggle; hence the name.

strapped on his horse, toes down
A cowboy's expression for someone who had been killed. During range wars many men were sent home in this manner. A loose horse would usually go home of his own accord, and when he carried such a gruesome burden, it served as a warning to the faction opposing the killers.

STRAPS
See buffalo tug, ropes, packsaddles and equipment, saddles and equipment, trunk strap, tug, whang, whang leather, whang strings.

stratum
In mining, a bed or layer of rock or earth.

strawberries
A logger's name for beans.

straw boss
A cowboy's title for the foreman under the general superintendent of a ranch.

straw bottom

See *hay bottom*.

straw line

In logging, a light line strung from head spar to tail spar, which pulls the transfer line, which in turn pulls the 2-inch steel cable skyline into position.

straw shed

A winter shelter for cattle made of posts and covered with straw.

stray man

See *rep*.

strays

A term applied to cattle visiting from other ranges; horses from other ranges are called *stray horses*, not merely *strays*.

stretch

A trader's word meaning *dead*; prone.

stretch hemp

A cowboy's expression meaning *to hang*.

stretchin' out

A method of roping an animal in which one cowhand ropes him by the forefeet while another ropes him by the hind feet, thus stretching the brute. A freighter's and trader's expression for starting a caravan of wagons moving over the trail.

stretchin' the blanket

A cowboy's expression for a windy or tall tale; lying.

Stretch out!

In freighting, a command from the wagon master to the teamsters to start their wagons.

strike

A trapper's term for a boisterous or strong man. In mining, the extension of a lode or deposit on a horizontal line. A valuable discovery. To find a vein of ore.

strike a lead

In mining, to come upon or discover a lead, lode, or vein, as of ore.

strike it rich

In mining, to find precious ore in abundance.

striker pilot

In steamboating, an apprentice pilot. An apprentice engineer is called a *striker*.

string

A cowboy's term for his rope. A rider's term for his mount of horses. The cowboy's string of horses is carefully made up of the different kinds necessary for his work: circle horses, cutting horses, roping horses, a night horse, and one or two broncs so that they may be learning cow work. Once a string has been turned over to the cowboy, it is the same as his own as long as he stays with the ranch; and no one, not even the boss, can ride one of his horses without his permission.

Each man is responsible for the condition of his own string, and while the boss never interferes with these horses, he had better not see them abused. A string is never split. If the rider quits or gets fired, the horses in his string are not used until he comes back or another rider takes his place. A rider taking a new job has a string of horses pointed out to him by the boss. He receives no information concerning them. Information is frequently taken as an offense, for it implies a lack of confidence in the rider's ability. When the boss takes a horse from a rider's string, this action tells the rider more strongly than words that the boss wants him to quit.

In logging, a section of logs fastened together to be floated down a river. In forming a string, care was taken not to put logs of the same length side by side but to break the joints and so make the string as strong as possible, to keep it from tearing apart as it went around bends in the river. In mining, a fuse.

string bet

In gambling, a type of bet in which the checks are "strung" along from one card to several others, usually consecutively, as from the deuce to the king. See *heel a string*.

stringing a greener

A cowboy's expression for playing tricks on a tenderfoot. There are many such tricks, and they constitute a favorite sport of the cow country.

stringing along
In gambling, betting all odd- or even-numbered cards to play one way.

stringing a whizzer
A cowboy's expression for telling a tall tale; also called *whizzing*.

stringing 'em out
In cattle driving, starting cattle moving onto the trail from the bed ground.

string of flats
A logger's name for a line of flatcars. Also, what he calls griddle cakes.

string up
A cowboy's expression meaning *to hang*.

strip
In logging, an area of land assigned to each individual working in timber.

stripper
A heifer; a cow without milk. A skinner of buffaloes or dead cattle.

strippers
In gambling, cards trimmed for dishonest dealing; see *humps*.

stroke
In steamboating, the stroke of an engine, the distance traveled by the crosshead of the piston in making a complete revolution of the wheel—equal to twice the length of the crank on the water-wheel shaft. Thus if the crank was 3 feet long, the stroke would be 6 feet. The lineal distance the piston traveled in a cylinder during half a revolution of a steamboat's paddle wheel.

stronger than (the) nuts
In gambling, a very crooked gambling game; literally, a game that shows a higher percentage for the operator than the shell game (the *nuts*); automatically true of all faro games today.

strong water
An Indian's term for whisky sold by traders.

struggle
A logger's name for a dance.

strychnine
What the miner calls whisky.

stub
A logger's name for a standing section of a tree broken off at a height of less than 20 feet from which the leaves and most of the branches have fallen.

stubble jumper
A cowboy's name for a sheep. A miner's name for a recruit from the farm.

stub-horn
A cowboy's name for an old bull whose horns are chipped and broken from many fights. He spends much of his time rubbing these horns on rocks and trees attempting to sharpen them for the next battle. Also, a man who has been scarred by many battles.

stuck
A word for a gambler who has gone broke trying to *call the turn*, or beat the faro bank.

stud bunch
A herd of mares and colts, averaging about twenty head, which a stallion holds in one bunch.

stuff
A cowman's general term for range stock, which may include yearlings, bulls, steers, weaners, cows with calves, and dry cows.

stull
In mining, a timber inclined or wedged at an incline between the hanging wall and the foot wall of a vein. A cross timber at the foot of a stope.

stumpage
In logging, the value of timber as it stands uncut in the woods. In a general sense, the standing timber itself.

stump detective
A logger's title for a man who measures or estimates the waste in stumps and tops of trees.

stump rancher

A small farmer in a wooded section.

stump shot

A logger's term for splinters that pull out in a stump and the butt end of a tree when the tree is felled.

stump sucker

A cowboy's term for a horse having the vice of biting or getting his teeth against something and "sucking wind."

STUPID

See boss-simple, feather-headed, full-grown in body only, hame-headed, his thinker is puny, job-simple, off his mental reservation, ought to be bored for the hollow horn, ought to be playing with a string of spools, yack.

SUCCESS

See breaking the medicine, get the bacon.

sudadero

A cowman's term for the leather lining of a saddle skirt; from the Spanish, meaning *handkerchief* or *sweat cloth*. The term is sometimes incorrectly applied to the *rosadero, q.v.*

sugan

A cowboy's and logger's term for a blanket for bedding, a heavy comforter often made from patches of pants, coats, or overcoats. A sugan usually weighs about 4 pounds—as the cowboy says, "a pound for each corner." Also called *soogan, soogin, suggan,* and *sougan.*

In her book *No Life for a Lady*, Agnes Morley Cleaveland tells a good story about sugans:

"It was a popular joke with us to tell some tenderfoot that we were sorry, but we had to confess that all our beds had soogins in them, and then watch the look of apprehension settle in the visitor's eye.

"One visitor put a certain cowboy properly in his place—an especially ignorant cowboy, I confess, but not too rare a specimen. The cowboy laughed uproariously at the visitor's unconcealed distaste for sleeping in a bed infested with soogins.

" 'You should laugh,' retorted the visitor, 'I happen to know that you slumber in bed.'

"The cowboy turned purple. 'No man can say that about me and get away with it!' he roared.

"Fortunately he had no gun. We rescued the visitor." Agnes Morley Cleaveland, *No Life for a Lady* [Boston, Houghton Mifflin & Company, 1941], 166.)

sugar eater

A cowboy's name for a pampered horse.

suicide gun

A .32-caliber gun, which the gunman thought lacked power. It was said that "when two men get into a smoking argument, the one with the .44 always kills his man, while the one with the .32 merely gives his man a skin complaint."

suicide horse

A cowboy's term for a blind bucker, a horse that goes insane from fear when ridden and is more dangerous to himself than to the rider, since he is likely to kill himself by bucking into or over obstacles.

suitcase rancher

A nonresident ranch owner who makes occasional visits to his ranch.

SUITCASES

See traveling bags.

SULK

See sull.

sulker

In rodeo, an unpredictable bronc. A contestant is indeed unlucky who draws a horse of this type. Such a horse will not leave the chute until he is good and ready. He will squat back on his haunches, bunching himself, after the chute gate is opened. No amount of coaxing will make him come out until he is ready to do so of his own accord. Suddenly he will leave with a mighty leap that causes most riders to break their balance across the cantle board of the saddle. Very seldom is the rider able to regain his seat and get with his mount. Another cowboy bites the dust, and the crowd gets a good laugh. (Bruce Clinton, "Buckin' Horses," *Western Horseman*, Vol. III, No. 3 [May-June, 1938], 28.)

sull

A cowboy's word meaning to sulk; generally applied to a cow or a horse that merely becomes sulky and refuses to move instead of offering resistance.

sulphide

In mining, the chemical union of sulphur with a metal.

summer name

A westerner's term for an alias. When a man chose to give a name rather than his true one, the West followed a strict code of showing no curiosity about his past. The nearest approach to curiosity would be to ask him facetiously, "What is your summer name?"

sump

In mining, a reservoir dug at the bottom of each shaft, below the bottom level, into which water from the shaft was run.

sunburst

See *sunset rowel*.

Sunday-go-to-meetin' clothes

What the cowboy calls his very best raiment.

Sunday horse

A horse with an easy gait, usually a single-footer with some style and one the cowboy saves to ride upon special occasions. He is generally a fancy, high-stepping, all-around saddler, but, as Whitey Blyth used to say, "He ain't worth a damn—only to ride down the road."

Sunday school

What the early-day logger called a poker game, because it was played on Sunday owing to the fact that the men worked all the other days of the week.

sundowner

A name for a man traveling west to avoid the sheriff.

sunfish

A bucking term used to describe the movements of a horse that twists his body in a crescent, alternately to the right and to the left, seeming to try to touch the ground with first one shoulder and then the other, letting the sunlight hit his belly.

sunfisher

A horse that sunfishes; see *sunfish*.

sun grinner

A cowboy's name for a Mexican.

sunned his moccasins

An expression for someone who has been thrown from a horse, especially when he landed with his feet in the air.

sun-specked jay

A cowboy's name for a rural resident.

sunset rowel

A spur wheel with many points set close together; also called *sunburst*.

sunshine rider

See *shadow rider*.

Supaway John.

An expression an early-day Indian used in asking for food when he came to a cow camp.

super

A logger's name for the superintendent.

supreme being

A logger's name for the superintendent.

surcingle

A belly band, or girth that passes under a horse's belly.

sure-thing bet

In faro, a type of bet that the sucker believes he cannot lose; the term is much used in connection with the "last turn." It is regarded by other faro players as a sucker term but is also used freely by other types of gamblers.

surface coal

A cowman's name for dried cow chips used for fuel; also called *surface fuel*.

surface fire

In logging, a fire that runs over the forest floor and burns only the surface litter, the loose debris, and the smaller vegetation.

surly

A cowboy's name for a bull.

swag

A cowboy's word variously used to mean *quantity, load, low place,* and *coulee.*

swallow-and-get-out trough

A cowboy's term for a hurry-up eating place. There is a story in the West that runs something like this: When a passenger train stopped at an eating station, an eastern lady rushed from it to one of those swallow-and-get-out troughs. The conductor notified the passengers that they had only about five minutes to eat because the train was late. So the lady just ordered a cup of coffee. When she got it, black and boiling hot, she remarked that she doubted if she could drink it in time to catch her train. A cowboy sitting next to her wanted to show her her true western hospitality, and so he shoved her his cup and said, "Here's one, lady, that's already saucered and blowed."

swallow dust

In cattle driving, to ride in the drag of a moving herd. See *drag ride.*

swallow-fork

An earmark made by hollowing the ear lengthwise, beginning halfway back, and cutting at a 45-degree angle toward the end. The result is a forked notch in the ear.

swallow-forkin'

A cowboy's expression for putting on airs or for dressing in one's best.

swallows his head

An expression describing a horse that bucks high and produces a decided curve in his back, with his head between his front feet and his tail between his hind ones.

swallowtail

An earmark made by trimming the tip of the ear into the shape of a bird's flaring tail.

swamp

A logger's term for clearing the ground of underbrush, fallen trees, and other obstructions preparatory to constructing a logging road, a landing, or a skid trail, or before felling and bucking.

swamp angel

What the cowboy calls a man from Loui-siana or Arkansas. What the logger calls a man who works in the swamps and also a stranger who comes to the lumber camp.

swamper

A cowboy's word for a cook's helper, for a janitor in a saloon, and also for a man who handles the brakes and helps the driver of a jerk-line string. A logger's word for a man who cuts roadways and also for one who lobs limbs from felled trees; these men have lowly jobs and receive the lowest pay. The word is also used to refer to a porter or a cleaner. A miner's word for the helper on an ore train and also for a man who cleans out the ore cars.

swamp gaboon

A logger's imaginary animal to which snowshoe tracks are attributed.

swamp seed

A cowboy's name for rice.

swap lead

To exchange shots in a gun battle.

swapping ends

An expression for a bucking movement peculiar to a bronc in which he quickly reverses his position, making a complete half-circle in the air.

sweat

A cowboy's term for working for one's board without other pay.

sweat board

In mining, a hand-and-shovel concrete mixer.

sweater

A word for someone sitting and watching a card game or for someone out of a job and hunting work.

sweating a game

An expression for sitting and watching a card game.

sweating a steer

In rodeo, tiring a particularly vicious steer by pulling the flank strap tight so that he will fret himself down and be easier to ride. It is a form of cheating.

Swede

A sawmill machine with rollers that catch the ends of the boards as they go by and send them on to another table.

Swede fiddle

On the middle northern range, a cowboy's name for an accordion. A logger's name for a crosscut saw.

Swedish condition powder

A logger's name for snoose, or snuff.

sweep

A logger's term for a gradual bend in a log, pole, or piling, considered a defect.

sweeten the pot

In gambling, to add chips to an unopened pot. See *fatten the kitty*.

swell-butted

A logger's expression for a tree greatly enlarged at the base.

swell fork

A saddle with leather swells, or projections, on each side of the fork below the horn. When riding a pitching horse, the rider can hook his knees under these projections to help him stay in the saddle.

swift wagon

An Indian's name for the stagecoach because of its speed in traveling.

swimming horse

A horse, selected because of his ability to swim, used in crossing rivers. Not all horses are good or steady swimmers, and during the trail days, when there were many rivers to cross, much depended upon a good swimming horse.

swimming the herd

In cattle driving, herding the cattle across water. If the river to be crossed was at medium stage and calm, there was usually no trouble in getting the leaders to take the water; but if the river was high and turbulent, much vigorous urging was required. Sometimes one or two cowboys would swim ahead on their horses to show the cattle that there was no danger. Occasionally the horse herd would cross to open the way. If the cattle reached swimming depth, they usually went ahead to the other side, unless some floating log or untoward event caused them to start milling in midstream.

There were instances where the lead cattle refused under all urging to take to the water of a swollen river, and several days elapsed before a crossing could be made.

swimming water

In cattle driving, water too deep to cross without swimming.

swindle stick

A logger's name for the scaler's rule.

swing

In logging, a donkey engine that relays logs from the woods to the loading points.

swing a wide loop

A cowboy's term meaning *to steal cattle* and also *to live a free life*.

swingdingle

A logging sled.

swing donkey

In logging, a donkey engine used to supplement a yarder over a long haul; the engine that skylines logs.

swinging brand

A cattle brand suspended from and connected to a quarter-circle.

swing kicker

In cattle driving, one of two horsemen, one on each side, behind the point men, whose job was to swing the main body of a driven herd.

swing line

A logger's name for the cable that guides a loading boom.

swing rider

One of the riders with a trail herd, riding about one-third of the way back from the point riders.

swing station

In stagecoaching, a relay station. Usually it was a one-story square log or adobe building with small windows; the roof was supported by rough framework. Usually the stock tender lived here alone, although at a few stations there were two men to furnish relays of horses to the incoming coaches. There was a large barn accommodating 30 to 50 horses. Since the fast horses of the coach lines were coveted by the Indians, the station was surrounded by a wall of turf 2 feet thick and pierced with loopholes for defense against attack. The barn was usually connected to the station by a similar turf wall. Such stations were usually placed about 12½ miles apart, and two or three were placed between one *home station (q.v.)* and the next.

swing team

In a six-horse team, the horses in the middle, or between the leaders and the wheelers.

switch

In gambling, to cut a deck of cards so as to replace it in its original order.

switch-tail

See *wring-tail.*

swivel dude

A cowboy's name for a gaudy fellow. Silk Kutner once said of one, "He's so pretty I feel like takin' off my hat ever' time I meet 'im."

T

"There ain't no hoss that can't be rode,
There ain't no man that can't be throwed"

tab

In faro, a printed score sheet on which players can record the behavior of various cards as they win or lose throughout the game; the case keeper records only one deal at a time. Marking this score sheet is called *keeping tabs.*

table stakes

In gambling, a limit placed on the betting before the game.

tack-berry buckle

A cinch buckle carrying two wraps of the latigo and hooking into the cinch ring.

tail crew

In logging, the men who anchor the *baloney (q.v.)* on the opposite end of the donkey.

tail down

In logging, to roll logs down a skidway.

tail end

In mining, the *tailings, q.v.*

tailing

Throwing an animal by the tail in lieu of a rope. When he is traveling rapidly, any animal can be sent heels over head by seizing his tail and giving it a pull to one side. This method was resorted to frequently with a wild longhorn, and a thorough tailing usually knocked the breath from him and so dazed him that he would behave for the rest of the day. The act requires both a quick and swift horse and a daring rider. (J. Frank Dobie, *Vaquero of the Brush Country* [Dallas, Southwest Press, 1929], 15.)

tailings

A cowboy's name for stragglers in a herd. In mining, those portions of washed ore that are regarded as too poor to be treated further. The term is used especially for the debris from stamp mills or other ore-dressing machinery, as distinguished from material that is to be smelted. Also called *tails.*

tailing up

Lifting weak cattle to their feet by their

tails. This method is used primarily after cattle are extricated from bog holes, or when they are too weak in winter to get to their feet.

tail off

In a sawmill, to receive lumber at the end of a processing machine. The *feeder* feeds the lumber to the machine, while the worker on the other end *tails off*, removing the lumber from the table onto a flat.

tail out

A cowboy's expression meaning *to depart* or *decamp*.

tail over the dashboard

A cowboy's description of someone in high spirits.

tail over the lines

A cowboy's description of someone hard to control.

tail pulling

A cowboy's expression for altering a horse's tail. The southern cowman lets the tails of his horses grow, perhaps to allow them to protect themselves from flies and insects, which are worse on southern ranges, or perhaps merely to follow a tradition. But on northern ranges since early days, it has been the custom to make some changes in the horse's tail. It became a practice at the end of the season to cut the tail off close to the bone. By doing this, the riders could distinguish them from the wild ones when they rode out the following spring to round up the saddle horses. With the aid of field glasses they could see the horses at a great distance, and if the bunch they spied wore long tails, they knew the horses were not the ones they were looking for and consequently were saved a long ride.

But cutting the tail made it grow out unnaturally heavy and bushy, giving it an ugly, misshapen appearance. To give the tail a lighter and dressier look, the cowhand began pulling or weeding out the hair. This improved the appearance so much that it became the fashion to pull rather than to cut the tail, and to this day a pulled tail is the sign that its possessor is a broken horse. To the northern cowboy, horses with long tails look like brood mares.

tail race

In mining, the channel in which *tailings* (*q.v.*), suspended in water, are conducted away.

tail rider

In cattle driving, one of the men at the rear of a herd on the drive; also called *drag rider, q.v.*

tail split

See *comet split*.

tail tree

In logging, a tree at the end of the run, to which the tackle is fastened in power skidding. Also, the number-two spar tree of a high-line installation.

tail water

In mining, the water in a *tail race, q.v.*

take a run

A cowboy's expression meaning *to run to a horse and mount him*.

take a squatter's right

To be thrown from a horse.

take a stick

A logger's expression meaning *to climb a pole*.

takeaway

What the logger calls the train that takes logs to the sawmill.

take five

A logger's expression meaning *to take five minutes*; to rest on the job long enough for a smoke.

take on

To put on flesh or fat; said of cattle.

take the big jump

A cowboy's expression meaning *to die*.

take the pins from under it

To throw an animal by roping it either by forefooting or by heeling.

take the slack out of his rope

A cowboy's expression for defeating someone or placing him at a disadvantage.

take to the tall timbers

To run away; to be on the dodge.

take to the tules

To run away; to be on the dodge. See *tule*.

take you to church

An expression used when a horse bucks violently and is doing his best to "make a Christian out of you."

TAKING A CHANCE

See grabbin' the brandin' iron by the hot end, playing a hand with his eyes shut.

taking leather

Grabbing the saddle while riding a bucking horse.

taking the bank

A freighter's expression for fording a stream and going up the opposite bank.

taking up a homestead

Thrown from a horse.

TALKING

See augurin' match, chew the cud, chin jaw, cow talk, coyotin' round the rim, diarrhea of the jawbone, flannelmouth, giggle talk, good comeback, hoof-and-mouth disease, leaky mouth, medicine tongue, more lip than a muley cow, mouthy, river talk, roll the guff, sagebrush philosopher, slack in the jaw, squaw talk, talking horse, talking load, talking talents, talk like a Texan, telling a windy, tongue oil, wagging his chin.

talking horse

Discussing horses, a favorite subject of conversation for a group of cowmen.

talking iron

A cowboy's name for his six gun.

talking load

A cowboy expression for being just drunk enough to be loquacious.

talking talents

A cowboy's term for the ability to talk freely.

talk like a Texan

To boast of one's work or accomplishments.

talk turkey

A westerner's expression meaning *to talk seriously*; to mean business.

tall

See *built high above his corns*.

tallier

In sheepshearing, a man who weighs the sacks of wool after shearing.

tallow

A cowman's word for *fat*; applied to both animals and humans; see *shore had tallow*.

tallow factory

An establishment in which cattle carcasses were cooked solely for the tallow they produced. Places of this sort were established in Texas after the Civil War, when cattle were plentiful and there were no markets for them.

TALL TALES

See build a high line, circular story, corral dust, peddler of loads, stretchin' the blanket, stringing a whizzer, telling a windy, Tie one to that! windies.

tally branding

Taking an inventory of cattle.

tally hand

See *tally man*.

tally man

A man appointed by the roundup captain to keep a record of the calves branded at the spring roundup. He was chosen for this position because of his honesty and clerical ability, and also sometimes because of his physical inability to do more strenuous work. He might be an older man, one recovering from an illness, or one hurt the previous day, but he was chosen primarily for his reputation for honesty. He had many opportunities to falsify his records, and upon his count depended an owner's estimate of the season's profits. Yet because of his own honesty and the ethics of the range, these things never entered his head. All the time calves were slithering to the fire, he chanted his tally, and as the number of unbranded calves grew smaller, the lines in his smudged and grimy book grew longer. At every lax moment he took the opportunity to sharpen a stub pencil, which was wearing down rapidly. Also called *tally hand*.

In logging, a man who makes a record of units being counted and measured.

tally sheet

The book or paper upon which the record was kept by the *tally man*, *q.v.*

tame ape

An early-day term for a logger.

tamping sticks

A packer's term for the sticks used in tamping hay into the corners of the aparejo.

tanglefoot

A word used by most outdoorsmen for whisky.

tank

A water reservoir made by damming a stream. An artificial water reservoir of wood, concrete, or metal. To cook cattle for their tallow.

Taos lightning

A trader's and trapper's term for a vile whisky made near Taos, New Mexico, in the early days; often shortened to *Taos* or *touse*.

tapadera

A wedge-shaped piece of leather covering the stirrup at the front and sides, but open at the rear. Made from heavy cowhide and occasionally reinforced by a wooden frame, it is used mostly in the brush country to protect the rider's feet and stirrups from brush. The word is usually shortened to *taps*. Also spelled *tapadero*. From the Spanish.

tapaojos

A blinder or eye cover for a horse or mule; a strip of leather about 3 inches wide, fastened to the headstall of the hackamore and long enough to extend across the brow of the animal. It is used on mean or unbroken horses being mounted for the first

time, and also on pack mules when they are being loaded, to keep them from getting excited. Americans do not use them extensively. (Harold W. Bentley, *Dictionary of Spanish Terms in English* [New York, Columbia University Press, 1932], 205.)

tapping the bank

In gambling, betting, by a gambler not connected with the house, an amount equaling the money backing the bank.

tarantula juice

A cowboy's name for whisky. In the words of Muley Metcalf, a few drinks of some of it would "have a man reelin' 'round like a pup tryin' to find a soft spot to lie down in," or, as another said, "knockin' 'round like a blind dog in a meat shop."

tar baby

In mining, a man who lubricates hoisting cables.

tarp

Short for *tarpaulin*, the early westerner's name for any canvas other than *pack covers* or *wagon sheets*. It usually referred to the piece of canvas in which he rolled his bed when not in use and with which he covered himself at night.

tarrabee

A hand-carved wooden machine used in spinning the threads for girths. Patterns vary, but all tarrabees work on the same principle. All have a hollow toward one end, and near this end a handle is inset to extend at right angles. The wood of a much-used twisting paddle takes on the appearance of satinwood; contact with oily hair and sweating hands give it a rich brown polish. (Brooks Taylor, "Girt Making," *Cattleman*, Vol. XXVII, No. 9 [February, 1941], 73–74.)

tasters

The little copper rollers in a spade bit. They have a taste that is pleasing to the horse and thus help him take the bit better.

tasting gravel

Thrown from a horse.

teakettle outfit

A logger's name for a small sawmill crew.

team roping

In rodeo, a recognized event for which a world's champion team is named, though it is not one of the five standard events. It is worked by two ropers, one roping the head of the steer and the other the hind legs, and is done in two ways, by team tying and by dally team roping. Also called *tied team roping.*

tear squeezer

What the cowboy calls anything sad, particularly a sad story.

techy as a teased snake

A cowboy's description of someone in a bad humor or of someone easy to anger.

teeth

See *nutcrackers.*

teeth in the saddle

A cowboy's description for a saddle that causes a horse a sore back. More riders lost their jobs over back-eating saddles than any other one thing. Some of the early-day saddles, as one cowboy said, "could eat out of a wire corral in one night."

teguas

Lightweight, comfortable rawhide moccasins, ankle-high, laced in front and undecorated; worn principally by Mexicans and Indians. Probably named for the Tegua Indians.

telegraph him home

A cowboy's expression for hanging a man in which the victim's own rope was used and a pole was borrowed from Western Union.

telephone

See *maw bell.*

tell box

In faro, one type of dealer's box with an intricate and effective internal mechanism that enabled the dealer not only to "tell" the location of the cards but also to manipulate the cards in order to deal seconds, etc.

telling a windy

A cowboy's expression for telling a tall tale or telling a lie.

telling off the riders

Giving directions to each rider about where to start his drive for the roundup; the job of the roundup captain. See *scattering the riders.*

telltale

In mining, a warning signal device.

ten-day miner

An itinerant miner; one who does not stay long at any one place.

tender

A cowboy's word for a horse that shows signs of getting saddle sores or sore feet.

TENDERFEET

See blanc-bec, early boughten, flat-heeled puncher, greenhorn, green pea, gunsel, Johnny-come-lately, juniper, lent, mail-order catalog on foot, mail-order cowboy, mangeur de lard, Monkey-Ward cowboy, new ground, pilgrim, punk, shorthorn, skim-milk cowboy, Some deck is shy a joker! tenderfoot.

tenderfoot

Originally, a cowman's name for an imported cow. Later, his name for a human being new to the country; both also called *pilgrim.*

tender-mouth

A horse that is very sensitive to the bit.

tenting

In sheep raising, placing young lambs and their mothers in tents during a cold spell in late spring after lambing.

tepee

Originally, a conical-shaped tent made of buffalo hides supported by poles and used by the Plains Indians. Later a cowman's word for his home.

tepee pole

One of several small poles skinned and used as supports for a teepee.

tequila

A liquor distilled from the juice of the maguey plant; named for Tequila, Mexico, where it was first made.

terrapin

A trapper's word for dog meat. A cowboy's word for a saddle. Also, a cowboy's word meaning *to travel slowly on foot*.

TEXANS

See beef head, rawhider.

texas

On western-river steamboats, a long, narrow cabin usually located on top of the skylight roof and surmounted by the pilothouse. The texas served as the quarters for the crew; the forward end was reserved for the captain, the middle section was assigned to the officers, and the rear end housed the Negro crewmen. The large, well-furnished captain's cabin served as office, living room, and, occasionally, dining room.

Texas butter

A cowboy's name for gravy made by adding some flour to grease in which steak has been fried, letting it bubble and brown, and then adding hot water and stirring until it thickens.

Texas cakewalk

A cowboy's name for a hanging.

Texas fever

See *Spanish fever*.

Texas gate

A makeshift gate made of barbed wire fastened to a pole.

Texas Panhandle

See *down in the skillet*.

Texas saddle

A heavy stock saddle usually having a high cantle, a high knobbed pommel, and two cinches.

Texas skirt

The square skirt used on Texas saddles.

texas tender

In steamboating, the man who cleaned and took care of the *texas, q.v.*

Texas tie

In roping, a method in which the roper keeps the home end of his rope tied hard to his saddle horn; so called because most Texans use this method.

Texas tree

The tree of a *Texas saddle, q.v.*

There goes horse and beaver!

An expression used by mountain men when they sustained a severe loss of any kind.

There's a one-eyed man in the game.

A warning. One of the most common superstitions in the early West was that bad luck would forever follow a man who played poker with a one-eyed gambler. This expression later came to mean, *Look out for a cheat*.

they

What the logger calls social workers.

THIEVES

See lépero, pack rat.

thimblerig

A swindle game of the early West, which later became known as the *shell-game*. The thimblerigger used a dried pea or a little rubber ball and three cup-shaped receptacles. Originally he favored three thimbles; hence the name. But in later years English-walnut shells or metal caps were used. The player was supposed to bet under which shell or cup the pea was resting after the rigger has moved them about a bit. The chances were that it was between two of the rigger's fingers. Soapy Smith became adept at this game.

thimblerigger

A *thimblerig (q.v.)* operator.

thin

See *snake on stilts*.

thinning

A logger's term for a cutting made in an immature stand for the purpose of increasing the rate of growth, improving the form or quality of the trees that remain, and increasing the total production of the stand.

third loader

In logging, the least-experienced member of a log-loading crew; it is his job to use the branding ax to stamp the ends of every log with the company ownership brand.

third rigger

In logging, the man in charge of preparing a secondary tail spar, the one that will next hold the sky line.

thirsty

See *dry*.

thirty years' gathering

What the cowboy calls his trinkets and plunder gathered through the years. In *No Life for a Lady* Agnes Morley Cleaveland tells a story of a cowboy on his way to a local roundup who stopped at her ranch for a meal. While he was eating, something stampeded his string of horses, and with them went the pack horse carrying his bedroll. The man leaped from his chair, shouting, "There goes the savin's of a lifetime!"

thorough braces

In stagecoaching, two straps of thick steer hide that suspended the heavy stagecoach body, allowing it to rock back and forth, and also served as shock absorbers for the horses. The thorough braces were fastened to C-shaped braces on both front and rear axles and absorbed far more shock than rigid springs.

The thorough braces made it possible for the heavily loaded stagecoaches to travel rapidly through rough country with reasonable comfort for the travelers and without killing the horses. They cushioned violent jerks on the traces caused by holes or obstructions in the road and eased the strain of the load on the team.

three-card monte

A Mexican game, with no similarity to monte. The operator of the game, known as the *thrower*, took three playing cards, called *rickets*, bent them slightly lengthwise for easier handling, and showed one of them to the players. Then he made a few hocus-pocus passes, threw the cards face downward upon the table, and invited the victims to guess which one they had seen. Rarely were these games honest. The sharp usually worked with one or two confederates, who would try the game once or twice and win or who supposedly aided the victim by ensuring where the particular card would be.

three-legged riding

A westerners expression for riding with a tight rein and sawing on the horse's mouth with the bit.

three-one

In faro, a system by which the player bets a given card to win after it has lost three times during the deal.

three-point

What the early trapper called his three-pound blanket, which was all the blanket he was allowed to carry.

three-quartering

A method of riding a bucking horse in which the rider grabs the reins or mane with his left hand and the horn of the saddle with his right. He puts his weight on his left knee against the horse's shoulder, and with his right spur hooked under the cinch, saddle skirt, or cantle, he lessens the jar and helps keep himself in the saddle.

three-quarter rig

A saddle with the cinch placed halfway between that of the center-fire and the rim-fire.

three-quarter seat

The leather seat covering of a saddle that extends only to the rear edge of the stirrup groove.

three saddles

A buster's term for three rides. The professional buster considers a horse broken after *three saddles*.

three-seven-seventy-seven (3-7-77)

These numbers, accompanied by skull and crossbones, were a warning issued by the early Montana vigilantes. They stood for *3 feet wide, 7 feet long, and 77 inches deep*, which pretty well described a grave. If the man so warned was wise, he lost no time leaving that part of the country.

three-up outfit

A small ranch that, as one cowboy said, "don't own 'nough beef to hold a barbecue."

three-up screw

A cowboy who worked on a small ranch where three horses were considered enough for a mount.

three walks

Part of the punishment the enlisted trapper received when he failed to answer the officer's "All's well!" He was fined 5 dollars and made to go on foot for three days— *three walks*.

throatlatch

The leather strap fastening the bridle under the horse's throat.

throat-tickling grub

A cowboy's name for the fancy food he never gets on the range.

through cattle

Cattle shipped or driven beyond local points to distant destinations.

through pouch

A pouch carried on a stagecoach to the final destination and not opened en route.

throw a long shadow

A cowboy's expression meaning *to be forceful*.

throw back

An expression for a bucking horse that hurls himself backward intentionally, the trick of a killer. To revert in type or character to an ancestral stock.

throw down

To cover someone with a gun; also, to shoot. The high hammer of the frontier six gun was not designed to be cocked by the thumb tip as are the hammers of modern double-action revolvers, but was to be cocked by hooking the whole thumb over it and simply closing the hand for the first shot. The recoil threw the gun muzzle up in the air, the thumb was hooked over the hammer, and the gun cocked itself by its own weight and level.

throw dust

A cowboy's expression meaning *to try to cover up* or *to deceive*.

throwed in his hand

A cowboy's expression for someone who quit or gave up. Originally, a gambler's expression for withdrawing from a game.

throw gravel in his boots

A cowboy's expression for shooting at someone's feet.

throw in

A cowboy's expression meaning *to go into partnership* or *to join in an enterprise*.

THROWING

See bedded, bust, California, colear, hogtie, tailing, take the pins from under it.

throwing the buckskin

A teamster's expression for using the whip.

throwing the game

In gambling, permitting a player to win by crooked dealing.

throwing over

A cowboy's expression for pushing stray cattle of outside brands toward their home range at the end of a roundup.

throwing the hitch

A packer's expression for making a diamond hitch.

throwing the pack

A packer's expression for a pack mule that starts bucking, loosening the pack rope and scattering the contents of the pack over the ground.

throwing the steel

A cowboy's expression for using the spurs freely.

throw lead

A cowboy's expression meaning *to shoot a gun*.

THROWN FROM A HORSE

See bite the dust, chase a cloud, chew gravel, dirtied his shirt, dumped, dusted, eatin' gravel, fartknocker, flung him away, forked end up, got busted, grassed him, grass hunting, Ketch my saddle! kissed the ground, landed, landed forked end up, landed on his sombrero, lost his hat and got off to look for it, lost his horse, met his shadow on the ground, pickin' daisies, piled, spilled, spread-eagle, sunned his moccasins, take a squatter's right, taking up a homestead, tasting gravel, turned the pack, went up to fork a cloud.

thrown tree

A trapper's term for a tree felled by beavers. Beavers would gnaw at cottonwood trees until they fell and then use them for food or to dam up the stream on which they were building a lodge. When the trapper saw a *thrown tree,* he knew that beavers were present.

throw one's leg

A cowboy's expression meaning *to be active and enterprising.*

throw out

In cattle driving, to stop a moving herd and leave the trail, as in, "*Throw out* the cattle and build camp."

throwout

A cowman's term for an animal cut from a herd. The word is also sometimes used for a dilapidated human being; I heard one cowman say of such a man, "He looks like a *throwout* from a footsore remuda."

throw smoke in his face

A cowboy's expression meaning *to shoot at someone.*

throw the lines away

A cowboy's expression meaning *to drive a team recklessly.*

thumb buster

A cowboy's name for the old-fashioned single-action six gun.

thumber

A man who removed the trigger and guard from his gun and shot by raising and releasing the hammer with his thumb. He did his shooting at close range and relied upon speed for his own safety.

thumbing

A cowboy's word for jabbing a horse with the thumbs to provoke bucking.

thumb whipping

A form of shooting similar to *slip shooting, q.v.* The gun is held in one hand and pointed at the target. The hammer is then worked rapidly with the thumb of the other hand by flipping it to full cock and then letting it slip from under the thumb.

thunder gust

What the early trader called a thunderstorm.

ticket

A logger's term for a doctor's certificate stating that the bearer is physically unable to work.

tick hole

In mining, a small unfilled cavity in a lode or the rock.

tickle fleece

An early trader's expression meaning *to scalp.*

Tie!

In packing, a signal from the off to the near packer that all slack has been rendered on the running rope. Also, a signal from the near to the off packer for the latter to secure the end of the rope on completion of the hitch.

tie cutter

See *tie man.*

Tied!

In packing, a signal from the near to the off packer, in slinging the load, that the square knot has been tied.

tied holster

A holster tied to the leg of the wearer to facilitate a quick draw; a good indication of a professional gunman. There was a saying in the old West that "the man who wears his holster tied down don't do much talking with his mouth."

tie-down man

A gunman who tied his holster to his leg.

tied reins

Bridle reins tied together at the ends.

tied team roping

See *team roping*.

tied to the ground

An expression for a horse whose rider has dropped the reins to the ground, knowing that the trained horse will be anchored just as surely as if he were actually tied.

tie-hard

A term the cowman frequently uses in speaking of a *tie man (q.v.)*, to distinguish him from a *dally man (q.v.)*.

tie judge

See *flagman*.

tie man

A roper who keeps the home end of his rope tied to the saddle horn. See *Texas tie*. In the early days, generally speaking, cowboys east of the Rockies *tied* and those west of the Rockies *dallied*. The tie man uses a shorter rope than the dally man, and the range he rides is open and level. He is usually an expert roper and has complete confidence in his ability to make a successful catch.

The Texan *ties* his rope, and when he ropes anything, he figures on hanging to it. The Californian keeps his rope untied, and when he ropes anything, he takes a *dally* around the saddle horn; then if his catch gets him into a jam, he can turn loose. The Texan does not say much about this practice, but the Californian knows what the Texan thinks, and he does not like those thoughts.

In logging, a man who cuts railroad ties; he is looked upon as the lowliest man in camp. Also called *tie cutter*, *tie peeler* and *tie whacker*. See *broadax brigade*. Also, a man who is no good for a real job at camp.

tie on

A cowboy's expression meaning *to rope*.

Tie one to that!

A phrase used by western storytellers at the conclusion of a wild tale, as if inviting the next man to tell a wilder one. The expression is now commonly used everywhere.

(W. S. Campbell [Stanley Vestal] to R.F.A.)

tie peeler

See *tie man*.

tie rope

A cowboy's term occasionally used for the *mecate*, q.v. Also, a short rope used for hog-tying.

tie whacker

A logger's name for a *tie man*, q.v. Also, the boob of the logging camp.

tiger

A cowboy's name for a convict; so called because he was caged and wore stripes. In gambling, a common name for faro. During the early 1830's a first-rate professional gambler carried his faro outfit in a fine mahogany box on which was painted a picture of a royal Bengal tiger. A representation of the animal was also carved on the ivory chips and painted on the oilcloth layout. The gamblers adopted the tiger as the presiding deity of the game, and faro soon became known throughout the country as the *tiger*. Many large gambling houses hung oil paintings of tigers above their faro tables.

tight-legging

Riding with the legs tightly gripping the sides of the horse, a manner of riding that disqualifies a rider under rodeo rules, since he is supposed to scratch his horse with the spurs throughout the ride.

tiller line

In steamboating, the wire line extending from the tillers to the drum of the pilot wheel which, when moved, caused the rudders to change position, steering the boat.

tillicums

A logger's word for acquaintances, friends, and relatives.

Tim-m-m-ber!

A logger's warning shout that timber is falling and that each man is to look out for himself; a traditional cry of danger.

timber beast

A logger.

timber belt

A belt or strip of timber.

timber break

In logging, logs that are broken in two when trees are felled across gullies, rocks, or stumps.

timber camp

A camp of men engaged in getting out timber.

timber cart

In logging, a high-wheeled cart for carrying lumber.

timber cattle

Cattle that range chiefly in timbered regions.

timber claim

A timbered area of public land secured upon condition that the claimant plant and cultivate a specific acreage of trees upon it.

timber cruise

In logging, a trip taken to seek out desirable tracts of timber.

timber cruiser

In logging, a man who seeks out desirable tracts of timber. A lumber estimator. Also called *tree looker*.

timber fall

In logging, an area where timber has been blown down by a storm; also called a *blow down* and *fallen timber*.

timber head

A logger.

timberhead

In steamboating, an upright post bolted inside a barge and extending about 1 foot above the gunwale, to which mooring lines were attached. On a lock wall such posts were called *mooring pins*. Modern steel barges have cast-steel *check posts* instead.

timber hunting

In logging, looking for desirable timber.

timber inspector

In logging, an official who inspects timber.

timberjack

A logger; a worker in the woods.

timber marking

In logging, selecting and indicating, usually by blaze or paintpot, trees to be cut or left standing; also called *spotting*.

timber pirate

In logging, a man who cuts and sells timber which is the property of another, or of the state or national government; also called *timber thief*.

timber raft

In logging, a raft of saw logs.

timber savage

A logger.

timber shanty

A shanty used by loggers engaged in timbering operations.

timber shoot

In logging, a chute down which logs are sent.

timber wheels

In logging, a pair of wheels, usually about 10 feet in diameter, used in transporting logs; also called *big wheels*, *katydid*, and *logging wheels*.

timber wolf

A gray wolf. A logger.

time

What most outdoor workingmen call wages.

TIME

See mañana, rodeo, rodeo events and stunts.

time judge

In rodeo, the timer of calf-roping and bulldogging contests. In the other events, his function corresponds to that of the referee of a prize fight.

timer

In rodeo, an official who times the contestants. There must be two or more timers who agree on the time of each contestant. The timers begin time when the contestant in a roping or steer-wrestling event comes out of the chute, or on the signal of the score-line judge. The timer also keeps time on the riding events and sounds a gun, buzzer, or whistle when the contestant has stayed aboard long enough to make a qualified ride.

tinaja

A trader's name for a water jar; from the Spanish.

tin-belly

A cowboy's name for a cheap, inferior spur.

tin coat

A logger's heavy, water-repellent coat.

tin dogs

A sheepherder's string of empty tin cans on a wire, they can make a frightening noise and are used to get sheep moving when they balk at something.

tin hat

A logger's water-repellent hat.

tinhorn

A gambler of a cheap, flashy, pretentious kind. Chuck-a-luck operators shake their dice in a small, churnlike affair of metal; hence the word, for the game is rather looked down on, and chuck-a-luck gamblers are never admitted to the aristocratic circle of faro dealers.

tin pants

A logger's water-repellent trousers.

tip

An earmark made by cutting off the tip of an ear, one-half as much as is removed by a crop.

tip the hole card

A cowboy's expression meaning *to give one's plans away*. See *hole card*.

tired

See *bushed*.

tiswin

A fermented intoxicating beverage made by the Apache Indians.

tobiano

A pinto horse with the white color originating at the back and rump and extending downward, with the borders of the markings generally smooth and regular. See *overo*. (George M. Glendenning, "Overos and Tobianos," *Western Horseman*, Vol. VII, No. 1 [January–February, 1942], 12.)

toe riding

Riding a horse with only the toes in the stirrups.

toggle

A block of wood about 4 inches wide, 3 inches thick, and 10 to 12 inches long, or a chain about the same length, used to keep a horse or a wild cow from running away. It was attached to a front foot by a piece of rope, rawhide, or hame strap; thus it would trail behind the animal, and if he tried to run, he would step on it with a hind foot. But if the animal merely walked, he soon learned to miss it with his hind foot or feet, and could travel fast enough to graze and travel with the homebound bunch.

tom

In mining, an inclined trough in which gold-bearing gravel is washed; also called *long tom* since it is longer than a rocker.

tom horn

A cowboy's term used in some sections for a rope.

tongue horses

In mountain country, the *wheel horses*— those directly before the vehicle—of a wagon team.

tongue oil

A cowboy's expression for talking ability.

tongue splitter

A rustler who cruelly split a calf's tongue to keep it from nursing and following its mother.

tonsil paint

A cowboy's name for whisky; also called *tonsil varnish*.

too handy with the rope

A cowboy's expression describing a cattle rustler.

tool chest

A bridle bit to which contrivances were added to make it cruel. The man who used one of them was soon cold-shouldered off the range.

tool nipper

A miner's name for a flunky who collects and distributes tools in a mine.

tools

What a logger calls his knife, fork, and spoon.

too much mustard

A cowboy's expression for a man who has the habit of bragging, picking quarrels, or otherwise making himself disagreeable.

too thick to drink and too thin to plow

What the cowboy calls muddy water that he is forced to drink. He may "have to chaw it 'fore he can swallow it," but if he's thirsty enough, it's "damned good water."

toothing

Looking into a horse's mouth to tell his age.

toothpick timber

A logger's contemptuous term for small trees, especially second-growth trees.

top

A cowboy's word for *best*. The best roper is the *top roper*; the best rider, the *top rider*; the best cutting horse, the *top cutter*; and so on (though the best shot is called *crack shot*). Also, to ride a bucking horse successfully.

In logging, to remove the upper portion of a standing tree to be used in yarding or to be loaded with power machinery.

top dirt

What the miner calls topsoil or surface soil.

top hand

A cowboy's term for a superior hand. A miner's name for a recruit from a farm.

topknot

What the early trapper called a scalp.

top layout

In monte, the two cards drawn from the top of the deck.

top load

In logging, a load of logs piled more than one tier high, as distinguished from a *bunk load*.

top loader

In logging, the member of a loading crew who stands on top of a load and directs the placement of logs as they are sent up.

top loadings

In logging, any extras put on lumber or log rafts, such as laths, shingles, or pickets.

top off

A cowboy's expression meaning *to ride first*; to take the rough edges off a horse.

TOPOGRAPHY

See arroyo, arroyo seco, badlands, baja, baldy, barranca, barrace pit, Bayou Salade, bench, blind canyon, boggy crossing, bog hole, boulder, box canyon, break, buckshot land, butte, cañada, canyon, cap rock, cedar brakes, charco, ciénaga, coulee, cross canyon, cutbank, draw, dry wash, fault, gulch, hogback, llano, Llano Estacado, loma, mal país, mesa, paso, pass, pothole, prairie, rincon, rivers, sag, savanna, slow country, swog, towhead, wash, zanja.

top out

To break a horse. Usually the expression implies that the horse has merely had the rough taken out of him but has not actually been broken.

topping

In logging, removing the crown of a living tree in order to use it for a spar for high-line assembling.

top railer

A cowboy's term for a man who sits on the top rail of a corral and gives advice about who should do the work and take the risks.

top screw

A cowboy's and logger's name for a foreman.

327

top the spars

In logging, to cut off treetops.

torch a squib

A miner's expression meaning *to light a fuse*.

torch basket

In steamboating, an iron coal basket about 1 foot in diameter and 18 inches deep, swung loosely between the prongs of a forked iron bar or standard that could be set in holes in the forward deck and swung far out over the water to allow live coals from burning wood to fall into the river, and not upon the deck.

tornado juice

A cowboy's name for whisky.

toro

A bull; sometimes used in the Southwest in early days, especially before ladies. From the Spanish.

tote team

In early-day logging, the horse and wagon or sleigh used to take supplies to a logging camp.

totin' stars on his duds

An expression describing a Texas cowman, whose clothing was almost always decorated with stars. An old saying of the range was, "For a Texas puncher not to be totin' stars on his duds is most as bad as votin' the Republican ticket."

touchin' leather

See *pulling leather*.

tough lay

A ranch employing a bunch of bad men or gunmen.

tour

What the miner calls a working shift.

touse

See *Taos lightning*.

tow

In river boating, one or more barges, rafts, or other river vessels hitched together and usually pushed by a steam-powered vessel. The barge moored immediately in front of a towing steamer was called the *tow barge*, and the barges in front of the tow barge were called *lead barges*. A barge towed alongside a towboat was said to be *slung under her arm*. When the barges were pulled behind the towboat, as was sometimes done in regions of floating ice, the barges were said to be *railroaded*.

towboat

A river steamboat designed primarily to push barges. See *tow*.

towhead

In river boating, a small island or alluvial obstruction causing a ripple on the river; an island with a low bluff point at the upriver end.

town clown

What a logger calls a small-town policeman.

Towns

See cow town, false front, honky-tonk town, pueblo, town with the hair on.

town with the hair on

A cowboy's expression for a wild and woolly or tough town, like those at the ends of the old cattle trails.

tow through

In logging, to push a raft of logs or lumber on a river with a steamboat.

trace

An early trapper's name for a trail.

tracker

An expert in tracking or reading *sign*, *q.v.*; also called *trailer*.

Tracking

See cut for sign, readin' sign, sliding the grove.

Tracks

See buffalo stamp, sign.

trade

In steamboating, the regular route over which a packet operated on a fixed schedule. Such a boat was called a *trade packet*, as distinguished from a *tramp packet*, which had no regular schedule. More recently, a general term for specific traffic, as *coal-tow-ing trade*.

trade gun

A gun made especially for the Hudson's Bay Company to trade to the Indians. The gun was of inferior quality.

TRADERS

See bourgeois, Comanchero, coureur de bois, courier, dubber, free trader, free trapper, freighters, fur trader, good trader, green hand, packers, patron.

trade whisky

Whisky used in trading with Indians. Later, any cheap whisky.

trading out

In rodeo, a contestant's practice of trading one position in a go-round for another.

trading post

See *estanco*.

trail

A path, usually a narrow one; hence packers moved the animals in their trains in single file. To follow in single file after a *bell horse*, *q.v.* In cattle driving, a route over which cattle were driven to market or shipping points. Famous cattle trails were the Chisholm Trail, the Western Trail and the Goodnight Trail.

trail blazer

A man who blazed, or marked, a trail through wilderness country.

trail boss

In cattle driving, the foreman of a trail herd. He had to know men and cattle; he had to be aggressive, quick to handle an emergency, and resourceful. It is said that a good trail boss fed his hands out of his herd, lost a few en route, and yet got to his destination with more cattle than he had when the owner counted them out as they left the home range. He belonged to the class of men who made cattle history in bossing the herds up the long trail north from Texas.

trail-broke

In cattle driving, cattle that have become used to the trail.

trail count

A count of cattle as they were strung off on a trail drive. After the cattle left the bed ground in the morning and were strung out in a thin line, the trail boss selected a man to be stationed on an imaginary line opposite him on the other side of a passing herd.

As the cattle passed between them, their forefingers rose and fell as they pointed directly to each animal that passed. As each hundred head was counted, each man dropped a pebble into a handy pocket, tied a knot in his horn string, or used some other form of counter. When the herd had passed, each man totaled his counters and announced to the other his tally for comparison. Generally their first count checked. If it did not and there was a very wide margin of difference, they rode to the head of the moving herd and started over again.

trail crew

A crew of men who drove cattle over the trail in early days.

trail crossing

In cattle driving, a river or other obstacle cattle had to cross on the trail.

trail cutter

In cattle driving, a man, usually employed by a stock association, whose job was to halt marching herds and inspect them for cattle that did not belong in the herd.

trail days

The days when long trails were thoroughfares for great herds of cattle moving from the range to market or shipping points. The trail days began soon after the Civil War and ended in the late 1880's, when the government gave out the last of the homesteading land and the railroads extended their lines south and west.

trail driver

A cowhand who drove cattle over the long trails, especially one of the interstate trails leading from Texas.

trail driving

Moving cattle on the trail. The act itself was called *driving*, but cattle were *trailed*, not *driven*; that is, they were kept headed in the direction the drovers wanted them to go as they grazed. In this manner they traveled 10 or 12 miles a day and fattened as they went. The only times they were driven were when they were leaving the familiar territory of the home range, when they were being tired down in an effort to avoid stampedes, and when the drovers were trying to get them to food and water in sections where these were scarce.

trailer

A man skilled in following a trail. In freighting, a smaller wagon carrying about 2 tons and fastened to the lead wagon by a short tongue. The tongue was fastened by a coupling pin fitted into a half-circle arrangement on the axle of the lead wagon.

trail hand

A man engaged in trailing cattle; also called *trail driver*. Every range-bred Texas boy was ambitious to "go up the trail." It gave him an opportunity to break the monotony of range life and offered him a chance to see the world.

trail herd

A bunch of cattle, guarded night and day, being trailed from one region to another. A trail herd usually traveled in single file, or two or three abreast, forming a long, sinuous line, which, if seen from above, would have looked like a huge serpent in slow motion.

Trail markings

See blaze, blind the trail, blind trail, cold trail, plain trail, sign.

Trails

See back trail, cattle driving, trace, trail, trail crossing, trail days, trail driving.

trail tree

In logging, the number-two spar of a sky-line hookup.

trail wagon

In freighting and cattle driving, a wagon fastened behind another wagon.

trail work

Trailing cattle from one range to another or up the trail to market.

trams

In mining, cars pushed along tracks to haul ore from the mine.

transom

In steamboating, a transverse bulkhead at the stern of the boat above water and on top of the end of the stern rake. Occasionally a *false transom* was built aft of the main transom; the rudder wells were usually built between the two.

trap

What the cowboy calls any freak saddle.

trap a squaw

A westerner's expression for a white man who married, or lived with, an Indian woman. A cowboy's expression meaning to get married.

trap corral

A corral used for capturing wild horses or cattle. The gate opens inward easily and closes behind so that the animals cannot escape.

trapper

A man who traps animals for their pelts. In mining, a door tender in a mine.

Trappers

See booshway, bossloper, bourgeois, coon, engagés, fur hunter, hiverannos, hunters, hunting, on his own hook, on the loose, partisan, skin trappers, trapper, voyageur, wah-kéitcha, white Indian, winterer.

trapper's butter

A trapper's term for marrow from the bones of a killed animal. Sometimes this was put into a gallon of water and heated nearly to the boiling point; then blood from the animal was stirred in until a thick broth was made.

Trapping

See beaver, beavering down, better count ribs than tracks, engagement, float-my-stick, fur country, gone beaver, grained, pro belle cutem, skin trade, thrown tree, trap the river clear, up to beaver.

trap sack

A trapper's term for the leather bag in which he carried beaver traps.

trap the river clear

A trapper's expression for trying to take all the beaver that would come to the bait.

travee

See *travois.*

TRAVELING BAGS

See boughten bag, coffin, cooster, go-easter, maleta, sacks.

traveling with the grass

In cattle driving, starting a herd of cattle north from southern Texas early in the spring when the northern ranges were still covered with snow. The grass at the starting place was already green, and as the herd slowly progressed northward, spring advanced and the grass turned green.

travels the lonesome places

A cowboy's expression for a man on the dodge, a man who "ain't on speakin' terms with the law."

travois

A Plains Indian vehicle made of two poles fastened together several feet apart and drawn by a horse, the backs of the poles trailing the ground. Between the poles was tied a platform, a skin, or a net on which the load was placed. Pronounced *travee* by early trappers and traders, some of whom adopted the method.

treasure box

In stagecoaching, an iron box for valuables and express carried beneath the driver's seat. It was always the main object of the road agent's demands.

treasure coach

A specially designed stagecoach, lined with steel to make it bulletproof and provided with portholes so that guards inside could stand off gangs of road agents. It was used for the transportation of gold dust, bullion, and other valuables to the railroads, and was always guarded by three to six messengers armed with sawed-off shotguns.

tree

The wooden frame of a saddle, which is covered with leather. The saddle usually takes its name from the shape of the tree or its maker, such as *California, Visalia, Frazier,* and *Ellenburg.*

TREE DISEASES

See conk wood, conky.

treeing the marshal

A cowboy's expression for bluffing a marshal. In the old days, on their return from a trip up the trail, cowboys liked to brag about how they made the marshal of the town at the end of the trail hide out.

tree looker

See *timber cruiser.*

tree ring

The metal ring to which the latigo straps are fastened.

TREES AND FORESTS

See advance growth, big sticks, big 'uns, basque, bottle-butted, brush, burn, crown, deadman, den tree, dry-ki, fat pine, fire scar, goose pen, high-lead tree, holiday, liner, lodgepole pine, logged-off land, logged-over land, logging, logs, piñon, piss fir, protection forest, quaker, ring, riñon, sapling, sawdust country, saw timber, sawing woods, scrub, second-growth forest, slash, snag, spar tree, strip, stumpage, swell-butted, thrown tree, timber belt, timber claim, toothpick timber, weed tree, widow-maker, windbreak, windfall, wolf tree.

tree squeak

An imaginary bird to which noise made by trees is attributed by loggers.

trey-deucer

In faro, a combination of a trey and a deuce drawn in a single turn.

tributer

A miner who works a *set,* or piece of ground, taking the proceeds as wages, after royalty deduction, but who works under the direction of the owners and holds no title as owner or lessee.

TRICKS

See come a dodge, horseplay, out-coyote, outfox, rim firing a horse, stringing a greener.

trigger is delicate

A cowboy's expression for a quick-tempered man or one quick to shoot over a grievance.

trigger itch

A cowboy's expression for a man quick to shoot.

trigueno

A word used in the Southwest for a brown horse; from the Spanish, meaning *brunette* or *swarthy*.

trimmer

A sawmill worker who cuts boards to specified lengths.

trimming his ears with a hat

Fanning a horse with a hat while riding.

trimming the herd

Cutting cattle from a herd; the expression was usually employed when a *trail cutter (q.v.)* inspected a herd.

trip

The rope used to release a load when stacking hay with a derrick. Also, the man who operates this rope and spots the hay for the stacker. A rope that is fastened to the front foot of a bad horse when he is being broken. Also called *trip rope*.

trip pilot

In steamboating, a pilot who held no regular job but was hired to take a boat over territory with which he was familiar, collected *trip wages*, and returned home or to headquarters to await another call.

tromper

In sheepshearing, a man who tramps the sheared wool into sacks.

trouble

A miner's word for a fault in a vein.

troublesome

See *hell with the hide off*.

trouble wagon

A wagon used on some early-day ranches to carry a couple of cowboys whose job it was to grease windmills, take care of pumps or pipes and water troughs, and haul salt.

trunk strap

A latigo strap that buckles. Also, a cowboy's term for ridicule.

Trustworthy

See worthiness.

trying to chin the moon

A cowboy's expression for a horse standing on his hind feet and pawing the air with his front ones, and also for a high bucker.

trying to find the long end of a square quilt

A cowboy's expression for herding sheep. The sheepherder's *sugan (q.v.)*, is square, and, according to the cowboy, sheepherders went crazy trying to find the longest side of their covers.

tucker bag

A cowboy's name for a bag for personal belongings; not commonly used.

Tucson bed

A cowboy's expression for sleeping in the open without cover.

tug

One of a pair of long straps of a harness that connects a horse to a load.

tule

In the Southwest, a word applied to the yucca and to certain kinds of reeds. When a man *takes to the tules*, he goes into hiding or is on the dodge.

tulles

Men or cattle native to the *tulares*, or tule country.

tumbleweed

The Russian thistle, which, when dry, breaks from its roots and rolls before the wind. These plants roll and jump great distances, scattering their seeds as they go. One old-timer said he "reckoned the Lord put tumblewoods here to show how the wind blows." Also, a cowboy's name for a man with a roving disposition.

tumbleweed wagon

A calaboose-type wagon used by early-day courts, such as Judge Parker's, to bring in prisoners gathered by the marshals.

tumbling brand

A cattle brand leaning in an oblique position.

tumpline

See *burden strap*.

tunnel

In mining, a horizontal excavation starting at the surface and driven across the country for the discovery of working of a lode or lodes.

tunnel disease

See *caisson disease*.

turkey

A logger's and northwestern cowboy's term for a pack of bedding or clothes. Also, a logger's term for a canvas bag for carrying tools.

turn

In logging, a unit of logs to be yarded; the number pulled by a single trip of the skidder carriage; a task done by a "cat," the size of which is measured by the elapsed time between the cat's departure from the landing to go into the brush for logs and its return to the landing with its load. In mining, the period during which ore is raised from a mine. In faro, the drawing of two cards from the dealer's box, one of which wins while the other loses; since neither the *soda card* nor the *hock card* has any action, there are twenty-five *turns* in a deal.

turn a wildcat

A cowboy's expression for a bucking horse.

turned his toes to the daisies

A cowboy's expression for someone who has died.

turned the cat

A cowboy's expression for a horse that has fallen after stepping into a prairie-dog hole.

turned the pack

A cowboy's expression for a horse that has thrown his rider. A packer's expression for a mule whose pack had twisted under his belly.

turned through himself

A cowboy's expression for a horse that has stopped quickly and turned in another direction.

turning the grass upside down

A cowboy's expression for plowing.

turn on his back

A trapper's expression meaning *to die*.

turn out

A trapper's expression meaning *to get up*. A cowboy's expression meaning *to turn horses loose*.

turnout

In logging, a wide place along a one-way road where vehicles can pass. Also, the release of logs from a boom.

turnout time

A cowboy's expression for the time in the spring when cattle are turned out to grass.

turtle

A member of the Cowboy's Turtle Association, the predecessor of the Rodeo Cowboy's Association.

twelve-hour leggin's

A cowboy's term occasionally used for chaps.

twenty-one

A card game in which each player tries to obtain cards whose spots total as near twenty-one as possible but not exceeding that number; also called *blackjack (q.v.)* and *vingt-et-un*.

twine

A cowboy's term for his rope.

twist a horse

To break a horse.

twister

A shortened form of *bronc twister*. A *twitch, q.v.* A tornado.

twist her tail

A miner's expression for cranking a liner machine or a drifting machine.

twist-horn

A longhorn; so called because of the many different twists and turns of his horns.

twisting down

In rodeo, twisting a steer's neck in bull-dogging until it falls on its side.

twisting out

A cowboy's expression for breaking a horse.

twist the tiger

To play faro; see *tiger*.

twitch

A small loop of cord with a stick through it, used to punish a held horse. The loop is placed vertically around the animal's upper lip and then tightened by twisting the stick. Also called *twister*; some claim that this is where the name *bronc twister* originated.

two-buckle boy

A cowboy's name for a farm hand.

two-gun man

A man who wore two guns and could shoot with either hand. This species was rare, even in the old West, and exists mostly in fiction. It was a rare case when two guns had any real advantage over one. Their apparent advantage was that they made the threat of an ace in the hole when a lone man stacked against a crowd. The two-gun man, when among strangers, had to be careful with the motion of both hands, and was thus handicapped in doing little things other men could do. He was, as a cowhand would say, "dressed to kill."

two jumps ahead of the sheriff

On the dodge. A reformed outlaw once told me that he "didn't really have to leave Texas. The sheriff came to the state line and jes' *begged* me to come back."

two-up driver

A driver of two spans, or four horses.

two whoops and a holler

A cowboy's expression for a short distance.

tying down

In rodeo, roping and catching an animal and tying it down by three of its feet against time. See *hog-tying*.

tying fast

In roping, tying the home end of the rope to the saddle horn. See *tie man*.

Tyler

In logging, one of the three most commonly used high-line systems, the others being the Lidgerwood and the North Bend.

U

"Tossin' your rope before buildin' a loop don't ketch the calf"

uncle

A logger's name for the superintendent.

uncorkin' a bronc

Taking off the rough edges in breaking a horse.

under a flag

A cowboy's expression for someone using an assumed name.

underbit

An earmark made by doubling the ear in and cutting a small piece, 1 inch long and usually 1/3 inch deep, out of the lower part of the ear.

underbrush

What the logger calls the brush growing in a forest.

underclerk

In steamboating, a subordinate clerk; also called *mud clerk*.

undercurrent

In mining, a shallow receptacle into which water is diverted from a sluice, with the object of catching finer gold particles.

undergrowth

A logger's term for small trees and scrubby plants growing under a forest canopy.

underhack

An earmark made by cutting up on the underside of the ear about 1 inch.

under-half-crop

An earmark made by splitting the ear from the tip, midway, about halfway back toward the head, and cutting off the lower half.

underhand pitch

In roping, a heel loop used on cattle. It can be used on foot in a corral, and was a favorite catch for mounted men working on roundup. It is about the only loop that can be whirled while working among cattle, and it is whirled very slowly, just enough to keep it moving. The loop is kept in motion at the right side of the thrower in a vertical plane, swinging up. When the object to be roped passes in front, the roper brings the rope around with a snap to give it carrying power and turns the loop loose over the back of his hand as it swings forward. This pitches the loop, standing up, under the animal's belly so that he can jump into it with his hind feet. The right hand continues to hold the rope, as is the case in most heeling and forefooting throws, and the slack is jerked up at once. (W. M. French, "Ropes and Roping," *Cattleman*, Vol. XXVI, No. 12 [May, 1940], 17–30.)

underhand stoping

In mining, work started at the top of a block of ore and progressing downward. The ore is allowed to slide into a chute in a winze, or raise, and from there into mine cars at the lower level.

underround

An earmark made by cutting a half-circle from the bottom of the ear.

underslope

An earmark made by cutting the ear about two-thirds of the way back from the tip straight to the center of the ear at its lower side.

undersplit

An earmark made by splitting the ear from the lower edge up to about the center.

under the gun

In poker, a situation in which a player must pass, bet, or check before other players do so.

underwears

A cowboy's name for sheep.

UNDISCERNING

See blind as a snubbing post, chuckleheaded as a prairie dog.

unhook

To unhitch a team from a wagon or other vehicle. The cowboy never uses the words *hitch* and *unhitch*.

unit

In logging, a working unit; the machinery and men necessary to gather and load the logs on railroad cars.

UNITS OF MEASURE

See bent, burro load, carga, chain, cheap stick, fanega, fathom, hand, jag, load, log scale, miner's inch, swag, vara.

unload

A term for a horse that bucks off its rider.

unravel some cartridges

A cowboy's expression meaning *to shoot*.

unrooster

To take off the rough edges in breaking a horse.

unshucked

A cowboy's word meaning *naked*. When the word was used in referring to a gun, as in *unshucked his gun*, it meant that the man had drawn it from the holster, thus making it a naked gun.

untie man

In rodeo, an arena employee who, after

the flagman has signaled that a tie has qualified, unties or releases the calf or steer from both the rope and the pigging string. Untie men usually work in pairs.

UNWELCOME

See his cinch is gettin' frayed, wedger in.

unwind

A term for a horse that starts bucking.

up and down as a cow's tail

A cowboy's expression meaning *honest and trustworthy.*

upcast

In mining, a ventilating shaft through which air ascends.

upper

A logger's term for a log or piece of lumber of superior grade.

upper deck

In steamboating, the deck above the boiler deck; also called *roof* and *hurricane deck.*

upraise

In mining, a raise, or steeply inclined passageway, connecting working places at different levels.

up the hill

A riverman's reference to shore. When a riverman went ashore, he went *up the hill,* whether it be in a city, along a mountainside, or across a prairie.

up the trail

Driving cattle up the trail; see *trail, trail days.*

up to beaver

A trapper's expression for cunning. Sometimes the beavers became so cautious that the trapper had difficulty catching them. He might even quit, admitting that he was not yet *up to beaver.*

up to Green River

A hunter's and trapper's expression for high quality or effectiveness. The knives used by the hunters and trappers were manufactured at the Green River (Wyoming) works, and had that name stamped upon the blades. Thus to say that something was *up to Green River* was to give it high praise. The phrase was also used in reference to thrusting a blade into someone up to the trade-mark.

use him to trim a tree

A cowboy's expression meaning *to hang someone.*

using his rope arm to hoist a glass

A cowboy's expression for someone drinking.

V

"The bigger the mouth the better it looks when shut"

vaca

In the Southwest, a cow; from the Spanish.

vacada

A drove of cows; from the Spanish.

valley tan

A trader's name for whisky made by the Mormons of Salt Lake Valley.

vamoose

A cowboy's word meaning *go;* an Americanized form of the Spanish *vamos!* The cowboy uses it to mean *get to hell out of here.*

van

A logger's name for the camp store, or *supply chest,* maintained by every owner or manager of logging operations at his camp in the woods.

vaquero

In the Southwest, a common word for any cowboy, but more particularly for a Mexican cowboy; from the Spanish.

vara

A trader's unit of measurement, a Spanish yard, or 33 inches.

varruga

A wattle; a mark usually made on the cheek or neck of an animal by cutting a strip of hide down about 2 inches and letting it hang. ·

Vaseline

A miner's name for nitroglycerin.

VEGETATION

See alegría, alfaloofee, amole, black chaparral, brush, brush country, buffalo grass, cactus, chaparral, chaparro, cholla, crazy weed, dogwood, greasewood, herbe salée, hickory, Indian medicine, Jim Hill mustard, Joshua tree, maguey, mesquital, mesquite, mesquite grass, motte, prairie wool, saguaro, shaved behind the skin, trees and forests, tule, tumbleweed, underbrush, undergrowth.

VEHICLES

See buckboard, candy wagon, cold-meat wagon, Concord, crotch, crotch tongue, hay sled, lodgepole vehicle, logging machinery and equipment, mining machinery and equipment, morphidite, pitching Betsy, skunk wagon, travois, treasure coach, wagons and equipment.

vein

In mining, a tabular deposit of ore or of mineral-bearing rock of varying thickness and irregular boundaries but with two dimensions many times greater than the third. A vein usually dips at a considerable angle from the horizontal, in contrast to a *bedded deposit*, which lies in a flat or gently sloping position.

VEINS

See lodes and veins, mines.

velvet

In gambling, the banker's money.

velvet couch

A cowboy's name for his bedroll.

vent brand

A cattle brand placed upon an animal that has been given an ownership brand and later sold. It has the effect of canceling the ownership brand, thus serving as the acknowledgment of a sale. It is usually placed on the same side of the animal as the original brand. Also, to put such a brand on cattle. From the Spanish *venta*, meaning *sale*. See *counter brand*.

verge staff

In steamboating, the forward jack staff on which the *jack*, or ensign, of the steamboat line is flown.

veta

A miner's name for the main vein of a deposit.

viga

A southwesterner's term for a rafter used to hold up a roof; from the Spanish.

viggerish

In dice, the house's cut.

vigilante

In the early days, one of a group of men who organized themselves into groups called *vigilance committees* to enforce the law and punish crime in regions where law or law enforcement seemed inadequate.

VIGILANTES

See hemp committee, stranglers, vigilante.

vinegaroon

A southwesterner's name for a whip scorpion, especially one of a large species; so called because of the odor it emits when it is frightened.

vingt-et-un

The original French name for the game now known in the United States as *blackjack (q.v.)* or *twenty-one*.

visa

A shortened form of *Visalia*, a saddle made on a Visalia tree.

visiting harness

What the cowman sometimes calls his town clothes.

voucher

What the early-day cowboy called an Indian scalp.

voyager

A traveler's name for a traveler.

voyageur

A man, usually a French Canadian, who signed on with the early-day fur companies because he liked the wild, carefree life his work afforded. Also called *engagé*.

vug

A miner's name for a cavity in the rock.

W

"It's sometimes safer to pull your freight than pull your gun"

W

A throw line used to break a wild horse to harness. It was tied to the forefoot of a horse and then run up through a ring in the bellyband and back to the wagon. If the horse started to run away, a pull on this rope would immediately trip him.

waddy

A cowboy's name for a hand who fills in or rounds out a ranch outfit in busy times. In the spring and fall when some ranches are shorthanded, they take on anyone who is able to ride a horse and keep him for a week or so; hence the word *waddy*, derived from *wad* or *wadding*—anything to fill in.

Some cowmen used the word to mean a rustler. Later, it was applied to any cowboy.

wagging his chin

A cowboy's expression for someone talking a lot.

wagon

The *chuck wagon* (*q.v.*), the cowboy's home during the roundup; also sometimes called *works*, *spread* or *layout*. All the various wagons upon the range were designated by their specific names, but when the cowman spoke of the *wagon*, every range man knew he was speaking of the chuck wagon.

wagon boss

The man in charge of the roundup. He stood out above the rank and file. One who knew the cow country could ride up to an outfit at a chuck wagon or in a branding pen for the first time and go straight to the boss, though he was hard at work and dressed like the others of the outfit. His appearance and attitude denoted leadership. He was a product of the hard school of the range. (John M. Hendrix, "Bosses," *Cattleman*, Vol. XXIII, No. 10 [March, 1937], 65–75.) He was usually quiet, with a certain measure of reserve, and had to have better than average intelligence in order to understand the nature of the cowhand. He had to arrange each man's work and place, day and night, without appearing to give orders; and this called for both tact and understanding. See *roundup captain*.

In freighting, the man in charge of the wagon train. He had to be courageous, firm, and genial, and his word was law. He selected the camp sites, directed the fording of streams, chose watering places, and gave orders to start in the morning and to halt at night.

In sheepherding, the *camp tender, q.v.*

wagon herder

A name for the sheepherder who preferred to spend time at his wagon rather than with his flock. Such a herder was looked upon with contempt.

wagon manners

A cowboy's expression for good behavior.

wagon master

A freighter's name for the wagon boss.

WAGONS AND EQUIPMENT

See ambulance, band wagon, bed wagon, blattin' cart, bull wagon, butcher-knife wagon, butt chain, caboose, cake wagon, calf wagon, carreta, carro, cat wagon, celerity wagon, chip wagon, chuck box, chuck wagon, Conestoga wagon, crumb castle, cuna, Dearborn, democrat wagon, doll baby, doll buggy, emigrant wagon, fence wagon, flapboard, floating wagon, fly, freight wagon, groanin' cart, growler, hayrack, hoodlum wagon, hooligan wagon, jerky, jewelry chest, jockey box, kitchen wagon, lead wagon, maniac den, mansion, mess wagon, Mormon brakes, Murphy wagon, pemina buggy, pie box, pie buggy, pie wagon, prairie schooner, range cradle, Red River cart, sand wagon, scoop wagon, sheep wagon, sheet, shotgun wagon, stage wagon, timber cart, tote team, trailer, trail wagon, trouble wagon, tumbleweed wagon, vehicles, wagon, wannigan, wheel house.

wagon-spoke rowel

A spur with an extra-long shank supporting widely spaced rowels that resemble the spokes of a wagon wheel.

wagon train

A caravan of people seeking new homes in the West. A caravan of traders.

WAGON TRAINS

See bull train, bull-wagon boss, caravan, emigrant train, grass train, mule train, wagon train.

wagon west

To migrate. The expression originated from the movement of settlers going west in wagons to settle the country.

wah-keitcha

An Indian's name for a French-Canadian fur trapper, meaning *bad medicine*.

WAITRESSES

See biscuit shooter, cookie pusher, hash slinger, hasler.

walk-a-heap

A western Indian's name for an Army infantryman.

walker

In logging, the superintendent of two or more logging camps; so called because he had to walk from one camp to another. Also called *walking boss*.

Walker pistol

An early frontier revolver made by Colt after the suggestions of Captain Samuel Walker, a Texas Ranger, and named for him.

walkin' beamin'

An expression for the seesaw motion of a bucking horse when he lands alternately on his front and hind feet.

walking

In steamboating, moving the boat over sand bars and shallow places by lowering huge spars on either side of the boat and setting them in the sand with the lower ends pointing downstream so that the pull on the lines would lift the boat and move it ahead. The lines were then hauled taut and thrown around the capstans, and the boat was *walked* over the bar. The process was often long and laborious and took one or two days to complete. Occasionally the paddle wheel was put into reverse; the object of this was to dam the river slightly and relieve the pressure on the bar. The water was sometimes backed in this way up to a height of 4 inches, which helped lift the boat enough to move it over the bar.

WALKING

See afoot, ankle express, footermans, high-heel, Indian file, ride shank's mare, set afoot, straddlin' down the road, terrapin, three walks.

walking boss

See *walker*.

walking brand

A cattle brand with lower designs like feet.

walking down

A method of capturing wild horses that calls for following them in relays fast enough to keep them in sight and give them no chance to rest or eat. After several days of such a chase the mustangs are exhausted enough that the riders can approach them and begin to control their turnings in any desired direction. This method has been known to be used by men on foot.

walking papers

What the logger calls a discharge from his job.

walking sheep

Herding sheep on foot rather than on horseback.

walking stick

A horse belonging to a long-legged puncher.

walking the boat

In river boating, moving a boat with poles. On each side of the boat eight or ten crewmen took their places on the narrow walkway. At the command of the patron the men would set their poles, put their shoulders against the knobs, stooping over so low that they could almost touch the deck with their hands, and proceed to *walk* the boat ahead. When they got as far as they could, they would run back to the bow and repeat the operation. This method required great stamina and strength.

walking the fence

A cowboy's expression for cattle that continually walk up and down the fence line in an effort to find a way to break out. Also, an expression for a nervous or impatient person.

walking the table

An early-day logger's way of expressing dissatisfaction with the quality of the food at the logging camp or the way the cook prepared it. If the boss did not do something about it, someone would shout, "Let's walk the table, boys!" Then some of the men would mount the table and walk down its length, kicking off food and dishes as they went. If the cook showed up, he would be met with a few well-directed cups or other utensils.

walking whisky vat

What the cowboy calls a heavy drinker.

walleyed

A cowboy's term for a horse with glass, blue, or "china" eyes and an irregular blaze.

wallflower

A logger's term for a beggar, especially a bum who begs drinks in a saloon.

wallow in velvet

A cowboy's expression meaning *to have plenty*. Often one hears a prosperous man spoken of as having " 'nough money to burn a wet mule," or having "a roll as big as a wagon hub."

Waltz with the lady!

A cowboy's shout of encouragement to a rider on a bucking horse.

wampum

An Indian's term for small shell beads used as money.

wampus cat

A logger's imaginary animal to which night noises are attributed.

wanigan

A logger's word for many things: the place where camp stores are kept, payroll charges for such stores, the caravan of supplies that accompanies a river drive, and a camp made by a crew of river drivers. It was also used for the cook's boat that followed a river drive; four times a day the boat was pulled to the bank, and the cook spread his table and blew his horn, which resounded through the woods, bringing the hungry loggers to their meal. A sheepherder's word for his supply wagon or his camp and house wagon; also called *wannigan wagon*. From the Indian.

wanted

An expression for a man on the dodge from the law.

war bag

A cowboy's sack or bag for personal belongings, in which he kept all the useless ditties and dofunnies he had gathered through the years. Here he kept his supply of makin's and cigarette papers, an extra spur, some whang leather, an extra cinch or bit, and perhaps a carefully wrapped picture of a girl or some tattered letters that had brought him news from the outside. Among this plunder, too, there would likely be a box of cartridges, a greasy deck of playing cards, a bill of sale for his private horse, and his "low-necked clothes."

warbles

Larvae of the *heel fly, q.v.* The eggs hatch on the hair of the cattle, and the tiny larvae burrow into the skin, causing itching and discomfort. Also called *cattle grubs* and *wolves.*

war bonnet

A cowboy's term for his hat; named for an Indian's headdress.

war bridle

A brutal hitch of rope placed in the mouth and around the lower jaw of a horse.

war dance

An Indian dance held before an excursion into battle; the dance simulated a battle.

warmed-up stock

A cowman's term for cattle beginning to fatten.

warm the blood

A cowman's expression for placing purebred bulls with inferior cows to breed up the stock.

Warnings

See All hands and the cook! Cuidado, Go 'way 'round 'em, Shep! Headache! Look out, cowboy! send up in smoke, shook a rope at him, telltale, three-seven-seventy-seven (3-7-77), Tim-m-m-ber! Whistling at point.

warpath

An Indian's term for a warlike expedition.

warp his backbone

A cowboy's expression for a horse that bucks with his back arched.

warping

In river boating, a means of moving a boat upstream by carrying a long line ahead of the boat in a skiff and making it fast to trees or rocks. The men on the boat then hauled on the line, pulling the boat until it reached the object to which the line was attached. The boat was then moored to the bank or held with poles until the line was again carried ahead and made fast, when the process was repeated. This method was used when some obstacle on the bank prevented the cordelle men from walking along the bank. River rapids that were too steep for the boat to negotiate unaided were also passed by this method. As soon as the boat reached the foot of a rapid, it was headed for the shore, and twelve or so crewmen left the boat and began running along the shore line. The lead crewman carried a pick, a spade, and a few stakes; the second carried a piece of timber a little smaller than a railroad tie; and the remainder carried a strong line that was uncoiled from the boat. Well beyond the head of the rapids the men planted a *deadman*; that is, they dug a trench 3 or 4 feet deep and large enough to hold the timber, with the long dimension at right angles to the river. The timber was buried and firmly staked down, and the line was fastened to it at its middle. The crew on the boat placed the other end of the line around the capstan, which was then slowly wound in under steam power. The operation was a very slow one, though usually less so than sparring over sand bars. See *sparring.*

warrior

A miner's name for an excavating drill.

warting

A scaly substance, sometimes more than 1 inch high, on the skin of cattle, caused by deep branding. It does no particular harm to the cattle, but is unsightly and a sign of poor branding.

wash

A westerner's name for a gulch or ravine.

washerwoman loop

In roping, a large, flat loop.

wash gold

In mining, gold that occurs in alluvial deposits, as distinguished from gold found in veins or lodes.

washies

A trapper's term for beaver excavations along a riverbank. Beavers' lodges were usually so placed that the animals ascended the stream some distance to arrive at the spot where they procured their food. They made their excursions under water, and along the way they dug excavations under the bank into which they swam to raise their heads above the surface in order to breathe without exposing themselves. Trappers sometimes caught beavers by pursuing them into these holes.

washing his profile

A cowboy's expression for washing his face.

washing out the canyon

A cowboy's expression for taking a bath.

washing stuff

In mining, any earthy deposits containing enough gold to pay for washing it.

Washoe canary

A miner's name for a burro; named for the Washoe region (later Nevada).

Washoe process

In mining, a silver-treatment process in which mercury and sometimes blue vitriol and salt are added to the ore, which is then ground in tubs or pans; named for the Washoe region (later Nevada), where it was first used.

wash off the war paint

A cowboy's expression for getting over an angry spell or backing down from a fight. One cowhand describing such an incident said, "When he looked into the danger end o' that scatter-gun, it didn't take 'im long to pull in his horns."

wash pan

In placer mining, a pan for washing pay gravel.

wash place

In mining, a place where ores are washed and separated from the waste, usually by hand jogs.

wasp nest

A cowboy's name for light bread.

wassup

A cowboy's name for an outlaw horse.

waste a loop

In roping, to throw a rope and miss the target.

wasted her

A cowboy's phrase when he has dashed off after a cow that has escaped from the herd and failed to bring her back.

watching the op'ra

A cowboy's expression for sitting on the top rail of the corral fence watching a fellow puncher ride a bad horse.

WATER

See beef tea, gypped, rivers, too thick to drink and too thin to plow, water hole, watering the herd.

water hole

A place for watering cattle. A cowboy's name for a saloon.

watering at night

On the dodge.

watering the herd

In cattle driving, the process of herding cattle to water. Watering a trail herd was quite an art. A good trail boss started slowing his herd some distance before he hit the river. As he brought them to the water, he spread them along the bank, heading the lead cattle downstream. As the others came up, they were headed upstream, so that all cattle, including the drags, got clear water because each succeeding group drank upstream from the preceding group. If the cattle were allowed to hit the river in a bunch, the lead cattle would be forced to the other side before they got sufficient water, and all the water would be muddied.

As a rule, cattle were watered only once a day, in the evening. Charles Goodnight once said that "the science of the trail is in grazing and watering the cattle, but the watering is the most important of the two."

watermelon under the saddle

An expression for a horse that arches his back excessively.

water rights

The right to a "piece of water" by priority of occupation.

water scrape

A trip across a region where there was no water.

water-shy

A cowboy's expression for a person not particular about body cleanliness. Rip Gunter, telling of an unusually dirty chuckwagon cook who was "considerably whiffy on the lee side," said, "He's always got his jowls full o' Climax, and ain't none particular where he unloads it, and his clothes are so stiff with beef blood and dry dough you'd have to chop 'em off."

We were kidding a certain puncher about being water-shy, and he answered right back: "I ain't afraid of water. In fact I like a little for a chaser once in a while."

water trap

A stout corral built in plain sight around a spring or watering place. It has a wide gate which is sprung after the animals enter for watering.

wattle

A mark of ownership made on the neck or the jaw of an animal by pinching up a quantity of skin and cutting it down but not entirely off. When the wound heals, a hanging flap of skin is left.

wave 'round

To wave a hat or other object in a semicircle from left to right, which, in the sign language of the plains, means that you are not wanted and are to stay away. On the range, when a rustler happened to have a maverick calf tied down at a branding fire and saw a rider approaching in the distance, he jerked his hat off and *waved the rider 'round*. If his warning was not heeded, he had the advantage of a .30-.30, which he was not afraid to use, and the "whine of a bullet is a hint in any man's language."

way pocket

The fourth pocket in the *mochila (q.v.)* of the pony-express rider, which was opened and closed en route by station keepers. The other three pockets were locked at the be-ginning of the trip and were only opened at four or five stops, such as forts.

way pouch

The pony-express rider's pouch in which mail was carried for destinations along the way.

Weak

See bed-slat ribs, paper-backed.

weak pen

A cowman's name for the pasture where sick animals were kept.

weaner

A cowboy's name for a calf old enough to wean. A cowboy's name for a young child.

Weaning devices

See blab, butterboard weaner, muzzle, spike weaner.

Weapons and ammunition

See armed to the teeth, artillery, belly gun, big fifty, black-eyed Susan, blowpipe, blue lightnin', blue whistler, buffalo gun, bull thrower, buscadero belt, cowboy change, credit, cutter, derringer, dewey, Dupont, equalizer, five beans in the wheel, flame thrower, forty-five, forty-four, fusil, galena, galena pills, gambler's gun, gun, hardware, Henry, hide-out gun, hog leg, hot lead, Indian hatchet, iron, knives, lead chuckler, lead plum, lead pusher, lightnin' stock, long tom, manstopper, meat in the pot, medicine iron, Navy, needle gun, nipple, no beans in the wheel, old cedar, old reliable, one-eyed scribe, paggamoggon, parlor gun, parrot-bill, peacemaker, pepperbox, persuader, plow handle, popgun, prairie belt, saddle gun, sawed-off shotgun, scalp taker, scatter-gun, Sharps, shooting iron, six gun, skull cracker, sleeve gun, slip gun, smokepole, smoke wagon, stingy gun, suicide gun, talking iron, thumb buster, trade gun, up to Green River, Walker pistol, Winchester, Worchestershire, yager.

wearin' callouses on his elbows

An expression for a cowboy spending his time in a saloon.

Weather

See blizzard, blue whistler, cayuse wind,

chinook, cow skinner, dancing devil, dry storm, duster, fence lifter, goose drowner, gully-washer, hell wind, Idaho brain storm, lay the dust, norther, Oklahoma rain, pogonip, sand auger, silver thaw, squaw wind, thunder gust, twister.

weaver

A bucking horse who has a peculiar weaving motion and whose feet never strike the ground in a straight line. This motion is most disconcerting to a rider.

webfoot

A cowboy's name for a man from Oregon; so called because of the long winter rains in that state. A logger's name for a man who works on the pond at the mill and sends logs up to the saws.

wedding

A miner's word for a collision of buckets and cars in a mine.

wedding ring

In trick roping, a stunt in which the roper swings a wide, horizontal loop around himself. It can be performed either on foot or on horseback, and it takes a strong wrist and arm and above-average skill.

wedge

In logging, an iron piece, sharpened on one end, driven into the saw cut with a large hammer to prevent the saw from binding and to direct the fall of the tree.

wedger in

What the cowboy calls an uninvited person or a meddler.

wedge rock

An expression first used by miners in the Comstock lode to designate rock too poor to be classed as *pay ore*, or even *second-class ore*, but better than waste. Today, a term for low-grade ore that usually assays under $5.00 a ton. When a car of good ore is placed on the cage to be hoisted, it is specially tagged. If it is waste rock, no tag is used. It became the custom to throw a wooden wedge on top of the car of very low grade ore; hence the term *wedge rock*.

wedges

In faro, cards trimmed with faro shears for use by dishonest dealers.

weed tree

A logger's name for a tree that has little or no commercial value.

weedy

An animal addicted to eating locoweed.

week on the bed wagon

An expression for a sick or injured cowboy meaning that he would not be able to ride again for about that long.

went under

A trapper's expression meaning *died* or *killed*.

went up to fork a cloud

An expression for a rider thrown high from a horse.

West

See *El Dorado*.

wet camp

A freighter's name for a camp near a creek, river, or other moving water.

wet herd

A herd of cattle made up entirely of cows.

wethers

Castrated male sheep. They are separated from the lambing flock at the beginning of the season.

wet stock

In early days, cattle or horses that were smuggled across the Rio Grande River after being stolen from their rightful owners in Mexico or Texas. Later the term was used for any stolen stock.

wet stuff

A cowboy's name for cows that are giving milk.

whacker

A shortened form of *bullwhacker, q.v.*

whale line

A cowboy's name for a rope.

whang

A cowboy's term for a buckskin thong. To tie.

whangdoodle

A cattle brand with a group of interlocking wings and with no central flying figure.

whang leather

A cowboy's term for a long, narrow strip of leather, usually rawhide, used for many purposes; also called *whit leather*.

whang strings

Long strings attached to the saddle and used for tying things to the saddle as well as for holding the saddle leathers together; another name for *saddle strings*, especially those made of buckskin.

wharf

In steamboating, a landing space where steamboats tied up, usually provided with ringbolts and generally paved, particularly in a city.

wharf boat

In steamboating, a boat moored to a floating warehouse at a wharf, usually at a larger town or freight-distribution point, which was used to transfer cargo and passengers. In the palmy days of steamboating these boats were found at nearly all towns of consequence and were usually privately owned and operated.

wheelers

In freighting and stagecoaching, the span of horses nearest the wheels of the vehicle. Theirs was the toughest job of the team. They had the greatest weight to pull and were the ones to receive the shock when a wheel struck an object in the road. Also called *wheel horses*.

wheel horses

See *wheelers*.

wheel house

A cowboy's term for a canvas-covered wagon.

wheelhouse

In steamboating, the structure over the wheel.

whey-belly

A cowboy's term for an inferior horse or for a pot-gutted animal.

Which way's the wagon?

The old-time trail driver's familiar greeting when he rode up to a trail outfit. The wagon was always the place where he sought company, food, or information.

while the gate's still open

A cowman's expression for opportunity.

whim

A miner's term for the windlass that hoists ore through the shaft to the surface.

whing-ding

A cowboy's term for playful bucking indulged in by both horse and rider in a spirit of fun. Also, his term for a party or social affair.

whip

An instrument for driving animals, usually a thong of plaited leather attached to a handle. Nearly every early-day driver worshiped his whip and considered it worth its weight in gold. In stagecoaching, a name for a coach driver. The *whip* of the Far West, though remembered for his picturesque qualities, was essentially a sober, dependable man. He was swaggering and rough-mannered, but generally keen. Though he was often profane, he was gentlemanly and accommodating to his passengers. Also called *whipster*. In mining, an apparatus for raising a bucket with rope and pulleys.

whip breaking

Training a horse, usually in a corral, by stinging his rump with a whip or the end of a rope every time he turned from the trainer. In time, from the pain, he would turn toward the trainer, and if the trainer backed away each time and dragged his whip, the horse would begin to understand what was wanted of him. Very few cowmen used this method.

whip out

In freighting, a teamster's term for beating animals with a whip when they became stuck to make them pull harder.

whipper in

A man who rode alongside a wagon with a black-snake whip to assist in breaking work horses to the wagon.

WHIPPING

See chapping, leggin' case, lodgepoling, pistol-whip, pour the bud into, puttin' the leggin's, throwing the buckskin, whip out, wiping him out.

whipping a tired pony out of Texas

On the dodge.

WHIPS

See black snake, bull whip, cow whip, cracker, persuader, popper, quirt, quista, romal, whip.

whipsaw

In logging, a thin, narrow saw set in a frame. To cut or get out timber with such a saw. In faro, to lose at two different bets in the same turn. Clever dealers know how to lead a player into this situation.

whipsawer

A man who uses a *whipsaw (q.v.)* in lumbering.

whipster

A stagecoach driver. See *whip*.

whirling

In roping, swinging the noose of a rope about the head until sufficient spread is developed to make a throw at the object to be roped. Whirling is never done in a corral, especially in a horse corral, because it alarms the animals.

WHISKY

See liquor.

whisky jack

A westerner's name for the Rocky Mountain jay.

whisky mill

A cowman's name for a frontier saloon.

whistle

A cowboy's name for anyone young and foolish.

whistle berries

A cowboy's name for beans.

whistle judge

In rodeo, an imposing westerner in the stand who blows a whistle at the end of 10 seconds in a bronc-riding contest.

whistle punk

In logging, the man who handles the signal wire that runs from the timber to the whistle of the donkey engine.

whistler

A cowman's name for a wind-broken horse.

whistling at point

In steamboating, blowing the whistle at sharp, wooded points or bends on the river; a matter of safety both for the boat coming up the river and for the one going down.

white-collar rancher

A nonresident ranch owner, or one who lives in the city.

whitefaces

Hereford cattle; also called *open-faced cattle*.

white house

A cowboy's name for the main house of the ranch or the owner's home; the "executive office" of the ranch.

white Indians

A name given to an early-day white trapper who had adopted the Indian way of life.

white mule

A logger's name for cheap corn whisky.

white-skin

A gambler's term for a spot card, as distinguished from a court card.

white-water bucko

A logger's name for one of the best of the river drivers.

whit leather

See *whang leather*.

whittler

A cowman's name for a good cutting horse.

whittle whanging

A cowboy's term for wrangling or quarreling.

whole shebang

A cowboy's term for a collective whole.

whoop-up

The original Fort Whoop-Up was a dive on the Canadian border north of Shelby, Montana. The boundary of the two countries ran down the middle of the building, and that fact came in handy, for the chief business at Whoop-Up was selling whisky to Indians. Later there grew a whole crop of Whoop-Ups, which worried the law-abiding Canucks far more than it did the Americans. The word *whoop-up* finally grew to mean a type of person rather than a place. "What tribes does he belong to?" someone would ask. "He's a whoop-up," would be the answer, and this was always funny. (Dan Cushman to R.F.A.)

wickiup

A hut made of branches of trees loosely interwoven, used by Indians of the West and Southwest. The word was sometimes used by a cowman in referring to his own house.

widow-maker

A cowman's name for an extra-bad horse; also, the name of the horse ridden by the legendary Pecos Bill. In logging, a falling tree or branch blown down by the wind or a tree limb partly broken off and threatening to fall; the most dangerous hazards of the woods. In mining, an excavating drill, another dangerous weapon.

wife

What a miner occasionally calls a fellow worker.

wiggle-tail

In mining, a machine used to drill holes for blasting; an old-fashioned power drill that makes much dust.

wigwam

An Indian dwelling, in the West usually cone-shaped, made of bark and mats or hides laid over stakes planted in the ground and converging at the top, where there was an opening for smoke to escape. The word was also used by the cowman in speaking of his residence.

WILD

See cimarrón, wild, woolly, and full o' fleas.

wild bunch

A westerner's term for a gang of outlaws. A group of horses that have not been handled enough to be controllable.

wildcat's ankle

A logger's expression for someone he regards highly.

wild-cow milking

In rodeo, an event in which a wild cow is turned loose in the arena and two cowboys dash after her on horseback. One rider ropes the animal, then the other dismounts and mugs her. After this, one roper runs on foot, carrying a pop bottle, and tries to obtain about an inch of milk in it. After securing the milk, he runs to the judges to display it. He does all this against time.

wildfire

A logger's term for a fire of any origin, burning out of control.

wild-horse race

In rodeo, an event recognized by the Rodeo Cowboy's Association for which no championship is given. In this event three unmounted cowboys must catch a wild horse, saddle him, and ride him across the finish line. The teams of riders compete against each other for first, second and third place.

wild mare's milk

A cowboy's term for whisky.

wild stuff

A cowman's term for wild cattle.

WILD-WEST SHOWS

See Bill-show.

wild willow west

A cowboy's term for a dude ranch.

wild, woolly, and full o' fleas

An early-day cowboy's expression for a genuine cowboy. The cowboy created the expression to impress the tenderfoot with his woolliness. The saying became so common that some people actually believed the cowboy had fleas, though he had no more love for fleas than any other man. As one said, he had "rather have graybacks than fleas 'cause after those seam squirrels graze, they bed down, but a flea's never satisfied. After he locates paydirt on one claim, he jumps to stake another, and he's a damned nimble prospector."

willow-tail

A horse, usually a mare, with a loose, coarse, heavy tail—an indication of poor breeding. Often shortened to *willow*.

Winchester

A breech-loading rifle, usually of a lever-loading, tubular-magazine type, first made by Oliver F. Winchester and manufactured by the Winchester Arms Company.

Winchester quarantine

A barrier created by force of arms. Such quarantines occurred many times in the early West, especially on the trail when a group of natives objected to a tick-infested trail herd passing through their range.

wind-belly

A cowboy's name for an orphan calf that is all belly, or, as the cowboy would say, "fat in the middle and pore at both ends."

windbreak

One or more rows of trees, a tall fence, or a natural formation on the windward side that provides shelter from wind.

wind-broken

A cowboy's expression for a horse with a respiratory disease that impairs his breathing.

windfall

A tree knocked down by the wind; also an area of such trees. Also called *blowdown*.

windfall bucker

A logger who salvages trees that have been blown down by the wind.

windies

A cowman's name for cattle that have to be driven out of canyons and onto the plains. These cattle are usually contrary and hard to drive, and by the time they have been coaxed out of the canyon, the cattle, the horses, and the cowboys are about exhausted; hence the name. Also, a word for boastful stories that contain no semblance of truth.

Windies

See tall tales.

windmiller

A man who cared for the windmills on a ranch. Only the larger ranches hired a man for this special duty. With a helper he was kept busy building new windmills and keeping the old ones in repair.

windmilling

A cowboy's word for a horse that is swapping ends as he bucks.

windmill monkey

A ranch hand who oiled and repaired windmills; so called because he had to do considerable climbing to do the job well.

windsucker

A cowboy's name for a steer that has been run and jerked around considerably.

wing fence

A fence on each side of a corral entrance that flares out for many feet to help direct the leaders of the entering herd into the opening of the pen.

winning out

In faro, betting on a card that won four times in one deal.

winnowing

A miner's term for panning gold.

win out

In faro, to win the fourth time after having already won three times during the deal.

winter drift

A cowboy's term for cattle that drifted south in winter to avoid the cold storms of the north.

winterer

A trapper's name for a man who had passed several winters in Indian country

winter horses

Horses kept at the home ranch for use in winter.

winter kill

A cowman's term for cattle that die from the winter cold and blizzards.

wintz

In mining, a winze; a passageway leading downward from a mine opening.

wipe out

An early-day trapper's term for a killing or massacre where all the enemy, such as Indians, were slain.

wipes

A cowboy's name for his neckerchief. It has more uses than almost anything else he wears and is not merely an ornamental necktie, as many folks think. The rodeo rider prefers bright colors in neckerchiefs, as he does in shirts; but the rangeman who wants to dodge the attention of either people or animals prefers neutral colors, since bright colors advertise him.

Folding his neckerchief diagonally, like the first garment he ever wore, he ties the two farthest corners in a square knot and hangs it on the peg he finds handiest—his neck. In this way he is never without it in case he needs it, and he generally does. Mostly he wears it draped loosely over his chest with the knot at the back. If the sun is at his back he reverses it to protect his neck. Riding in the drag of a herd, he pulls it over his nose and mouth so that he can breathe without being suffocated by the dust that is kicked up. It is a protection against cold wind and stinging sleet. Pulled up under his eyes, it guards against snow blindness.

If he is riding in a stiff wind and does not have bonnet strings on his hat, he ties it on with his bandanna; sometimes, when the weather is cold, he uses it for an ear muff, and when it is hot, he wears it wet under his hat to keep his head cool. When he is thirsty and is caught in country where there is no running water, he spreads it over a muddy water hole to use as a strainer to drink through.

When he washes his face at the water hole in the morning, he carries his towel with him, tied around his neck. In the branding pen, when the sweat is running down into his eyes, this mop is hanging handy, and it also makes a rag for holding the handle of a hot branding iron.

Perhaps he uses it as a blindfold in saddling a snaky bronc, or as a piggin' string when he runs across a calf that has been overlooked in branding. He sometimes uses it to hobble his horse; one end tied to the lower jaw of a gentle horse serves as an Indian bridle that will do in a pinch. It has been used as a sling for a broken arm, a tourniquet, and a bandage for a wound. Men have been handcuffed with neckerchiefs, and more than one cowboy has been buried out on the plains with one spread over his face to keep the dirt from touching it.

It can be used as a saddlebag, a mosquito net, or a trail marker; it has been used as a flag for signaling, a dishcloth, a recoil pad, a gun sling, a basket, and a sponge; and the highwayman has used it as a mask.

wiping him out

A cowboy's expression for quirting a horse.

wiping stick

A stick with which the trapper cleaned his rifle.

WIRE

See California buckskin, fences, Mormon buckskin, silk.

wire-edged

A cowman's term meaning *skittery* or *nervous.*

wire edges

A lumberman's term for the partial separation of the grain of a piece of timber, caused either by improper seasoning or by dull knives.

wire road

In early days a road or trail following government telegraph lines.

wisdom bringer

A cowboy's name for a schoolteacher. Since most of these teachers were imported from the East, the cowman did not have much respect for their knowledge. To him, anyone who did not know cows "couldn't teach a settin' hen to cluck."

WISE

See savvy, wrinkles on his horns.

wish book

A cowboy's term for a mail-order catalog. Many cowboys got their education from one of these books, and by studying the pictures they knew what practically everything on earth was before they ever saw the real article. The women of the ranch did their wishful window-shopping from its pages, and it was not uncommon to see some cowboy thumbing through its thickness, lingering with a look of wonder over the pages picturing women's personal wearing apparel.

witch's bridle

A cowboy's term for tangles in a horse's mane.

witch stick

What the miner calls a divining rod.

wobblies

A logger's name for members of the Industrial Workers of the World, a word invented by members of the organization on the Pacific Coast; hence any excessively earnest labor agitator. Also called *wobs.*

wobbly horrors

A logger's term for the jim-jams that bedevil an employer who fears labor trouble.

wobs

A shortened form of *wobblies, q.v.*

Wo-ha-a-a!

In freighting, a call of the ox drivers.

wohaw

An Indian's name for cattle. The first cattle the Indians saw under the white man's control were the ox teams of the early freighters. Listening with wonder to the strange words of the bullwhackers as they shouted, "Whoa!" "Haw!" and "Gee!" they thought these words were the names of the animals, and began calling cattle *wohaws.* Rarely did a trail herd pass through the Indian country on its march

north that it was not stopped to receive a demand for *wohaw.* This demand became so common that the cattlemen themselves began to use the word, and it became a part of their vocabulary.

wolf

The predatory animal of the cattle country. What the cowboy calls a cattle grub hatched from the eggs of the *heel fly, q.v.*

WOLF

See buffalo wolf, loafer, lobo, wolf.

wolfer

A man hired by a rancher to trap and hunt wolves on his range. He matched wits with this most cunning of animals for the bounty paid both by the rancher and by the county in which he worked.

wolf tree

A logger's name for an old tree that shuts off light needed by younger trees growing under it; a forest tree whose size and position cause it to prevent the growth of small trees around it by usurping their space, light, and nourishment.

WOMEN

See calico, calico queen, catalog woman, Cattle Kate, chippy, Cousin Anne, Cousin Jenny, cow bunny, dragging her rope, dulce, esposa, filly girls, heart-and-hand woman, live dictionary, long-haired partner, Montgomery Ward woman sent west on approval, painted cat, pink pretties, puncture lady, running mate, sage hen, shanty queen, slack puller.

wompoo

A Wyoming cowboy's term for the bucking of a horse.

wood

A cowboy's name for a saddle.

wood bee

A party of loggers or other woodsmen organized to gather and prepare fuel for some needy person.

wood boat

In steamboating, a boat used to transfer wood from the shore to a steamer. Flatboats or scows capable of carrying 20 to 40

cords of wood were loaded at the woodyards in readiness for the expected steamer.
Since wood already loaded in the scow was
worth more, a higher price was paid for
it by steamboatmen, and contracts were
made ahead. The date of the boat's arrival
was determined, and the wood boat was in
readiness, day or night, with two men on
board. When the steamboat arrived, the
wood boat ran alongside and tied up to it,
and, while the steamer was on her way
upriver, thirty or forty men pitched or carried the wood aboard.

wood butcher

A logger's name for a carpenter, especially a poor one.

wooden island

A riverman's term for an island of floating timber or debris in the river.

wooden piston

A miner's name for a wooden shovel.

wood'er down

In logging, to load as many logs as possible on a truck; the expression used by log-
truck drivers at the log landing.

wood harp

A logger's name for a crosscut saw.

wood hawk

In steamboating, a man who operated
woodyards along the river to supply the
boats with fuel.

wood head

A logger.

wood hick

A logger.

wooding

In steamboating, loading wood on the
boat. When the boat touched the shore to
take on wood, the mate called "Woodpile!"
and every available man jumped ashore,
grabbed a load of wood, and took it on
board. In a very short time the work was
done, and the boat was on its way. Also
called *wooding up*.

The most serious problem with which
the Missouri River navigator had to deal
was that of procuring fuel. Steamboats were

built to burn nothing but wood, and the
heavy growth of trees along the river made
this form of fuel ideal. But the most common wood along the rivers was cottonwood,
which did not make the best fuel. If it was
green, it was next to impossible to maintain
steam with it without the aid of rosin.
Often it would not last long enough to
carry the boat from one wooding place to
the next.

In the early years the fuel was cut by the
crew itself as the boat proceeded on her
voyage. But as the traffic became more regular, woodyards were established, either by
the boatowners or by people who cut wood
for sale.

wooding station

A place or station where steamboats took
on wood.

wooding up

See *wooding*.

wood monkey

A man responsible for supplying wood
for a ranch or a roundup camp.

woodpecker

A logger's name for a poor wood
chopper; also called *beaver*.

wood pussy

A cowboy's name for a skunk.

wood rat

A woodsman.

woods crew

The crew of a logging train.

wood sheller

A cowboy's name for a cutter of fence
posts and branding fuel.

WOODSMEN

See bushwhacker, hunters, loggers, trappers, wood rat, wood tick.

wood tick

A woodsman.

wool-blind

A sheep whose wool has grown over its
eyes, shutting out its sight.

wooled sheep

Unshorn sheep.

wool in his teeth

A sheepherder's expression for a person of low principle, implying that he was a sheep-killing cur.

woollies

A common name for sheep.

woolsey

A cowboy's name for a cheap hat, usually made of wool. Ross Santee told a good story about a cowhand named Shorty who let a cow-town merchant sell him a cheap hat so much too large for him that he had to stuff five lampwicks under the sweatband to make it fit.

" 'It's pourin' rain when I leaves town, [says Shorty] and the old hat weighs a ton. I ain't any more than started when it's down over both ears, an' by the time I hit Seven Mile it's leakin' like a sieve. I'm riding a bronc that's pretty snuffy, an' every time I raises the lid enough to get a little light, I see him drop one ear. I finally decides to take the lamp-wicks out altogether. I'm tryin' to raise the lid enough to see somethin' besides the saddle-horn when the old bronc bogs his head. I make a grab for leather when he leaves the ground, but I might as well have a gunny-sack tied over my head, for I can't see nothin'. When he comes down the second time I'm way over on one side. When he hits the ground the third jump, I ain't with him. I'm sittin' in the middle of the wash with both hands full of sand. I finally lifts the lid enough to see the old bronc headin' for the ranch. He's wide open and kickin' at his paunch.' " (Ross Santee, *Men and Horses* [New York, The Century Company, 1921], 115.)

wool tier

In sheepshearing, a man who ties wool into sacks after the shearing.

wool tramper

In sheepshearing, a man who tramps fleece into wool sacks.

wool with the handle on

A cowboy's name for a mutton chop.

wooshers

A cowboy's name for hogs.

Worchestershire

A cowboy's name for a Winchester rifle.

wore 'em low

An expression for a man who wore his gun low where it was easily accessible and indicated that he was willing to stand or fall by his ability to use it. Very often the expression was used to mean that his gun was for hire and that he was a professional gunman. Duke Noel used to say of one such man, "That hogleg hangin' at his side ain't no watch charm, and he don't pack that hardware for bluff nor balance."

work

A cowboy's term meaning *to handle cattle*. To round up stock, to brand calves, and to gather beeves is to *work cattle*. The word is also used for handling and training a horse.

work by the mile

A logger's term for doing piecework in which the workman is paid according to the amount of timber he bucks.

work horse

A cowboy's name for a horse used in harness, to distinguish it from a riding horse.

working ahead of the roundup

A cowman's expression for an industrious rancher or cowhand who built a herd rapidly by driving his cattle on the range ahead of the larger outfits and claiming all unbranded stock. See *sooner*.

working brands

Changing brands from one type to another by using a running iron; the practice of a rustler.

working the bed ground

In sheepherding, getting the mothers and lambs together, the duty of the sheep wrangler.

working the herd

Gathering cattle in circle on roundup for the purpose of cutting out the beef, the breeding specimens, or other types desired.

The expression was used for cutting a large bunch into one or more smaller herds.

work over

To change a brand. To take the buck out of a horse.

works

In logging, a name for the company and equipment engaged in the removal of a section of timber.

WORTHINESS

See full sixteen hands high, square, straight as a wagon tongue, up and down as a cow's tail, wildcat's ankle.

worthless as a four-card flush

A cowboy's expression for anything worthless or beyond repair.

WOUNDED

See as full of arrows as a porcupine, boogered up, gut-shot, singed.

wrangatang

What the cowboy occasionally called the day wrangler.

wrangle

To herd horses.

wrangle horse

A horse kept near camp and used to drive up the saddle horses.

wrangler

A herder of the saddle horses. It was the duty of this man or boy to see that the horses were kept together and at hand when wanted for work. A corruption of the Spanish *caverango, q.v.*

The wrangler's job was considered the most menial in cow work, and he did not stand very high in a cow camp. He rode the sorriest horse in the outfit and was the butt of all the jokes of a dozen cowhands. Yet his job was a training school, and many a good cowboy got his start in a wrangler's job.

By studying the characteristics of the va-

rious horses, he saved himself much work and grief. He knew which horses were likely to be bunch quitters, which were fighters, and which were afraid of their own shadows. The arrival of stray men with their strings added to his cares, and he had more horses to get acquainted with. Although it could rarely be said, the greatest praise that could be bestowed upon a wrangler was that "he never lost a horse."

WRANGLERS

See caverango, cavvy man, dew wrangler, dude wrangler, horse pestler, horse rustler, jingler, wrangatang, wrangler, wrango.

wrango

A shortened form of *wrangler, q.v.*

wrastle

What the logger calls a dance.

wrastling calves

A common expression for flanking calves for branding.

wreck pan

The receptacle for the dirty dishes after a meal in a cow camp. See *round pan.*

wring-tail

A cowboy's name for a horse of nervous disposition that has been ridden to exhaustion and spurred to make him go, causing him to develop the habit of wringing his tail as he runs. Jerking on the bits also develops the habit. No real cowman likes to ride such a horse, for he makes the rider nervous. Also called *switch-tail.*

wrinkle-horn

A cowboy's name for an old steer whose horns have become wrinkled and scaly.

wrinkles his spine

An expression for a bucking horse.

wrinkles on his horns

A cowboy's expression for a person possessing wisdom or one who has had much experience.

X

"Faint heart never filled a flush"

xerga
In packing, a saddle cloth placed between the *salea (q.v.)* and the packsaddle.

Y

"Nobody ever drowned himself in sweat"

yack
A cowboy's name for a stupid person.

yager
A rifle with a short barrel and a large bore popular in early days in the South and Southwest.

Yakima
An Indian pony.

yaks
A name given by the northern cowboy to the Mexican cattle that went up the trail; so called because they came from Yaqui Indian country.

yamping
A cowboy's term for ordinary stealing; petty theft.

Yankee
See *blue belly*.

yannigan
A canvas bag or kit used by the logger; also called *yannigan bag* and *turkey*.

yannigan bag
What a cowboy sometimes called the bag he used for his personal belongings.

yard
In logging, to accumulate logs either in a yard or at a skidway.

yarder
A logger's name for a man who brings logs to a *yard, q.v.* Also, a machine, usually a donkey engine, that moves logs to a yard.

yard the grub
A logger's expression meaning *to eat*.

yawl
In river boating, a flat-bottomed rowboat used in conjunction with larger boats, such as keelboats or steamboats, for messenger service or short trips.

yearling
A year-old calf or colt. A cowboy's word for a child.

yegua
A *broomtail (q.v.)* mare; from the Spanish.

yellow-bellies
Cattle of Mexican breed, splotched on flank and belly with a yellowish color.

yellow legs
A name given the early soldier of the frontier because of the yellow leggings he wore.

yo
A sheepherder's name for a ewe.

yoke

A wooden or metal frame fastened around a cow's neck to prevent her from crawling through a fence. In freighting, a wooden neck yoke used on bull teams. In logging, the heavy U-shaped part of a block by which the block is attached to a tree, stump, or other object.

Yoke up!

In freighting, the wagon master's com mand to the driver of the ox teams to yoke up for moving out.

yoking

What a miner calls a collision of buckets or cars in a mine.

younker

A cowman's name for a young one; a child.

yucca country

A general term for the Southwest.

Z

"Never call a man a liar because he knows more'n you do"

zalea

See *salea.*

zanja

An arroyo. An irrigation ditch. From the Spanish.

zanjero

A man who digs irrigation ditches. From the Spanish.

zapato

A word sometimes used in the Southwest for a shoe or boat. From the Spanish.

zebra dun

A horse of dun color with a more or less distinct dorsal stripe over the entire length of his top line, often with a transverse shoulder stripe and sometimes with zebra stripes on the legs.

zorrillas

Cattle of the early longhorn breed; so called in the border country because of their color, black with a line back, white freckles frequently appearing on the sides and belly. From the Spanish, meaning *pole-cats.*

Adios, and may you never get your spurs tangled up